P9-BZC-075

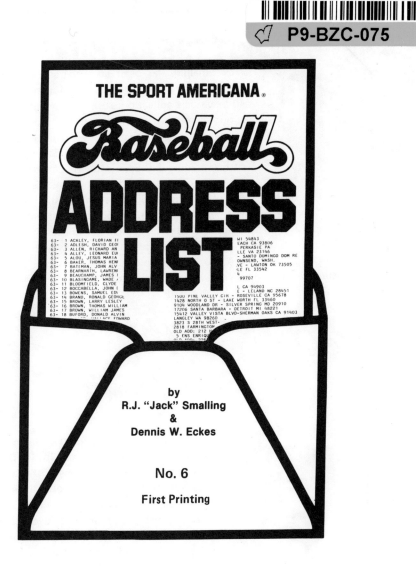

THE SPORT AMERICANA®

Baseball

ADDRESS LIST

by
R.J. "Jack" Smalling
&
Dennis W. Eckes

No. 6

First Printing

The Sport Americana Baseball Address List, Number 6, is copyrighted ©, 1990, by Dennis W. Eckes and R. J. Smalling. All rights reserved. No part of this publication may be reproduced, stored in a retrieval system or transmitted in any form or by any means, electronic, mechanical, photocopying, recording, or otherwise, without prior permission in writing from the publisher. Printed in the U.S.A., 1990. Published by Edgewater Book Company, Inc., Box 40238, Cleveland, Ohio 44140, in conjunction with Den's Collectors Den.

ISBN 0-937424-48-X

ABOUT THE AUTHORS

Jack Smalling has been an autograph collector for 28 years and a card collector for more than 40 years. His collection of big league autographs is one of the best in the country. Reproductions of many of these signatures appear in this publication. He was educated at Iowa State University, obtaining a B.S. in Modern Languages and an M. Ed. in School Administration. His athletic activities have included officiating for 30 years — football, basketball and baseball. After a successful high school baseball career, he played 13 years at the semi-pro level. A teaching and coaching career of 15 years ended in 1979 when he joined Gateway Insurance Services in Ames, IA, to sell commercial and personal lines of insurance. He and his wife, Marge, have four sons.

Denny Eckes has been an avid fan of baseball for as long as he can remember. In 1976, he founded Den's Collectors Den, one of the largest and most reputable sports memorabilia establishments in the country. Mr. Eckes holds a B.S. degree in chemistry and an M.B.A. degree in quantative methods, both from the University of Maryland. Before the establishment of Den's Collectors Den, he held positions as research chemist, information analyst, scheduling engineer, and program manager for a large engineering firm. Among his other published works are *The Sport Americana Baseball Card Price Guide, The Sport Americana Football, Hockey, Basketball and Boxing Card Price Guide, The Sport Americana Alphabetical Baseball Card Checklist, The Sport Americana Baseball Card Team Checklist, The Sport Americana Memorabilia and Autograph Price Guide,* and *The Sport Americana Price Guide to the Non-Sports Cards.* In all, Mr. Eckes has authored nearly 40 successful books.

THE SPORT AMERICANA
BASEBALL ADDRESS LIST
NO. 6

TABLE OF CONTENTS

AUTOGRAPHS — BASEBALL CARDS
RESEARCH MATERIAL

LIVING PLAYER 3x5 AUTOGRAPHS

1910 to 1940 debut - 100 different - $31.00 ppd. (600 different available for $.30 @ plus $1 UPS)
1941 to 1990 debut - 100 different - $23.00 ppd. (2000 different available for $.22 @ plus $1 UPS)

All are my choice. Larger quantities of the first three groups are available.

DECEASED PLAYER 3x5 AUTOGRAPHS

25 different - $17.50 ppd.
50 different - $34.00 ppd.
100 different - $80.50 ppd.
200 different - $176.00 ppd.
350 different - $360.00 ppd.
500 different - $573.00 ppd.
700 different - $900.00 ppd.

Note: The deceased player lots are assembled by picking the most recently deceased players first. Consequently as the quantity increases, the price increases at a greater rate to reflect the higher priced 3x5s included.

DECEASED PLAYER 3x5 AUTOGRAPHS BY YEARS

YR DIED	25 Diff.	50 Diff.	100 Diff.
'88-90	$17.25	$31.00	$56.00
'85-87	$25.50	$46.00	$83.50
'82-84	$33.50	$61.00	$111.00
'79-81	$41.50	$76.00	$138.50
Pre-79	$49.75	$91.00	$166.00

(All above prices are postpaid. All lots are my choice.)

INDESTRUCTO BOXES

Size #7 (Holds 730 cards)
10 for $5.75 ppd.
25 for $11.00 ppd.
50 for $19.50 ppd.
100 for $35.00 ppd.

SALE LIST

My latest sale list of autographed gum cards, 3x5s and 8x10s is available for $.50 postage.

PUBLICATION SALE LIST

My latest sale list of yearbooks, programs, magazines and press guides from all sports is available for $.50 postage.

PRICES QUOTED HERE

All prices in this ad are subject to change without notice

DEBUT LISTS

A complete set of 80 debut lists from 1910-1989 is $7.00 ppd. These list the numbers for each player listed in this book.

HIGH SCHOOL/COLLEGE RESEARCH

In order to aid my research for the whereabouts of players I've compiled lists of the high schools and colleges attended by the players. Debut years 1977 through 1987 are available for $3.00 postpaid each. Each list shows all players who debuted in a given year along with birth data, high school and college.

ADDRESS CORRECTIONS

Address corrections to this book will be provided on the following basis only. Send the face of the returned letter along with a self addressed stamped envelope. No more than five at a time. Only corrections to addresses shown as valid will be provided.

BUYING COLLECTIONS

I am looking to buy collections of baseball 3x5 autographs and baseball cards. If you really want to sell, send me your collection along with your phone number. I'll give you a call with my offer. I seldom have to send them back!

R.J. "Jack" SMALLING
2308 Van Buren Avenue
Ames, Iowa 50010

READY TO USE LABELS

Ready to use adhesive labels of this book are available for $300.00 postpaid. Over 6000 labels, these addresses reflect all the current up-to-date changes that are available. Available as 3-up or on magnetic tape. They can be coded to your specifications and sorted in zip code order, if you wish.

PUBLICATIONS WANTED

STREET & SMITH
FOOTBALL: 1950
BASKETBALL: 1957

NATIONAL LEAGUE GREEN BOOK
1934, 1935, 1937

AMERICAN LEAGUE RED BOOK
1938, 1939, 1941

BASEBALL PRESS GUIDES WANTED

68 NYN, 67 Bal, 64 Mil, 63 Bal, 63 Det, 63 KCA, 63 Phi, 63 Pit, 62 LAA, 62 Phi, 62 Pit, 61 Cle, 61 KCA, 61 Min, 61 Was, 61 Mil, 61 Phi, 61 Pit, 60 Bal, 60 Bos, 60 Was, 60 Mil, 60 Phi, 60 Pit, 59 Det, 59 Was, 59 Mil, 59 Phi, 59 Pit, 59 StL, 58 KCA, 58 NYA, 58 Was, 58 Mil, 58 Phi, 58 Pit, 58 SFG, 57 Bal, 57 Bos, 57 NYA, 57 Was, 57 Chi, 57 Mil, 57 NYN, 57 Phi, 57 Pit. Need many prior to 56.

BASEBALL YEARBOOKS WANTED

10 Pit, 19 Cin, 34 ChA, 34 Det, 34 ChN, 35 ChN, 36 ChN, 37 SLA, 37 ChN, 38 ChN, 39 ChN, 40 ChN, 41 ChN, 42 ChN, 45 SLA, 47 Was, 49 Was, 50 Was, 56 KCA, 57 KCA, 58 Cle, 58 KCA, 58 Cin, 69 NYA, 61 Cin, 62 Cle, 62 KCA, 62 NYA, 62 Cin, 62 SFG, 63 NYN, 64 NYN, 64 Phi, 65 NYA, 65 HoA, 66 KCA, 66 HoA, 67 KCA, 67 NYN, 71 Bos, 71 Pit, 72 Mon, 73 Bos, 74 NYN, 77 Sea, 80 Tor, 80 NYN, 81 Tor, 82 Tor, 83 KCR, 83 Oak, 84 Mon, 86 Tor, 86 NYN, 87 Tor, 87 Cin.

ORGANIZATIONAL GUIDES WANTED
MINOR LEAGUE PRESS GUIDES WANTED

I need major league organizational guides and minor league press guides to aid in my research for this book. If you have any of these guides, please write.

FOOTBALL PROGRAMS WANTED

I collect football programs from Iowa State, Iowa, Iowa Seahawks, Drake, Iowa State Teachers, State College of Iowa and Northern Iowa. If you have any programs, old or new, let me know.

ADDRESS LISTS #1, #2, #3, & #4

While they last, previous editions are available as follows: #1-1980 $1.00; #2-1982 $4.50; #3-1984 $4.50; #4-1986 $5.00. Add shipping as follows: Book Rate $1.50; UPS $2.25; First Class $2.75.

PREFACE

This book concentrates on the personal signatures or autographs of baseball players. We attempt to provide the background, explanations, and wherewithal for a collector to begin or augment his collection. Many illustrations taken from what we believe are authenic signatures are presented for your observation. Some helpful hints are provided so that your autograph hunting pursuits may be simplified and fruitful.

When reading and using this book, please keep in mind the moral and legal rights of the ballplayers themselves. Some are more cooperative than others, some have more time to comply with your requests than others, but all are entitled to respect, privacy, and the right to affix or not affix his signature based on his own personal thoughts or moods.

There might be nothing more distinctive and personal that a person may do throughout his life than write his own name. This signature, how it changes from childhood to senility, its thin or broad stroke, its clarity, neatness, and readability is a reflexion of the character, mood, and personality of the signer. Perhaps for these reasons, a person's signature has become his universally accepted mark for identification, acknowledgement, and legal and contractual agreement.

As these addresses are under constant update because of the transient nature of the society in which we live, we should appreciate any information you can provide concerning the validity of the information and addresses contained herein. Please send all correspondence concerning address corrections, changes of address or death notices to:

R.J. "Jack" Smalling
2308 Van Buren Avenue
Ames, IA 50010

We hope this edition of the Sport Americana Baseball Address List provides a useful, interesting and enjoyable tool for your autograph and baseball historical pursuits.

Sincerely,

Jack Smalling
Denny Eckes

THE
AUTOGRAPH
COLLECTOR'S MAGAZINE

**Serving Collectors
in All 50 States
and 40
Countries**

Each issue features stories and news concerning the world of historical documents and letters, signed cards, photos and First Day Covers. Topics include entertainment, sports, politics, aviation, science, military, literary, business, invention.

Plus 200 VIP Addresses in Each Issue!
$25⁰⁰ year United States
$30⁰⁰ Canada & Mexico
$35⁰⁰ Foreign

Now 10 issues a year!

THE AUTOGRAPH
COLLECTOR'S MAGAZINE
P.O. Box 55328
Stockton, CA 95205
(209) 473-0570 • (209) 942-2131

2

AUTHENTICITY

One of the enjoyable features of collecting autographs is knowing that one possesses an original mark made by another human being, a human being who for one reason or another has distinguished him or herself in the eyes of the collector. Facsimile autographs, autographs signed by someone other than the one whose name appears on the autograph, or photographs or copies of autographs do not comply with the definition of a true autograph; hence, they are of no value to the collector.

The only way one can be absolutely sure that an autograph is authentic is to personally witness the signer as he affixes his autograph. Practically speaking, were directly obtained autographs the only ones collected, logistic problems would prevent anyone from having but a modest collection. While authenticity can only be assured by directly obtaining autographs, many sources offer a high probability that an autograph is valid.

Knowing how a person's signature is supposed to look is a first step toward ascertaining authenticity. Facsimile autographs to compare with ones you are attempting to validate can be found on baseball cards, in books or magazines, or quite possibly, from the many facsimile autographs found in the text of this book. The reputation of the secondary source (dealer, friend, other collector) from whom you are obtaining the autograph is of utmost importance. Unfortunately, even the most reputable source may be unaware that he possesses a non-legitimate autograph.

Obtaining an autograph from a logical source increases the probability that an autograph is authentic. Other variables being equal, a resident of Boston is much more likely to have a valid autograph of a Red Sox player than is a resident of Butte, MT. A seventy-year old is much more likely to possess an autographed Babe Ruth ball than is a twelve-year old. Autographs obtained from the estate or from personal friends of the autographer are highly likely to be authentic. Autographs from financial or legal documents, such as cancelled checks or contracts, or any notarized communications can be considered authentic.

HOW TO OBTAIN AUTOGRAPHS

Although the text of this book is intended to provide the information necessary to obtain autographs through the mail, there are other ways to obtain autographs of ballplayers. There are basically two general categories by which you can obtain an autograph—first hand or directly, where you actually watch the ballplayer affix his signature, and second hand or indirectly, where you are not present at the time the ballplayer signs the autograph. As autograph collectors place such a high concern on authenticity, obtaining autographs first hand is preferential. Practically speaking, some autographs are impossible to obtain first hand, while many others are near impossible or at best very difficult to obtain first hand; hence, most collectors obtain a considerable portion of their collections via the indirect method.

OBTAINING AUTOGRAPHS FIRST HAND

The most obvious place to obtain a ballplayer's autograph is at the ballpark. The traditional crowd around the clubhouse awaiting the departure of their favorite players after the game, pens and papers in hands, is still perhaps the most viable means to obtain autographs. Many clubs provide special nights at the ballparks where, before the game, fans are encouraged to chat, photograph, and obtain autographs from the local team members who are available for these activities for the time periods specified.

Local merchants sometimes sponsor promotional activities at their establishments and feature a ballplayer as the guest celebrity. The ballplayer is normally available to sign autographs, and the merchants might well provide a medium (photo, postcard, etc.) for obtaining the autograph.

Other opportunities arise at hotels, airports, celebrity dinners or other public places where a ballplayer might chance to be during the course of his normal routine. However, we must emphasize again the necessity for patience and politeness when requesting an autograph in person from a ballplayer. Quite often time may allow only a few or no signatures to be signed before the ballplayer's schedule requires him to halt the autograph activities.

More and more over the past few years, the many sports collectibles conventions and shows held across the country have been featuring guest baseball players. These shows provide excellent opportunities for obtaining autographs from some of the most popular ballplayers.

Each year the Baseball Hall of Fame in Cooperstown, NY, holds induction ceremonies for newly elected members. Not only do the newly elected members attend, but also many of the members who have been previously elected are in attendance. There is probably no other time or place that occurs during the year when one can obtain, in person, as many living HOFer autographs as on induction day in Cooperstown.

OBTAINING AUTOGRAPHS INDIRECTLY

Most collectors, by necessity, obtain the bulk of their collections indirectly. Trading with other collectors, purchasing from dealers, purchasing from private parties, or bidding at auction from estate liquidations, hobby paper ads, or at sports collectibles conventions are the most prevalent methods which do not involve the sports personality himself. The most common way to obtain an autograph from the sports personality without the presence of the sports personality is through the mail. It is for this purpose that the SPORT AMERICANA BASEBALL ADDRESS LIST is most useful.

Autograph collecting is a reasonably popular hobby. It is not uncommon to find other collectors with autograph interests similar to yours. It is also not uncommon to find collectors who posses more than one autograph of the same player, a duplicate which they can be convinced to part with in exchange for an autograph which they desire but do not possess— one which you yourself may have in duplicate. These conditions form the basis for trade negotiations from which both parties can obtain satisfaction. Most trading is not quite this simple; however, the underlying motives of all tradings are to obtain something you do not posses and desire to have for something you have but do not place such a high value on as you do the item you desire to obtain.

4

Dealers in autographed material exist just as they do for any collectible. Many specialize in particular types of autographs. In any event, these dealers have acquired autograph material and are willing to sell it at a given price (a price which may or may not be negotiable). These dealers can be found at sports collectibles conventions, at local flea markets, and from advertisements in the hobby papers or autograph oriented periodicals (including this book).

A check of your local newspapers, particular the auction section of the Sunday editions, is an excellent way to become aware of estate and private party autograph sales and auctions. The auction method offers you the opportunity to obtain autographs you desire for amounts less than you might pay to a dealer. In fact, because of the scarcity of certain autographs, the auction method may be the only available way to obtain a particular autograph. In such cases a fair market value might not be known, and the auction offers a means to arrive at a price based on the value of the autograph to the collector.

OBTAINING AUTOGRAPHS THROUGH THE MAIL

A large number of active and retired baseball players honor autograph requests made through the mail. One of the prime purposes of compiling this book is to provide the collector with the wherewithal to obtain autographs he or she desires through the mails. The authors do not profess to know all players who will comply with your autograph requests nor those who will not comply. The authors also do not promote or sanction any harassment or excessive requests on your part of the ballplayers contacted through the addresses found in this Address List. To the contrary, we emphatically suggest a polite, patient and respectful course in obtaining autographs through the mail.

Ballplayers, particularly active players during the baseball season, have schedules much tighter and more regimented than the normal 9 to 5 worker. Mail they receive may not be opened for lengthy periods. Many schedule limited time periods that they devote to autograph requests. Quite possibly, dependent on the number of autograph requests a particular player receives, your autograph request might not be answered for a considerable period of time. Be patient. The authors know of cases where years have elapsed before an autograph request was returned.

Like everyone else, ballplayers are human beings and appreciate politeness. Words such as "please" and "thank you" are as pleasantly received and as revered by ballplayers as they are by parents of teenagers (fortunately, ballplayers hear them much more often). Excessive requests, imperative tones, and impoliteness are justifiably scorned.

Some ballplayers do not honor autograph requests, either in person or through the mail. Some do not even accept mail, and your letter may come back marked "refused." Some change their autographing philosophies over the years, becoming more liberal or conservative in their autographing habits. Whatever a player's thoughts or ideas are on accepting or rejecting autograph requests, they should be respected.

The mechanics of obtaining autographs through the mail are quite simple. Send the request, postpaid, to the ballplayer, including a politely written request outlining what you are asking of the ballplayer, any material that you wish to have autographed, and a SASE (self-addressed stamped envelope) large enough to contain the material you wish to be autographed and returned to you. Never send an autograph request postage due. To do so is presumptuous, in poor taste and completely uncalled for.

Do not send an unreasonable amount of material for autographing. A limit of three items per request has become the accepted practice of collectors. An exception to this limit is considered permissible if you have duplicates of the item you wish to have autographed, and you would like to give the ballplayer the opportunity to keep one of the duplicates for his own enjoyment. Ballplayers like most of us enjoy seeing and having interesting photos or other material concerning themselves, particularly if the item is novel or the ballplayer has never before seen it. Many collectors use this method. as a gesture of good faith and intent when requesting autographs through the mail. However, the limit of three items you wish to have signed and returned to you, exclusive of the items you wish to present to the ballplayer at his option to keep, is still the accepted standard.

It is not considered unreasonable to request a short personalization with an autograph; for example, "To John from...", or "Best Wishes to Gayle from...", etc. Requesting a two-page letter or an answer to a question that requires a dissertation is unreasonable. Do not do it.

Always include a SASE with sufficient postage to cover the material you expect might be returned to you. The SASE alleviates the need for the ballplayer to package and address your reply himself; it enables you to pay, as you should, for return postage; and it assures that the reply will be sent to the party requesting it (assuming you can competently write your own address on an envelope).

VALUES

Like other collectibles, there is a definite price structure for the autographs of ballplayers. We should like to present a discussion of values within a context of scarcity and desirability, which when all results are in, are the prime determinants of value for any collectible.

LIVING OR DECEASED

Like artists and martyrs, the values of whose accomplishments during their lifetimes are magnified and glorified after death, the value of ballplayers' autographs increases considerably after death. The deceased ballplayer can no longer, of course, sign autographs; hence, the supply of the autographs of this player ceases at this point in time. All autographs of deceased ballplayers must be obtained second hand after death, making authenticity questionable.

HALL OF FAME MEMBERS

The pinnacle of success for a ballplayer is election to baseball's Hall of Fame. This honor is limited to the most skillful and proficient players and those others who have made the most significant contributions to the game. The autographs of these men are among the most desireable and have, other factors being equal, the highest value to collectors.

POPULARITY AND NOTORIETY

While popularity can generally be measured by ballplaying skills, there are certainly exceptions. Many ballplayers whose skills on the field were limited have achieved success and notoriety in others walks of life (William A. "Billy" Sunday, Joe Garagiola, Chuck Connors, Jim Thorpe to name but a few). The more popular the ballplayer, whether his popularity was derived by playing skills or by some other means, the higher the value placed on his autograph.

CONDITION AND TYPE OF AUTOGRAPH

Autographs, like other collectibles, exist in various physical conditions — from the weakest, broken pencil autograph to the boldest, unbroken, indelible ink signature. The higher value is placed on the better condition autograph of the same person. Many types of media are available on which to obtain autographs. There are the relatively bland cuts and 3 X 5 varieties at one end of the spectrum and the most elaborate pieces of one-of-a-kind items autographed by the player portrayed at the other end. In between there is a myriad of possible forms and designs that the autograph medium may take. The same autograph has a higher value based on the more interesting, enjoyable and attractive medium on which the autograph is written.

NEW IN THIS EDITION OF THE ADDRESS LIST

The Address List contains over 10,000 entries. The players new to the big leagues in 1988 and 1989 have been added with their corresponding debut years and numbers. Address corrections have been made and obituary data has been supplied for those who have died since the last edition. In total, nearly 2,000 additions and corrections have been made.

MAJOR LEAGUE TEAM ADDRESSES

BASEBALL COMMISSIONER'S OFFICE
Fay Vincent, Commissioner
350 Park Avenue
New York, NY 10022
(212) 371-2211

AMERICAN LEAGUE OFFICE
Robert W. Brown, President
350 Park Avenue, 18th Floor
New York, NY 10022
(212) 339-7600

BALTIMORE ORIOLES
Lawrence Lucchino, President and CEO
Memorial Stadium
Baltimore, MD 21218
(301) 243-9800

BOSTON RED SOX
Jean R. Yawkey, Majority Owner, Chairwoman
Fenway Park
4 Yawkey Way
Boston, MA 02215
(617) 267-9440

CALIFORNIA ANGELS
Gene Autry, Chairman, President
Anaheim Stadium
P.O. Box 2000
Anaheim, CA 92803
(714) 937-6700

CHICAGO WHITE SOX
Jerry Reinsdorf, Chairman
Eddie Einhorn, President
Comiskey Park
324 West 35th Street
Chicago, IL 60616
(312) 924-1000

CLEVELAND INDIANS
Richard E. Jacobs, Chairman
Hank Peters, President
Cleveland Stadium
Cleveland, OH 44114
(216) 861-1200

DETROIT TIGERS
James A. Campbell, Chairman
Glenn E. (Bo) Schembechler, President
Tiger Stadium
2121 Trumbull Avenue
Detroit, MI 48216
(313) 962-4000

KANSAS CITY ROYALS
Ewing Kauffman, Chairman
Joseph R. Burke, President
Royals Stadium
P.O. Box 419969
Kansas City, MO 64141
(816) 921-2200

MILWAUKEE BREWERS
Allan H. "Bud" Selig, President
Milwaukee County Stadium
201 South 46th Street
Milwaukee, WI 53214
(414) 933-4114

MINNESOTA TWINS
Carl R. Pohlad, Owner
Jerry Bell, Jr., President
Hubert H. Humphrey Metrodome
501 Chicago Avenue South
Minneapolis, Minnesota 55415
(612) 375-1366

NEW YORK YANKEES
George M. Steinbrenner, Principal Owner
Yankee Stadium
East 161st Street and River Avenue
Bronx, NY 10451
(212) 293-4300

OAKLAND A'S
Walter A. Haas, Jr., Owner
Walter J. (Wally) Haas, President
Oakland-Alameda County Coliseum
P.O. Box 2220
Oakland, CA 94621
(415) 638-4900

SEATTLE MARINERS
Jeffrey Smulyan, Chairman
The Kingdome
P.O. Box 4100
Seattle, WA 98104
(206) 628-3555

TEXAS RANGERS
Michael H. Stone, President
Arlington Stadium
P.O. Box 1111
Arlington, TX 76010
(817) 273-5222

TORONTO BLUE JAYS
N. E. Hardy, Chairman
Exhibition Stadium
P.O. Box 3200
Toronto, Ontario, Canada M5V 3B3
(416) 341-1000

NATIONAL LEAGUE OFFICE
Bill White, President
350 Park Avenue
New York, NY 10022
(212) 339-7700

ATLANTA BRAVES
William C. Batholomay, Chairman
Stanley H. Kasten, President
Atlanta-Fulton County Stadium
P.O. Box 4064
Atlanta, GA 30312
(404) 522-7630

CHICAGO CUBS
Donald C. Grenesko, Chairman
Wrigley Field
1060 West Addison Street
Chicago, IL 60613
(312) 404-CUBS

CINCINNATI REDS
Marge Schott, President
Riverfront Stadium
100 Riverfront Stadium
Cincinnati, OH 45202
(513) 421-4510

HOUSTON ASTROS
John J. McMullen, Chairman
The Astrodome
P.O. Box 288
Houston, TX 77001
(713) 799-9500

LOS ANGELES DODGERS
Peter O'Malley, President
Dodger Stadium
1000 Elysian Park Avenue
Los Angeles, CA 90012
(213) 224-1500

MONTREAL EXPOS
Charles R. Bronfman, Chairman
Claude R. Brochu, President
Olympic Stadium
P.O. Box 500, Station 'M'
Montreal, Quebec, Canada H1V 3P2
(514) 253-3434

NEW YORK METS
Nelson Doubleday, Chairman
William A. Shea Stadium
126th Street & Roosevelt Avenue
Flushing, NY 11368
(212) 507-6387

PHILADELPHIA PHILLIES
William Y. Giles, President
Veterans Stadium
P.O. Box 7575
Philadelphia, PA 19101
(215) 463-6000

PITTSBURGH PIRATES
Douglas C. Danforth, Chairman
Carl F. Bargar, President
Three Rivers Stadium
P.O. Box 7000
Pittsburgh, PA 15212
(412) 323-5000

ST. LOUIS CARDINALS
August A. Busch III, Chairman
Fred L. Kuhlmann, President
Busch Stadium
P.O. Box 8787
250 Stadium Plaza
St. Louis, MO 63102
(314) 421-4040

SAN DIEGO PADRES
Joan Kroc, Chairwoman
Dick Freeman, President
San Diego/Jack Murphy Stadium
P.O. Box 2000
San Diego, CA 92120
(619) 283-7294

SAN FRANCISCO GIANTS
Robert A. Lurie, Chairman
Al Rosen, President
Candlestick Park
San Francisco, CA 94124
(415) 468-3700

TRIPLE A LEAGUE TEAM ADDRESSES

AMERICAN ASSOCIATION
Randy A. Mobley, President
P.O. Box 608
Grove City, OH 43123
(614) 871-1300

BUFFALO BISONS
Robert E. Rich, Sr., Chairman
Robert E. Rich, Jr., President
Pilot Field
P.O. Box 450
Buffalo, NY 14205
(716) 878-8215

DENVER ZEPHYRS
John Dikeou, Chairman
Robert Howsam, Jr., President
Mile High Stadium
2850 West 20th Avenue
Denver, CO 80211
(303) 433- 2032

INDIANAPOLIS INDIANS
Henry R. Warren. Jr., Chairman
Max B. Schumacher, President
Owen J. Bush Stadium
1501 West 16th Street
Indianapolis, IN 46202
(317) 269-3545

IOWA CUBS
Ken Grandquist, President
Sec Taylor Stadium
2nd & Riverside Drive
Des Moines, Iowa 50309
(515) 243-6111

LOUISVILLE REDBIRDS
Daniel C. Ulmer., Jr., Chairman
Gene P. Gardner, President
Cardinal Stadium
P.O. Box 36407
Louisville, KY 40233
(502) 367-9121

NASHVILLE SOUNDS
Larry Schmittou, President
Herschel Greer Stadium
P.O. Box 23290
Nashville, IN 37202
(615) 242-4371

OKLAHOMA CITY 89ers
Jeffrey H. Loria, Chairman
Bobby Murcer, President
All Sports Stadium
P.O. Box 75089
Oklahoma City, OK 73147
(405) 946-8989

OMAHA ROYALS
Irving Cherry, Chairman, President
Rosenblatt Stadium
P.O. Box 3665
Omaha, NE 68103
(402) 734-2550

INTERNATIONAL LEAGUE
Harold Cooper, President
P.O. Box 608
Grove City, OH 43123
(614) 871-1300

COLUMBUS CLIPPERS
Donald A. Borror, Chairman
Richard Smith, President
Cooper Stadium
1155 West Mound Street
Columbus, OH 43223
(614) 462-5250

PAWTUCKET RED SOX
Bernard G. Mondor, Chairman
Mike Tamburro, President
McCoy Stadium
P.O. Box 2365
Pawtucket, RI 02861
(401) 724-7300

RICHMOND BRAVES
R. E. 'Ted' Turner, Chairman
The Diamond
P.O. Box 6667
Richmond, VA 23230
(804) 359-4444

ROCHESTER RED WINGS
Anna B. Silver, Chairperson
Fred Strauss, President
Silver Stadium
500 Norton Street
Rochester, NY 14621
(716) 467-3000

SCRANTON/WILKES-BARRE RED BARONS
Bill Terlecky, General Manager
Lackawanna County Stadium
P.O. Box 3449
Scranton, PA 18505
(717) 969-2255

SYRACUSE CHIEFS
Robert Johnson, Chairman
Donald R. Waful, President
MacArthur Stadium
Syracuse, NY 13208
(315) 474-7833

TIDEWATER TIDES
Richard J. Davis, President
Met Park
P.O. Box 12111
Norfolk, VA 23502
(804) 461-5600

TOLEDO MUD HENS
Charles Bracken, President
Lucas County Recreation Center
2901 Key Street
Maumee, OH 43537
(419) 893-9481

PACIFIC COAST LEAGUE
William S. Cutler, President
2101 East Broadway No. 35
Tempe, Arizona 85282
(602) 967-7679

ALBUQUERQUE DUKES
Robert Lozinak, Chairman
Pat McKernan, President
Albuquerque Sports Stadium
P.O. Box 26267
Albuquerque, NM 87125
(505) 243-1791

CALGARY CANNONS
Russel A. Parker, Chairman, President
Foothills Stadium
P. O. Box 3690, Station B
Calgary, Alberta, Canada T2M 4M4
(403) 284-1111

COLORADO SPRINGS SKY SOX
David G. Elmore, Chairman
Fred Whitacre, President
Sky Sox Stadium
4385 Tutt Boulevard
Colorado Springs, CO 80922
(719) 597-1449

EDMONTON TRAPPERS
Peter Pocklington, Chairman
Mel Kowalchuk, President
John Ducey Park
10233 96th Avenue
Edmonton, Alberta, Canada T5K 0A5
(403) 429-2934

LAS VEGAS STARS
Larry Koentopp, Chairman, President
Cashman Field
850 Las Vegas Blvd. North
Las Vegas, NV 89101
(702) 386-7200

PHOENIX FIREBIRDS
Martin Stone, Chairman, President
Phoenix Municipal Stadium
5999 East Van Buren Street
Phoenix, AZ 85008
(602) 275-0500

PORTLAND BEAVERS
Joe Buzas, Chairman, President
Portland Civic Stadium
1844 SW Morrison Avenue
Portland, OR 97207
(503) 233-2837

TACOMA TIGERS
Michael A. Tucci, Chairman
Stan Naccarato, President
Cheney Stadium
P.O. Box 11087
Tacoma, WA 98401
(206) 752-7707

TUCSON TOROS
Richard M. Holtzman, Chairman, President
Hi Corbett Field
P.O. Box 27045
Tucson, AZ 85726
(602) 215-2621

VANCOUVER CANADIANS
John Winter, President
Nat Bailey Stadium
4601 Ontario Street
Vancouver, B.C. Canada V5V 3H4
(604) 872-5232

ASK YOUR LOCAL BOOKSTORE ATTENDANT TO SHOW
YOU THE COMPLETE LINE OF SPORT AMERICANA
REFERENCE BOOKS AVAILABLE TO THE COLLECTOR
OF SPORTS MEMORABILIA, AUTOGRAPHS AND CARDS.

HOW TO USE THE SPORT AMERICANA BASEBALL ADDRESS LIST

The Address List is composed of four sections:

1. Players in the Baseball Hall of Fame
2. Players who debuted from 1910 to 1989
3. Coaches with no Major League playing or managerial experience who debuted from 1910 to 1989
4. Umpires who debuted from 1910 to 1989

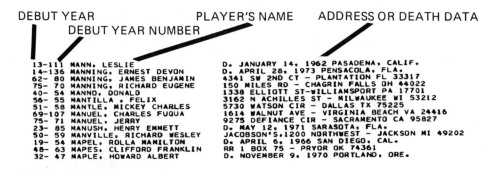

DEBUT YEAR   PLAYER'S NAME   ADDRESS OR DEATH DATA
     DEBUT YEAR NUMBER

```
13-111  MANN, LESLIE                    D. JANUARY 14, 1962 PASADENA, CALIF.
14-136  MANNING, ERNEST DEVON           D. APRIL 28, 1973 PENSACOLA, FLA.
62- 80  MANNING, JAMES BENJAMIN         4341 SW 2ND CT - PLANTATION FL 33317
75- 70  MANNING, RICHARD EUGENE         150 MILES RD - CHAGRIN FALLS OH 44022
40- 54  MANNO, DONALD                   1338 ELLIOTT ST-WILLIAMSPORT PA 17701
56- 55  MANTILLA , FELIX                3162 N ACHILLES ST - MILWAUKEE WI 53212
51- 58  MANTLE, MICKEY CHARLES          5730 WATSON CIR - DALLAS TX 75225
69-107  MANUEL, CHARLES FUQUA           1614 WALNUT AVE - VIRGINIA BEACH VA 24416
75- 71  MANUEL, JERRY                   9275 DEFIANCE CIR - SACRAMENTO CA 95827
23- 85  MANUSH, HENRY EMMETT            D. MAY 12, 1971 SARASOTA, FLA.
50- 59  MANVILLE, RICHARD WESLEY        JACOBSON'S,1200 NORTHWEST - JACKSON MI 49202
19- 54  MAPEL, ROLLA HAMILTON           D. APRIL 6, 1966 SAN DIEGO, CAL.
48- 63  MAPES, CLIFFORD FRANKLIN        RR 1 BOX 75 - PRYOR OK 74361
32- 47  MAPLE, HOWARD ALBERT            D. NOVEMBER 9, 1970 PORTLAND, ORE.
```

The address portion of the listing contains the known current address of the player if the player is now living or information as follows:

> ADDRESS NOT KNOWN—An old address is given for players for whom a current address is not known. In many cases, the year the address was last valid is shown in the data. Birth information is given if no other data is available. If no information is known about a player except his name, a blank space will appear in the address portion of the listing.

> DECEASED PLAYERS—The date and place of a player's death will be listed for deceased players. Incomplete death data is given for some players because complete information is not known. The abbreviation D. with no other information in the address portion of the listing indicates that a player is reportedly deceased, but that no other data is available.

PLEASE NOTE:

> Managers who never appeared in a big league game are listed with the year they first managed in the big leagues.
> Only those coaches who never appeared in a big league game are listed in the coaches section.
> The abbreviations used for states on addresses are standard U.S. Postal Service abbreviations.
> B. indicates born, D. indicates deceased, and other abbreviations are self-explanatory as they are used in normal written communications.

As this nation is known to be a nation of transients, one can expect that the addresses of a considerable number of the ballplayers listed will become invalid over the course of the next year or two.

BASEBALL HALL OF FAME MEMBERS

HOF177 AARON, HENRY LOUIS	1611 ADAMS DR SW - ATLANTA GA 30311
HOF 14 ALEXANDER, GROVER CLEVELAND	D. NOVEMBER 4, 1950 ST. PAUL, NEB.
HOF181 ALSTON, WALTER EMMONS 'SMOKEY'	D. OCTOBER 1, 1984 OXFORD, OHIO
HOF 17 ANSON, ADRIAN CONSTANTINE 'CAP'	D. APRIL 14, 1922 CHICAGO, ILL.
HOF185 APARICIO, LUIS ERNEST	CALLE 67 #26-82 - MARACAIBO VENEZUELA S.A.
HOF 95 APPLING, LUCIUS BENJAMIN 'LUKE'	RR 7, BRAGG RD - CUMMINGS GA 30130
HOF147 AVERILL, HOWARD EARL	D. AUGUST 16, 1983 EVERETT, WASH.
HOF 74 BAKER, JOHN FRANKLIN 'HOME RUN'	D. JUNE 28, 1963 TRAPPE, MD.
HOF119 BANCROFT, DAVID JAMES	D. OCTOBER 9, 1972 SUPERIOR, WIS.
HOF158 BANKS, ERNEST	P.O. BOX 24302 - LOS ANGELES CA 90024
HOF203 BARLICK, ALBERT JOSEPH	2071 NORTH SIXTH - SPRINGFIELD IL 62702
HOF 63 BARROW, EDWARD GRANT	D. DECEMBER 15, 1953 PORT CHESTER, N. Y.
HOF120 BECKLEY, JACOB PETER	D. JUNE 25, 1918 KANSAS CITY, MO.
HOF141 BELL, JAMES 'COOL PAPA'	3034 JAMES COOL PAPA BELL AVE - ST. LOUIS MO 63106
HOF201 BENCH, JOHN LEE	661 REISLING KNOLL - CINCINNATI OH 45226
HOF 64 BENDER, CHARLES ALBERT 'CHIEF'	D. MAY 22, 1954 PHILADELPHIA, PA.
HOF127 BERRA, LAWRENCE PETER 'YOGI'	19 HIGHLAND AVE - MONTCLAIR NJ 07042
HOF142 BOTTOMLEY, JAMES LEROY	D. DECEMBER 11, 1959 SAINT LOUIS, MO.
HOF115 BOUDREAU, LOUIS	15600 ELLIS AVENUE - DOLTON IL 60419
HOF 29 BRESNAHAN, ROGER PATRICK	D. DECEMBER 4, 1944 TOLEDO, O.
HOF190 BROCK, LOUIS CLARK	12595 DURBIN DRIVE - SAINT LOUIS MO 63141
HOF 30 BROUTHERS, DENNIS 'DAN'	D. AUGUST 3, 1932 EAST ORANGE, N. J.
HOF 56 BROWN, MORDECAI PETER CENTENNIAL	D. FEBRUARY 14, 1948 TERRE HAUTE, IND.
HOF 6 BULKELEY, MORGAN G.	D. NOVEMBER 6, 1922 HARTFORD, CONN.
HOF 39 BURKETT, JESSE CAIL	D. MAY 27, 1953 WORCESTER, MASS.
HOF111 CAMPANELLA, ROY	6213 CAPISTRANO - WOODLAND HILLS CA 91367
HOF 85 CAREY, MAX GEORGE	D. MAY 30, 1976 MIAMI, FLA.
HOF 15 CARTWRIGHT, ALEXANDER JOY	D. JULY 12, 1892 HONOLULU, HAWAII
HOF 16 CHADWICK, HENRY	D. APRIL 20, 1908 BROOKLYN, N. Y.
HOF 40 CHANCE, FRANK LEROY	D. SEPTEMBER 15, 1924 LOS ANGELES, CAL.
HOF178 CHANDLER, ALBERT BENJAMIN 'HAPPY'	191 ELM STREET - VERSAILLES KY 40383
HOF152 CHARLESTON, OSCAR MCKINLEY	D. OCTOBER 11, 1954 PHILADELPHIA, PA.
HOF 41 CHESBRO, JOHN DWIGHT	D. NOVEMBER 6, 1931 CONWAY, MASS.
HOF 31 CLARKE, FRED CLIFFORD	D. AUGUST 14, 1960 WINFIELD, KAN.
HOF 91 CLARKSON, JOHN GIBSON	D. FEBRUARY 4, 1909 CAMBRIDGE, MASS.
HOF135 CLEMENTE, ROBERTO WALKER	D. DECEMBER 31, 1972 SAN JUAN, P. R.

HOF 1 COBB, TYRUS RAYMOND	D. JULY 17, 1961 ATLANTA, GA.
HOF 50 COCHRANE, GORDON STANLEY 'MICKEY'	D. JUNE 2, 1962 LAKE FOREST, ILL.
HOF 18 COLLINS, EDWARD TROWBRIDGE SR.	D. MARCH 25, 1951 BOSTON, MASS.
HOF 32 COLLINS, JAMES JOSEPH	D. MARCH 6, 1943 BUFFALO, N. Y.
HOF116 COMBS, EARLE BRYAN	D. JULY 21, 1976 RICHMOND, KY.
HOF 19 COMISKEY, CHARLES ALBERT	D. OCTOBER 26, 1931 EAGLE RIVER, WIS.
HOF143 CONLAN, JOHN BERTRAND 'JOCKO'	D. APRIL 16, 1989 SCOTTSDALE, ARIZ.
HOF 65 CONNOLLY, THOMAS HENRY	D. APRIL 28, 1961 NATICK, MASS.
HOF153 CONNOR, ROGER	D. JANUARY 4, 1931 WATERBURY, CONN.
HOF112 COVELESKI, STANLEY ANTHONY	D. MARCH 20, 1984 SOUTH BEND, IND.
HOF 82 CRAWFORD, SAMUEL EARL	D. JUNE 15, 1968 HOLLYWOOD, CALIF.
HOF 80 CRONIN, JOSEPH EDWARD	D. SEPTEMBER 7, 1984 OSTERVILLE, MASS.
HOF 20 CUMMINGS, WIILLIAM ARTHUR 'CANDY'	D. MAY 17, 1924 TOLEDO, O.
HOF108 CUYLER, HAZEN SHIRLEY 'KIKI'	D. FEBRUARY 11, 1950 ANN ARBOR, MICH.

HOF199 DANDRIDGE, RAYMOND
HOF 66 DEAN, JAY HANNA 'DIZZY'
HOF 33 DELAHANTY, EDWARD JAMES
HOF 71 DICKEY, WILLIAM MALCOLM
HOF159 DIHIGO, MARTIN
HOF 75 DIMAGGIO, JOSEPH PAUL
HOF194 DOERR, ROBERT PERSHING
HOF186 DRYSDALE, DONALD SCOTT
HOF 34 DUFFY, HUGH

P.O. BOX 1139 - PALM BAY FL 32906
D. JULY 17, 1974 RENO, NEV.
D. JULY 2, 1903 FORT ERIE, ONT.
7611 CHOCTAW ROAD - LITTLE ROCK AR 72205
D. MAY 22, 1971 CIENFUEGOS, CUBA
2150 BEACH ST - SAN FRANCISCO CA 94123
33705 ILLAMO AGNESS RD - AGNESS OR 97406
2 LACERRA CIR - RANCHO MIRAGE CA 92270
D. OCTOBER 19, 1954 BOSTON, MASS.

HOF136 EVANS, WILLIAM GEORGE
HOF 42 EVERS, JOHN JOSEPH
HOF 21 EWING, WILLIAM BUCKINGHAM 'BUCK'
HOF 96 FABER, URBAN CHARLES 'RED'
HOF 87 FELLER, ROBERT WILLIAM ANDREW
HOF187 FERRELL, RICHARD BENJAMIN 'RICK'
HOF 92 FLICK, ELMER HARRISON
HOF144 FORD, EDWARD CHARLES 'WHITEY'
HOF174 FOSTER, ANDREW "RUBE"
HOF 59 FOXX, JAMES EMORY
HOF117 FRICK, FORD CHRISTOPHER
HOF 51 FRISCH, FRANK FRANCIS
HOF102 GALVIN, JAMES F. 'PUD'
HOF 22 GEHRIG, HENRY LOUIS 'LOU'
HOF 57 GEHRINGER, CHARLES LEONARD
HOF128 GIBSON, JOSH
HOF175 GIBSON, ROBERT
HOF167 GILES, WARREN CHRISTOPHER
HOF129 GOMEZ, VERNON LOUIS 'LEFTY'

D. JANUARY 23, 1956 MIAMI, FLA.
D. MARCH 28, 1947 ALBANY, N. Y.
D. OCTOBER 20, 1906 CINCINNATI, O.
D. SEPTEMBER 25, 1976 CHICAGO, ILL.
BOX 157 - GATES MILLS OH 44040
2199 GOLFVIEW #203 - TROY MI 48084
D. JANUARY 9, 1971 BEDFORD, O.
38 SCHOOLHOUSE LANE - LAKE SUCCESS NY 11020
D. DECEMBER 9, 1930 KANKAKEE, ILL.
D. JULY 21, 1967 MIAMI, FLA.
D. APRIL 8, 1978 BRONXVILLE, N. Y.
D. MARCH 12, 1973 WILMINGTON, DEL.
D. MARCH 7, 1902 PITTSBURGH, PA.
D. JUNE 2, 1941 RIVERDALE, N. Y.
32301 LAHSER RD - BIRMINGHAM MI 48010
D. JANUARY 20, 1947 PITTSBURGH, PA.
215 BELLEVIEW BLVD SOUTH - BELLEVIEW NE 68005
D. FEBRUARY 7, 1979 CINCINNATI, O.
D. FEBRUARY 17, 1989 GREENBRAE, CALIF.

SPORT AMERICANA PUBLICATIONS

The Number One Publisher of Reference Works for Sports Memorabilia and Trading Card Collectors

Baseball Card Price Guide No. 12 . . . .$ 14.95

Football Card Price Guide No. 7 . . . .$ 14.95

Football, Hockey, Basketball & Boxing
    Card Price Guide No. 6 . . . .$ 14.95

Baseball Address List No. 6 . . . .$ 12.95

Price Guide to the Non-Sports Cards,
    No. 3, Part 2 . . . .$ 12.95

Alphabetical Baseball Card Checklist No. 4 . . . .$ 12.95

Price Guide to Baseball Collectibles No. 2 . . . .$ 14.95

Team Baseball Card Checklist No. 5 . . . .$ 12.95

ADD POSTAGE & HANDLING (P&H) TO ALL ITEMS
PRICES SUBJECT TO CHANGE WITHOUT NOTICE

MasterCard VISA

POSTAGE & HANDLING SCHEDULE
$ .01 to $ 20.00 add $ 2.00
$ 20.01 to $ 29.99 add $ 2.50
$ 30.00 to $ 49.99 add $ 3.00
$ 50.00 or more add $ 4.00

MARYLAND RESIDENTS ADD 5% SALES TAX
CANADIAN ORDERS — BOOKS ONLY
Canadian orders, orders outside the contiguous
United States, APO and FPO add 25% additional
U.S. FUNDS ONLY

SEND
ONLY $ 1.00
for DEN'S
BIG CATALOGUE
CATALOGUE
sent FREE
with each ORDER

DEN'S
COLLECTORS
DEN

HOME OF
SPORT
AMERICANA

Dept. BAL

P.O. BOX 606, LAUREL, MD 20725

HOF 109 GOSLIN, LEON ALLEN 'GOOSE'	D. MAY 15, 1971 BRIDGETON, N. J.
HOF 81 GREENBERG, HENRY BENJAMIN	D. SEPTEMBER 4, 1986 BEVERLY HILLS, CALIF.
HOF 43 GRIFFITH, CLARK CALVIN	D. OCTOBER 27, 1955 WASHINTON, D. C.
HOF 97 GRIMES, BURLEIGH ARLAND	D. DECEMBER 6, 1985 CLEAR LAKE, WIS.
HOF 52 GROVE, ROBERT MOSES 'LEFTY'	D. MAY 22, 1975 NORWALK, O.
HOF 121 HAFEY, CHARLES JAMES 'CHICK'	D. JULY 2, 1973 CALISTOGA, CAL.
HOF 118 HAINES, JESSE JOSEPH 'POP'	D. AUGUST 5, 1978 DAYTON, O.
HOF 86 HAMILTON, WILLIAM ROBERT	D. DECEMBER 16, 1940 WORCESTER, MASS.
HOF 130 HARRIDGE, WILLIAM	D. APRIL 9, 1971 EVANSTON, ILL.
HOF 148 HARRIS, STANLEY RAYMOND 'BUCKY'	D. NOVEMBER 8, 1977 BETHESDA, MD.
HOF 76 HARTNETT, CHARLES LEO 'GABBY'	D. DECEMBER 20, 1972 PARK RIDGE, ILL.
HOF 61 HEILMANN, HARRY EDWIN	D. JULY 9, 1951 DETROIT, MICH.
HOF 149 HERMAN, WILLIAM JENNINGS BRYAN	3111 GARDEN EAST #33 - PALM BEACH GARDENS FL 33410
HOF 122 HOOPER, HARRY BARTHOLOMEW	D. DECEMBER 18, 1974 SANTA CRUZ, CALIF.
HOF 27 HORNSBY, ROGERS	D. JANUARY 5, 1963 CHICAGO, ILL.
HOF 113 HOYT, WAITE CHARLES	D. AUGUST 25, 1984 CINCINNATI, O.
HOF 154 HUBBARD, ROBERT CAL	D. OCTOBER 16, 1977 ST PETERSBURG, FLA.
HOF 53 HUBBELL, CARL OWEN	D. NOVEMBER 21, 1988 SCOTTSDALE, ARIZ.
HOF 98 HUGGINS, MILLER JAMES	D. SEPTEMBER 25, 1929 NEW YORK, N. Y.
HOF 197 HUNTER, JAMES AUGUSTUS 'CATFISH'	RR 1 BOX 895 - HERTFORD NC 27944
HOF 137 IRVIN, MONFORD MERRILL 'MONTE'	104 SYCAMORE CIRCLE - HOMOSASSA FL 32646
HOF 179 JACKSON, TRAVIS CALVIN	D. JULY 27, 1987 WALDO, ARK.
HOF 35 JENNINGS, HUGH AMBROSE	D. FEBRUARY 1, 1928 SCRANTON, PA.
HOF 7 JOHNSON, BYRON BANCROFT 'BAN'	D. MARCH 28, 1931 ST. LOUIS, MO.
HOF 2 JOHNSON, WALTER PERRY	D. DECEMBER 10, 1946 WASHINGTON, D. C.
HOF 150 JOHNSON, WILLIAM JULIUS 'JUDY'	D. JUNE 14, 1989 WILMINGTON, DEL.
HOF 164 JOSS, ADRIAN 'ADDIE'	D. APRIL 14, 1911 TOLEDO, O.
HOF 170 KALINE, ALBERT WILLIAM	945 TIMBERLAKE DR - BLOOMFIELD HILLS MI 48013
HOF 99 KEEFE, TIMOTHY J.	D. APRIL 23, 1933 CAMBRIDGE, MASS.
HOF 23 KEELER, WILLIAM HENRY 'WEE WILLIE'	D. JANUARY 1, 1923 BROOKLYN, N. Y.
HOF 182 KELL, GEORGE CLYDE	BOX 158 - SWIFTON AR 72471
HOF 123 KELLEY, JOSEPH JAMES	D. AUGUST 14, 1943 BALTIMORE, MD.
HOF 138 KELLY, GEORGE LANGE	D. OCTOBER 13, 1984 BURLINGAME, CALIF.
HOF 36 KELLY, MICHAEL JOSEPH	D. NOVEMBER 8, 1894 BOSTON, MASS.
HOF 188 KILLEBREW, HARMON CLAYTON	BOX 626 - ONTARIO OR 97914
HOF 151 KINER, RALPH MCPHERRAN	48 271 SILVER SPUR TRAIL - PALM DESERT CA 92260
HOF 171 KLEIN, CHARLES HERBERT	D. MARCH 28, 1958 INDIANAPOLIS, IND.
HOF 67 KLEM, WILLIAM J.	D. SEPTEMBER 16, 1951 MIAMI, FLA.
HOF 131 KOUFAX, SANFORD 'SANDY'	1000 ELYSIAN PARK AVE - LOS ANGELES CA 90012
HOF 8 LAJOIE, NAPOLEON	D. FEBRUARY 7, 1959 DAYTONA BEACH, FLA.
HOF 28 LANDIS, KENESAW MOUNTAIN	D. NOVEMBER 25, 1944 CHICAGO, ILL.

HOF 155 LEMON, ROBERT GRANVILLE	1141 CLAIBORNE DR-LONG BEACH CA 90807
HOF 132 LEONARD, WALTER FENNER 'BUCK'	605 ATLANTIC AVE - ROCKY MOUNT NC 27801
HOF 156 LINDSTROM, FRED CHARLES	D. OCTOBER 4, 1981 CHICAGO, ILL.
HOF 160 LLOYD, JOHN HENRY	D. MARCH 19, 1964
HOF 195 LOMBARDI, ERNEST NATALI	D. SEPTEMBER 26, 1977 SANTA CRUZ, CALIF.
HOF 161 LOPEZ, ALFONSO RAMON	3601 BEACH DR - TAMPA FL 33609
HOF 77 LYONS, THEODORE AMAR	D. JULY 25, 1986 SULPHUR, LA.
HOF 9 MACK, CORNELIUS ALEXANDER 'CONNIE'	D. FEBRUARY 8, 1956 GERMANTOWN, PA.
HOF 165 MACPHAIL, LELAND STANFORD 'LARRY'	D. OCTOBER 1, 1975 MIAMI, FLA.
HOF 145 MANTLE, MICKEY CHARLES	42 CENTRAL PARK SOUTH - NEW YORK NY 10019

HOF100	MANUSH, HENRY EMMETT 'HEINIE'	D. MAY 12, 1971 SARASOTA, FLA.
HOF 72	MARANVILLE, WALTER JAMES VINCENT	D. JANUARY 5, 1954 NEW YORK, N. Y.
HOF183	MARICHAL, JUAN ANTONIO SANCHEZ	3178 NW 19TH ST - MIAMI FL 33125
HOF124	MARQUARD, RICHARD WILLIAM 'RUBE'	D. JUNE 1, 1980 BALTIMORE, MD.
HOF166	MATHEWS, EDWIN LEE	13744 RECUERDO DR - DEL MAR CA 92014
HOF 3	MATHEWSON, CHRISTOPHER	D. OCTOBER 7, 1925 SARANAC LAKE, N. Y.
HOF168	MAYS, WILLIE HOWARD	51 MT VERNON LN - ATHERTON CA 94025
HOF 83	MCCARTHY, JOSEPH VINCENT	D. JANUARY 13, 1978 BUFFALO, N. Y.
HOF 44	MCCARTHY, THOMAS FRANCIS MICHAEL	D. AUGUST 5, 1922 BOSTON, MASS.
HOF196	MCCOVEY, WILLIE LEE	P.O. BOX 620342 - WOODSIDE CA 94062
HOF 45	MCGINNITY, JOSEPH JEROME	D. NOVEMBER 14, 1929 BROOKLYN, N. Y.
HOF 10	MCGRAW, JOHN JOSEPH	D. FEBRUARY 25, 1934 NEW ROCHELLE, N. Y.
HOF 88	MCKECHNIE, WILLIAM BOYD	D. OCTOBER 29, 1965 BRADENTON, FLA.
HOF110	MEDWICK, JOSEPH MICHAEL	D. MARCH 21, 1975 ST. PETERSBURG, FLA.
HOF176	MIZE, JOHN ROBERT	BOX 112 - DEMOREST GA 30535
HOF205	MORGAN, JOSEPH LEONARD	5588 FERNHOFF ROAD - OAKLAND CA 94619
HOF114	MUSIAL, STANLEY FRANK	85 TRENT DR - LADUE MO 63124
HOF 58	NICHOLS, CHARLES AUGUSTUS 'KID'	D. APRIL 11, 1953 KANSAS CITY, MO.
HOF 37	OROURKE, JAMES HENRY	D. JANUARY 8, 1919 BRIDGEPORT, CONN.
HOF 60	OTT, MELVIN THOMAS	D. NOVEMBER 21, 1958 NEW ORLEANS, LA.
HOF125	PAIGE, LEROY 'SATCHEL'	D. JUNE 8, 1982 KANSAS CITY, MO.

HOF206	PALMER, JAMES ALVIN	BOX 145 - BROOKLANDVILLE MD 21022
HOF 54	PENNOCK, HERBERT JEFFERIS	D. JANUARY 30, 1948 NEW YORK, N. Y.
HOF 46	PLANK, EDWARD STEWART	D. FEBRUARY 24, 1926 GETTYSBURG, PA.
HOF 24	RADBOURN, CHARLES 'HOSS'	D. FEBRUARY 5, 1897 BLOOMINGTON, ILL.
HOF189	REESE, HAROLD HENRY 'PEE WEE'	3211 BEALS BRANCH RD - LOUISVILLE KY 40206
HOF 93	RICE, EDGAR CHARLES 'SAM'	D. OCTOBER 13, 1974 ROSSMOR, MD.
HOF105	RICKEY, WESLEY BRANCH	D. DECEMBER 9, 1965 COLUMBIA, MO.
HOF 94	RIXEY, EPPA	D. FEBRUARY 28, 1963 TERRACE PARK, O.
HOF157	ROBERTS, ROBIN EVAN	504 TERRACE HILL DR - TEMPLE TERRACE FL 33617
HOF184	ROBINSON, BROOKS CALBERT	1506 SHERBROOK RD - LUTHERVILLE MD 21093
HOF180	ROBINSON, FRANK	15557 AQUA VERDE DR - LOS ANGELES CA 90077
HOF 89	ROBINSON, JACK ROOSEVELT	D. OCTOBER 24, 1972 STAMFORD, CONN.
HOF 38	ROBINSON, WILBERT	D. AUGUST 8, 1934 ATLANTA, GA.
HOF 90	ROUSH, EDD J	D. MARCH 21, 1988 BRADENTON, FLA.
HOF106	RUFFING, CHARLES HERBERT 'RED'	D. FEBRUARY 17, 1986 MAYFIELD HEIGHTS, O.
HOF162	RUSIE, AMOS WILSON	D. DECEMBER 6, 1942 SEATTLE, WASH.
HOF 4	RUTH, GEORGE HERMAN 'BABE'	D. AUGUST 16, 1948 NEW YORK, N. Y.
HOF 78	SCHALK, RAYMOND WILLIAM	D. MAY 19, 1970 CHICAGO, ILL.

HOF204	SCHOENDIENST, ALBERT FRED 'RED'	331 LADUE WOODS COURT - CREVE COEUR MO 63141
HOF163	SEWELL, JOSEPH WHEELER	D. MARCH 6, 1990 MOBILE, ALA.
HOF 68	SIMMONS, ALOYSIUS HARRY	D. MAY 26, 1956 MILWAUKEE, WIS.
HOF 25	SISLER, GEORGE HAROLD	D. MARCH 26, 1973 ST. LOUIS, MO.
HOF191	SLAUGHTER, ENOS BRADSHER 'COUNTRY'	RURAL ROUTE 2 - ROXBORO NC 27573
HOF172	SNIDER, EDWIN DONALD 'DUKE'	3037 LAKEMONT DR - FALLBROOK CA 92028
HOF139	SPAHN, WARREN EDWARD	RR 2 - HARTSHORNE OK 74547
HOF 26	SPALDING, ALBERT GOODWILL	D. SEPTEMBER 9, 1915 SAN DIEGO, CALIF.
HOF 11	SPEAKER, TRISTRAM E.	D. DECEMBER 8, 1958 LAKE WHITNEY, TEX.
HOF200	STARGELL, WILVER DORNEL	113 ASHLEY PLACE - STONE MOUNTAIN GA 30083
HOF103	STENGEL, CHARLES DILLON 'CASEY'	D. SEPTEMBER 29, 1975 GLENDALE, CAL.

HOF 73	TERRY, WILLIAM HAROLD	D. JANUARY 9, 1989 JACKSONVILLE, FLA.
HOF146	THOMPSON, SAMUEL L.	D. NOVEMBER 7, 1922 DETROIT, MICH.
HOF 47	TINKER, JOSEPH BERT	D. JULY 27, 1948 ORLANDO, FLA.
HOF 55	TRAYNOR, HAROLD JOSEPH 'PIE'	D. MARCH 16, 1972 PITTSBURGH, PA.
HOF 79	VANCE, CLARENCE ARTHUR 'DAZZY'	D. FEBRUARY 16, 1961 HOMOSASSA SPRINGS, FLA.
HOF192	VAUGHAN, JOSEPH FLOYD 'ARKY'	D. AUGUST 30, 1952 EAGLEVILLE, CALIF.
HOF 48	WADDELL, GEORGE EDWARD 'RUBE'	D. APRIL 1, 1914 SAN ANTONIO, TEX.
HOF 5	WAGNER, JOHN PETER 'HONUS'	D. DECEMBER 6, 1955 CARNEGIE, PA.
HOF 69	WALLACE, RHODERICK JOHN 'BOBBY'	D. NOVEMBER 3, 1960 TORRANCE, CAL.
HOF 49	WALSH, EDWARD AUGUSTIN	D. MAY 26, 1959 POMPANO BEACH, FLA.
HOF107	WANER, LLOYD JAMES	D. JULY 22, 1982 OKLAHOMA CITY, OKLA.
HOF 62	WANER, PAUL GLEE	D. AUGUST 29, 1965 SARASOTA, FLA.
HOF101	WARD, JOHN MONTGOMERY	D. MARCH 4, 1925 AUGUSTA, GA.
HOF126	WEISS, GEORGE MARTIN	D. AUGUST 13, 1972 GREENWICH, CONN.
HOF140	WELCH, MICHAEL FRANCIS 'MICKEY'	D. JULY 30, 1941 NASHUA, N. H.
HOF 84	WHEAT, ZACHARY DAVIS	D. MARCH 11, 1972 SEDALIA, MO.
HOF193	WILHELM, JAMES HOYT 'HOYT'	3102 NORTH HIMES AVENUE - TAMPA FL 33607
HOF198	WILLIAMS, BILLY LEO	3227 RANDOLPH AVENUE - OAKLAND CA 94602
HOF104	WILLIAMS, THEODORE SAMUEL	P.O. BOX 5127 - CLEARWATER FL 34618
HOF169	WILSON, LEWIS ROBERT 'HACK'	D. NOVEMBER 23, 1948 BALTIMORE, MD.
HOF 12	WRIGHT, GEORGE	D. AUGUST 31, 1937 BOSTON, MASS.
HOF 70	WRIGHT, WILLIAM HENRY 'HARRY'	D. OCTOBER 3, 1895 ATLANTIC CITY, N. J.
HOF133	WYNN, EARLY	P.O. BOX 218 - NOKOMIS FL 34274
HOF202	YASTRZEMSKI, CARL MICHAEL	4621 SOUTH OCEAN BLVD - HIGHLAND BEACH FL 33431
HOF173	YAWKEY, THOMAS AUSTIN	D. JULY 9, 1976 BOSTON, MASS.
HOF 13	YOUNG, DENTON TRUE	D. NOVEMBER 4, 1955 NEWCOMERSTOWN, O.
HOF134	YOUNGS, ROSS MIDDLEBROOK	D. OCTOBER 22, 1927 SAN ANTONIO, TEX.

Billy Williams

Yours very truly,
Geo Wright

Harry Wright
#39 Eliot Street
Boston, Mass.

PLAYERS DEBUTING FROM 1910 TO 1989

54-	1 AARON, HENRY LOUIS	1611 ADAMS DR SW - ATLANTA GA 30311
62-	1 AARON, TOMMIE LEE	D. AUGUST 16, 1984 ATLANTA, GA.
77-	1 AASE, DONALD WILLIAM	5055 VIA RICARDO - YORBA LINDA CA 92686
89-	1 ABBOTT, JAMES ANTHONY	OLD ADD: 923 MAXINE STREET - FLINT MI 48503
10-	1 ABBOTT, ODY CLEON	D. APRIL 13, 1933 WASHINGTON, D. C.
73-	1 ABBOTT, WILLIAM GLENN	4413 DAWSON - NORTH LITTLE ROCK AR 72116
50-	1 ABER, ALBERT JULIUS	7009 MEADOWBROOK AVE - CLEVELAND OH 44144
52-	1 ABERNATHIE, WILLIAM EDWARD	3395 SEPULVEDA - SAN BERNARDINO CA 92404
42-	1 ABERNATHY, TALMADGE LAFAYETTE 'TED'	225 SPRING STREET - THOMASVILLE NC 27360
55-	1 ABERNATHY, THEODORE WADE	2211 ARMSTRONG PK RD - GASTONIA NC 28052
46-	1 ABERNATHY, VIRGIL WOODROW 'WOODY'	507 SOUTH KENTUCKY AVE - CHESNEE SC 29323
47-	1 ABERSON, CLIFFORD ALEXANDER	D. JUNE 23, 1973 VALLEJO, CAL.
87-	1 ABNER, SHAWN WESLEY	OLD ADD: 105 BEECHWOOD DRIVE - MECHANICSBURG PA 17055
49-	1 ABRAMS, CALVIN ROSS	BOX 974 - AMAGANSETT NY 11930
23-	1 ABRAMS, GEORGE ALLEN	D. DECEMBER 5, 1986 CLEARWATER, FLA.
85-	1 ABREGO, JOHNNY RAY	563 WASATCH DRIVE - FREMONT CA 94536
42-	2 ABREU, JOSEPH LAWRENCE	26090 REGAL AVE - HAYWARD CA 94544
83-	1 ACKER, JAMES JUSTIN	BOX AA - FREER TX 78357
56-	1 ACKER, THOMAS JAMES	314 EVERS ST - WYCKOFF NJ 07481
63-	1 ACKLEY, FLORIAN FREDERICK 'FRITZ'	417 WEST 5TH ST - HAYWARD WI 54843
13-	1 ACOSTA, BALMADERO PEDRO 'CY'	D. NOVEMBER 17, 1963 MIAMI, FLA.
72-	1 ACOSTA, CECILIO 'CY'	AUG RAMIREZ 1420,COL GAB LEYVA-CULIACAN SINALOA MEX.
70-	1 ACOSTA, EDUARDO ELIXBET	22822 BOLTANA - MISSION VIEJO CA 92675
20-	1 ACOSTA, JOSE	OLD ADD: VUENA VISTA - MARIANAO CUBA
31-	1 ADAIR, JAMES AUBREY	D. DECEMBER 9, 1982 DALLAS, TEXAS
58-	1 ADAIR, KENNETH JERRY	D. MAY 31, 1987 TULSA, OKLA.
70-	2 ADAIR, MARION DANNE 'BILL'	1535 PINELLAS POINT S-ST PETERSBURG FL 33705
41-	1 ADAMS, ACE TOWNSEND	1005 SUMMETT DR-ALBANY GA 31705
46-	2 ADAMS, CHARLES DWIGHT 'RED'	1780 LAMBETH LANE - CONCORD CA 94518
14-	1 ADAMS, DANIEL LESLIE	D. OCTOBER 6, 1964 ST. LOUIS, MO.
22-	1 ADAMS, EARL JOHN 'SPARKY'	D. FEBRUARY 24, 1989 POTTVILLE, PA.
39-	1 ADAMS, ELVIN CLARK 'BUSTER'	74390 ALLESANDRO #5 - PALM DESERT CA 92260
75-	1 ADAMS, GLENN CHARLES	RR 1 - SEDAN NM 88436
69-	1 ADAMS, HAROLD DOUGLAS 'DOUG'	1129 HARMONY CIR NE - JANESVILLE WI 53545
48-	1 ADAMS, HERBERT LOREN	903 SOUTH WILLISTON - WHEATON IL 60187
12-	1 ADAMS, JAMES IRVIN 'WILLIE'	D. JUNE 18, 1937 ALBANY, N.Y.
10-	2 ADAMS, JOHN BERTRAM	D. JUNE 24, 1940 LOS ANGELES, CALIF.
14-	2 ADAMS, KARL TUTWILER	D. SEPTEMBER 17, 1967 EVERETT, WASH.
47-	2 ADAMS, RICHARD LEROY	4650 DULIN ROAD #136 - FALLBROOK CA 92028
82-	1 ADAMS, RICKY LEE	10195 BOLTON - MONTCLAIR CA 91763
31-	2 ADAMS, ROBERT ANDREW	D. MARCH 6, 1970 JACKSONVILLE, FLA.
25-	1 ADAMS, ROBERT BURDETTE	357 WALTON ST - LEMOYNE PA 17043
46-	3 ADAMS, ROBERT HENRY	3828 PUEBLO WAY - SCOTTSDALE AZ 85251
77-	2 ADAMS, ROBERT MELVIN JR.	7653 DESOTO AVE - CANOGA PARK CA 91304
72-	2 ADAMS, ROBERT MICHAEL 'MIKE'	3828 PUEBLO WAY - SCOTTSDALE AZ 85251
23-	2 ADAMS, SPENCER DEWEY	D. NOVEMBER 25, 1970 FT. LAUDERDALE, FLA.
67-	1 ADAMSON, JOHN MICHAEL 'MIKE'	4408 SKY GLEN CT - MOORPARK CA 93021
50-	2 ADCOCK, JOSEPH WILBUR	BOX 385 - COUSHATTA LA 71019
50-	3 ADDIS, ROBERT GORDON	7466 HOLLYCROFT LN - MENTOR OH 44060
83-	2 ADDUCI, JAMES DAVID	10429 SOUTH LAMON - OAK LAWN IL 60453
39-	2 ADERHOLT, MORRIS WOODROW	D. MARCH 18, 1955 SARASOTA, FLA.
28-	1 ADKINS, GRADY EMMETT	D. MARCH 31, 1966 LITTLE ROCK, ARK.
42-	3 ADKINS, JOHN DEWEY	2627 WESTWOOD BLVD-LOS ANGELES CA 90064
42-	4 ADKINS, RICHARD EARL	D. SEPTEMBER 22, 1955 ELECTRA, TEX.
63-	2 ADLESH, DAVID GEORGE	9770 AVENIDA MONTEREY - CYPRESS CA 90630
87-	2 AFENIR, MICHAEL TROY	804 CHERRY COURT - SAN MARCOS CA 92069
62-	2 AGEE, TOMMIE LEE	OLD ADD: 9441 43RD AVE - EAST ELMHURST NY 11369
54-	2 AGGANIS, HARRY	D. JUNE 27, 1955 CAMBRIDGE, MASS.
12-	1 AGLER, JOSEPH ABRAM	D. APRIL 26, 1971 MASSILLON, O.
13-	2 AGNEW, SAMUEL LESTER	D. JULY 19, 1951 SONOMA, CALIF.
81-	1 AGOSTO, JUAN R	VIA LETICIA 4LS8 - CAROLINA PR 00630
80-	1 AGUAYO, LUIS (MURIEL)	BOX 9036, SABANA BRANCH - VEGA BAJA PR 00764
85-	2 AGUILERA, RICHARD WARREN	%FRATTO,6506 HALM AVENUE - LOS ANGELES CA 90056
55-	2 AGUIRRE, HENRY JOHN	31101 SUNSET DR - FRANKLIN MI 48025
77-	3 AIKENS, WILLIE MAYS	P.O. BOX 1141 - SENECA SC 29678
79-	1 AINGE, DANIEL RAY	10 ORDWAY ROAD - WELLESLEY MA 02181
10-	3 AINSMITH, EDWARD WILBUR	D. SEPTEMBER 6, 1981 FORT LAUDERDALE, FLA.
11-	1 AITCHISON, RALEIGH LEONIDAS	D. SEPTEMBER 26, 1958 COLUMBUS, KAN.
12-	3 AITON, GEORGE WILSON 'BILL'	D. AUGUST 16, 1976 VAN NUYS, CALIF.
64-	1 AKER, JACK DELANE	38 PUCADILLY ROAD - GREAT NECK NY 11023
86-	1 AKERFELDS, DARREL WAYNE	17336 EAST RICE CIRCLE #F - AURORA CO 80015
12-	4 AKERS, ALBERT EARL 'JERRY'	D. MAY 15, 1979 BAY PINES, FLA.
29-	1 AKERS, THOMAS ERNEST 'BILL'	D. APRIL 13, 1962 CHATTANOOGA, TENN.
88-	1 ALBA, GIBSON ROBERTO	PROYECTO 7 NO. 5, JARD. METRO. - SANTIAGO DOM. REP.
58-	2 ALBANESE, JOSEPH PETER	54 LONGFELLOW DR - COLONIA NJ 07067
78-	1 ALBERTS, FRANCIS BURT. 'BUTCH'	3063 AMBERLEA LN - BALDWINSVILLE NY 13027
10-	4 ALBERTS, FREDERICK JOSEPH 'CY'	D. AUGUST 27, 1917 FORT WAYNE, IND.
41-	2 ALBOSTA, EDWARD JOHN	5360 FORT RD-SAGINAW MI 48601
49-	2 ALBRECHT, EDWARD ARTHUR	D. 1979 CENTERVILLE, ILL.
47-	3 ALBRIGHT, JOHN HAROLD	5433 HEWLETT DR - SAN DIEGO CA 92115
73-	2 ALBURY, VICTOR	6205 ALCOT CT - TAMPA FL 33624
76-	1 ALCALA, SANTO	RAMON MOTA #18 - SAN PEDRO DE MACORIS DOM. REP.
67-	2 ALCARAZ, ANGEL LUIS	1968 ADD: BOX 423 - HUMACAO PR 00661
14-	3 ALCOCK, JOHN FORBES 'SCOTTY'	D. JANUARY 30, 1973 WOOSTER, O.
43-	1 ALDERSON, DALE LEONARD	D. FEBRUARY 12, 1982 GARDEN GROVE, CALIF.
86-	2 ALDRETE, MICHAEL PETER	231 VIA DEL PINAR - MONTEREY CA 93940
87-	3 ALDRICH, JAY ROBERT	OLD ADD: 168 SALISBURY ROAD - WAYNE NJ 07470
17-	1 ALDRIDGE, VICTOR EDDINGTON	D. APRIL 17, 1973 TERRE HAUTE, IND.
41-	3 ALENO, CHARLES	601 MARION CT-DELAND FL 32720
29-	2 ALEXANDER, DAVID DALE	D. MARCH 2, 1979 GREENEVILLE, TENN.
71-	1 ALEXANDER, DOYLE LAFAYETTE	6412 SADDLE RIDGE ROAD - ARLINGTON TX 76016
75-	2 ALEXANDER, GARY WAYNE	5701 BOWCROFT ST - LOS ANGELES CA 90016
11-	2 ALEXANDER, GROVER CLEVELAND	D. NOVEMBER 4, 1950 ST. PAUL, NEB.
37-	1 ALEXANDER, HUGH	49 CITRUS DRIVE - PALM HARBOR FL 34684
73-	3 ALEXANDER, MATTHEW	2419 STONEWALL - SHREVEPORT LA 71103
55-	3 ALEXANDER, ROBERT SOMERVILLE	468 CANCAN COURT - FALLBROOK CA 92028
12-	5 ALEXANDER, WALTER ERNEST	D. DECEMBER 29, 1978 FORT WORTH, TEXAS
88-	1 ALICEA, LUIS RENE	5767 CYPRESS CIRCLE - TALLAHASSEE FL 32303

86-	3	ALLANSON, ANDREW NEAL	P.O. BOX 91718 - CLEVELAND OH 44101
79-	2	ALLARD, BRIAN MARSHALL	110 RICHARD ST - HENRY IL 61537
14-	4	ALLEN, ARTEMUS WARD 'NICK'	D. OCTOBER 16, 1939 HINES, ILL.
62-	3	ALLEN, BERNARD KEITH	9120 MOHICAN TRAIL - NEGLEY OH 44441
26-	1	ALLEN, ETHAN NATHAN	STRATFORD HILL APTS #40C-CHAPEL HIL NC 27514
10-	5	ALLEN, FLETCHER MANSON 'SLEP'	D. OCTOBER 16, 1959 LUBBOCK, TEX.
12-	6	ALLEN, FRANK LEON	D. JULY 30, 1933 GAINESVILLE, ALA.
66-	1	ALLEN, HAROLD ANDREW 'HANK'	15 STATON DR - UPPER MARLBORO MD 20870
19-	1	ALLEN, HORACE TANNER 'PUG'	D. JULY 5, 1981 CANTON, N. C.
83-	3	ALLEN, JAMES BRADLEY 'JAMIE'	1203 FOLSOM AVE - YAKIMA WA 98902
14-	5	ALLEN, JOHN MARSHALL	D. SEPTEMBER 24, 1967 HAGERSTOWN, MD.
32-	1	ALLEN, JOHN THOMAS	D. MARCH 29, 1959 ST. PETERSBURG, FLA.
80-	2	ALLEN, KIM BRYANT	1651 N. RIVERSIDE AVE #614 - RIALTO CA 92376
69-	2	ALLEN, LLOYD CECIL	OLD ADD: 1678 MARGUERITE AVE - CORONA DEL MAR CA 92625
79-	3	ALLEN, NEIL PATRICK	1402 ARMSTRONG - KANSAS CITY KS 66102
63-	3	ALLEN, RICHARD ANTHONY	P.O. BOX 204 - SELLERSVILLE PA 18960
19-	2	ALLEN, ROBERT	B. 1896
37-	2	ALLEN, ROBERT EARL	1888 WEST AMES CIR-CHESAPEAKE VA 23321
61-	1	ALLEN, ROBERT GRAY	515 WOODLAWN - HENDERSON TX 75652
83-	4	ALLEN, RODERICK BERNET	721 WEST CHAPARRAL DRIVE - MURRAY UT 84123
72-	3	ALLEN, RONALD FREDRICK	917 WINONA DR - YOUNGSTOWN OH 44511
79-	4	ALLENSON, GARY MARTIN	2037 SAN MARCOS #329 - WINTER HAVEN FL 33880
63-	4	ALLEY, LEONARD EUGENE 'GENE'	10236 STEUBEN DRIVE - GLEN ALLEN VA 23060
54-	3	ALLIE, GAIR ROOSEVELT	1802 TOWN OAK DRIVE - SAN ANTONIO TX 78232
75-	3	ALLIETTA, ROBERT GEORGE	25 ROBINSON RD - FALMOUTH MA 02540
11-	1	ALLISON, MACK PENDLETON	D. MARCH 13, 1964 ST. JOSEPH, MO.
13-	3	ALLISON, MILO HENRY	D. JUNE 18, 1957 KENOSHA, WIS.
58-	3	ALLISON, WILLIAM ROBERT 'BOB'	P.O. BOX 64268 - EAGAN MN 55164
89-	2	ALLRED, DALE LEBEAU 'BEAU'	SAFFORD AZ 85546
33-	1	ALMADA, MELO BALDOMERO	D. AUGUST 13, 1988 HERMOSILLO, SONORA MEXICO
11-	4	ALMEIDA, RAFAEL D.	D. MARCH, 1968 HAVANA, CUBA
74-	1	ALMON, WILLIAM FRANCIS	88 CLAFLIN COURT - WARWICK RI 02886
50-	4	ALOMA, LUIS BARBA	8414 NORTH MARMORA - MORTON GROVE IL 60053
88-	3	ALOMAR, ROBERTO	URB. MONSERRATE B-56, BOX 367 - SALINAS PR 00751
64-	2	ALOMAR, SANTOS CONDES 'SANDY'	P.O. BOX 367 - SALINAS PR 00751
88-	4	ALOMAR, SANTOS JR.	URB. MONSERRATE B-56, BOX 367 - SALINAS PR 00751
58-	4	ALOU, FELIPE ROJAS	BOX 1287 - SANTO DOMINGO DOMINICAN REP.
63-	5	ALOU, JESUS MARIA	APARTADO POSTAL 539/2 LAFARIA - SANTO DOMINGO DOM REP.
60-	1	ALOU, MATEO ROJAS	APARTADO POSTAL 30063 - SANTO DOMINGO DOMINICAN REP.
54-	4	ALSTON, THOMAS EDISON	1A LAKESPRING COURT - GREENSBORO NC 27405
36-	1	ALSTON, WALTER EMMONS 'SMOKEY'	D. OCTOBER 1, 1984 OXFORD, O.
77-	4	ALSTON, WENDELL 'DEL'	17 LAMBERT RD - WHITE PLAINS NY 10605
82-	2	ALTAMARINO, PORFIRIO	B. MAY 17, 1952 ESTELI, NICARAGUA
20-	2	ALTEN, ERNEST MATTHIAS	D. SEPTEMBER 9, 1981 NAPA, CALIF.
16-	1	ALTENBURG, JESSE HOWARD	D. MARCH 12, 1973 LANSING, MICH.
59-	1	ALTMAN, GEORGE LEE	3601 BRIAR LANE - HAZEL CREST IL 60429
55-	4	ALTOBELLI, JOSEPH	54 GRECIAN GARDENS DRIVE #B - ROCHESTER NY 14626
58-	5	ALUSIK, GEORGE JOSEPH	581 GARDEN AVE - WOODRIDGE NJ 07095
68-	1	ALVARADO, LUIS CESAR	BOX 853 - LAJAS PR 00667
89-	3	ALVAREZ, HOUSTON	CALLE 868 CON AV 3A #868 20 - MARACAIBO VENEZUELA S.A.
73-	4	ALVAREZ, JESUS ORLANDO	CUMMUNIDAD DOLORES 37 - RIO GRANDE PR 00745
81-	2	ALVAREZ, JOSE LINO	2830 SW 120TH ROAD - MIAMI FL 33175
58-	6	ALVAREZ, OSWALDO GONZALES 'OSSIE'	SANTUARIO 3137,COL. CHAPALITA-GUADALAJARA JALISCO MEX.
60-	2	ALVAREZ, ROGELIO	5010 NW 183RD ST - CAROL CITY FL 33055
62-	4	ALVIS, ROY MAXWELL 'MAX'	806 HUNTERWOOD DR - JASPER TX 75951
65-	1	ALYEA, BRANT RYERSON	P.O. BOX 25 - COLUMBUS NC 28722
54-	5	AMALFITANO, JOHN JOSEPH 'JOE'	3432 PECK AVE #202 - SAN PEDRO CA 90731
58-	7	AMARO, RUBEN	2333 BRICKELL AVE #616 - MIAMI FL 33129
37-	3	AMBLER, WAYNE HARPER	305 TOURNAMENT RD - PONTE VEDRA BEACH FL 32082
84-	1	AMELUNG, EDWARD ALLEN	44 CANDLEWOOD WAY - BUENA PARK CA 90621
55-	5	AMOR, VINCENTE ALVAREZ	3905 WEST 8TH COURT - HIALEAH FL 33012
52-	2	AMOROS, EDMUNDO ISASI 'SANDY'	3712 WEST CASS STREET #14 - TAMPA FL 33609
15-	1	ANCKER, WALTER	D. FEBRUARY 13, 1954 ENGLEWOOD, N.J.
75-	4	ANDERSEN, LARRY EUGENE	17016 NE 2ND PL - BELLEVUE WA 98004
41-	4	ANDERSON, ALFRED WALTON	D. JUNE 23, 1985 ALBANY, GA.
48-	2	ANDERSON, ANDY HOLM	D. JULY 18, 1982 SEATTLE, WASH.
37-	4	ANDERSON, ARNOLD REVOLA 'RED'	D. AUGUST 7, 1972 SIOUX CITY, IA.
88-	5	ANDERSON, BRADY KEVIN	17736 ST. ANDREWS DRIVE - POWAY CA 92064
83-	5	ANDERSON, DAVID CARTER	5044 VIA DONALDO - YORBA LINDA CA 92686
71-	2	ANDERSON, DWAIN CLEAVEN	1807 FALLBROOK DRIVE - DANVILLE CA 94526
46-	4	ANDERSON, FERRELL JACK 'ANDY'	D. MARCH 12, 1978 JOPLIN, MO.
14-	6	ANDERSON, GEORGE ANDREW JENDRUS	D. MAY 28, 1962 CLEVELAND, O.
59-	2	ANDERSON, GEORGE LEE 'SPARKY'	P.O.BOX 6415 - THOUSAND OAKS CA 91360
32-	2	ANDERSON, HAROLD	D. MAY 1, 1974 ST. LOUIS, MO.
57-	1	ANDERSON, HARRY WALTER	4823 KENNETT PIKE - GREENVILLE DE 19807
78-	2	ANDERSON, JAMES LEA	16434 HALSEY STREET - GRANADA HILLS CA 91344
58-	8	ANDERSON, JOHN CHARLES	OLD ADD: BOX 49 - BROWNING MT 59417
82-	3	ANDERSON, KARL ADAM 'BUD'	196 WEST CYPRUS LANE - WESTBURY NY 11590
89-	4	ANDERSON, KENT MCKAY	RURAL ROUTE 1 BOX 380 - TIMMONSVILLE SC 29161
74-	2	ANDERSON, LAWRENCE DENNIS	378 CASTAIC - SHELL BEACH CA 93449
71-	3	ANDERSON, MICHAEL ALLEN	RR ONE - TIMMONSVILLE SC 29161
61-	2	ANDERSON, NORMAN CRAIG	RR 7, 6 WILLOWBROOK DR EAST - BETHLEHEM PA 18015
86-	5	ANDERSON, RICHARD ARLEN	3818 100TH STREET SE - EVERETT WA 98204
79-	5	ANDERSON, RICHARD LEE	D. JUNE 23, 1989 WILMINGTON, CALIF.
86-	4	ANDERSON, RICHARD LEE	2015 RAINBOW DRIVE NE - LANCASTER OH 43130
57-	2	ANDERSON, ROBERT CARL	4209 EAST 104TH - TULSA OK 74137
87-	4	ANDERSON, SCOTT RICHARD	605 ELDORO DRIVE - ARLINGTON TX 76006
17-	2	ANDERSON, WALTER CARL	1811 MORNINGSIDE DR SE - GRAND RAPIDS MI 49506
25-	2	ANDERSON, WILLIAM EDWARD	D. MARCH 13, 1983 MEDFORD, MASS.
10-	6	ANDERSON, WINGO CHARLIE	D. DECEMBER 19, 1950 FORT WORTH, TEX.
55-	6	ANDRE, JOHN EDWARD	D. NOVEMBER 25, 1976 CENTERVILLE, MASS.
46-	5	ANDRES, ERNEST HENRY	5714 GARDEN LAKES DRIVE - BRADENTON FL 34203
75-	5	ANDREW, KIM DARRELL	10052 DENSMORE AVE - SEPULVEDA CA 91343
25-	3	ANDREWS, ELBERT DEVORE	D. NOVEMBER 25, 1979 GREENWOOD, S. C.
76-	2	ANDREWS, FRED	8239 SOUTH KINGSTON - CHICAGO IL 60617
47-	4	ANDREWS, HERBERT CARL 'HUB'	2305 2ND ST - DODGE CITY KS 67801
31-	3	ANDREWS, IVY PAUL	D. NOVEMBER 23, 1970 DORA, ALA.
73-	5	ANDREWS, JOHN RICHARD	9292 GORDON AVE - LAHABRA CA 90631

ORIGINAL PAINTING OF JOCKO CONLAN ART POST CARD

66-	2	ANDREWS, MICHAEL JAY	29 PAUL AVE - PEABODY MA 01960
37-	5	ANDREWS, NATHAN HARDY	RR 3 BOX 271 - KING NC 27021
75-	6	ANDREWS, ROBERT PATRICK	1280 MOUNTBATTEN CT - CONCORD CA 94518
39-	3	ANDREWS, STANLEY JOSEPH	3840 IRONWOOD LN #403 - BRADENTON FL 33505
31-	4	ANDRUS, WILLIAM MORGAN	D. MARCH 12, 1982 WASHINGTON, D. C.
76-	3	ANDUJAR, JOAQUIN	400 RANDAL WAY #106 - SPRING TX 77388
72-	4	ANGELINI, NORMAN STANLEY	16196 EAST BAILS PL - AURORA CO 80012
29-	3	ANGLEY, THOMAS SAMUEL	D. OCTOBER 26, 1952 WICHITA, KAN.
36-	2	ANKENMAN, FRED NORMAN 'PAT'	D. JANUARY 13, 1989 HOUSTON, TEXAS
89-	5	ANTHONY, ERIC TODD	OLD ADD: HOUSTON TX
44-	1	ANTOLICK, JOSEPH	723 2ND ST - CATASAUQUA PA 18032
48-	3	ANTONELLI, JOHN AUGUST	12 WOODBURY PLACE - ROCHESTER NY 14618
44-	2	ANTONELLI, JOHN LAWRENCE	D. APRIL 18, 1990 MEMPHIS, TENN.
53-	1	ANTONELLO, WILLIAM JAMES	4054 VALENTINE CT - ST PAUL MN 55112
56-	2	APARICIO, LUIS ERNEST	CALLE 67 #26-82 - MARACAIBO VENEZUELA S.A.
73-	6	APODACA, ROBERT JOHN	BOX 7845 - COLUMBIA SC 29202
80-	3	APONTE, LUIS EDUARDO	RES LAS GIRASOLES #17A,ST ELENA-BARQUISIMETO LARA VENEZ
89-	6	APPIER, ROBERT KEVIN 'KEVIN'	OLD ADD: LANCASTER CA 93534
15-	2	APPLETON, EDWARD SAMUEL	D. JANUARY 27, 1932 ARLINGTON, TEX.
27-	1	APPLETON, PETER WILLIAM	D. JANUARY 18, 1974 TRENTON, N.J.
30-	1	APPLING, LUCIUS BENJAMIN 'LUKE'	RR 7, BRAGG RD - CUMMINGS GA 30130
86-	6	AQUINO, LUIS ANTONIO	30 S.O. 1506 CAPARRA TERRACE - RIO PIEDRAS PR 00921
14-	7	ARAGON, ANGEL VALDES SR. 'JACK'	D. JANUARY 24, 1952 NEW YORK, N.Y.
41-	5	ARAGON, ANGEL VALDES JR. 'JACK'	D. APRIL 4, 1988 CLEARWATER, FLA.
23-	3	ARCHDEACON, MAURICE BRUCE	D. SEPTEMBER 5, 1954 ST. LOUIS, MO.
36-	3	ARCHER, FREDERICK MARVIN	D. OCTOBER 31, 1981 CHARLOTTE, N. C.
61-	3	ARCHER, JAMES WILLIAM	1414 OLEANDER DR - TARPON SPRINGS FL 33589
38-	1	ARCHIE, GEORGE ALBERT	820 MARQUETTE DRIVE - NASHVILLE TN 37205
68-	2	ARCIA, JOSE RAIMUNDO	7325 NW 3RD ST - MIAMI FL 33125
61-	4	ARDELL, DANIEL MIERS	1966 PORT CLARIDGE - NEWPORT BEACH CA 92660
47-	5	ARDIZOIA, RINALDO JOSEPH 'RUGGER'	130 SANTA ROSA AVE - SAN FRANCISCO CA 94112
48-	4	ARFT, HENRY IRVIN	109 SUNNYSIDE LANE - BALLWIN MO 63021
59-	3	ARIAS, RODOLFO MARTINEZ 'RUDY'	3911 NW 11TH ST - MIAMI FL 33126
31-	5	ARLETT, RUSSELL LORIS 'BUZZ'	D. MAY 16, 1964 MINNEAPOLIS, MINN.
65-	2	ARLICH, DONALD LOUIS	7877 SOUTH 73RD ST - COTTAGE GROVE MN 55016
69-	3	ARLIN, STEPHEN RALPH	6338 CAMINO CORTO - SAN DIEGO CA 92120
76-	4	ARMAS, ANTONIO RAFAEL	LOS MERCEDES #37,P.PIRITU EDO. - ANZOATEQUI VENEZ
73-	7	ARMBRISTER, EDISON ROSANDER	MCQUAY ST, BOX 2003 - NASSAU BAHAMAS W.I.
34-	1	ARMBRUST, ORVILLE MARTIN	D. OCTOBER 2, 1967 MOBILE, ALA.
46-	6	ARMSTRONG, GEORGE NOBLE	16 FRANKLIN ST - EAST ORANGE NJ 07017
11-	5	ARMSTRONG, HOWARD ELMER	D. MARCH 8, 1926 CANISTEO, N.Y.
88-	6	ARMSTRONG, JACK WILLIAM	711 HATTON COURT - NEPTUNE NJ 07753
80-	4	ARMSTRONG, MICHAEL DENNIS	BOX 846 - HALIFAX VA 24558
89-	7	ARNDT, LARRY WAYNE	505 WEST SMITH STREET - GIBSONBURG OH 43431
71-	4	ARNOLD, CHRISTOPHER PAUL	2219 EL CAPITAN - ARCADIA CA 91006
88-	7	ARNOLD, SCOTT GENTRY	2936 RUNNYMEADE WAY - LEXINGTON KY 40503
86-	7	ARNOLD, TONY DALE	1224 ELBY - IRVING TX 75061
36-	4	ARNOVICH, MORRIS	D. JULY 20, 1959 SUPERIOR, WIS.
86-	8	ARNSBERG, BRADLEY JEFF	2450 HILLCREST ROAD - MEDFORD OR 97504
43-	2	ARNTZEN, ORIE EDGAR	D. JANUARY 28, 1970 CEDAR RAPIDS, IA.
61-	5	ARRIGO, GERALD WILLIAM	3740 REDTHORNE DR - AMELIA OH 45102
75-	7	ARROYO, FERNANDO	4917 FIRST PARKWAY - SACRAMENTO CA 95823
55-	7	ARROYO, LUIS ENRIQUE	BOX 354 - PENUELAS PR 00724
71-	5	ARROYO, RUDOLPH	828 SIERRA VISTA - MOUNTAIN VIEW CA 94040
86-	9	ASADOOR, RANDALL CARL	1459 WEST MESA - FRESNO CA 93711
38-	2	ASBELL, JAMES MARION	D. JULY 6, 1967 SAN MATEO, CAL.
28-	2	ASBJORNSON, ROBERT ANTHONY	D. JANUARY 21, 1970 WILLIAMSPORT, PA.
25-	4	ASH, KENNETH LOWTHER	D. NOVEMBER 15, 1979 CLARKSBURG, W. VA.
48-	5	ASHBURN, RICH	PHILLIES ANNOUNCER - ARDMORE PA 19003
73-	8	ASHBY, ALAN DEAN	3151 COUNTRY CLUB BLVD - SUGARLAND TX 77478
76-	5	ASHFORD, THOMAS STEVEN 'TUCKER'	502 MAPLE ST - COVINGTON TN 38019
57-	3	ASPROMONTE, KENNETH JOSEPH	% COORS, 10400 HARWIN - HOUSTON TX 77036
56-	3	ASPROMONTE, ROBERT THOMAS	251 SUGARBERRY CIR - HOUSTON TX 77024
76-	6	ASSELSTINE, BRIAN HANLY	1488 COUNTRY CT - SANTA YNEZ CA 93460
86-	10	ASSENMACHER, PAUL ANDRE	6404 BALFOUR - ALLEN PARK MI 48101
45-	1	ASTROTH, JOSEPH HENRY	151 SOUTH MOYER RD - CHALFONT PA 18914
83-	6	ATHERTON, KEITH ROWE	ROUTE 198 BLAKES - MATHEWS VA 23020
50-	5	ATKINS, JAMES CURTIS	RR 14 BOX 3635 - CULLMAN AL 35055
27-	2	ATKINSON, HUBERT BURLEY 'LEFTY'	D. FEBRUARY 12, 1961 CHICAGO, ILL.
76-	7	ATKINSON, WILLIAM CECIL GLENN	RR 2 - CHATHAM ONT. N7M 5S2 CAN.
26-	2	ATTREAU, RICHARD GILBERT	D. JULY 5, 1964 CHICAGO, ILL.
52-	3	ATWELL, MAURICE DAILEY 'TOBY'	BOX 686 - PURCELLVILLE VA 22132
36-	5	ATWOOD, WILLIAM FRANKLIN	3100 EL PASO-SNYDER TX 79549
71-	6	AUERBACH, FREDERICK STEVEN 'RICK'	4724 ABARGO ST - WOODLAND HILLS CA 91364
88-	8	AUGUST, DONALD GLENN	24442 DIAMANTE - MISSION VIEJO CA 92692
73-	9	AUGUSTINE, DAVID RALPH	OLD ADD: 14850 SW 280TH ST #25-HOMESTEAD FL
75-	8	AUGUSTINE, GERALD LEE	569 WEST 13442 HALES PK CT-HALES CORNER WI 53130
33-	2	AUKER, ELDEN LEROY	15 SAILFISH RD - VERO BEACH FL 32960
47-	6	AULDS, LEYCESTER DOYLE	YANCEY STAR RT BOX 16 - HONDO TX 78861
76-	8	AULT, DOUGLAS REAGAN	2990 BONAVENTURE CIRCLE - PALM HARBOR FL 33563
65-	3	AUST, DENNIS KAY	P.O. BOX 75559 - TAMPA FL 33675
70-	3	AUSTIN, RICK GERALD	BOX 347 - BROOKFIELD MO 64628
76-	9	AUTRY, ALBERT	1119 PRINCETON - MODESTO CA 95350
24-	1	AUTRY, MARTIN GORDON	D. JANUARY 26, 1950 SAVANNAH, GA.
56-	4	AVERILL, EARL DOUGLAS	1806 19TH DR NE - AUBURN WA 98002
29-	4	AVERILL, HOWARD EARL	D. AUGUST 16, 1983 EVERETT, WASH.
49-	3	AVILA, ROBERTO FRANCISCO GONZALEZ	NAVEGANTES FR-19 REFORMA - VERACRUZ VERACRUZ MEX.
77-	5	AVILES, RAMON ANTONIO	JARDINES DEMONICO,CALLE 2 C19 - MANATI PR 00701
50-	6	AVREA, JAMES EPHERIUM	927 GLENSTONE - DALLAS TX 75232
74-	3	AYALA, BENIGNO 'BENNIE'	BOX 814 - BAYAMON PR 00619
47-	7	AYERS, WILLIAM OSCAR	D. SEPTEMBER 24, 1980 NEWNAN, GA.
13-	4	AYERS, YANCEY WYATT 'DOC'	D. MAY 26, 1968 PULASKI, VA.
53-	2	AYLWARD, RICHARD JOHN	D. JUNE 11, 1983 SPRING VALLEY, CALIF.
60-	3	AZCUE, JOSE JOAQUIN	7609 WEST 115TH ST - OVERLAND PARK KS 66210
79-	6	BABCOCK, ROBERT ERNEST	4652 OLD PITTSBURG RD - NEW CASTLE PA 16101
52-	4	BABE, LOREN ROLLAND	D. FEBRUARY 14, 1984 OMAHA, NEB.
34-	2	BABICH, JOHN CHARLES	6111 ROSALIND AV - RICHMOND CA 94803
15-	3	BABINGTON, CHARLES PERCY	D. MARCH 22, 1957 PROVIDENCE, R.I.

```
81-  3 BABITT, MACK NEAL 'SHOOTY'        2530 MATHEWS ST - BERKELEY CA 94702
80-  5 BACKMAN, WALTER WAYNE             160 SE 39TH - HILLSBORO OR 97123
17-  3 BACON, EDGAR SUTER                D. OCTOBER 2, 1963 FRANKFORT, KY.
75-  9 BACSIK, MICHAEL JAMES             935 GREEN RIDGE DR - DUNCANVILLE TX 75137
53-  3 BACZEWSKI, FREDERICK JOHN         D. NOVEMBER 14, 1976 CULVER CITY, CALIF.
12-  7 BADER, LORE VERNE 'KING'          D. JUNE 2, 1973 LEROY, KAN.
29-  5 BADGRO, MORRIS HIRAM 'RED'        1010 EAST TEMPERANCE ST - KENT WA 98031
26-  3 BAECHT, EDWARD JOSEPH             D. AUGUST 15, 1957 QUARRY TWP., ILL.
77-  6 BAEZ, JOSE ANTONIO                40 BOORAEM AVENUE - JERSEY CITY NJ 07307
12-  8 BAGBY, JAMES CHARLES JACOB SR.    D. JULY 28, 1954 MARIETTA, GA.
38-  3 BAGBY, JAMES CHARLES JACOB JR.    D. SEPTEMBER 2, 1988 MARIETTA, GA.
23-  4 BAGWELL, WILLIAM MALLORY          D. OCTOBER 5, 1976 CHOUDRANT, LA.
66-  3 BAHNSEN, STANLEY RAYMOND          780 NE 76TH ST - BOCA RATON FL 33431
46-  7 BAHR, EDSON GARFIELD              OLD ADD: STAR RT 1 BOX 51 - ONALASKA WA
14-  8 BAICHLEY, GROVER CLEVELAND        D. JUNE 30, 1956 SAN JOSE, CALIF.
86- 11 BAILES, SCOTT ALAN                2101 KIRKWOOD - SPRINGFIELD MO 65804
19-  3 BAILEY, ABRAHAM LINCOLN           D. SEPTEMBER 27, 1939 JOLIET, ILL.
17-  4 BAILEY, ARTHUR EUGENE             D. NOVEMBER 14, 1973 HOUSTON, TEX.
16-  2 BAILEY, FRED MIDDLETON            D. AUGUST 16, 1972 HUNTINGTON, W. VA.
11-  6 BAILEY, HARRY LEWIS               D. OCTOBER 27, 1967 SEATTLE, WASH.
81-  4 BAILEY, HOWARD L.                 12596 LAKE SHORE DRIVE - GRAND HAVEN MI 49417
59-  4 BAILEY, JAMES HOPKINS             4375 STONEWALL TELL RD - COLLEGE PARK GA 30349
84-  2 BAILEY, JOHN MARK                 OLD ADD: 829 SOUTH LINK - SPRINGFIELD MO 65804
53-  4 BAILEY, LONAS EDGAR 'ED'          642 BROOME RD - KNOXVILLE TN 37919
62-  5 BAILEY, ROBERT SHERWOOD           7065 SEAWIND DR - LONG BEACH CA 90803
67-  3 BAILEY, STEVEN JOHN               1005 EUCLID AVE - LORAIN OH 44052
75- 10 BAILOR, ROBERT MICHAEL            15221 TRICIA LANE - LAMIRADA CA 90638
45-  2 BAIN, HERBERT LOREN               OLD ADD: 1926 ARTHUR ST NE - MINNEAPOLIS MN
80-  6 BAINES, HAROLD DOUGLAS            P.O. BOX 335 - SAINT MICHAELS MD 21663
76- 10 BAIR, CHARLES DOUGLAS 'DOUG'      6401 PHEASANT RD - LOVELAND OH 45140
17-  5 BAIRD, ALBERT WELLS               D. NOVEMBER 27, 1976 SHREVEPORT, LA.
15-  4 BAIRD, HOWARD DOUGLASS            D. JUNE 13, 1967 THOMASVILLE, GA.
62-  6 BAIRD, ROBERT ALLEN               D. APRIL 11, 1974 CHATTANOOGA, TENN.
64-  3 BAKENHASTER, DAVID LEE            3710 ROME CORNERS ROAD - GALENA OH 43021
38-  4 BAKER, ALBERT JONES               D. NOVEMBER 6, 1982 KENEDY, TEXAS
78-  3 BAKER, CHARLES JOSEPH             1521 CHALGROVE DR - CORONA CA 91720
82-  4 BAKER, DAVID GLENN                2216 HIGHWAY S23 - LACONA IA 50139
14-  9 BAKER, DELMAR DAVID               D. SEPTEMBER 11, 1973 SAN ANTONIO, TEX.
84-  3 BAKER, DOUGLAS LEE                2251 S23 HIGHWAY - LACONA IA 50139
53-  5 BAKER, EUGENE WALTER              2202 E. 48TH ST - DAVENPORT IA 52807
43-  3 BAKER, FLOYD WILSON               3033 IDLEWOOD AVE-YOUNGSTOWN OH 44511
69-  4 BAKER, FRANK                      383 GIRARD AVE - SOMERSET NJ 08873
70-  4 BAKER, FRANK WATTS                BOX 3066 - MERIDIAN MS 39301
12-  9 BAKER, HOWARD FRANCIS             D. JANUARY 16, 1964 BRIDGEPORT, CONN.
76- 11 BAKER, JACK EDWARD                4536 SWALLOW PL - BIRMINGHAM AL 35213
11-  7 BAKER, JESSE ORMAND               D. SEPTEMBER 26, 1972 TACOMA, WASH.
68-  3 BAKER, JOHNNIE B. 'DUSTY'         633 STONEGATE DRIVE SOUTH - SAN FRANCISCO CA 94080
19-  4 BAKER, MICHAEL MYRON 'JESSE'      D. JULY 29, 1976 WEST LOS ANGELES, CALIF.
27-  3 BAKER, NEAL VERNON                D. JANUARY 5, 1982 HOUSTON, TEX.
78-  4 BAKER, STEVEN BYRNE               27527 EASY ACRES DRIVE - EUGENE OR 97405
35-  1 BAKER, THOMAS CALVIN              2002 GOULD ST-FORT WORTH TX 76106
63-  6 BAKER, THOMAS HENRY               D. MARCH 9, 1980 PORT TOWNSEND, WASH.
11-  8 BAKER, TRACY LEE                  D. MARCH 14, 1975 PLACERVILLE, CAL.
40-  1 BAKER, WILLIAM PRESLEY            P.O. BOX 825 - FAIR BLUFF NC 28439
38-  5 BALAS, MITCHELL FRANCIS           CHAMBERLAIN ROAD - WESTFORD MA 01886
74-  4 BALAZ, JOHN LARRY                 2624 WORDEN STREET #184 - SAN DIEGO CA 92110
81-  5 BALBONI, STEPHEN CHARLES          126 WOOD GLEN LANE - LEES SUMMIT MO 64063
56-  5 BALCENA, ROBERT RUDOLPH           D. JANUARY 4, 1990 SAN PEDRO, CALIF.
61-  6 BALDSCHUN, JACK EDWARD            492 BADER ST - GREEN BAY WI 54302
66-  4 BALDWIN, DAVID GEORGE             4025 PULITZER PLACE #308 - SAN DIEGO CA 92122
53-  6 BALDWIN, FRANK DEWITT             6359 BEAVER PIKE - BEAVER OH 45613
27-  4 BALDWIN, HENRY CLAY               D. FEBRUARY 24, 1964 PHILADELPHIA, PA.
24-  2 BALDWIN, HOWARD EDWARD 'HARRY'    D. JANUARY 23, 1958 BALTIMORE, MD.
78-  5 BALDWIN, REGINALD CONRAD          763 LIEBOLD - DETROIT MI 48217
75- 11 BALDWIN, RICK ALAN                3713 WINDWOOD PLACE - MODESTO CA 95355
75- 12 BALDWIN, ROBERT HARVEY 'BILLY'    878 PACKARD DR - AKRON OH 44320
11-  9 BALENTI, MICHAEL RICHARD          D. AUGUST 4, 1955 ALTUS, OKLA.
66-  5 BALES, WESLEY OWEN 'LEE'          7223 AUGUSTINE - HOUSTON TX 77036
87-  5 BALLARD, JEFFREY SCOTT            4828 RIMROCK ROAD - BILLINGS MT 59102
28-  3 BALLENGER, PELHAM ASHBY           D. DECEMBER 8, 1948 GREENVILLE COUNTY, S. C.
82-  5 BALLER, JAY SCOT                  RR 1 BOX 296B,FREEMANSVILLE RD - READING PA 19607
71-  7 BALLINGER, MARK ALAN              %D.BALLINGER,.176 DALE - NEWBURY PARK CA 91320
25-  5 BALLOU, NOBLE WINFIELD 'WIN'      D. JANUARY 30, 1963 SAN FRANCISCO, CAL.
62-  7 BALSAMO, ANTHONY FRED             160-15 86TH ST - HOWARD BEACH NY 11414
51-  1 BAMBERGER, GEORGE IRVIN           455 N. BATH CLUB BLVD - NORTH REDINGTON BEACH FL 33708
48-  6 BAMBERGER, HAROLD EARL            RR 1 BOX 317 - BIRDSBORO PA 19508
15-  5 BANCROFT, DAVID JAMES             D. OCTOBER 9, 1972 SUPERIOR, WIS.
81-  6 BANDO, CHRISTOPHER MICHAEL        35640 BRUSHWOOD DR - SOLON OH 44139
66-  6 BANDO, SALVATORE LEONARD          104 WEST JUNIPER LN - MEQUON WI 53092
73- 10 BANE, EDWARD NORMAN               3129 EAST TARO LANE - PHOENIX AZ 85024
69-  5 BANEY, RICHARD LEE                1412 DAMON AVE - ANAHEIM CA 92802
47-  8 BANKHEAD, DANIEL ROBERT           D. MAY 2, 1976 HOUSTON, TEX.
86- 12 BANKHEAD, MICHAEL SCOTT           2020 GUM TREE ROAD - ASHEBORO NC 27203
53-  7 BANKS, ERNEST                     P.O. BOX 24302 - LOS ANGELES CA 90024
62-  8 BANKS, GEORGE EDWARD              D. MARCH 1, 1985 SPARTANBURG, S. C.
15-  6 BANKSTON, WILBORN EVERETT 'BILL'  D. FEBRUARY 26, 1970 GRIFFIN, GA.
74-  5 BANNISTER, ALAN                   455 SELVA LAKE CIRCLE - ATLANTIC BEACH FL 32233
77-  7 BANNISTER, FLOYD FRANKLIN         6701 EAST CABALLO DRIVE - PARADISE VALLEY AZ 85253
47-  9 BANTA, JOHN KAY                   3215 EAST 30TH AVE - HUTCHINSON KS 67502
14- 10 BARBARE, WALTER LAWRENCE          D. OCTOBER 28, 1965 GREENVILLE, S.C.
43-  4 BARBARY, DONALD ODELL 'RED'       402 WEST CURTIS - SIMPSONVILLE SC 29681
26-  4 BARBEE, DAVID MONROE              D. JULY 1, 1968 ALBEMARLE, N. C.
60-  4 BARBER, STEPHEN DAVID             3084 E. VAN BUSKIRK CIR - LAS VEGAS NV 89121
70-  5 BARBER, STEVEN LEE                1517 CUSHMAN DR - SIERRA VISTA AZ 85635
15-  7 BARBER, TYRUS TURNER              D. OCTOBER 20, 1968 MILAN, TENN.
66-  7 BARBIERI, JAMES PATRICK           13619 EAST 5TH AVE - SPOKANE WA 99216
57-  4 BARCLAY, CURTIS CORDELL           D. MARCH 27, 1985 MISSOULA, MONT.
72-  5 BARE, RAYMOND DOUGLAS             OLD ADD: 911 NORTH IVY ST - JENKS OK 74037
81-  7 BARFIELD, JESSE LEE               4208 CANTERWOOD DRIVE - HOUSTON TX 77068
```

89- 8	BARFIELD, JOHN DAVID	1009 SOUTH WOLFE - LITTLE ROCK AR 72202
22- 2	BARFOOT, CLYDE RAYMOND	D. MARCH 11, 1971 HIGHLAND PARK, CAL.
83- 7	BARGAR, GREG ROBERT	23005 KATHRYN AVENUE - TORRANCE CA 90505
76- 12	BARKER, LEONARD HAROLD	1339 BEECHWOOD HILLS CT NW - ATLANTA GA 30327
60- 5	BARKER, RAYMOND HAROLD	% GENERAL MOTORS - MARTINSBURG WV 25401
84- 4	BARKLEY, JEFFREY CARVER	264 THIRD AVE NE - HICKORY NC 28601
37- 6	BARKLEY, JOHN DUNCAN 'RED'	1200 LAWRENCE DR - WACO TX 76710
75- 13	BARLOW, MICHAEL ROSWELL	%SHEFTIC,4524 FRANCIS RD - CAZENOVIA NY 13035
53- 8	BARMES, BRUCE RAYMOND	509 MCDONALD AVE - CHARLOTTE NC 28203
37- 7	BARNA, HERBERT PAUL 'BABE'	D. MAY 18, 1972 CHARLESTON, W. VA.
27- 5	BARNABE, CHARLES EDWARD	D. AUGUST 16, 1977 WACO, TEX.
27- 6	BARNES, EMILE DEERING 'RED'	D. JULY 3, 1959 MOBILE, ALA.
23- 5	BARNES, EVERETT DUANE 'EPPIE'	D. NOVEMBER 17, 1980 MINEOLA, N. Y.
57- 5	BARNES, FRANK	1508 BRAZIL - GREENVILLE MS 38701
29- 6	BARNES, FRANK SAMUEL 'LEFTY'	D. SEPTEMBER 27, 1967 HOUSTON, TEX.
15- 8	BARNES, JESSE LAWRENCE	D. SEPTEMBER 9, 1961 SANTA ROSA, N.MEX.
26- 5	BARNES, JOHN FRANCIS 'HONEY'	D. JUNE 18, 1981 LOCKPORT, N. Y.
34- 3	BARNES, JUNIE SHOAF	D. DECEMBER 31, 1963 JACKSONVILLE, N. C.
72- 6	BARNES, LUTHER OWEN	6190 CULVER DRIVE SE - SALEM OR 97301
82- 6	BARNES, RICHARD MONROE	4357 DAVIS ROAD - LAKE WORTH FL 33461
24- 3	BARNES, ROBERT AVERY	BOX 68 - LACON IL 61540
21- 1	BARNES, SAMUEL THOMAS	D. FEBRUARY 19, 1981 MONTGOMERY, ALA.
19- 5	BARNES, VIRGIL JENNINGS	D. JULY 24, 1958 WICHITA, KAN.
83- 8	BARNES, WILLIAM HENRY 'SKEETER'	6626 RAVENAL CT - CINCINNATI OH 45213
15- 9	BARNEY, EDMUND J.	D. OCTOBER 4, 1967 RICE LAKE, WIS.
43- 5	BARNEY, REX EDWARD	MEMORIAL STADIUM - BALTIMORE MD 21218
20- 3	BARNHART, CLYDE LEE	D. JANUARY 21, 1980 HAGERSTOWN, MD.
24- 4	BARNHART, EDGAR VERNON	D. SEPTEMBER 14, 1984 COLUMBIA, MO.
28- 4	BARNHART, LESLIE EARL	D. OCTOBER 7, 1971 SCOTTSDALE, ARIZ.
44- 3	BARNHART, VICTOR DEE	RR 5 - HAGERSTOWN MD 21741
39- 4	BARNICLE, GEORGE BERNARD	9981 88TH ST NORTH - SEMINOLE FL 33543
65- 4	BARNOWSKI, EDWARD ANTHONY	311 RED OAK DRIVE - WILLIAMSVILLE NY 14221
82- 7	BAROJAS, SALOME ROMERO	B. JUNE 16, 1957 COROVA, VERACRUZ, MEXICO
60- 6	BARONE, RICHARD ANTHONY	403 GLENFORD PARK CT - SAN JOSE CA 95136
71- 8	BARR, JAMES LELAND	6335 OAK HILL DRIVE - ROSEVILLE CA 95661
35- 2	BARR, ROBERT ALEXANDER	BARRINGTON MOBILE HOMES-BARRINGTON NH 03825
74- 6	BARR, STEVEN CHARLES	OLD ADD: 550 AVENUE NORTH SE - WINTER HAVEN FL 33880
61- 7	BARRAGAN, FACUNDO ANTHONY 'CUNO'	1824 ST. ANN COURT - CARMICHAEL CA 95608
79- 7	BARRANCA, GERMAN MICHAEL	CALLE PINO SUAREZ #1642 - VERACRUZ VERACRUZ MEX.
37- 8	BARRETT, CHARLES HENRY 'RED'	410 MONTICELLO DR - WILSON NC 27893
39- 5	BARRETT, FRANCIS JOSEPH	434 NORTH 3RD ST-LEESBURG FL 32748
42- 5	BARRETT, JOHN JOSEPH	D. AUGUST 17, 1974 SEABROOK BEACH, N. H.
82- 8	BARRETT, MARTIN GLENN	3140 CLAMDIGGER - LAS VEGAS NV 89117
23- 6	BARRETT, ROBERT SCHLEY	D. JANUARY 18, 1982 ATLANTA, GA.
88- 9	BARRETT, THOMAS LOREN	2201 EAST MESQUITE STREET - LAS VEGAS NV 89101
88- 10	BARRETT, TIMOTHY WAYNE	P.O. BOX 138 - OTWELL IN 47564
33- 3	BARRETT, TRACEY SOUTER 'DICK'	D. NOVEMBER 7, 1966 SEATTLE, WASH.
21- 2	BARRETT, WILLIAM JOSEPH	D. JANUARY 26, 1951 CAMBRIDGE, MASS.
74- 7	BARRIOS, FRANCISCO XAVIER	D. APRIL 9, 1982 HERMOSILLO SONORA MEXICO
82- 9	BARRIOS, JOSE MANUEL	6484 SW 25TH ST - MIAMI FL 33155
29- 7	BARRON, DAVID IRENUS 'RED'	D. OCTOBER 4, 1982 ATLANTA, GA.
14- 11	BARRON, FRANK JOHN	D. SEPTEMBER 18, 1964 PLEASANTS CO., W. VA.
12- 10	BARRY, HARDIN	D. NOVEMBER 5, 1969 CARSON CITY, NEV.
69- 6	BARRY, RICHARD DONOVAN	OLD ADD: 47275 MIO MIO LOOP - KANEOHE HI 96744
27- 7	BARTELL, RICHARD WILLIAM	1118 ISLAND DR - ALAMEDA CA 94501
44- 4	BARTHELSON, ROBERT EDWARD	40 MEADOWLARK LN - NORTHFORD CT 06472
28- 5	BARTHOLOMEW, LESTER JUSTIN	D. SEPTEMBER 19, 1972 MADISON, WIS.
52- 5	BARTIROME, ANTHONY JOSEPH	1104 PALMA SOLA BLVD - BRADENTON FL 34209
43- 6	BARTLEY, BOYD OWEN	7500 NOREAST DR - FORT WORTH TX 76118
38- 6	BARTLING, IRVING HENRY	D. JUNE 12, 1973 WESTLAND, MICH.
65- 5	BARTON, ROBERT WILBUR	1298 MCCLELLAND STREET - SAN MARCOS CA 92069
31- 6	BARTON, VINCENT DAVID	D. SEPTEMBER 13, 1973 TORONTO, ONT.
45- 3	BARTOSCH, DAVID ROBERT	10712 SW 42ND - PORTLAND OR 97219
48- 7	BASGALL, ROMANUS 'MONTY'	2745 ST. ANDREWS DRIVE - SIERRA VISTA AZ 85635
12- 11	BASHANG, ALBERT C.	D. JUNE 23, 1967 CINCINNATI, O.
36- 6	BASHORE, WALTER FRANKLIN	D. SEPTEMBER 26, 1984 SEBRING, FLA.
44- 5	BASINSKI, EDWIN FRANK	6585 SW 67TH ST - PORTLAND OR 97223
11- 10	BASKETTE, JAMES BLAINE	D. JULY 30, 1947 ATHENS, TENN.
82- 10	BASS, KEVIN CHARLES	1971 BYERS DR - MENLO PARK CA 94025
61- 8	BASS, NORMAN DELANEY	8814 THIRD AVE - INGLEWOOD CA 90305
77- 8	BASS, RANDY WILLIAM	RR 3 BOX 23C - LAWTON OK 73501
39- 6	BASS, RICHARD WILLIAM	P.O. BOX 291 - GREENWOOD FL 32443
18- 1	BASS, WILLIAM CAPERS 'DOC'	D. JANUARY 12, 1970 MACON, GA.
13- 5	BASSLER, JOHN LANDIS	D. JUNE 29, 1979 SANTA MONICA, CALIF.
23- 7	BATCHELDER, JOSEPH EDMUND	D. MAY 5, 1989 BEVERLY, MASS.
63- 7	BATEMAN, JOHN ALVIN	3301 OLD SAPULPA ROAD #61 - SAND SPRINGS OK 74063
69- 7	BATES, CHARLES RICHARD 'DICK'	P.O. BOX 116 - WOODBINE IA 51579
27- 8	BATES, CHARLES WILLIAM	D. JANUARY 29, 1980 TOPEKA, KANS.
70- 6	BATES, DELBERT OAKLEY	8336 133RD NE - REDMOND WA 98052
39- 7	BATES, HUBERT EDGAR	D. APRIL 29, 1987 LONG BEACH, CALIF.
13- 6	BATES, RAYMOND	D. AUGUST 15, 1970 TUCSON, ARIZ.
89- 9	BATES, WILLIAM DERRICK	14307 SELLERS ROAD - HOUSTON TX 77060
86- 13	BATHE, WILLIAM DAVID	11027 KENTUCKY AVENUE - WHITTIER CA 90603
73- 11	BATISTA, RAFAEL	BOX 211 - SAN PEDRO DE MACORIS DOMINICAN REP.
89- 10	BATISTE, KEVIN WADE	3624 AVENUE M - GALVESTON TX 77550
16- 3	BATSCH, WILLIAM MCKINLEY	D. DECEMBER 31, 1963 CANTON, O.
12- 12	BATTEN, GEORGE BERNARD	D. AUGUST 4, 1972 NEW PORT RICHEY, FLA.
55- 8	BATTEY, EARL JESSE	2501 SW 3RD STREET - OCALA FL 32674
27- 9	BATTLE, JAMES MILTON	D. SEPTEMBER 30, 1965 CHICO, CAL.
76- 13	BATTON, CHRISTOPHER SEAN	6109 WEST 77TH ST - LOS ANGELES CA 90045
47- 10	BATTS, MATTHEW DANIEL	838 NORTH ALLYSON - BATON ROUGE LA 70815
48- 8	BAUER, HENRY ALBERT	12705 WEST 108TH ST - OVERLAND PARK KS 66210
18- 2	BAUER, LOUIS WALTER	D. FEBRUARY 4, 1979 POMONA, N. J.
36- 7	BAUERS, RUSSELL LEE	1924 GARDNER RD-WESTCHESTER IL 60156
11- 11	BAUMANN, CHARLES JOHN 'PADDY'	D. NOVEMBER 20, 1969 INDIANAPOLIS, IND.
55- 9	BAUMANN, FRANK MATTHEW	7712 SUNRAY LN - ST LOUIS MO 63123
49- 4	BAUMER, JAMES SLOAN	303 PAOLI WOODS - PAOLI PA 19301
12- 13	BAUMGARDNER, GEORGE WASHINGTON	D. DECEMBER 13, 1970 BARBOURSVILLE, W. VA.

78- 6 BAUMGARTEN, ROSS	1020 BLUFF RD - GLENCOE IL 60022
20- 4 BAUMGARTNER, HARRY E.	D. DECEMBER 3, 1930 AUGUSTA, GA.
53- 9 BAUMGARTNER, JOHN EDWARD	237 KENT LANE - BIRMINGHAM AL 35209
14- 13 BAUMGARTNER, STANWOOD FULTON	D. OCTOBER 4, 1955 PHILADELPHIA, PA.
47- 11 BAUMHOLTZ, FRANK CONRAD	4327 JENNINGS RD - CLEVELAND OH 44109
60- 7 BAUTA, EDUARDO GALVEZ	810 SOUTH RIDGEWOOD #302 - DAYTONA BEACH FL 32014
88- 11 BAUTISTA, JOSE JOAQUIN	RESTAURACION #26 - BANI DOMINICAN REP.
59- 5 BAXES, DIMITRIOS SPEROS 'JIM'	6211 HUNTLEY AVE - GARDEN GROVE CA 92645
56- 6 BAXES, MICHAEL	303 WICKMAN DR - MILL VALLEY CA 94941
70- 7 BAYLOR, DON EDWARD	733 SAPPHIRE STREET - VENTURA CA 93004
19- 6 BAYNE, WILLIAM LEAR	D. MAY 27, 1981 ST. LOUIS, MO.
13- 7 BEALL, JOHN WOOLF	D. JUNE 13, 1926 BELTSVILLE, MD.
75- 14 BEALL, ROBERT BROOKS	513 BIRCHWOOD RD - HILLSBORO OR 97123
24- 5 BEALL, WALTER ESAU	D. JANUARY 28, 1959 SUITLAND, MD.
56- 7 BEAMON, CHARLES ALONZO SR.	1717 WOODLAND AVE #3 - EAST PALO ALTO CA 94303
78- 7 BEAMON, CHARLES ALONZO JR.	421 OAKLAND AVE #6 - OAKLAND CA 94611
30- 2 BEAN, BEVERIC BENTON 'BELVE'	D. JUNE 1, 1988 COMANCHE, TEXAS
87- 6 BEAN, WILLIAM DARO	1102 EAST JOANA - SANTA ANA CA 92701
84- 5 BEANE, WILLIAM LAMAR	1720 KNOLL FIELD WAY - ENCINITAS CA 92024
80- 7 BEARD, CHARLES DAVID 'DAVE'	813 EAST BLOOMINGDALE #284 - BRANDON FL 33511
48- 9 BEARD, CRAMER THEODORE 'TED'	10517 STELOR CT - INDIANAPOLIS IN 46256
74- 8 BEARD, MICHAEL RICHARD	OLD ADD: 5901 JFK BLVD #1603 - NORTH LITTLE ROCK AR
54- 6 BEARD, RALPH WILLIAM	1367 BERKSHIRE DR - WEST PALM BEACH FL 33406
47- 12 BEARDEN, HENRY EUGENE 'GENE'	BOX 176 - HELENA AR 72342
76- 14 BEARE, GARY RAY	2752 ELYSSEE ST - SAN DIEGO CA 92123
63- 8 BEARNARTH, LAWRENCE DONALD	85-18 143RD LN - SEMINOLE FL 33542
77- 9 BEASLEY, LEWIS PAIGE 'TEX'	RR 1 BOX 65 - BOWLING GREEN VA 22427
78- 8 BEATTIE, JAMES LOUIS	9610 SE 34TH ST - MERCER ISLAND WA 98040
14- 14 BEATTY, DESMOND A.	D. OCTOBER 6, 1969 NORWAY, ME.
89- 11 BEATTY, GORDON BLAINE 'BLAINE'	RURAL ROUTE 1 BOX 143C - VICTORIA TX 77901
63- 9 BEAUCHAMP, JAMES EDWARD	BOX 1790 - PHENIX CITY AL 36867
41- 6 BEAZLEY, JOHN ANDREW	D. APRIL 21, 1990 NASHVILLE, TENN.
26- 6 BECK, CLYDE EUGENE	D. JULY 15, 1988 TEMPLE CITY, CALIF.
14- 15 BECK, ERNEST GEORGE B	D. OCTOBER 29, 1973 SOUTH BEND, IND.
65- 6 BECK, RICHARD HENRY	EAST 527 PARKHILL DRIVE - SPOKANE WA 99208
24- 5 BECK, WALTER WILLIAM 'BOOM BOOM'	D. MAY 7, 1987 CHAMPAIGN, ILL.
13- 8 BECK, ZINN BERTRAM	D. MARCH 19, 1981 WEST PALM BEACH, FLA.
11- 12 BECKER, CHARLES S.	D. JULY 30, 1928 WASHINGTON, D.C.
43- 7 BECKER, HEINZ REINHARD	302 CLARENDON DR-DALLAS TX 75208
36- 8 BECKER, JOSEPH EDWARD	2800 21ST PLACE - VERO BEACH FL 32960
15- 10 BECKER, MARTIN HENRY	D. SEPTEMBER 25, 1957 CINCINNATI, O.
65- 7 BECKERT, GLENN ALFRED	870 VIRGINA LAKE CT - PALATINE IL 60067
27- 10 BECKMAN, JAMES JOSEPH	6989 BENNETT ROAD - CINCINNATI OH 45230
39- 8 BECKMANN, WILLIAM ALOYSIUS	D. JANUARY 2, 1990 FLORISSANT, MO.
79- 8 BECKWITH, THOMAS JOSEPH 'JOE'	2057 COUNTRY SQUIRE RD - AUBURN AL 36830
55- 10 BECQUER, JULIO VELLEGAS	829 VINCENT AVE - MINNEAPOLIS MN 55411
62- 9 BEDELL, HOWARD WILLIAM	1187 CRESTWOOD DR - POTTSTOWN PA 19464
25- 6 BEDFORD, WILLIAM EUGENE	D. OCTOBER 6, 1977 SAN ANTONIO, TEXAS
22- 3 BEDGOOD, PHILIP BURLETTE	D. NOVEMBER 8, 1927 FORT PIERCE, FLA.
12- 14 BEDIENT, HUGH CARPENTER	D. JULY 21, 1965 JAMESTOWN, N.Y.
30- 3 BEDNAR, ANDREW JACKSON	D. NOVEMBER 26, 1937 GRAHAM, TEX,
81- 8 BEDROSIAN, STEPHEN WAYNE	5490 CHEISENWOOD DRIVE - DULUTH GA 30136
44- 6 BEELER, JOSEPH SAM 'JODIE'	3709 NABHOLTZ - MESQUITE TX 75150
68- 4 BEENE, FREDERICK RAY	BOX 143 - OAKHURST TX 77359
83- 9 BEENE, RAMON ANDREW 'ANDY'	9919 ILA - DALLAS TX 75220
48- 10 BEERS, CLARENCE SCOTT	4701 ANDERSON RD #30 - HOUSTON TX 77045
83- 10 BEGENNA, RICHARD KIPP	9451 TONI DRIVE - CUTLER RIDGE FL 33157
38- 7 BEGGS, JOSEPH STANLEY	D. JULY 19, 1983 INDIANAPOLIS, IND.
24- 7 BEGLEY, JAMES LAWRENCE	D. FEBRUARY 22, 1957 SAN FRANCISCO, CAL.
21- 3 BEHAN, CHARLES FREDERICK 'PETIE'	D. JANUARY 21, 1957 BRADFORD, PA.
70- 7 BEHNEY, MELVIN BRIAN	241 GROVE AVE - VERONA NJ 07042
46- 8 BEHRMAN, HENRY BERNARD	D. JANUARY 20, 1987 NEW YORK, N. Y.
34- 4 BEJMA, ALOYSIUS FRANK 'OLLIE'	4510 WEST WASHINGTON #107 - SOUTH BEND IN 46619
65- 8 BELANGER, MARK HENRY	2028 POT SPRING RD - TIMONIUM MD 21093
50- 7 BELARDI, CARROLL WAYNE	1467 PHANTOM AVE - SAN JOSE CA 95125
87- 7 BELCHER, TIMOTHY WAYNE	SPRING STREET - SPARTA OH 43350
89- 12 BELINDA, STANLEY PETER	454 SYLVAN DRIVE - STATE COLLEGE PA 16803
62- 10 BELINSKY, ROBERT 'BO'	P.O. BOX 671 - WAIALUA HI 96791
72- 6 BELL, DAVID GUS 'BUDDY'	6485 HUNTERS TRAIL - CINCINNATI OH 45243
50- 8 BELL, DAVID RUSSELL 'GUS'	%MINUTEMAN,920 RACE STREET - CINCINNATI OH 45202
85- 7 BELL, ERIC ALVIN	1601 COUCHMAN LANE - MODESTO CA 95355
39- 9 BELL, FERN LEE	1975 ADD: 122 WEST 59TH PL - LOS ANGELES CA
58- 9 BELL, GARY	AMERICAN SPORTS,1436 N. FLORES - SAN ANTONIO TX 78212
24- 8 BELL, HERMAN S. 'HI'	D. JUNE 7, 1949 GLENDALE, CAL.
86- 14 BELL, JAY STUART	9752 QUAIL HOLLOW COURT - PENSACOLA FL 32514
71- 9 BELL, JERRY HOUSTON	339 KEATON AVENUE - OLD HICKORY TN 37138
81- 9 BELL, JORGE ANTONIO	BARIO REST. CLE T #179-SAN PEDRO DE MACORIS DOM. REP.
89- 13 BELL, JUAN (MATHEY)	CALLE T #174 BO. RESTAURACION-SP DE MACORIS DOM. REP.
76- 15 BELL, KEVIN ROBERT	OLD ADD: ALGONQUIN - ROLLING MEADOWS IL
23- 8 BELL, LESTER ROWLAND	D. NOVEMBER 26, 1985 HARRISBURG, PA.
12- 15 BELL, RALPH A.	D. OCTOBER 18, 1959 BURLINGTON, IA.
35- 3 BELL, ROY CHESTER 'BEAU'	D. SEPTEMBER 14, 1977 COLLEGE STATION, TEXAS
86- 15 BELL, TERENCE WILLIAM	4317 FERNMONT STREET - KETTERING OH 45440
52- 6 BELL, WILLIAM SAMUEL	D. OCTOBER 11, 1962 DURHAM, N. C.
57- 6 BELLA, JOHN 'ZEKE'	24 TAYLOR DR - COS COB CT 06807
89- 14 BELLE, ALBERT JOJUAN 'JOEY'	4378 THURGOOD CIRCLE - SHREVEPORT LA 71109
82- 11 BELLIARD, RAFAEL LEONIDAS	DOMINGO CASTELLANO 17,GURABITO-SANTIAGO DOMINICAN REP.
75- 15 BELLOIR, ROBERT EDWARD	335 MIMOSA DRIVE - FAYETTEVILLE GA 30214
67- 4 BENCH, JOHN LEE	661 REISLING KNOLL - CINCINNATI OH 45226
78- 9 BENEDICT, BRUCE EDWIN	335 QUIET WATER LANE - DUNWOODY GA 30338
89- 15 BENES, ANDREW CHARLES	4001 WOODCASTLE ROAD - EVANSVILLE IN 47711
31- 7 BENES, JOSEPH ANTHONY	D. MARCH 7, 1975 ELMHURST N. Y.
25- 7 BENGE, RAYMOND ADELPHIA	RR1 BOX 134A - JEWETT TX 75846
23- 9 BENGOUGH, BERNARD OLIVER	D. DECEMBER 22, 1968 PHILADELPHIA, PA.
71- 10 BENIQUEZ, JUAN JOSE	CALLE 99A BLK.87 #12 - CAROLINA PR 00630
39- 10 BENJAMIN, ALFRED STANLEY 'STAN'	46 ALLEN ST - GREENFIELD MA 01301
89- 16 BENJAMIN, MICHAEL PAUL	BELLFLOWER CA 90706
14- 16 BENN, HOMER OMER	D. JUNE 4, 1967 MENDOTA, WIS.

64- 4	BENNETT, DAVID HANS	408 FAIRCHILD ST - YREKA CA 96097
62- 11	BENNETT, DENNIS JOHN	630 NORTH 5TH - KLAMATH FALLS OR 97601
27- 11	BENNETT, FRANCIS ALLEN	D. MARCH 18, 1966 WILMINGTON, DEL.
23- 10	BENNETT, HERSCHELL EMMETT	D. SEPTEMBER 9, 1964 SPRINGFIELD, MO.
28- 6	BENNETT, JAMES FRED	D. MAY 12, 1975 ATKINS, ARK.
18- 3	BENNETT, JOSEPH HARLEY	D. NOVEMBER 21, 1957 JOEL, MO.
23- 11	BENNETT, JOSEPH ROSENBLUM	D. JULY 11, 1987 MORRO BAY, CALIF.
34- 5	BENSON, ALLEN WILBERT	HURLEY SD 57036
43- 8	BENSON, VERNON ADAIR	BOX 127-GRANITE QUARRY NC 28072
13- 9	BENTLEY, JOHN NEEDLES	D. OCTOBER 24, 1969 OLNEY, MD.
78- 10	BENTON, ALFRED LEE 'BUTCH'	OLD ADD: 895 VIL LAKES#102 - ST PETERSBURG FL
34- 6	BENTON, JOHN ALTON 'AL'	D. APRIL 14, 1968 LYNWOOD, CAL.
10- 7	BENTON, JOHN CLEBON 'RUBE'	D. DECEMBER 12, 1937 DOTHAN, ALA.
23- 12	BENTON, LAWRENCE JAMES	D. APRIL 3, 1953 CINCINNATI, O.
22- 4	BENTON, SIDNEY WRIGHT	D. MARCH 8, 1977 FAYETTEVILLE, ARK.
22- 5	BENTON, STANLEY 'RABBIT'	D. JUNE 7, 1984 DALLAS, TEXAS
11- 13	BENZ, JOSEPH LOUIS	D. APRIL 23, 1957 CHICAGO, ILL.
87- 8	BENZINGER, TODD ERIC	3502 BEHMER ROAD - CINCINNATI OH 45245
12- 16	BERAN, DENNIS MARTIN	D. APRIL 28, 1943 BOSTON, MASS.
39- 11	BERARDINO, JOHN	1719 AMBASSADOR AVE - BEVERLY HILLS CA 90210
54- 7	BERBERET, LOUIS JOSEPH	4025 MARDON AVE - LAS VEGAS NV 89118
78- 11	BERENGUER, JUAN BAUTISTA	868 SWEETWATER ISLAND CIRCLE - LONGWOOD FL 32779
80- 8	BERENYI, BRUCE MICHAEL	BOX 133 - SHERWOOD OH 43556
23- 13	BERG, MORRIS 'MOE'	D. MAY 29, 1972 BELLEVILLE, N. J.
44- 7	BERGAMO, AUGUST SAMUEL	D. AUGUST 19, 1974 GROSSE POINTE CITY, MICH.
14- 17	BERGER, CLARENCE EDWARD	D. JUNE 30, 1959 WASHINGTON, D. C.
22- 6	BERGER, JOHN HENNE	D. MAY 7, 1979 LAKE CHARLES, LA.
13- 10	BERGER, JOSEPH AUGUST	D. MARCH 5, 1956 ROCK ISLAND, ILL.
32- 3	BERGER, LOUIS WILLIAM 'BOZE'	11914 RENWOOD LN - ROCKVILLE MD 20852
30- 4	BERGER, WALTER ANTONE	D. NOVEMBER 30, 1988 REDONDO BEACH, CALIF.
11- 11	BERGHAMMER, MARTIN ANDREW	D. DECEMBER 21, 1957 PITTSBURGH, PA.
16- 4	BERGMAN, ALFRED HENRY	D. JUNE 21, 1961 FORT WAYNE, IND.
75- 16	BERGMAN, DAVID BRUCE	728 CANTERBURY COURT - GROSSE POINTE WOODS MI 48236
24- 9	BERLY, JOHN CHAMBERS	D. JUNE 26, 1977 HOUSTON, TEX.
18- 4	BERMAN, ROBERT LEON	D. AUGUST 2, 1988 BRIDGEPORT, CONN.
77- 10	BERNAL, VICTOR HUGO	4632 ABNER ST - LOS ANGELES CA 90032
78- 12	BERNARD, DWIGHT VERN	RURAL ROUTE 1 - BELLE RIVE IL 62810
79- 9	BERNAZARD, ANTONIO (GARCIA)	SANTA AV D-25,URB SANTA ELVIRA-CAGUAS PR00625
76- 16	BERNHARDT, JUAN RAMON	PROL. SERGIO A. BERA #13-SAN PEDRO DE MACORIS DOM REP.
18- 5	BERNHARDT, WALTER JACOB	D. JULY 26, 1958 WATERTOWN, N. Y.
53- 10	BERNIER, CARLOS RODRIGUEZ	D. APRIL 6, 1989 JUANA DIAZ, P.R.
48- 11	BERO, JOHN GEORGE	D. MAY 11, 1985 GARDENA, CALIF.
77- 11	BERRA, DALE ANTHONY	517 RIDGEWOOD AVENUE - GLEN RIDGE NJ 07028
46- 9	BERRA, LAWRENCE PETER 'YOGI'	19 HIGHLAND AVE - MONTCLAIR NJ 07042
34- 7	BERRES, RAYMOND	111 HAWTHORNE RD - TWIN LAKES WI 53181
89- 17	BERROA, GERONIMO EMILIANO	HUMANITARIA #20 ENS. MARGARA - SANTO DOMINGO DOM. REP.
62- 12	BERRY, ALLEN KENNETH 'KEN'	3421 BRIARWOOD LN - TOPEKA KS 66611
25- 8	BERRY, CHARLES FRANCIS	D. SEPTEMBER 6, 1972 EVANSTON, ILL.
48- 12	BERRY, CORNELIUS JOHN 'CONNIE'	407 INKSTER AVE - KALAMAZOO MI 49001
42- 6	BERRY, JONAS ARTHUR	D. SEPTEMBER 27, 1958 ANAHEIM, CAL.
21- 4	BERRY, JOSEPH HOWARD JR	D. APRIL 29, 1976 PHILADELPHIA, PA.
87- 9	BERRYHILL, DAMON SCOTT	8 CAMSHIP - LAGUNA NIGUEL CA 92677
64- 5	BERTAINA, FRANK LOUIS	2340 HILLTOP COURT - SANTA ROSA CA 95405
60- 8	BERTELL, RICHARD GEORGE	25332 REMESA DR - MISSION VIEJO CA 92675
53- 11	BERTOIA, RENO PETER	3400 ERSKINE ST #906 - WINDSOR ONTARIO CAN.
36- 9	BERTRAND, ROMAN MATHIAS	1909 MOUNT HOOD - THE DALLES OR 97058
56- 8	BESANA, FREDERICK CYRIL	222 DIAMOND OAKS DR - ROSEVILLE CA 95678
40- 2	BESSE, HERMAN	D. AUGUST 13, 1972 LOS ANGELES, CAL.
55- 11	BESSENT, FRED DONALD 'DON'	OLD ADD: 5139 110TH STREET - JACKSONVILLE FL 32244
83- 11	BEST, KARL JOHN	11132 SE 129TH - KIRKLAND WA 98034
78- 13	BESWICK, JAMES WILLIAM	12519 DOMINGO RD NE - ALBUQUERQUE NM 87123
10- 8	BETCHER, FRANKLIN LYLE	D. NOVEMBER 27, 1981 WYNNEWOOD, PA.
64- 6	BETHEA, WILLIAM LAMAR	4001 WYLDWOOD - AUSTIN TX 78739
65- 9	BETHKE, JAMES CHARLES	419 NORTH OAKLEY ST - KANSAS CITY MO 64123
28- 7	BETTENCOURT, LAWRENCE JOSEPH	D. SEPTEMBER 15, 1978 NEW ORLEANS, LA.
84- 6	BETTENDORF, JEFFREY ALLEN	916 WEST LIME - LOMPOC CA 93436
20- 5	BETTS, WALTER MARTIN 'HUCK'	D. JUNE 13, 1987 MILLSBORO, DEL.
14- 18	BETZEL, CHRISTIAN FREDERICK ALBERT	D. FEBRUARY 7, 1965 WEST HOLLYWOOD,FLA
71- 11	BEVACQUA, KURT ANTHONY	2607 PIRINEOS WAY #101 - CARLSBAD CA 92008
52- 7	BEVAN, HAROLD JOSEPH	D. OCTOBER 5, 1968 NEW ORLEANS, LA.
44- 8	BEVENS, FLOYD CLIFFORD 'BILL'	5067 8TH NE - SALEM OR 97303
42- 7	BEVIL, LOUIS EUGENE	D. FEBRUARY 1, 1973 DIXON, ILL.
17- 6	BEZDEK, HUGH FRANCIS	D. SEPTEMBER 19, 1952 ATLANTIC CITY, N.J.
82- 12	BIANCALANA, ROLAND AMERICO 'BUDDY'	4120 SAN SAVERA DR NORTH - JACKSONVILLE FL 32217
75- 17	BIANCO, THOMAS ANTHONY	OLD ADD: 4 CURVEWOOD RD - PORT WASHINGTON NY 11050
49- 5	BIASATTI, HENRY ARCADO	9024 ALLEN RD - ALLEN PARK MI 48101
72- 9	BIBBY, JAMES BLAIR	RR 6 BOX 402 - MADISON HEIGHTS VA 24572
88- 12	BICHETTE, ALPHONSE DANTE	2560 113TH STREET NORTH - LAKE PARK FL 33410
48- 13	BICKFORD, VERNON EDGELL	D. MAY 8, 1960 RICHMOND, VA.
48- 14	BICKNELL, CHARLES STEPHEN	6981 FORDS STATION RD - GERMANTOWN TN 38138
84- 7	BIELECKI, MICHAEL JOSEPH	1932 EASTFIELD RD - BALTIMORE MD 21222
20- 6	BIEMILLER, HARRY LEE	D. MAY 25, 1965 ORLANDO, FLA.
16- 5	BIGBEE, CARSON LEE	D. OCTOBER 17, 1964 PORTLAND, ORE.
20- 7	BIGBEE, LYLE RANDOLPH	D. AUGUST 5, 1942 PORTLAND, ORE.
29- 8	BIGELOW, ELLIOT ALLARDICE	D. AUGUST 10, 1933 TAMPA, FLA.
88- 13	BIGGIO, CURTIS ALAN	829 RINGWOOD AVENUE - HASKELL NJ 07420
32- 4	BIGGS, CHARLES ORVAL	D. MAY 24, 1954 FRENCH LICK, IND.
70- 9	BIITTNER, LARRY DAVID	169 CRESTVIEW CT - BARRINGTON IL 60010
49- 6	BILBREY, JAMES MELVIN	D. DECEMBER 26, 1985 TOLEDO, O.
37- 9	BILDILLI, EMIL	D. SEPTEMBER 16, 1946 HARTFORD CITY, IND.
49- 7	BILKO, STEPHEN THOMAS	D. MARCH 7, 1978 WILKES-BARRE, PA.
83- 12	BILLARDELLO, DANN JAMES	1157 HYACINTH PLACE W - WEST PALM BEACH FL 33414
68- 5	BILLINGHAM, JOHN EUGENE	8945 LAKE IRMA POINTE - ORLANDO FL 32817
27- 12	BILLINGS, HASKELL CLARK	D. DECEMBER 26, 1983 GREENBRAE, CALIF.
13- 11	BILLINGS, JOHN AUGUSTUS 'JOSH'	D. DECEMBER 30, 1981 SANTA MONICA, CALIF.
68- 6	BILLINGS, RICHARD ARLIN	1917 CREEKWOOD DR - ARLINGTON TX 76010
44- 9	BINKS, GEORGE EUGENE	4803 BELMONT RD - DOWNERS GROVE IL 60515
44- 10	BIRAS, STEPHEN ALEXANDER	D. APRIL 21, 1965 ST. LOUIS, MO.

MANTLE & WILLIAMS

Two of the most prized autographs
of living Hall of Famers are shown here
on both their Perez-Steele Art Post Cards
and their Great Moments cards

73- 12 BIRD, JAMES DOUGLAS 'DOUG'	OLD ADD: 5542-3 MALT DRIVE - FORT MYERS FL 33907
21- 5 BIRD, JAMES EDWARD 'RED'	D. MARCH 23, 1972 MURFREESBORO, ARK.
86- 16 BIRKBECK, MICHAEL LAURENCE	1705 WEST HILL DRIVE - ORRVILLE OH 44667
33- 4 BIRKOFER, RALPH JOSEPH	D. MARCH 16, 1971 CINCINNATI, O.
55- 12 BIRRER, WERNER JOSEPH 'BABE'	115 RANCH TRAIL WEST - WILLIAMSVILLE NY 14221
85- 4 BIRTSAS, TIMOTHY DEAN	43 ROBERTSON COURT - CLARKSTON MI 48016
42- 8 BISCAN, FRANK STEPHEN	D. MAY 22, 1959 ST. LOUIS, MO.
25- 9 BISCHOFF, JOHN GEORGE	D. DECEMBER 28, 1981 GRANITE CITY, ILL.
52- 8 BISHOP, CHARLES TULLER	2705 ADDISON DR - DORAVILLE GA 30040
23- 14 BISHOP, JAMES MORTON	D. SEPTEMBER 20, 1973 MEXICO, MO.
14- 19 BISHOP, LLOYD CLIFTON	D. JUNE 17, 1968 WICHITA, KAN.
24- 10 BISHOP, MAX FREDERICK	D. FEBRUARY 4, 1962 WAYNESBORO, PA.
83- 13 BISHOP, MICHAEL DAVID	497 EAST NEWLOVE #D - SANTA MARIA CA 93454
21- 6 BISHOP, WILLIAM HENRY	D. FEBRUARY 14, 1956 ST. JOSEPH, MO.
12- 17 BISLAND, RIVINGTON MARTIN	D. JANUARY 11, 1973 SALZBURG, AUSTRIA
28- 8 BISSONETTE, DELPHIA LOUIS	D. JUNE 9, 1972 AUGUSTA, ME.
42- 9 BITHORN, HIRAM GABRIEL	D. JANUARY 1, 1952 EL MANTE, MEX.
86- 17 BITTIGER, JEFFREY SCOTT	821 HUDSON AVENUE - SECAUCUS NJ 07094
35- 4 BIVIN, JAMES NATHANIEL	D. NOVEMBER 7, 1982 PUEBLO, COLO.
83- 14 BJORKMAN, GEORGE ANTON	3216 BANDOLINO LANE - PLANO TX 75075
14- 20 BLACK, DAVID	D. OCTOBER 27, 1936 PITTSBURGH, PA.
43- 9 BLACK, DONALD PAUL	D. APRIL 21, 1959 CUYAHOGA FALLS, O.
81- 10 BLACK, HARRY RALSTON 'BUD'	75-707 HWY 111 #C-6 - PALM DESERT CA 92260
11- 15 BLACK, JOHN FALCNOR	D. MARCH 19, 1962 RUTHERFORD, N. J.
24- 11 BLACK, JOHN WILLIAM 'BILL'	D. JANUARY 14, 1968 PHILADELPHIA, PA.
52- 9 BLACK, JOSEPH	1904 GREYHOUND TOWERS - PHOENIX AZ 85077
52- 10 BLACK, WILLIAM CARROLL	1233 MT OLIVE AVE - UNIVERSITY CITY MO 63130
62- 13 BLACKABY, ETHAN ALLEN	2308 EAST ORANGEWOOD - PHOENIX AZ 85020
12- 18 BLACKBURN, EARL STUART	D. AUGUST 4, 1966 MANSFIELD, O.
15- 11 BLACKBURN, FOSTER EDWIN 'BABE'	D. MARCH 9, 1984 NEWPORT RICHEY, FLA.
48- 15 BLACKBURN, JAMES RAY	D. OCTOBER 26, 1969 CINCINNATI, O.
58- 10 BLACKBURN, RONALD HAMILTON	RR 10 BOX 67 - MORGANTON NC 28655
10- 9 BLACKBURNE, RUSSELL AUBREY 'LENA'	D. FEBRUARY 29, 1968 RIVERSIDE, N. J.
28- 9 BLACKERBY, GEORGE FRANKLIN	OLD ADD: 1334 AVENUE B #173 - YUMA AZ 85364
42- 10 BLACKWELL, EWELL	20 MOY TOY LANE - BREVARD NC 28712
17- 8 BLACKWELL, FREDRICK WILLIAM	D. DECEMBER 8, 1975 MORGANTOWN, KY.
74- 9 BLACKWELL, TIMOTHY P	1933 MAPLEBROOK - EL CAJON CA 92021
22- 7 BLADES, FRANCIS RAYMOND	D. MAY 18, 1979 LINCOLN, ILL.
69- 8 BLADT, RICHARD ALAN	OLD ADD: 620 SOUTH WATER ST - SILVERTON OR 97381
25- 10 BLAEHOLDER, GEORGE FRANKLIN	D. DECEMBER 29, 1947 GARDEN GROVE, CALIF.
41- 7 BLAEMIRE, RAE BERTRUM	D. DECEMBER 23, 1975 CHAMPAIGN, ILL.
29- 9 BLAIR, CLARENCE VICK	D. JULY 1, 1982 TEXARKANA, TEX.
74- 10 BLAIR, DENNIS HERMAN	612 FAIRWAY - REDLANDS CA 92373
42- 11 BLAIR, LOUIS NATHAN 'BUDDY'	700 FILHOIL - MONROE LA 71203
64- 7 BLAIR, PAUL L. D.	OLD ADD: DAMCO, 307 5TH AVE,6TH FLR.-NEW YORK NY 10016
51- 2 BLAKE, EDWARD JAMES	208 WILLOW CREEK COURT - BELLEVILLE IL 62223
20- 8 BLAKE, JOHN FREDERICK 'SHERIFF'	D. OCTOBER 31, 1982 BECKLEY, W. VA.
34- 8 BLAKELY, LINCOLN HOWARD	D. SEPTEMBER 28, 1976 OAKLAND, CALIF.
55- 13 BLANCHARD, JOHN EDWIN	15541 LARKIN DR - MINNETONKA MN 55343
35- 5 BLANCHE, PROSPER ALBERT 'AL'	81 EVERETT ST - ARLINGTON MA 02174
72- 9 BLANCO, DAMASO	OLD ADD: 659 CATAMARAN ST #2 - FOSTER CITY CA
65- 10 BLANCO, GILBERT HENRY	OLD ADD: 360 EAST MONTE VISTA RD - PHOENIX AZ 85004
70- 10 BLANCO, OSVALDO CARLOS	OLD ADD: DE LOZADA B1 E16,SAN JOSE DE AVILAVZ
10- 10 BLANDING, FRED JAMES	D. JULY 16, 1950 SALEM, VA.
22- 8 BLANKENSHIP, HOMER	D. JUNE 22, 1974 LONGVIEW, TEX.
88- 14 BLANKENSHIP, KEVIN DEWAYNE	450 VIA DEL LEON - PLACENTIA CA 92670
88- 15 BLANKENSHIP, LANCE ROBERT	850 CLAREWOOD COURT - CONCORD CA 94518
22- 9 BLANKENSHIP, THEODORE	D. JANUARY 14, 1945 ATOKA, OKLA.
72- 10 BLANKS, LARVELL	408 WATERS AVE - DEL RIO TX 78840
34- 9 BLANTON, DARRELL ELIJAH 'CY'	D. SEPTEMBER 13, 1945 NORMAN, OKLA.
55- 14 BLASINGAME, DONALD LEE	9795 EAST MISSION LN - SCOTTSDALE AZ 85258
63- 10 BLASINGAME, WADE ALLEN	5207 RIVERHILL RD NE - MARIETTA GA 30067
64- 8 BLASS, STEPHEN ROBERT	1756 QUIGG DR - PITTSBURGH PA 15241
71- 12 BLATERIC, STEPHEN LAWRENCE	1662 SOUTH UTICA - DENVER CO 80219
48- 16 BLATNIK, JOHN LOUIS	68615 CHERMONT RD, BOX 246 - LANSING OH 43934
42- 12 BLATTNER, ROBERT GARNETT	RR 73 BOX 205 - LAKE OZARK MO 65049
87- 10 BLAUSER, JEFFREY MICHAEL	5715 RIVER RUN CIRCLE - ROCKLIN CA 95677
59- 6 BLAYLOCK, GARY NELSON	BOX 241 - MALDEN MO 63863
50- 9 BLAYLOCK, MARVIN EDWARD	2200 ANDOVER CT #602 - LITTLE ROCK AR 72207
56- 9 BLAYLOCK, ROBERT EDWARD	RR 2 BOX 460 - MULDROW OK 74948
65- 11 BLEFARY, CURTIS LEROY	1808 SW 4TH COURT - FORT LAUDERDALE FL 33312
60- 9 BLEMKER, RAYMOND 'BUDDY'	2363 DUNDEE DR - HENDERSON KY 42420
72- 11 BLESSITT, ISAIAH 'IKE'	19712 ANGLIN - DETROIT MI 48234
23- 15 BLETHEN, CLARENCE WALDO	D. APRIL 11, 1973 FREDERICK, MD.
42- 13 BLOCK, SEYMOUR 'CY'	4 OLDFIELD LN - LAKE SUCCESS NY 11020
85- 5 BLOCKER, TERRY FENNELL	823 PINEY WOODS ROAD - COLUMBIA SC 29210
69- 9 BLOMBERG, RONALD MARK	11660 MOUNTAIN LAUREL DR - ROSWELL GA 30075
37- 10 BLOODWORTH, JAMES HENRY	BOX 232-APALACHICOLA FL 32320
63- 11 BLOOMFIELD, CLYDE STALCUP 'BUD'	RR 8 BOX 592 - ROGERS AR 72756
24- 12 BLOTT, JACK LEONARD	D. JUNE 11, 1964 ANN ARBOR, MICH.
89- 18 BLOWERS, MICHAEL ROY	22211 42ND AVENUE EAST - SPANAWAY WA 98387
21- 7 BLUE, LUZERNE ATWELL	D. JULY 28, 1958 ALEXANDRIA, VA.
69- 10 BLUE, VIDA	P.O. BOX 1449 - PLEASANTON CA 94556
22- 10 BLUEGE, OSWALD LOUIS	D. OCTOBER 15, 1985 EDINA, MINN.
32- 5 BLUEGE, OTTO ADAM	D. JUNE 28, 1977 CHICAGO, ILL.
14- 21 BLUEJACKET, JAMES	D. MARCH 26, 1947 PEKIN, ILL.
18- 6 BLUHM, HARVEY FRED 'RED'	D. MAY 7, 1952 FLINT, MICH.
22- 11 BLUME, CLINTON WILLIS	D. JUNE 12, 1973 ISLIP, N. Y.
70- 11 BLYLEVEN, RIKALBERT BERT	18992 CANYON DR - VILLA PARK CA 92667
53- 12 BLYZKA, MICHAEL JOHN	1615 EAST 13TH ST #1 - CHEYENNE WY 82001
60- 10 BOAK, CHESTER ROBERT "CHET"	D. NOVEMBER 28, 1983 EMPORIUM, PA.
13- 12 BOARDMAN, CHARLES LOUIS	D. AUGUST 10, 1968 SACRAMENTO, CALIF.
68- 7 BOBB, MARK RANDALL 'RANDY'	D. JUNE 13, 1982 CARNELIAN BAY, CALIF.
63- 12 BOCCABELLA, JOHN DOMINIC	1035 LEA DR - SAN RAFAEL CA 94903
33- 5 BOCEK, MILTON FRANK	2342 SOUTH 61ST CT - CICERO IL 60650
74- 11 BOCHTE, BRUCE ANTON	6475 SOUTH MAXWELTON RD - CLINTON WA 98236
78- 14 BOCHY, BRUCE DOUGLAS	14035 BARRYMORE STREET - SAN DIEGO CA 92129
46- 10 BOCKMAN, JOSEPH EDWARD 'EDDIE'	1400 MILBRAE AVE #2 - MILLBRAE CA 94030

26

86- 18	BOCKUS, RANDY WALTER	9313 CHESTNUT STREET - EAST SPARTA OH 44626
80- 9	BODDICKER, MICHAEL JAMES	56 CARTER DRIVE - FRAMINGHAM MA 01701
11- 16	BODIE, FRANK STEPHAN 'PING'	D. DECEMBER 12, 1961 SAN FRANCISCO, CALIF.
17- 9	BOECKEL, NORMAN DOXIE	D. FEBRUARY 16, 1924 TORREY PINES, CALIF.
12- 19	BOEHLER, GEORGE HENRY	D. JUNE 23, 1958 LAWRENCEBURG, IND.
12- 20	BOEHLING, JOHN JOSEPH	D. SEPTEMBER 8, 1941 RICHMOND, VA.
67- 5	BOEHMER, LEONARD JOSEPH	3570 HIGHWAY P - WENTZVILLE MO 63385
32- 6	BOERNER, LAWRENCE HYER	D. OCTOBER 16, 1969 STAUNTON, VA.
85- 6	BOEVER, JOSEPH MARTIN	5141 TOWNE SOUTH ROAD - ST.LOUIS MO 63128
20- 9	BOGART, JOHN RENZIE	D. DECEMBER 7, 1986 CLARENCE, N. Y.
82- 13	BOGENER, TERRY WAYNE	2134 COVINGTON CIRCLE - WICHITA KS 67212
28- 10	BOGGS, RAYMOND JOSEPH	1135 HILL AVE - GRAND JUNCTION CO 81501
76- 17	BOGGS, THOMAS WINSTON	67 EMANUEL CIRCLE - HOT SPRINGS NATIONAL AR 71909
82- 14	BOGGS, WADE ANTHONY	14615 VILLAGE GLEN CIRCLE - TAMPA FL 33606
68- 8	BOGLE, WARREN FREDERICK	11605 SW 103RD AVE - MIAMI FL 33156
13- 13	BOHEN, LEO IGNATIUS 'PAT'	D. APRIL 8, 1942 NAPA, CALIF.
16- 6	BOHNE, SAMUEL ARTHUR	D. MAY 23, 1977 PALO ALTO, CALIF.
82- 15	BOHNET, JOHN KELLY	224 PANORAMA DR - BENICIA CA 94510
74- 12	BOISCLAIR, BRUCE ARMAND	29064 W. SADDLE BROOK - AGOURA CA 91301
78- 15	BOITANO, DANNY JON	15400 WINCHESTER BLVD #43-LOS GATOS CA 95030
51- 3	BOKELMANN, RICHARD WERNER	629 NORTH BELMONT AV - ARLINGTON HEIGHTS IL 60004
33- 6	BOKEN, ROBERT ANTHONY	D.OCTOBER 6, 1988 LAS VEGAS, NEV.
36- 10	BOKINA, JOSEPH	1901 EAST 25TH ST-CHATTANOOGA TN 37404
15- 12	BOLAND, BERNARD ANTHONY	D. SEPTEMBER 12, 1973 DETROIT, MICH.
34- 10	BOLAND, EDWARD JOHN	1655 S. HIGHLAND AVE #J196 - CLEARWATER FL 33516
14- 22	BOLD, CHARLES DICKENS	D. JULY 29, 1978 CHELSEA, MASS.
19- 7	BOLDEN, WILLIAM HORACE	D. DECEMBER 8, 1966 JEFFERSON CITY, TENN.
26- 7	BOLEN, STEWART O'NEAL	D. AUGUST 30, 1969 JACKSON, ALA.
62- 14	BOLES, CARL THEODORE	18020 CASTLEWOOD CT - HAYWARD CA 94541
27- 13	BOLEY, JOHN PETER 'JOE'	D. DECEMBER 30, 1962 MAHANOY CITY, PA.
50- 10	BOLGER, JAMES CYRIL	5524 SIDNEY RD - CINCINNATI OH 45238
61- 9	BOLIN, BOBBY DONALD	BOX EAST - SIX MILE SC 29682
54- 8	BOLLING, FRANK ELMORE	171 FENWICK RD - MOBILE AL 36608
39- 12	BOLLING, JOHN EDWARD	BOX 9266 - PANAMA CITY BEACH FL 32407
52- 11	BOLLING, MILTON JOSEPH	2752 FONTAINEBLEAU DR SOUTH - MOBILE AL 36606
65- 12	BOLLO, GREGORY GENE	15207 REGINA ST - ALLEN PARK MI 48101
50- 11	BOLLWEG, DONALD RAYMOND	513 TIMBER RIDGE DR #206 - CAROL STREAM IL 60188
28- 11	BOLTON, CECIL GLENFORD	419 SOUTH MAIN ST - GREENVILLE MS 38701
87- 11	BOLTON, THOMAS EDWARD	RURAL ROUTE 1, NOLENSVILLE ROAD - BRENTWOOD TN 37027
31- 12	BOLTON, WILLIAM CLIFTON	D. APRIL 21, 1979 LEXINGTON, N. C.
78- 16	BOMBACK, MARK VINCENT	3573 COUNTY STREET - SOMERSET MA 02726
60- 11	BOND, WALTER FRANKLIN	D. SEPTEMBER 14, 1967 HOUSTON, TEX.
86- 18	BONDS, BARRY LAMAR	175 LYNDHURST AVENUE - SAN CARLOS CA 94070
68- 9	BONDS, BOBBY LEE	175 LYNDHURST - SAN CARLOS CA 94070
37- 11	BONETTI, JULIO G	D. JUNE 17, 1952 BELMONT, CAL.
27- 14	BONEY, HENRY TATE	BOX 906 - LAKE WORTH FL 33460
38- 8	BONGIOVANNI, ANTHONY THOMAS 'NINO'	416 ROSEWOOD AVE - SAN JOSE CA 95117
40- 3	BONHAM, ERNEST EDWARD 'TINY'	D. SEPTEMBER 15, 1949 PITTSBURGH, PA.
71- 13	BONHAM, WILLIAM GORDON	1605 SYCAMORE WAY - SOLVANG CA 93463
62- 13	BONIKOWSKI, JOSEPH PETER	6701 OLD REID RD - CHARLOTTE NC 28210
81- 11	BONILLA, JUAN GUILLERMO	RR 3 BOX 262 - QUINCY FL 32351
86- 20	BONILLA, ROBERTO MARTIN ANTONIO	2648 BAINBRIDGE AVENUE - BRONX NY 10458
13- 14	BONIN, ERNEST LUTHER	D. JANUARY 3, 1965 SYCAMORE, O.
77- 12	BONNELL, ROBERT BARRY	2102 179TH COURT NE - REDMOND WA 98052
80- 10	BONNER, ROBERT AVERILL	39 CEDAR TERRACE - HILTON NY 14468
44- 11	BONNESS, WILLIAM JOHN	D. DECEMBER 3, 1977 CLEVELAND, O.
20- 10	BONO, ADLAI WENDELL 'GUS'	D. DECEMBER 3, 1948 DEARBORN, MICH.
34- 11	BONURA, HENRY JOHN 'ZEKE'	D. MARCH 9, 1987 NEW ORLEANS, LA.
13- 15	BOOE, EVERETT LITTLE	D. MAY 21, 1969 KENNEDY, TEX.
83- 15	BOOKER, GREGORY SCOTT	14261 DALHOUSIE RD - SAN DIEGO CA 92129
66- 8	BOOKER, RICHARD LEE	BOX 59 - BRODKNEAL VA 24528
87- 12	BOOKER, RODERICK STEWART	526 WEST ALTADENA DRIVE - ALTADENA CA 91001
28- 12	BOOL, ALBERT	D. SEPTEMBER 27, 1981 LINCOLN, NEB.
81- 12	BOONE, DANIEL HUGH	320 MINNESOTA - EL CAJON CA 92020
22- 12	BOONE, ISAAC MORGAN 'IKE'	D. AUGUST 1, 1958 NORTHPORT, ALA.
19- 8	BOONE, JAMES ALBERT 'DANNY'	D. MAY 11, 1968 TUSCALOOSA, ALA.
13- 16	BOONE, LUTE JOSEPH	D. JULY 29, 1982 PITTSBURGH, PA.
48- 17	BOONE, RAYMOND OTIS	15420 OLDE HWY 80 #137 - EL CAJON CA 92021
72- 12	BOONE, ROBERT RAYMOND	18571 VILLA DR - VILLA PARK CA 92667
62- 16	BOOZER, JOHN MORGAN	D. JANUARY 24, 1986 LEXINGTON, S. C.
69- 11	BORBON, PEDRO RODRIGUEZ	LAS PALMAS,CORRAZOND DEJESUS #2-SANTO DOMINGO DOM. REP.
34- 12	BORDAGARAY, STANLEY GEORGE 'FRENCHY'	395 CRESTWOOD AV - VENTURA CA 93003
88- 16	BORDERS, PATRICK LANCE	1135 SOUTH LAKESHORE BLVD - LAKE WALES FL 33853
80- 11	BORDI, RICHARD ALBERT 'RICH'	206 ARROYO DR - SOUTH SAN FRANCISCO CA 94080
80- 12	BORDLEY, WILLIAM CLARKE	3605 WEST HIDDEN LANE #321 - PALOS VERDES CA 90274
72- 13	BORGMANN, GLENN DENNIS	16 LUNDY TER - BUTLER NJ 07405
82- 16	BORIS, PAUL STANLEY	12 WOODLAND DR - COLINIA NJ 07067
64- 9	BORK, FRANK BERNARD	5754 STRATHMORE LANE - DUBLIN OH 43017
50- 12	BORKOWSKI, ROBERT VILARIAN	1031 GERHARD ST - DAYTON OH 45404
60- 12	BORLAND, THOMAS BRUCE	624 CHEROKEE DR - STILLWATER OK 74074
44- 12	BOROM, EDWARD JONES 'RED'	827 HIGHLAND OAKS - DALLAS TX 75232
57- 7	BOROS, STEPHEN	13121 DECANT - POWAY CA 92064
42- 14	BOROWY, HENRY LUDWIG	210 WEST PASSAIC AVENUE - BLOOMFIELD NJ 07003
12- 21	BORTON, WILLIAM BAKER 'BABE'	D. JULY 29, 1954 BERKELEY, CALIF.
66- 9	BOSCH, DONALD JOHN	1600 MCKINLEY RD - NAPA CA 94558
76- 18	BOSETTI, RICHARD ALAN 'RICK'	1233 HILL ST - ANDERSON CA 96007
86- 21	BOSIO, CHRISTOPHER LOUIS	10425 AMBASSADOR DRIVE - RANCHO CORDOVA CA 95670
77- 13	BOSLEY, THADDIS	OLD ADD: 1965 VALLEY ROAD - OCEANSIDE CA 92054
66- 10	BOSMAN, RICHARD ALLAN	3058 LANDMARK BLVD #1202 - PALM HARBOR FL 33563
28- 13	BOSS, ELMER HARLEY	D. MAY 15, 1964 NASHVILLE, TENN.
45- 4	BOSSER, MELVIN EDWARD	RR 14 BOX 291 - CROSSVILLE TN 38555
15- 13	BOSTICK, HENRY LANDERS	D. SEPTEMBER 16, 1968 DENVER, COLO.
75- 18	BOSTOCK, LYMAN WESLEY	D. SEPTEMBER 24, 1978 GARY, IND.
84- 8	BOSTON, DARYL LAMONT	1016 VALLEY LANE - CINCINNATI OH 45229
64- 10	BOSWELL, DAVID WILSON	309 ROXBURY CT - JOPPA MD 21085
67- 6	BOSWELL, KENNETH GEORGE	2301 MATTERHORN LN - AUSTIN TX 78704
82- 17	BOTELHO, DEREK WAYNE	OLD ADD: 4900 NW 5TH AVE - BOCA RATON FL 33432
37- 12	BOTTARINI, JOHN CHARLES	D. OCTOBER 8, 1976 SPRING, N. MEX.

79- 10 BOTTING, RALPH WAYNE	1521 NORTH MYERS - BURBANK CA 91506
22- 13 BOTTOMLEY, JAMES LEROY	D. DECEMBER 11, 1959 SAINT LOUIS, MO.
62- 17 BOTZ, ROBERT ALLEN	4592 MONCHES RD - COLGATE WI 53017
56- 10 BOUCHEE, EDWARD FRANCIS	2036 SPRUCE AVE - DES PLAINES IL 60018
14- 23 BOUCHER, ALEXANDER FRANCIS	D. JUNE 23, 1974 TORRANCE, CALIF.
14- 24 BOUCHER, MEDRIC CHARLES FRANCIS	D. MARCH 12, 1974 MARTINEZ, CALIF.
38- 9 BOUDREAU, LOUIS	15600 ELLIS AVENUE - DOLTON IL 60419
61- 10 BOULDIN, CARL EDWARD	37 AUDUBON - FORT THOMAS KY 41075
80- 13 BOURJOS, CHRISTOPHER	3451 NORTH NEWCASTLE - CHICAGO IL 60634
71- 14 BOURQUE, PATRICK DANIEL	2013 EAST HARVARD DR - TEMPE AZ 85283
62- 18 BOUTON, JAMES ALAN	6 MYRON CT - TEANECK NJ 07666
70- 12 BOWA, LAWRENCE ROBERT	1029 MORRIS AVENUE - BRYN MAWR PA 19010
14- 25 BOWDEN, DAVID TIMON	D. OCTOBER 25, 1949 EMORY, GA.
19- 9 BOWEN, EMMONS JOSEPH 'CHICK'	D. AUGUST 9, 1948 NEW HAVEN, CONN.
77- 14 BOWEN, SAMUEL THOMAS	1405 KNOX VALLEY DRIVE - BRENTWOOD TN 37027
63- 13 BOWENS, SAMUEL EDWARD	RR 4 BOX 27 NATIONAL AVE - LELAND NC 28451
49- 8 BOWERS, GROVER BILL	P. O. BOX 401 - WYNNE AR 72396
35- 6 BOWERS, STEWART COLE	1620 RIDGWAY RD - HAVERTOWN PA 19083
31- 9 BOWLER, GRANT TIERNEY	D. JUNE 25, 1968 DENVER, COLO.
43- 10 BOWLES, CHARLES JAMES	3004 NORTH CENTER ST-HICKORY NC 28601
22- 14 BOWLES, EMMETT JEROME	D. SEPTEMBER 3, 1959 FLAGSTAFF, ARIZ.
67- 7 BOWLIN, LOIS WELDON 'HOSS'	BOX 1026 - LIVINGSTON AL 35470
76- 19 BOWLING, STEPHEN SHADDON	1784 WEST 63RD - TULSA OK 74132
14- 26 BOWMAN, ALVAH EDSON	D. OCTOBER 11, 1979 LONGVIEW, TEXAS
20- 11 BOWMAN, ELMER WILHELM	D. DECEMBER 17, 1985 LOS ANGELES, CALIF.
61- 11 BOWMAN, ERNEST FERRELL 'BUDDY'	ROUTE 17, EAST SHORE APT #8 - JOHNSON CITY TN 37601
32- 7 BOWMAN, JOSEPH EMIL	2001 WEST 83RD ST - LEAWOOD KS 66206
39- 13 BOWMAN, ROBERT JAMES	D. SEPTEMBER 4, 1972 BLUEFIELD, W. VA.
55- 15 BOWMAN, ROBERT LEROY	2911 VIA CARMEN - SAN JOSE CA 95124
49- 9 BOWMAN, ROGER CLINTON	1538 20TH STREET - SANTA MONICA CA 90404
10- 11 BOWSER, JAMES H. 'RED'	B. 1886 GREENSBURG, PA.
58- 11 BOWSFIELD, EDWARD OLIVER 'TED'	OLD ADD: 17 DORADO PLACE - ROLLING HILLS CA 90274
32- 18 BOYD, DENNIS RAY 'OIL CAN'	1611 20TH ST. - MERIDIAN MS 39301
69- 12 BOYD, GARY LEE	15227 CHANERA AVE - GARDENA CA 90249
10- 12 BOYD, RAYMOND C.	D. FEBRUARY 11, 1920 HOUTONVILLE, ILL.
51- 4 BOYD, ROBERT RICHARD	2811 NORTH VASSAR AVE - WICHITA KS 67220
55- 16 BOYER, CLETIS LEROY	100 ALETA DRIVE - BELLEAIR BEACH FL 34635
49- 10 BOYER, CLOYD VICTOR	RR 2 BOX 70-A-1 - JASPER MO 64755
55- 17 BOYER, KENTON LLOYD	D. SEPTEMBER 7, 1982 ST. LOUIS, MO.
78- 17 BOYLAND, DORIAN SCOTT 'DOE'	OLD ADD: 1205 SW 18TH - PORTLAND OR 97205
26- 8 BOYLE, JAMES JOHN	D. DECEMBER 24, 1958 CINCINNATI, O.
12- 22 BOYLE, JOHN BELLEW	D. APRIL 3, 1971 FORT LAUDERDALE, FLA.
29- 10 BOYLE, RALPH FRANCIS 'BUZZ'	D. NOVEMBER 12, 1978 CINCINNATI, O.
38- 10 BOYLES, HARRY	101 SIOUX RD #473 - PHARR TX 78577
66- 11 BRABENDER, EUGENE MATHEW	10969 AMENDA ROAD - MAZOMANIA WI 53560
37- 13 BRACK, GILBERT HERMAN 'GIB'	D. JANUARY 20, 1960 GREENVILLE, TEX.
64- 11 BRADEY, DONALD EUGENE	3686 OAKLEAF ROAD - WEST BLOOMFIELD MI 48033
66- 12 BRADFORD, CHARLES WILLIAM 'BUDDY'	6440 SPRING PARK AVE - LADERA HEIGHTS CA90056
43- 11 BRADFORD, HENRY VICTOR 'VIC'	259 STONEY POINT RD - PARIS KY 40361
77- 15 BRADFORD, LARRY	4998 GREENTREE TRAIL - COLLEGE PARK GA 30349
56- 11 BRADFORD, WILLIAM D	BOX 3043 - FAIRFIELD BAY AR 72153
48- 18 BRADLEY, FREDERICK LANGDON	4540 SOUTH LAYMAN AVE - PICO RIVERA CA 90660
46- 11 BRADLEY, GEORGE WASHINGTON	D. OCTOBER 19, 1982 LAWRENCEBURG, TENN.
27- 15 BRADLEY, HERBERT THEODORE	D. OCTOBER 16, 1959 CLAY CENTER, KAN.
10- 13 BRADLEY, HUGH FREDERICK	D. JANUARY 26, 1949 WORCESTER, MASS.
16- 7 BRADLEY, JOHN THOMAS	D. MARCH 18, 1969 TULSA, OKLA.
81- 13 BRADLEY, MARK ALLEN	OLD ADD: 413 PIERCE STREET - ELIZABETHTOWN KY 42701
83- 16 BRADLEY, PHILIP POOLE	207 MEADOW DRIVE - MACOMB IL 61455
84- 9 BRADLEY, SCOTT WILLIAM	30 ESSEX ROAD - ESSEX FALLS NJ 07021
83- 17 BRADLEY, STEVEN BERT 'BERT'	96 NORTH GOULD ROAD - COLUMBUS OH 43209
69- 13 BRADLEY, THOMAS WILLIAM	6306 WHISPERING OAKS DR - JACKSONVILLE FL 32211
17- 10 BRADSHAW, DALLAS CARL	D. DECEMBER 11, 1939 HERRIN, ILL.
52- 12 BRADSHAW, GEORGE THOMAS	258 BRUNSWICK AVENUE WEST - HOLDEN BEACH NC 28462
29- 11 BRADSHAW, JOE SIAH	D. JANUARY 30, 1985 TAVARES, FLA.
89- 19 BRADY, BRIAN PHELAN	67 SCHOOL STREET - MALVERNE NY 11565
20- 12 BRADY, CLIFFORD FRANCIS	D. SEPTEMBER 25, 1974 BELLEVILLE, ILL.
15- 14 BRADY, CORNELIUS JOSEPH 'NEAL'	D. JUNE 19, 1947 FORT MITCHELL, KY.
56- 12 BRADY, JAMES JOSEPH	4454 MAYWOOD DRIVE - JACKSONVILLE FL 32211
46- 12 BRADY, ROBERT JAY	42 OVERLAND ST - MANCHESTER CT 06040
12- 23 BRADY, WILLIAM A.	
40- 4 BRAGAN, ROBERT RANDALL	1901 INDIAN CREEK DR - FORT WORTH TX 76107
86- 22 BRAGGS, GLENN ERICK	2876 STATE STREET - SAN BERNARDINO CA 92405
14- 27 BRAINARD, FREDERICK	D. APRIL 17, 1959 GALVESTON, TEX.
15- 15 BRAITHWOOD, ALFRED	D. NOVEMBER 24, 1949 ROWLESBURG, W. VA.
28- 14 BRAME, ERVIN BECKHAM	D. NOVEMBER 22, 1949 HOPKINSVILLE, KY.
35- 7 BRAMHALL, ARTHUR WASHINGTON	D. SEPTEMBER 4, 1985 MADISON, WIS.
44- 13 BRANCA, RALPH THEODORE JOSEPH	NAT. PENSION, 1025 WESTCHESTER - WHITE PLAINS NY 10604
39- 14 BRANCATO, ALBERT	108 GREEN VALLEY RD-UPPER DARBY PA 19082
62- 19 BRANCH, HARVEY ALFRED	4995 JOLLY DR - MEMPHIS TN 38101
41- 8 BRANCH, NORMAN DOWNS	D. NOVEMBER 21, 1971 NAVASOTA, TEX.
79- 11 BRANCH, ROY	5322 TERRY AVE - SAINT LOUIS MO 63120
63- 14 BRAND, RONALD GEORGE	1500 PINE VALLEY CIR - ROSEVILLE CA 95678
66- 13 BRANDON, DARRELL G	196 OLD FARM RD - HANOVER MA 02339
28- 15 BRANDT, EDWARD ARTHUR	D. NOVEMBER 1, 1944 SPOKANE, WASH.
56- 13 BRANDT, JOHN GEORGE 'JACKIE'	611 OSAGE DR - PAPILLION NE 68046
41- 9 BRANDT, WILLIAM GEORGE	D. MAY 16, 1968 FORT WAYNE, IND.
28- 16 BRANNAN, OTIS OWEN	D. JUNE 6, 1967 LITTLE ROCK, ARK.
27- 16 BRANOM, EDGAR DUDLEY 'DUD'	D. FEBRUARY 4, 1980 SUN CITY, ARIZ.
80- 14 BRANT, MARSHALL LEE	604 SCOTLAND DRIVE - SANTA ROSA CA 95409
88- 17 BRANTLEY, JEFFREY HOKE	4761 MERRYWOOD CIRCLE - BIRMINGHAM AL 35226
86- 23 BRANTLEY, MICHAEL CHARLES 'MICKEY'	102 SUMMIT - CATSKILL NY 12414
21- 8 BRATCHE, FREDERICK OSCAR	D. JANUARY 7, 1962 MASSILLON, O.
24- 13 BRATCHER, JOSEPH WARLICK	D. OCTOBER 13, 1977 FORT WORTH, TEX.
64- 12 BRAUN, JOHN PAUL	1014 AMSTERDAM AVE - MADISON WI 53716
71- 15 BRAUN, STEPHEN RUSSELL	12605 JAMES ROAD - MINNETONKA MN 55343
69- 14 BRAVO, ANGEL ALFONSO	OLD ADD: CALLE CAMINO NUEVO #208-MARACAIBO VZ
21- 9 BRAXTON, EDGAR GARLAND	D. FEBRUARY 25, 1966 NORFLOK, VA.
41- 10 BRAY, CLARENCE WILBUR 'BUSTER'	D. SEPTEMBER 4, 1982 EVANSVILLE, IND.

21- 10	BRAZILL, FRANK LEO	D. NOVEMBER 3, 1976 OAKLAND, CALIF.
43- 12	BRAZLE, ALPHA EUGENE	D. OCTOBER 24, 1973 GRAND JUNCTION , COL.
83- 18	BREAM, SIDNEY EUGENE	2516 ELKRIDGE DRIVE - WEXFORD PA 15090
69- 15	BREAZEALE, JAMES LEO	717 BOLLING LANE - HOUSTON TX 77076
40- 5	BRECHEEN, HARRY DAVID	1134 SOUTH HIGHSCHOOL - ADA OK 74820
29- 12	BRECKINRIDGE, WILLIAM ROBERTSON	D. AUGUST 23, 1958 TULSA, OKLA.
69- 16	BREEDEN, DANNY RICHARD	111 "B" AVENUE - LOXLEY AL 36551
71- 16	BREEDEN, HAROLD NOEL	RR1 BOX 311 - LEESBURG GA 31763
60- 13	BREEDING, MARVIN EUGENE	BOX 1061 - DECATUR AL 35601
80- 15	BREINING, FRED LAWRENCE	1218 33RD AVE - SAN FRANCISCO CA 94122
37- 14	BREMER, HERBERT FREDERICK	D. NOVEMBER 28, 1979 COLUMBUS, GA.
14- 28	BRENEGAN, OLAF SELMAR	D. APRIL 20, 1956 GALESVILLE, WIS.
81- 14	BRENLY, ROBERT EARL	936 ORANGE ST - COSHOCTON OH 43812
10- 14	BRENNAN, ADDISON FOSTER	D. JANUARY 7, 1962 KANSAS CITY, MO.
33- 7	BRENNAN, JAMES DONALD 'DON'	D. APRIL 2L, 1953 BOSTON, MASS.
81- 15	BRENNAN, THOMAS MARTIN	5500 OAK CENTER DR - OAK LAWN IL 60453
88- 18	BRENNAN, WILLIAM RAYMOND	678 SIOUX DRIVE - MACON GA 31210
65- 13	BRENNEMAN, JAMES LEROY	OLD ADD: 1855 EAST ROSE #12A - ORANGE CA 92667
12- 24	BRENNER, DELBERT HENRY	D. APRIL 11, 1971 ST. LOUIS PARK, MINN.
13- 17	BRENTON, LYNN DAVIS	D. OCTOBER 14, 1968 LOS ANGELES, CALIF.
32- 8	BRENZEL, WILLIAM RICHARD	D. JUNE 12, 1979 OAKLAND, CALIF.
14- 29	BRESSLER, RAYMOND BLOOM 'RUBE'	D. NOVEMBER 7, 1966 MT. WASHINGTON, O.
56- 14	BRESSOUD, EDWARD FRANCIS	10455 CRESTON DR - LOS ALTOS CA 94022
13- 18	BRETON, JOHN FREDERICK 'JIM'	D. MAY 30, 1973 BELOIT, WIS.
73- 13	BRETT, GEORGE HOWARD	OLD ADD: 3201 WEST 98TH - LEAWOOD KS 06206
24- 14	BRETT, HERBERT JAMES	D. NOVEMBER 25, 1974 ST PETERSBURG, FLA.
67- 8	BRETT, KENNETH ALLEN	501 JOHN STREET - MANHATTAN BEACH CA 90266
39- 15	BREUER, MARVIN HOWARD	1106 JOYCE AVE-ROLLA MO 65401
84- 10	BREWER, ANTHONY BRUCE	659 WILDWOOD LANE - PALO ALTO CA 94303
44- 14	BREWER, JACK HERNDON	28271 WEST WORCESTER ROAD - SUN CITY CA 92381
60- 14	BREWER, JAMES THOMAS	D. NOVEMBER 16, 1987 TYLER, TEXAS
86- 24	BREWER, MICHAEL QUINN	2260 BRENTWOOD COURT - EAST PALO ALTO CA 94303
54- 9	BREWER, THOMAS AUSTIN	409 STATE RD - CHERAW SC 29520
43- 13	BREWSTER, CHARLES LAWRENCE	RURAL ROUTE 2 BOX 982 - BLACKSHEAR GA 31516
61- 12	BRICE, ALAN HEALEY	7807 16TH AVE NW - BRADENTON FL 33505
58- 12	BRICKELL, FRITZ DARRELL	D. OCTOBER 15, 1965 WICHITA, KAN.
26- 9	BRICKELL, GEORGE FREDERICK 'FRED'	D. APRIL 8, 1961 WICHITA, KAN.
13- 19	BRICKLEY, GEORGE VINCENT	D. FEBRUARY 23, 1947 EVERETT, MASS.
52- 13	BRICKNER, RALPH HAROLD	3967 ROBINHILL DR - CINCINNATI OH 45211
51- 5	BRIDEWESER, JAMES EHRENFELD	D. AUGUST 25, 1989 EL TORO, CALIF.
51- 6	BRIDGES, EVERETT LAMAR 'ROCKY'	2445 E. GATEWAY RD - COUER D'ALENE ID 83814
59- 7	BRIDGES, MARSHALL	1937 CAMELLIA LANE - JACKSON MS 39204
30- 5	BRIDGES, THOMAS JEFFERSON DAVIS	D. APRIL 19, 1968 NASHVILLE, TENN.
12- 25	BRIEF, ANTHONY VINCENT 'BUNNY'	D. FEBRUARY 10, 1963 MILWAUKEE, WIS.
75- 19	BRIGGS, DANIEL LEE	231 FRANCE ST - SONOMA CA 95476
64- 13	BRIGGS, JOHN EDWARD	432 E. 27TH - PATERSON NJ 07514
56- 15	BRIGGS, JOHN TIFT	8724 SHERRY DR - ORANGEVALE CA 95662
58- 13	BRIGHT, HARRY JAMES	2048 50TH AVE - SACRAMENTO CA 95827
65- 14	BRILES, NELSON KELLEY	1324 CLEARVIEW DRIVE - GREENSBURG PA 15501
88- 19	BRILEY, GREGORY	RURAL ROUTE 5 BOX 141 - GREENVILLE NC 27834
22- 15	BRILLHEART, JAMES BENSON	D. SEPTEMBER 2, 1972 RADFORD, VA.
12- 26	BRINKER, WILLIAM HUTCHINSON	D. FEBRUARY 5, 1965 ARCADIA, CAL.
69- 17	BRINKMAN, CHARLES ERNEST	2911 WESTRIDGE #3 - CINCINNATI OH 45238
61- 13	BRINKMAN, EDWIN ALBERT	7106 WYANDOTTE DR - CINCINNATI OH 45238
52- 14	BRINKOPF, LEON CLARENCE	915 SOUTH MINNESOTA - CAPE GIRARDEAU MO 63701
47- 13	BRISSIE, LELAND VICTOR 'LOU'	1908 WHITEPINE DR - NORTH AUGUSTA SC 29841
66- 14	BRISTOL, JAMES DAVID 'DAVE'	RURAL ROUTE 1 BOX 456 - ANDREWS NC 28901
37- 15	BRITTAIN, AUGUST SCHUSTER	D. FEBRUARY 16, 1974 WILMINGTON, N. C.
50- 13	BRITTIN, JOHN ALBERT	1036 FRANCELLA CT - SPRINGFIELD IL 62702
67- 9	BRITTON, JAMES ALAN	10455 SW 112TH ST - MIAMI FL 33176
13- 20	BRITTON, STEPHEN GILBERT	D. JUNE 20, 1983 PARSONS, KAN.
79- 12	BRIZZOLARA, ANTHONY JOHN	1638 PRINCESS CIR NE - ATLANTA GA 30345
34- 13	BROACA, JOHN JOSEPH	D. MAY 16, 1985 LAWRENCE, MASS.
71- 17	BROBERG, PETER SVEN	220 MONTEREY RD - PALM BEACH FL 33480
82- 19	BROCK, GREGORY ALLEN	201 SOUTH 46TH STREET - MILWAUKEE WI 53214
17- 11	BROCK, JOHN RAY	D. OCTOBER 27, 1951 CLAYTON, MO.
61- 14	BROCK, LOUIS CLARK	12595 DURBIN DR - ST LOUIS MO 63141
52- 15	BRODOWSKI, RICHARD STANLEY	90 FORD ST - LYNN MA 01904
59- 8	BROGLIO, ERNEST GILBERT	2838 VIA CARMEN - SAN JOSE CA 95124
72- 14	BROHAMER, JOHN ANTHONY	1236 LEXINGTON DR - VISTA CA 92083
44- 15	BRONDELL, KENNETH LEROY	7029 DECELIS PLACE - VAN NUYS CA 91406
10- 15	BRONKIE, HERMAN CHARLES	D. MAY 27, 1968 SOMERS, CONN.
59- 9	BRONSTAD, JAMES WARREN	693 QUAIL RIDGE ROAD - ALEDO TX 76008
75- 20	BROOKENS, EDWARD DWAIN	RR 1 - FAYETTEVILLE PA 17222
79- 13	BROOKENS, THOMAS DALE	120 HILLSIDE DR - FAYETTEVILLE PA 17222
80- 16	BROOKS, HUBERT	1502 SPRING AVE - COMPTON CA 90221
25- 11	BROOKS, JONATHAN JOSEPH 'MANDY'	D. JUNE 17, 1962 KIRKWOOD, MO.
69- 18	BROOKS, ROBERT	1130 WEST 252ND ST - HARBOR CITY CA 90710
40- 6	BROSKIE, SIGMUND THEODORE	D. MAY 17, 1975 CANTON, O.
54- 10	BROSNAN, JAMES PATRICK	7742 WEST CHURCHILL ST - MORTON GROVE IL 60053
69- 19	BROSSEAU, FRANKLIN LEE	41 ISLAND RD - SAINT PAUL MN 55110
16- 8	BROTTEM, ANTON CHRISTIAN 'TONY'	D. AUGUST 5, 1929 CHICAGO, ILL.
80- 17	BROUHARD, MARK STEVEN	6289 JACKIE AVE - WOODLAND HILLS CA 91367
55- 18	BROVIA, JOSEPH JOHN	142 ACADIA ST - SANTA CRUZ CA 95060
20- 13	BROWER, FRANK WILLARD	D. NOVEMBER 20, 1960 BALTIMORE, MD.
31- 10	BROWER, LOUIS LESTER	308 SUNRISE RD - ROSWELL NM 88201
86- 25	BROWER, ROBERT RICHARD	2110 GUNNELL FARMS DRIVE - VIENNA VA 22180
51- 7	BROWN, ALTON LEO	253 CONSUL AVE - VIRGINIA BEACH VA 23462
11- 17	BROWN, CARROLL WILLIAM 'BOARDWALK'	D. FEBRUARY 8, 1977 BURLINGTON, N. J.
11- 18	BROWN, CHARLES ROY 'CURLY'	D. JUNE 10, 1968 SPRING HILL, KAN.
28- 17	BROWN, CLINTON HAROLD	D. DECEMBER 31, 1955 ROCKY RIVER,O.
73- 14	BROWN, CURTIS	3745 HAYWOOD ST - SACRAMENTO CA 95838
83- 19	BROWN, CURTIS STEVEN	104 EAST HEMINGWAY CIRCLE - COCONUT CREEK FL 33063
81- 16	BROWN, DARRELL WAYNE	5843 FIFTH AVE - LOS ANGELES CA 90043
14- 30	BROWN, DELOS HIGHT	D. DECEMBER 21, 1964 CARBONDALE, ILL.
15- 16	BROWN, DONALD G	1917 ADD: 712 ELLAS ST - BEATRICE NE
13- 21	BROWN, DRUMMOND NICOL	D. JANUARY 27, 1927 PLATTE CO., MO.
20- 14	BROWN, EDWARD WILLIAM	D. SEPTEMBER 10, 1956 VALLEJO, CAL.

29

69- 20 BROWN, EDWIN RANDOLPH 'RANDY'	P.O. BOX 326 - PLYMOUTH FL 32768
11- 19 BROWN, ELMER YOUNG	D. JANUARY 23, 1955 INDIANAPOLIS, IND.
51- 8 BROWN, HECTOR HAROLD 'HAL'	BOX 1626 - GREENSBORO NC 27402
69- 21 BROWN, ISAAC 'IKE'	LINCOLN CT #A-4 - LAKELAND FL 33805
70- 13 BROWN, JACKIE GENE	RR 3 BOX 50B - HOLDENVILLE OK 74848
37- 16 BROWN, JAMES ROBERSON	D. DECEMBER 29, 1977 BATH, N. C.
75- 21 BROWN, JERALD RAY 'JAKE'	D. DECEMBER 18, 1981 HOUSTON, TEXAS
84- 11 BROWN, JOHN CHRISTOPHER	5015 BRIGHTON AVE - LOS ANGELES CA 90062
86- 26 BROWN, JOHN KEVIN	MCINTYRE GA 31054
37- 17 BROWN, JOHN LINDSAY	D. JANUARY 1, 1967 SAN ANTONIO, TEX.
68- 10 BROWN, JOPHERY CLIFFORD	3008 WEST 81ST ST - INGLEWOOD CA 90305
27- 17 BROWN, JOSEPH HENRY	D. MARCH 7, 1950 LOS ANGELES, CALIF.
88- 20 BROWN, KEITH EDWARD	2584 NEAL LANE - REDDING CA 96003
63- 15 BROWN, LARRY LESLEY	13158 LAMIRADA CIRCLE - WEST PALM BEACH FL 33414
76- 20 BROWN, LEON	7537 SOUTH LAROSA - TEMPE AZ 85283
25- 12 BROWN, LLOYD ANDREW	D. JANUARY 14, 1974 OPALOCKA, FLA.
35- 8 BROWN, MACE STANLEY	305 NORTH HOLDEN ROAD-GREENSBORO NC 27410
84- 12 BROWN, MARK ANTHONY	59 CHURCH ST - NORTH WALPOLE NH 03608
88- 21 BROWN, MARTY LEO	619 PINE STREET - ROLLA MO 65401
83- 20 BROWN, MICHAEL CHARLES	312 COPCO LANE - SAN JOSE CA 95123
82- 20 BROWN, MICHAEL GARY	8712 PINE NEEDLES CT - VIENNA VA 22180
22- 16 BROWN, MYRL LINCOLN	D. FEBRUARY 23, 1981 HARRISBURG, PA.
43- 14 BROWN, NORMAN	106 EAST MAIN ST-BENNETTSVILLE SC 29512
65- 15 BROWN, OLLIE LEE	8462 COUNTRY CLUB DR - BUENA PARK CA 90621
69- 22 BROWN, OSCAR LEE	19113 GUNLOCK AVE - CARSON CA 90746
61- 15 BROWN, PAUL DWAYNE	RR 4 - HOLDENVILLE OK 74848
57- 8 BROWN, RICHARD ERNEST	D. APRIL 12, 1970 BALTIMORE, MD.
14- 31 BROWN, ROBERT M.	B. 1891
30- 6 BROWN, ROBERT MURRAY	%M.REMONDINI,123 RICHARD DRIVE - HANOVER MA 02339
46- 13 BROWN, ROBERT WILLIAM	1324 THOMAS PL - FORT WORTH TX 76107
79- 14 BROWN, ROGERS LEE 'BOBBY'	OLD ADD: BOX 874 - EASTVILLE VA 23307
81- 17 BROWN, SCOTT EDWARD	RR 1 BOX 1058 - DEQUINCY LA 70633
83- 21 BROWN, STEPHEN ELBERT	1203 WEST 8TH STREET - DAVIS CA 95616
78- 18 BROWN, THOMAS DALE	248 GLORIA DR - BATON ROUGE LA 70815
44- 16 BROWN, THOMAS MICHAEL	315 SHADY PL - BRENTWOOD TN 37027
63- 16 BROWN, THOMAS WILLIAM	9104 WOODLAND DR - SILVER SPRING MD 20910
25- 13 BROWN, WALTER GEORGE 'JUMBO'	D. OCTOBER 2, 1966 FREEPORT, N. Y.
47- 14 BROWN, WALTER IRVING	RR ORIENTAL PARK - BEMUS POINT NY 14712
47- 15 BROWN, WILLARD JESSE	2217 BRECKENRIDGE - HOUSTON TX 77026
63- 17 BROWN, WILLIAM JAMES 'GATES'	17206 SANTA BARBARA - DETROIT MI 48221
12- 27 BROWN, WILLIAM VERNA	D. MAY 15, 1965 LUBBOCK, TEX.
65- 16 BROWNE, BYRON ELLIS	OLD ADD: 1015 NORTH 31ST ST - BATON ROUGE LA 7080
35- 9 BROWNE, EARL JAMES	98 POTTS LANE - KING GEORGE VA 22485
86- 27 BROWNE, JEROME AUSTIN	2A PRINCE STREET - CHRISTIANSTED VI 00820
62- 20 BROWNE, PRENTICE ALMONT 'PIDGE'	187-23 CASPER DR - SPRING TX 77373
60- 15 BROWNING, CALVIN DUANE	1000 CAMELOT - CLINTON OK 73601
10- 16 BROWNING, FRANK	D. MAY 19, 1948 SAN ANTONIO, TEX.
84- 13 BROWNING, THOMAS LEO	5312 VANDERBILT ROAD - MOUNT JULIET TN 37122
67- 10 BRUBAKER, BRUCE ELLSWORTH	2026 BAHAMA ROAD - LEXINGTON KY 40509
32- 9 BRUBAKER, WILBUR LEE 'BILL'	D. APRIL 2, 1978 LAGUNA HILLS, CALIF.
59- 10 BRUCE, ROBERT JAMES	RR 4 BOX 363X - CANYON LAKE TX 78130
61- 16 BRUCKBAUER, FRED JOHN	404 MCHUGH - HOLMEN WI 54636
37- 18 BRUCKER, EARLE FRANCIS SR	D. MAY 8, 1981 SAN DIEGO, CALIF.
48- 19 BRUCKER, EARLE FRANCIS JR.	629 MUNDY TERRACE - EL CAJON CA 92020
21- 11 BRUGGY, FRANK LEO	D. APRIL 5, 1959 ELIZABETH, N. J.
78- 19 BRUHERT, MICHAEL EDWIN	143-35 95TH AVE - JAMAICA NY 11435
87- 13 BRUMLEY, ANTHONY MICHAEL 'MIKE'	OLD ADD: 2618 WEST QUINCY CIR - BROKEN ARROW OK 74012
64- 14 BRUMLEY, TONY MIKE 'MIKE'	2621 WEST VANDALIA STREET - BROKEN ARROW OK 74012
81- 18 BRUMMER, GLENN EDWARD	RR 2 BOX 175 - MOUNTAIN GROVE MO 65711
81- 19 BRUNANSKY, THOMAS ANDREW	1319 SOUTH HILLWARD AVE - WEST COVINA CA 91791
49- 11 BRUNER, JACK RAYMOND	1641 NORTH 76TH - LINCOLN NE 68505
39- 16 BRUNER, WALTER ROY	D. NOVEMBER 30, 1986 ST. MATTHEWS, KY.
56- 16 BRUNET, GEORGE STUART	1511 EAST DIANA AVENUE - ANAHEIM CA 92805
76- 21 BRUNO, THOMAS MICHAEL	OLD ADD: 4609 LINSCOTT - DOWNERS GROVE IL
66- 15 BRUNSBERG, ARLO ADOLPH	1164 128TH AVE NORTH - BLAINE MN 55434
77- 16 BRUSSTAR, WARREN SCOTT	3320 REDWOOD RD - NAPA CA 94558
53- 13 BRUTON, WILLIAM HARON	6122 WEST OUTER DR - DETROIT MI 48235
61- 17 BRYAN, BILLY RONALD	3001 HICKORY LANE - OPELIKA AL 36801
35- 10 BRYANT, CLAIBORNE HENRY	1380 NW 43RD TER #102-FORT LAUDERDALE FL33313
79- 15 BRYANT, DEREK ROSZELL	PASEO DE LAS VILLAS #72 - GUAYAMOS SONORA MEX.
66- 16 BRYANT, DONALD RAY	OLD ADD: 4023 SW 328TH - FEDERAL WAY WA 98003
85- 7 BRYANT, RALPH WENDELL	RR 4 BOX 374 - LEESBURG GA 31763
67- 11 BRYANT, RONALD RAYMOND	2318 SHIRE LN - DAVIS CA 95616
86- 28 BRYDEN, THOMAS RAY	11133 51ST AVENUE SOUTH #10 - SEATTLE WA 98178
70- 14 BRYE, STEPHEN ROBERT	681 ROCK ISLAND CIRCLE - DANVILLE CA 94526
22- 17 BUBSER, HAROLD FRED	D. JUNE 22, 1959 MELROSE PARK, ILL.
48- 20 BUCHA, JOHN GEORGE	1215 NORTH MINK RD - DANIELSVILLE PA 18038
85- 8 BUCHANAN, ROBERT GORDON	4704 HIGHWAY 30 - ELY IA 52227
61- 18 BUCHEK, GERALD PETER	3950A WILMINGTON AVE - ST. LOUIS MO 63116
34- 14 BUCHER, JAMES QUINTER	RR 1 BOX 599 - PALMYRA PA 17078
18- 7 BUCKEYE, GARLAND MAIERS	D. NOVEMBER 14, 1975 STONE LAKE, WIS.
16- 9 BUCKLES, JESS ROBERT	D. AUGUST 2, 1975 WESTMINSTER, CAL.
84- 14 BUCKLEY, KEVIN JOHN	34 CALVIN ST - BRAINTREE MA 02184
69- 23 BUCKNER, WILLIAM JOSEPH	3 MCDONALD CIR - ANDOVER MA 01810
78- 20 BUDASKA, MARK DAVID	702 WASHINGTON STREET #43 - MARINA DEL REY CA 90292
56- 17 BUDDIN, DONALD THOMAS	BOX 186 - FOUNTAIN INN SC 29644
46- 14 BUDNICK, MICHAEL JOE	307 WEST BLAINE - SEATTLE WA 98119
85- 9 BUECHELE, STEVEN BERNARD	1730 MIRAMAR - FULLERTON CA 92631
13- 22 BUES, ARTHUR FREDERICK	D. NOVEMBER 7, 1954 WHITEFISH BAY, WIS.
63- 18 BUFORD, DONALD ALVIN	15412 VALLEY VISTA BLVD-SHERMAN OAKS CA 91403
53- 14 BUHL, ROBERT RAY	146 ORANGE BLOSSOM LANE SW - WINTER HAVEN FL 33880
87- 14 BUHNER, JAY CAMPBELL	1511 DAVON LANE - HOUSTON TX 77058
87- 15 BUICE, DEWAYNE ALLISON	1866 PARKCREST DRIVE - COSTA MESA 92627
45- 5 BUKER, CYRIL OWEN	108 CENTRAL AVE - GREENWOOD WI 54437
54- 11 BULLARD, GEORGE DONALD	7 DYER COURT - DANVERS MA 01923
77- 17 BULLING, TERRY CHARLES 'BUD'	OLD ADD: 15591 ASTER ST - WESTMINSTER CA
85- 10 BULLOCK, ERIC JERALD	17503 HARWICK COURT - CARSON CA 90746
36- 11 BULLOCK, MALTON JOSEPH	D. JUNE 27, 1988 PASCAGOULA, MISS.

GEORGE ALTMAN

SANDY ALOMAR

BERT BLYLEVEN

SCOTT BRADLEY

STEVE CARLTON

ORLANDO CEPEDA

JACK CLARK

SAM DENTE

DOM DIMAGGIO

BUMBRY

CABALLERO

72- 15 BUMBRY, ALONZO BENJAMIN — 28 TREMBLANT CT - LUTHERVILLE MD 21093
63- 19 BUNKER, WALLACE EDWARD — 502 FIRST ST - LANGLEY WA 98260
55- 19 BUNNING, JAMES PAUL DAVID — 4 FAIRWAY DRIVE - SOUTHGATE KY 41071
69- 24 BURBACH, WILLIAM DAVID — BOX 3 - DICKEYVILLE WI 53808
55- 20 BURBRINK, NELSON EDWARD — 9895 88TH WAY NORTH - SEMINOLE FL 33543
69- 25 BURCHART, LARRY WAYNE — OLD ADD: 6305 SOUTH 114TH EAST AVE - TULSA OK 74133
62- 21 BURDA, EDWARD ROBERT 'BOB' — 8737 EAST KEIM DR - SCOTTSDALE AZ 85253
62- 22 BURDETTE, FREDDIE THOMASON — 1200 KINGSTON CT #G5 - ALBANY GA 31707
50- 14 BURDETTE, SELVA LEWIS 'LOU' — 2019 BENEVA ROAD - SARASOTA FL 34232
10- 17 BURG, JOSEPH PETER — D. APRIL 28, 1969 JOLIET, ILL.
49- 12 BURGESS, FORREST HARRILL 'SMOKEY' — 717 CAROLEEN RD - FOREST CITY NC 28043
54- 12 BURGESS, THOMAS ROLAND — 3201 WALNUT ST NE - ST PETERSBURG FL 33704
68- 11 BURGMEIER, THOMAS HENRY — 13118 WALMER - OVERLAND PARK KS 66209
43- 15 BURGO, WILLIAM ROSS — D. OCTOBER 19, 1988
42- 15 BURICH, WILLIAM MAX — 1175 LAMOREE RD #62 - SAN MARCOS CA 92069
10- 18 BURK, CHARLES SANFORD — D. OCTOBER 11, 1934 BROOKLYN, N.Y.
56- 18 BURK, MACK EDWIN — 5710 GLEN PINES - HOUSTON TX 77069
15- 17 BURKAM, CHAUNCEY DEPEW — D. MAY 9, 1964 KALAMAZOO, MICH.
36- 12 BURKART, ELMER ROBERT — 139 OTHORIDGE - LUTHERVILLE MD 21093
76- 22 BURKE, GLENN LAWRENCE — 641 61ST STREET - OAKLAND CA 94609
58- 14 BURKE, LEO PATRICK — 1729 WOODBURN DRIVE - HAGERSTOWN MD 21740
23- 16 BURKE, LESLIE KINGSTON — D. MAY 6, 1975 DANVERS, MASS.
24- 15 BURKE, PATRICK EDWARD — D. JULY 7, 1965 ST. LOUIS, MO.
27- 18 BURKE, ROBERT JAMES — D. FEBRUARY 8, 1971 JOLIET, ILL.
77- 18 BURKE, STEVEN MICHAEL — 4656 HIBISCUS RD - STOCKTON CA 95205
85- 11 BURKE, TIMOTHY PHILIP — 4715 SOUTH 162ND AVENUE - OMAHA NE 68135
10- 19 BURKE, WILLIAM IGNATIUS — D. FEBRUARY 9, 1967 WORCESTER, MASS.
87- 16 BURKETT, JOHN DAVID — 104 CRANDON CIRCLE - BEAVER PA 15009
45- 6 BURKHART, WILLIAM KENNETH 'KEN' — 3708 SPLENDOR DRIVE, RR 7 - KNOXVILLE TN 37918
87- 17 BURKS, ELLIS RAY — 2709 GALEMEADOW DRIVE - FORT WORTH TX 76133
74- 13 BURLESON, RICHARD PAUL 'RICK' — 270 EAST MIRA VERDE DR - LAHABRA HEIGHTS CA 90631
27- 19 BURNETT, JOHN HENDERSON — D. AUGUST 12, 1959 TAMPA, FLA.
56- 19 BURNETTE, WALLACE HARPER — RR 1 BOX 168 - BLAIRS VA 24527
23- 17 BURNS, DENNIS — D. MAY 21, 1969 TULSA, OKLA.
12- 28 BURNS, EDWARD JAMES — D. JUNE 1, 1942 MONTEREY, CALIF.
14- 32 BURNS, GEORGE HENRY — D. JANUARY 7, 1978 KIRKLAND, WASH.
11- 20 BURNS, GEORGE JOSEPH — D. AUGUST 15, 1966 GLOVERSVILLE, N.Y.
30- 7 BURNS, JOHN IRVING — D. APRIL 18, 1975 BOSTON, MASS.
10- 20 BURNS, JOSEPH FRANCIS — D. JULY 12, 1987 BEVERLY, MASS.
24- 16 BURNS, JOSEPH FRANCIS — D. JANUARY 7, 1986 TRENTON, N. J.
43- 16 BURNS, JOSEPH JAMES — D. JUNE 24, 1974 BRYN MAWR, PA.
78- 21 BURNS, ROBERT BRITT — 2162 BANEBERRY DRIVE - BIRMINGHAM AL 35244
88- 22 BURNS, TODD ERIC — 1210 WEST SHARON LANE - SCHAUMBURG IL 60193
55- 21 BURNSIDE, PETER WILLITS — 1945 CHESTNUT - WILMETTE IL 60091
78- 22 BURNSIDE, SHELDON JOHN — 4351 BLOOR ST #34 - ETOBICKE ONT. M9C 2A4 CAN.
46- 15 BURPO, GEORGE HARVIE — 8981 EAST PALMS DR - TUCSON AZ 85715
14- 33 BURR, ALEXANDER THOMSON — D. NOVEMBER 1, 1918 FRANCE
62- 23 BURRIGHT, LARRY ALLEN — 1239 EAST PALM DR - GLENDORA CA 91740
73- 15 BURRIS, BERTRAM RAY 'RAY' — 2304 WOODSONG TRAIL - ARLINGTON TX 76016
48- 21 BURRIS, PAUL ROBERT — 12816 MAYES ROAD - HUNTERSVILLE NC 28078
70- 15 BURROUGHS, JEFFREY ALAN — 6155 LAGUNA CT - LONG BEACH CA 90803
43- 17 BURROWS, JOHN — D. APRIL 27, 1987 COAL RUN, O.
19- 10 BURRUS, MAURICE LENNON 'DICK' — D. DECEMBER 2, 1972 ELIZABETH CITY, N. C.
58- 15 BURTON, ELLIS NARRINGTON — 8044 ROSE STREET #4 - PARAMOUNT CA 90723
75- 22 BURTON, JIM SCOTT — 9606 LONE OAK COURT - MATTHEWS NC 28105
50- 15 BURTSCHY, EDWARD FRANK 'MOE' — 620 PEDRETTE APT A-6 - CINCINNATI OH 45238
85- 12 BURTT, DENNIS ALLEN — 135 WEST STADIUM DRIVE - STOCKTON CA 95204
60- 16 BURWELL, RICHARD MATTHEW — P. O. BOX 1825 - TWIN FALLS ID 83301
20- 15 BURWELL, WILLIAM EDWIN — D. JUNE 11, 1973 ORMOND BEACH, FLA.
50- 16 BUSBY, JAMES FRANKLIN — RR 1 BOX 76A - MILLEN GA 30442
41- 11 BUSBY, PAUL MILLER — 2011 35TH AVE-MERIDIAN MS 39301
72- 16 BUSBY, STEVEN LEE — OLD ADD: BOX 783 - BLUE SPRINGS MO
43- 18 BUSCH, EDGAR JOHN — D. JANUARY 17, 1987 SHILOH VALLEY TWP,ST. CLAIR CO,ILL.
65- 17 BUSCHHORN, DONALD LEE — 17804 EAST 26TH ST - INDEPENDENCE MO 64057
23- 18 BUSH, GUY TERRELL — D. JULY 2, 1985 SHANNON, MISS.
12- 29 BUSH, LESLIE AMBROSE 'JOE' — D. NOVEMBER 1, 1974 FORT LAUDERDALE, FLA.
82- 21 BUSH, ROBERT RANDALL 'RANDY' — OLD ADD: 38 OLYMPIC COURT - NEW ORLEANS LA 70114
27- 20 BUSHEY, FRANCIS CLYDE — D. MARCH 18, 1972 TOPEKA, KAN.
26- 10 BUSKEY, JOSEPH HENRY — D. APRIL 11, 1949 CUMBERLAND, MD.
77- 19 BUSKEY, MICHAEL THOMAS — 500 KING DRIVE #1012 - DALY CITY CA 94015
73- 16 BUSKEY, THOMAS WILLIAM — 476 ALLEGHENY DR - HARRISBURG PA 17111
71- 18 BUSSE, RAYMOND EDWARD — OLD ADD: 501 MYRTLE LN SOUTH - DAYTONA BEACH FL
36- 13 BUTCHER, ALBERT MAXWELL 'MAX' — D. SEPTEMBER 15, 1957 LOGAN, W. VA.
11- 21 BUTCHER, HENRY JOSDPH — D. DECEMBER 28, 1979 HAZEL CREST, ILL.
80- 18 BUTCHER, JOHN DANIEL — 302 WINCHESTER COURT - LAKE BLUFF IL 60044
80- 19 BUTERA, SALVATORE PHILIP — 1944 SAINT ANDREWS PLACE - LONGWOOD FL 32779
43- 19 BUTKA, EDWARD LUKE — 131 WEST COLLEGE ST-CANONSBURG PA 15317
40- 7 BUTLAND, WILBURN RUE 'BILL' — 2735 CRUFT-TERRE HAUTE IN 47803
11- 22 BUTLER, ARTHUR EDWARD — D. OCTOBER 7, 1984 FALL RIVER, MASS.
81- 20 BUTLER, BRETT MORGAN — 215 FRASHER WAY - DULUTH GA 30136
62- 24 BUTLER, CECIL DEAN — RR4 - DALLAS GA 30132
33- 8 BUTLER, CHARLES THOMAS — D. MAY 10, 1964 BRUNSWICK, GA.
26- 11 BUTLER, JOHN STEPHEN — D. APRIL 29, 1967 LONG BEACH, CAL.
69- 26 BUTLER, WILLIAM FRANKLIN — HC 3 BOX 122 - CROSS JUNCTION VA 22625
62- 25 BUTTERS, THOMAS ARDEN — 46 APPLETON PL - DURHAM NC 27705
38- 11 BUXTON, RALPH STANLEY — 942 PARADISE BLVD - HAYWARD CA 94541
45- 7 BUZAS, JOSEPH JOHN — BOX 5010 - READING PA 19612
58- 16 BUZHARDT, JOHN WILLIAM — RR 2 BOX 1684 - PROSPERITY SC 29127
43- 20 BYERLY, ELDRED WILLIAM 'BUD' — 8611 SAPPINGTON RD-ST LOUIS MO 63126
87- 18 BYERS, RANDELL PARKER — 31 WALDEN DRIVE(P.O. BOX 304) - BRIDGETON NJ 08302
50- 17 BYRD, HARRY GLADWIN — D. MAY 14, 1985 DARLINGTON, S. C.
77- 20 BYRD, JEFFREY ALAN — 12514 MUTH VALLEY ROAD - LAKESIDE CA 92040
29- 13 BYRD, SAMUEL DEWEY — D. MAY 11, 1981 MESA, ARIZ.
29- 14 BYRNE, GERALD WILFORD — D. AUGUST 11, 1955 LANSING, MICH.
43- 21 BYRNE, THOMAS JOSEPH — 442 PINEVIEW AVE-WAKE FOREST NC 27587
43- 22 BYRNES, MILTON JOHN — D. FEBRUARY 1, 1979 ST. LOUIS, MO.
80- 20 BYSTROM, MARTIN EUGENE — P.O. BOX 26 - GEIGERTOWN PA 19523
44- 17 CABALLERO, RALPH JOSEPH 'PUTSY' — 6773 MILNE ST - NEW ORLEANS LA 70119

72- 17	CABELL, ENOS MILTON	1002 GOLDFINCH AVENUE - SUGAR LAND TX 77478
13- 23	CABRERA, ALFREDO A	D. HAVANA, CUBA
89- 20	CABRERA, FRANCISCO (PAULINO)	OLD ADD: SANTO DOMINGO DOMINICAN REPUBLIC
77- 21	CACEK, CRAIG THOMAS	8916 GLORIA AVE - SEPULVEDA CA 91343
87- 19	CADARET, GREGORY JAMES	5665 CAROLINE DRIVE - LAKEVIEW MI 48850
15- 18	CADORE, LEON JOSEPH	D. MARCH 16, 1958 SPOKANE, WASH.
12- 30	CADY, FORREST LEROY 'HICK'	D. MARCH 3, 1946 CEDAR RAPIDS, IA.
37- 19	CAFEGO, THOMAS	D. OCTOBER 29, 1961 DETROIT, MICH.
56- 20	CAFFIE, JOSEPH CLIFFORD	P.O. BOX 1932 - WARREN OH 44482
78- 23	CAGE, WAYNE LEVELL	RR 1 BOX 62 - CHOUDRANT LA 71227
68- 12	CAIN, LESLIE	4516 CYPRESS AVE - RICHMOND CA 91804
32- 10	CAIN, MERRITT PATRICK 'SUGAR'	D. APRIL 3, 1975 ATLANTA, GA.
49- 13	CAIN, ROBERT MAX	161 EAST 226TH ST - EUCLID ON 44123
34- 15	CAITHAMER, GEORGE THEODORE	D. JUNE 1, 1954 CHICAGO, ILL.
84- 15	CALDERON, IVAN	OLD ADD: 334 EST. 34 BUZON - LOIZA PR 00672
50- 18	CALDERONE, SAMUEL FRANCIS	1000 SOUTH COOPER ST - BEVERLY NJ 08010
28- 18	CALDWELL, BRUCE	D. FEBRUARY 15, 1959 WEST HAVEN, CONN.
25- 14	CALDWELL, CHARLES WILLIAM	D. NOVEMBER 1, 1957 PRINCETON, N. J.
28- 19	CALDWELL, EARL WELTON	D. SEPTEMBER 15, 1981 MISSION, TEXAS
71- 19	CALDWELL, RALPH MICHAEL 'MIKE'	1645 BROOK RUN DR - RALEIGH NC 27614
10- 21	CALDWELL, RAYMOND BENJAMIN	D. AUGUST 17, 1967 SALAMANCA, N. Y.
84- 16	CALHOUN, JEFFREY WILTON	1212 PARK ST - MCCOMB MS 39648
13- 24	CALHOUN, WILLIAM DAVITTE	D. FEBRUARY 11, 1955 SANDERSVILLE, GA.
41- 12	CALIGIURI, FREDERICK JOHN	BOX 429 - RIMERSBURG PA 16248
22- 18	CALLAGHAN, MARTIN FRANCIS	D. JUNE 24, 1975 NORWOOD, MASS.
83- 22	CALLAHAN, BENJAMIN FRANKLIN	BOX 676 - DOBSON NC 27017
10- 22	CALLAHAN, DAVID JOSEPH	D. OCTOBER 28, 1969 OTTAWA, ILL.
39- 17	CALLAHAN, JOSEPH THOMAS	D. MAY 24, 1949 SOUTH BOSTON, MASS.
13- 25	CALLAHAN, LEO DAVID	D. MAY 2, 1982 ERIE, PA.
15- 19	CALLAHAN, RAYMOND JAMES	D. JANUARY 23, 1973 OLYMPIA, WASH.
13- 26	CALLAHAN, WESLEY LEROY	D. SEPTEMBER 13, 1953 DAYTON,O.
21- 12	CALLAWAY, FRANK BURNETT	D. AUGUST 21, 1987 KNOXVILLE, TENN.
58- 17	CALLISON, JOHN WESLEY	2316 OAKDALE ST - GLENSIDE PA 19038
63- 20	CALMUS, RICHARD LEE	3823 SOUTH 28TH WEST AVE - TULSA OK 74107
83- 23	CALVERT, MARK	RR 4 BOX 314J - BROKEN ARROW OK 74012
42- 16	CALVERT, PAUL LEO EMILE	364 CHATELAINE ST #7 - SHERBROOKE QUE J1G 1Z6 CAN.
13- 27	CALVO, JACINTO 'JACK'	D. JUNE 15, 1965 MIAMI, FLA.
80- 21	CAMACHO, ERNEST CARLOS	OLD ADD: 746 ST REGIS - AVON LAKE OH 44012
70- 16	CAMBRIA, FREDERICK DENNIS	12 IRIS CT - NORTHPORT NY 11768
43- 23	CAMELLI, HENRY RICHARD	6 LARCH RD-WELLESLEY MA 02181
33- 9	CAMILLI, ADOLF LOUIS	2831 HACIENDA ST - SAN MATEO CA 94403
60- 17	CAMILLI, DOUGLAS JOSEPH	872 ORIOLE DRIVE SE - WINTER HAVEN FL 33880
69- 27	CAMILLI, LOUIS STEVEN	4700 OAHU DR NE - ALBUQUERQUE NM 87111
87- 20	CAMINITI, KENNETH GENE	5129 CORDOY LANE - SAN JOSE CA 95124
17- 12	CAMP, HOWARD LEE	D. MAY 8, 1950 EASTABOGA, ALA.
76- 23	CAMP, RICK LAMAR	6 CANTEY PLACE NW - ATLANTA GA 30327
48- 22	CAMPANELLA, ROY	6213 CAPISTRANO - WOODLAND HILLS CA 91367
64- 15	CAMPANERIS, DAGOBERTO 'BERT'	P.O. BOX 8232 - SCOTTSDALE AZ 85252
43- 24	CAMPANIS, ALEXANDER SEBASTIAN	3113 CORONADO DR - FULLERTON CA 92632
66- 17	CAMPANIS, JAMES ALEXANDER	17082·CASCADES AVE - YORBA LINDA CA 92686
28- 20	CAMPBELL, ARCHIBALD STEWART	630 MARGRAVE DRIVE - RENO NV 89502
30- 8	CAMPBELL, BRUCE DOUGLAS	4011 BAYSIDE RD - FORT MYERS BEACH FL 33931
40- 8	CAMPBELL, CLARENCE 'SOUP'	SPARTA VA 22552
77- 22	CAMPBELL, DAVID ALLEN	OLD ADD: RR 10 LYNN TER #2 - JOHNSON CITY TN 37601
67- 12	CAMPBELL, DAVID WILSON	9978 WALDGROVE PLACE - SAN DIEGO CA 92131
62- 26	CAMPBELL, JAMES ROBERT	1924 KNOLLWOOD LN - LOS ALTOS CA 94022
70- 17	CAMPBELL, JAMES ROBERT	RR 1 BOX 194 - LAMAR SC 29069
33- 10	CAMPBELL, JOHN MILLARD 'WHITEY'	100 SILVER BEACH #4 - DAYTONA BEACH FL 32081
67- 13	CAMPBELL, JOSEPH EARL	2151 SMALLHOUSE RD - BOWLING GREEN KY 42101
87- 21	CAMPBELL, MICHAEL THOMAS	6412 SOUTHWEST HINDS - SEATTLE WA 98116
41- 13	CAMPBELL, PAUL MCLAUGHLIN	BOX 1724 - FAIRFIELD GLADE TN 38555
64- 16	CAMPBELL, RONALD THOMAS	2254 LAUREL HILLS DRIVE NW - CLEVELAND TN 37311
33- 11	CAMPBELL, WILLIAM GILTHORPE 'GILLY'	D. FEBRUARY 21, 1973 LOS ANGELES, CAL.
73- 17	CAMPBELL, WILLIAM RICHARD	217 BEAUMONT LN - BARRINGTON IL 60010
77- 23	CAMPER, CARDELL	175 EAST EASTON #33 - RIALTO CA 92376
69- 28	CAMPISI, SALVATORE JOHN	3303 LAKEWOOD DR - HOLIDAY FL 33590
51- 9	CAMPOS, FRANCISCO JOSE LOPEZ	2840 NW 4TH ST - MIAMI FL 33125
88- 23	CAMPUSANO, SILVESTRE	CLEM GUZMAN #5 CASA 19,MANOGUAYABO-STO DOMINGO DOM REP.
89- 21	CANALE, GEORGE ANTHONY	3386 KELLY LANE EXT. SW - ROANOKE VA 24018
18- 8	CANAVAN, HUGH EDWARD	D. SEPTEMBER 4, 1967 BOSTON, MASS.
86- 29	CANDAELE, CASEY TODD	1001 EAST MAPLE - LOMPOC CA 93436
75- 23	CANDELARIA, JOHN ROBERT	25732 BUCKLESTONE COURT - LAGUNA HILLS CA 92633
43- 25	CANDINI, MILO CAIN	641 MANOR - MANTECA CA 95336
83- 24	CANDIOTTI, THOMAS CAESER	1700 FOUNTAIN SPRINGS CIRCLE - DANVILLE CA 94526
77- 24	CANEIRA, JOHN CASCAES	18 SPRUCE ST - NAUGATUCK CT 06770
85- 13	CANGELOSI, JOHN ANTHONY	183 SE 4TH AVENUE - HIALEAH FL 33010
60- 18	CANNIZZARO, CHRISTOPHER JOHN	576 DOLORES - SAN LEANDRO CA 94577
77- 25	CANNON, JOSEPH JEROME	6426 WAGNER RD - PENSACOLA FL 32505
89- 22	CANO, JOSE (SORIANO)	VILLA DOLORES 2DA #41 - SAN PEDRO DE MACORIS DOM. REP.
85- 14	CANSECO, JOSE	4525 SHERIDAN AVENUE - MIAMI BEACH FL 33140
25- 15	CANTRELL, DEWEY GUY	D. JANUARY 31, 1961 MCALESTER, OKLA.
27- 21	CANTWELL, BENJAMIN CALDWELL	D. DECEMBER 4, 1962 SALEM, MO.
16- 10	CANTWELL, MICHAEL JOSEPH	D. JANUARY 9, 1953 OTEEN, N.C.
88- 24	CAPEL, MICHAEL LEE	23103 HARPERGATE DRIVE - SPRING TX 77373
76- 24	CAPILLA, DOUGLAS EDMOND	3254 KILO AVENUE - SAN JOSE CA 95124
81- 21	CAPPUZZELLO, GEORGE ANGELO	1625 DOWN LAND DR - WINDERMERE FL 32786
71- 20	CAPRA, LEE WILLIAM 'BUZZ'	7112 RIVERSIDE DR - BERWYN IL 60402
82- 22	CAPRA, NICK LEE	3201 SOUTH UTICA - DENVER CO 80236
44- 18	CAPRI, PATRICK NICHOLAS	D. JUNE 14, 1989 NEW YORK, N.Y.
12- 31	CAPRON, RALPH EARL	D. SEPTEMBER 19, 1980 LOS ANGELES, CALIF.
30- 9	CARAWAY, CECIL BRADFORD PATRICK 'PAT'	D. JUNE 9, 1974 EL PASO, TEX.
69- 29	CARBO, BERNARDO	1637 FORT STREET - WYANDOTTE MI 48192
46- 16	CARDEN, JOHN BRUTON	D. FEBRUARY 8, 1949 MEXIA, TEX.
63- 21	CARDENAL, JOSE DOMEC	5701 NORTH SHERIDAN - CHICAGO IL 60660
60- 19	CARDENAS, LEONARDO LAZARO 'CHICO'	OLD ADD: 5369 BAHAMA TER #7 - CINCINNATI OH 45223
63- 22	CARDINAL, CONRAD SETH 'RANDY'	3810 VERDE WAY - NORTH LAS VEGAS NV 89030
43- 26	CARDONI, ARMAND JOSEPH 'BEN'	D. APRIL 2, 1969 JESSUP, PA.
57- 9	CARDWELL, DONALD EUGENE	P.O. BOX 454 - CLEMMONS NC 27012

67- 14	CAREW, RODNEY CLINE	5144 EAST CRESCENT DR - ANAHEIM CA 92807
52- 16	CAREY, ANDREW ARTHUR	1601 DOVE STREET #220 - NEWPORT BEACH CA 92660
10- 23	CAREY, MAX GEORGE	D. MAY 30, 1976 MIAMI, FLA.
35- 11	CAREY, THOMAS FRANCIS ALOYSIUS	D. FEBRUARY 21, 1970 ROCHESTER, N. Y.
32- 11	CARLETON, JAMES OTTO 'TEX'	D. JANUARY 11, 1977 FORT WORTH, TEX.
41- 14	CARLIN, JAMES ARTHUR	1215 33RD ST-BIRMINGHAM AL 35218
67- 15	CARLOS, FRANCISCO MANUEL 'CISCO'	OLD ADD: 1229 SESMAS ST - DUARTE CA 91010
48- 23	CARLSEN, DONALD HERBERT	3600 EAST EASTER AVE - LITTLETON CO 80122
17- 13	CARLSON, HAROLD GUST	D. MAY 28, 1930 CHICAGO, ILL.
20- 16	CARLSON, LEON ALTON	D. SEPTEMBER 15, 1961 JAMESTOWN, N. Y.
11- 23	CARLSTROM, ALBIN OSCAR 'SWEDE'	D. APRIL 23, 1935 ELIZABETH, N.J.
65- 18	CARLTON, STEVEN NORMAN	90 BALSAM - OLDSMAR FL 33557
27- 22	CARLYLE, HIRAM CLEO	D. NOVEMBER 12, 1967 LOS ANGELES, CAL.
25- 16	CARLYLE, ROY EDWARD	D. NOVEMBER 22, 1956 NORCROSS, GA.
83- 25	CARMAN, DONALD WAYNE	6 COOPER RUN DRIVE - CHERRY HILL NJ 08003
59- 11	CARMEL, LEON JAMES 'DUKE'	10 PHEASANT VALLEY DR - CORAM NY 11727
41- 15	CARNETT, EDWIN ELLIOTT	1010 INDIAN CREEK DR - LEBANON MO 65536
88- 25	CARPENTER, CRIS HOWELL	1760 LAKEVIEW CIRCLE - GAINESVILLE GA 30501
43- 27	CARPENTER, LEWIS EMMETT	D. APRIL 25, 1979 MARIETTA, GA.
16- 11	CARPENTER, PAUL CALVIN	D. MARCH 14, 1968 NEWARK, O.
40- 9	CARPENTER, ROBERT LOUIS	9321 SOUTH SACRAMENTO AVE - EVERGREEN PARK IL 60642
65- 19	CARPIN, FRANK DOMINIC	5202 RIVERSIDE DR - RICHMOND VA 23225
39- 18	CARRASQUEL, ALEJANDRO ALEXANDER	D. AUGUST 19, 1969 CARACAS, VENEZUELA
50- 19	CARRASQUEL, ALFONSO COLON 'CHICO'	1432 NORTH LAWNDALE AVE - CHICAGO IL 60657
59- 12	CARREON, CAMILO GARCIA	D. SEPTEMBER 2, 1987 TUCSON, ARIZ.
87- 22	CARREON, MARK STEVEN	4450 EAST COOPER STREET - TUCSON AZ 85711
70- 18	CARRITHERS, DONALD GEORGE	9367 SUNNY GLADE COURT - ELK GROVE CA 95624
64- 17	CARROLL, CLAY PALMER	3131 MOUNTAIN CREEK RD #681 - CHATTANOOGA TN 37455
19- 11	CARROLL, DORSEY LEE 'DIXIE'	D. OCTOBER 13, 1984 JACKSONVILLE, FLA.
29- 15	CARROLL, EDGAR FLEISCHER	D. OCTOBER 13, 1984 ROSSVILLE, MD.
25- 17	CARROLL, OWEN THOMAS	D. JUNE 8, 1975 ORANGE, N. J.
16- 12	CARROLL, RALPH ARTHUR 'DOC'	D. JUNE 27, 1983 WORCESTER, MASS.
55- 22	CARROLL, THOMAS EDWARD	OLD ADD: 114-69 207TH ST - ST. ALBANS NY 11411
74- 14	CARROLL, THOMAS MICHAEL	RR 1 BOX 857 - WATERFORD VA 22190
10- 24	CARSON, ALBERT JAMES	D. NOVEMBER 26, 1962 SAN DIEGO, CALIF.
34- 16	CARSON, WALTER LLOYD 'KIT'	D. JUNE 21, 1983 LONG BEACH, CALIF.
53- 15	CARSWELL, FRANK WILLIS	3517 STANFORD - HOUSTON TX 77006
44- 19	CARTER, ARNOLD LEE	8102 PEBBLE BROOK LN - LOUISVILLE KY 40219
74- 15	CARTER, GARY EDMUND	15 HUNTLY DRIVE - PALM BEACH GARDENS FL 33418
26- 12	CARTER, JOHN HOWARD 'HOWIE'	430 EAST 86TH ST - NEW YORK NY 10028
83- 26	CARTER, JOSEPH CHRIS	1800 NE 51ST - OKLAHOMA CITY OK 73111
25- 18	CARTER, OTIS LEONARD 'BLACKIE'	D. SEPTEMBER 10, 1978 GREENVILLE, S. C.
14- 34	CARTER, PAUL WARREN 'NICK'	D. SEPTEMBER 11, 1984 LAKE PARK, GA.
31- 11	CARTER, SOLOMON MOBLEY	2402 GALE PL - EL DORADO AR 71730
89- 23	CARTER, STEVEN JEROME	25 RUCKER DRIVE - RUCKERSVILLE VA 22968
63- 23	CARTY, RICARDO ADOLFO JACABO 'RICO'	5 ENS ENRIQUILLO-SAN PEDRO DE MACORIS DOM. REP.
85- 15	CARY, CHARLES DOUGLAS	3323 CASA GRANDE DRIVE - SAN RAMON CA 94583
47- 16	CARY, SCOTT RUSSELL	RR 4 - BRONSON MI 49028
58- 18	CASALE, JERRY JOSEPH	635 HARMON COVE TOWERS - SECAUCUS NJ 07094
65- 20	CASANOVA, ORTIZ PAULINO 'PAUL'	OLD ADD: 413 CHERRY - SYRACUSE NY 13210
34- 17	CASCARELLA, JOSEPH THOMAS	7111 PARK HEIGHTS AVE - BALTIMORE MD 21215
37- 20	CASE, GEORGE WASHINGTON	D. JANUARY 23, 1989 TRENTON, N. J.
35- 12	CASEY, HUGH THOMAS	D. JULY 3, 1951 ATLANTA, GA.
69- 30	CASH, DAVID	402 FREELAND STREET - PITTSBURGH PA 15210
58- 19	CASH, NORMAN DALTON	D. OCTOBER 12, 1986 BEAVER ISLAND, MICH.
73- 18	CASH, RONALD FOREST	820 GREENFOREST DRIVE - SMYRNA GA 30080
11- 24	CASHION, JAY CARL	D. NOVEMBER 17, 1935 LAKE MILLICENT, WIS.
73- 19	CASKEY, CRAIG DOUGLAS	836 YVONNE PL - ANAHEIM CA 92801
49- 14	CASSINI, JACK DEMPSEY	2498 LEISURE WORLD - MESA AZ 85206
34- 18	CASTER, GEORGE JASPER	D. DECEMBER 18, 1955 LAKEWOOD, CAL.
42- 17	CASTIGLIA, JAMES VINCENT	5301 WESTBARD CIR #313 - WASHINGTON DC 20016
47- 17	CASTIGLIONE, PETER PAUL	1320 NE 26TH TERRACE - POMPANO BEACH FL 33062
78- 24	CASTILLO, ANTHONY BELTRAN	10300 JOYCE CT - SAN JOSE CA 95127
88- 26	CASTILLO, ANTONIO JOSE	EL MOLINO VIA SANARE - QUIBOR, LARA VENEZUELA S. A.
80- 22	CASTILLO, ESTEBAN MANUEL 'MANNY'	COSTA RICA 112,ENS. OZAMA - SANTO DOMINGO DOM. REP.
86- 30	CASTILLO, JUAN	CALLE ELIA CAMARENA 100-SAN PEDRO DE MACORIS DOM. REP.
81- 22	CASTILLO, MARTIN HORACE	2669 BAYLOR ST - ANAHEIM CA 92801
82- 23	CASTILLO, MONTE CARMELO	189 AUDUBON AVENUE #3N - NEW YORK NY 10032
77- 26	CASTILLO, ROBERT ERNIE	2837 SIERRA ST - LOS ANGELES CA 90031
79- 16	CASTINO, JOHN ANTHONY	6624 GLEASON RD - EDINA MN 55435
43- 28	CASTINO, VINCENT CHARLES	D. MARCH 6, 1967 SACRAMENTO, CAL.
73- 20	CASTLE, DONALD HARDY	24 COUNTRY CLUB DRIVE - SENATOBIA MS 38668
10- 25	CASTLE, JOHN FRANCIS	D. APRIL 13, 1929 PHILADELPHIA, PA.
34- 19	CASTLEMAN, CLYDELL	BOX 140601 - DONELSON TN 37214
54- 13	CASTLEMAN, FOSTER EPHRAIM	8250 GRAVES ROAD - CINCINNATI OH 45243
23- 19	CASTNER, PAUL HENRY	D. MARCH 3, 1986 ST. PAUL, MINN.
74- 16	CASTRO, WILLIAMS RADHAMES	5231 RAVEN DR - GREENDALE WI 53129
64- 18	CATER, DANNY ANDERSON	500 EAST ANDERSON LANE #176L - AUSTIN TX 78752
12- 33	CATHER, THEODORE P.	D. APRIL 9, 1945 ELKTON, MD.
42- 18	CATHEY, HARDIN	561 ELAINE DR - NASHVILLE TN 37211
83- 27	CATO, JOHN KEEFE	98 MARYTON ROAD - WHITE PLAINS NY 10603
17- 14	CATON, JAMES HOWARD 'BUSTER'	D. JANUARY 8, 1948 ZANESVILLE, O.
79- 17	CAUDILL, WILLIAM HOLLAND	1200 MANHATTAN BLVD - MANHATTAN BEACH CA 90266
46- 17	CAULFIELD, JOHN JOSEPH	D. DECEMBER 16, 1986 SAN FRANCISCO, CALIF.
18- 9	CAUSEY, CECIL ALGERNON 'RED'	D. NOVEMBER 11, 1960 TAMPA, FLA.
55- 23	CAUSEY, JAMES WAYNE	2905 PAYNTER DR - RUSTON LA 71270
19- 12	CAVANAUGH, JOHN J.	D. JANUARY 14, 1961 NEW BRUNSWICK, N. J.
34- 20	CAVARRETTA, PHILIP JOSEPH	2206 PORTSIDE PASSAGE - PALM HARBOR FL 33563
22- 19	CAVENEY, JAMES CHRISTOPHER 'IKE'	D. JULY 6, 1949 SAN FRANCISCO, CAL.
11- 25	CAVET, TILLER 'PUG'	D. AUGUST 4, 1966 SAN LUIS OBISPO, CALIF.
55- 24	CECCARELLI, ARTHUR EDWARD	63 HALL DR - ORANGE CT 06477
88- 27	CECENA, JOSE ISABEL	OLD ADD: CIUDAD OBREGON MEXICO
44- 20	CECIL, REX HOLSTON	D. OCTOBER 30, 1966 LONG BEACH, CAL.
70- 19	CEDENO, CESAR EUGENITO	9919 SAGE DOWNE - HOUSTON TX 77034
42- 19	CENTER, MARVIN EARL 'PETE'	BOX 64 - CAMPTON KY 41301
58- 20	CEPEDA, ORLANDO MANUEL	3 SOMMER RIDGE DRIVE #156 - ROSEVILLE CA 95678
75- 25	CERONE, RICHARD 'RICK'	63 EISENHOWER - CRESSKILL NJ 07626
85- 16	CERUTTI, JOHN JOSEPH	43 SOUTH MAIN AVENUE - ALBANY NY 12208

51- 10	CERV, ROBERT HENRY	2601 WINCHESTER S. - LINCOLN NE 68512
71- 21	CEY, RONALD CHARLES	22714 CREOLE RD - WOODLAND HILLS CA 91364
60- 20	CHACON, ELIO RODRIGUEZ	OLD ADD: AVE ANDALUCIA,ED. MARICAY-CARACAS VZ
86- 31	CHADWICK, RAY CHARLES	607 GADDIS STREET - DURHAM NC 27702
29- 16	CHAGNON, LEON WILBUR	D. JULY 30, 1953 AMESBURY, MASS.
51- 11	CHAKALES, ROBERT EDWARD	206 MORELAND DR - RICHMOND VA 23229
73- 21	CHALK, DAVID LEE	6126 SUMMER CREEK CIR - DALLAS TX 75231
10- 26	CHALMERS, GEORGE W.	D. AUGUST 5, 1960 BRONX, N. Y.
79- 18	CHAMBERLAIN, CRAIG PHILIP	10408 SANTA CLARA STREET - CYPRESS CA 90630
32- 12	CHAMBERLAIN, WILLIAM VINCENT	13 CENTER DRIVE - MATTAPOISETT MA 02739
34- 21	CHAMBERLIN, JOSEPH JEREMIAH	D. JANUARY 28, 1983 SAN FRANCISCO, CALIF.
83- 28	CHAMBERS, ALBERT EUGENE	1303 NORTH 14TH ST - HARRISBURG PA 17103
48- 24	CHAMBERS, CLIFFORD DAY	10237 PRAIRIE RD - BOISE ID 83702
37- 21	CHAMBERS, JOHNNIE MONROE	D. MAY 11, 1977 PALATKA, FLA.
10- 27	CHAMBERS, WILLIAM CHRISTOPHER	D. MARCH 27, 1962 FORT WAYNE, IND.
71- 22	CHAMBLISS, CARROLL CHRISTOPHER 'CHRIS'	19 ORATAM ROAD - UPPER SADDLE RIVER NJ 07458
69- 31	CHAMPION, BUFORD BILLY	304 NE LOWER CREEK DR - LENOIR NC 28645
76- 25	CHAMPION, ROBERT MICHAEL 'MIKE'	17965 FIESTA WAY - TUSTIN CA 92680
63- 24	CHANCE, ROBERT	2258 OAK RIDGE DR - CHARLESTON WV 25311
61- 19	CHANCE, WILMER DEAN	9505 W. SMITHVILLE WESTERN - WOOSTER OH 44691
47- 18	CHANDLER, EDWARD OLIVER	5811 SOUTH HALM AVENUE - LOS ANGELES CA 90056
37- 22	CHANDLER, SPURGEON FERDINAND 'SPUD'	D. JANUARY 9, 1990 ST. PETERSBURG, FLA.
69- 32	CHANEY, DARREL LEE	2235 ST. THOMAS WAY - SUWANEE GA 30174
13- 28	CHANEY, ESTEY CLEON	D. FEBRUARY 5, 1952 CLEVELAND, O.
10- 28	CHANNELL, LESTER CLARK	D. MAY 7, 1954 DENVER, COLO.
75- 24	CHANT, CHARLES JOSEPH	13426 SUNFLOWER CT - SUNNYMEAD CA 92388
20- 17	CHAPLIN, BERT EDGAR	D. AUGUST 15, 1978 SANFORD, FLA.
28- 21	CHAPLIN, JAMES BAILEY 'TINY'	D. MARCH 25, 1939 NATIONAL CITY, CAL.
35- 13	CHAPMAN, CALVIN LOUIS	D. APRIL 1, 1983 BATESVILLE, MISS.
33- 12	CHAPMAN, EDWIN VOLNEY	RURAL ROUTE 2 - LAMBERT MS 38643
39- 19	CHAPMAN, FREDERICK WILLIAM	112 NORTH RIDGE AVE - KANNAPOLIS NC 28081
34- 22	CHAPMAN, GLENN JUSTICE	D. NOVEMBER 5, 1988 RICHMOND, IND.
12- 34	CHAPMAN, HARRY E.	D. OCTOBER 21, 1918 NEVADA, MO.
24- 17	CHAPMAN, JOHN JOSEPH	D. NOVEMBER 3, 1953 PHILADELPHIA, PA.
79- 19	CHAPMAN, KELVIN KEITH	300 ROAD NORTH - REDWOOD VALLEY CA 94570
12- 35	CHAPMAN, RAYMOND JOHNSON	D. AUGUST 17, 1920 NEW YORK, N.Y.
38- 12	CHAPMAN, SAMUEL BLAKE	11 ANDREW DR #39 - TIBURON CA 94920
30- 10	CHAPMAN, WILLIAM BENJAMIN 'BEN'	401 SHADESWOOD CIR - BIRMINGHAM AL 35226
78- 25	CHAPPAS, HARRY PERRY	1440 NW 52ND AVE - LAUDERHILL FL 33313
13- 29	CHAPPELL, LAVERNE ASHFORD 'LARRY'	D. NOVEMBER 8, 1918 SAN FRANCISCO, CALIF.
80- 23	CHARBONEAU, JOSEPH	OLD ADD: 450 HARVARD AVE #412 - SANTA CLARA CA 95051
62- 27	CHARLES, EDWIN DOUGLAS	57 PARK TERRACE EAST #B58 - NEW YORK NY 10034
88- 28	CHARLTON, NORMAN WOOD	16615 FRONT ROYALS STREET - SAN ANTONIO TX 78247
40- 10	CHARTAK, MICHAEL GEORGE	D. JULY 25, 1967 OAKDALE, IA.
64- 19	CHARTON, FRANK LANE "PETE"	27 VINCINDA LN - HARRIMAN TN 37748
36- 14	CHASE, KENDALL FAY	D. JANUARY 16, 1985 ONEONTA, N. Y.
30- 11	CHATHAM, CHARLES L. 'BUSTER'	D. DECEMBER 15, 1975 WACO, TEXAS
66- 18	CHAVARRIA, OSWALDO QUIJANO	5771 WINCH STREET - NORTH BARNEBY B.C. CAN.
67- 16	CHAVEZ, NESTOR ISAIAS SILVA	D. MARCH 16, 1969 MARACAIBO, VENEZ.
73- 22	CHEADLE, DAVID BEARD	1142 RED MILL BLVD - VIRGINIA BEACH VA 23454
10- 29	CHEEK, HARRY G.	D. JUNE 25, 1956 PARAMUS, N. J.
20- 18	CHEEVES, VIRGIL EARL 'CHIEF'	D. MAY 5, 1979 DALLAS, TEXAS
35- 14	CHELINI, ITALO VINCENT	D. AUGUST 25, 1972 SAN FRANCISCO, CAL.
11- 26	CHENEY, LAURANCE RUSSELL	D. JANUARY 6, 1969 DAYTONA BEACH, FLA.
57- 10	CHENEY, THOMAS EDGAR	P.O. BOX 313 - SYLVESTER GA 31791
37- 23	CHERVINKO, PAUL	D. JUNE 3, 1976 DANVILLE, ILL.
48- 25	CHESNES, ROBERT VINCENT	D. MAY 23, 1979 EVERETT, WASH.
45- 8	CHETKOVICH, MITCHELL	D. AUGUST 24, 1971 GRASS VALLEY, CAL.
77- 27	CHEVEZ, ANTONIO SILVIO	TELIA D PTO. - LEON NICARAGUA C.A.
82- 24	CHIFFER, FLOYD JOHN	4325 LEVELSIDE AVE - LAKESIDE CA 90712
30- 12	CHILD, HARRY PATRICK	D. NOVEMBER 8, 1972 ALEXANDRIA, VA.
85- 17	CHILDRESS, RODNEY OSBORNE 'ROCKY'	5 MEADOWGLEN COURT - SANTA ROSA CA 95404
71- 23	CHILES, RICHARD FRANCIS	4501 SAN RAMON DR - DAVIS CA 95616
35- 15	CHIOZZA, DINO JOSEPH	D. APRIL 23, 1972 MEMPHIS, TENN.
34- 23	CHIOZZA, LOUIS PEO	D. FEBRUARY 28, 1971 MEMPHIS, TENN.
41- 16	CHIPMAN, ROBERT HOWARD	D. NOVEMBER 8, 1973 HUNTINGTON, N.Y.
45- 9	CHIPPLE, WALTER JOHN	D. JUNE 8, 1988 TONAWANDA, N. Y.
79- 20	CHISM, THOMAS RAYMOND	OLD ADD: 1311 ELSON ROAD - CHESTER PA 19013
50- 20	CHITI, HARRY	5968 AUSTIN COVE - MEMPHIS TN 38134
58- 21	CHITTUM, NELSON BOYD	616 BONITA PARKWAY - HENDERSONVILLE TN 37075
70- 20	CHLUPSA, ROBERT JOSEPH	OLD ADD: RURAL ROUTE 1 - SOUND BEACH NY 11789
60- 21	CHOATE, DONALD LEON	7105 STATE STREET REAR - EAST SAINT LOUIS IL 62203
10- 30	CHOUINARD, FELIX GEORGE	D. APRIL 28, 1955 HINES, ILL.
10- 31	CHOUNEAU, WILLIAM 'CHIEF'	D. SEPTEMBER 17, 1948 CLOQUET, MINN.
37- 24	CHOZEN, HARRY KENNETH	2208 20TH ST - LAKE CHARLES LA 70601
79- 21	CHRIS, MICHAEL	12437 WOODGREEN ST - LOS ANGELES CA 90066
57- 11	CHRISLEY, BARBRA O'NEIL 'NEIL'	106 SHALOTT COURT - GREENWOOD SC 29646
19- 13	CHRISTENBURY, LLOYD REID	D. DECEMBER 13, 1944 BIRMINGHAM, ALA.
71- 24	CHRISTENSEN, BRUCE RAY	BOX 178 - MORONI UT 84646
84- 17	CHRISTENSEN, JOHN LAWRENCE	2223 E. COMMONWEALTH AVE - FULLERTON CA 92631
26- 13	CHRISTENSEN, WALTER NIELS	D. DECEMBER 20, 1984 MENLO PARK, CALIF.
79- 22	CHRISTENSON, GARY RICHARD	1610 WASHINGTON AVE - NEW HYDE PARK NY 11040
73- 23	CHRISTENSON, LARRY RICHARD	250 SOUTH 17TH #601 - PHILADELPHIA PA 19103
68- 13	CHRISTIAN, ROBERT CHARLES	D. FEBRUARY 20, 1974 SAN DIEGO, CAL.
84- 18	CHRISTIANSEN, CLAY C.	RURAL ROUTE 3 - COLUMBUS KS 66725
38- 13	CHRISTMAN, MARQUETTE JOSEPH	D. OCTOBER 9, 1976 ST. LOUIS, MO.
83- 29	CHRISTMAS, STEPHEN RANDALL	OLD ADD: 5860 MATTOX ST - ORLANDO FL 32809
59- 13	CHRISTOPHER, JOSEPH O'NEAL	4055 NORTH SHERIDAN ROAD - CHICAGO IL 60613
45- 10	CHRISTOPHER, LOYD EUGENE	747 GOLDEN GATE AVE - RICHMOND CA 94801
42- 20	CHRISTOPHER, RUSSELL ORMAND	D. DECEMBER 5, 1954 POINT RICHMOND, CAL.
50- 21	CHURCH, EMORY NICHOLAS 'BUBBA'	3304 AFTON CIRCLE - BIRMINGHAM AL 35243
66- 19	CHURCH, LEONARD	D. APRIL 22, 1988 RICHARDSON, TEXAS
57- 12	CHURN, CLARENCE NOTTINGHAM 'CHUCK'	BOX 39 - GREENBUSH VA 23357
24- 18	CHURRY, JOHN	D. FEBRUARY 8, 1970 ZANESVILLE, O.
51- 12	CIAFFONE, LAWRENCE THOMAS	240 LAKE ST - BROOKLYN NY 11223
87- 23	CIARDI, MARK THOMAS	21 MITCHELL AVENUE - PISCATAWAY NJ 08854
83- 30	CIAS, DARRYL RICHARD	12330 LITHUANIA ST - GRANADA HILLS CA 91344
29- 17	CICERO, JOSEPH FRANCIS	D. MARCH 30, 1983 CLEARWATER, FLA.

57- 13 CICOTTE, ALVA WARREN	D. NOVEMBER 29, 1982 WESTLAND, MICH.
44- 21 CIESLAK, THADDEUS WALTER 'TED'	6244 SOUTH 20TH ST - MILWAUKEE WI 53221
45- 11 CIHOCKI, ALBERT JOSEPH	124 WEST GREEN - NANTICOKE PA 18634
32- 13 CIHOCKI, EDWARD JOSEPH	D. NOVEMBER 9, 1987 NEWARK, DEL.
65- 21 CIMINO, PETER WILLIAM	14 FILLMORE ST - BRISTOL PA 19007
56- 21 CIMOLI, GINO NICHOLAS	30 LINDA VISTA - TIBURON CA 94920
43- 29 CIOLA, LOUIS ALEXANDER	2105 8TH AVE NW-AUSTIN MN 55912
61- 20 CIPRIANI, FRANK DOMINICK	62 BARLOW - LACKAWANNA NY 14218
37- 25 CISAR, GEORGE JOSEPH	2520 SOUTH 56TH COURT-CICERO IL 60650
61- 21 CISCO, GALEN BERNARD	02396 GLYNWOOD ROAD - ST MARYS OH 45885
28- 22 CISSELL, CHALMER WILLIAM 'BILL'	D. MARCH 15, 1949 CHICAGO, ILL.
83- 31 CITARELLA, RALPH ALEXANDER	29 EAST SHERMAN AVE - COLONIA NJ 07067
26- 14 CLABAUGH, JOHN WILLIAM 'MOOSE'	D. JULY 11, 1984 TUCSON, ARIZ.
20- 19 CLAIRE, DAVID MATTHEW	D. JANUARY 7, 1956 LAS VEGAS, NEV.
11- 27 CLANCY, ALBERT HARRISON	D. OCTOBER 17, 1951 LAS CRUCES, N. MEX.
77- 28 CLANCY, JAMES	6147 ROBROY ST - OAK FOREST IL 60452
24- 19 CLANCY, JOHN WILLIAM 'BUD'	D. SEPTEMBER 26, 1968 OTTUMWA, IA.
22- 20 CLANTON, UCAL CURT	D. FEBRUARY 24, 1960 ANTLERS, OKLA.
76- 26 CLAREY, DOUGLAS WILLIAM	506 NEW ARDEN BLVD - LOS ANGELES CA 90004
47- 19 CLARK, ALFRED ALOYSIUS 'ALLIE'	250 NORTH STEVENS AVE - SOUTH AMBOY NJ 08879
27- 23 CLARK, BAILEY EARL	D. JANUARY 16, 1938 WASHINGTON, D. C.
81- 23 CLARK, BRYAN DONALD	700 STARKEY ROAD #511 - LARGO FL 33541
22- 21 CLARK, DANIEL CURRAN	D. MAY 23, 1937 MERIDIAN, MISS.
86- 32 CLARK, DAVID EARL	RURAL ROUTE 3 BOX 248 - TUPELO MS 38801
13- 30 CLARK, GEORGE MYRON	D. NOVEMBER 14, 1940 SIOUX CITY, IA.
67- 17 CLARK, GLEN ESTER	3110 EAST 14TH - AUSTIN TX 78702
75- 26 CLARK, JACK ANTHONY	4478 DEER RIDGE ROAD - DANVILLE CA 94526
48- 26 CLARK, JAMES	OLD ADD: 1002 S.BARRINGTON AVE - LOS ANGELES CA 90049
71- 25 CLARK, JAMES	23611 MEADCLIFF PLACE - DIAMOND BAR CA 91765
11- 28 CLARK, JAMES FRANCIS	D. MARCH 20, 1969 BEAUMONT, TEX.
88- 29 CLARK, JERALD DWAYNE	618 SYCAMORE STREET - CROCKETT TX 75838
38- 14 CLARK, JOHN CARROLL 'CAP'	D. FEBRUARY 16, 1957 FAYETTEVILLE, N. C.
51- 13 CLARK, MELVIN EARL	BOX 97 - WEST COLUMBIA SC 29169
52- 17 CLARK, MICHAEL JOHN	3 ASPEN AVE - BELLMAWR NJ 08030
58- 22 CLARK, PHILIP JAMES	228 PINEKNOLL ROAD - SYLVESTER GA 31791
67- 18 CLARK, RICKEY CHARLES	16132 MEADOWBROOK - DETROIT MI 48240
79- 23 CLARK, ROBERT CALE	1030 PERVISITO ST - PERRIS CA 92370
20- 20 CLARK, ROBERT WILLIAM	D. MAY 18, 1944 CARLSBAD, N. M.
66- 20 CLARK, RONALD BRUCE	700 STARKEY RD #511 - LARGO FL 33541
88- 30 CLARK, TERRY LEE	15234 HARTSVILLE - LAPUENTE CA 91744
~~86- 22 CLARK, WILLIAM~~	~~6526 VIRGILIAN STREET - NEW ORLEANS LA~~
45- 12 CLARK, WILLIAM OTIS 'OTEY'	2735 EAST BASS LAKE RD - GRAND RAPIDS MN 55744
24- 20 CLARK, WILLIAM WATSON 'WATTY'	D. MARCH 4, 1972 CLEARWATER, FLA.
21- 13 CLARKE, ALAN THOMAS	D. MARCH 11, 1975 CHEVERLY, MD.
65- 22 CLARKE, HORACE MEREDITH	BOX 891 - FREDERIKSTED VI 00840
44- 22 CLARKE, RICHARD GREY	2122 GLENWOOD ST - KANNAPOLIS NC 28081
23- 20 CLARKE, RUFUS RIVERS	D. FEBRUARY 8, 1983 COLUMBIA, S. C.
83- 32 CLARKE, STANLEY MARTEN	37 EAST LAKE STREET - TOLEDO OH 43608
20- 21 CLARKE, SUMPTER MILLS	D. MARCH 16, 1962 KNOXVILLE, TENN.
55- 25 CLARKE, VIBERT ERNESTO 'WEBBO'	D. JUNE 14, 1970 CRISTOBAL, CANAL ZONE
29- 18 CLARKE, WILLIAM STUART 'STU'	D. AUGUST 26, 1985 HAYWARD, CALIF.
52- 18 CLARKSON, JAMES BUSTER 'BUS'	D. JANUARY 31, 1989 JEANNETTE, PA.
27- 24 CLARKSON, WILLIAM HENRY	D. AUGUST 27, 1971 RALEIGH, N. C.
42- 21 CLARY, ELLIS	206 WEST ALDEN ST-VALDOSTA GA 31603
87- 24 CLARY, MARTIN KEITH	254 PARE - CLAWSON MI 48017
33- 13 CLASET, GOWELL SYLVESTER	D. MARCH 8, 1981 ST. PETERSBURG, FLA.
13- 31 CLAUSS, ALBERT STANLEY	D. SEPTEMBER 13, 1952 NEW HAVEN, CONN.
43- 30 CLAY, DAIN ELMER	462 PARKWAY - CHULA VISTA CA 92010
88- 31 CLAY, DANNY BRUCE	OLD ADD: 10216 AMBOY AVENUE - PACOIMA CA 91331
77- 29 CLAY, KENNETH EARL	1665 GOLDENTREE PLACE - CHARLOTTESVILLE VA 22901
79- 24 CLEAR, MARK ALAN	14653 HALSEY - OLATHE KS 66062
45- 13 CLEARY, JOSEPH CHRISTOPHER	135 WEST 225 STREET - NEW YORK NY 10463
39- 20 CLEMENS, CHESTER SPURGEON	423 CRESPI - SAN CLEMENTE CA 92672
14- 35 CLEMENS, CLEMENT LAMBERT	D. NOVEMBER 18, 1967 ST PETERSBURG, FLA.
60- 22 CLEMENS, DOUGLAS HORACE	RR 2 BOX 174 - NEW HOPE PA 18938
84- 19 CLEMENS, WILLIAM ROGER	~~1818 BROOKCHESTER - KATY TX 77450~~
39- 21 CLEMENSEN, WILLIAM MELVILLE	7555 MYRTLE VISTA AVE - SACRAMENTO CA 95831
55- 26 CLEMENTE, ROBERTO WALKER	D. DECEMBER 31, 1972 SAN JUAN, P. R.
85- 18 CLEMENTS, PATRICK BRIAN	125 PARMAC ROAD #5 - CHICO CA 95926
71- 26 CLEMONS, LANCE LEVIS	1346 LODGE CIR - SPRING HILL FL 33512
14- 36 CLEMONS, ROBERT BAXTER	D. APRIL 5, 1964 LOS ANGELES, CALIF.
16- 13 CLEMONS, VERNE JAMES	D. MAY 5, 1959 BAY PINES, FLA.
61- 22 CLENDENON, DONN ALVIN	1201 EAST 57TH STREET #5 - SIOUX FALLS SD 57106
69- 33 CLEVELAND, REGINALD LESLIE	OLD ADD: 1 EDGEWOOD DR NW - CALGARY ALBERTA T3A 2T3
54- 14 CLEVENGER, TRUMAN EUGENE 'TEX'	74 NORTH CARMELITA - PORTERVILLE CA 93257
80- 24 CLIBURN, STANLEY GENE	112 SPANISH MOSS DRIVE - CLINTON MS 39056
84- 20 CLIBURN, STEWART WALKER	5720 MEDALLION DR - JACKSON MS 39211
34- 24 CLIFT, HARLOND BENTON	915 NORTH 15TH AVE #5 - YAKIMA WA 98902
34- 25 CLIFTON, HERMAN EARL 'FLEA'	4077 RACE RD - CINCINNATI OH 45211
60- 23 CLINE, TYRONE ALEXANDER	676 AYERS - CHARLESTON SC 29412
70- 21 CLINES, EUGENE ANTHONY	245 DARLENE ST - YORK PA 17402
60- 24 CLINTON, LUCIEN LOUIS	330 N. ARMOUR - WICHITA KS 67206
61- 23 CLONINGER, TONY LEE	RR 2 BOX 381-A - IRON STATION NC 28080
66- 21 CLOSTER, ALAN EDWARD	6518 JESSUP ROAD - RICHMOND VA 23234
24- 21 CLOUGH, EDGAR GEORGE	D. JANUARY 30, 1944 HARRISBURG, PA.
26- 15 CLOWERS, WILLIAM PERRY	D. JANUARY 13, 1978 SWEENY, TEX.
86- 34 CLUTTERBUCK, BRYAN RICHARD	OLD ADD: 2360 OLTESVIG LANE - HIGHLAND MI 48031
73- 24 CLYDE, DAVID EUGENE	402 HICKORY POST - HOUSTON TX 77024
43- 31 CLYDE, THOMAS KNOX	3612 GARDEN BROOK DR - DALLAS TX 75234
46- 18 COAN, GILBERT FITZGERALD	P.O. BOX 668 - BREVARD NC 28712
56- 22 COATES, JAMES ALTON	BOX 57 - LANCASTER VA 22503
29- 19 COBB, HERBERT EDWARD	D. JANUARY 8, 1980 TARBORO, N. C.
18- 10 COBB, JOSEPH STANLEY	D. DECEMBER 24, 1947 ALLENTOWN, PA.
39- 22 COBLE, DAVID LAMAR	D. OCTOBER 15, 1971 ORLANDO, FLA.
83- 33 COCANOWER, JAMES STANLEY 'JAIME'	1609 STONEHENGE - LITTLE ROCK AR 72212
15- 20 COCHRAN, ALVAH JACKSON	D. MAY 23, 1947 ATLANTA, GA.
18- 11 COCHRAN, GEORGE LESLIE	D. MAY 21, 1960 HARBOR CITY, CALIF.

86- 35	COCHRANE, DAVID CARTER	5362 EUCALYPTUS HILL ROAD - YORBA LINDA CA 92686
25- 19	COCHRANE, GORDON STANLEY 'MICKEY'	D. JUNE 2, 1962 LAKE FOREST, ILL.
13- 32	COCREHAM, EUGENE	D. DECEMBER 27, 1945 LULING, TEX.
82- 25	CODIROLI, CHRISTOPHER ALLEN	5421 SILVERLODE DRIVE - PLACERVILLE CA 95667
12- 36	COFFEY (JOHN JOSEPH SMITH) 'JACK'	D. DECEMBER 4, 1962 NEW YORK, N. Y.
37- 25	COFFMAN, GEORGE DAVID	1120 BEACON PKWY EAST #202 - BIRMINGHAM AL 35209
87- 25	COFFMAN, KEVIN REESE	203 EDINBURGH - VICTORIA TX 77904
27- 25	COFFMAN, SAMUEL RICHARD 'DICK'	D. MARCH 24, 1972 ATHENS, ALA.
67- 19	COGGINS, FRANKLIN	106 ARMSTEDD CIR - GRIFFIN GA 30223
72- 18	COGGINS, RICHARD ALLEN	OLD ADD: 3801 PARKVIEW - IRVINE CA 92713
31- 12	COHEN, ALTA ALBERT	1 CLARIDGE DR - VERONA NJ 07044
26- 16	COHEN, ANDREW HOWARD	D. OCTOBER 29, 1988 EL PASO, TEXAS
55- 27	COHEN, HYMAN	737 CEDAR POINT PLACE - WESTLAKE VILLAGE CA 91362
34- 26	COHEN, SYDNEY HARRY	D. APRIL 9, 1988 EL PASO, TEXAS
58- 23	COKER, JIMMIE GOODWIN	BOX TWO - THROCKMORTON TX 76083
55- 28	COLAVITO, ROCCO DOMENICO	OLD ADD: TEMPLE PA 19560
78- 26	COLBERN, MICHAEL MALLOY	1059 EAST FAIRMONT - TEMPE AZ 85282
66- 22	COLBERT, NATHAN	OLD ADD: 17369 RUETTE ABETO - SAN DIEGO CA 92128
70- 22	COLBERT, VINCENT NORMAN	1417 'E' STREET SE - WASHINGTON DC 20003
69- 34	COLBORN, JAMES WILLIAM	2932 SOLIMAR BEACH DR - VENTURA CA 93001
21- 14	COLE, ALBERT GEORGE	D. MAY 30, 1975 SAN MATEO, CAL.
50- 22	COLE, DAVID BRUCE	104 WILLCOX DRIVE - WILLIAMSPORT MD 21795
38- 15	COLE, EDWARD WILLIAM	OLD ADD: 6853 LARMANDA - DALLAS TX 75231
51- 14	COLE, RICHARD ROY	3149 MADEIRA AVE - COSTA MESA CA 92626
61- 24	COLEMAN, CLARENCE 'CHOO CHOO'	OLD ADD: 726 CORNELIA COURT - ORLANDO FL 32807
12- 37	COLEMAN, CURTIS HANCOCK	D. JULY 1, 1980 NEWPORT, ORE.
77- 30	COLEMAN, DAVID LEE	4303 DELHI DR - DAYTON OH 45432
49- 15	COLEMAN, GERALD FRANCIS	1004 HAVENHURST DR - LAJOLLA CA 92037
59- 14	COLEMAN, GORDON CALVIN	8698 ZENITH CT - CINCINNATI OH 45231
65- 23	COLEMAN, JOSEPH HOWARD	2372 CHANDLER AVE - FORT MYERS FL 33907
42- 22	COLEMAN, JOSEPH PATRICK	1751 CORAL WAY - NORTH FORT MYERS FL 33917
32- 14	COLEMAN, PARKE EDWARD 'ED'	D. AUGUST 5, 1964 OREGON CITY, ORE.
47- 20	COLEMAN, RAYMOND LEROY	BOX 8 - HORNBROOK CA 96044
13- 33	COLEMAN, ROBERT HUNTER	D. JULY 16, 1959 BOSTON, MASS.
85- 19	COLEMAN, VINCENT MAURICE	1864 HERMITAGE - IMPERIAL MO 63052
55- 29	COLEMAN, WALTER GARY	207 PAWLING AVE - TROY NY 12180
14- 37	COLES, CADWALLADER R.	D. JUNE 30, 1942 MIAMI, FLA.
58- 24	COLES, CHARLES EDWARD	BOX 32 - JEFFERSON PA 15344
83- 34	COLES, DARNELL	OLD ADD: 4282 WEST GAIL DRIVE - CHANDLER AZ 85226
72- 19	COLETTTA, CHRISTOPHER MICHAEL	%JOHN COLETTA,1819 SE 26TH TER - CAPE CORAL FL 33904
11- 31	COLLAMORE, ALLAN EDWARD	D. AUGUST 8, 1980 BATTLE CREEK, MI.
27- 26	COLLARD, EARL CLINTON 'HAP'	D. JULY 14, 1968 JAMESTOWN, N. Y.
31- 13	COLLIER, ORLIN EDWARD	D. SEPTEMBER 9, 1944 MEMPHIS, TENN.
13- 34	COLLINS, CYRIL WILSON	D. FEBRUARY 28, 1941 KNOXVILLE, TENN.
75- 27	COLLINS, DAVID SCOTT	95 SPRINGWOOD DRIVE - SPRINGBORO OH 45066
77- 31	COLLINS, DONALD EDWARD	BOX 208 - LYONS GA 30436
39- 23	COLLINS, EDWARD TROWBRIDGE JR.	BOX 206 - KENNETT SQUARE PA 19348
20- 22	COLLINS, HARRY WARREN 'RIP'	D. MAY 27, 1968 BRYAN, TEX.
31- 14	COLLINS, JAMES ANTHONY 'RIP'	D. APRIL 16, 1970 NEW HAVEN, N. Y.
14- 38	COLLINS, JOHN EDGAR "ZIP"	D. DECEMBER 19, 1983 MANASSAS, VA.
10- 32	COLLINS, JOHN FRANCIS 'SHANO'	D. SEPTEMBER 10, 1955 NEWTON, MASS.
48- 27	COLLINS, JOSEPH EDWARD	D. AUGUST 30, 1989 UNION, N.J.
65- 24	COLLINS, KEVIN MICHAEL	97 W. ELMWOOD ST - CLAWSON MI 48017
23- 21	COLLINS, PHILIP EUGENE	D. AUGUST 14, 1960 CHICAGO, ILL.
40- 11	COLLINS, ROBERT JOSEPH	D. APRIL 19, 1969 PITTSBURGH, PA.
19- 14	COLLINS, THARON LESLIE 'PAT'	D. MAY 19, 1960 KANSAS CITY, KAN.
10- 33	COLLINS, WILLIAM SHIRLEY	D. JUNE 26, 1961 SAN BERNARDINO, CALIF.
51- 15	COLLUM, JACK DEAN	523 11TH AVE - GRINNELL IA 50112
42- 23	COLMAN, FRANK LOYD	D. FEBRUARY 19, 1983, LONDON, ONT.
70- 23	COLPAERT, RICHARD CHARLES	47412 ELDON - UTICA MI 48087
70- 24	COLSON, LOYD ALBERT	RR ONE - GOULD OK 73544
68- 14	COLTON, LAWRENCE ROBERT	OLD ADD: 4015 SW 52ND AVE - PORTLAND OR 97221
73- 25	COLUCCIO, ROBERT PASQUALI	417 WILDCAT STREET SE - OLYMPIA WA 98503
80- 25	COMBE, GEOFFREY WADE	2384 E. AVENIDA OTONO - THOUSAND OAKS CA 91362
24- 22	COMBS, EARLE BRYAN	D. JULY 21, 1976 RICHMOND, KY.
47- 21	COMBS, MERRILL RUSSELL	D. JULY 8, 1981 RIVERSIDE, CALIF.
89- 24	COMBS, PATRICK DENNIS	6565 WESTWICK AVENUE - HOUSTON TX 77072
45- 14	COMELLAS, JORGE	13015 SW 50TH ST - MIAMI FL 33165
67- 20	COMER, HARRY WAYNE	RR 1 BOX 4F - SHENANDOAH VA 22849
78- 27	COMER, STEVEN MICHAEL	20500 SUMMERVILLE RD - EXCELSIOR MN 55331
54- 15	COMMAND, JAMES DALTON	1743 MATILDA ST NE - GRAND RAPIDS MI 49503
26- 17	COMORSKY, ADAM ANTHONY	D. MARCH 2, 1951 SWOYERSVILLE, PA.
11- 30	COMPTON, ANNA SEBASTIAN 'PETE'	D. FEBRUARY 3, 1978 KANSAS CITY, MO.
11- 31	COMPTON, HARRY LEROY 'JACK'	D. JULY 4, 1974 LANCASTER, O.
70- 25	COMPTON, MICHAEL LYNN	8624 LEIGHTON DR - TAMPA FL 33614
72- 20	COMPTON, ROBERT CLINTON	OLD ADD: 45 KENT ST - MONTGOMERY AL
84- 21	COMSTOCK, KEITH MARTIN	9615 EAST DESERT TRAIL - SCOTTSDALE AZ 85260
13- 35	COMSTOCK, RALPH REMICK	D. SEPTEMBER 13, 1966 TOLEDO, O.
48- 28	CONATSOR, CLINTON ASTOR	26701 QUAIL CREEK #191 - LAGUNA HILLS CA 92653
70- 26	CONCEPCION, DAVID ISMAEL	URB. LOS CAOBOS BOTALON 5D, 5 PISO-MARACAY VENEZ
80- 26	CONCEPCION, ONIX (CARDONA)	PARCELA 61AA-BO.HIGUILLAR - DORADO PR 00646
62- 28	CONDE, RAMON LUIS	BOX 57 - JUANA DIAZ PR 00665
86- 36	CONE, DAVID BRIAN	3612 BIRCHWOOD DRIVE - KANSAS CITY MO 64137
15- 21	CONE, ROBERT EARL	D. MAY 24, 1955 GALVESTON, TEX.
40- 12	CONGER, RICHARD	D. FEBRUARY 16, 1970 LOS ANGELES, CAL.
64- 20	CONIGLIARO, ANTHONY RICHARD	D. FEBRUARY 24, 1990 SALEM, MASS.
69- 35	CONIGLIARO, WILLIAM MICHAEL	ROSEMARY RD - NAHANT MA 01908
20- 23	CONKWRIGHT, ALLEN HOWARD	8787 CENTER DRIVE - LAMESA CA 92041
34- 27	CONLAN, JOHN BERTRAND 'JOCKO'	D. APRIL 16, 1989 SCOTTSDALE, ARIZ.
52- 19	CONLEY, DONALD EUGENE 'GENE'	12 RIDGE ROAD - FOXBORO MA 02035
14- 39	CONLEY, JAMES PATRICK 'SNIPE'	D. JANUARY 7, 1978 DESOTO, TEX.
58- 25	CONLEY, ROBERT BURNS	OLD ADD: 75 TOWNE SQUARE DR - NEWPORT NEWS VA 23607
23- 22	CONLON, ARTHUR JOSEPH	D. AUGUST 5, 1987 FALMOUTH, MASS.
83- 35	CONNALLY, FRITZIE LEE	714 CARDINAL CIRCLE - PASADENA TX 77502
21- 15	CONNALLY, GEORGE WALTER 'SARGE'	D. JANUARY 27, 1978 TEMPLE, TEXAS
25- 20	CONNALLY, MERVIN THOMAS	D. JUNE 12, 1964 BERKELEY, CAL.
31- 15	CONNATSER, BROADUS MILBURN 'BRUCE'	D. JANUARY 27, 1971 TERRE HAUTE, IND.

31- 16	CONNELL, EUGENE JOSEPH	D. AUGUST 31, 1937 WAVERLY, N. Y.
26- 18	CONNELL, JOSEPH BERNARD	D. SEPTEMBER 21, 1977 TREXLERTOWN, PA.
20- 24	CONNELLY, THOMAS MARTIN	D. FEBRUARY 18, 1941 HINES, ILL.
45- 15	CONNELLY, WILLIAM WIRT	D. NOVEMBER 27, 1980 RICHMOND, VA.
29- 20	CONNOLLY, EDWARD JOSEPH	D. NOVEMBER 14, 1963 PITTSFIELD, MASS.
64- 21	CONNOLLY, EDWARD JOSEPH JR.	14 HIGHRIDGE ROAD - WILBRAHAM MA 01095
13- 36	CONNOLLY, JOSEPH ALOYSIUS	D. SEPTEMBER 1, 1943 SPRINGFIELD, R.I.
21- 16	CONNOLLY, JOSEPH GEORGE	D. MARCH 30, 1960 SAN FRANCISCO, CALIF.
15- 22	CONNOLLY, THOMAS FRANCIS	D. MAY 14, 1966 BOSTON, MASS.
49- 16	CONNORS, KEVIN JOSEPH 'CHUCK'	STAR ROUTE 3-4400 BOX 73 - TEHACHAPI CA 93561
37- 27	CONNORS, MERVYN JAMES	1131 ADDISON ST-BERKELEY CA 94702
66- 23	CONNORS, WILLIAM JOSEPH	895 N. VILLAGE DR #101 - ST. PETERSBURG FL 33702
78- 28	CONROY, TIMOTHY JAMES	416 LUZERNE DR - MONROEVILLE PA 15146
23- 23	CONROY, WILLIAM FREDERICK 'PEP'	D. JANUARY 23, 1970 CHICAGO, ILL.
35- 16	CONROY, WILLIAM GORDON	7194 CRAIL CT - CITRUS HEIGHTS CA 95610
53- 16	CONSOLO, WILLIAM ANGELO	1266 WILLSBROOK CT - WESTLAKE VILLAGE CA91360
56- 23	CONSTABLE, JAMES LEE	RR 14 - BOX 540 - JONESBORO TN 37659
50- 23	CONSUEGRA, SANDALIO SIMEON	3255 FLAGLER STREET #14 - MIAMI FL 33125
80- 27	CONTRERAS, ARNALDO JUAN 'NARDIE'	1540 RIVER LN - TAMPA FL 33603
11- 32	CONWAY, CHARLES CONNELL	D. SEPTEMBER 12, 1968 YOUNGSTOWN, O.
41- 17	CONWAY, JACK CLEMENTS	3545 PINE - WACO TX 76708
20- 25	CONWAY, JEROME PATRICK	D. APRIL 16, 1980 HOLYOKE, MASS.
15- 23	CONWAY, OWEN SYLVESTER	D. MARCH 12, 1942 PHILADELPHIA, PA.
18- 12	CONWAY, RICHARD DANIEL 'RIP'	D. DECEMBER 3, 1971 ST PAUL, MINN.
11- 33	CONWELL, EDWARD JAMES	D. MAY 1, 1926 NORWOOD PARK, ILL.
50- 24	CONYERS, HERBERT LEROY	D. SEPTEMBER 16, 1964 CLEVELAND, O.
13- 37	CONZELMAN, JOSEPH HARRISON	D. APRIL 17, 1979 MOUNTAIN BROOK, ALA.
50- 25	COOGAN, DALE ROGER	D. MARCH 8, 1989 MISSION VIEJO CALIF.
88- 32	COOK, DENNIS BRYAN	5017 CEDAR CREEK - DICKINSON TX 77539
41- 18	COOK, EARL DAVIS	RR 4 - STOUFFVILLE ONTARIO CAN.
85- 20	COOK, GLEN PATRICK	2834 ENGLISH COLONY DRIVE - WEBSTER TX 77598
13- 38	COOK, LUTHER ALMUS 'DOC'	D. JUNE 30, 1973 LAWRENCEBURG, TENN.
86- 37	COOK, MICHAEL HORACE	518 SARAH STREET - CHARLESTON SC 29407
59- 15	COOK, RAYMOND CLIFFORD 'CLIFF'	605 WILLIAMSBURG MANOR - ARLINGTON TX 76014
15- 24	COOK, ROLLIN EDWARD	D. AUGUST 11, 1975 TOLEDO, O.
70- 27	COOK, RONALD WAYNE	913 FLANAGAN - LONGVIEW TX 75602
30- 13	COOKE, ALLEN LINDSEY 'DUSTY'	D. NOVEMBER 21, 1987 RALEIGH, N. C.
89- 25	COOLBAUGH, SCOTT RICHARD	6214 HICKORY HOLLOW - SAN ANTONIO TX 78239
14- 40	COOMBS, CECIL LYSANDER	D. NOVEMBER 25, 1975 FORT WORTH, TEX.
63- 25	COOMBS, DANIEL BERNARD	14130 CLEOBROOK - HOUSTON TX 77070
33- 14	COOMBS, RAYMOND FRANKLIN 'BOBBY'	BOX 782 - OGUNQUIT ME 03907
17- 15	COONEY, JAMES EDWARD	34 WOODSIA RD - SAUNDERSTOWN RI 02874
21- 17	COONEY, JOHN WALTER	D. JULY 8, 1986 SARASOTA, FLA.
31- 17	COONEY, ROBERT DANIEL	D. MAY 4, 1976 GLEN FALLS, N. Y.
12- 38	COOPER, ARLEY WILBUR	D. AUGUST 7, 1973 ENCINO, CALIF.
48- 29	COOPER, CALVIN ASA	330 POPLAR ST - CLINTON SC 29325
71- 27	COOPER, CECIL CELESTER	1431 MISTY BEND - KATY TX 77450
13- 39	COOPER, CLAUDE WILLIAM	D. JANUARY 21, 1974 PLAINVIEW, TEX.
81- 24	COOPER, DONALD JAMES	2122 SEWARD DRIVE - SARASOTA FL 34234
80- 28	COOPER, GARY NATHANIEL	127 OGLESBY AVE - GARDEN CITY GA 31408
14- 41	COOPER, GUY EVANS	D. AUGUST 2, 1951 SANTA MONICA, CALIF.
38- 16	COOPER, MORTON CECIL	D. NOVEMBER 17, 1958 LITTLE ROCK, ARK.
46- 19	COOPER, ORGE PATTERSON 'PAT'	4424 HOBBS HILL DRIVE - CHARLOTTE NC 28215
40- 13	COOPER, WILLIAM WALKER 'WALKER'	10567 SADDLE HORN - SCOTTSDALE AZ 85258
35- 17	COPELAND, MAYS	D. NOVEMBER 29, 1982 INDIO, CALIF.
35- 18	COPPOLA, HENRY PETER	42 PLEASANT STREET-MILFORD MA 01757
87- 26	CORA, JOSE MANUEL	CALLE 17, F12 VILLA NUEVA - CAGUAS PR 00625
80- 29	CORBETT, DOUGLAS MITCHELL	108 STONEBROOK CT - LONGWOOD FL 32779
36- 15	CORBETT, EUGENE LOUIS	BOX 904 - SALISBURY MD 21801
88- 33	CORBETT, SHERMAN STANLEY	8205 TRAINER HALE ROAD - CONVERSE TX 78109
71- 28	CORBIN, ALTON RAY	922 LIBERTY ST - LIVE OAK FL 32060
45- 16	CORBITT, CLAUDE ELLIOTT	D. MAY 1, 1978 CINCINNATI, O.
15- 25	CORCORAN, ARTHUR ANDREW	D. JULY 27, 1958 CHELSEA, MASS.
10- 34	CORCORAN, MICHAEL JOSEPH 'MICKEY'	D. DECEMBER 9, 1950 BUFFALO, N.Y.
77- 32	CORCORAN, TIMOTHY MICHAEL	4349 FRIAR CIRCLE - LAVERNE CA 91750
18- 13	COREY, EDWARD NORMAN	D. SEPTEMBER 17, 1970 KENOSHA, WIS.
79- 25	COREY, MARK MUNDELL	BOX 161 - EVERGREEN CO 80439
25- 21	CORGAN, CHARLES HOWARD	D. JUNE 13, 1928 WAGONER, OKLA.
11- 34	CORHAN, ROY GEORGE	D. NOVEMBER 24, 1958 SAN FRANCISCO, CALIF.
69- 36	CORKINS, MICHAEL PATRICK	1274 BRADLEY STREET - RIVERSIDE CA 92506
78- 29	CORNEJO, NEIVES MARDIE	1510 EAST FORTUNA - WICHITA KS 67216
84- 22	CORNELL, JEFFERY RAY	5207 MCCOY - KANSAS CITY MO 64133
77- 33	CORNUTT, TERRY STANTON	179 WEST HAZEL - ROSEBURG OR 97470
64- 22	CORRALES, PATRICK	2499 PEACHTREE ROAD NE - ATLANTA GA 30305
85- 21	CORREA, EDWIN JOSEPH	OLD ADD: BUZON 755 RUTA 649 - CAROLINA PR 00630
72- 21	CORRELL, VICTOR CROSBY	P.O. BOX 904 - NASHVILLE GA 31639
10- 35	CORRIDEN, JOHN MICHAEL SR. 'RED'	D. SEPTEMBER 28, 1959 INDIANAPOLIS, IND.
46- 20	CORRIDEN, JOHN MICHAEL JR	5441 EAST 17TH ST - INDIANAPOLIS IN 46218
88- 34	CORSI, JAMES BERNARD	36 ANTHONY CIRCLE - NEWTONVILLE MA 02160
77- 34	CORT, BARRY LEE	OLD ADD: 8707 SEAHAWK LN - TAMPA FL
23- 24	CORTAZZO, JOHN FRANK 'SHINE'	D. MARCH 4, 1963 PITTSBURGH, PA.
51- 16	CORWIN, ELMER NATHAN 'AL'	1412 SHERWOOD - GENEVA IL 60134
35- 19	COSCARART, JOSEPH MARVIN	127A SPATH RD - SEQUIM WA 98382
38- 17	COSCARART, PETER JOSEPH	2808 JULINDA WAY - ESCONDIDO CA 92025
80- 30	COSEY, DONALD RAY	139 BYXBEE ST - SAN FRANCISCO CA 94132
72- 22	COSGROVE, MICHAEL JOHN	3827 WEST BELMONT - PHOENIX AZ 85051
66- 24	COSMAN, JAMES HARRY	6520 ROBBINS RIDGE LN - MEMPHIS TN 38119
13- 40	COSTELLO, DANIEL FRANCIS	D. MARCH 26, 1936 PITTSBURGH, PA.
88- 35	COSTELLO, JOHN REILLY	224 BEDELL STREET - OCEANSIDE NY 11572
26- 19	COTE, WARREN PETER 'PETE'	D. OCTOBER 17, 1987 MIDDLETON, MASS.
26- 20	COTTER, EDWARD CHRISTOPHER	D. JUNE 14, 1959 HARTFORD, CONN.
22- 22	COTTER, HARVEY LOUIS	D. AUGUST 6, 1955 LOS ANGELES, CAL.
11- 35	COTTER, RICHARD RAPHAEL	D. APRIL 4, 1945 BROOKLYN, N. Y.
59- 16	COTTIER, CHARLES KEITH	7129 LAKE BALLINGER WAY - EDMONDS WA 98020
84- 23	COTTO, HENRY	JUAN J. GARCIA ED. 21 #201 - CAGUAS PR 00625
11- 36	COTTRELL, ENSIGN STOVER	D. FEBRUARY 27, 1947 SYRACUSE, N.Y.
17- 16	COUCH, JOHN DANIEL	D. DECEMBER 8, 1975 PALO ALTO, CALIF.

Ray Dandridge

Monte Irvin

Al Kaline

Ralph Kiner

Stan Musial

Edd Roush

Billy Williams

HALL OF FAME OUTFIELDERS

Dandridge, Irvin, Kaline, Kiner, Musial, Roush, Williams and Yastrzemski are featured on these Perez-Steele autographed Art Post Cards

Carl Yastrzemski

83- 36	COUCHEE, MICHAEL EUGENE	16900 CYPRESS WAY - LOS GATOS CA 95030
60- 25	COUGHTRY, JAMES MARLAN	4232 SAN VICENTE - CHINO CA 91709
69- 37	COULTER, THOMAS LEE 'SKIP'	809 TRENTON ST - TORONTO OH 43964
14- 42	COUMBE, FREDERICK NICHOLAS 'FRITZ'	D. MARCH 21, 1978 PARADISE, CALIF.
51- 17	COURTNEY, CLINTON DAWSON	D. JUNE 16, 1975 ROCHESTER, N. Y.
19- 15	COURTNEY, HENRY SEYMOUR	D. DECEMBER 11, 1954 LYME, CT.
23- 25	COUSINEAU, ED 'D'	D. JULY 14, 1951 WATERTOWN, MASS.
12- 39	COVELESKI, STANLEY ANTHONY	D. MARCH 20, 1984 SOUTH BEND, IND.
44- 23	COVINGTON, CHESTER ROGERS	D. JUNE 11, 1976 PEMBROKE PARK, FLA.
13- 41	COVINGTON, CLARENCE CALVERT 'TEX'	D. JANUARY 4, 1963 DENISON, TEX.
56- 24	COVINGTON, JOHN WESLEY 'WES'	905 10145 119TH STREET - EDMONTON ALBERTA T5K 1Z2 CAN.
11- 37	COVINGTON, WILLIAM WILKES	D. DECEMBER 10, 1931 DENISON, TEX.
63- 26	COWAN, BILLY ROLAND	1539 VIA CORONEL-PALOS VERDES ESTATES CA90274
74- 17	COWENS, ALFRED EDWARD	5723 KENISTON AVE - LOS ANGELES CA 90043
82- 26	COWLEY, JOSEPH ALAN	146 RUGBY RD - LEXINGTON KY 40504
83- 37	COX, DANNY BRADFORD	306 FEAGIN MILL RD - WARNER ROBINS GA 31093
25- 22	COX, ELMER JOSEPH 'DICK'	D. JUNE 1, 1966 MORRO BAY, CALIF.
22- 23	COX, ERNEST THOMPSON	D. APRIL 29, 1974 BIRMINGHAM, ALA.
28- 23	COX, GEORGE MELVIN	1525 NORTH WHARTON - SHERMAN TX 75090
55- 30	COX, GLENN MELVIN	P.O. BOX 432 - LOS MOLINOS CA 96055
73- 26	COX, JAMES CHARLES	916 SOUTH VALE - BLOOMINGTON IL 61701
80- 31	COX, JEFFREY LINDON	2727 VANDERHOOF DR - WEST COVINA CA 91791
66- 25	COX, JOSEPH CASEY	630 GRAND AVE - LONG BEACH CA 90814
73- 27	COX, LARRY EUGENE	D. FEBRUARY 17, 1990 BELLEFONTAINE, O.
26- 21	COX, LESLIE WARREN	D. OCTOBER 14, 1934 SAN ANGELO, TEX.
20- 26	COX, PLATEAU REX	D. OCTOBER 15, 1984 ROANOKE, VA.
68- 15	COX, ROBERT JOE	4030 RIVER RIDGE CHASE - MARIETTA GA 30067
70- 28	COX, TERRY LEE	216 HOLLAND - CARLSBAD NM 88220
36- 16	COX, WILLIAM DONALD	45 CIRCLE DR-CHARLESTON IL 61920
41- 19	COX, WILLIAM RICHARD	D. MARCH 30, 1978 HARRISBURG, PA.
77- 35	COX, WILLIAM TED	113 WEST PRATT DR - MIDWEST CITY OK 73110
14- 43	COYNE, "TOOTS"	
45- 17	COZART, CHARLES RHUBIN	RR 2 BOX 212-A - HUDSON NC 28638
12- 40	CRABB, JAMES ROY	D. MARCH 30, 1940 LEWISTON, MONT.
10- 36	CRABLE, GEORGE E	B. 1886 BROOKLYN, N.Y.
29- 21	CRABTREE, ESTEL CRAYTON	D. JANUARY 4, 1967 LOGAN, O.
55- 31	CRADDOCK, WALTER ANDERSON	D. JULY 6, 1980 PARMA HEIGHTS OHIO
37- 28	CRAFT, HARRY FRANCIS	716 GLEN HAVEN DR - CONROE TX 77301
16- 14	CRAFT, MAURICE MONTAGUE 'MOLLY'	D. OCTOBER 25, 1978 LOS ANGELES, CALIF.
31- 18	CRAGHEAD, HOWARD OLIVER	D. JULY 15, 1962 SAN ZIELOE, CAL.
64- 23	CRAIG, PETER JOEL	OLD ADD: 801 SILVERLEAF PLACE - RALEIGH NC 27609
79- 26	CRAIG, RODNEY PAUL 'ROCKY'	OLD ADD: 23230 SESAME ST - TORRANCE CA
55- 32	CRAIG, ROGER LEE	26658 SAN FELIPE RD - WARNER SPRING CA 92086
69- 38	CRAM, GERALD ALLEN	2748 NORTH 121ST AVENUE - OMAHA NE 68164
29- 22	CRAMER, ROGER MAXWELL 'DOC'	5 HILLIARD DR - MANAHAWKIN NJ 08050
12- 41	CRAMER, WILLIAM WENDELL	D. SEPTEMBER 11, 1966 FORT WAYNE, IND.
49- 17	CRANDALL, DELMAR WESLEY	25 ROCK CLIFF PLACE - POMONA CA 91766
14- 44	CRANE, SAMUEL BYREN	D. NOVEMBER 12, 1955 PHILADELPHIA, PA.
37- 29	CRAWFORD, CHARLES LOWRIE 'LARRY'	94 OAK HILLS DRIVE - HANOVER PA 17331
29- 23	CRAWFORD, CLIFFORD RANKIN 'PAT'	812 SHEPARD STREET - MOREHEAD CITY NC 28557
45- 18	CRAWFORD, GLENN MARTIN	D. JANUARY 2, 1972 SAGINAW, MICH.
73- 28	CRAWFORD, JAMES FREDERICK	OLD ADD: 48621 I-94 S'CE DR DR-BELLKEVILLE MI
15- 26	CRAWFORD, KENNETH DANIEL	D. NOVEMBER 11, 1976 PITTSBURGH, PA.
52- 20	CRAWFORD, RUFUS 'JAKE'	2928 WESTBROOK - FORT WORTH TX 76111
80- 32	CRAWFORD, STEVE RAY	RR 2 BOX 7-8 - SALINA OK 74365
64- 24	CRAWFORD, WILLIE MURPHY	P.O. BOX 491054 - LOS ANGELES CA 90049
43- 32	CREEDEN, CORNELIUS STEPHEN	D. NOVEMBER 30, 1969 SANTA ANA, CAL.
31- 19	CREEDON, PATRICK FRANCIS	622 NORTH MAIN ST - BROCKTON MA 02401
45- 19	CREEL, JACK DALTON	7119 OAK ARBOR - HOUSTON TX 77088
82- 27	CREEL, STEVEN KEITH	527 TRAIL RIDGE DR - DUNCANVILLE TX 75116
47- 22	CREGER, BERNARD ODELL	15 GREENWELL CT - LYNCHBURG VA 24502
27- 27	CREMINS, ROBERT ANTHONY	415 MANOR RIDGE RD - PELHAM NY 10803
38- 18	CRESPI, FRANK ANGELO JOSEPH 'CREEPY'	D. MARCH 1, 1990 FLORISSANT, MO.
48- 30	CRESS, WALKER JAMES	14177 WINTERSET - GREENWELL SPRINGS LA 70739
87- 27	CREWS, STANLEY TIMOTHY 'TIM'	8103 19TH AVENUE - TAMPA FL 33619
69- 39	CRIDER, JERRY STEPHEN	OLD ADD: 821 KENSINGTON DR - ORLANDO FL 32801
87- 28	CRIM, CHARLES ROBERT	25800 SAND CYN - CANYON COUNTRY CA 91350
51- 18	CRIMIAN, JOHN MELVIN	3012 GREEN ST - CLAYMONT DE 19703
78- 30	CRIPE, DAVID GORDON	40657 OAKLAND AVE - HEMET CA 92343
77- 36	CRISCIONE, DAVID GERALD	87 HAMLET ST - FREDONIA NY 14063
42- 24	CRISCOLA, ANTHONY PAUL	4025 BAYARD-SAN DIEGO CA 92109
10- 37	CRISP, JOSEPH SHELBY	D. FEBRUARY 5, 1939 KANSAS CITY, MO.
51- 19	CRISTANTE, LEO DANTE	D. AUGUST 24, 1977 DEARBORN, MICH.
24- 23	CRITZ, HUGH MELVILLE	D. JANUARY 10, 1980 GREENWOOD, MISS.
44- 24	CROCKER, CLAUDE ARTHUR	MERRIE OAKS - CLINTON SC 29325
74- 18	CROMARTIE, WARREN LIVINGSTON	%BOOTH,1751 NW 36TH ST - MIAMI FL 33142
37- 30	CROMPTON, HERBERT BRYAN	D. AUGUST 5, 1963 MOLINE, ILL.
54- 16	CRONE, RAYMOND HAYES	610 COX STREET - CEDAR HILL TX 75104
29- 24	CRONIN, JAMES JOHN	D. JUNE 10, 1983 RICHMOND, CALIF.
26- 22	CRONIN, JOSEPH EDWARD	D. SEPTEMBER 7, 1984 OSTERVILLE, MASS.
28- 24	CRONIN, WILLIAM PATRICK	D. OCTOBER 26, 1966 NEWTON, MASS.
70- 29	CROSBY, EDWARD CARLTON	11463 ANTICOST WAY - CYPRESS CA 90630
75- 28	CROSBY, KENNETH STEWART	BOX 680306 - PARK CITY UT 84068
32- 15	CROSETTI, FRANK PETER JOSEPH	65 WEST MONTEREY AV - STOCKTON CA 95204
42- 25	CROSS, JOFFRE JAMES 'JEFF'	6154 LONGMONT DRIVE - HOUSTON TX 77057
12- 42	CROSSIN, FRANK PATRICK	D. DECEMBER 6, 1965 KINGSPORT, TN.
30- 14	CROUCH, JACK ALBERT	D. AUGUST 25, 1972 LEESBURG, FLA.
39- 24	CROUCH, WILLIAM ELMER	D. DECEMBER 26, 1980 HOWELL, MICH.
10- 38	CROUCH, WILLIAM HENRY	D. DECEMBER 22, 1945 HIGHLAND PARK, MICH.
88- 36	CROUCH, ZACHARY QUINN	3122 TORY - SACRAMENTO CA 95827
39- 25	CROUCHER, FRANK DONALD	D. MAY 21, 1980 HOUSTON, TEXAS
23- 26	CROUSE, CLYDE ELLSWORTH 'BUCK'	D. OCTOBER 23, 1983 MUNCIE, IND.
82- 28	CROW, DONALD LEROY	7605 WESTBROOK AVE - YAKIMA WA 98908
26- 23	CROWDER, ALVIN FLOYD 'GEN'	D. APRIL 3, 1972 WINSTON-SALEM, N. C.
52- 21	CROWE, GEORGE DANIEL	OLD ADD: 3820 SE 73RD STREET - OCALA FL 32671
15- 27	CROWELL, MINOT JOY 'CAP'	D. SEPTEMBER 30, 1962 CENTRAL FALLS, R.I.
28- 25	CROWLEY, EDGAR JEWEL	D. APRIL 14, 1970 BIRMINGHAM, ALA.
69- 40	CROWLEY, TERRENCE MICHAEL	10626 ANGLOHILL RD - COCKEYSVILLE MD 21030

45- 20 CROWSON, THOMAS WOODROW WILSON 'WOODY D. AUGUST 14, 1947 MAYODAN, N. C.
14- 45 CRUISE, WALTON EDWIN   D. JANUARY 9, 1975 SYLACAUGA ALA.
17- 17 CRUM, CALVIN CARL   D. DECEMBER 7, 1945 TULSA, OKLA.
45- 21 CRUMLING, EUGENE LEON   RR 24 BOX 809 - YORK PA 17406
24- 24 CRUMP, ARTHUR ELLIOTT   D. SEPTEMBER 7, 1976 RALEIGH, N. C.
20- 27 CRUMPLER, RAY MAXTON   D. OCTOBER 6, 1969 FAYETTEVILLE, N. C.
14- 46 CRUTCHER, RICHARD LOUIS   D. JUNE 19, 1952 FRANKFORT, KY.
13- 42 CRUTHERS, CHARLES PRESTON 'PRESS'   D. DECEMBER 27, 1976 KENOSHA, WISC.
73- 29 CRUZ, CIRILO 'TOMMY'   CALLE H-E-8 - ARROYO PR 00615
73- 30 CRUZ, HECTOR LUIS   CALLE H-E-8 - ARROYO PR 00615
75- 29 CRUZ, HENRY ACOSTA   OLD ADD: MONTRE BRISAS CALLE T-0-6 - FAJARDO PR 00648
70- 30 CRUZ, JOSE DELAN   B-15 JARDINES LAFAYETTE - ARROYO PR 00615
77- 37 CRUZ, JULIO LOUIS   40 ORCAS KEY - BELLEVUE WA 98006
78- 31 CRUZ, TODD RUBEN   868 WEST OLIVE STREET - COLTON CA 92324
78- 32 CRUZ, VICTOR MANUEL   ALEXANDER FLEMING NO. 67 - SANTO DOMINGO DOMINICAN REP.
74- 19 CUBBAGE, MICHAEL LEE   BOX 126 - RUCKERSVILLE VA 22968
35- 20 CUCCINELLO, ALFRED EDWARD   106 LWGION PLACE - MALVERNE NY 11565
30- 15 CUCCINELLO, ANTHONY FRANCIS   3610 BEACH DR - TAMPA FL 33629
43- 33 CUCCURULLO, ARTHUR JOSEPH 'COOKIE'   D. JANUARY 23, 1983 WEST ORANGE, N. J.
77- 38 CUELLAR, BOBBY   705 EAST SIXTH STREET - ALICE TX 78332
50- 26 CUELLAR, CHARLES JESUS PATRICK   3209 GRACE ST - TAMPA FL 33607
59- 17 CUELLAR, MIGUEL 'MIKE'   BOX 50016 - LEVITTOWN PR 00950
61- 25 CUETO, DAGOBERTO CONCEPCION   EL COROJO - SAN LUIS PINAR DEL RIO CUBA
14- 47 CUETO, MANUEL MELO   D. JUNE 29, 1942 REGLA, HAVANA CUBA
43- 34 CULBERSON, DELBERT LEON 'LEON'   D. SEPTEMBER 17, 1989 ROME, GA.
62- 29 CULLEN, JOHN PATRICK   164 ALEXANDER AVE - NUTLEY NJ 07110
66- 26 CULLEN, TIMOTHY LEO   789 SOLANA DR - LAFAYETTE CA 94549
38- 19 CULLENBINE, ROY JOSEPH   24638 MEADOW LN - MOUNT CLEMENS MI 48043
36- 17 CULLER, RICHARD BROADUS   D. JUNE 16, 1964 CHAPEL HILL, N. C.
26- 24 CULLOP, HENRY 'NICK'   D. DECEMBER 8, 1978 WESTERVILLE, O.
13- 43 CULLOP, NORMAN ANDREW 'NICK'   D. APRIL 15, 1961 TAZEWELL, VA.
25- 23 CULLOTON, BERNARD ALOYSIUS 'BUD'   D. NOVEMBER 9, 1976 KINGSTON, N. Y.
83- 38 CULMER, WILFRED HILLARD   BOX N9762 - NASSAU BAHAMAS W.I.
42- 26 CULP, BENJAMIN BALDY   3827 KAREN ST-PHILADELPHIA PA 19114
63- 27 CULP, RAY LEONARD   7400 WATERLINE - AUSTIN TX 78731
10- 39 CULP, WILLIAM EDWARD   D. SEPTEMBER 3, 1969 ARNOLD, PA.
66- 24 CULVER, GEORGE RICHARD   4800 TREANNA AVENUE #2A - BAKERSFIELD CA 93301
68- 16 CUMBERLAND, JOHN SHELDON   36 ARLINGTON AVENUE - WESTBROOK ME 04092
26- 25 CUMMINGS, JOHN WILLIAM   D. OCTOBER 5, 1962 WEST MIFFLIN, PA.
89- 26 CUMMINGS, STEVEN BRENT   11010 SAGECREST - HOUSTON TX 77089
29- 25 CUNNINGHAM, BRUCE LEE   D. MARCH 8, 1984 HAYWARD, CALIF.
16- 15 CUNNINGHAM, GEORGE HAROLD   D. MARCH 10, 1972 CHATTANOOGA, TENN.
54- 17 CUNNINGHAM, JOSEPH ROBERT   BOX 8787 - ST.LOUIS MO 63102
31- 20 CUNNINGHAM, RAYMOND LEE   1007 CHRISTINE - HOUSTON TX 77017
10- 40 CUNNINGHAM, WILLIAM JAMES   D. FEBRUARY 21, 1946 SCHENECTADY, N. Y.
21- 18 CUNNINGHAM, WILLIAM ALOYSIUS   D. SEPTEMBER 26, 1953 COLUSA, CAL.
75- 30 CURRENCE, DELANCY LAFAYETTE   1238 STANLEY DR - ROCK HILL SC 29730
16- 16 CURRIE, MURPHY ARCHIBALD   D. JUNE 22, 1939 ASHEBORO, N.C.
55- 33 CURRIE, WILLIAM CLEVELAND   ARLINGTON GA 31713
47- 23 CURRIN, PERRY GILMORE   1967 ADD: 1615 SIGMON NW - ROANOKE VA 24017
60- 26 CURRY, GEORGE ANTHONY 'TONY'   BOX 7054 - NASSAU BAHAMAS W.I.
11- 38 CURRY, GEORGE JAMES   D. OCTOBER 5, 1963 STRATFORD, CONN.
88- 37 CURRY, STEPHEN THOMAS   OLD ADD: 207 46TH STREET WEST - BRADENTON FL 33529
61- 26 CURTIS, JACK PATRICK   RR 3 BOX 458 - GRANITE FALLS NC 28630
70- 31 CURTIS, JOHN DUFFIELD   858 ANDROMEDA LN - FOSTER CITY CA 94404
43- 35 CURTIS, VERNON EUGENE   724 21ST ST - CAIRO IL 62914
43- 36 CURTRIGHT, GUY PAXTON   1620 BENTWOOD DR - SUN CITY CENTER FL 33570
51- 20 CUSICK, JOHN PETER   D. NOVEMBER 17, 1989 ENGLEWOOD, N.J.
12- 43 CUTSHAW, GEORGE WILLIAM   D. AUGUST 22, 1973 SAN DIEGO, CALIF.
21- 19 CUYLER, HAZEN SHIRLEY 'KIKI'   D. FEBRUARY 11, 1950 ANN ARBOR, MICH.
22- 24 CVENGROS, MICHAEL JOHN   D. AUGUST 2, 1970 HOT SPRINGS, ARK.
14- 48 CYPERT, ALFRED BOYD   D. JANUARY 9, 1973 WASHINGTON, D.C.
73- 31 DACQUISTO, JOHN FRANCIS   3440 FIR ST - SAN DIEGO CA 92104
75- 31 DADE, LONNIE PAUL   OLD ADD: 15829 SE 171ST PL - RENTON WA 98055
43- 37 DAGENHARD, JOHN DOUGLAS   10511 HALBRENT AVE - MISSION HILLS CA 91345
32- 16 DAGLIA, PETER GEORGE   D. MARCH 11, 1952 WILLITS, CAL.
55- 34 DAGRES, ANGELO GEORGE   GREENTREE LN RFD - ROWLEY MA 01969
63- 28 DAHL, JAY STEVEN   D. JUNE 20, 1965 SALISBURY, N. C.
35- 21 DAHLGREN, ELLSWORTH TENNEY 'BABE'   17 WOODLYN LN - BRADBURY CA 91010
56- 25 DAHLKE, JEROME ALEXANDER 'JOE'   3643 HALLBROOK ST - MEMPHIS TN 38127
29- 26 DAILEY, SAMUEL LAURENCE   D. DECEMBER 2, 1979 COLUMBIA, MO.
61- 27 DAILEY, WILLIAM GARLAND   RR 1 BOX M8 - DUBLIN VA 24084
67- 21 DAL CANTON, JOHN BRUCE   624 RAY DR - CARNEGIE PA 15106
11- 39 DALE, EMMETT EUGENE 'GENE'   D. MARCH 20, 1958 ST. LOUIS, MO.
89- 27 DALENA, PETER MARTIN   4951 NORTH THORNE - FRESNO CA 93704
55- 35 DALEY, BUDDY LEO   RR 62-C BOX 205 - LANDER WY 82520
12- 44 DALEY, JOHN FRANCIS   D. AUGUST 31, 1988 MANSFIELD, OHIO
11- 40 DALEY, JUD LAWRENCE   D. JANUARY 26, 1967 GADSDEN, ALA.
55- 36 DALEY, PETER HARVEY   4019 CALLE MIRA MONTE - NEWBURY PARK CA 91320
37- 31 DALLESSANDRO, NICHOLAS DOMINIC 'DOM'   D. APRIL 29, 1988 INDIANAPOLIS, IND.
60- 27 DALRYMPLE, CLAYTON ERROL   710 BRUCE LANE - CHICO CA 95928
15- 28 DALRYMPLE, WILLIAM DUNN   D. JULY 14, 1967 SAN DIEGO, CALIF.
10- 41 DALTON, TALBOT PERCY 'JACK'   OLD ADD: 2 PROSPECT AVE - CATONSVILLE MD
13- 44 DALY, THOMAS DANIEL   D. NOVEMBER 7, 1946 MEDFORD, MASS.
63- 29 DAMASKA, JACK LLOYD   252 BLACKHAWK RD - BEAVER FALLS PA 15010
15- 29 DAMRAU, HARRY ROBERT   D. AUGUST 21, 1957 STATEN ISLAND, N. Y.
28- 26 DANEY, ARTHUR LEE   D. MARCH 11, 1988 SCOTTSDALE, ARIZ.
11- 41 DANFORTH, DAVID CHARLES   D. SEPTEMBER 19, 1970 BALTIMORE, MD.
57- 14 DANIEL, CHARLES EDWARD   1640 BABS RD - MEMPHIS TN 38116
37- 32 DANIEL, HANDLEY JACOB 'JAKE'   990 NEW HUTCHINSON MILL RD - LAGRANGE GA 30240
57- 15 DANIELS, BENNIE   P.O. BOX 4444 - COMPTON CA 90221
10- 42 DANIELS, BERNARD ELMER 'BERT'   D. JUNE 6, 1958 CEDAR GROVE, N.J.
45- 22 DANIELS, FREDERICK CLINTON   522 SALISBURY RD - STATESVILLE NC 28677
52- 22 DANIELS, HAROLD JACK   3715 ELMRIDGE DR - EVANSVILLE IN 47711
86- 38 DANIELS, KALVOSKI   OLD ADD: 151 IGNICI DRIVE #2L - WARNER ROBINS GA 31093
15- 30 DANNER, HENRY FREDERICK 'BUCK'   D. SEPTEMBER 21, 1949 BOSTON, MASS.
33- 15 DANNING, HARRY   212 FOX CHAPEL COURT - VALPARAISO IN 46383
28- 27 DANNING, IKE   D. MARCH 28, 1983 SANTA MONICA, CALIF.

41

44- 25 DANTONIO, JOHN JAMES 'FATS'   430 SOUTH CLARK ST - NEW ORLEANS LA 70119
42- 27 DAPPER, CLIFFORD ROLAND   733 BURMA RD-FALLBROOK CA 92028
74- 20 DARCY, PATRICK LEONARD   515 SOUTH COLUMBUS BLVD - TUCSON AZ 85711
14- 49 DARINGER, CLIFFORD CLARENCE   D. DECEMBER 12, 1971 SACRAMENTO, CALIF.
14- 50 DARINGER, ROLLA HARRISON   D. MAY 23, 1974 SEYMOUR, IND.
46- 21 DARK, ALVIN RALPH   103 CRANBERRY WAY - EASLEY SC 29640
83- 39 DARLING, RONALD MAURICE   19 WOODLAND STREET - MILLBURY MA 01527
54- 18 DARNELL, ROBERT JACK   509 MAPLE DR - SPRINGDALE AR 72764
77- 39 DARR, MICHAEL EDWARD   OLD ADD: 5862 "B" FULLERTON AVE - BUENA PARK CA 90621
34- 28 DARROW, GEORGE OLIVER   D. MARCH 24, 1983 SUN CITY, ARIZ.
62- 30 DARWIN, ARTHUR BOBBY LEE   17509 ALORA STREET - CERRITOS CA 90701
78- 33 DARWIN, DANIEL WAYNE   302 SOUTH FM 372 - VALLEY VIEW TX 76272
88- 38 DASCENZO, DOUGLAS CRAIG   316 CHESTNUT STREET - HILLER PA 15444
24- 25 DASHIELL, JOHN WALLACE 'WALLY'   D. MAY 20, 1972 PENSACOLA, FLA.
13- 45 DASHNER, LEE CLAIRE   D. DECEMBER 16, 1960 EL DORADO, KAN.
45- 23 DASSO, FRANCIS JOSEPH NICHOLAS   1413 MADISON - WENATCHEE WA 98801
89- 28 DATZ, JEFFREY WILLIAM   86 SOUTH MAIN STREET - MULLICA HILL NJ 08062
15- 31 DAUBERT, HARRY J.   D. JANUARY 8, 1944 DETROIT, MICH.
10- 43 DAUBERT, JACOB ELSWORTH   D. OCTOBER 9, 1924 CINCINNATI, O.
76- 27 DAUER, RICHARD FREMONT   6880 GALA - HIGHLAND CA 92346
51- 21 DAUGHERTY, HAROLD RAY   OLD ADD: 66 ELDRED AVENUE - BEDFORD OH 44014
87- 29 DAUGHERTY, JOHN MICHAEL   8633 SOMERSET AVE - SAN DIEGO CA 92123
37- 33 DAUGHTERS, ROBERT FRANCIS   D. AUGUST 22, 1988 SOUTHBURY, CONN.
83- 40 DAULTON, DARREN ARTHUR   RURAL ROUTE 3 BOX 21 - ARKANSAS CITY KS 67005
12- 45 DAUSS, GEORGE AUGUST 'HOOKS'   D. JULY 27, 1963 ST. LOUIS, MO.
53- 17 DAVALILLO, POMPEYO ROMERO 'YO-YO'   L. DE CORREA,CORREO NUEVA GRANDA - CARACAS VENEZ
63- 30 DAVALILLO, VICTOR JOSE   CLE TRUJILLO 7,MARIPEREZ,Q.V.-CARACAS VENEZ
69- 41 DAVANON, FRANK GERALD   5751 CHEENA - HOUSTON TX 77096
20- 28 DAVENPORT, CLAUDE EDWIN   D. JUNE 13, 1976 CORPUS CHRISTI, TEX.
14- 51 DAVENPORT, DAVID W.   D. OCTOBER 16, 1954 EL DORADO, ARK.
58- 26 DAVENPORT, JAMES HOUSTON   1016 HEWITT DR - SAN CARLOS CA 94070
21- 20 DAVENPORT, JOUBERT LUM   D. APRIL 21, 1961 DALLAS, TEX.
77- 40 DAVEY, MICHAEL GERARD   SOUTH 5118 MADELIA - SPOKANE WA 99203
62- 31 DAVIAULT, RAYMOND JOSEPH ROBERT   12116 ONTARIO E. - POINTES AUX TREMBLES QUE CAN.
84- 24 DAVID, ANDRE ANTER   OLD ADD: 1428 CALLE LINDA - SAN DIMAS CA 91773
18- 14 DAVIDSON, CLAUDE BOUCHER   D. APRIL 18, 1956 WEYMOUTH, MASS.
86- 39 DAVIDSON, JOHN MARK   P.O. BOX 1001 - MOORESVILLE NC 28115
89- 29 DAVIDSON, ROBERT BANKS   496 WARMSPRINGS DRIVE - FAYETTEVILLE NC 28303
65- 25 DAVIDSON, THOMAS EUGENE 'TED'   515 DE ARMOND PLACE - SANTA MARIA CA 93454
59- 18 DAVIE, GERALD LEE   19380 SAVAGE ROAD - BELLEVILLE MI 48111
14- 52 DAVIES, LLOYD GARRISON 'CHICK'   D. SEPTEMBER 5, 1973 MIDDLETOWN, CONN.
84- 25 DAVIS, ALVIN GLENN   OLD ADD: 14945 SE 60TH STREET - BELLEVUE WA 98006
65- 26 DAVIS, ARTHUR WILLARD 'BILL'   6638 KNOX AVE SOUTH - MINNEAPOLIS MN 55423
63- 31 DAVIS, BRYSHEAR BARNETT 'BROCK'   2080 WEST ONTARIO AVE - CORONA CA 91720
81- 25 DAVIS, CHARLES THEODORE 'CHILI'   4227 DON ORTEGA PLACE - LOS ANGELES CA 90008
34- 29 DAVIS, CURTIS BENTON   D. OCTOBER 12, 1965 COVINA, CAL.
88- 39 DAVIS, DOUGLAS RAYMOND   RURAL ROUTE 4 - BLOOMSBURG PA 17815
84- 26 DAVIS, ERIC KEITH   6606 DENVER AVE #1 - LOS ANGELES CA 90044
12- 46 DAVIS, FRANK TALMADGE 'DIXIE'   D. FEBRUARY 4, 1944 RALEIGH, N.C.
12- 47 DAVIS, GEORGE ALLEN   D. JUNE 4, 1961 BUFFALO, N.Y.
82- 29 DAVIS, GEORGE EARL 'STORM'   OLD ADD: P.O. BOX 14025 - SAVANNAH GA 31416
26- 26 DAVIS, GEORGE WILLIS 'KIDDO'   D. MARCH 4, 1983 BRIDGEPORT, CONN.
83- 41 DAVIS, GERALD EDWARD   72 THERESA STREET - TRENTON NJ 08618
84- 27 DAVIS, GLENN EARLE   1410 BRIAR GREEN COURT - RICHMOND TX 77469
32- 17 DAVIS, HARRY ALBERT   2002 LINE STREET - SHREVEPORT LA 71104
59- 19 DAVIS, HERMAN THOMAS 'TOMMY'   9767 WHIRLAWAY - ALTA LOMA CA 91701
19- 16 DAVIS, ISAAC MARION   D. APRIL 2, 1984 TUCSON, ARIZ.
62- 32 DAVIS, JACKE SYLVESTA   1131 LYNNWOOD DR - CARTHAGE TX 75633
54- 19 DAVIS, JAMES BENNETT   3327 COUNTRYSIDE DR - SAN MATEO CA 94403
81- 26 DAVIS, JODY RICHARD   RR 1 BEN HILL DR - OAKWOOD GA 30566
85- 22 DAVIS, JOEL CLARK   4117 PACKARD DRIVE - JACKSONVILLE FL 32216
41- 20 DAVIS, JOHN HUMPHREY 'RED'   P.O. BOX 2742 - LAUREL MS 39440
87- 30 DAVIS, JOHN KIRK   9840 AOLA - NORTHRIDGE CA 91324
15- 32 DAVIS, JOHN WILBUR 'BUD'   D. MAY 26, 1967 LIGHTFOOT, VA.
40- 14 DAVIS, LAWRENCE COLUMBUS 'CRASH'   4767 CHAMPION CT - GREENSBORO NC 27410
80- 33 DAVIS, MARK WILLIAM   1620 READING BLVD - WYOMISSING PA 19610
80- 34 DAVIS, MICHAEL DWAYNE   10027 VALLATA COURT - SPRING VALLEY CA 92077
80- 35 DAVIS, ODIE ERNEST   1014 MONTANA ST - SAN ANTONIO TX 78203
46- 22 DAVIS, OTIS ALLEN   3078 EASTLAND BLVD #202A - CLEARWATER FL 33519
36- 18 DAVIS, RAY THOMAS 'PEACHES'   1802 BEECH ST-DUNCAN OK 73533
77- 41 DAVIS, RICHARD EARL   2415 WEST ALONDRA - COMPTON CA 90220
52- 23 DAVIS, ROBERT BRANDON 'BRANDY'   222 CHELTENHAM RD - NEWARK DE 19712
58- 27 DAVIS, ROBERT EDWARD   37 WEST 12TH ST - NEW YORK NY 10003
73- 32 DAVIS, ROBERT JOHN EUGENE   BOX 132 - LOCUST GROVE OK 74352
62- 33 DAVIS, RONALD EVERETTE   10811 SHAWNBROOK - HOUSTON TX 77071
78- 34 DAVIS, RONALD GENE   8103 COYTON - HOUSTON TX 77061
79- 27 DAVIS, STEVE MICHAEL   1377 ANTONIO LANE - SAN JOSE CA 95117
85- 23 DAVIS, STEVEN KENNON   2400 88TH STREET - VANCOUVER WA 98665
49- 18 DAVIS, THOMAS OSCAR 'TOD'   D. DECEMBER 31, 1978 WEST COVINA, CALIF.
85- 24 DAVIS, TRENCH NEAL   OLD ADD: 916 SEAGULL AVE - BALTIMORE MD 21225
28- 28 DAVIS, VIRGIL LAWRENCE 'SPUD'   D. AUGUST 14, 1984 BIRMINGHAM, ALA.
83- 42 DAVIS, WALLACE MCARTHUR 'BUTCH'   112 PRICE STREET - WILLIAMSTON NC 27892
60- 28 DAVIS, WILLIAM HENRY 'WILLIE'   OLD ADD: 4419 BUENA VISTA #203 - DALLAS TX 75202
38- 20 DAVIS, WOODROW WILSON   BOX 87-ODUM GA 31555
69- 42 DAVISON, MICHAEL LYNN   578 PROSPECT - HUTCHINSON MN 55350
83- 43 DAWLEY, WILLIAM CHESTER   RR 2, KENDALL ROAD EXT - LISBON CT 06417
76- 28 DAWSON, ANDRE NOLAN   10301 SW 144TH STREET - MIAMI FL 33176
24- 26 DAWSON, RALPH FENTON 'JOE'   D. JANUARY 4, 1978 LONGVIEW, TEX.
13- 46 DAWSON, REXFORD PAUL   D. OCTOBER 20, 1958 INDIANAPOLIS, IND.
69- 43 DAY, CHARLES FREDERICK 'BOOTS'   11972 CHARTER OAK PKWY - ST. LOUIS MO 63146
24- 27 DAY, CLYDE HENRY 'PEA RIDGE'   D. MARCH 21, 1934 KANSAS CITY, MO.
83- 44 DAYETT, BRIAN KELLY   10 HEMLOCK TERRACE EXT - DEEP RIVER CT 06417
82- 30 DAYLEY, KENNETH GRANT   1601 MOUNT HOOD ST - THE DALLES OR 97058
12- 48 DEAL, CHARLES ALBERT   D. SEPTEMBER 16, 1979 COVINA, CALIF.
47- 24 DEAL, ELLIS FERGUSON 'COT'   4710 HEMLOCK CIRCLE - OKLAHOMA CITY OK 73162
39- 26 DEAL, LINDSAY FRED   D. APRIL 18, 1979 LITTLE ROCK, ARK.
36- 19 DEAN, ALFRED LOVILL 'CHUBBY'   D. DECEMBER 21, 1970 RIVERSIDE, N. J.
41- 21 DEAN, JAMES HARRY   D. JUNE 1, 1960 ROCKMART, GA.

30- 16 DEAN, JAY HANNA 'DIZZY'	D. JULY 17, 1974 RENO, NEV.
34- 30 DEAN, PAUL DEE	D. MARCH 17, 1981 SPRINGDALE, ARK.
67- 22 DEAN, TOMMY DOUGLAS	RR2 - IUKA MS 38852
24- 28 DEAN, WAYLAND OGDEN	D. APRIL 10, 1930 HUNTINGTON, W. VA.
27- 28 DEAR, PAUL STANFORD 'BUDDY'	BOX 2475 - CHRISTIANSBURG VA 24073
77- 42 DEBARR, DENNIS LEE	33843 JULIET CIRCLE - FREMONT CA 94555
16- 17 DEBERRY, JOHN HERMAN 'HANK'	D. SEPTEMBER 10, 1951 SAVANNAH, TENN.
20- 29 DEBERRY, JOSEPH GADDY	D. OCTOBER 9, 1944 SOUTHERN PINES, N. C.
17- 18 DEBUS, ADAM JOSEPH	D. MAY 13, 1977 CHICAGO, ILL.
62- 34 DEBUSSCHERE, DAVID ALBERT	90 3RD ST - GARDEN CITY NY 11530
22- 25 DECATUR, ARTHUR RUE	D. APRIL 25, 1966 TALLADEGA, ALA.
73- 33 DECINCES, DOUGLAS VERNON	2 LEESBURG COURT - NEWPORT BEACH CA 92660
83- 45 DECKER, DEE MARTIN 'MARTY'	920 GATE LANE - PILOT HILL CA 95664
69- 44 DECKER, GEORGE HENRY 'JOE'	4111 NORTH AZALEA LANE - BOISE ID 83703
16- 18 DEDE, ARTHUR RICHARD	D. SEPTEMBER 6, 1971 KEENE, N.H.
35- 22 DEDEAUX, RAOUL MARTIAL 'ROD'	1430 SOUTH EASTMAN AVE - LOS ANGELES CA 90023
83- 46 DEDMON, JEFFREY LINDEN	21102 SOUTH BROADWELL - TORRANCE CA 90502
15- 33 DEE, MAURICE LEO 'SHORTY'	D. AUGUST 12, 1971 JAMAICA PLAINS, MASS.
84- 28 DEER, ROBERT GEORGE	421 ST. MARY PLACE - SANTA ROSA CA 95405
63- 32 DEES, CHARLES HENRY	23412 DORSET PL - HARBOR CITY CA 90710
17- 19 DEFATE, CLYDE HERBERT 'TONY'	D. SEPTEMBER 3, 1963 NEW ORLEANS, LA.
78- 35 DEFREITES, ARTURO SIMON	HERMONOS MIRABEL #21 - SAN PEDRO DE MACORIS DOM. REP.
61- 28 DEGERICK, MICHAEL ARTHUR	353 RIDGEDALE AVE - EAST HANOVER NJ 07936
74- 21 DEIDEL, JAMES LAWRENCE	OLD ADD: 2545 SOUTH PATTON CT - DENVER CO
40- 15 DEJAN, MIKE DAN	D. FEBRUARY 2, 1953 WEST LOS ANGELES, CALIF.
74- 22 DEJESUS, IVAN	GAUTHIER #1753,SANTIAGO IGLESAIS - RIO PIEDRAS PR 00921
88- 40 DEJESUS, JOSE LUIS	7E6 VILLA DEL CARMEN - CIDRA PR 00639
82- 31 DEJOHN, MARK STEPHEN	966 WORTHINGTON RIDGE - BERLIN CT 06037
45- 24 DEKONING, WILLIAM CALLAHAN	D. JULY 26, 1979 PALM HARBOR, FLA.
44- 26 DELACRUZ, TOMAS	D. SEPTEMBER 6, 1958 HAVANA, CUBA
60- 29 DELAHOZ, MIGUEL ANGEL	1367 SW 14TH STREET - MIAMI FL 33145
32- 18 DELANCEY, WILLIAM PINKNEY	D. NOVEMBER 28, 1946 PHOENIX, ARIZ.
24- 29 DELANEY, ARTHUR DEWEY	D. MAY 2, 1970 HAYWARD, CALIF.
75- 32 DELAROSA, JESUS	20 #28 LOS MINOS - SANTO DOMINGO DOMINICAN REP.
83- 47 DELEON, JOSE	216 BRIGHTON AVENUE - PERTH AMBOY NJ 08861
81- 27 DELEON, LUIS ANTONIO	SAN ANTON 120,CLE E.CABRERRA - PONCE PR 00731
77- 43 DELGADO, LUIS FELIPE	VILLA DEL CARMEN, BOX 879 - AY HATILLO PR 00659
52- 24 DELGRECO, ROBERT GEORGE	625 SOUTHVIEW DR - PITTSBURGH PA 15226
12- 49 DELHI, LEE WILLIAM 'FLAME'	D. MAY 9, 1966 GREENBRAE, CALIF.
55- 37 DELIS, JUAN FRANCISCO	1963 ADD:3A #24508, REPARTO DOLORES - HAVANA
29- 27 DELKER, EDWARD ALBERTS	1 SOUTH FRONT ST - ST CLAIR PA 17970
12- 50 DELL, WILLIAM GEORGE 'WHEEZER'	D. AUGUST 24, 1966 INDEPENDENCE, CALIF.
33- 16 DELMAS, ALBERT CHARLES	D. DECEMBER 4, 1979 HUNTINGTON BEACH, CALIF.
52- 25 DELOCK, IVAN MARTIN 'IKE'	433 CYPRESS WAY EAST - NAPLES FL 33942
88- 41 DELOSSANTOS, LUIS MANUEL	575 WEST 172ND STREET - NEW YORK NY 10032
74- 23 DELOSSANTOS, RAMON	ARZ. FDEZ DE NAVARRETE #177 - -SANTO DOMINGO DOM. REP.
43- 38 DELSAVIO, GARTON ORVILLE	48 ROOSEVELT DR-BLAUVELT NY 10913
48- 31 DELSING, JAMES HENRY	1569 WALPOLE DR - CHESTERFIELD MO 63017
51- 22 DEMAESTRI, JOSEPH PAUL	50 FAIRWAY - NOVATO CA 94947
12- 51 DEMAREE, ALBERT WENTWORTH	D. MAY 2, 1962 LONG BEACH, CALIF.
32- 19 DEMAREE, JOSEPH FRANKLIN	D. AUGUST 30, 1958 LOS ANGELES, CAL.
48- 32 DEMARS, WILLIAM LESTER	661 POINSETTIA #207 - CLEARWATER FL 33515
57- 16 DEMERIT, JOHN STEPHEN	550 WEST WALTERS ST - PORT WASHINGTON WI 53074
74- 24 DEMERY, LAWRENCE CALVIN	OLD ADD: 4077 CARRIAGE HOUSE CT - EAST POINT GA 30344
56- 26 DEMETER, DONALD LEE	1521 SW 56TH ST - OKLAHOMA CITY OK 73119
59- 20 DEMETER, STEVEN	2805 MARIONCLIFF DR - PARMA OH 44134
74- 25 DEMOLA, DONALD JOHN	500-184A PECONIC - LAKE RONKONKOMA NY 11779
10- 44 DEMOTT, BENYEW HARRISON	D. JULY 5, 1963 SOMERVILLE, N.J.
51- 23 DEMPSEY, CORNELIUS FRANCIS 'CON'	1530 CORDILLERAS RD - REDWOOD CITY CA 94062
69- 45 DEMPSEY, JOHN RIKARD 'RICK'	5641 MASON AVE - WOODLAND HILLS CA 91364
82- 32 DEMPSEY, MARK STEVEN	OLD ADD: 30 E. LANE AVE - DAYTON OH 45406
67- 23 DENEHY, WILLIAM FRANCIS	1520 SAYBROOK RD - MIDDLETOWN CT 06457
82- 33 DENMAN, BRIAN JOHN	33 PARKHURST BOULEVARD - BUFFALO NY 14223
23- 27 DENNEHEY, THOMAS FRANCIS 'TOD'	D. AUGUST 8, 1977 PHILADELPHIA, PA.
42- 28 DENNING, OTTO GEORGE	3434 WEST MELROSE-CHICAGO IL 60618
65- 22 DENNIS, DONALD RAY	RR2 - UNIONTOWN KS 66779
74- 26 DENNY, JOHN ALLEN	OLD ADD: 14551 BURNLEA ST - CHESTERFIELD MO 63017
89- 30 DENSON, ANDREW	1718 AVONLEA AVENUE - CINCINNATI OH 45237
73- 34 DENT, RUSSELL EARL 'BUCKY'	5540 EAST COACH HOUSE CIRCLE - BOCA RATON FL 33432
47- 25 DENTE, SAMUEL JOSEPH	19 REDMAN TER - WEST CALDWELL NJ 07006
43- 39 DEPHILLIPS, ANTHONY ANDREW	26 TIMBERLINE CIRCLE - PORT JEFFERSON NY 11777
80- 36 DERNIER, ROBERT EUGENE	9509 EAST 77TH ST - RAYTOWN MO 64138
10- 45 DERRICK, CLAUD LESTER	D. JULY 15, 1974 CLAYTON, GA.
70- 32 DERRICK, JAMES MICHAEL	107 OLIVER - WEST COLUMBIA CAYCE SC 29033
31- 21 DERRINGER, PAUL	D. NOVEMBER 17, 1987 SARASOTA, FLA.
56- 27 DERRINGTON, CHARLES JAMES 'JIM'	10509 BRYSON AVE - SOUTH GATE CA 90281
44- 27 DERRY, ALVA RUSSELL 'RUSS'	PRINCETON MO 64673
80- 37 DESA, JOSEPH	D. DECEMBER 20, 1986 SAN JUAN, P. R.
30- 17 DESAUTELS, EUGENE ABRAHAM	2802 MANSFIELD AV - FLINT MI 48503
84- 29 DESHAIES, JAMES JOSEPH	OLD ADD: 24 CHASE STREET - MASSENA NY 13662
32- 20 DESHONG, JAMES BROOKLYN	99 SOUTH 31ST ST - HARRISBURG PA 17109
16- 19 DESJARDIEN, PAUL RAYMOND 'SHORTY'	D. MARCH 7, 1956 MONROVIA, CALIF.
87- 31 DESTRADE, ORESTES	3015 SOUTHWEST 92ND PLACE - MIAMI FL 33165
80- 38 DETHERAGE, ROBERT WAYNE	OLD ADD: 2325 NORTH BENTON - SPRINGFIELD MO 65803
30- 18 DETORE, GEORGE FRANCIS	RR 1 - NEW HARTFORD NY 13413
73- 35 DETTORE, THOMAS ANTHONY	1120 MCEWEN AVE - CANONSBURG PA 15317
42- 29 DETWEILER, ROBERT STERLING 'DUCKY'	312 HOLT ST-FEDERALSBURG MD 21632
46- 23 DEUTSCH, MELVIN ELLIOTT	RR 2 BOX 373A - CALDWELL TX 77836
32- 21 DEVENS, CHARLES	1 POST OFFICE SQUARE #900 - BOSTON MA 02110
87- 32 DEVEREAUX, MICHAEL	2236 WEST DOUBLEGROVE STREET - WEST COVINA CA 91790
73- 36 DEVINE, PAUL ADRIAN	271 TIMBER LAUREL LANE - LAWRENCEVILLE GA 30245
18- 15 DEVINE, WILLIAM PATRICK 'MICKEY'	D. OCTOBER 1, 1957 ALBANY, N. Y.
20- 30 DEVINEY, JOHN HAROLD 'HAL'	D. JANUARY 4, 1933 WESTWOOD, MASS.
24- 30 DEVIVEIROS, BERNARD JOHN	3520 REDDING ST - OAKLAND CA 94619
44- 28 DEVLIN, JAMES RAYMOND	130 WORMAN ST, ESPY - BLOOMSBURG PA 17815
13- 47 DEVOGT, REX EUGENE	D. NOVEMBER 9, 1935 ALMA, MICH.
87- 33 DEWILLIS, JEFFREY ALLEN	3105 YOST ROAD - PEARLAND TX 77581
77- 44 DIAZ, BAUDILIO JOSE 'BO	LA VEGA #40 - CUA - ESTADO MIRANDA VENEZUELA S.A.

82- 34 DIAZ, CARLOS ANTHONY	1204 NORTH C STREET - LOMPOC CA 93436
86- 40 DIAZ, EDGAR SERRANO	CALLE DIAMANTE #32 VILLA BLANCA - CAGUAS PR 00625
87- 34 DIAZ, MARIO RAFAEL	OLD ADD: URB. JAIME C. RODRIGUEZ STR 2 - YABUCOA PR
83- 48 DIAZ, MICHAEL ANTHONY	1032 BANYAN WAY - PACIFICA CA 94044
88- 42 DIBBLE, ROBERT KEITH	54 SUMMIT FARMS ROAD - SOUTHINGTON CT 06489
24- 31 DIBUT, PEDRO	D. DECEMBER 4, 1979 HIALEAH, FLA.
64- 25 DICKEN, PAUL FRANKLIN	7253 ST ANDREWS RD - LAKE WORTH FL 33460
23- 28 DICKERMAN, LEO LOUIS	D. APRIL 30, 1982 ATKINS, ARK.
17- 20 DICKERSON, GEORGE CLARK	D. JULY 9, 1938 LOS ANGELES, CALIF.
35- 23 DICKEY, GEORGE WILLARD 'SKEETS'	D. JUNE 16, 1976 DEWITT, ARK.
28- 29 DICKEY, WILLIAM MALCOLM	7611 CHOCTAW ROAD - LITTLE ROCK AR 72205
36- 20 DICKMAN, GEORGE EMERSON	D. APRIL 27, 1981 NEW YORK, N. Y.
36- 21 DICKSHOT, JOHN OSCAR	1530 JENKINSON CT - WAUKEGAN IL 60085
63- 33 DICKSON, JAMES EDWARD	685 FRANKLIN - ASTORIA OR 97103
39- 27 DICKSON, MURRY MONROE	D. SEPTEMBER 21, 1989 KANSAS CITY, KAN.
10- 46 DICKSON, WALTER R.	D. DECEMBER 9, 1918 ARDMORE, OKLA.
69- 46 DIDIER, ROBERT DANIEL	544 SW 335TH STREET - FEDERAL WAY WA 98023
42- 30 DIEHL, GEORGE KRAUSE	D. AUGUST 24, 1986 KINGSPORT, TENN.
47- 26 DIERING, CHARLES EDWARD ALLEN	1 NOB HILL DR - ST LOUIS MO 63138
64- 26 DIERKER, LAWRENCE EDWARDS	8318 NORTH TAHOE - HOUSTON TX 77040
33- 17 DIETRICH, WILLIAM JOHN	D. JUNE 20, 1978 PHILADELPHIA, PA.
27- 29 DIETRICK, WILLIAM ALEXANDER	D. MAY 6, 1946 BETHESDA, MD.
40- 16 DIETZ, LLOYD ARTHUR 'DUTCH'	D. OCTOBER 29, 1972 BEAUMONT, TEX.
66- 28 DIETZ, RICHARD ALLEN	406 LEYSWOOD DRIVE - GREENVILLE SC 29607
54- 20 DIETZEL, LEROY LOUIS	2331 CARTWIGHT PL - CHARLOTTE NC 28208
48- 33 DIFANI, CLARENCE JOSEPH 'JAY'	808 NORTH MILL - FESTUS MO 63028
34- 31 DIGGS, REESE WILSON	D. OCTOBER 30, 1978 BALTIMORE, MD.
69- 47 DILAURO, JACK EDWARD	168 EAST MOHAWK - MALVERN OH 44644
59- 21 DILLARD, DAVID DONALD 'DON'	RR1 - WATERLOO SC 29384
88- 43 DILLARD, GREGORY LEE	1290 RIDER AVENUE - SALINAS CA 93905
75- 33 DILLARD, STEPHEN BRADLEY	6217 48TH DR EAST - BRADENTON FL 33508
17- 21 DILLHOEFER, WILLIAM MARTIN 'PICKLES'	D. FEBRUARY 22, 1922 ST. LOUIS, MO.
14- 54 DILLINGER, HARLEY HUGH	D. JANUARY 8, 1959 CLEVELAND, O.
46- 24 DILLINGER, ROBERT BERNARD	15380 RHODODENDRON DR-CANYON COUNTY CA 91351
67- 24 DILLMAN, WILLIAM HOWARD	204 IRON ROCK COURT - LANGHORNE PA 19047
63- 34 DILLON, STEPHEN EDWARD	130 WEST 228TH ST - BRONX NY 10463
74- 27 DILONE, MIGUEL ANGEL	CALLE EL SOL #190 - SANTIAGO DOMINICAN REP.
40- 17 DIMAGGIO, DOMINIC PAUL	162 POINT RD - MARION MA 02738
36- 22 DIMAGGIO, JOSEPH PAUL	2150 BEACH ST - SAN FRANCISCO CA 94123
37- 34 DIMAGGIO, VINCENT PAUL	D. OCTOBER 3, 1986 NORTH HOLLYWOOD, CALIF.
88- 44 DIMICHELE, FRANK LAWRENCE	812 TASKER STREET - PHILADELPHIA PA 19148
77- 45 DIMMEL, MICHAEL WAYNE	1705 BIG CANYON TRAIL - CARROLLTON TX 75007
75- 34 DINEEN, KERRY MICHAEL	702 ELDER AVE - CHULA VISTA CA 92010
45- 25 DINGES, VANCE GEORGE	274 SOUTH HIGH ST - HARRISONBURG VA 22801
73- 37 DIORIO, RONALD MICHAEL	2 WHITE OAK LN - WATERBURY CT 06705
51- 24 DIPIETRO, ROBERT LOUIS PAUL	909 CARRIAGE HILL DR - YAKIMA WA 98902
81- 28 DIPINO, FRANK MICHAEL	8082 WILD LEMON LANE - MANLIUS NY 13104
89- 31 DISARCINA, GARY THOMAS	6 PATRICK AVENUE - BILLERICA MA 01866
69- 48 DISTASO, ALEC JOHN	25156 AVENIDA RONDEL - VALENCIA CA 91355
84- 30 DISTEFANO, BENITO JAMES	16 LOCUST DR - THIELLS NY 10984
18- 17 DISTEL, GEORGE ADAM 'DUTCH'	D. FEBRUARY 12, 1967 MADISON, IND.
54- 21 DITMAR, ARTHUR JOHN	14 CINNAMON FERN LANE - MYRTLE BEACH SC 29577
52- 26 DITTMER, JOHN DOUGLAS	200 NORTH MAIN ST - ELKADER IA 52043
16-101 DIVIS, EDWARD G. 'MOXIE'	D. DECEMBER 19, 1955 LAKEWOOD, OHIO
53- 18 DIXON, JOHN CRAIG 'SONNY'	7920 STEELE CREEK ROAD - CHARLOTTE NC 28217
84- 31 DIXON, KENNETH JOHN	40 CLINTON HILL COURT - BALTIMORE MD 21228
25- 24 DIXON, LEO MOSES	D. APRIL 11, 1984 CHICAGO, ILL.
77- 46 DIXON, THOMAS EARL	2945 SOUTH DELANEY ST - ORLANDO FL 32806
12- 52 DOAK, WILLIAM LEOPOLD	D. NOVEMBER 26, 1954 BRADENTON, FLA.
24- 32 DOBB, JOHN KENNETH	973 HAMPDEN RD - MUSKEGON MI 49441
59- 22 DOBBEK, DANIEL JOHN	4042 SE YAMHILL - PORTLAND OR 97214
29- 28 DOBENS, RAYMOND JOSEPH	D. APRIL 21, 1980 STUART, FLA.
39- 28 DOBERNIC, ANDREW JOSEPH 'JESS'	2906 MISSOURI - SAINT LOUIS MO 63118
66- 29 DOBSON, CHARLES THOMAS	2604 LACLEDE STATION RD - MAPLEWOOD MO 63143
39- 29 DOBSON, JOSEPH GORDON	7605 MOWRY STREET - JACKSONVILLE FL 32256
67- 25 DOBSON, PATRICK EDWARD	5318 SW 26TH AVENUE - CAPE CORAL FL 33914
47- 27 DOBY, LAWRENCE EUGENE	NISHUANE RD 45 - MONTCLAIR NJ 07042
45- 26 DOCKINS, GEORGE WOODROW	BOX 3 - CLYDE KS 66938
12- 53 DODD, ORAN A. 'ONA'	D. MARCH 31, 1929 NEWPORT, ARK.
86- 41 DODD, THOMAS MARION	3735 NORTHEAST SHAVER - PORTLAND OR 97212
12- 54 DODGE, JOHN LEWIS	D. JUNE 19, 1916 MOBILE, ALA.
21- 21 DODGE, SAMUEL EDWARD	D. APRIL 5, 1966 UTICA, N. Y.
86- 42 DODSON, PATRICK NEAL	844 GLENWAY DRIVE - INGLEWOOD CA 90302
37- 35 DOERR, ROBERT PERSHING	33705 ILLAMO-AGNESS RD - AGNESS OR 97406
74- 28 DOHERTY, JOHN MICHAEL	109 WAKEFIELD ST - READING MA 01867
14- 55 DOLAN, LEON MARK 'BIDDY'	D. JULY 15, 1950 INDIANAPOLIS, IND.
30- 19 DOLJACK, FRANK JOSEPH	D. JANUARY 23, 1948 CLEVELAND, O.
35- 24 DOLL, ARTHUR JAMES	D. APRIL 28, 1978 CALUMET CITY, ILL.
23- 29 DONAHUE, JOHN FREDERICK	D. OCTOBER 3, 1949 BOSTON, MASS.
43- 40 DONAHUE, JOHN STEPHEN MICHEAL	812 NORTH SALEM LANE - CARPENTERSVILLE IL 60110
38- 21 DONALD, RICHARD ATLEY	RR 2 BOX 132-CHOUDRANT LA 71227
12- 55 DONALDS, EDWARD ALEXANDER	D. JULY 3, 1950 COLUMBUS, O.
66- 30 DONALDSON, JOHN DAVID	3331 BENARD AVE - CHARLOTTE NC 28206
29- 29 DONDERO, LEONARD PETER	BOX 2224 - FREMONT CA 94536
11- 42 DONNELLY, EDWARD	D. NOVEMBER 28, 1957 RUTLAND, VT.
59- 23 DONNELLY, EDWARD VINCENT	823 ROPER - HOUSTON TX 77034
44- 29 DONNELLY, SYLVESTER URBAN 'BLIX'	D. JUNE 20, 1976 OLIVIA, MINN.
61- 29 DONOHUE, JAMES THOMAS	16 HUNTLEIGH DOWNS - ST LOUIS MO 63131
21- 22 DONOHUE, PETER JOSEPH	D. FEBRUARY 23, 1988 FORT WORTH, TEXAS
79- 28 DONOHUE, THOMAS JAMES	33 RUGBY ROAD - WESTBURY NY 11590
55- 38 DONOSO, LINO GALATA	1971 ADD: CALLE SANTA MARIA - HAVANA CUBA
50- 27 DONOVAN, RICHARD EDWARD	61 DEEP RUN RD - COHASSET MA 02025
42- 31 DONOVAN, WILLARD EARL	1611 SOUTH 10TH AVE-MAYWOOD IL 60153
85- 25 DOPSON, JOHN ROBERT	3337 OLD GAMBER ROAD - FINKSBURG MD 21048
82- 35 DORAN, WILLIAM DONALD	1522 RAMBLING STONE - RICHMOND TX 77459
22- 26 DORAN, WILLIAM JAMES	D. MARCH 9, 1978 SANTA MONICA, CALIF.
47- 28 DORISH, HARRY	68 ELEY ST - KINGSTON PA 18704
23- 30 DORMAN, CHARLES WILLIAM	D. NOVEMBER 15, 1928 SAN FRANCISCO, CAL.

28- 30	DORMAN, DWIGHT DEXTER	D. DECEMBER 7, 1974 ANAHEIM, CAL.
87- 35	DORSETT, BRIAN RICHARD	OLD ADD: 3123 EMERALD ROAD - TERRE HAUTE IN 47805
40- 18	DORSETT, CALVIN LEAVELLE	D. OCTOBER 22, 1970 ELK CITY, OKLA.
80- 39	DORSEY, JAMES EDWARD	335 ELM STREET - SEEKONK MA 02771
11- 43	DORSEY, JEREMIAH	B. 1885 OAKLAND, CALIF.
79- 29	DOTSON, RICHARD ELLIOTT	4240 PALOMINO CIR %HICKS - RENO NV 89509
61- 30	DOTTER, GARY RICHARD	1639 HURSCH - WICHITA FALLS TX 76302
57- 17	DOTTERER, HENRY JOHN 'DUTCH'	10592 DAVITT AVE - GARDEN GROVE CA 92643
21- 23	DOUGLAS, ASTYANAX SAUNDERS	D. JANUARY 26, 1975 EL PASO, TEXAS
57- 18	DOUGLAS, CHARLES WILLIAM 'WHAMMY'	135 ASH ST - HUBERT NC 28539
45- 27	DOUGLAS, JOHN FRANKLIN	D. FEBRUARY 11, 1984 MIAMI, FLA.
12- 56	DOUGLAS, PHILIPS BROOKS	D. AUGUST 1, 1952 SEQUATCHIE VALLEY, TENN.
15- 34	DOUGLASS, HOWARD LAWRENCE 'LARRY'	D. NOVEMBER 4, 1949 JELLICO, TENN.
23- 31	DOUTHIT, TAYLOR LEE	D. MAY 28, 1986 FREMONT, CALIF.
10- 47	DOWD, JAMES JOSEPH 'SKIP'	D. DECEMBER 20, 1960 HOLYOKE, MASS.
19- 17	DOWD, RAYMOND BERNARD	D. APRIL 4, 1962 NORTHAMPTON, MASS.
87- 36	DOWELL, KENNETH ALLEN	2720 CASTRO WAY - SACRAMENTO CA 95818
64- 27	DOWLING, DAVID BARCLAY	1802 24TH - LONGVIEW WA 98632
61- 31	DOWNING, ALPHONSO ERWIN	2800 NEILSON WAY #412 - SANTA MONICA CA 90405
73- 38	DOWNING, BRIAN JAY	4861 SILVER SPURS - YORBA LINDA CA 92686
72- 23	DOWNS, DAVID RALPH	925 EAST 1050 NORTH - BOUNTIFUL UT 84010
86- 43	DOWNS, KELLY ROBERT	925 EAST 1050 NORTH - BOUNTIFUL UT 84010
78- 36	DOYLE, BRIAN REED	1310 MEADOW CIR NE - WINTER HAVEN FL 33880
43- 41	DOYLE, HOWARD JAMES 'DANNY'	322 SOUTH PAYNE - STILLWATER OK 74074
10- 48	DOYLE, JAMES FRANCIS	D. FEBRUARY 1, 1912 SYRACUSE, N.Y.
83- 49	DOYLE, JEFFREY DONALD	845 NORTHWEST TENTH - CORVALLIS OR 97330
25- 25	DOYLE, JESSE HERBERT	D. APRIL 15, 1961 BELLEVILLE, ILL.
69- 49	DOYLE, PAUL SINNOTT	5832 WOODBORO DR - HUNTINGTON BEACH CA 92649
70- 33	DOYLE, ROBERT DENNIS 'DENNY'	6756 WINTERSET GARDENS-WINTER HAVEN FL 33880
35- 25	DOYLE, WILLIAM CARL	D. SEPTEMBER 4, 1951 KNOXVILLE, TENN.
86- 44	DOZIER, THOMAS DEAN	3804 DON WAY - RICHMOND CA 94806
47- 29	DOZIER, WILLIAM JOSEPH 'BUZZ'	2609 BRAEMER - WACO TX 76710
86- 45	DRABEK, DOUGLAS DEAN	1803 TRAVIS - VICTORIA TX 77901
56- 28	DRABOWSKY, MYRON WALTER 'MOE'	530 AUDUBON PLACE - HIGHLAND PARK IL 60035
69- 50	DRAGO, RICHARD ANTHONY	OLD ADD: P.O. BOX 353 - SANIBEL ISLAND FL 33957
11- 44	DRAKE, DELOS DANIEL	D. OCTOBER 3, 1965 FINDLAY, O.
45- 28	DRAKE, LARRY FRANCIS	D. JULY 14, 1985 HOUSTON, TEXAS
22- 27	DRAKE, LOGAN GAFFNEY	D. JUNE 1, 1940
60- 30	DRAKE, SAMUEL HARRISON	4415 SPRINGDALE DR - LOS ANGELES CA 90043
56- 29	DRAKE, SOLOMON LOUIS	1732 CORNING ST - LOS ANGELES CA 90035
39- 30	DRAKE, THOMAS KENDALL	D. JULY 2, 1988 BIRMINGHAM, ALA.
82- 36	DRAVECKY, DAVID FRANCIS	806 PARK HARBOUR DRIVE - BOARDMAN OH 44512
31- 22	DREESEN, WILLIAM RICHARD	D. NOVEMBER 9, 1971 MOUNT VERNON, N. Y.
44- 30	DREISEWERD, CLEMENT JOHN	45 SNIPE ST - NEW ORLEANS LA 70124
44- 31	DRESCHER, WILLIAM CLAYTON	D. MAY 15, 1968 CONGERS, N. Y.
25- 26	DRESSEN, CHARLES WALTER	D. AUGUST 10, 1966 DETROIT, MICH.
14- 56	DRESSEN, LEO AUGUST	D. JUNE 30, 1931 DILLER, NEB.
75- 35	DRESSLER, ROBERT ALAN	OLD ADD: 3002 N. 46TH ST - PHOENIX AZ 85018
88- 45	DREW, CAMERON STEWARD	31 HIGHBRIDGE ROAD - YARDVILLE NJ 08620
44- 32	DREWS, FRANK JOHN	D. APRIL 22, 1972 BUFFALO, N. Y.
46- 25	DREWS, KARL AUGUST	D. AUGUST 15, 1963 DANIA, FLA.
73- 39	DRIESSEN, DANIEL	BOX 1001 - HILTON HEAD ISLAND SC 29928
70- 34	DRISCOLL, JAMES BERNARD	28 HIBBARD ROAD - NEWTON MA 02158
17- 22	DRISCOLL, JOHN LEO 'PADDY'	D. JUNE 28, 1968 CHICAGO, ILL.
16- 20	DRISCOLL, MICHAEL COLUMBUS	D. MARCH 22, 1953 FOXBORO, MASS.
13- 48	DROHAN, THOMAS F.	D. SEPTEMBER 17, 1926 KEWANEE, ILL.
49- 19	DROPO, WALTER	7 GRANT ROAD - MARBLEHEAD MA 01945
57- 19	DROTT, RICHARD FRED	D. AUGUST 16, 1985 GLENDALE HEIGHTS, ILL.
87- 37	DRUMMOND, TIMOTHY DARNELL	HIGHWAY 925S BOX 335E - WALDORF MD 20601
78- 37	DRUMRIGHT, KEITH ALAN	OLD ADD: 422 EAST DOWNING - SPRINGFIELD MO 65807
56- 30	DRYSDALE, DONALD SCOTT	2 LACERRA CIR - RANCHO MIRAGE CA 92270
44- 33	DUBIEL, WALTER JOHN 'MONK'	D. OCTOBER 25, 1969 HARTFORD, CONN.
89- 32	DUBOIS, BRIAN ANDREW	159 RIDGE STREET - BRAIDWOOD IL 60402
87- 38	DUCEY, ROBERT THOMAS	47 ELGIN STREET NORTH - CAMBRIDGE ONT. N1R 5H1 CAN.
63- 35	DUCKWORTH, JAMES RAYMOND	14205 JENNINGS VISTA TRAIL - LAKESIDE CA 92040
29- 30	DUDLEY, ELISE CLISE 'CLISE'	D. JANUARY 12, 1989 MONCKS CORNER, S. C.
41- 22	DUDRA, JOHN JOSEPH	D. OCTOBER 24, 1965 PANA, ILL.
77- 47	DUES, HAL JOSEPH	DRAWER R - DICKINSON TX 77539
22- 28	DUFF, CECIL ELBA 'LARRY'	D. NOVEMBER 10, 1969 BEND, ORE.
61- 32	DUFFALO, JAMES FRANCIS	4109 CHILDRESS #101 - MESQUITE TX 75150
67- 26	DUFFIE, JOHN BROWN	3453 GLEN RD - DECATUR GA 30032
13- 49	DUFFY, BERNARD ALLEN	D. FEBRUARY 9, 1962 ABILENE, TEX.
70- 35	DUFFY, FRANK THOMAS	1740 EAST SILVER STREET - TUCSON AZ 85719
28- 31	DUGAN, DANIEL PHILLIP	D. JUNE 25, 1968 GREEN BROOK, N. J.
17- 23	DUGAN, JOSEPH ANTHONY	D. JULY 7, 1982 NORWOOD, MASS.
30- 20	DUGAS, AUGUSTIN JOSEPH	46 SOUTH "A" ST - TAFTVILLE CT 06380
13- 50	DUGEY, OSCAR JOSEPH	D. JANUARY 1, 1966 DALLAS, TEX.
11- 45	DUGGAN, JAMES ELMER	D. DECEMBER 5, 1951 INDIANAPOLIS, IND.
69- 51	DUKES, JAN NOBLE	959 HELENA DRIVE - SUNNYVALE CA 94087
67- 27	DUKES, THOMAS EARL	325 MONTE VISTA RD - ARCADIA CA 91007
59- 24	DULIBA, ROBERT JOHN	RURAL ROUTE 2 BOX 545 - ESTILL SPRINGS TN 37330
15- 35	DUMONT, GEORGE HENRY	D. OCTOBER 13, 1956 MINNEAPOLOS, MINN.
77- 48	DUMOULIN, DANIEL LYNN	304 IVY DR - KOKOMO IN 46902
23- 32	DUMOVICH, NICHOLAS	D. DECEMBER 12, 1979 LAGUNA HILLS, CALIF.
83- 50	DUNBAR, THOMAS JEROME	558 SOUTH PALM DRIVE - AIKEN SC 29801
64- 28	DUNCAN, DAVID EDWIN	455 WEST RAPA - TUCSON AZ 85704
15- 36	DUNCAN, LOUIS BAIRD 'PAT'	D. JULY 17, 1960 COLUMBUS, O.
85- 26	DUNCAN, MARIANO	INGENIO ANGELINA #137 - SAN PEDRO DE MACORIS DOM REP.
77- 49	DUNCAN, TAYLOR MCDOWELL	83 HAMPTON STREET - ASHEVILLE NC 28803
13- 51	DUNCAN, VERNON VAN DYKE	D. JUNE 1, 1954 DAYTONA BEACH, FLA.
70- 36	DUNEGAN, JAMES WILLIAM	7536 NORTH 12TH STREET - PHOENIX AZ 85020
26- 27	DUNHAM, LELAND HUFFIELD	D. MAY 11, 1961 ATLANTA, GA.
53- 19	DUNLAP, GRANT LESTER	6401 EL PATO COURT - CARLSBAD CA 92007
29- 31	DUNLAP, WILLIAM JAMES	D. NOVEMBER 29, 1980 READING, PA.
13- 52	DUNLOP, GEORGE HENRY	D. DECEMBER 12, 1972 MERIDEN, CONN.
52- 27	DUNN, JAMES WILLIAM	1656 SUMMIT DR - GADSDEN AL 35901
74- 29	DUNN, RONALD RAY	OLD ADD: 236 E. CALIMYRNA ST - FRESNO CA 93726
87- 39	DUNNE, MICHAEL DENNIS	4900 LINDA CURVE - BARTONVILLE IL 61607
70- 37	DUNNING, STEVEN JOHN	23 PLYMOUTH - IRVINE CA 92714

85- 27	DUNSTON, SHAWON DONNELL	6145 NORTH SHERIDAN #157 - CHICAGO IL 60660
76- 29	DUPREE, MICHAEL DENNIS	5164 E. ASHLAN #129 - FRESNO CA 93727
81- 29	DURAN, DANIEL JAMES	201 DEL NORTE - SUNNYVALE CA 94086
54- 22	DUREN, RINOLD GEORGE	7606 WEST HAMPSTEAD DRIVE - MIDDLETON WI 53562
72- 24	DURHAM, DONALD GARY	2627 PENNINGTON BEND RD - NASHVILLE TN 37214
29- 32	DURHAM, EDWARD FANT	D. APRIL 27, 1976 CHESTER, S. C.
54- 23	DURHAM, JOSEPH VANN	9715 MENDOZA RD - RANDALLSTOWN MD 21133
80- 40	DURHAM, LEON	3932 DICKSON AVE - CINCINNATI OH 45229
57- 20	DURNBAUGH, ROBERT EUGENE	1638 NORTH CENTRAL DR - DAYTON OH 45432
25- 27	DURNING, GEORGE DEWEY	D. APRIL 18, 1986 TAMPA, FLA.
17- 24	DURNING, RICHARD KNOTT	D. SEPTEMBER 23, 1948 CASTLE POINT, N. Y.
25- 28	DUROCHER, LEO ERNEST	OLD ADD: 1400 E.PALM CANYON #210-PALM SPRINGS CA 92262
44- 34	DURRETT, ELMER CHARLES 'RED'	RR 3 BOX 93 - WAXAHACHIE TX 75165
22- 29	DURST, CEDRIC MONTGOMERY	D. FEBRUARY 16, 1971 SAN DIEGO, CAL.
41- 23	DUSAK, ERVIN FRANK	241 EAST PRAIRIE AVE - LOMBARD IL 60148
56- 31	DUSER, CARL ROBERT	3021 CORMWALL RD - BETHLEHEM PA 18017
63- 36	DUSTAL, ROBERT ANDREW	725 ELEVENTH STREET, OCEAN - MARATHON FL 33050
73- 40	DWYER, JAMES EDWARD	7607 WEST 159TH PL - TINLEY PARK IL 60477
37- 36	DWYER, JOSEPH MICHAEL	56 HIGH ST - WEST ORANGE NJ 07052
80- 41	DYBZINSKI, JEROME MATTHEW	OLD ADD: 89 245 DERBY - NAPERVILLE IL 60540
51- 35	DYCK, JAMES ROBERT	1704 SECOND STREET - CHENEY WA 99004
14- 57	DYER, BENJAMIN FRANKLIN	D. AUGUST 7, 1959 KENOSHA, WIS.
68- 17	DYER, DONALD ROBERT 'DUFFY'	742 WEST LAS PALMARITAS - PHOENIX AZ 85021
22- 30	DYER, EDWIN HAWLEY	D. APRIL 20, 1964 HOUSTON, TEX.
89- 33	DYER, MICHAEL LAWRENCE	2044 BENWOOD STREET - COVINA CA 91724
18- 18	DYKES, JAMES JOSEPH	D. JUNE 15, 1976 PHILADELPHIA, PA.
85- 28	DYKSTRA, LENNY KYLE	908 RASHFORD DRIVE - PLACENTIA CA 92670
59- 25	EADDY, DONALD JOHNSON	%J.EADDY,3440 POINSETTIA-GRAND RAPIDS MI49508
15- 37	EAKLE, CHARLES EMORY	D. JUNE 15, 1959 BALTIMORE, MD.
84- 32	EARL, WILLIAM SCOTT	BOX 63 - NORTH VERNON IN 47265
60- 31	EARLEY, ARNOLD CARL	4341 CAPTAINS LN - FLINT MI 48507
38- 22	EARLEY, THOMAS FRANCIS ALOYSIUS	D. APRIL 5, 1988 NANTUCKET ISLAND, MASS.
86- 46	EARLEY, WILLIAM ALBERT	OLD ADD: 3120 ROOSEVELT AVE - CINCINNATI OH 45211
39- 31	EARLY, JACOB WILLARD	D. MAY 31, 1985 MELBOURNE, FLA.
28- 32	EARNSHAW, GEORGE LIVINGSTON	D. DECEMBER 1, 1976 LITTLE ROCK, ARK.
73- 41	EASLER, MICHAEL ANTHONY	407 BLUFF COURT - SAN ANTONIO TX 78216
87- 40	EASLEY, KENNETH LOGAN	RURAL ROUTE 1 BOX 35 - KIMBERLY ID 83341
15- 38	EAST, CARLTON WILLIAM	D. JANUARY 15, 1953 WHITESBURG, GA.
41- 24	EAST, GORDON HUGH	D. NOVEMBER 2, 1981 CHARLESTON, S. C.
49- 20	EASTER, LUSCIOUS LUKE	D. MARCH 29, 1979 EUCLID, O.
28- 33	EASTERLING, PAUL	% TATTNALL, BOX 860 - REIDSVILLE GA 30453
74- 30	EASTERLY, JAMES MORRIS 'JAMIE'	1306 PLANTATION - CROCKETT TX 75835
44- 35	EASTERWOOD, ROY CHARLES	D. AUGUST 24, 1984 GRAHAM, TEXAS
55- 39	EASTON, JOHN DAVID	SCOTCH RD BOX 418 RR1 - PENNINGTON NJ 08534
74- 31	EASTWICK, RAWLINS JACKSON	224 CHESTNUT STREET - HADDONFIELD NJ 08033
79- 30	EATON, CRAIG	3307 BALTUSROL LN - LAKE WORTH FL 33467
44- 36	EATON, ZEBULON VANCE	D. DECEMBER 17, 1989 WEST PALM BEACH, FLA.
88- 46	EAVE, GARY LOUIS	1609 KING AVENUE - BASTROP LA 71220
35- 26	EAVES, VALLIE ENNIS	D. APRIL 19, 1960 NORMAN, OKLA.
13- 53	EAYRS, EDWIN	D. NOVEMBER 30, 1969 WARWICK, R.I.
15- 39	ECCLES, HARRY JOSIAH	D. JUNE 28, 1955 JAMESTOWN, N.Y.
39- 32	ECHOLS, JOHN GRESHAM	D. NOVEMBER 13, 1972 ATLANTA, GA.
75- 36	ECKERSLEY, DENNIS LEE	263 MORSE RD - SUDBURY MA 01776
30- 21	ECKERT, ALBERT GEORGE	D. APRIL 20, 1974 MILWAUKEE, WIS.
19- 18	ECKERT, CHARLES WILLIAM	D. AUGUST 22, 1986 TREVOSE, PA.
32- 32	ECKHARDT, OSCAR GEORGE 'OX'	D. APRIL 22, 1651 YORKTOWN, TEX.
70- 38	EDDY, DONALD EUGENE	BOX 537 - ROCKWELL IA 50469
79- 31	EDDY, STEVEN ALLEN	6599 EAST THOMAS ROAD #1045 - SCOTTSDALE AZ 85251
81- 30	EDELEN, BENNY JOE	BOX 13 - GRACEMONT OK 73042
32- 33	EDELEN, EDWARD JOSEPH	D. FEBRUARY 1, 1982 LAPLATA, MD.
55- 40	EDELMAN, JOHN ROGERS	922 MONTE VISTON DR - WEST CHESTER PA 19380
76- 30	EDEN, EDWARD MICHAEL 'MIKE'	OLD ADD: 6705 NORTH HINES AVE - TAMPA FL 33614
87- 41	EDENS, THOMAS PATRICK	RURAL ROUTE 2 BOX 2424 - FRUITLAND ID 83619
79- 32	EDGE, CLAUDE LEE 'BUTCH'	3728 MARCONI AVENUE - SACRAMENTO CA 95821
66- 31	EDGERTON, WILLIAM ALBERT	2838 FIR LANE - SOUTH BEND IN 46615
12- 57	EDINGTON, JACOB FRANK 'STUMP'	D. NOVEMBER 29, 1969 BASTROP, LA.
80- 42	EDLER, DAVID DELMAR	1504 SOUTH 34TH AVE - YAKIMA WA 98902
13- 54	EDMONDSON, EDWARD EARL	D. MAY 10, 1971 LEESBURG, FLA.
22- 31	EDMONDSON, GEORGE HENDERSON	D. JULY 11, 1973 WACO, TEX.
69- 52	EDMONDSON, PAUL MICHAEL	D. FEBRUARY 13, 1970 SANTA BARBARA, CALIF
15- 40	EDWARDS, ALBERT	B. 1896 FREEPORT, N.Y.
46- 26	EDWARDS, CHARLES BRUCE	D. APRIL 25, 1975 SACRAMENTO, CALIF.
78- 38	EDWARDS, DAVID LEONARD	15544 PRAIRIE AVENUE - RIVERSIDE CA 92504
25- 29	EDWARDS, FOSTER HAMILTON	D. JANUARY 4, 1980 ORLEANS, MASS.
41- 25	EDWARDS, HENRY ALBERT	D. JUNE 22, 1978 SANTA ANA, CALIF.
62- 35	EDWARDS, HOWARD RODNEY 'DOC'	4717 HUMPHREY ROAD - GREAT VALLEY NY 14741
22- 32	EDWARDS, JAMES CORBETTE 'JIM JOE'	D. JANUARY 19, 1965 CALHOUN COUNTY, MISS.
61- 33	EDWARDS, JOHN ALBAN	10118 SPRINGWOOD FOREST DR - HOUSTON TX 77055
81- 31	EDWARDS, MARSHALL LYNN	15544 PRAIRIE AVE - RIVERSIDE CA 92504
77- 50	EDWARDS, MICHAEL LEWIS	OLD ADD: 3216 WADSWORTH AVE - LOS ANGELES CA 90011
34- 32	EDWARDS, SHERMAN STANLEY	1223 WEST FIRST - ELDORADO AR 71730
89- 34	EDWARDS, WAYNE MAURICE	9738 AQUEDUCT AVENUE - SEPULVEDA CA 91343
63- 37	EGAN, RICHARD WALLIS	3508 CHEROKEE DRIVE - CARSON CITY NV 89701
65- 28	EGAN, THOMAS PATRICK	184 EAST MYRNA LANE - TEMPE AZ 85284
27- 30	EGGERT, ELMER ALBERT	D. APRIL 9, 1971 ROCHESTER, N. Y.
15- 41	EHMKE, HOWARD JONATHAN	D. MARCH 17, 1959 PHILADELPHIA, PA.
24- 33	EHRHARDT, WELTON CLAUDE 'RUBE'	D. APRIL 27, 1980 CHICAGO HEIGHTS, ILL.
12- 58	EIBEL, HENRY HACK	D. OCTOBER 16, 1945 MACON, GA.
78- 39	EICHELBERGER, JUAN TYRONE	14674 SILVERSET ST - POWAY CA 92064
82- 37	EICHHORN, MARK ANTHONY	132 WINGFOOT COURT - APTOS CA 95003
25- 30	EICHRODT, FREDERICK GEORGE	D. JULY 14, 1965 INDIANAPOLIS, IND.
88- 47	EILAND, DAVID WILLIAM	26 COTTONWOOD PLACE - ZEPHYRHILLS FL 34248
64- 29	EILERS, DAVID LOUIS	1500 LEE - BRENHAM TX 77833
44- 37	EISENHART, JACOB HENRY 'HANK'	D. DECEMBER 20, 1987 HUNTINGDON, PA.
82- 38	EISENREICH, JAMES DONALD	2006 11TH AVENUE SOUTH - ST. CLOUD MN 56301
35- 27	EISENSTAT, HARRY	3333 WARRENSVILLE CTR #214 - SHAKER HEIGHTS OH 44122
49- 21	ELDER, GEORGE REZIN	40200 BROOKSIDE AVE - CHERRY VALLEY CA 92223
13- 55	ELDER, HENRY KNOX 'HEINIE'	D. NOVEMBER 13, 1958 LONG BEACH, CALIF.

Red
Ruffing

YANKEE GREATS

Autographed Perez-Steele Art Post Cards picture Yankee Hall of Famers Ruffing, Hoyt, DiMaggio, Dickey and Berra

Waite
Hoyt

Joe
DiMaggio

Bill
Dickey

Yogi
Berra

66- 32 ELIA, LEE CONSTANTINE   1201 NORWOOD AVE - CLEARWATER FL 33516
43- 42 ELKO, PETER   133 MADISON ST -WILKES BARRE PA 18702
17- 25 ELLER, HORACE OWEN 'HOD'   D. JULY 18, 1961 INDIANAPOLIS, IND.
19- 19 ELLERBE, FRANCIS ROGERS   D. JULY 8, 1988 LATTA, S. C.
74- 32 ELLINGSEN, HAROLD BRUCE   5873 DANELAND - LAKEWOOD CA 90713
62- 36 ELLIOT, LAWRENCE LEE   13278 STONE CANYON RD #B - POWAY CA 92064
23- 33 ELLIOTT, ALLEN CLIFFORD   D. MAY 6, 1979 ST. LOUIS, MO.
21- 24 ELLIOTT, CARTER WARD   D. MAY 21, 1959 PALM SPRINGS, CAL.
11- 46 ELLIOTT, EUGENE BIRMINGHOUSE   D. JANUARY 5, 1976 HUNTINGDON, PA.
10- 49 ELLIOTT, HAROLD B. 'ROWDY'   D. FEBRUARY 12, 1934 SAN FRANCISCO, CALIF.
29- 33 ELLIOTT, HAROLD WILLIAM   D. APRIL 25, 1963 HONOLULU, HAW.
53- 20 ELLIOTT, HARRY LEWIS   1154 RANDOM - EL CAJON CA 92020
47- 30 ELLIOTT, HERBERT GLENN   D. JULY 27, 1969 PORTLAND, ORE.
23- 34 ELLIOTT, JAMES THOMPSON   D. JANUARY 7, 1970 TERRE HAUTE, IND.
72- 25 ELLIOTT, RANDY LEE   P.O. BOX 834 - SOMIS CA 93066
39- 33 ELLIOTT, ROBERT IRVING   D. MAY 4, 1966 SAN DIEGO, CAL.
68- 18 ELLIS, DOCK PHILIP   121 E. 139TH ST - LOS ANGELES CA 90061
67- 28 ELLIS, JAMES RUSSELL   13608 AVE 224 - TULARE CA 93274
69- 53 ELLIS, JOHN CHARLES   15 WHITNEY LN - EAST LYME CT 06333
71- 29 ELLIS, ROBERT WALTER   1204D UNIVERSITY VILLAGE - EAST LANSING MI 48823
62- 37 ELLIS, SAMUEL JOSEPH   6111 WHITEWAY - TEMPLE TERRACE FL 33617
20- 31 ELLISON, GEORGE RUSSELL   D. JANUARY 20, 1978 SAN FRANCISCO, CALIF.
16- 21 ELLISON, HERBERT SPENCER 'BABE' D. AUGUST 11, 1955 SAN FRANCISCO, CALIF.
58- 28 ELLSWORTH, RICHARD CLARK   1099 WEST MORRIS - FRESNO CA 93705
88- 48 ELLSWORTH, STEVEN CLARK   1099 WEST MORRIS - FRESNO CA 93705
24- 34 ELMORE, VERDO WILSON   D. AUGUST 5, 1969 BIRMINGHAM, ALA.
23- 35 ELSH, EUGENE ROY   D. NOVEMBER 12, 1978 PHILADELPHIA, PA.
86- 47 ELSTER, KEVIN DANIEL   5801 MARSHALL DRIVE - HUNTINGTON BEACH CA 92649
53- 21 ELSTON, DONALD RAY   2436 MAPLE ST - NORTHBROOK IL 60062
41- 26 EMBREE, CHARLES WILLIAM 'RED'   5500 N. BANK RD - CRESCENT CITY CA 95531
23- 36 EMBRY, CHARLES AKIN 'SLIM'   D. OCTOBER 10, 1947 NASHVILLE, TENN.
11- 47 EMERSON, CHESTER ARTHUR   D. JULY 2, 1971 AUGUSTA, ME.
63- 38 EMERY, CALVIN WAYNE   RR 1 BOX 24 - CENTRE HALL PA 16828
24- 35 EMERY, HERRICK SMITH 'SPOKE'   D. JUNE 2, 1975 CAPE CANAVERAL, FLA.
16- 22 EMMER, FRANK WILLIAM   D. OCTOBER 18, 1963 HOMESTEAD, FLA.
23- 37 EMMERICH, ROBERT G.   D. NOVEMBER 22, 1948 BRIDGEPORT, CONN.
45- 29 EMMERICH, WILLIAM PETER 'SLIM'   257 EAST FAIRVIEW ST - ALLENTOWN PA 18103
46- 27 ENDICOTT, WILLIAM FRANKLIN   14219 OAK KNOLL ROAD - SONORA CA 95370
12- 59 ENGEL, JOSEPH WILLIAM   D. JUNE 12, 1969 CHATTANOOGA, TENN.
85- 29 ENGEL, STEVEN MICHAEL   1657 TRILLIUM COURT - READING OH 45215
25- 31 ENGLE, CHARLES AUGUST   D. OCTOBER 12, 1983 SAN ANTONIO, TEX.
81- 32 ENGLE, RALPH DAVID 'DAVE'   5343 CASTLE HILLS DRIVE - SAN DIEGO CA 92109
81- 33 ENGLE, RICHARD DOUGLAS   2634 JACKSON PIKE - BATAVIA OH 45103
32- 24 ENGLISH, CHARLES DEWIE   1600 SOUTH BALDWIN AVENUE #22 - ARCADIA CA 91006
27- 31 ENGLISH, ELWOOD GEORGE   14 NORTH ELEVENTH ST - NEWARK OH 43055
31- 23 ENGLISH, GILBERT RAYMOND   RR 2 BOX 356 - TRINITY NC 27370
46- 28 ENNIS, DELMAR   712 WOODSIDE RD - JENKINTOWN PA 19046
26- 28 ENNIS, RUSSELL ELWOOD   D. JANUARY 29, 1949 SUPERIOR, WIS.
76- 31 ENRIGHT, GEORGE ALBERT   6046 LAKE WORTH RD #969-LAKE WORTH FL 33463
17- 26 ENRIGHT, JOHN PERCY   D. AUGUST 18, 1975 POMPANO BEACH, FLA.
12- 60 ENS, ANTON 'MUTZ'   D. JUNE 28, 1950 ST. LOUIS, MO.
22- 33 ENS, JEWEL WINKLEMEYER   D. JANUARY 17, 1950 SYRACUSE, N. Y.
74- 33 ENYART, TERRY GENE   520 SEAL AVE - PIKETON OH 45661
14- 58 ENZENROTH, CLARENCE HERMAN 'JACK' D. FEBRUARY 21, 1944
14- 59 ENZMANN, JOHN   D. MARCH 14, 1984 RIVERHEAD, N. Y.
87- 42 EPPARD, JAMES GERHARD   332 ASHBY STREET - AZUSA CA 91702
38- 23 EPPERLY, ALBERT PAUL   2621 IOWA ST - DAVENPORT IA 52803
35- 28 EPPS, AUBREY LEE   D. NOVEMBER 13, 1984 ACKERMAN, MISS.
38- 24 EPPS, HAROLD FRANKLIN   4500 CYPRESSWOOD #406 - SPRING TX 77379
66- 33 EPSTEIN, MICHAEL PETER   9985 OAKWILDE AVENUE - STOCKTON CA 95212
77- 51 ERARDI, JOSEPH GREGORY 'GREG'   42 WESTGATE ROAD - MASSAPEQUA PARK NY 11762
47- 31 ERAUTT, EDWARD LORENZ   7252 WAITE DR - LAMESA CA 92041
50- 28 ERAUTT, JOSEPH MICHAEL   D. OCTOBER 6, 1976 PORTLAND, ORE.
58- 29 ERICKSON, DON LEE   2717 INTERLACHEN - SPRINGFIELD IL 62704
14- 60 ERICKSON, ERIC GEORGE ADOLPH   D. MAY 19, 1965 JAMESTOWN, N. Y.
53- 22 ERICKSON, HAROLD JAMES   333 BAYSHORE DR - OSPREY FL 33559
35- 29 ERICKSON, HENRY NELS   D. DECEMBER 13, 1964 LOUISVILLE, KY.
41- 27 ERICKSON, PAUL WALFORD   363 BOYD ST - FOND DU LAC WI 54935
29- 34 ERICKSON, RALPH LIEF   3307 QUAIL MEADOWS DRIVE - SANTA MARIA CA 93455
78- 40 ERICKSON, ROGER FARRELL   2506 ARROWHEAD DRIVE - SPRINGFIELD IL 62702
47- 32 ERMER, CALVIN COOLIDGE   1009 PANORAMA DR - CHATTANOOGA TN 37421
57- 21 ERNAGA, FRANK JOHN   50 NORTH ROOP ST - SUSANVILLE CA 96130
38- 25 ERRICKSON, RICHARD MERRIWELL   2976 DOUGLAS LANE - VINELAND NJ 08360
48- 34 ERSKINE, CARL DANIEL   6214 SOUTH MADISON AVE - ANDERSON IN 46013
83- 51 ESASKY, NICHOLAS ANDREW   1048 JUMPERS RIDGE - MARIETTA GA 30064
54- 24 ESCALERA, SATURNINO CUADRADO 'NINO' 201 DK2O VALLE ARRIBE HEIGHTS - CAROLINA PR 00620
82- 39 ESCARREGA, ERNESTO   APARTADO POSTAL 48G - LOS MOCHIS SINOLOA MEX.
15- 42 ESCHEN, JAMES GODRICH   D. SEPTEMBER 27, 1960 SLOATSBURG, N.Y.
42- 32 ESCHEN, LAWRENCE EDWARD   346 36TH AVE NE - ST. PETERSBURG FL 33704
88- 49 ESCOBAR, ANGEL RUBEN   OLD ADD: CARICUAO, CARACAS VENEZUELA S.A.
11- 48 ESMOND, JAMES J.   D. JUNE 26, 1948 TROY, N.Y.
82- 40 ESPINO, JUAN   EUGENIO M. DE CESTOS #50 - BONAO DOMINICAN REP.
74- 34 ESPINOSA, ARNULFO ACEVEDO 'NINO' D. DECEMBER 25, 1987 VILLA ALTAGRACIA, DOMINICAN REP.
84- 33 ESPINOZA, ALVARO ALBERTO   URB. MICHELENA C/93 #86-74 - VALENCIA VENEZUELA S.A.
52- 28 ESPOSITO, SAMUEL   NCSU,CASE CENTER BOX 8501 - RALEIGH NC 27695
83- 52 ESPY, CECIL EDWARD   P.O. BOX 14464 - SAN DIEGO CA 92114
58- 30 ESSEGIAN, CHARLES ABRAHAM   15639 BRONCO DRIVE - CANYON COUNTRY CA 91351
79- 33 ESSER, MARK GERALD   4 JACKSON DR - POUGHKEEPSIE NY 12603
73- 42 ESSIAN, JAMES SARKIS   134 ECKFORD - TROY MI 48098
35- 30 ESTALELLA, ROBERTO MENDEZ   3297 WEST 14TH LN - HIALEAH FL 33012
64- 30 ESTELLE, RICHARD HARRY   2221 TAYLOR AVE - POINT PLEASANT NJ 08742
51- 26 ESTOCK, GEORGE JOHN   595 RAY STREET - SEBASTIAN FL 32958
60- 32 ESTRADA, CHARLES LEONARD   459 NORTH TASSAJARA - SAN LUIS OBISPO CA 93401
71- 30 ESTRADA, FRANCISCO (SOTO)   MANUEL DOBLADO PTE 605-A - NAVAJOA SONORA MEX.
29- 35 ESTRADA, OSCAR   D. JANUARY 2, 1978 HAVANA, CUBA
62- 38 ETCHEBARREN, ANDREW AUGUSTE   1102 CROFTER - WALNUT CA 91789
43- 43 ETCHISON, CLARENCE HAMPTON 'BUCK' D. JANUARY 24, 1980 EAST NEW MARKET, MD.

67- 29 ETHERIDGE, BOBBY LAMAR	2633 WILLOW DRIVE - GREENVILLE MS 38701
38- 26 ETTEN, NICHOLAS RAYMOND TOM	21 SPINNING WHEEL RD - HINSDALE IL 60521
22- 34 EUBANKS, UEL MELVIN	D. NOVEMBER 21, 1954 DALLAS, TEX.
85- 30 EUFEMIA, FRANK ANTHONY	71 DELFORD AVENUE - BERGENFIELD NJ 07621
17- 27 EUNICK, FERNANDES BOWEN	D. DECEMBER 9, 1959 BALTIMORE, MD.
39- 34 EVANS, ALFRED HUBERT	D. APRIL 6, 1979 WILSON, N. C.
78- 41 EVANS, BARRY STEVEN	OLD ADD: 30 LOW STREET - MCDONOUGH GA 30253
69- 54 EVANS, DARRELL WAYNE	31918 FOXFIELD DRIVE - WESTLAKE VILLAGE CA 91361
72- 26 EVANS, DWIGHT MICHAEL	10120 CASABA AVENUE - CHATSWORTH CA 91311
15- 43 EVANS, JOSEPH PATTON	D. AUGUST 9, 1953 GULFPORT, MISS.
36- 23 EVANS, RUSSELL EDISON 'RED'	D. JUNE 14, 1982 LAKEVIEW, ARK.
32- 25 EVANS, WILLIAM ARTHUR	D. JANUARY 8, 1952 WICHITA, KANS.
16- 23 EVANS, WILLIAM JAMES	D. DECEMBER 21, 1946 BURLINGTON, N. C.
49- 22 EVANS, WILLIAM LAWRENCE	D. NOVEMBER 30, 1983 GRAND JUNCTION, COLO.
69- 55 EVERITT, EDWARD LEON	RR 1 BOX 417 - MARSHALL TX 75670
13- 56 EVERS, JOSEPH FRANCIS	D. JANUARY 4, 1949 ALBANY, N.Y.
41- 28 EVERS, WALTER ARTHUR 'HOOT'	637 SOUTH RIPPLE CREEK - HOUSTON TX 77057
21- 25 EWING, REUBEN	D. OCTOBER 5, 1970 WEST HARTFORD, CONN.
73- 43 EWING, SAMUEL JAMES	RR 4, POWELL RD - LEWISBURG TN 37091
19- 20 EWOLDT, ARTHUR LEE	D. DECEMBER 8, 1977 DES MOINES, IA.
43- 44 EYRICH, GEORGE LINCOLN	565 SOUTH 15TH ST-READING PA 19602
23- 38 EZZELL, HOMER ESTELL	D. AUGUST 3, 1976 SAN ANTONIO, TEX.
14- 61 FABER, URBAN CHARLES 'RED'	D. SEPTEMBER 25, 1976 CHICAGO, ILL.
16- 24 FABRIQUE, ALBERT LAVERNE 'BUNNY'	D. JANUARY 10, 1960 ANN ARBOR, MICH.
53- 23 FACE, ELROY LEON	608 DELLA DR #5F - NORTH VERSAILLES PA 15137
80- 43 FAEDO, LEONARDO LAGO 'LENNY'	2920 COLLINS ST - TAMPA FL 33607
19- 21 FAETH, ANTHONY JOSEPH	D. DECEMBER 22, 1982 ST. PAUL, MINN.
43- 45 FAGAN, EVERETT JOSEPH	D. FEBRUARY 16, 1983 MORRISTOWN, N.J.
18- 19 FAHEY, FRANCIS RAYMOND	D. MARCH 19, 1954 BOSTON, MASS.
12- 61 FAHEY, HOWARD SIMPSON	D. OCTOBER 24, 1971 CLEARWATER, FLA.
71- 31 FAHEY, WILLIAM ROGER	5740 MONA LN - DALLAS TX 75236
51- 27 FAHR, GERALD WARREN 'RED'	816 WEST PARK ST - PARAGOULD AR 72450
14- 62 FAHRER, CLARENCE WILLIE 'PETE'	D. JUNE 10, 1967 FREMONT, MICH.
47- 33 FAIN, FERRIS ROY	E08997,BOX 2000 J111A - VACAVILLE CA 95696
19- 22 FAIRCLOTH, JAMES LAMAR 'RAGS'	D. OCTOBER 5, 1953 TUCSON, ARIZ.
68- 19 FAIREY, JAMES BURKE	218 STRAWBERRY ST - CLEMSON SC 29361
58- 31 FAIRLY, RONALD RAY	OLD ADD: 23140 PARK SORRENTO - CALABASAS PARK CA 91302
75- 37 FALCONE, PETER FRANK	3179 BOLERO DR - ATLANTA GA 30341
20- 32 FALK, BIBB AUGUST	D. JUNE 8, 1989 AUSTIN, TEXAS
25- 32 FALK, CHESTER EMANUEL 'CHET'	D. JANUARY 7, 1982 AUSTIN, TEXAS
31- 24 FALLENSTIN, EDWARD JOSEPH	D. NOVEMBER 24, 1971 ORANGE, N.J.
37- 37 FALLON, GEORGE DECATUR	71 PLAINVIEW DR - STRATFORD CT 06497
84- 34 FALLON, ROBERT JOSEPH	2114 NORTH 44TH AVE - HOLLYWOOD FL 33021
14- 63 FALSEY, PETER JAMES	D. MAY 23, 1976 LOS ANGELES, CALIF.
45- 30 FANNIN, CLIFFORD BRYSON	D. DECEMBER 11, 1966 SANDUSKY, O.
54- 25 FANNING, WILLIAM JAMES 'JIM'	BOX 500 STATION M - MONTREAL QUEBEC H1V 3P2 CAN.
63- 39 FANOK, HARRY MICHAEL	12373 OLD STATE ROAD - CHARDON OH 44024
49- 23 FANOVICH, FRANK JOSEPH	3 FAIRGREEN AVENUE - NEW SMYRNA BEACH FL 32069
86- 48 FANSLER, STANLEY ROBERT	RURAL ROUTE 2 BOX 550-1 - ELKINS WV 26241
10- 50 FANWELL, HARRY CLAYTON	D. JULY 15, 1965 BALTIMORE, MD.
70- 39 FANZONE, CARMEN	5114 RANCHITO AVE - SHERMAN OAKS CA 91423
61- 34 FARLEY, ROBERT JACOB	RR 3 BOX 190 - MONTOURSVILLE PA 17754
71- 32 FARMER, EDWARD JOSEPH	13538 SOUTH LECLAIRE - CRESTWOOD IL 60445
16- 25 FARMER, FLOYD HASKELL 'JACK'	D. MAY 21, 1970 COLUMBIA, LA.
82- 41 FARR, JAMES ALFRED	RR 1 BOX 98 - ATHENS PA 18810
84- 35 FARR, STEVEN MICHAEL	RURAL ROUTE 1 BOX 33 - PORT TOBACCO MD 20677
25- 33 FARRELL, EDWARD STEPHEN 'DOC'	D. DECEMBER 20, 1966 LIVINGSTON, N. J.
87- 43 FARRELL, JOHN EDWARD	12 HIGHLAND AVENUE - MONMOUTH BEACH NJ 07750
14- 64 FARRELL, JOHN J.	D. MARCH 24, 1918 CHICAGO, ILL.
43- 46 FARRELL, MAJOR KERBY	D. DECEMBER 17, 1975 NASHVILLE, TENN.
56- 32 FARRELL, RICHARD JOSEPH	D. JUNE 11, 1977 GREAT YARMOUTH, ENGLAND
68- 20 FAST, DARCY RAE	127 SUNNYSIDE DRIVE - CENTRALIA WA 98531
53- 24 FASZHOLZ, JOHN EDWARD	7108 GENEVA - AUSTIN TX 78723
62- 39 FAUL, WILLIAM ALVAN	RR1 BOX 7 - PLEASANT PLAIN OH 45162
27- 32 FAULKNER, JAMES LEROY	D. JUNE 2, 1962 WEST PALM BEACH, FLA.
44- 38 FAUSETT, ROBERT SHAW	503 SOUTHWEST PARKWAY #711 - COLLEGE STATION TX 77840
11- 49 FAUST, CHARLES VICTOR	D. JUNE 18, 1915 FORT STEILACOOM, WASH.
16- 26 FAUTSCH, JOSEPH ROAMON	D. MARCH 16, 1971 NEW HOPE, MINN.
62- 40 FAZIO, ERNEST JOSEPH	2626 NICHOLSON ST - SAN LEANDRO CA 94577
52- 29 FEAR, LUVERN CARL	D. SEPTEMBER 6, 1976 SPENCER, IA.
51- 28 FEDEROFF, ALFRED	10150 MORTONVIEW - TAYLOR MI 48080
34- 33 FEHRING, WILLIAM PAUL 'DUTCH'	1735 POPPY AVE - MENLO PARK CA 94023
38- 27 FEINBERG, EDWARD	D. APRIL 20, 1986 HOLLYWOOD, FLA.
85- 31 FELDER, MICHAEL OTIS	322 SOUTH 17TH STREET - RICHMOND CA 94804
42- 33 FELDERMAN, MARVIN WILFRED	10633 HYACINTH LANE - MORENO VALLEY CA 92388
41- 29 FELDMAN, HARRY	D. MARCH 16, 1962 FORT SMITH, ARK.
23- 39 FELIX, AUGUST GUENTHER	D. MAY 12, 1960 MONTGOMERY, ALA.
89- 35 FELIX, JUNIOR FRANCISCO	DONA ANTONIA #42, VILLA ELINA-GUAYUBIN DOMINICAN REP.
58- 32 FELLER, JACK LELAND	LUKES POINT DRIVE - QUINCY MI 49082
36- 24 FELLER, ROBERT WILLIAM ANDREW	BOX 157 - GATES MILLS OH 44040
15- 44 FELSCH, OSCAR EMIL 'HAPPY'	D. AUGUST 17, 1964 MILWAUKEE, WIS.
68- 21 FELSKE, JOHN FREDRICK	600 LIVINGSTON - MCHENRY IL 60050
79- 34 FELTON, TERRY LANE	BOX 533 - BAKER LA 70714
21- 26 FENNER, HORACE ALFRED 'HOD'	D. NOVEMBER 20, 1954 DETROIT, MICH.
72- 27 FENWICK, ROBERT RICHARD	OLD ADD: 2626 9TH AVENUE NORTH - ANOKA MN 55303
42- 34 FERENS, STANLEY	BOX 261-YUKON PA 15698
18- 20 FERGUSON, JAMES ALEXANDER	D. APRIL 28, 1976 SEPULVEDA, CALIF.
70- 40 FERGUSON, JOE VANCE	1184 WEST 11TH STREET - SAN PEDRO CA 90731
44- 39 FERGUSON, ROBERT LESTER	ROLLING RIDGE APTS #38 - WETUMPKA AL 36092
87- 44 FERMIN, FELIX JOSE	CALLE CAPOTILLO #24 - MAO, VALVERDE, DOMINICAN REP.
40- 19 FERNANDES, EDWARD PAUL	D. NOVEMBER 27, 1968 HAYWARD, CAL.
83- 53 FERNANDEZ, CHARLES SIDNEY 'SID'	748 KALANIPUU STREET - HONOLULU HI 96825
67- 30 FERNANDEZ, FRANK	37 COUGHLAN AVE - STATEN ISLAND NY 10310
42- 35 FERNANDEZ, FROILAN 'NANNY'	26229 MONTE VISTA-LOMITA CA 90717
56- 33 FERNANDEZ, HUMBERTO PEREZ 'CHICO'	3322 24TH ST - DETROIT MI 48208
68- 22 FERNANDEZ, LORENZO MARTO	1310 SW 97TH AVE - MIAMI FL 33175
83- 54 FERNANDEZ, OCTAVIO ANTONIO 'TONY'	CALLE N#3,B.RESTAURACION-SAN PEDRO DE MACORIS DOM. REP.
63- 40 FERRARA, ALFRED JOHN	BOX 69263 - LOS ANGELES CA 90069

55- 41 FERRARESE, DONALD HUGH	14140 GAYHEAD RD - APPLE VALLEY CA 92307
66- 34 FERRARO, MICHAEL DENNIS	6195-B LAUREL LANE - TAMARAC FL 33319
35- 31 FERRAZZI, WILLIAM JOSEPH	13 ARI WOODS - KEYSTONE HEIGHTS FL 32656
85- 32 FERREIRA, ANTHONY ROSS	3756 LOFTON PLACE - RIVERSIDE CA 92501
29- 36 FERRELL, RICHARD BENJAMIN 'RICK'	2199 GOLFVIEW #203 - TROY MI 48084
27- 33 FERRELL, WESLEY CHEEK	D. DECEMBER 9, 1976 SARASOTA, FLA.
74- 35 FERRER, SERGIO	P.AREILAGE NX-8,LEVITTOWN LAKES - TOA BAJA PR 00632
41- 30 FERRICK, THOMAS JEROME	517 HARRINGTON RD-HAVERTOWN PA 19083
79- 35 FERRIS, ROBERT EUGENE	9718 IRONMASTER DR - BURKE VA 22015
45- 31 FERRISS, DAVID MEADOW 'BOO'	510 ROBINSON DR - CLEVELAND MS 38732
10- 51 FERRY, JOHN FRANCIS	D. AUGUST 29, 1954 PITTSFIELD, MASS.
37- 38 FETTE, LOUIS HENRY WILLIAM	D. JANUARY 3, 1981 WARRENSBURG, MO.
89- 36 FETTERS, MICHAEL LEE	91-847 PAALOHA STREET - EWA BEACH HI 96706
17- 28 FEWSTER, WILSON LLOYD 'CHICK'	D. APRIL 16, 1945 BALTIMORE, MD.
81- 34 FIALA, NEIL STEPHEN	3102 NORTH HIMES - TAMPA FL 33607
44- 40 FICK, JOHN RALPH	D. JUNE 9, 1958 SOMERS POINT, N. J.
76- 32 FIDRYCH, MARK STEVEN	260 WEST STREET - NORTHBORO MA 01532
32- 26 FIEBER, CLARENCE THOMAS 'LEFTY'	D. AUGUST 20, 1985 REDWOOD CITY, CALIF.
85- 33 FIELDER, CECIL GRANT	426 REDCOAT LANE - ARLINGTON TX 76018
86- 49 FIELDS, BRUCE ALAN	OLD ADD: 1003 GORDON AVENUE - LANSING MI 48910
73- 44 FIFE, DANNY WAYNE	5854 MISTY HILL DRIVE - CLARKSTON MI 48016
74- 36 FIGUEROA, EDUARDO	CALLE 41 A-N15 - SANTA JUANITA PR 00619
80- 44 FIGUEROA, JESUS MARIA	SANTA CRUZ VILLA MELLA KM 8 - SANTO DOMINGO DOM. REP.
40- 20 FILE, LAWRENCE SAMUEL	550 OCEAN PINES - BERLIN MD 21811
82- 42 FILER, THOMAS CARSON	9748 SUSAN RD - PHILADELPHIA PA 19115
44- 41 FILIPOWICZ, STEPHEN CHARLES	D. FEBRUARY 21, 1975 WILKES-BARRE, PA.
34- 34 FILLEY, MARCUS LUCIUS	1011 HOOSICK ROAD - TROY NY 12180
15- 45 FILLINGIM, DANA	D. FEBRUARY 3, 1961 TUSKEGEE, ALA.
82- 43 FILSON, WILLIAM PETER 'PETE'	1034 10TH AVE - FOLSOM PA 19033
83- 55 FIMPLE, JOHN JOSEPH	5328 CROXTON WAY - SACRAMENTO CA 95842
79- 36 FINCH, JOEL D	68571 OAK SPRING RD - EDWARDSBURG MI 49112
16- 27 FINCHER, WILLIAM ALLEN	D. MAY 7, 1946 SHREVEPORT, LA.
47- 34 FINE, THOMAS MORGAN	13130 BLANCO RD #1001 - SAN ANTONIO TX 78216
68- 23 FINGERS, ROLAND GLEN	11582 AVENIDA SIRVITA - SAN DIEGO CA 92128
54- 26 FINIGAN, JAMES LEROY	D. MAY 16, 1981 QUINCY, ILL.
35- 32 FINK, HERMAN ADAM	D. AUGUST 24, 1980 SALISBURY, N. C.
86- 50 FINLEY, CHARLES EDWARD	OLD ADD: RURAL ROUTE 1 BOX 165 - WEST MONROE LA 71291
43- 47 FINLEY, ROBERT EDWARD	D. JANUARY 2, 1986 WEST COVINA, CALIF.
89- 37 FINLEY, STEVEN ALLEN	OLD ADD: PADUCAH KY
30- 22 FINN, CORNELIUS FRANCIS 'MICKEY'	D. JULY 7, 1933 ALTOONA, PA.
12- 62 FINNERAN, JOSEPH IGNATIUS 'HAPPY'	D. FEBRUARY 3, 1942 ORANGE, N.J.
31- 25 FINNEY, HAROLD WILSON	RR 2 BOX 195 - LAFAYETTE AL 36862
31- 26 FINNEY, LOUIS KLOPSCHE	D. APRIL 22, 1966 LAFAYETTE, ALA.
68- 24 FIORE, MICHAEL GARY JOSEPH	17 SILVER ST - MALVERNE NY 11565
81- 35 FIREOVID, STEPHEN JOHN	OLD ADD: RURAL ROUTE 5 - BRYAN OH 43506
81- 36 FIROVA, DANIEL MICHAEL	1606 GRANT - LAREDO TX 78040
19- 23 FISBURN, SAMUEL	D. APRIL 11, 1965 BETHLEHEM, PA.
30- 23 FISCHER, CHARLES WILLIAM 'CARL'	D. DECEMBER 10, 1963 MEDINA, N. Y.
62- 41 FISCHER, HENRY WILLIAM	2304 PEBBLE BEACH DR - LAKE WORTH FL 33467
87- 45 FISCHER, JEFFREY THOMAS	124 GREGORY PLACE - WEST PALM BEACH FL 33405
41- 31 FISCHER, REUBEN WALTER	RR 1 BOX 1517 - HUDSON WI 54016
86- 51 FISCHER, TODD RICHARD	12581 MCGREGOR BLVD - FORT MYERS FL 33919
13- 57 FISCHER, WILLIAM CHARLES	D. SEPTEMBER 4, 1945 RICHMOND, VA.
56- 34 FISCHER, WILLIAM CHARLES	139 UPLAND DRIVE - COUNCIL BLUFFS IA 51501
77- 52 FISCHLIN, MICHAEL THOMAS	4410 CIRCULO DE LAS CHACRAS - TUCSON AZ 85718
88- 50 FISHEL, JOHN ALAN	2957 SHAMROCK AVENUE - BREA CA 92621
11- 50 FISHER, AUGUSTUS HARRIS	D. APRIL 8, 1972 PORTLAND, ORE.
85- 34 FISHER, BRIAN KEVIN	629 JASPER ST - AURORA CO 80011
19- 24 FISHER, CLARENCE HENRY	D. NOVEMBER 2, 1965 POINT PLEASANT, W. VA.
45- 32 FISHER, DONALD RAYMOND	D. JULY 29, 1973 MAYFIELD HEIGHTS, O.
59- 26 FISHER, EDDIE GENE	408 CARDINAL CIRCLE SOUTH - ALTUS OK 73521
64- 31 FISHER, FREDERICK BROWN 'FRITZ'	3703 BARCELONA DRIVE - TOLEDO OH 43615
23- 40 FISHER, GEORGE ALOYS 'SHOWBOAT'	BARACUDA AVE S. (BOX 203) - AVON MN 56310
51- 29 FISHER, HARRY DEVEREAUX	D. SEPTEMBER 20, 1981 WATERLOO, ONT.
10- 52 FISHER, JOHN GUS 'RED'	D. JANUARY 1, 1940 LOUISVILLE, KY.
59- 27 FISHER, JOHN HOWARD 'JACK'	1647 SOUTH 11TH STREET - BETHLEHEM PA 18017
55- 42 FISHER, MAURICE WAYNE	15920 LUCERNE RD - FREDERICKTOWN OH 43019
10- 53 FISHER, RAYMOND LYLE	D. NOVEMBER 3, 1982 ANN ARBOR, MICH.
12- 63 FISHER, ROBERT TAYLOR	D. AUGUST 4, 1963 JACKSONVILLE, FLA.
67- 31 FISHER, THOMAS GENE	OLD ADD: 8233 HUMMINGBIRD CT - INDIANAPOLIS IN 46256
16- 28 FISHER, WILBUR MCCULLOUGH	D. OCTOBER 24, 1960 WELCH, W. VA.
69- 56 FISK, CARLTON ERNEST	16612 CATAWBA RD - LOCKPORT IL 60441
14- 65 FISKE, MAXIMILIAN PATRICK	D. MAY 15, 1928 CHICAGO, ILL.
14- 66 FITTERY, PAUL CLARENCE	D. JANUARY 28, 1974 CARTERSVILLE, GA.
28- 34 FITZBERGER, CHARLES CASPAR	D. JANUARY 25, 1965 BALTIMORE, MD.
48- 33 FITZGERALD, EDWARD RAYMOND	431 CHRISTOPHER DR - FOLSOM CA 95630
22- 35 FITZGERALD, HOWARD CHUMNEY	D. FEBRUARY 26, 1959 EAGLE FALLS, TEX.
58- 33 FITZGERALD, JOHN FRANCIS	RR 7 BOX 492 INGRASSIA RD - MIDDLETOWN NY 10940
11- 51 FITZGERALD, JUSTIN HOWARD 'MIKE'	D. JANUARY 17, 1945 SAN MATEO, CALIF.
83- 56 FITZGERALD, MICHAEL ROY	3641 MANOR DR - LAKEWOOD CA 90712
88- 51 FITZGERALD, MICHAEL PATRICK	1607 EAST 37TH STREET - SAVANNAH GA 31404
31- 27 FITZGERALD, RAYMOND FRANCIS	D. SEPTEMBER 6, 1977 WESTFIELD, MASS.
24- 36 FITZKE, PAUL FREDERICK HERMAN	D. JUNE 30, 1950 SACRAMENTO, CAL.
66- 35 FITZMAURICE, SHAUN EARLE	12107 MOUNTAIN LAUREL DRIVE - RICHMOND VA 23236
69- 57 FITZMORRIS, ALAN JAMES	3545 MOUNT EVEREST AVE - SAN DIEGO CA 92111
15- 46 FITZPATRICK, EDWARD HENRY	D. OCTOBER 23, 1965 BETHLEHEM, PA.
25- 34 FITZSIMMONS, FREDERICK LANDIS	D. NOVEMBER 18, 1979 YUCCA VALLEY, CALIF.
19- 25 FITZSIMMONS, THOMAS WILLIAM	D. DECEMBER 20, 1971 OAKLAND, CALIF.
14- 67 FLACK, MAX JOHN	D. JULY 31, 1975 BELLEVILLE, ILL.
45- 33 FLAGER, WALTER LEONARD	3306 SUNNYVIEW - SALEM OR 97303
17- 29 FLAGSTEAD, IRA JAMES	D. MARCH 13, 1940 OLYMPIA, WASH.
41- 32 FLAIR, ALBERT DELL	D. JULY 25, 1988 NEW ORLEANS, LA.
75- 38 FLANAGAN, MICHAEL KENDALL	6 WYNDHAM COURT - TIMONIUM MD 21093
13- 58 FLANIGAN, CHARLES JAMES	D. JANUARY 8, 1930 SAN FRANCISCO, CALIF.
46- 29 FLANIGAN, RAYMOND ARTHUR	1416 GLENDALE RD - BALTIMORE MD 21239
54- 27 FLANIGAN, THOMAS ANTHONY	114 EAST 40TH - COVINGTON KY 41015
77- 53 FLANNERY, JOHN MICHAEL	6152 TURNER GROVE DRIVE - LAKEWOOD CA 90713
79- 37 FLANNERY, TIMOTHY EARL	1835 BEL AIR TER - ENCINITAS CA 92024

27- 34 FLASKAMPER, RAYMOND HAROLD	D. FEBRUARY 3, 1978 SAN ANTONIO, TEX.
64- 32 FLAVIN, JOHN THOMAS	2027 CALIMYRNA AVE #101 - FRESNO CA 93711
48- 36 FLEITAS, ANGEL FELIX HUSTA	689 EBONY STREET - MELBOURNE FL 32935
40- 21 FLEMING, LESLIE FLETCHERD 'BILL'	2750 WEST HOLCOMB LN - RENO NV 89511
39- 35 FLEMING, LESLIE HARVEY 'BILL'	D. MARCH 5, 1980 CLEVELAND, TEXAS
89- 38 FLETCHER, DARRIN GLEN	RURAL ROUTE 1 BOX 408 - OAKWOOD IL 61832
34- 35 FLETCHER, ELBURT PRESTON	131 OTIS AVE - MILTON MA 02186
14- 68 FLETCHER, OLIVER FRANK	D. OCTOBER 7, 1974 ST. PETERSBURG, FLA.
81- 37 FLETCHER, SCOTT BRIAN	2063 PANOLA RD,%O.BELLAMY - ELLENWOOD GA 30049
62- 42 FLETCHER, THOMAS WAYNE	RR 1 BOX 408 - OAKWOOD IL 61858
55- 43 FLETCHER, VANOIDE	P.O. BOX 368 - YADKINVILLE NC 27055
43- 48 FLICK, LEWIS MILLER	114 MAPLE STREET #2 - WEBER CITY VA 24251
17- 30 FLINN, DON RAPHIEL	D. MARCH 9, 1959 WACO, TEX.
78- 42 FLINN, JOHN RICHARD	173 RIVO ALTO CANAL - LONG BEACH CA 90803
42- 36 FLITCRAFT, HILDRETH MILTON 'HILLY'	50 EAST AVENUE(BOX 260) - WOODSTOWN NJ 08098
34- 36 FLOHR, MORITZ HERMAN 'MORT'	5522 ORDWAY LANE - CANISTEO NY 14823
56- 35 FLOOD, CURTIS CHARLES	4139 CLOVERDALE AVE - LOS ANGELES CA 90008
26- 29 FLORENCE, PAUL ROBERT	D. MAY 28, 1986 GAINESVILLE, FLA.
77- 54 FLORES, GILBERTO	BDA SALAZAR 1 #38 - PONCE PR 00731
42- 37 FLORES, JESSE SANDOVAL	1930 EL PORTAL DR - LAHABRA CA 90632
51- 30 FLOWERS, BENNETT	901 TREMONT RD - WILSON NC 27895
40- 22 FLOWERS, CHARLES WESLEY	D.
23- 41 FLOWERS, D'ARCY RAYMOND 'JAKE'	D. DECEMBER 27, 1962 CLEARWATER, FLA.
44- 42 FLOYD, LESLIE ROE 'BUBBA'	13610 BROOKGREEN DRIVE - DALLAS TX 75240
68- 25 FLOYD, ROBERT NATHAN	OLD ADD: 1319 HALIFAX - MESA AZ 85203
15- 47 FLUHRER, JOHN L.	D. JULY 17, 1946 COLUMBUS, O.
10- 54 FLYNN, JOHN ANTHONY	D. MARCH 23, 1935 PROVIDENCE, R.I.
75- 39 FLYNN, ROBERT DOUGLAS	428 MCKENNA CT - LEXINGTON KY 40505
36- 25 FLYTHE, STUART MCGUIRE	D. OCTOBER 18, 1963 DURHAM, N. C.
58- 34 FODGE, EUGENE ARLEN	1505 NORTH CHICAGO ST - SOUTH BEND IN 46628
53- 25 FOILES, HENRY LEE	BOX 1021 - VIRGINIA BEACH VA 23451
78- 43 FOLEY, MARVIS EDWIN	4058 LANCASTER DRIVE - SARASOTA FL 34241
28- 35 FOLEY, RAYMOND KIRWIN	D. MARCH 22, 1980 VERO BEACH, FLA.
83- 57 FOLEY, THOMAS MICHAEL	11723 SW 95TH TERRACE - MIAMI FL 33186
70- 41 FOLI, TIMOTHY JOHN	105 WILLOW BEND LANE - ORMOND BEACH FL 32074
70- 42 FOLKERS, RICHARD NEVIN	7100 3RD AVENUE NORTH - ST. PETERSBURG FL 33710
51- 31 FONDY, DEE VIRGIL	1422 BELLA VISTA CIR - REDLANDS CA 92373
21- 27 FONSECA, LEWIS ALBERT	D. NOVEMBER 26, 1989 ELY, IOWA
83- 58 FONTENOT, SILTON RAY	904 LAKE RIDGE LN - LAKE CHARLES LA 70605
71- 33 FOOR, JAMES EMERSON	42 SOUTH SCHLUETER - ST LOUIS MO 63135
73- 45 FOOTE, BARRY CLIFTON	5300 CASTLEBROOK DR - RALEIGH NC 27604
85- 35 FORD, CURTIS GLENN	520 WOODLYNN CROSSING - BALLWIN MO 63021
75- 40 FORD, DARNELL GLENN 'DANNY'	P.O. BOX 17968 - ANAHEIM HILLS CA 92817
78- 44 FORD, DAVID ALAN	OLD ADD: .3585 WEST 49TH ST - CLEVELAND OH 44102
50- 29 FORD, EDWARD CHARLES 'WHITEY'	38 SCHOOLHOUSE LANE - LAKE SUCCESS NY 11020
36- 26 FORD, EUGENE MATTHEW	D. SEPTEMBER 7, 1970 EMMETSBURG, IA.
19- 26 FORD, HORACE HILLS 'HOD'	D. JANUARY 29, 1977 WINCHESTER, MASS.
73- 46 FORD, PERCIVAL EDMUND WENTWORTH	D. JULY 8, 1980 NASSAU BAHAMAS
70- 43 FORD, THEODORE HENRY	430 NORTH 4TH STREET - VINELAND NJ 08360
24- 37 FOREMAN, AUGUST	D. FEBRUARY 13, 1953 NEW YORK, N. Y.
52- 30 FORNIELES, JOSE MIGUEL 'MIKE'	29 OAK SQUARE AVE - BRIGHTON MA 02135
70- 44 FORSCH, KENNETH ROTH	7445 STONE CREEK LN - ANAHEIM CA 92807
74- 37 FORSCH, ROBERT HERBERT	428 HICKORY GLEN LN - ST LOUIS MO 63141
71- 34 FORSTER, TERRY JAY	3504 MOUNT LAURENCE - SAN DIEGO CA 92117
15- 48 FORSYTHE, CLARENCE D	B. ST. LOUIS, MO.
16- 29 FORTUNE, GARRETT REESE	D. SEPTEMBER 23, 1955 WASHINGTON, D. C.
64- 33 FOSNOW, GERALD EUGENE 'JERRY'	253 WHOOPING LOOP - ALTAMONTE SPRINGS FL 32701
21- 28 FOSS, GEORGE DUEWARD	D. NOVEMBER 10, 1969 MIAMI, FLA.
61- 35 FOSS, LAWRENCE CURTIS	P.O. BOX 775027 - STEAMBOAT SPRINGS CO 80477
88- 52 FOSSAS, EMILIO ANTHONY 'TONY'	OLD ADD: 12 ST. PETERS STREET - BOSTON MA 02130
67- 32 FOSSE, RAYMOND EARL	7950 WEST BATES RD - TRACY CA 95376
67- 33 FOSTER, ALAN BENTON	1515 STALKER CT - EL CAJON CA 92020
10- 55 FOSTER, EDWARD CUNNINGHAM	D. JANUARY 15, 1937 WASHINGTON, D.C.
13- 59 FOSTER, GEORGE 'RUBE'	D. MARCH 1, 1976 BOKOSHE, OKLA.
69- 58 FOSTER, GEORGE ARTHUR	BOX 11098 - GREENWICH CT O6830
63- 41 FOSTER, LARRY LYNN	BOX 97 - WHITEHALL MI 49461
71- 35 FOSTER, LEONARD NORRIS	36 JACOB PRICE APTS - COVINGTON KY 41012
70- 45 FOSTER, ROY	OLD ADD: 1321 E. 276TH STREET - EUCLID OH 44132
22- 36 FOTHERGILL, ROBERT ROY 'FATTY'	D. MARCH 20, 1938 DETROIT, MICH.
73- 47 FOUCAULT, STEVEN RAYMOND	1525 SW 87TH AVENUE - MIAMI FL 33174
12- 64 FOURNIER, JOHN FRANK	D. SEPTEMBER 5, 1973 TACOMA, WASH.
24- 38 FOWLER, JESSE	D. SEPTEMBER 23, 1973 COLUMBIA, S. C.
54- 28 FOWLER, JOHN ARTHUR 'ART'	3046 EAST MAIN EXTENSION - SPARTANBURG SC 29301
23- 42 FOWLER, JOSEPH CHESTER 'CHET'	D. OCTOBER 8, 1988 DALLAS, TEXAS
41- 33 FOWLER, RICHARD JOHN	D. MAY 22, 1972 ONEONTA, N. Y.
82- 44 FOWLKES, ALAN KIM	OLD ADD: 1333 N. 68TH ST #224 - SCOTTSDALE AZ 85257
42- 38 FOX, CHARLES FRANCIS	50 MOUNDS ROAD #612 - SAN MATEO CA 94402
33- 18 FOX, ERVIN 'PETE'	D. JULY 5, 1966 DETROIT, MICH.
44- 43 FOX, HOWARD FRANCIS	D. OCTOBER 9, 1955 SAN ANTONIO, TEX.
47- 35 FOX, JACOB NELSON 'NELLIE'	D. DECEMBER 1, 1975 BALTIMORE, MD.
60- 33 FOX, TERRENCE EDWARD	317 SUGAR MILL ROAD - NEW IBERIA LA 70560
25- 35 FOXX, JAMES EMORY	D. JULY 21, 1967 MIAMI, FLA.
66- 36 FOY, JOSEPH	D. OCTOBER 12, 1989 BRONX, N.Y.
53- 26 FOYTACK, PAUL EUGENE	5590 TADWORTH PL - WEST BLOOMFIELD MI 48033
72- 28 FRAILING, KENNETH DOUGLAS	4137 PRESCOTT - SARASOTA FL 33582
60- 34 FRANCIS, EARL COLEMAN	28 QUAIL HILL RD - PITTSBURGH PA 15214
22- 37 FRANCIS, RAY JAMES	D. JULY 14, 1932 ATLANTA, GA.
84- 36 FRANCO, JOHN ANTHONY	54 BAY 46TH ST - BROOKLYN NY 11214
82- 45 FRANCO, JULIO CESAR	CF 16 B.LIBRE ING CONS-SAN PEDRO DE MACORIS DOM. REP.
56- 36 FRANCONA, JOHN PATSY 'TITO'	2206 MERCER RD - NEW BRIGHTON PA 15066
81- 38 FRANCONA, TERRY JON	1912 EAST CAMPBELL TERRACE - TUCSON AZ 85718
27- 35 FRANKHOUSE, FREDERICK MELOY	D. AUGUST 17, 1989 PORT ROYAL, PA.
44- 44 FRANKLIN, JAMES WILFORD 'JACK'	105 WATER OAK COURT - PANAMA CITY BEACH FL 32407
71- 36 FRANKLIN, JOHN WILLIAM 'JAY'	OLD ADD: 2305 STRYKER AVE - VIENNA VA
41- 34 FRANKLIN, MURRAY ASHER	D. MARCH 16, 1978 HARBOR CITY, CALIF.
39- 36 FRANKS, HERMAN LOUIS	2745 COMANCHE DR-SALT LAKE CITY UT 84108
86- 52 FRASER, WILLIAM PATRICK 'WILLIE'	17 EDGEWOOD DRIVE - NEWBURGH NY 12550
31- 28 FRASIER, VICTOR PATRICK	D. JANUARY 10, 1977 JACKSONVILLE, TEX.

51

78- 45	FRAZIER, GEORGE ALLEN	1235 SOUTH 120TH EAST AVE #16 - TULSA OK 74128
47- 36	FRAZIER, JOSEPH FILMORE	519 FAIRWAY DR - BROKEN ARROW OK 74012
29- 37	FREDERICK, JOHN HENRY	D. JUNE 18, 1977 TIGARD, ORE.
42- 39	FREED, EDWIN CHARLES	840 MCDOW DR-ROCK HILL SC 29730
70- 46	FREED, ROGER VERNON	2450 MISSION ST #4 - SAN MARINO CA 91108
61- 36	FREEHAN, WILLIAM ASHLEY	4248 SUNNINGDALE - BLOOMFIELD HILLS MI 48013
21- 29	FREEMAN, ALEXANDER VERNON 'BUCK'	D. FEBRUARY 21, 1953 FORT SAM HOUSTON, TEXAS
21- 30	FREEMAN, HARVEY BAYARD	D. JANUARY 10, 1970 KALAMAZOO, MICH.
52- 31	FREEMAN, HERSHELL BASKIN	5437 SAN MARINO PL - ORLANDO FL 32807
72- 29	FREEMAN, JIMMY LEE	2144 SOUTH FULTON PL - TULSA OK 74114
27- 36	FREEMAN, JOHN EDWARD	D. APRIL 14, 1958 WASHINGTON, D. C.
89- 39	FREEMAN, LAVEL MAURICE	2501 GARDENDALE ROAD - SACRAMENTO CA 95822
59- 28	FREEMAN, MARK PRICE	6 BROOKSIDE DR - LITTLETON CO 80120
86- 53	FREEMAN, MARVIN	7314 SOUTH LOWE STREET - CHICAGO IL 60621
55- 44	FREESE, EUGENE LEWIS	6504 GLENDALE - METAIRIE LA 70003
53- 27	FREESE, GEORGE WALTER	3341 SW MARIGOLD ST - PORTLAND OR 97219
25- 36	FREEZE, CARL ALEXANDER 'JAKE'	D. APRIL 9, 1983 SAN ANGELO, TEX.
61- 37	FREGOSI, JAMES LOUIS	5730 MIDNIGHT PASS ROAD #408B - SARASOTA FL 34242
41- 35	FREIBURGER, VERNON DONALD	15490 DEVONSHIRE CIR - WESTMINSTER CA 92683
22- 38	FREIGAU, HOWARD EARL	D. JULY 18, 1932 CHATTANOOGA, TENN.
74- 38	FREISLEBEN, DAVID JAMES	2119 PEACH LN - PASADENA TX 77502
32- 27	FREITAS, ANTONIO	5648 GREENACRES WAY - ORANGEVALE CA 95662
17- 31	FRENCH, FRANK ALEXANDER 'PAT'	D. JULY 13, 1984 BATH, ME.
29- 38	FRENCH, LAWRENCE ROBERT	D. FEBRUARY 9, 1987 SAN DIEGO, CALIF.
20- 33	FRENCH, RAYMOND EDWARD	D. APRIL 3, 1978 ALAMEDA, CALIF.
65- 29	FRENCH, RICHARD JAMES 'JIM'	6960 GLORIA DR - PENNGROVE CA 94951
23- 43	FRENCH, WALTER EDWARD	D. MAY 13, 1984 MOUNTAIN HOME, ARK.
29- 39	FREY, BENJAMIN RUDOLPH	D. NOVEMBER 1, 1937 JACKSON, MICH.
80- 45	FREY, JAMES GOTTFRIED	1805 REUTER RD - TIMONIUM MD 21093
33- 19	FREY, LINUS REINHARD 'LONNY'	14424 127TH AVE SE - SNOHOMISH WA 98290
89- 40	FREY, STEVEN FRANCIS	1414 SECOND STREET PIKE - SOUTHAMPTON PA 18966
73- 48	FRIAS, JESUS MARIA 'PEPE'	CALLE 4 #9 - SAN PEDRO DE MACORIS DOM. REP.
19- 27	FRIBERG, GUSTAF BERNHARD	D. DECEMBER 8, 1958 LYNN, MASS.
52- 32	FRICANO, MARION JOHN	D. MAY 18, 1976 TIJUANA, MEX.
23- 44	FRIDAY, GRIER WILLIAM 'SKIPPER'	D. AUGUST 25, 1962 GASTONIA, N. C.
52- 33	FRIDLEY, JAMES RILEY	540 JOSMINE NW AVE - PORT CHARLOTTE FL 33952
20- 34	FRIED, ARTHUR EDWIN 'CY'	D. OCTOBER 10, 1970 SAN ANTONIO, TEX.
32- 28	FRIEDRICHS, ROBERT GEORGE	2091 NEEB ROAD - CINCINNATI OH 45238
49- 24	FRIEND, OWEN LACEY	2917 HALSTED - WICHITA KS 67204
51- 32	FRIEND, ROBERT BARTMESS	4 SALEM CIR - FOX CHAPEL PA 15238
41- 36	FRIERSON, ROBERT LAWRENCE 'BUCK'	RR 1 BOX 257 - ARTHUR CITY TX 75411
10- 56	FRILL, JOHN EDMUND	D. SEPTEMBER 28, 1918 WESTERLY, R. I.
34- 37	FRINK, FREDERICK FERDINAND	2830 JEFFERSON STREET - COCONUT GROVE FL 33133
19- 28	FRISCH, FRANK FRANCIS	D. MARCH 12, 1973 WILMINGTON, DEL.
67- 34	FRISELLA, DANIEL VINCENT	D. JANUARY 1, 1977 PHOENIX, ARIZ.
13- 60	FRITZ, HARRY KOCH	D. NOVEMBER 4, 1974 COLUMBUS, O.
75- 41	FRITZ, LAURENCE JOSEPH	2632 SCHRAGE AVE - WHITING IN 46394
55- 45	FROATS, WILLIAM JOHN	OLD ADD: 16 ASHTON RD - YONKERS NY 10705
82- 46	FROBEL, DOUGLAS STEPHEN	63 GLENRIDGE RD - OTTAWA ONT. K2G 2Z8 CAN.
87- 46	FROHWIRTH, TODD GERARD	6608 WEST CHAMBERS STREET - MILWAUKEE WI 53210
77- 55	FROST, CARL DAVID 'DAVE'	2206 OCANA DR - LONG BEACH CA 90815
78- 46	FRY, JERRY RAY	77 RUTH COURT - SPRINGFIELD IL 62704
23- 45	FRY, JOHNSON	D. APRIL 7, 1959 CARMI, ILL.
40- 23	FRYE, CHARLES ANDREW	D. MAY 25, 1945 HICKORY, N. C.
66- 37	FRYMAN, WOODROW THOMPSON	RR 1 BOX 21 - EWING KY 41039
42- 40	FUCHS, CHARLES RUDOLPH	D. JUNE 10, 1969 WEEHAWKEN, N. J.
29- 40	FUCHS, EMIL EDWIN	D. DECEMBER 5, 1961 BOSTON, MASS.
83- 59	FUENTES, MICHAEL JAY	1300 NW 122ND TERRACE - PEMBROKE PINES FL 33026
69- 59	FUENTES, MIGUEL	D. JANUARY 29, 1970 LOIZA ALDEA, P. R.
65- 30	FUENTES, RIGOBERTO PEAT 'TITO'	1080 HATTERAS - FOSTER CITY CA 94404
21- 31	FUHR, OSCAR LAWRENCE	D. MARCH 27, 1975 DALLAS, TEX.
22- 39	FUHRMAN, ALFRED GEORGE 'OLLIE'	D. JANUARY 11, 1969 PEORIA, ILL.
21- 32	FULGHUM, JAMES LAVOISIER 'DOT'	D. NOVEMBER 11, 1947 MIAMI, FLA.
79- 38	FULGHUM, JOHN THOMAS	301 S. BRYANT AVE #C200 - EDMOND OK 73034
15- 49	FULLER, FRANK EDWARD	D. OCTOBER 29, 1965 WARREN, MICH.
73- 49	FULLER, JAMES H	4215 HAITI LANE - PASADENA TX 77505
74- 39	FULLER, JOHN EDWARD	34521 CALLE MONTE - CAPISTRANO BEACH CA 92624
64- 34	FULLER, VERN GORDON	%REGISTRY,7901 24TH AVE SOUTH - MINNEAPOLIS MN 55420
21- 33	FULLERTON, CURTIS HOOPER	D. JANUARY 2, 1975 WINTHROP, MASS.
28- 36	FULLIS, CHARLES PHILIP 'CHICK'	D. MARCH 28, 1946 ASHLAND, PA.
87- 47	FULTON, WILLIAM DAVID	217 DOROTHY DRIVE - PITTSBURGH PA 15235
81- 39	FUNDERBURK, MARK CLIFFORD	4910 SILVER OAKS VILLAGE - ORLANDO FL 32808
29- 41	FUNK, ELIAS CALVIN 'LIZ'	D. JANUARY 17, 1968 OKLAHOMA CITY, OKLA.
60- 35	FUNK, FRANKLIN RAY	4452 EAST BELLVIEW ST - PHOENIX AZ 85008
86- 54	FUNK, THOMAS JAMES	2905 NE 56TH TERRACE - KANSAS CITY MO 64119
46- 30	FURILLO, CARL ANTHONY	D. JANUARY 21, 1989 STONY CREEK MILLS, PA.
22- 40	FUSSELL, FREDERICK MORRIS	D. OCTOBER 23, 1966 SYRACUSE, N. Y.
52- 34	FUSSELMAN, LESTER LEROY	D. MAY 21, 1970 CLEVELAND, O.
35- 33	GABLER, FRANK HAROLD	D. NOVEMBER 1, 1967 LONG BEACH, CAL.
59- 29	GABLER, JOHN RICHARD	8606 WEST 81ST ST - OVERLAND PARK KS 66204
58- 35	GABLER, WILLIAM LOUIS	729 POPE - ST. LOUIS MO 63147
45- 34	GABLES, KENNETH HARLIN	D. JANUARY 2, 1960 WALNUT GROVE, MO.
39- 37	GABRIELSON, LEONARD HILBOURNE	1387 GLEN DR - SAN LEANDRO CA 94577
60- 36	GABRIELSON, LEONARD GARY	24230 HILLVIEW DR - LOS ALTOS HILLS CA 94022
38- 28	GADDY, JOHN WILSON	D. MAY 3, 1966 ALBEMARLE, N. C.
51- 33	GAEDEL, EDWARD CARL	D. JUNE 19, 1961 CHICAGO, ILL.
81- 40	GAETTI, GARY JOSEPH	OLD ADD: 1420 JONQUIL STREET - CENTRALIA IL 62801
82- 47	GAFF, BRENT ALLEN	RURAL ROUTE 2 BOX 110 - ALBION IN 46701
36- 27	GAFFKE, FABIAN SEBASTIAN	4305 SOUTH PENNSYLVANIA AVE-MILWAUKEE WI 53207
63- 42	GAGLIANO, PHILIP JOSEPH	730 OAKHILL LANE - MANCHESTER MO 63021
65- 31	GAGLIANO, RALPH MICHAEL	845 DICKINSON ST - MEMPHIS TN 38107
83- 60	GAGNE, GREGORY CARPENTER	8318 17TH AVE SOUTH - BLOOMINGTON MN 55420
14- 69	GAGNIER, EDWARD J.	D. SEPTEMBER 13, 1946 DETROIT, MICH.
22- 41	GAGNON, HAROLD DENNIS 'CHICK'	D. APRIL 30, 1970 WILMINGTON, DEL.
60- 37	GAINES, ARNESTA JOE	4759 MELDON AVE - OAKLAND CA 94619
21- 34	GAINES, WILLARD ROLAND 'NEMO'	D. JANUARY 26, 1979 WARRENTON, VA.
85- 36	GAINEY, TELMANCH 'TY'	131 JERICHO ST - CHERAW SC 29520
34- 38	GALAN, AUGUST JOHN	1345 NOB HILL - PINOLE CA 94564

85- 37	GALARRAGA, ANDRES JOSE PADOVANI	BARRIO NUEVO CHAPELLIN CLEJON SOLEDAD #5-CARACAS VENEZ
77- 56	GALASSO, ROBERT JOSE	915 REED ROAD NE - SMYRNA GA 30080
33- 20	GALATZER, MILTON	D. JANUARY 29, 1976 SAN FRANCISCO, CALIF.
78- 47	GALE, RICHARD BLACKWELL	3 YORK DRIVE - DURHAM NH 03824
34- 39	GALEHOUSE, DENNIS WARD	121 HUFFMAN AVE - DOYLESTOWN OH 44230
70- 47	GALLAGHER, ALAN MITCHELL	1852 BEVERLY AVE - CLOVIS CA 93612
87- 48	GALLAGHER, DAVID THOMAS	STRIDELL, 177 APPLEGATE DRIVE - TRENTON NJ 08690
62- 43	GALLAGHER, DOUGLAS EUGENE	1690 MAPLE LN - FREMONT OH 43420
32- 29	GALLAGHER, EDWARD MICHAEL	D. DECEMBER 22, 1981 HYANNIS PORT, MASS.
15- 50	GALLAGHER, JOHN CARROLL	D. MARCH 30, 1952 NORFOLK, VA.
23- 46	GALLAGHER, JOHN LAURENCE	D. SEPTEMBER 10, 1984 GLADWYN, PA.
39- 38	GALLAGHER, JOSEPH EMMETT	2525 MCCUE #121 - HOUSTON TX 77056
22- 42	GALLAGHER, LAWRENCE KIRBY 'GIL'	D. JANUARY 6, 1957 WASHINGTON, D. C.
72- 30	GALLAGHER, ROBERT COLLINS	315 FAIR AVE - SANTA CRUZ CA 95060
42- 41	GALLE, STANLEY JOSEPH	7 NORTH REED AVE - MOBILE AL 36604
85- 38	GALLEGO, MICHAEL ANTHONY	22235 CAMINITO ZARAGOZA - LAGUNA HILLS CA 92653
12- 65	GALLIA, MELVIN ALLYS 'BERT'	D. MARCH 19, 1976 DEVINE, TEX.
31- 29	GALLIVAN, PHILIP JOSEPH	D. NOVEMBER 24, 1969 ST. PAUL, MINN.
19- 29	GALLOWAY, CLARENCE EDWARD 'CHICK'	D. NOVEMBER 7, 1969 CLINTON, S. C.
12- 66	GALLOWAY, JAMES CATO 'BAD NEWS'	D. MAY 3, 1950 FORT WORTH, TEX.
86- 55	GALVEZ, BALVINO	BATEY LABOMBA DIV PORV'IR-SAN PEDRO DE MACORIS DOM REP.
30- 34	GALVIN, JAMES JOSEPH	D. SEPTEMBER 30, 1969 MARIETTA, GA.
72- 31	GAMBLE, JOHN ROBERT	3740 AMADOR WAY - RENO NV 89502
35- 34	GAMBLE, LEE JESSE	237 JENKS AVE-PUNXATAWNEY PA 15767
69- 60	GAMBLE, OSCAR CHARLES	108 TENSAW RD - MONTGOMERY AL 36117
10- 57	GANDIL, CHARLES ARNOLD 'CHICK'	D. DECEMBER 12, 1970 CALISTOGA, CALIF.
16- 30	GANDY, ROBERT BRINKLEY	D. JUNE 19, 1945 JACKSONVILLE, FLA.
87- 49	GANT, RONALD EDWIN	512 MONTERREY - VICTORIA TX 77904
39- 39	GANTENBEIN, JOSEPH STEPHEN	535 ORANGE AVE - SOUTH SAN FRANCISCO CA 94080
76- 33	GANTNER, JAMES ELMER	BOX 156 - EDEN WI 53019
27- 37	GANZEL, FOSTER PIRIE 'BABE'	D. FEBRUARY 6, 1978 JACKSONVILLE FLA.
46- 31	GARAGIOLA, JOSEPH HENRY	6221 EAST HUNTRESS DR - PARADISE VALLEY AZ 85253
44- 45	GARBARK, NATHANIEL MICHAEL 'MIKE'	2015 QUEENS ROAD #1 - CHARLOTTE NC 28207
34- 40	GARBARK, ROBERT MICHAEL	267 JEFFERSON ST - MEADVILLE PA 16335
69- 61	GARBER, HENRY EUGENE 'GENE'	771 STONEMILL DRIVE - ELIZABETHTOWN PA 17022
56- 37	GARBER, ROBERT MITCHELL	101 ACACIA LN - REDWOOD CITY CA 94062
84- 37	GARBEY, BARBARO GARBEY	OLD ADD: 181-10 NW 56TH ST - MIAMI FL 33178
52- 35	GARBOWSKI, ALEXANDER	110 ELLIOTT ST - YONKERS NY 10705
76- 34	GARCIA, ALFONSO RAFAEL 'KIKO'	OLD ADD: 526A NORTH CIVIC DRIVE - WALNUT CREEK CA 94596
78- 48	GARCIA, DAMASO DOMINGO	SANCHEZ NO. 104 - MOCA DOMINICAN REP.
81- 41	GARCIA, DANIEL RAPHAEL	72 MEADE AVENUE - BETHPAGE NY 11714
77- 57	GARCIA, DAVID	15420 OLDE HWY 80 #129 - EL CAJON CA 92021
48- 37	GARCIA, EDWARD MIGUEL 'MIKE'	D. JANUARY 13, 1986 FAIRVIEW PARK, O.
87- 50	GARCIA, LEONARDO ANTONIO	JUAN SALTITOPA #28 E.BOLIVAL-SANTIAGO DOMINICAN REP.
87- 51	GARCIA, MIGUEL ANGEL	CARLOS DELGADO CHALBAUD BLQ6 LETRA C #6-CARACAS VENEZ
73- 50	GARCIA, PEDRO MODESTO	OLD ADD: BARRIOS PUENTO DE JOBOS-GUAYAMA PR
72- 32	GARCIA, RALPH	725 EL CENTAURO DR - EL PASO TX 79922
48- 38	GARCIA, RAMON GARCIA	FALGUERAS 256 - HAVANA CUBA
54- 29	GARCIA, VINICIO UZCANGA	R. CAMPOAMOR 805,COL ANAHUAC-MONTEREY NUEVO LEON MEX.
45- 35	GARDELLA, ALFRED STEVE	3761 NW 35TH STREET - COCONUT CREEK FL 33066
44- 46	GARDELLA, DANIEL LEWIS	16 MORSEMERE PL - YONKERS NY 10701
81- 42	GARDENHIRE, RONALD CLYDE	7701 QUAIL - WICHITA KS 67212
23- 47	GARDINER, ARTHUR CECIL	D. OCTOBER 21, 1954 COPIAGUE, N. Y.
75- 42	GARDNER, ARTHUR JUNIOR	RR 2 BOX 41 - WALNUT GROVE MS 39189
45- 36	GARDNER, GLENN MILESO	D. JULY 7, 1964 ROCHESTER, N. Y.
11- 52	GARDNER, HARRY RAY	D. AUGUST 2, 1961 CANBY, ORE.
89- 41	GARDNER, MARK ALLAN	489 BURGAN STREET - CLOVIS CA 93612
29- 42	GARDNER, RAYMOND VINCENT	D. MAY 3, 1968 FREDERICK, MD.
65- 32	GARDNER, RICHARD FRANK 'ROB'	OLD ADD: 129 CHAPIN ST - BINGHAMTON NY 13905
84- 38	GARDNER, WESLEY BRIAN	305 RUTH STREET - BENTON AR 72015
54- 30	GARDNER, WILLIAM FREDERICK	35 DAYTON RD - WATERFORD CT 06385
36- 28	GARIBALDI, ARTHUR EDWARD	D. OCTOBER 20, 1967 SACRAMENTO, CAL.
62- 44	GARIBALDI, BOB ROY	2143 OREGON AVENUE - STOCKTON CA 95204
31- 30	GARLAND, LOUIS LYMAN	BOX 492 - IDAHO FALLS ID 83401
73- 51	GARLAND, MARCUS WAYNE	8529 NEWSON STATION ROAD - NASHVILLE TN 37221
69- 62	GARMAN, MICHAEL DOUGLAS	3806 AIRPORT AVE - CALDWELL ID 83605
32- 30	GARMS, DEBS C.	D. DECEMBER 16, 1984 GLEN ROSE, TEXAS
73- 52	GARNER, PHILIP MASON	2451 LAKE VILLAGE DRIVE - KINGWOOD TX 77339
68- 26	GARR, RALPH ALLAN	7819 CHASEWAY DR - MISSOURI CITY TX 77459
82- 48	GARRELTS, SCOTT WILLIAM	206 EAST ELM - BUCKLEY IL 60918
15- 51	GARRETT, CLARENCE RAYMOND	D. FEBRUARY 11, 1977 MOUNDSVILLE, W. VA.
70- 48	GARRETT, GREGORY	OLD ADD: 14963 SANDRA - SAN FERNANDO CA 91340
66- 38	GARRETT, HENRY ADRIAN 'ADE'	BOX 201 - MANCHACA TX 78652
69- 63	GARRETT, RONALD WAYNE	716 DEAN AVE - SARASOTA FL 33577
64- 35	GARRIDO, GIL GONZALO	SHERIFF DEPT.,556 N. MCDONOUGH - DECATUR GA 30030
46- 32	GARRIOTT, CECIL VIRGIL	24612 VISTA VERDE DRIVE - MURRIETTA CA 92362
28- 30	GARRISON, CLIFFORD WILLIAM	RURAL ROUTE 1 BOX 710G - ESPARTO CA 95627
43- 49	GARRISON, ROBERT FORD	5075 65TH AVENUE NORTH - PINELLAS PARK FL 34665
31- 31	GARRITY, FRANCIS JOSEPH 'HANK'	D. SEPTEMBER 3, 1962 BOSTON, MASS.
48- 39	GARVER, NED FRANKLIN	BOX 114 - NEY OH 43549
69- 64	GARVEY, STEVEN PATRICK	13162 CAMINITO POINT DEL MAR - DEL MAR CA 92014
77- 58	GARVIN, THEODORE JARED 'JERRY'	75 ZACA LANE #100 - SAN LUIS OBISPO CA 93401
69- 65	GASPAR, RODNEY EARL	28771 PEACH BLOSSOM - MISSION VIEJO CA 92692
44- 47	GASSAWAY, CHARLES CASON	10925 WESTWOOD LAKE DR - MIAMI FL 33165
55- 46	GASTALL, THOMAS EVERETT	D. SEPTEMBER 20, 1956 CHESAPEAKE BAY, MD.
20- 35	GASTON, ALEXANDER NATHANIEL	D. FEBRUARY 8, 1979 SANTA MONICA, CALIF.
67- 36	GASTON, CLARENCE EDWIN 'CITO'	1421 GLEN BURNIE ROAD - MISSISSAUGA ONT. L5G 3C7 CAN.
24- 39	GASTON, NATHANIEL MILTON 'MILT'	5064 WHITE OAK COURT - BRADENTON FL 34207
78- 49	GATES, JOSEPH DANIEL	1517 EAST NINETEENTH AVE - GARY IN 46407
81- 43	GATES, MICHAEL GRANT	4005 PATTE ANN - MEMPHIS TN 38116
63- 43	GATEWOOD, AUBREY LEE	5 PINE TREE LOOP - NORTH LITTLE ROCK AR 72116
78- 50	GAUDET, JAMES JENNINGS	969 UNDERWOOD DRIVE - MACON GA 31210
25- 35	GAUTREAU, WALTER PAUL 'DOC'	D. AUGUST 23, 1970 SALT LAKE CITY, UTAH
36- 29	GAUTREAUX, SIDNEY ALLEN	D. APRIL 19, 1980 MORGAN CITY, LA.
20- 36	GAW, GEORGE JOSEPH 'CHIPPY'	D. MAY 26, 1968 BOSTON, MASS.
23- 48	GAZELLA, MICHAEL	D. SEPTEMBER 11, 1978 ODESSA, TEX.
47- 37	GEARHART, LLOYD WILLIAM	206 HOME AVE - XENIA OH 45385
23- 49	GEARIN, DENNIS JOHN 'DINTY'	D. MARCH 11, 1959 PROVIDENCE, R. I.

42- 42	GEARY, EUGENE FRANCIS JOSEPH 'HUCK'	D. JANUARY 27, 1981 CUBA, N. Y.
18- 21	GEARY, ROBERT NORTON	D. JANUARY 31, 1980 CINCINNATI, O.
71- 37	GEBHARD, ROBERT HENRY	117 MARQUETTE AVE -NORTH MANKATO MN 56001
47- 38	GEBRIAN, PETER	811 SW SOUTHWEST DRIVE #207 - STUART FL 34997
72- 33	GEDDES, JAMES LEE	RURAL ROUTE 4, 6524 SEEDS ROAD - GROVE CITY OH 43123
39- 40	GEDEON, ELMER JOHN	D. APRIL 20, 1944 - ST. POL, FRANCE
13- 61	GEDEON, ELMER JOSEPH	D. MAY 19, 1941 SAN FRANCISCO, CALIF.
80- 46	GEDMAN, RICHARD LEO	32 LAFAYETTE - WORCESTER MA 01608
39- 41	GEE, JOHN ALEXANDER	D. JANUARY 23, 1988 CORTLAND, N. Y.
23- 50	GEHRIG, HENRY LOUIS 'LOU'	D. JUNE 2, 1941 RIVERDALE, N. Y.
24- 40	GEHRINGER, CHARLES LEONARD	32301 LAHSER RD - BIRMINGHAM MI 48010
37- 39	GEHRMAN, PAUL ARTHUR	D. OCTOBER 23, 1986 BEND, ORE.
58- 36	GEIGER, GARY MERLE	OLD ADD: 7327 SOUTH 69TH EAST CT - TULSA OK 74133
78- 51	GEISEL, JOHN DAVID 'DAVE'	59 COSHWAY PLACE - TONAWANDA NY 14150
69- 66	GEISHERT, VERNON WILLIAM	RR 4 - RICHLAND CENTER WI 53581
29- 43	GELBERT, CHARLES MAGNUS	D. JANUARY 13, 1967 EASTON, PA.
64- 36	GELNAR, JOHN RICHARD	GENERAL DELIVERY - MANGUM OK 73547
22- 43	GENEWICH, JOSEPH EDWARD	D. DECEMBER 21, 1985 LOCKPORT, N. Y.
50- 30	GENOVESE, GEORGE MICHAEL	11474 ERWIN ST - HOLLYWOOD CA 91606
57- 22	GENTILE, JAMES EDWARD	1016 NEPTUNE - EDMOND OK 73034
43- 50	GENTILE, SAMUEL CHRISTOPHER	123 CENTRAL AVE-EVERETT MA 02149
69- 67	GENTRY, GARY EDWARD	205 STAR ROUTE TWO - CAVE CREEK AZ 85331
54- 31	GENTRY, HARVEY WILLIAM	109 EATON LN - BRISTOL TN 37620
43- 51	GENTRY, JAMES RUFFUS	4929 FULP ST - WINSTON SALEM NC 27105
55- 47	GEORGE, ALEX THOMAS	1001 ROMANY ROAD - KANSAS CITY MO 64113
35- 35	GEORGE, CHARLES PETER 'GREEK'	RURAL ROUTE 2 BOX 46 - BRUNSWICK GA 31520
11- 53	GEORGE, THOMAS EDWARD 'LEFTY'	D. MAY 13, 1955 YORK, PA.
38- 29	GEORGY, OSCAR JOHN	905 VOURAY STREET #C - KENNER LA 70065
36- 30	GERAGHTY, BENJAMIN RAYMOND	D. JUNE 18, 1963 JACKSONVILLE, FLA.
62- 45	GERARD, DAVID FREDERICK	318 DOONE PL - FAIRLESS HILLS PA 19030
85- 39	GERBER, CRAIG STUART	4297 PERSHING AVENUE - SAN BERNARDINO CA 92407
14- 70	GERBER, WALTER	D. JUNE 19, 1951 COLUMBUS, O.
62- 46	GERBERMAN, GEORGE ALOIS	1501 MICHAEL - EL CAMPO TX 77437
88- 53	GEREN, ROBERT PETER	2710 BAY CANYON COURT - SAN DIEGO CA 92117
74- 40	GERHARDT, ALLEN RUSSELL 'RUSTY'	2003 HEATHERWAY - ARLINGTON TX 76012
86- 56	GERHART, HAROLD KENNETH 'KEN'	707 ELLIOT STREET - MURFREESBORO TN 37130
43- 52	GERHEAUSER, ALBERT	D. MAY 28, 1972 SPRINGFIELD, MO.
27- 38	GERKEN, GEORGE HERBERT	D. OCTOBER 23, 1977 ARCAIDA, CALIF.
45- 37	GERKIN, STEPHEN PAUL	D. NOVEMBER 8, 1978 BAY PINES, FLA.
38- 30	GERLACH, JOHN GLENN	5721 DOGWOOD PL - MADISON WI 53705
19- 30	GERNER, EDWIN FREDERICK	D. MAY 15, 1970 PHILADELPHIA, PA.
52- 36	GERNERT, RICHARD EDWARD	1420 ROSE VIRGINIA RD - READING PA 19615
69- 68	GERONIMO, CESAR FRANCISCO	TEFADA FLO. #56 - SANTO DOMINGO DOMINICAN REP.
13- 62	GERVAIS, LUCIEAN EDWARD 'LEFTY'	D. OCTOBER 19, 1950 LOS ANGELES, CALIF.
45- 38	GETTEL, ALLEN JONES	5620 PARLIAMENT DR - VIRGINIA BEACH VA 23452
10- 58	GEYER, JACOB BOWMAN 'RUBE'	D. OCTOBER 12, 1962 WAHKON, MINN.
24- 41	GEYGAN, JAMES EDWARD 'CHAPPIE'	D. MARCH 16, 1966 COLUMBUS, O.
16- 31	GHARRITY, EDWARD PATRICK 'PATSY'	D. OCTOBER 10, 1966 BELOIT, WIS.
83- 61	GHELFI, ANTHONY PAUL	3414 GENEVA LANE - LACROSSE WI 54601
58- 37	GIALLOMBARDO, ROBERT PAUL	60 BAY 41ST STREET - BROOKLYN NY 11214
11- 54	GIANNINI, JOSEPH FRANCIS	D. SEPTEMBER 26, 1942 SAN FRANCISCO, CALIF.
25- 38	GIARD, JOSEPH OSCAR	D. JULY 10, 1956 WORCESTER, MASS.
60- 38	GIBBON, JOSEPH CHARLES	RR 2 - NEWTON MS 39345
84- 39	GIBBONS, JOHN MICHAEL	95 DUNCAN ST #A - BOLLING AIR FORCE BASE DC 20366
62- 47	GIBBS, JERRY DEAN 'JAKE'	225 OXFORD CIRCLE - OXFORD MS 38655
24- 42	GIBSON, CHARLES GRIFFIN	713 RIDGECREST RD - LAGRANGE GA 30241
13- 63	GIBSON, FRANK GILBERT	D. APRIL 27, 1961 AUSTIN, TEX.
67- 36	GIBSON, JOHN RUSSELL 'RUSS'	495 GARDNERS NOOK RD - SWANSEA MA 02777
79- 39	GIBSON, KIRK HAROLD	1082 OAK POINTE DR - PONTIAC MI 48054
88- 54	GIBSON, PAUL MITCHELL	OLD ADD: 27 SURREY DRIVE - CENTER MORICHES NY 11934
59- 30	GIBSON, ROBERT	215 BELLEVIEW BLVD SOUTH - BELLEVIEW NE 68005
83- 62	GIBSON, ROBERT LOUIS	261 POWELL ROAD - SPRINGFIELD PA 19064
26- 30	GIBSON, SAMUEL BRAXTON	D. JANUARY 31, 1983 HIGH POINT, N. C.
37- 40	GICK, GEORGE EDWARD	3 BRADY CT - LAFAYETTE IN 47905
87- 52	GIDEON, BYRON BRETT	P.O. BOX 822 - GEORGETOWN TX 78627
75- 43	GIDEON, JAMES LESLIE	5623 BRAESVALLEY - HOUSTON TX 77035
13- 64	GIEBEL, JOSEPH HENRY	D. MARCH 17, 1981 SILVER SPRING, MD.
39- 42	GIEBELL, FLOYD GEORGE	RR 1 BOX 111, LAURELWOOD DR - WILKESBORO NC 28697
54- 32	GIEL, PAUL ROBERT	13400 MCGINTZ RD - MINNEAPOLIS MN 55343
59- 31	GIGGIE, MCANDREW THOMAS	89 MCANDREW RD - BRAINTREE MA 02184
67- 37	GIGON, NORMAN PHILLIP	205 PAXINOSA RD EAST - EASTON PA 18042
67- 38	GIL, TOMAS GUSTAVO 'GUS'	URB. LAUDAVETA,VEREDA 15#1 - CARACAS VENEZUELA S.A.
42- 43	GILBERT, ANDREW	803 WALNUT DR-LATROBE PA 15650
40- 24	GILBERT, CHARLES MADER	D. AUGUST 13, 1983 NEW ORLEANS, LA.
59- 32	GILBERT, DREW EDWARD 'BUDDY'	1913 BELCARO DR - KNOXVILLE TN 37918
50- 31	GILBERT, HAROLD JOSEPH 'TOOKIE'	D. JUNE 23, 1967 NEW ORLEANS, LA.
72- 34	GILBERT, JOE DENNIS	1952 NORTH BOWIE ST - JASPER TX 75951
14- 71	GILBERT, LAWRENCE WILLIAM	D. FEBRUARY 17, 1965 NEW ORLEANS, LA.
85- 40	GILBERT, MARK DAVID	OLD ADD: 3151 N. COURSE LN #201 - POMPANO BEACH FL 3306
28- 38	GILBERT, WALTER JOHN	D. SEPTEMBER 8, 1959 DULUTH, MINN.
72- 35	GILBREATH, RODNEY JOE	1438 RIDGELAND WAY - LILBURN GA 30247
71- 38	GILBRETH, WILLIAM FREEMAN	690 EAST NORTH 16TH ST - ABILENE TX 79601
59- 33	GILE, DONALD LOREN	570 SEAHORSE LANE - REDWOOD CITY CA 94065
81- 44	GILES, BRIAN JEFFREY	8607 GLEN HAVEN ST - SAN DIEGO CA 92125
20- 37	GILHAM, GEORGE LEWIS	D. APRIL 25, 1937 LANSDOWNE, PA.
11- 55	GILHOOLEY, FRANK PATRICK	D. JULY 11, 1959 TOLEDO, O.
19- 31	GILL, EDWARD JAMES	27 FEDERICO CIR - STOUGHTON MA 02072
37- 41	GILL, GEORGE LLOYD	RAYMOND MS 39154
23- 51	GILL, HAROLD EDWARD	D. AUGUST 1, 1932 BROCKTON, MASS.
27- 39	GILL, JOHN WESLEY	D. DECEMBER 26, 1984 NASHVILLE, TENN.
40- 25	GILLENWATER, CARDEN EDISON	49 COUNTRY CLUB DR - LARGO FL 33543
23- 52	GILLENWATER, CLARAL LEWIS	D. FEBRUARY 26, 1978 PENSACOLA, FLA.
22- 44	GILLESPIE, JOHN PATRICK	D. FEBRUARY 15, 1954 VALLEJO, CAL.
42- 44	GILLESPIE, PAUL ALLEN	D. AUGUST 11, 1970 ANNISTON, ALA.
44- 48	GILLESPIE, ROBERT WILLIAM	123 CAROL RD - WINSTON SALEM NC 27106
53- 28	GILLIAM, JAMES WILLIAM 'JUNIOR'	D. OCTOBER 8, 1978 INGLEWOOD, CALIF.
67- 39	GILLIFORD, PAUL GANT	7 WOODLAND DR - MALVERN PA 19355
27- 40	GILLIS, GRANT	D. FEBRUARY 4, 1981 THOMASVILLE, ALA.

DAVE DRAVECKY

SHAWON DUNSTON

SHAWON DUNSTON

LEO DUROCHER

CARL ERSKINE

SID FERNANDEZ

HERMAN FRANKS

JOE HAUSER

#18   CHRIS JAMES   OF

CHRIS JAMES

DOUG JONES

14- 72 GILMORE, ERNEST GROVER	D. NOVEMBER 25, 1919 SIOUX CITY, IA.
44- 49 GILMORE, LEONARD PRESTON	RR 2 BOX 213C - JONES OK 73049
68- 27 GILSON, HAROLD	OLD ADD: 1509 JULIE ST #B - BERKELEY CA 94703
15- 52 GINGRAS, JOSEPH ELZEAD JOHN	D. SEPTEMBER 6, 1947 JERSEY CITY, N.J.
14- 73 GINN, TINSLEY RUCKER	D. AUGUST 30, 1931 ATLANTA, GA.
48- 40 GINSBERG, MYRON NATHAN 'JOE'	243 COLDWAY DRIVE #B9 - PUNTA GORDA FL 33950
44- 50 GIONFRIDDO, ALBERT FRANCIS	64 BRISTOL PLACE - GOLETA CA 93117
53- 29 GIORDANO, THOMAS ARTHUR	1026 CARLL DR - BAYSHORE NY 11706
10- 59 GIRARD, CHARLES AUGUST	D. AUGUST 6, 1936 BROOKLYN, N. Y.
89- 42 GIRARDI, JOSEPH ELLIOTT	812 OAKWOOD BOULEVARD - EAST PEORIA IL 61611
36- 31 GIULIANI, ANGELO JOHN	1985 NORFOLK AVE - ST PAUL MN 55116
62- 48 GIUSTI, DAVID JOHN	524 CLAIR DR - PITTSBURGH PA 15241
46- 33 GLADD, JAMES WALTER	D. NOVEMBER 8, 1977 LONG BEACH, CALIF.
83- 63 GLADDEN, CLIFTON DANIEL 'DAN'	888 BROOK GROVE LN - CUPERTINO CA 95014
61- 38 GLADDING, FRED EARL	4721 MACMONT CIR - POWELL TN 37819
44- 51 GLADU, ROLAND EDWIN	OLD ADD: 4368 BERRIE - MONTREAL QUEBEC
20- 38 GLAISER, JOHN BURKE	D. MARCH 7, 1959 HOUSTON, TEX.
25- 39 GLASS, THOMAS JOSEPH	D. DECEMBER 15, 1981 GREENSBORO, N. C.
13- 65 GLAVENICH, LUKE FRANK	D. MAY 22, 1935 STOCKTON, CALIF.
49- 25 GLAVIANO, THOMAS GIATANO	23905 HITCHING POST RD - SONORA CA 95370
87- 53 GLAVINE, THOMAS MICHAEL	89 TREBLE COVE ROAD - BILLERICA MA 01862
20- 39 GLAZNER, CHARLES FRANKLIN 'WHITEY'	D. JUNE 6, 1989 ORLANDO, FLA.
20- 40 GLEASON, JOSEPH PAUL	18 EXCHANGE - PHELPS NY 14532
63- 44 GLEASON, ROY WILLIAM	1115 WILCOX AVE - MONTEREY PARK CA 91754
16- 32 GLEASON, WILLIAM PATRICK	D. JANUARY 9, 1957 HOLYOKE, MASS.
79- 40 GLEATON, JERRY DON	121 GARMAN DR - EARLY TX 76801
36- 32 GLEESON, JAMES JOSEPH	545 EAST 129TH TER - KANSAS CITY MO 64145
19- 32 GLEICH, FRANK ELMER	D. MARCH 27, 1949 COLUMBUS, O.
20- 41 GLENN, BURDETTE 'BOB'	D. JUNE 3, 1977 RICHMOND, CALIF.
15- 53 GLENN, HARRY MELVILLE	D. OCTOBER 12, 1918 ST. PAUL, MINN.
60- 39 GLENN, JOHN	32 EDGEWATER BEACH APTS - BEVERLY NJ 08010
32- 31 GLENN, JOSEPH CHARLES	D. MAY 6, 1985 TUNKHANNOCK, PA.
30- 25 GLIATTO, SALVADOR MICHAEL	6031D ARBOLEDA WAY - DALLAS TX 75248
14- 74 GLOCKSON, NORMAN STANLEY	D. AUGUST 5, 1955 MAYWOOD, ILL.
39- 43 GLOSSOP, ALBAN	120 SOUTH RUBY LANE - FAIRVIEW HEIGHTS IL 62208
75- 44 GLYNN, EDWARD PAUL	157 SAN CARLOS STREET - TOMS RIVER NJ 08757
49- 26 GLYNN, WILLIAM VINCENT	6916 51ST - SAN DIEGO CA 92120
74- 41 GODBY, DANNY RAY	RR 2 BOX 28A - CHAPMANVILLE WV 25508
72- 36 GODDARD, JOSEPH HAROLD	302 RIDGE PARK DR - BECKLEY WV 25801
22- 45 GOEBEL, EDWIN	D. AUGUST 12, 1959 BROOKLYN, N. Y.
60- 40 GOETZ, JOHN HARDY	3253 MYDDLETON - TROY MI 48084
72- 37 GOGGIN, CHARLES FRANCIS	6008 ROBERT E. LEE DR - NASHVILLE TN 37215
70- 49 GOGOLEWSKI, WILLIAM JOSEPH	1522 GRAHAM AVE - OSHKOSH WI 54901
60- 41 GOLDEN, JAMES EDWARD	8630 SW 10TH - TOPEKA KS 66606
10- 60 GOLDEN, ROY KRAMER	D. OCTOBER 4, 1961 NORWOOD, O.
28- 39 GOLDMAN, JONAH JOHN	D. AUGUST 17, 1980 PALM BEACH, FLA.
49- 27 GOLDSBERRY, GORDON FREDERICK	22772 BAY FRONT LN - LAKE FOREST CA 92630
26- 31 GOLDSMITH, HAROLD EUGENE	%GENE GOLDSMITH,8 GRANDVIEW TER - ESSEX CT 06426
32- 32 GOLDSTEIN, ISADORE	944 FLANDERS T - DELRAY BEACH FL 33446
43- 53 GOLDSTEIN, LESLIE ELMER 'LONNIE'	6516 SABROSA CT WEST - FORT WORTH TX 76133
62- 49 GOLDY, PURNAL WILLIAM	1318 CHERRYVILLE RD - LITTLETON CO 80120
41- 37 GOLETZ, STANLEY	OLD ADD: 14513 SOUTH ROBINSON - OKLAHOMA CITY OK 73170
49- 28 GOLIAT, MIKE MITCHEL	2650 GREEN LAWN DR - SEVEN HILLS OH 44131
72- 38 GOLTZ, DAVID ALLAN	RR 6 BOX 230 - FERGUS FALLS MN 56537
22- 46 GOLVIN, WALTER GEORGE	D. JUNE 11, 1973 GARDENA, CALIF.
35- 36 GOMEZ, JOSE LUIS RODRIGUEZ 'CHILE'	GUATEMALA 2950, COL. GUERRERO - NUEVA LAREDO TAM. MEX.
74- 42 GOMEZ, LUIS JOSE	676 CHESTERFIELD DRIVE - LAWRENCEVILLE GA 30245
44- 52 GOMEZ, PRESTON MARTINEZ	23 BELCOURT DRIVE SOUTH - NEWPORT BEACH CA 92660
84- 40 GOMEZ, RANDALL SCOTT 'ROCKY'	1200 EAST HILLSDALE #44B - FOSTER CITY CA 94404
53- 30 GOMEZ, RUBEN	T2-8 IQUAZA PARK GARDENS-RIO PIEDRAS PR 00928
30- 26 GOMEZ, VERNON LOUIS 'LEFTY'	D. FEBRUARY 17, 1989 GREENBRAE, CALIF.
60- 42 GONDER, JESSE LEMAR	5937 WHITNEY ST - OAKLAND CA 94609
79- 41 GONZALES, DANIEL DAVID	OLD ADD: 12319 CULLMAN AVE-WHITTIER CA 90604
18- 22 GONZALES, EUSEBIO MIGUEL	D. FEBRUARY 14, 1976 HAVANA, CUBA
37- 42 GONZALES, JOE MADRID	30715 COCOS PALM AVE - HOMELAND CA 92348
77- 59 GONZALES, JULIO CESAR	BO. RIO CANAS, BOX 86 - CAGUAS PR 00625
49- 29 GONZALES, JULIO ENRIQUE	OLD ADD: CALIXTO GARCIA 37 - ORIENTE CUBA
84- 41 GONZALES, RENE ADRIAN	755 ORANGEWOOD - COVINA CA 91723
55- 48 GONZALES, WENCESLAO O'REILLY 'VINCE'	D. MARCH 11, 1981 CIUDAD DEL CARMEN,CAMP.MEX
60- 43 GONZALEZ, ANDRES ANTONIO 'TONY'	8011 SW 196TH TER - MIAMI FL 33189
84- 42 GONZALEZ, DENIO MARIANO	CALLE SAN LUIS #131, GUALEY - SANTO DOMINGO DOM. REP.
88- 55 GONZALEZ, GERMAN JOSE	OLD ADD: RIO CARIBE VENEZUELA S.A.
72- 39 GONZALEZ, JOSE FERNANDO	URB VISTA ANGEL CALLE 4-A-48-ARECIBO PR 00612
85- 41 GONZALEZ, JOSE RAFAEL	CALLE ANTERA MOTA #35 - PUERTO PLATA DOMINICAN REP.
89- 43 GONZALEZ, JUAN ALBERTO	EXT. CATONI A-9 - VEGA BAJA PR 00763
12- 67 GONZALEZ, MIGUEL ANGEL CORDERO 'MIKE'	D. FEBRUARY 19, 1977 HAVANA, CUBA
76- 35 GONZALEZ, ORLANDO EUGENE	OLD ADD: 2352 SW 26TH LN - MIAMI FL
63- 45 GONZALEZ, PEDRO	104 GEN CABRAL - SAN PEDRO DE MACORIS DOM. REP.
29- 44 GOOCH, CHARLES FURMAN	D. MAY 30, 1982 LANHAM, MD.
21- 35 GOOCH, JOHN BEVERLEY	D. MAY 15, 1975 NASHVILLE, TENN.
15- 54 GOOCH, LEE CURRIN	D. MAY 18, 1966 RALEIGH, N.C.
10- 61 GOOD, RALPH NELSON	D. NOVEMBER 24, 1965 WATERVILLE, ME.
28- 40 GOODELL, JOHN HENRY WILLIAM 'BILL'	10 LITTLE DEER, BELLA VISTA - BENTONVILLE AR 72714
84- 43 GOODEN, DWIGHT EUGENE	6755 30TH STREET SOUTH - ST PETERSBURG FL 33712
35- 37 GOODMAN, IVAL RICHARD	D. NOVEMBER 25, 1984 CINCINNATI, O.
47- 39 GOODMAN, WILLIAM DALE	D. OCTOBER 1, 1984 SARASOTA, FLA.
70- 50 GOODSON, JAMES EDWARD 'ED'	RR 2 BOX 12-O - INDEPENDENCE VA 24348
14- 75 GOODWIN, CLAIRE VERNON 'PEP'	D. FEBRUARY 15, 1972 OAKLAND, CALIF.
75- 45 GOODWIN, DANNY KAY	3628 MEADOWGLEN VILLAGE LN #G - ATLANTA GA 30340
48- 41 GOODWIN, JAMES PATRICK	11533 FRANCETTA LN - ST. LOUIS MO 63138
16- 33 GOODWIN, MARVIN MARDO	D. OCTOBER 21, 1925 HOUSTON, TES.
46- 34 GOOLSBY, RAYMOND DANIEL	548 LAKE DOE BLVD - APOPKA FL 32703
65- 33 GOOSSEN, GREGORY BRYANT	12321 BLIX ST - NORTH HOLLYWOOD CA 91607
55- 49 GORBOUS, GLEN EDWARD	D. JUNE 12, 1990 CALGARY, ALBERTA
86- 57 GORDON, DONALD THOMAS	87-13 95TH STREET - WOODHAVEN NY 11421
38- 31 GORDON, JOSEPH LOWELL	D. APRIL 14, 1978 SACRAMENTO, CALIF.
77- 60 GORDON, MICHAEL WILLIAM	161 BISHOP ST - BROCKTON MA 02401
41- 38 GORDON, SIDNEY	D. JUNE 17, 1975 NEW YORK, N.Y.

56

88- 56	GORDON, THOMAS	1052 HIGHLANDS AVENUE - AVON PARK FL 33828
21- 36	GORDONIER, RAYMOND CHARLES	D. NOVEMBER 15, 1960 ROCHESTER, N. Y.
54- 33	GORIN, CHARLES PERRY	2617 FISET DR - AUSTIN TX 78731
77- 61	GORINSKI, ROBERT JOHN	BOX 133 - CALUMET PA 15621
52- 37	GORMAN, HERBERT ALLEN	D. APRIL 5, 1953 SAN DIEGO, CAL.
37- 43	GORMAN, HOWARD PAUL	D. APRIL 29, 1984 HARRISBURG, PA.
52- 38	GORMAN, THOMAS ALOYSIUS	474 WEST VLY STRM BLVD - VALLEY STREAM NY 11581
39- 44	GORMAN, THOMAS DAVID	D. AUGUST 11, 1986 CLOSTER, N. J.
81- 45	GORMAN, THOMAS PATRICK	2523 NORTH BOONES FERRY RD - WOODBURN OR 97071
41- 39	GORNICKI, HENRY FRANK	5510 TAMBERLANE DRIVE - PALM BEACH GARDENS FL 33418
40- 26	GORSICA, JOHN JOSEPH PERRY	BOX 1518 - BECKLEY WV 25801
57- 23	GORYL, JOHN ALBERT	3282 YOTHERS RD - APOPKA FL 32703
63- 46	GOSGER, JAMES CHARLES	1527 LYONS STREET - PORT HURON MI 48060
21- 37	GOSLIN, LEON ALLEN 'GOOSE'	D. MAY 15, 1971 BRIDGETON, N. J.
62- 50	GOSS, HOWARD WAYNE	9817 HOUGHTON AVENUE - SANTE FE SPRINGS CA 90670
72- 40	GOSSAGE, RICHARD MICHAEL 'GOOSE'	10565 VIACHA WAY - SAN DIEGO CA 92124
13- 66	GOSSETT, JOHN STAR 'DICK'	D. OCTOBER 6, 1962 MASSILLON, O.
60- 44	GOTAY, JULIO ENRIQUE	JUAN JOSE CARTAGENA ST #L34 - PONCE PR 00731
82- 49	GOTT, JAMES WILLIAM	1840 LOS ROBLES AVE - SAN MARINO CA 91108
12- 68	GOULAIT, THEODORE LEE	D. JULY 15, 1936 ST. CLAIR, MICH.
16- 34	GOULD, ALBERT FRANK	D. AUGUST 8, 1982 SAN JOSE, CALIF.
44- 53	GOULISH, NICHOLAS EDWARD	D. MAY 15, 1984 YOUNGSTOWN, O.
10- 62	GOWDY, HARRY 'HANK'	D. AUGUST 1, 1966 COLUMBUS, O.
72- 41	GOWELL, LAWRENCE CLYDE	45 SEVENTH ST - AUBURN ME 04210
89- 44	GOZZO, MAURO PAUL	156 NEWTON STREET - KENSINGTON CT 06037
69- 69	GRABARKEWITZ, BILLY CORDELL	5440 HARVEST HILL #225 - DALLAS TX 75230
58- 38	GRABER, RODNEY BLAINE	4674 MOUNT ARMET DR - SAN DIEGO CA 92117
29- 45	GRABOWSKI, ALFONS FRANCIS	D. OCTOBER 29, 1966 MEMPHIS, N. Y.
24- 43	GRABOWSKI, JOHN PATRICK	D. MAY 23, 1946 ALBANY, N. Y.
32- 33	GRABOWSKI, REGINALD JOHN	D. APRIL 2, 1955 SYRACUSE, N. Y.
38- 32	GRACE, JOSEPH LAVERNE	D. SEPTEMBER 18, 1969 MURPHYSBORO, ILL.
88- 57	GRACE, MARK EUGENE	OLD ADD: 14882 FOXCROFT - TUSTIN CA 92680
78- 52	GRACE, MICHAEL LEE	3514 SHELBY - PONTIAC MI 48054
29- 46	GRACE, ROBERT EARL	D. DECEMBER 22, 1980 PHOENIX, ARIZ.
13- 67	GRAF, FREDERICK GOTTLIEB	D. OCTOBER 4, 1979 CHATTANOOGA, TENN.
57- 24	GRAFF, MILTON EDWARD	3602 TANGLEWOOD DRIVE - BRYAN TX 77802
34- 41	GRAHAM, ARTHUR WILLIAM 'SKINNY'	D. JULY 10, 1967 ARLINGTON, MASS.
10- 63	GRAHAM, BERT	D. JUNE 17, 1971 COTTONWOOD, ARIZ.
79- 42	GRAHAM, DANIEL JAY	BOX 728 - WINKELMAN AZ 85298
14- 76	GRAHAM, DAWSON FRANK 'TINY'	D. DECEMBER 29, 1962 NASHVILLE, TENN.
46- 35	GRAHAM, JOHN BERNARD	1521 INTERLACHEN #258K - SEAL BEACH CA 90740
24- 44	GRAHAM, KYLE	D. DECEMBER 1, 1973 OAK GROVE, ALA.
83- 64	GRAHAM, LEE WILLIAM	OLD ADD: BOX 1012 - BELLEVIEW FL 32620
22- 47	GRAHAM, ROY VINCENT	D. APRIL 26, 1933 MANILLA, PHILLIPINES
63- 47	GRAHAM, WAYNE LEON	13218 SOUTH THORNTREE - HOUSTON TX 77015
66- 39	GRAHAM, WILLIAM ALBERT	RR 2 BOX 275 - FLEMINGSBURG KY 41041
68- 28	GRAMLY, BERT THOMAS 'TOM'	16485 REDWOOD CIR, RR 1 - MCKINNEY TX 75069
54- 34	GRAMMAS, ALEXANDER PETER	3432 OAKDALE DR - BIRMINGHAM AL 35223
27- 41	GRAMPP, HENRY ERCHARDT	D. MARCH 24, 1986 NEW YORK, N. Y.
68- 29	GRANGER, WAYNE ALLEN	BOX 134, ALDRICH AVE - HUNTINGTON MA 01050
23- 53	GRANT, GEORGE ADDISON	D. MARCH 25, 1986 MONTGOMERY, ALA.
42- 45	GRANT, JAMES CHARLES	D. JULY 8, 1970 ROCHESTER, MINN.
23- 54	GRANT, JAMES RONALD	D. NOVEMBER 30, 1985 DES MOINES, IOWA
58- 39	GRANT, JAMES TIMOTHY 'MUDCAT'	1020 SOUTH DUNSMUIR - LOS ANGELES CA 90019
84- 44	GRANT, MARK ANDREW	123 FAIRLANE DR - JOLIET IL 60435
83- 65	GRANT, THOMAS RAYMOND	BOX 113 - MENDON MA 01756
22- 48	GRANTHAM, GEORGE FARLEY	D. MARCH 16, 1954 KINGMAN, ARIZ.
83- 66	GRAPENTHIN, RICHARD RAY	RURAL ROUTE 1 - LINN GROVE IA 51033
48- 42	GRASMICK, LOUIS JUNIOR	6715 QUAD AVE - BALTIMORE MD 21237
46- 36	GRASSO, NEWTON MICHAEL 'MICKEY'	D. OCTOBER 15, 1975 MIAMI FLA.
45- 39	GRATE, DONALD	1245 NW 203RD ST - MIAMI FL 33169
26- 32	GRAVES, JOSEPH EBENEZER	D. DECEMBER 22, 1980 SALEM, MASS.
27- 42	GRAVES, SAMUEL SIDNEY 'SID'	D. DECEMBER 26, 1983 BIDDEFORD, ME.
64- 37	GRAY, DAVID ALEXANDER	2755 WEST SAINT TROPAZ - TUCSON AZ 85713
77- 62	GRAY, GARY GEORGE	BOX 98 - LAPLACE LA 70068
88- 58	GRAY, JEFFREY EDWARD	OLD ADD: 120 EAST PASSAGE - COLUMBIA SC 29212
54- 35	GRAY, JOHN LEONARD	6320 SW 138TH COURT #206 - MIAMI FL 33183
82- 50	GRAY, LORENZO	3263 PALM AVE #A - LYNWOOD CA 90262
37- 44	GRAY, MILTON MARSHALL	D. JUNE 30, 1969 QUINCY, FLA.
45- 40	GRAY, PETER	203 PHILLIPS ST - NANTICOKE PA 18634
58- 40	GRAY, RICHARD BENJAMIN	503 SOUTH HAMPTON - ANAHEIM CA 92804
24- 45	GRAY, SAMUEL DAVID	D. APRIL 16, 1953 MCKINNEY, TEX.
12- 69	GRAY, STANLEY OSCAR	D. OCTOBER 11, 1964 SNYDER, TEX.
46- 37	GRAY, THEODORE GLENN	21 EAST WASHINGTON - CLARKSTON MI 48016
59- 34	GRBA, ELI	OLD ADD: 6533 7TH AVE #21 - PHOENIX AZ 85013
54- 36	GREASON, WILLIAM HENRY	4536 HILLMAN DR SW - BIRMINGHAM AL 35221
84- 45	GREEN, CHRISTOPHER DEWAYNE	3740 59TH AVE WEST - BRADENTON FL 33507
81- 46	GREEN, DAVID ALEJANDRO	COLINIA MANAGUA GRUPO H#47 - MANAGUA NICARAGUA C.A.
59- 35	GREEN, ELIJAH JERRY 'PUMPSIE'	BERKELEY H.S. 2246 MILVA-BERKELEY CA 94704
59- 36	GREEN, FRED ALLAN	BOX 161 - TITUSVILE NJ 08560
86- 58	GREEN, GARY ALLEN	4185 SOUTH PARADISE ROAD #1032 - LAS VEGAS NV 89109
57- 25	GREEN, GENE LEROY	D. MAY 23, 1981 ST. LOUIS, MO.
60- 45	GREEN, GEORGE DALLAS 'DALLAS'	RURAL ROUTE 1 BOX 227A - WEST GROVE PA 19390
35- 38	GREEN, HARVEY GEORGE	D. JULY 24, 1970 FRANKLIN, LA.
24- 46	GREEN, JOSEPH HENRY	D. FEBRUARY 4, 1972 BRYN MAWR, PA.
28- 41	GREEN, JULIUS FOUST 'JUNE'	D. MARCH 19, 1974 GLENDORA, CALIF.
57- 26	GREEN, LEONARD CHARLES	18693 SUNSET ST - DETROIT MI 48234
63- 48	GREEN, RICHARD LARRY	525 38TH - RAPID CITY SD 57701
30- 27	GREENBERG, HENRY BENJAMIN	D. SEPTEMBER 4, 1986 BEVERLY HILLS, CALIF.
43- 42	GREENE, ALTAR ALPHONSE	18294 MARLOWE - DETROIT MI 48235
89- 45	GREENE, IRA THOMAS 'TOMMY'	P.O. BOX 224 - BRUNSWICK NC 28424
24- 47	GREENE, NELSON GEORGE	D. APRIL 6, 1983 LEBANON, PA.
24- 48	GREENFIELD, KENT	D. MARCH 14, 1978 GUTHRIE, KY.
52- 39	GREENGRASS, JAMES RAYMOND	2930 OCTAVIA CIR - MARIETTA GA 30062
85- 42	GREENWELL, MICHAEL LEWIS	954 EAST HYACINTH STREET - NORTH FORT MYERS FL 33903
54- 37	GREENWOOD, ROBERT CHANDLER	OLD ADD: 35800 MOLINA COURT - FREMONT CA 94536
77- 63	GREER, BRIAN	OLD ADD: 914 CARLSON DRIVE - BREA CA 92621
13- 68	GREGG, DAVID CHARLES	D. NOVEMBER 12, 1965 CLARKSTON, WASH.

```
43- 54  GREGG, HAROLD DANA                          KEOUGHS RR 1 #1 - BISHOP CA 93514
11- 56  GREGG, SYLVEANUS AUGUSTUS 'VEAN'            D. JULY 29, 1964 ABERDEEN, WASH.
87- 54  GREGG, WILLIAM THOMAS                       3924 OLD VINEYARD ROAD #35 - WINSTON SALEM NC 27104
12- 70  GREGORY, FRANK ERNST                        D. NOVEMBER 5, 1955 BELOIT, WIS.
64- 38  GREGORY, GROVER LEROY 'LEE'                 6456 NORTH TEILMAN - FRESNO CA 93705
11- 57  GREGORY, HOWARD WATTERSON                   D. MAY 30, 1970 TULSA, OKLA.
32- 34  GREGORY, PAUL EDWIN                         P.O. BOX 921 - STARKVILLE MS 39759
71- 39  GREIF, WILLIAM BRILEY                       807 EAST 31ST - AUSTIN TX 78705
40- 27  GREMP, LOUIS EDWARD 'BUDDY'                 205 FLOYD AVENUE #2 - MODESTO CA 95350
19- 33  GREVELL, WILLIAM                            D. JUNE 21, 1923 PHILADELPHIA, PA.
70- 51  GRICH, ROBERT ANTHONY                       206 PROSPECT AVE - LONG BEACH CA 90803
20- 42  GRIESENBECK, CARLOS PHILIPPE TIMOTHY        D. MARCH 25, 1953 SAN ANTONIO, TEX.
70- 52  GRIEVE, THOMAS ALAN                         3206 HERITAGE CT - ARLINGTON TX 76016
46- 38  GRIFFETH, LEON CLIFFORD                     BOX 335 - PATTERSON NY 12563
73- 53  GRIFFEY, GEORGE KENNETH 'KEN'               3942 MACK ROAD #9 - FAIRFIELD OH 45014
89- 46  GRIFFEY, GEORGE KENNETH, JR. 'KEN'          5385 CROSS BRIDGE DRIVE - WESTCHESTER OH 45069
76- 36  GRIFFIN, ALFREDO CLAUDINO                   B#3 B HATOMAYOR ING CONS-SAN PEDRO DE MACORIS DOM. REP.
70- 53  GRIFFIN, DOUGLAS LEE                        992 WILLOW BROOK COURT - WINTER HAVEN FL 33884
17- 32  GRIFFIN, FRANCIS ARTHUR 'PUG'               D. OCTOBER 12, 1951 COLORADO SPRINGS COLO.
19- 34  GRIFFIN, IVY MOORE                          D. AUGUST 25, 1957 GAINESVILLE, FLA.
11- 58  GRIFFIN, JAMES LINTON 'HANK'                D. FEBRUARY 11, 1950 TERRELL, TEX.
28- 42  GRIFFIN, MARTIN JOHN                        D. NOVEMBER 19, 1951 LOS ANGELES, CAL.
79- 44  GRIFFIN, MICHAEL LEROY                      1620 GROVE AVE - WOODLAND CA 95695
14- 77  GRIFFIN, PATRICK RICHARD                    D. JUNE 7, 1927 YOINGSTOWN, O.
69- 70  GRIFFIN, THOMAS JAMES                       13147 AVENIDA LAVELENCIA - POWAY CA 92064
22- 49  GRIFFITH, BARTHOLOMEW JOSEPH                D. MAY 5, 1973 BISHOP, CALIF.
63- 49  GRIFFITH, ROBERT DERRELL 'DERRELL'         201 EAST CENTRAL - ANADARKO OK 73005
13- 69  GRIFFITH, THOMAS HERMAN                     D. APRIL 13, 1967 CINCINNATI, O.
56- 38  GRIGGS, HAROLD LLOYD                        OLD ADD: 2781 NE 2ND AVE - POMPANO BEACH FL 33064
23- 55  GRIGSBY, DENVER CLARENCE                    D. NOVEMBER 10, 1973 SAPULPA, OKLA.
66- 40  GRILLI, GUIDO JOHN                          4636 LORECE - MEMPHIS TN 38117
75- 46  GRILLI, STEPHEN JOSEPH                      3040 WALPOLE LN - BALDWINSVILLE NY 13027
54- 38  GRIM, ROBERT ANTON                          7118 CODY STREET - SHAWNEE MISSION KS 66203
16- 35  GRIMES, BURLEIGH ARLAND                     D. DECEMBER 6, 1985 CLEAR LAKE, WIS.
31- 32  GRIMES, EDWARD ADELBERT                     D. OCTOBER 4, 1974 CHICAGO, ILL.
38- 33  GRIMES, OSCAR RAY JR.                       25151 BROOKPARD RD #203 - NORTH OLMSTED OH 44070
20- 43  GRIMES, OSCAR RAY SR.                       D. MAY 25, 1953 MINERVA, O.
20- 44  GRIMES, ROY AUSTIN                          D. SEPTEMBER 13, 1954 HANOVERTON, O.
16- 36  GRIMM, CHARLES JOHN                         D. NOVEMBER 15, 1983 SCOTTSDALE, ARIZ.
89- 47  GRIMSLEY, JASON ALAN                        RURAL ROUTE 6 BOX 195 - CLEVELAND TX 77327
51- 34  GRIMSLEY, ROSS ALBERT                       1538 FRAYSER BLVD - MEMPHIS TN 38127
71- 40  GRIMSLEY, ROSS ALBERT II                    39 JUDGES LN - TOWSON MD 21204
12- 71  GRINER, DONALD DEXTER 'DAN'                 D. JUNE 3, 1950 BISHOPVILLE, S.C.
34- 42  GRISSOM, LEO THEO                           GENERAL DELIVERY - PARKER AZ 85344
89- 48  GRISSOM, MARQUIS DEON                       RED OAK GA 30272
46- 39  GRISSOM, MARVIN EDWARD                      13975 NOBLE WAY - RED BLUFF CA 96080
52- 40  GROAT, RICHARD MORROW                       320 BEACH ST - PITTSBURGH PA 15218
56- 39  GROB, CONRAD GEORGE                         5047 ENCHANTED VALLEY RD - CROSS PLAINS WI 53528
41- 40  GRODZICKI, JOHN                             5927 RIVERSIDE DRIVE - DAYTONA BEACH FL 32019
12- 72  GROH, HENRY KNIGHT 'HEINIE'                 D. AUGUST 22, 1968 CINCINNATI,O.
19- 35  GROH, LEWIS CARL                            D. OCTOBER 20, 1960 ROCHESTER, N. Y.
41- 41  GROMEK, STEPHEN JOSEPH                      21455 CORSAUT - BIRMINGHAM MI 48010
55- 50  GROSS, DONALD JOHN                          9007 LIGHTHOUSE DRIVE - LAKE MI 48632
25- 40  GROSS, EWELL 'TURKEY'                       D. JANUARY 22, 1936 DALLAS, TEX.
73- 54  GROSS, GREGORY EUGENE                       16 RABBIT RUN ROAD - MALVERN PA 19355
83- 67  GROSS, KEVIN FRANK                          OLD ADD: 402 4TH STREET - FILLMORE CA 93015
76- 37  GROSS, WAYNE DALE                           45 LEONARD COURT - DANVILLE CA 94526
30- 28  GROSSKLOS, HOWARD HOFFMAN 'HOWDIE'          310 LLWYD'S LANE - VERO BEACH FL 32960
52- 41  GROSSMAN, HARLEY JOSEPH                     1032 OAKWOOD LN - EVANSVILLE IN 47710
63- 50  GROTE, GERALD WAYNE                         OLD ADD: RR 10 BOX 243 - SAN ANTONIO TX 78213
47- 40  GROTH, ERNEST WILLIAM                       BLACKHAWK-NEGLY RD - BEAVER FALLS PA 15010
46- 40  GROTH, JOHN THOMAS                          177 QUEENS LN - PALM BEACH FL 33480
40- 28  GROVE, ORVAL LEROY                          2743 POPE AVE - SACRAMENTO CA 95821
25- 41  GROVE, ROBERT MOSES 'LEFTY'                 D. MAY 22, 1975 NORWALK, O.
13- 70  GROVER, CHARLES BERT                        D. MAY 24, 1971 EMMETT TWP., CALHOUN CO.,MICH
16- 37  GROVER, ROY ARTHUR                          D. FEBRUARY 7, 1978 MILWAUKIE, ORE.
12- 73  GRUBB, HARVEY HARRISON                      D. JANUARY 25, 1970 CORPUS CHRISTI, TEX.
72- 42  GRUBB, JOHN MAYWOOD                         3920 COGBILL RD - RICHMOND VA 23234
20- 45  GRUBBS, THOMAS DILLARD                      D. JANUARY 28, 1986 MOUNT STERLING, KY.
31- 33  GRUBE, FRANKLIN THOMAS                      D. JULY 2, 1945 NEW YORK, N. Y.
84- 46  GRUBER, KELLY WAYNE                         7601 BASIL COVE - AUSTIN TX 78750
55- 51  GRUNWALD, ALFRED HENRY                      7120 BOTHWELL RD - RESEDA CA 91335
38- 34  GRYSKA, SIGMUND STANLEY                     4527 SOUTH DRAKE-CHICAGO IL 60632
61- 39  GRZENDA, JOSEPH CHARLES                     GOULDSBORO PA 18424
82- 51  GUANTE, CECILIO (MAGALLANE)                 JALISCO 67 SIMON BOLIVAR-SANTO DOMINGO DOMINICAN REP.
84- 47  GUBICZA, MARK STEVEN                        593 MONASTERY AVE - PHILADELPHIA PA 19128
29- 47  GUDAT, MARVIN JOHN                          D. MARCH 2, 1954 LOS ANGELES, CAL.
37- 45  GUERRA, FERMIN ROMERO 'MIKE'                4025 NW 3RD ST - MIAMI FL 33126
73- 55  GUERRERO, MARIO MIGUEL                      CALLE DUARTE #450 - SANTO DOMINGO DOMINICAN REP.
78- 53  GUERRERO, PEDRO                             535 S. PLYMOUTH BLVD - LOS ANGELES CA 90020
84- 48  GUETTERMAN, ARTHUR LEE 'LEE'                RR 7 BOX 190A MARTEL EST. EAST - LENOIR CITY TN 37771
75- 47  GUIDRY, RONALD AMES                         109 CONWAY - LAFAYETTE LA 70507
85- 43  GUILLEN, OSWALDO JOSE                       CLE SAN JOSE #52,EL RODEO DEL TUY-MIRANDO VENEZ
64- 39  GUINDON, ROBERT JOSEPH                      THORNHILL INN - JACKSON NH 03846
68- 30  GUINN, DRANNON EUGENE 'SKIP'                6060 MONTEVERDE DRIVE - SAN JOSE CA 95120
46- 41  GUINTINI, BENJAMIN JOHN                     OLD ADD: 735 SHADOW RIDGE #4 - ROSEVILLE CA 95678
40- 29  GUISE, WITT ORISON                          D. AUGUST 13, 1968 NORTH LITTLE ROCK, ARK.
16- 38  GUISTO, LOUIS JOSEPH                        D. OCTOBER 15, 1989 NAPA, CALIF.
78- 54  GULDEN, BRADLEY LEE                         BOX 254 (LIME STREET) - CARVER MN 55315
70- 54  GULLETT, DONALD EDWARD                      RURAL ROUTE 2 - MALONETON KY 41158
23- 56  GULLEY, THOMAS JEFFERSON                    D. NOVEMBER 24, 1966 ST. CHARLES, ARK.
30- 29  GULLIC, TEDD JOSEPH                         BOX 703 - WEST PLAINS MO 65775
79- 45  GULLICKSON, WILLIAM LEE                     300 BRENTVALE LANE - BRENTWOOD TN 37027
82- 52  GULLIVER, GLENN JAMES                       8123 CORTLAND - ALLEN PARK MI 48101
35- 39  GUMBERT, HARRY EDWARD                       BOX 377 - WIMBERLEY TX 78676
82- 53  GUMPERT, DAVID LAWRENCE                     921 CHAMBERS ST - SOUTH HAVEN MI 49090
36- 33  GUMPERT, RANDALL PENNINGTON                 MONOCACY STATION PA 19542
16- 39  GUNKEL, WOODROW WILLIAM 'RED'               D. APRIL 19, 1954 NORTH CHICAGO, ILL.
```

11- 59	GUNNING, HYLAND	D. MARCH 28, 1975 TOGUS, ME.
70- 55	GURA, LARRY CYRIL	P.O. BOX 94 - LITCHFIELD PARK AZ 85340
11- 60	GUST, ERNEST HERMAN FRANK	D. OCTOBER 26, 1945 MAUPIN, ORE.
39- 45	GUSTINE, FRANK WILLIAM	1130 GREENTREE RD - PITTSBURGH PA 15220
72- 43	GUTH, CHARLES HENRY 'BUCKY'	202 MORRIS DR - SALISBURY MD 21801
89- 49	GUTHRIE, MARK ANDREW	BOX 394 - VENICE FL 34284
67- 40	GUTIERREZ, CESAR DARIO	PINTO A MISERIA #100 - CARACAS VENEZUELA S.A.
83- 68	GUTIERREZ, JOAQUIN FERNANDO	AMBERES 3ER CALLEJON # 29-35-CARTAGENA COLOMBIA S.A.
36- 34	GUTTERIDGE, DONALD JOSEPH	804 LAKEVIEW DR - PITTSBURG KS 66762
85- 44	GUZMAN, JOSE ALBERTO	BO. PLAYA #28 - SANTA ISABEL PR 00757
69- 71	GUZMAN, SANTIAGO DONOVAN	ENS RESTAUROSIN M4TA#12-SAN PEDRO DE MACORIS DOM. REP.
81- 47	GWOSDZ, DOUGLAS WAYNE	14503 ROYAL HILL DR - HOUSTON TX 77083
82- 54	GWYNN, ANTHONY KEITH	3524 DELTA - LONG BEACH CA 90810
87- 55	GWYNN, CHRISTOPHER KARLTON	3524 DELTA AVENUE - LONG BEACH CA 90810
33- 21	GYSELMAN, RICHARD RENALD	5212 54TH AV SOUTH - SEATTLE WA 98118
37- 46	HAAS, BERTHOLD JOHN	4604 KENSINGTON AVE - TAMPA FL 33629
15- 55	HAAS, BRUNO PHILIP	D. JUNE 5, 1952 SARASOTA, FLA.
76- 38	HAAS, BRYAN EDMUND 'MOOSE'	9961 EAST DOUBLETREE RANCH RD - SCOTTSDALE AZ 85258
57- 27	HAAS, GEORGE EDWIN 'EDDIE'	100 HILLMONT DR, RR 10 - PADUCAH KY 42001
25- 42	HAAS, GEORGE WILLIAM 'MULE'	D. JUNE 30, 1974 NEW ORLEANS, LA.
51- 35	HABENICHT, ROBERT JULIUS	D. DECEMBER 24, 1980 RICHMOND, VA.
85- 45	HABYAN, JOHN GABRIEL	122 PLUNKETT ST - BRENTWOOD NY 11717
32- 35	HACK, STANLEY CAMFIELD	D. DECEMBER 15, 1979 DIXON, ILL.
71- 41	HACKER, RICHARD WARREN	930 EAST MAIN - BELLEVILLE IL 62220
48- 43	HACKER, WARREN LOUIS	BOX 41 - LENZBURG IL 62255
52- 42	HADDIX, HARVEY	2105 CHEVIOT HILLS DRIVE - SPRINGFIELD OH 45505
26- 33	HADLEY, IRVING DARIUS 'BUMP'	D. FEBRUARY 15,1963 LYNN, MASS.
58- 41	HADLEY, KENT WILLIAM	549 HYDE - POCATELLO ID 83201
15- 56	HAEFFNER, WILLIAM BERNHARD	D. JANUARY 27, 1982 DELAWARE CO., PA.
43- 55	HAEFNER, MILTON ARNOLD 'MICKEY'	504 JACKSON-NEW ATHENS IL 62264
24- 49	HAFEY, CHARLES JAMES 'CHICK'	D. JULY 2, 1973 CALISTOGA, CAL.
35- 40	HAFEY, DANIEL ALBERT 'BUD'	D. JULY 27, 1986 SACRAMENTO, CALIF.
39- 46	HAFEY, THOMAS FRANCIS	7747 TERRACE DR - EL CERRITO CA 94532
11- 61	HAGEMAN, KURT MORITZ 'CASEY'	D. APRIL 1, 1964 NEW BEDFORD, PA.
83- 69	HAGEN, KEVIN EUGENE	OLD ADD: 15232 SE 272ND #15 - KENT WA 98031
68- 31	HAGUE, JOE CLARENCE	13202 LARKBROOK - SAN ANTONIO TX 78233
69- 72	HAHN, DONALD ANTONE	1046 BOISE DR - CAMPBELL CA 95008
52- 43	HAHN, FREDERICK ALOYS	D. AUGUST 16, 1984 VALHALLA, N.Y.
40- 30	HAHN, RICHARD FREDERICK	1616 ORIOLE AVE - ORLANDO FL 32803
19- 36	HAID, HAROLD AUGUSTINE	D. AUGUST 13, 1952 LOS ANGELES, CAL.
23- 57	HAINES, HENRY LUTHER 'HINKEY'	D. JANUARY 9, 1979 SHARON HILL, PA.
18- 23	HAINES, JESSE JOSEPH 'POP'	D. AUGUST 5, 1978 DAYTON, O.
73- 56	HAIRSTON, JERRY WAYNE	3770 FIRST STREET WEST - BIRMINGHAM AL 35207
69- 73	HAIRSTON, JOHN LOUIS	3612 4TH ST WEST - BIRMINGHAM AL 35207
51- 36	HAIRSTON, SAMUEL	3800 CENTERPLACE WEST - BIRMINGHAM AL 35207
13- 71	HAISLIP, JAMES CLIFTON	D. JANUARY 22, 1970 DALLAS, TEX.
41- 42	HAJDUK, CHESTER	6838 CONCORD LN-NILES IL 60648
19- 37	HALAS, GEORGE STANLEY	D. OCTOBER 31, 1983 CHICAGO, ILL.
31- 34	HALE, ARVEL ODELL	D. JUNE 9, 1980 EL DORADO, ARK.
14- 78	HALE, GEORGE WAGNER	D. NOVEMBER 1, 1945 WICHITA, KAN.
74- 43	HALE, JOHN STEVEN	2715 CLEMSON COURT - BAKERSFIELD CA 93306
55- 52	HALE, ROBERT HOUSTON	200 THOMAS PARKWAY #3M - PARK RIDGE IL 60068
20- 46	HALE, SAMUEL DOUGLAS	D. SEPTEMBER 6, 1974 WHEELER, TEX.
89- 50	HALE, WALTER WILLIAM 'CHIP'	867 AUBREY APRK COURT #2 - HERMOSA BEACH CA 90254
15- 57	HALEY, RAYMOND TIMOTHY	D. OCTOBER 8, 1973 BRADENTON, FLA.
74- 44	HALICKI, EDWARD LOUIS	273 HICKORY ST - KEARNEY NJ 07032
81- 48	HALL, ALBERT	1628 SPAULDING RD - BIRMINGHAM AL 35211
86- 59	HALL, ANDREW CLARK 'DREW'	RR 1 BOX 195 - RUSH KY 41168
11- 62	HALL, HERBERT ERNEST	D. JULY 18, 1948 SEATTLE, WASH.
18- 24	HALL, HERBERT SILAS	D. JULY 1, 1970 FRESNO, CAL.
43- 56	HALL, IRVIN GLADSTONE	1153 DEANWOOD RD - BALTIMORE MD 21234
63- 51	HALL, JIMMIE RANDOLPH	4001 LADY MARIAN DRIVE - WILSON NC 27893
48- 44	HALL, JOHN SYLVESTER	300 BELL DR - MIDWEST CITY OK 73110
10- 64	HALL, MARCUS	D. FEBRUARY 24, 1915 JOPLIN, MO.
81- 49	HALL, MELVIN	RR 1 ROUTE 90 - CAYAGA NY 13034
52- 44	HALL, RICHARD WALLACE	2131 FOLKSTONE RD - TIMONIUM MD 21093
49- 30	HALL, ROBERT LEWIS	D. MARCH 12, 1983 ST. PETERSBURG, FLA.
68- 32	HALL, THOMAS EDWARD	3592 LILLIAN AVENUE - RIVERSIDE CA 92504
13- 72	HALL, WILLIAM BERNARD	D. AUGUST 15, 1947 NEWPORT, KY.
54- 39	HALL, WILLIAM LEE	D. JANUARY 1, 1986 MOULTRIE, GA.
25- 43	HALLAHAN, WILLIAM ANTHONY	D. JULY 8, 1981 BINGHAMTON, N. Y.
61- 40	HALLER, THOMAS FRANK	75315 MONTECITO DRIVE - INDIAN WELLS CA 92210
40- 31	HALLETT, JACK PRICE	D. JUNE 11, 1982 TOLEDO, O.
16- 40	HALLIDAY, NEWTON REESE	D. APRIL 6, 1918 GREAT LAKES, ILL.
11- 63	HALLINAN, EDWARD S	D. AUGUST 24, 1940 SAN FRANCISCO, CALIF.
14- 79	HALT, ALVA WILLIAM	D. JANUARY 22, 1973 SANDUSKY, O.
22- 50	HAMANN, ELMER JOSEPH 'DOC'	D. JANUARY 11, 1973 MILWAUKEE, WIS.
71- 42	HAMBRIGHT, ROGER DEE	OLD ADD: 523 NORTH 39 TH ST - SPRINGFIELD OR
26- 34	HAMBY, JAMES SANFORD	1117 SOUTH 11TH ST - SPRINGFIELD IL 62703
88- 59	HAMILTON, DARRYL QUINN	757 WEST MCKINLEY STREET - BATON ROUGE LA 70802
72- 44	HAMILTON, DAVID EDWARD	9464 CHERRY HILLS LN - SAN RAMON CA 94583
11- 64	HAMILTON, EARL ANDREW	D. NOVEMBER 17, 1968 ANAHEIM, CALIF.
62- 51	HAMILTON, JACK EDWIN	HCR 2 BOX 1035 - HOLLISTER MO 65672
86- 60	HAMILTON, JEFFREY ROBERT	OLD ADD: 6216 KNOLLWOOD - FLINT MI 48507
61- 41	HAMILTON, STEVE ABSHER	RR 5 - MOREHEAD KY 40351
52- 45	HAMILTON, THOMAS BALL	D. NOVEMBER 29, 1973 TYLER, TEX.
57- 28	HAMLIN, KENNETH LEE	RURAL ROUTE 1 BOX 280 - GERMFASK MI 49836
33- 22	HAMLIN, LUKE DANIEL 'HOT POTATO'	D. FEBRUARY 18, 1978 CLARE, MICH.
70- 56	HAMM, PETER WHITFIELD	525 LOCKHART BULCH RD - SANTA CRUZ CA 95060
81- 50	HAMMAKER, CHARLTON ATLEE	2739 STUBB BLUFF RD - KNOXVILLE TN 37932
82- 55	HAMMOND, STEVEN BEN	OLD ADD: 2555 FOX HALL LN - COLLEGE PARK GA 30349
15- 58	HAMMOND, WALTER CHARLES 'JACK'	D. MARCH 4, 1942 KENOSHA, WIS.
44- 54	HAMNER, GRANVILLE WILBUR	OLD ADD: 410 EAST SHORE DR - CLEARWATER FL 33515
46- 42	HAMNER, RALPH CONANT	BOX 236 - BRADLEY AR 71826
45- 41	HAMNER, WESLEY GARVIN 'GAR'	RR 2 BOX 91 - MECHANICSVILLE VA 23111
74- 45	HAMPTON, ISAAC BERNARD 'IKE'	1604 LEE ST - CAMDEN SC 29020
55- 53	HAMRIC, ODBERT HERMAN 'BERT'	D. AUGUST 8, 1984 SPRINGBORO, O.

ID	Name	Address / Status
43- 57	HAMRICK, RAYMOND BERNARD	3125 SHANE DRIVE - RICHMOND CA 94806
40- 32	HANCKEN, MORRIS MEDLOCK 'BUDDY'	BOX 288 - HOUSTON TX 77001
49- 31	HANCOCK, FRED JAMES	D. MARCH 12, 1986 CLEARWATER, FLA.
78- 55	HANCOCK, RONALD GARRY	2217 GREEN HILLS DR - VALRICO FL 33594
70- 57	HAND, RICHARD ALLEN	4227 OAK SPRINGS DRIVE - ARLINGTON TX 76016
11- 65	HANDIBOE, ALOYSIUS JAMES 'MIKE'	D. JANUARY 31, 1953 SAVANNAH, GA.
46- 43	HANDLEY, EUGENE LOUIS	8656 FRESNO DR #506A - HUNTINGTON BEACH CA 92646
36- 35	HANDLEY, LEE ELMER	D. APRIL 8, 1970 PITTSBURGH, PA.
64- 40	HANDRAHAN, JAMES VERNON 'VERN'	36 NEWLAND CRESCENT - CHARLOTTETOWN PEI C1A 4H5 CAN.
65- 34	HANDS, WILLIAM ALFRED	WILLOW TERRACE - ORIENT NY 11957
53- 31	HANEBRINK, HARRY ALOYSIUS	10400 RENFREW DR - ST LOUIS MO 63137
22- 51	HANEY, FRED GIRARD	D. NOVEMBER 9, 1977 BEVERLY HILLS, CALIF.
66- 41	HANEY, WALLACE LARRY	BOX 97 - BARBOURSVILLE VA 22923
14- 80	HANFORD, CHARLES JOSEPH	D. JULY 19, 1963 TRENTON, N.J.
27- 43	HANKINS, DONALD WAYNE	D. MAY 16, 1963 WINSTON-SALEM, N. C.
61- 42	HANKINS, JAY NELSON	9309 EAST 84TH TER - RAYTOWN MO 64138
13- 73	HANLEY, JOSEPH PATRICK	D. MAY 1, 1961 ELMHURST, N. Y.
75- 48	HANNA, PRESTON LEE	5555 MAYFAIR DR - PENSACOLA FL 32506
18- 25	HANNAH, JAMES HARRISON 'TRUCK'	D. APRIL 27, 1982 FOUNTAIN VALLEY, CALIF.
76- 39	HANNAHS, GERALD ELLIS	26 LORNA DR - LITTLE ROCK AR 72205
62- 52	HANNAN, JAMES JOHN	3907 CHERRY HILL WAY - ANNANDALE VA 22003
39- 47	HANNING, LOY VERNON	D. JULY 8, 1986 ANACONDA, MO.
44- 55	HANSEN, ANDREW VIGGO	362 YORKTOWN CIR - ATLANTIS FL 33462
51- 34	HANSEN, DOUGLAS WILLIAM	16706 EAST ROCKY KNOLL RD - HACIENDA HEIGHTS CA 91745
74- 46	HANSEN, ROBERT JOSEPH	19 NORTH KELSEY AVE - EVANSVILLE IN 47711
58- 42	HANSEN, RONALD LAVERN	13602 ALLISTON DR - BALDWIN MD 21013
30- 30	HANSEN, ROY EMIL FREDERICK 'SNIPE'	D. SEPTEMBER 11, 1978 CHICAGO, ILL.
18- 26	HANSEN, ROY INGLOF	D. FEBRUARY 9, 1977 BELOIT, WIS.
43- 58	HANSKI, DONALD THOMAS	D. SEPTEMBER 2, 1957 WORTH, ILL.
21- 38	HANSON, EARL SYLVESTER 'OLLIE'	D. AUGUST 19, 1951 CLIFTON, N.J.
88- 60	HANSON, ERIK BRIAN	735 RIDGE ROAD - KINNELON NJ 07405
13- 74	HANSON, HARRY	B. ST. LOUIS, MO.
42- 46	HANYZEWSKI, EDWARD MICHAEL	RR 1 BOX 120 - VERGAS MN 56587
23- 58	HAPPENNY, JOHN CLIFFORD	D. DECEMBER 29, 1988 CORAL SPRINGS, FLA.
28- 43	HARDER, MELVIN LEROY	130 CENTER ST #6A - CHARDON OH 44024
18- 27	HARDGROVE, WILLIAM HENRY 'PAT'	D. JANUARY 26, 1973 JACKSON, MISS.
67- 41	HARDIN, JAMES WARREN	235 BEMONTE ROAD - WEST PALM BEACH FL 33405
52- 46	HARDIN, WILLIAM EDGAR	1930 WEST SAN MARCOS BLVD #409 - SAN MARCOS CA 90269
13- 75	HARDING, CHARLES HAROLD	D. OCTOBER 30, 1971 BOLD SPRINGS, TENN.
58- 43	HARDY, CARROLL WILLIAM	3052 FULTON CIRCLE - BOULDER CO 80301
51- 38	HARDY, FRANCIS JOSEPH 'RED'	5620 NORTH 12TH ST - PHOENIX AZ 85014
74- 47	HARDY, HOWARD LAWRENCE 'LARRY'	2402 DRAWBRIDGE RD - ARLINGTON TX 76012
89- 51	HARDY, JOHN GRAYDON	9713 NORTH NEW RIVER CANAL RD - PLANTATION FL 33324
65- 35	HARGAN, STEVEN LOWELL	2502 MORANGO TRAIL - PALM SPRINGS CA 92262
80- 47	HARGESHEIMER, ALAN ROBERT	116 SOUTH DONALD - ARLINGTON HEIGHTS IL 60004
79- 46	HARGIS, GARY LYNN	157 GEMINI AVE - LOMPOC CA 93436
13- 76	HARGRAVE, EUGENE FRANKLIN 'BUBBLES'	D. FEBRUARY 23, 1969 CINCINNATI, O.
23- 59	HARGRAVE, WILLIAM MCKINLEY 'PINKY'	D. OCTOBER 3, 1942 FT. WAYNE, IND.
23- 60	HARGREAVES, CHARLES RUSSELL	D. MAY 9, 1979 NEPTUNE, N. J.
74- 48	HARGROVE, DUDLEY MICHAEL 'MIKE'	RR 3 BOX 94C - PERRYTON TX 79070
88- 61	HARKEY, MICHAEL ANTHONY	23930 STRANGE CREEK DRIVE - DIAMOND BAR CA 91765
10- 65	HARKNESS, FREDERICK HARVEY 'SPECS'	D. MAY 18, 1952 COMPTON, CALIF.
61- 43	HARKNESS, THOMAS WILLIAM 'TIM'	OLD ADD: 222 PEARSON RD #42 - OSHAWA ONT. L1G 7C6 CAN.
75- 49	HARLOW, LARRY DUANE	OLD ADD: 1002 TOWNSEND AVE - AZTEC NM
41- 43	HARMAN, WILLIAM BELL	9 GUYENNE RD - WILMINGTON DE 19807
54- 40	HARMON, CHARLES BYRON	6035A RIDGEACRE DR - CINCINNATI OH 45237
67- 42	HARMON, TERRY WALTER	OAKWOOD DR - MEDFORD NJ 08055
88- 62	HARNISCH, PETER THOMAS	2 CORNFIELD LANE - COMMACK NY 11725
79- 47	HARPER, BRIAN DAVID	6 SILVERLEAF DR - ROLLING HILLS CA 90274
16- 41	HARPER, GEORGE WASHINGTON	D. AUGUST 18, 1978 MAGNOLIA, ARK.
13- 77	HARPER, HARRY CLAYTON	D. APRIL 23, 1963 LAYTON, N.J.
15- 59	HARPER, JOHN WESLEY	D. JUNE 18, 1927 HALSTEAD, KAN.
80- 48	HARPER, TERRY JOE	1685 DORRIS RD - DOUGLAS GA 30134
62- 53	HARPER, THOMAS	5 COW HILL ROAD - SHARON MA 02067
11- 66	HARPER, WILLIAM HOMER	D. JUNE 17, 1951 SOMERVILLE, TENN.
69- 74	HARRAH, COLBERT DALE 'TOBY'	6120 TEN MILE BRIDGE ROAD - FORT WORTH TX 76115
69- 75	HARRELL, JOHN ROBERT	756 ERIE CIR - MILPITAS CA 95035
12- 74	HARRELL, OSCAR MARTIN 'SLIM'	D. APRIL 30, 1971 HILLSBORO, TEX.
35- 41	HARRELL, RAYMOND JAMES	D. JANUARY 28, 1984 ALEXANDRIAS, LA.
55- 54	HARRELL, WILLIAM	253 MOUNT HOPE DRIVE - ALBANY NY 12202
65- 36	HARRELSON, DERRELL MCKINLEY 'BUD'	25 FALCON DR - HAUPPAUGE NY 11787
63- 52	HARRELSON, KENNETH SMITH 'HAWK'	150 CROSSWAYS PARK WEST - WOODBURY NY 11797
68- 33	HARRELSON, WILLIAM CHARLES	2440 SPRUCE - BAKERSFIELD CA 93301
13- 78	HARRINGTON, ANDREW FRANCIS	D. NOVEMBER 12, 1938 MALDEN, MASS.
25- 44	HARRINGTON, ANDREW MATTHEW	D. JANUARY 26, 1979 BOISE, IDAHO
63- 53	HARRINGTON, CHARLES MICHAEL 'MIKE'	RR 7 BOX 626 - HATTIESBURG MS 39401
53- 32	HARRINGTON, WILLIAM WOMBLE	17 CLEVELAND SCHOOL RD - GARNER NC 27529
67- 43	HARRIS, ALONZO	7753 S. HOOPER - LOS ANGELES CA 90001
25- 46	HARRIS, ANTHONY SPENCER	D. JULY 3, 1982 MINNEAPOLIS, MINN.
14- 81	HARRIS, BENJAMIN FRANKLIN	D. APRIL 29, 1927 ST. LOUIS, MO.
55- 55	HARRIS, BOYD GAIL	9008 WEIR STREET - MANASSAS VA 22110
41- 44	HARRIS, CHALMER LUMAN 'LUM'	RR 1 BOX 280 - VINCENT AL 35178
48- 45	HARRIS, CHARLES 'BUBBA'	P. O. BOX 159 - NOBLETON FL 34263
25- 45	HARRIS, DAVID STANLEY	D. SEPTEMBER 18, 1973 ATLANTA, GA.
81- 51	HARRIS, GREG ALLEN	11248 BARBI LANE - LOS ALAMITOS CA 90720
88- 63	HARRIS, GREGORY WADE	RURAL ROUTE 2 BOX 290 - PITTSBORO NC 27312
36- 36	HARRIS, HERBERT BENJAMIN	545 WOODMAR TERRACE - CRYSTAL LAKE IL 60014
68- 34	HARRIS, JAMES WILLIAM	114 WEST BRANDYWINE CIRCLE - WILMINGTON NC 28403
79- 48	HARRIS, JOHN THOMAS	3609 LINKWOOD - CLOVIS NM 88101
14- 82	HARRIS, JOSEPH	D. DECEMBER 10, 1959 RENTON, PA.
88- 64	HARRIS, LEONARD ANTHONY	3210 NW TENTH AVENUE - MIAMI FL 33127
40- 33	HARRIS, MAURICE ALFRED 'MICKEY'	D. APRIL 15, 1971 FARMINGTON, MICH.
38- 35	HARRIS, ROBERT ARTHUR	BOX 492 - NORTH PLATTE NE 69101
41- 45	HARRIS, ROBERT NED	D. DECEMBER 18, 1976 WEST PALM BEACH, FLA.
19- 38	HARRIS, STANLEY RAYMOND 'BUCKY'	D. NOVEMBER 8, 1977 BETHESDA, MD.
89- 52	HARRIS, TYRONE EUGENE 'GENE'	1267 NE 16TH AVENUE - OKEECHOBEE FL 33472
72- 45	HARRIS, VICTOR LANIER	5420 GARTH AVENUE - LOS ANGELES CA 90056

UNCUT CELEBRATION SHEET NUMBER 1
AUTOGRAPHED BY EIGHT PLAYERS

AUTOGRAPHED JOCKO CONLAN

AUTOGRAPHED ROY CAMPANELLA

70- 58 HARRIS, WALTER FRANCIS 'BUDDY'   2305 CAROL LN - NORRISTOWN PA 19403
23- 61 HARRIS, WILLIAM MILTON   D. AUGUST 21, 1965 INDIAN TRAIL, N. C.
57- 29 HARRIS, WILLIAM THOMAS   322 SOUTH REED - KENNEWICK WA 99336
65- 37 HARRISON, CHARLES WILLIAM   RURAL ROUTE 2 BOX 777E - ABILENE TX 79602
55- 56 HARRISON, ROBERT LEE   253 BRIERLEY WAY - INDIANAPOLIS IN 46032
72- 46 HARRISON, RORIC EDWARD   24621 VIA ALVARADO - MISSION VIEJO CA 92692
65- 38 HARRISON, THOMAS JAMES   6822 SHERMAN WAY - BELL CA 90203
20- 47 HARRISS, WILLIAM JENNINGS BRYAN 'SLIM' D. SEPTEMBER 19, 1963 TEMPLE, TEXAS
45- 42 HARRIST, EARL   BOX 238 - SIMSBORO LA 71275
37- 47 HARSHANEY, SAMUEL   419 THELMA DR-SAN ANTONIO TX 78212
48- 46 HARSHMAN, JOHN ELVIN   2227 COMMONWEALTH - SAN DIEGO CA 92104
15- 60 HARSTAD, OSCAR THEANDER   D. NOVEMBER 14, 1985 CORVALLIS, ORE.
80- 49 HART, JAMES MICHAEL 'MIKE'   409 LARKSPUR - PORTAGE MI 49081
63- 54 HART, JAMES RAY   6769 CEDAR BOULEVARD - NEWARK CA 94560
89- 53 HART, JOHN HENRY   307 EAST VANDERBILT STREET - ORLANDO FL 32804
84- 49 HART, MICHAEL LAWRENCE   16552 WEST CRESCENT DR - NEW BERLIN WI 53151
43- 59 HART, WILLIAM WOODROW   D. JULY 29, 1968 LYKINS,PA.
65- 39 HARTENSTEIN, CHARLES OSCAR   6815 DEPAUL COVE - AUSTIN TX 78723
12- 75 HARTER, FRANKLIN PIERCE   D. APRIL 14, 1959 BREESE, ILL.
14- 83 HARTFORD, BRUCE DANIEL   D. MAY 25, 1975 LOS ANGELES, CAL.
39- 48 HARTJE, CHRISTIAN HENRY   D. JUNE 26, 1946 SEATTLE, WASH.
11- 67 HARTLEY, GROVER ALLEN   D. OCTOBER 19, 1964 DAYTONA BEACH, FLA.
89- 54 HARTLEY, MICHAEL EDWARD   1415 CASCADE PLACE - EL CAJON CA 92021
62- 54 HARTMAN, J. C.   3425 ROSEDALE ST - HOUSTON TX 77004
59- 37 HARTMAN, ROBERT LOUIS   2732 LINCOLN RD - KENOSHA WI 53140
22- 52 HARTNETT, CHARLES LEO 'GABBY'   D. DECEMBER 20, 1972 PARK RIDGE, ILL.
13- 79 HARTRANFT, RAYMOND CHARLES   D. FEBRUARY 10, 1955 CHESTER CO., PA.
73- 57 HARTS, GREGORY RUDOLPH   OLD ADD: 160 WOODARD AVE SE - ATLANTA GA
50- 32 HARTSFIELD, ROY THOMAS   OLD ADD: 150 HUNTER'S COVE - ROSWELL GA 30076
47- 41 HARTUNG, CLINTON 'HONDO'   1018 EAST FULTON - SINTON TX 78387
76- 40 HARTZELL, PAUL FRANKLIN   610 NEWPORT CENTER RD #1290 - NEWPORT BEACH CA 92660
28- 44 HARVEL, LUTHER RAYMOND   D. APRIL 10, 1986 KANSAS CITY, MO.
87- 56 HARVEY, BRYAN STANLEY   RURAL ROUTE 1 BOX 144K - CATAWBA NC 28609
16- 42 HASBROOK, ROBERT LYNDON 'ZIGGY'   D. FEBRUARY 9, 1976 GARLAND, TEX.
45- 43 HASENMAYER, DONALD IRVIN   721 GOLF DRIVE - WARRINGTON PA 18976
40- 34 HASH, HERBERT HOWARD   RR ONE BOX 3 - BOSTON VA 22713
33- 23 HASLIN, MICHAEL JOSEPH 'MICKEY'   171 GEORGE AV - PLAINS PA 18705
36- 37 HASSETT, JOHN ALOYSIUS 'BUDDY'   114 STONY RIDGE DR-HILLSDALE NJ 07642
78- 56 HASSEY, RONALD WILLIAM   5935 EAST PLACITA ESQUINA - TUCSON AZ 85718
71- 43 HASSLER, ANDREW EARL   OLD ADD: BOX 17101 - TUCSON AZ
28- 45 HASSLER, JOSEPH FREDERICK   D. SEPTEMBER 4, 1971 DUNCAN, OKLA.
37- 48 HASSON, CHARLES EUGENE 'GENE'   5205 SAN BERARDINO RD #513 - MONTCLAIR CA 91763
19- 39 HASTY, ROBERT KELLER   D. MAY 28, 1972 DALLAS, GA.
79- 49 HATCHER, MICHAEL VAUGHN 'MICKEY'   720 SOUTH DOBSON #59 - MESA AZ 85202
84- 50 HATCHER, WILLIAM AUGUSTUS   P.O. BOX 207 - WILLIAMS AZ 86046
50- 33 HATFIELD, FRED JAMES   STAR ROUTE 1 BOX 3025 - TALLAHASSEE FL 32304
45- 44 HATHAWAY, RAY WILSON   25 LEISURE MOUNT RD - ASHEVILLE NC 28804
46- 44 HATTEN, JOSEPH HILARIAN   D. DECEMBER 16, 1988 REDDING, CALIF.
35- 42 HATTER, CLYDE MELNO   D. OCTOBER 16, 1937 YOSEMITE, KY.
46- 45 HATTON, GRADY EDGEBERT   BOX 97 - WARREN TX 77664
12- 76 HAUGER, JOHN ARTHUR   D. AUGUST 2, 1944 REDWOOD CITY, CALIF.
43- 60 HAUGHEY, CHRISTOPHER FRANCIS   OLD ADD: 46728 CRAWFORD ST #25 - FREMONT CA 94539
47- 42 HAUGSTAD, PHILIP DONALD   RR 4 BOX 180 - BLACK RIVER FALLS WI 54615
10- 66 HAUSER, ARNOLD GEORGE   D. MAY 22, 1956 AURORA, ILL.
22- 53 HAUSER, JOSEPH JOHN   919 NORTH 5TH STREET #14 - SHEBOYGAN WI 53081
75- 50 HAUSMAN, THOMAS MATTHEW   3165 WESTFIELD CIR - LAS VEGAS NV 89121
44- 56 HAUSMANN, CLEMENS RAYMOND   D. AUGUST 29, 1972 BAYTOWN, TEX.
44- 57 HAUSMANN, GEORGE JOHN   218 FAWN VALLEY - BOERNE TX 78006
81- 52 HAVENS, BRADLEY DAVID   1304 MONTROSE AVENUE - ROYAL OAK MI 48073
51- 39 HAWES, ROY LEE   RURAL ROUTE 5 - RINGGOLD GA 30736
11- 68 HAWK, EDWARD   D. MARCH 26, 1936 NEOSHO, MO.
82- 56 HAWKINS, MELTON ANDREW 'ANDY'   P.O. BOX 8812 - WACO TX 76714
60- 46 HAWKINS, WYNN FIRTH   5326 COTTAGE LN - CORTLAND OH 44410
21- 39 HAWKS, NELSON LOUIS 'CHICK'   D. MAY 26, 1973 SAN RAFAEL, CAL.
15- 61 HAWORTH, HOMER HOWARD   D. JANUARY 28, 1953 TROUTDALE, ORE.
70- 59 HAYDEL, JOHN HAROLD 'HAL'   304 LYNWOOD DR - HOUMA LA 70360
58- 44 HAYDEN, EUGENE FRANKLIN   1597 ALAMO DR #188 - VACAVILLE CA 95688
82- 57 HAYES, BEN JOSEPH   3501 10TH ST NE - ST PETERSBURG FL 33704
88- 65 HAYES, CHARLES DEWAYNE   OLD ADD: RR 11 BOX 28 - HATTIESBURG MS 39401
33- 24 HAYES, FRANKLIN WITMAN   D. JUNE 22, 1955 POINT PLEASANT, N. J.
35- 43 HAYES, JAMES MILLARD   6180 ROCKLAND RD - LITHONIA GA 30058
27- 44 HAYES, MINTER CARNEY'JACKIE'   D. FEBRUARY 9, 1983 BIRMINGHAM, ALA.
81- 53 HAYES, VON FRANK   OLD ADD: 312 N. GULF BLVD #C-TADIAN ROCK BEACH FL 34635
80- 50 HAYES, WILLIAM ERNEST   8 SOUTH ASH ST - NORTH PLATTE NE 69101
39- 49 HAYNES, JOSEPH WALTER   D. JANUARY 6, 1967 HOPKINS, MINN.
86- 61 HAYWARD, RAYMOND ANTON   327 HAMPTON - LONGVIEW TX 75601
68- 35 HAYWOOD, WILLIAM KIERNAN   4 MARINE DRIVE - HARLINGEN TX 78550
44- 58 HAYWORTH, MYRON CLAUDE 'RED'   507 OAK VIEW RD - HIGH POINT NC 27260
26- 35 HAYWORTH, RAYMOND HALL   219 SHULER CIRCLE - THOMASVILLE NC 27360
80- 51 HAZEWOOD, DRUNGO LARUE   5130 DEL NORTE BLVD - SACRAMENTO CA 95820
55- 57 HAZLE, ROBERT SIDNEY   164 DORSET DR - COLUMBIA SC 29210
40- 35 HEAD, EDWARD MARVIN   D. JANUARY 31, 1980 BASTROP, LA.
23- 62 HEAD, RALPH   D. OCTOBER 8, 1962 MUSCADINE, ALA.
30- 31 HEALEY, FRANCIS JEREMIAH   71 PENACOOK STREET - SPRINGFIELD MA 01104
69- 76 HEALY, FRANCIS XAVIER   1 PRIMROSE LN - HOLYOKE MA 01040
15- 62 HEALY, THOMAS FITZGERALD   D. JANUARY 15, 1974 CLEVELAND, O.
54- 41 HEARD, JEHOSIE   6465 3RD AVE SOUTH - BIRMINGHAM AL 35212
10- 67 HEARN, BUNN 'BUNNY'   D. OCTOBER 11, 1959 WILSON, N.C.
10- 68 HEARN, EDMUND   D. SEPTEMBER 8, 1952 SAWTELLE, CALIF.
86- 62 HEARN, EDWARD JOHN   12458 CRAIG - OVERLAND PARK KS 66213
26- 36 HEARN, ELMER LAFAYETTE 'BUNNY'   D. MARCH 31, 1974 VENICE, FLA.
47- 43 HEARN, JAMES TOLBERT   1678 BEVERLY WOOD CT - CHAMBLEE GA 30341
85- 46 HEARRON, JEFFREY VERNON   13176 EAST HEDDA DR - CERRITOS CA 90701
36- 38 HEATH, JOHN GEOFFREY 'JEFF'   D. DECEMBER 9, 1975 SEATTLE, WASH.
82- 57 HEATH, KELLY MARK   202 WOODSTOCK DR - GREENVILLE NC 27834
78- 57 HEATH, MICHAEL THOMAS   12137 FRUITWOOD DRIVE - RIVERVIEW FL 33569
31- 35 HEATH, MINOR WILSON 'MICKEY'   D. JULY 30, 1986 DALLAS, TEXAS
20- 48 HEATH, SPENCER PAUL   D. JANUARY 25, 1930 CHICAGO, ILL.

35- 44	HEATH, THOMAS GEORGE	D. FEBRUARY 26, 1967 LOS GATOS, CAL.
65- 40	HEATH, WILLIAM CHRIS	2111 PLANTATION DR - RICHMOND TX 77469
83- 70	HEATHCOCK, RONALD JEFFREY 'JEFF'	OLD ADD: 12861 ASPENWOOD LANE - GARDEN GROVE CA 92640
18- 28	HEATHCOTE, CLIFTON EARL	D. JANUARY 19, 1939 YORK, PA.
82- 59	HEATON, NEAL	611 BLUE POINT RD - HOLTSVILLE NY 11742
75- 51	HEAVERLO, DAVID WALLACE	3720 WEST LAKESHORE DR - MOSES LAKE WA 98837
31- 36	HEBERT, WALLACE ANDREW	3408 WESTWOOD RD - WEST LAKE LA 70665
68- 36	HEBNER, RICHARD JOSEPH 'RICHIE'	6 THERAULT STREET - WALPOLE MA 02081
12- 77	HECHINGER, MICHAEL VINCENT	D. AUGUST 13, 1967 CHICAGO, ILL.
13- 80	HEDGEPETH, HARRY MALCOLM	D. JULY 30, 1966 RICHMOND, VA.
65- 41	HEDLUND, MICHAEL DAVID	2412 KLINGER RD - ARLINGTON TX 76016
79- 50	HEEP, DANIEL WILLIAM	327 TEAKWOOD LN - SAN ANTONIO TX 78216
34- 43	HEFFNER, DONALD HENRY	D. AUGUST 1, 1989 PASADENA, CALIF.
63- 55	HEFFNER, ROBERT FREDERICK	910 NORTH TWELFTH - ALLENTOWN PA 18102
45- 45	HEFLIN, RANDOLPH RUTHERFORD	115 23RD STREET NW #25 - HICKORY NC 28601
41- 46	HEGAN, JAMES EDWARD	D. JUNE 17, 1984 SWAMPSCOTT, MASS.
64- 41	HEGAN, JAMES MICHAEL 'MIKE'	9648 OLD BARN RD - MEQUON WI 53092
85- 47	HEGMAN, ROBERT HILMER	RURAL ROUTE 5 - SAINT CLOUD MN 56301
18- 29	HEHL, HERMAN JACOB 'JAKE'	D. JULY 4, 1961 BROOKLYN, N. Y.
69- 77	HEIDEMANN, JACK SEALE	1303 CHAPPELL HILL - BRENHAM TX 77833
14- 84	HEILMANN, HARRY EDWIN	D. JULY 9, 1951 SOUTHFIELD, MICH.
42- 47	HEIM, VAL RAYMOND	1050 LOUDON - SUPERIOR NE 68978
20- 49	HEIMACH, FRED AMOS	D. JUNE 1, 1973 FORT MYERS, FLA.
83- 71	HEIMUELLER, GORMAN JOHN	8134 CALABAR AVENUE - PLAYA DEL REY CA 90291
21- 40	HEINE, WILLIAM HENRY 'BUD'	D. SEPTEMBER 2, 1976 FORT LAUDERDALE, FLA.
88- 66	HEINKEL, DONALD ELLIOTT	1012 SHERATON DRIVE - RACINE WI 53402
37- 49	HEINTZELMAN, KENNETH ALPHONSE	406 S. CHURCH - SAINT PETERS MO 63376
73- 58	HEINTZELMAN, THOMAS KENNETH	406 SOUTH CHURCH - ST PETERS MO 63376
34- 44	HEISE, CLARENCE EDWARD 'LEFTY'	5 WEST NIGHTINGALE STREET - APOPKA FL 32712
57- 30	HEISE, JAMES EDWARD	4021 HARGILL DR - ORLANDO FL 32806
67- 44	HEISE, ROBERT LOWELL	361 INNOCENT WAY - COPPEROPOLIS CA 95228
61- 44	HEISER, LEROY BARTON	1038 GROVE HILL RD - BALTIMORE MD 21227
60- 47	HEIST, ALFRED MICHAEL	P.O. BOX 70 - COOKSON OK 74427
18- 30	HEITMANN, HENRY ANTON	D. DECEMBER 15, 1958 BROOKLYN, N. Y.
56- 40	HELD, MELVIN NICHOLAS	BOX 204 - EDON OH 43518
54- 42	HELD, WOODSON GEORGE	BIG DIAMOND RANCH - DUBOIS WY 82513
38- 36	HELF, HENRY HARTZ	D. OCTOBER 27, 1984 AUSTIN, TEXAS
15- 63	HELFRICH, EMORY WILBUR 'TY'	D. MARCH 18, 1955 PLEASANTVILLE, N.J.
64- 42	HELMS, TOMMY VANN	5427 BLUE SKY DR - CINCINNATI OH 45247
43- 61	HELTZEL, WILLIAM WADE 'HEINIE'	RR 2-YORK PA 17403
61- 45	HEMAN, RUSSELL FREDRICK	1410 NORTH MARLES DR - SANTA ANA CA 92706
14- 85	HEMINGWAY, EDSON MARSHALL	D. JULY 5, 1969 EAST GRAND RAPIDS, MICH
89- 55	HEMOND, SCOTT MATHEW	263 FLORIDA AVENUE - DUNEDIN FL 33928
28- 46	HEMSLEY, RALSTON BURDETT 'ROLLIE'	D. JULY 31, 1972 WASHINGTON, D. C.
49- 32	HEMUS, SOLOMON JOSEPH 'SOLLY'	6565 WEST LOOP SOUTH #555 - BELLAIRE TX 77401
30- 32	HENDERSON WILLIAM MAXWELL	D. OCTOBER 6, 1966 PENSACOLA, FLA.
21- 41	HENDERSON, BERNARD	D. JUNE 4, 1966 LINDEN, TEXAS
81- 54	HENDERSON, DAVID LEE	BOX 21 - SOUTH DOD PALOS CA 93665
14- 86	HENDERSON, EDWARD J.	D. JANUARY 15, 1964 NEW YORK, N. Y.
74- 49	HENDERSON, JOSEPH LEE	OLD ADD: 125 INQUERO LN #38 - EL PASO TX
65- 42	HENDERSON, KENNETH JOSEPH	947 WILLOWLEAF DR #1305 - SAN JOSE CA 95128
79- 51	HENDERSON, RICKEY HENLEY	10561 ENGLEWOOD DR - OAKLAND CA 94621
77- 64	HENDERSON, STEPHEN CURTIS	5003 BEEKMAN COURT - TAMPA FL 33624
61- 46	HENDLEY, CHARLES ROBERT 'BOB'	645 WIMBISH - MACON GA 31204
71- 44	HENDRICK, GEORGE ANDREW	20893 STARSHINE ROAD - WALNUT CA 91789
23- 63	HENDRICK, HARVEY LEE	D. OCTOBER 29, 1941 COVINGTON, TENN.
10- 69	HENDRICKS, EDWARD	D. NOVEMBER 28, 1930 JACKSON, MICH.
68- 37	HENDRICKS, ELROD JEROME	3709 BROWNBROOK COURT - RANDALLSTOWN MD 21133
45- 46	HENDRICKSON, DONALD WILLIAM	D. JANUARY 19, 1977 NORFOLK, VA.
11- 69	HENDRIX, CLAUDE RAYMOND	D. MARCH 22, 1944 ALLENTOWN, PA.
11- 70	HENDRYX, TIMOTHY GREEN	D. AUGUST 14, 1957 CORPUS CHRISTI, TEX.
86- 63	HENGEL, DAVID LEE	1501 QUINTANA WAY - FREMONT CA 94538
19- 40	HENION, LAFAYETTE MARION	D. JULY 22, 1955 SAN LUIS OBISPO, CALIF.
82- 60	HENKE, THOMAS ANTHONY	RR SIX - JEFFERSON CITY MO 65101
54- 43	HENLEY, GAIL CURTICE	10150 DAINES DR - TEMPLE CITY CA 91780
21- 42	HENLINE, WALTER JOHN 'BUTCH'	D. OCTOBER 9, 1957 SARASOTA, FLA.
87- 57	HENNEMAN, MICHAEL ALAN	1515 WESTVALE DRIVE - FESTUS MO 63028
37- 50	HENNESSEY, GEORGE	D. JANUARY 15, 1988 PRINCETON, N. J.
13- 81	HENNESSY, LESTER BAKER	D. NOVEMBER 20, 1976 NEW YORK, N. Y.
69- 78	HENNIGAN, PHILLIP WINSTON	P.O. BOX 1212 - CENTER TX 75935
14- 87	HENNING, ERNEST HERMAN 'PETE'	D. NOVEMBER 9, 1939 DYER, IND.
73- 59	HENNINGER, RICHARD LEE	OLD ADD: 2112 GERMANTOWN COURT - PLANO TX 75075
24- 50	HENRICH, FRANK WILDE 'FRITZ'	D. MAY 1, 1959 PHILADELPHIA, PA.
57- 31	HENRICH, ROBERT EDWARD	1531 VIA LOS COYOTES - LAHABRA CA 90631
37- 51	HENRICH, THOMAS DAVID	1347 ALBINO TRAIL - DEWEY AZ 86327
11- 71	HENRIKSEN, OLAF	D. OCTOBER 17, 1962 NORWOOD, MASS.
84- 51	HENRY, DWAYNE ALLEN	502 HAMPSTEAD ROAD - MIDDLETOWN DE 19709
44- 59	HENRY, EARL CLIFFORD	BOX 43 - WHITE COTTAGE OH 43791
21- 43	HENRY, FRANK JOHN 'DUTCH'	D. AUGUST 23, 1968 EAST CLEVELAND, O.
22- 54	HENRY, FREDERICK MARSHALL	D. OCTOBER 12, 1987 WENDELL, N.C.
36- 39	HENRY, JAMES FRANCIS	D. AUGUST 15, 1976 MEMPHIS, TENN.
10- 70	HENRY, JOHN PARK	D. NOVEMBER 24, 1941 FORT HUACHUCA, ARIZ.
61- 47	HENRY, RONALD BAXTER	3329 EAST BAYARD AVE #405 - DENVER CO 80209
66- 42	HENRY, WILLIAM FRANCIS	190 BOULEVARD - KENILWORTH NJ 07033
52- 47	HENRY, WILLIAM RODMAN	302 CHRISTINE - HOUSTON TX 77017
33- 25	HENSHAW, ROY KNIKELBINE	4221 GARDEN AVE - WESTERN SPRINGS IL 60558
35- 45	HENSIEK, PHILIP FRANK	D. FEBRUARY 21, 1972 ST. LOUIS, MO.
86- 64	HENSLEY, CHARLES FLOYD	OLD ADD: P.O. BOX 439 - TULARE CA 93277
66- 43	HEPLER, WILLIAM LEWIS	10271 BLOSSOM LAKE DR - SEMINOLE FL 33542
63- 56	HERBEL, RONALD SAMUEL	105 CHINOOK LANE #F - STEILACOOM WA 98388
13- 82	HERBERT, ERNIE ALBERT	D. JANUARY 13, 1968 DALLAS, TEX.
15- 64	HERBERT, FREDERICK	D. MAY 29, 1963 TICE, FLA.
50- 34	HERBERT, RAYMOND ERNEST	32629 FIVE MILE RD - LIVONIA MI 48150
87- 58	HEREDIA, UBALDO JOSE	CLE ESPIRITO SANTO ISLA MARG.-NUEVA ESPARTA VENEZ
26- 37	HERMAN, FLOYD CAVES 'BABE'	D. NOVEMBER 27, 1987 GLENDALE, CALIF.
31- 37	HERMAN, WILLIAM JENNINGS BRYAN	3111 GARDEN EAST #33-PALM BEACH GARDENS FL 33410
23- 64	HERMANN, ALBERT BARTEL	D. AUGUST 20, 1980 LEWES, DEL.
43- 62	HERMANSKI, EUGENE VICTOR	100 HALLOCK AVE,FOX HALL #14 - MIDDLESEX NJ 08846

67- 45	HERMOSO, ANGEL REMIGIO	CALLE BOUKTON #7 - CARABOBO VENEZ
74- 50	HERNAIZ, JESUS RAFAEL	24 ST BLOCK 76 #47 VILLA - CAROLINA PR 00630
71- 45	HERNANDEZ, ENZO OCTAVIO	VEREDA NORTH 5E-4,GUANTRA-PUERTA LACRUZ ANZ, VENEZ
89- 56	HERNANDEZ, FRANCIS XAVIER 'XAVIER'	3549 LAY AVENUE - GROVES TX 77619
56- 41	HERNANDEZ, GREGORIO EVELIO	3004 SW 113TH AVE - MIAMI FL 33165
77- 65	HERNANDEZ, GUILLERMO 'WILLIE'	BO ESPINA CALLE C BOX 125 - AGUADA PR 00602
65- 43	HERNANDEZ, JACINTO ZULUETA 'JACKIE'	13390 NE SEVENTH AVENUE #103 - NORTH MIAMI FL 33181
74- 51	HERNANDEZ, KEITH	255 EAST 49TH #28D - NEW YORK NY 10017
82- 61	HERNANDEZ, LEONARDO JESUS	URB. EL MILAGRO,CALLE SUCRE 38 - EDO MIRANDA VENEZ
86- 65	HERNANDEZ, MANUEL ANTONIO	EUGENIO A. ALFIONADA #35 - LAROMANA DOMINICAN REP.
79- 52	HERNANDEZ, PEDRO JULIO	JULIO A. GARCIA #43 - LA ROMANA DOMINICAN REP.
67- 46	HERNANDEZ, RAMON GONZALEZ	REPARTO, ROSAMARIA CLE 5F-19-CAROLINA PR00630
72- 47	HERNANDEZ, RODOLFO 'RUDY'	CARVAJAL #1802 NORTE - MAZATLAN SINOLOA MEX.
60- 48	HERNANDEZ, RUDOLPH ALBERT	8 CALLE RODRIGUEZ SERRA - CONDADO PR 00907
42- 48	HERNANDEZ, SALVADOR JOSE RAMOS	D. JANUARY 3, 1986 HAVANA, CUBA
84- 52	HERNANDEZ, TOBIAS RAFAEL	IRA CALLE GUAMACHITO #47-49 - CALABOZO, GUARICO VENEZ
74- 52	HERNDON, LARRY DARNELL	6915 SKYLINE BLVD - HILLSBOROUGH CA 94010
79- 53	HERR, THOMAS MITCHELL	1077 OLDE FORGE CROSSING - LANCASTER PA 17601
11- 72	HERRELL, WALTER WILLIAM	D. JANUARY 23, 1949 FRONT ROYAL, VA.
67- 47	HERRERA, JOSE CONCEPCION	MARAVEN ADRI 12,CEN.COM. LAGUNILLAS - E. ZULIA VENEZ
58- 45	HERRERA, JUAN FRANCISCO 'PANCHO'	2930 NW 21ST AVE - MIAMI FL 33142
51- 40	HERRERA, PROCOPIO RODRIGUEZ 'TITO'	APDO POSTAL 257-CIUDAD SATELITE, EDO MEX.
25- 47	HERRERA, RAMON 'MIKE'	D. FEBRUARY 3, 1978 HAVANA, CUBA
56- 42	HERRIAGE, WILLIAM TROY	3204 TAMWORTH COURT - MODESTO CA 95350
54- 44	HERRIN, THOMAS EDWARD	BOX 550 - SAN JOSE CA 95125
29- 48	HERRING, ARTHUR L.	296 HIGHWAY DR - MARION IN 46952
12- 78	HERRING, HERBERT LEE	D. APRIL 22, 1964 TUCSON, ARIZ.
15- 65	HERRING, WILLIAM FRANCIS	D. SEPTEMBER 10, 1962 HONESDALE, PA.
67- 48	HERRMANN, EDWARD MARTIN	2774 ARISTOTLE DRIVE - SAN DIEGO CA 92139
32- 36	HERRMANN, LEROY GEORGE	D. JULY 3, 1972 LIVERMORE, CAL.
18- 31	HERRMANN, MARTIN JOHN	D. SEPTEMBER 11, 1956 CINCINNATI, O.
62- 55	HERRNSTEIN, JOHN ELLETT	603 SEMINOLE RD - CHILLICOTHE OH 45602
62- 56	HERRSCHER, RICHARD FRANKLIN 'RICK'	4024 DRUID - DALLAS TX 75205
56- 43	HERSH, EARL WALTER	3201 MURKLE RD - WESTMINSTER MD 21157
61- 48	HERSHBERGER, NORMAN MICHAEL 'MIKE'	4130 MEADOWVIEW DR - CANTON OH 44709
38- 37	HERSHBERGER, WILLARD MCKEE	D. AUGUST 3, 1940 BOSTON, MASS.
83- 72	HERSHISER, OREL LEONARD QUINTON	1199 MADIA STREET - PASADENA CA 91103
52- 48	HERTWECK, NEAL CHARLES	3030 ST CLAIRE RD - WINSTON SALEM NC 27106
64- 43	HERTZ, STEVE ALLAN	10211 SW 96TH TER - MIAMI FL 33156
56- 44	HERZOG, DORREL NORMAN ELVERT 'WHITEY'	9426 SAPPINGTON ESTATES DRIVE - ST. LOUIS MO 63127
84- 53	HESKETH, JOSEPH THOMAS	3690 SALISBURY AVE - BLASDELL NY 14219
16- 43	HESSELBACHER, GEORGE EDWARD	D. FEBRUARY 18, 1980 RYDAL, PA.
45- 47	HETKI, JOHN EDWARD	4004 STARY DR - PARMA OH 44134
89- 57	HETZEL, ERIC PAUL	RURAL ROUTE 3 BOX 249 - CROWLEY LA 70526
35- 46	HEUSSER, EDWARD BURLETON	D. MARCH 1, 1956 AURORA, COLO.
20- 50	HEVING, JOHN ALOYSIUS	D. DECEMBER 24, 1968 SALISBURY, N. C.
30- 33	HEVING, JOSEPH WILLIAM	D. APRIL 11, 1970 COVINGTON, KY.
73- 60	HEYDEMAN, GREGORY GEORGE	1717 MILITARY AVENUE - SEASIDE CA 93955
64- 44	HIATT, JACK E	STAR ROUTE BOX 341 - PINE AZ 85544
89- 58	HIBBARD, JAMES GREGORY 'GREG'	313 ROYAL STREET - GULFPORT MS 39503
67- 49	HIBBS, JAMES KERR	2821 SOUTH MAIN STREET - VENTURA CA 93003
42- 49	HICKEY, JAMES ROBERT	163 CHESTER ST - EAST HARTFORD CT 06108
81- 55	HICKEY, KEVIN JOHN	5715 SOUTH MASON - CHICAGO IL 60638
15- 66	HICKMAN, DAVID JAMES	D. DECEMBER 30, 1958 BROOKLYN, N. Y.
62- 57	HICKMAN, JAMES LUCIUS	BOX 355 - HENNING TN 38041
65- 44	HICKMAN, JESWE OWENS	1801 JEWEL STREET - PINEVILLE LA 71360
56- 45	HICKS, CLARENCE WALTER 'BUDDY'	7600 COOLGROVE DR - DOWNEY CA 90240
64- 45	HICKS, JAMES EDWARD	3717 EUCLID AVE - EAST CHICAGO IN 46312
59- 38	HICKS, WILLIAM JOSEPH 'JOE'	2707 BROOKMERE RD - CHARLOTTESVILLE VA 22901
37- 52	HIGBE, WALTER KIRBY	D. MAY 6, 1985 COLUMBIA, S. C.
22- 55	HIGBEE, MAHLON JESSE	D. APRIL 7, 1968 DEPAUW, IND.
49- 33	HIGDON, WILLIAM TRAVIS	D. AUGUST 30, 1986 PASCAGOULA, MISS.
66- 44	HIGGINS, DENNIS DEAN	2204 ANDERSON DR - JEFFERSON CITY MO 65101
89- 59	HIGGINS, MARK DOUGLAS	3700 CARLYLE CLOSE #940 - MOBILE AL 36609
30- 34	HIGGINS, MICHAEL FRANKLIN 'PINKY'	D. MARCH 21, 1969 DALLAS, TEX.
22- 56	HIGH, ANDREW AIRD	D. FEBRUARY 22, 1981 TOLEDO, O.
19- 41	HIGH, CHARLES EDWIN	D. SEPTEMBER 11, 1960 PORTLAND, ORE.
13- 83	HIGH, HUGH JENKEN	D. NOVEMBER 16, 1962 ST. LOUIS CO., MO.
85- 48	HIGUERA, TEODORO VALENZUELA	OLD ADD: CIUDAD DE JUAREZ CHIHUAHUA MEX.
31- 38	HILCHER, WALTER FRANK	D. NOVEMBER 21, 1962 MINNEAPOLIS, MINN.
31- 39	HILDEBRAND, ORAL CLYDE	D. SEPTEMBER 8, 1977 SOUTHPORT, IND.
13- 84	HILDEBRAND, PALMER MARION	D. JANUARY 25, 1960 NORTH CANTON, O.
69- 79	HILGENDORF, THOMAS EUGENE	P.O. BOX 124 - CAMANCHE IA 52730
15- 67	HILL, CARMEN PROCTOR 'BUNKER'	D. JANUARY 1, 1990 INDIANAPOLIS, IND.
17- 33	HILL, CLIFFORD JOSEPH 'RED'	D. AUGUST 11, 1938 EL PASO, TEX.
57- 32	HILL, DAVID BURNHAM	827 WEST WOODCHASE DRIVE - KNOXVILLE TN 37922
83- 73	HILL, DONALD EARL	5607 E. NAPLES CANAL ST - LONG BEACH CA 90803
69- 80	HILL, GARRY ALTON	3538 BACK CREEK CHURCH RD - CHARLOTTE NC 28213
89- 60	HILL, GLENALLEN	111 MCPHERSON STREET - SANTA CRUZ CA 95060
15- 68	HILL, HERBERT LEE	D. SEPTEMBER 2, 1970 FARMERS BRANCH, TEX.
69- 81	HILL, HERMAN ALEXANDER	D. DECEMBER 14, 1970 MAGALLANES, VEN.
35- 47	HILL, JESSE TERRILL	245 SOUTH EL MOLINO #208 - PASADENA CA 91101
39- 50	HILL, JOHN CLINTON	D. SEPTEMBER 20, 1970 DECATUR, GA.
88- 67	HILL, KENNETH WADE	43 KINGS HILL DRIVE - LYNN MA 01905
73- 61	HILL, MARC KEVIN	804 LINCOLN - ELSBERRY MO 63343
87- 59	HILLEGAS, SHAWN PATRICK	RURAL ROUTE 1 BOX 39A - SOUTH FORK PA 15956
61- 49	HILLER, CHARLES JOSEPH	11060 HARBOR SIDE DRIVE - LARGO FL 34643
46- 46	HILLER, FRANK WALTER	D. JANUARY 8, 1987 WEST CHESTER, PA.
20- 51	HILLER, HARVEY MAX 'HOB'	D. DECEMBER 27, 1956 LEHIGHTON, PA.
65- 45	HILLER, JOHN FREDERICK	RURAL ROUTE 1 BOX 85B - HERMANSVILLE MI 49847
24- 51	HILLIS, MALCOLM DAVID 'MACK'	D. JUNE 16, 1961 CAMBRIDGE, MASS.
55- 58	HILLMAN, DARIUS DUTTON 'DAVE'	849 MIMOSA DR - KINGSPORT TN 37660
14- 88	HILLY, WILLIAM EDWARD	D. JULY 25, 1953 EUREKA, MO.
72- 48	HILTON, JOHN DAVID 'DAVE'	330 EAST PASADENA STREET - PHOENIX AZ 85012
61- 50	HIMSL, AVITUS BERNARD 'VEDIE'	5127 WEST HUTCHINSON - CHICAGO IL 60641
77- 66	HINDS, SAMUEL RUSSELL	2165 SAN JOSE - CLOVIS CA 93612
34- 45	HINKLE, DANIEL GORDON 'GORDIE'	D. MARCH 19, 1972 HOUSTON, TEX.
51- 41	HINRICHS, PAUL EDWIN	1982 BRETT DRIVE - MADISONVILLE KY 42431

10- 71	HINRICHS, WILLIAM LOUIS	D. AUGUST 18, 1972 SELMA, CALIF.
82- 62	HINSHAW, GEORGE ADDISON	543 EVERGREEN STREET - INGLEWOOD CA 90302
64- 46	HINSLEY, JERRY DEAN	3115 EL CAMINO REAL #31 - LAS CRUCES NM 88001
28- 47	HINSON, JAMES PAUL	D. SEPTEMBER 23, 1960 MUSKOGEE, OKLA.
61- 51	HINTON, CHARLES EDWARD	6330 16TH ST NW - WASHINGTON DC 20011
71- 46	HINTON, RICHARD MICHAEL	OLD ADD: 730 AGAVE PLACE - TUCSON AZ 85718
87- 60	HINZO, THOMAS LEE	82 MILLAN COURT - CHULA VISTA CA 92010
66- 45	HIPPAUF, HERBERT AUGUST	1781 KIMBERLY DR - SUNNYVALE CA 94087
71- 47	HISER, GENE TAYLOR	1450 CALDWELL LANE - HOFFMAN ESTATES IL 60194
68- 38	HISLE, LARRY EUGENE	P.O. BOX 84 %FERGUSON - PORTSMOUTH OH 45662
51- 42	HISNER, HARLEY PARNELL	RR 2 BOX 253A - MONROEVILLE IN 46773
38- 38	HITCHCOCK, JAMES FRANKLIN	D. JUNE 23, 1959 MONTGOMERY, ALA.
42- 50	HITCHCOCK, WILLIAM CLYDE	1117 WEST COLLINWOOD CIR-OPELIKA AL 36801
17- 34	HITT, BRUCE SMITH	D. NOVEMBER 10, 1973 PORTLAND, ORE.
49- 34	HITTLE, LLOYD ELDON	2031 WEST ELM STREET - LODI CA 95242
31- 40	HOAG, MYRIL OLIVER	D. JULY 28, 1971 HIGH SPRINGS, FLA.
54- 45	HOAK, DONALD ALBERT	D. OCTOBER 9, 1969 PITTSBURGH, PA.
61- 52	HOBAUGH, EDWARD RUSSELL	527 5TH AVE - FORD CITY PA 16226
57- 33	HOBBIE, GLEN FREDERICK	RR 2, NORTHWOOD HEIGHTS - HILLSBORO IL 62049
81- 56	HOBBS, JOHN DOUGLAS	3 WADE DR - CHERRY HILL NJ 08034
13- 85	HOBBS, WILLIAM LEE	D. JANUARY 5, 1945 HAMILTON, O.
75- 52	HOBSON, CLELL LAVERN 'BUTCH'	1422 CLARENDON AVENUE - BESSEMER AL 35020
20- 52	HOCK, EDWARD FRANCIS	D. NOVEMBER 21, 1963 PORTSMOUTH, O.
75- 53	HOCKENBERY, CHARLES MARION	308 SPRUCE STREET - ONALASKA WI 54650
38- 39	HOCKETT, ORIS LEON	D. MARCH 23, 1969 HAWTHORNE, CAL.
34- 46	HOCKETTE, GEORGE EDWARD	D. JANUARY 20, 1974 PLANTATION, FLA.
25- 48	HODAPP, URBAN JOHN	D. JUNE 14, 1980 CINCINNATI, O.
51- 43	HODERLEIN, MELVIN ANTHONY	535 CINTI BATAVIA PIKE - CINCINNATI OH 45244
20- 53	HODGE, CLARENCE CLEMET 'SHOVEL'	D. DECEMBER 31, 1967 FORT WALTON BEACH, FLA.
84- 54	HODGE, ED OLIVER	RR 2, WILLIAMS ROAD #2 - SEYMOUR TN 37865
42- 51	HODGE, EDWARD BURTON 'BERT'	RR 19-KNOXVILLE TN 37920
71- 48	HODGE, HAROLD MORRIS 'GOMER'	501 WISCONSIN STREET - SPINDALE NC 28160
43- 63	HODGES, GILBERT RAYMOND	D. APRIL 2, 1972 WEST PALM BEACH, FLA.
73- 62	HODGES, RONALD WRAY	RURAL ROUTE 5 BOX 97 - ROCKY MOUNT VA 24151
39- 51	HODGIN, ELMER RALPH	3203 FARMINGTON DR-GREENSBORO NC 27407
80- 52	HODGSON, PAUL JOSEPH DENIS	110 CHANDLER DRIVE - FREDERICTON NEW BRUN. E3B 5S7 CAN.
46- 47	HODKEY, ALOYSIUS JOSEPH 'ELI'	5163 BROADWAY - LORAIN OH 44052
52- 49	HOEFT, WILLIAM FREDERICK	36427 SHERWOOD - LIVONIA MI 48154
63- 57	HOERNER, JOSEPH WALTER	6344 TIDEWATER DR - FLORISSANT MO 63033
40- 36	HOERST, FRANK JOSEPH	31 VILLAGE LANE - MOUNT LAUREL NJ 08054
11- 73	HOFF, CHESTER CORNELIUS	1114 ATLANTIC AVENUE #3 - DAYTONA BEACH FL 32018
44- 60	HOFFERTH, STEWART EDWARD	BOX 283 - KOUTS IN 46347
29- 49	HOFFMAN, CLARENCE CASPER 'DUTCH'	D. DECEMBER 6, 1962 BELLEVILLE, ILL.
15- 69	HOFFMAN, EDWARD ADOLPH 'TEX'	D. MAY 19, 1947 NEW ORLEANS, LA.
80- 53	HOFFMAN, GLENN EDWARD	217 NORTH DALE ST - ANAHEIM CA 92801
79- 54	HOFFMAN, GUY ALAN	1111 WALNUT STREET - OTTAWA IL 61350
64- 47	HOFFMAN, JOHN EDWARD	2315 NW 85TH - SEATTLE WA 98117
42- 52	HOFFMAN, RAYMOND LAMONT	3509 SILVER LACE LANE #53 - BOYNTON BEACH FL 33436
39- 52	HOFFMAN, WILLIAM JOSEPH	3234 NORTH 25TH ST-PHILADELPHIA PA 19129
49- 35	HOFMAN, ROBERT GEORGE	14 BROOK HOLLOW - OAKLAND NJ 07436
19- 42	HOFMANN, FRED	D. NOVEMBER 19, 1964 ST. HELENA, CAL.
14- 89	HOGAN, GEORGE A.	D. FEBRUARY 28, 1922 BARTLESVILLE, OKLA.
25- 49	HOGAN, JAMES FRANCIS 'SHANTY'	D. APRIL 7, 1967 BOSTON, MASS.
21- 44	HOGAN, KENNETH SYLVESTER	D. JANUARY 2, 1980 CLEVELAND, O.
11- 74	HOGAN, WILLIAM HENRY 'HAPPY'	D. SEPTEMBER 28, 1974 SAN JOSE, CALIF.
11- 75	HOGG, CARTER BRADLEY	D. APRIL 2, 1935 BUENA VISTA, GA.
34- 47	HOGG, WILBERT GEORGE 'BERT'	D. NOVEMBER 5, 1973 DETROIT, MICH.
29- 50	HOGSETT, ELON CHESTER 'CHIEF'	115 WEST 16TH ST - HAYS KS 67601
52- 50	HOGUE, CALVIN GREY	1050 BERKSHIRE RD - DAYTON OH 45419
48- 47	HOGUE, ROBERT CLINTON	D. DECEMBER 22, 1987 MIAMI, FLA.
27- 45	HOHMAN, WILLIAM HENRY	D. OCTOBER 29, 1968 BALTIMORE, MD.
10- 72	HOHNHURST, EDWARD HENRY	D. MARCH 26, 1916 COVINGTON, KY.
89- 61	HOILES, CHRISTOPHER ALLEN	8688 JERRY CITY ROAD - WAYNE OH 43466
44- 61	HOLBOROW, WALTER ALBERT	D. JULY 14, 1986 FORT LAUDERDALE, FLA.
35- 48	HOLBROOK, JAMES MARBURY 'SAMMY'	1914 11TH STREET #113 - MERIDIAN MS 39301
45- 48	HOLCOMBE, KENNETH EDWARD	32 BOTANY DR - ASHEVILLE NC 28805
34- 48	HOLDEN, JOSEPH FRANCIS	424 SOUTH 2ND ST - ST CLAIR PA 17970
13- 86	HOLDEN, WILLIAM PAUL	D. SEPTEMBER 14, 1971 PENSACOLA, FLA.
72- 49	HOLDSWORTH, FREDRICK WILLIAM	47300 WEST MAIN ST - NORTHVILLE MI 48167
14- 90	HOLKE, WALTER HENRY	D. OCTOBER 12, 1954 ST LOUIS, MO.
20- 54	HOLLAHAN, WILLIAM JAMES	D. NOVEMBER 27, 1965 NEW YORK, NEW YORK
77- 67	HOLLAND, ALFRED WILLIS	28 ACORN HILL DRIVE - VOORHEES NJ 08043
26- 38	HOLLAND, HOWARD ARTHUR 'MUL'	D. FEBRUARY 16, 1969 WESTCHESTER, VA.
32- 37	HOLLAND, ROBERT CLYDE 'DUTCH'	D. JUNE 16, 1967 LUMBERTON, N.C.
39- 53	HOLLAND, WILLIAM DAVID	504 CASHWELL PL - GOLDSBORO NC 27530
79- 55	HOLLE, GARY CHARLES	820 FIFTH AVE - WATERVLIET NY 12189
28- 48	HOLLEY, EDWARD EDGAR	D. OCTOBER 26, 1986 PADUCAH, KY.
21- 45	HOLLING, CARL	D. JULY 28, 1962 SONOMA, CAL.
35- 49	HOLLINGSWORTH, ALBERT WAYNE	10812 SLAUGHTER CREEK - AUSTIN TX 78748
22- 57	HOLLINGSWORTH, JOHN BURNETT 'BONNIE'	D. JANUARY 4, 1990 SHANNONDALE, TENN.
49- 36	HOLLMIG, STANLEY ERNEST	D. DECEMBER 4, 1981 SAN ANTONIO, TEXAS
18- 32	HOLLOCHER, CHARLES JACOB	D. AUGUST 14, 1940 STRATMAN, MO.
53- 33	HOLLOMAN, ALVA LEE 'BOBO'	D. MAY 1, 1987 ATHENS, GA.
29- 51	HOLLOWAY, JAMES MADISON	RR 1 BOX 3285 - MARINGOUIN LA 70757
22- 58	HOLLOWAY, KENNETH EUGENE	D. SEPTEMBER 25, 1968 THOMASVILLE, GA.
77- 68	HOLLY, JEFFREY OWEN	2601 ALVORD ST - REDONDO BEACH CA 90278
24- 52	HOLM, ROSCOE ALBERT 'WATTIE'	D. MAY 19, 1950 EVERLY, IA.
43- 64	HOLM, WILLIAM FRED	D. JULY 27, 1977 EAST CHICAGO, IND.
88- 68	HOLMAN, BRIAN SCOTT	OLD ADD: 1650 PARK PLACE - WICHITA KS 67203
68- 39	HOLMAN, GARY RICHARD	SVL BOX 7080 - VICTORVILLE CA 92392
80- 54	HOLMAN, RANDY SCOTT	OLD ADD: 750 MOBILE AVE #48 - CAMARILLO CA 93010
89- 62	HOLMAN, SHAWN LEROY	ROUTE 3, EDGEWOOD ROAD - SEWICKLEY PA 15143
18- 33	HOLMES, ELWOOD MARTER	D. APRIL 15, 1954 CAMDEN, N. J.
42- 53	HOLMES, THOMAS FRANCIS	1 PINE DR-WOODBURY NY 11797
30- 35	HOLSHAUSER, HERMAN ALEXANDER	90 WINECOFF AVE NE - CONCORD NC 28025
25- 50	HOLT, JAMES EMMETT MADISON 'RED'	D. FEBRUARY 2, 1961 BIRMINGHAM, ALA.
68- 40	HOLT, JAMES WILLIAM	RR 3 BOX 335 - GRAHAM NC 27253
80- 55	HOLT, ROGER BOYD	1615 SAILFISH AVE - FRUITLAND PARK FL 32731

65- 46 HOLTGRAVE, LAVERN GEORGE 'VERN'	389 NORTH 8TH ST - BREESE IL 62230
85- 49 HOLTON, BRIAN JOHN	33 WHITE PINE COURT - HUNT VALLEY MD 21030
65- 47 HOLTZMAN, KENNETH DALE	933 PROVIDENCE - BUFFALO GROVE IL 60089
77- 69 HONEYCUTT, FREDERICK WAYNE 'RICK'	207 FORREST ROAD - FORT OGLETHORPE GA 30742
25- 51 HOOD, ALBIE LARRISON	D. OCTOBER 14, 1988 CHESAPEAKE, VA.
73- 63 HOOD, DONALD HARRIS	708 FIRESTONE DR - FLORENCE SC 29501
20- 55 HOOD, WALLACE JAMES SR.	D. MAY 2, 1965 HOLLYWOOD, CAL.
49- 37 HOOD, WALLACE JAMES JR.	966 EILINITA AVE - GLENDALE CA 91208
57- 34 HOOK, JAMES WESLEY 'JAY'	768 SUFFIELD - BIRMINGHAM MI 48009
35- 50 HOOKS, ALEXANDER MARCUS	BOX 123-EDGEWOOD TX 75117
50- 35 HOOPER, ROBERT NELSON	D. MARCH 17, 1980 NEW BRUNSWICK, N. J.
74- 53 HOOTEN, MICHAEL LEON	461 NORTH 11TH ST - COOS BAY OR 97420
71- 49 HOOTON, BURT CARLTON	3619 GRANBY COURT - SAN ANTONIO TX 78217
52- 51 HOOVER, RICHARD LLOYD	D. APRIL 12, 1981 LAKE PLACID, FLA.
43- 65 HOOVER, ROBERT JOE	D. SEPTEMBER 2, 1965 LOS ANGELES, CAL.
75- 54 HOPKINS, DONALD	7984 BEARCREEK DRIVE - CINCINNATI OH 45249
68- 41 HOPKINS, GAIL EASON	131 SOUTH ROSE STREET - LODI CA 95240
34- 49 HOPKINS, MEREDITH HILLIARD 'MARTY'	D. NOVEMBER 20, 1963 DALLAS, TEX.
27- 46 HOPKINS, PAUL HENRY	131 MAIN ST - DEEP RIVER CT 06417
39- 54 HOPP, JOHN LEONARD	1914 AVENUE N - SCOTTSBLUFF NE 69361
46- 48 HOPPER, JAMES MCDANIEL	D. JANUARY 23, 1982 CHARLOTTE, N. C.
13- 87 HOPPER, WILLIAM BOOTH	D. JANUARY 14, 1965 ALLEN PARK, MICH.
24- 53 HORAN, JOSEPH PATRICK 'SHAGS'	D. FEBRUARY 13, 1969 LOS ANGELES, CAL.
61- 53 HORLEN, JOEL EDWARD	3718 CHARTWELL DRIVE - SAN ANTONIO TX 78230
87- 61 HORN, SAMUEL LEE	7463 BLACK OAK RD - SAN DIEGO CA 92114
29- 52 HORNE, BERLYN DALE 'TRADER'	D. FEBRUARY 3, 1983 FRANKLIN, O.
78- 58 HORNER, JAMES ROBERT 'BOB'	209 STEEPLECHASE DRIVE - IRVING TX 75062
15- 70 HORNSBY, ROGERS	D. JANUARY 5, 1963 CHICAGO, ILL.
12- 79 HORSEY, HANSON	D. DECEMBER 1, 1949 MILLINGTON, MD.
17- 35 HORSTMAN, OSCAR THEODORE	D. MAY 11, 1977 SALINA, KAN.
64- 48 HORTON, ANTHONY DARRIN	17001 LIVORNO DR - PACIFIC PALISADES CA 90272
84- 55 HORTON, RICKY NEAL	OLD ADD: 15703 LAMAR RIDGE ROAD - CHESTERFIELD MO 63017
63- 58 HORTON, WILLIAM WATTERSN	%REID,15124 WARWICK - DETROIT MI 48223
53- 34 HOSKINS, DAVID TAYLOR	D. APRIL 2, 1970 FLINT, MICH.
70- 60 HOSLEY, TIMOTHY KENNETH	401 WEST HENRY ST - SPARTANBURG SC 29301
56- 46 HOST, EUGENE EARL	1415 FULTON ST - NASHVILLE TN 37206
44- 62 HOSTETLER, CHARLES CLOYD	D. FEBRUARY 18, 1971 FORT COLLINS, COLO.
81- 57 HOSTETLER, DAVID ALAN	424 WEST NORMAN - ARCADIA CA 91006
71- 50 HOTTMAN, KENNETH	8559 BANFF VISTA - ELK GROVE CA 95624
12- 80 HOUCK, BYRON SIMON	D. JUNE 17, 1969 SANTA CRUZ, CALIF.
70- 61 HOUGH, CHARLES OLIVER	2266 SHADE TREE CIR - BREA CA 92621
47- 44 HOUK, RALPH GEORGE	3000 PLANTATION ROAD - WINTER HAVEN FL 33884
50- 36 HOUSE, HENRY FRANKLIN 'FRANK'	2564 DOLLY RIDGE RD - BIRMINGHAM AL 35243
67- 50 HOUSE, PATRICK LORY	4205 GREEN MEADOWS DR - MERIDIAN ID 83642
71- 51 HOUSE, THOMAS ROSS	12794 VIA FELINO - DEL MAR CA 92014
13- 88 HOUSE, WILLARD EDWIN	D. NOVEMBER 16, 1923 KANSAS CITY, MO.
80- 56 HOUSEHOLDER, PAUL WESLEY	BOX 236 - NORTH MONMOUTH ME 04265
10- 73 HOUSER, BENJAMIN FRANKLIN	D. JANUARY 15, 1952 AUGUSTA, ME.
14- 91 HOUSER, JOSEPH WILLIAM	D. JANUARY 3, 1953 ORLANDO, FLA.
45- 49 HOUTTEMAN, ARTHUR JOSEPH	1755 WEST BUELL RD - LAKE ORION MI 48035
69- 82 HOVLEY, STEPHEN EUGENE	205 1/2 SOUTH LOMITA AVENUE - OJAI CA 93023
18- 34 HOVLIK, EDWARD C.	D. MARCH 20, 1955 PAINESVILLE, O.
63- 59 HOWARD, BRUCE ERNEST	8705 MISTY CREEK DRIVE - SARASOTA FL 34241
12- 81 HOWARD, DAVID AUSTIN	D. JANUARY 26, 1956 DALLAS, TEX.
72- 50 HOWARD, DOUGLAS LYNN	OLD ADD: 352 SOUTH 1200 EAST - SALT LAKE CITY
18- 35 HOWARD, EARL NYCUM	D. APRIL 4, 1937 EVERETT, PA.
55- 59 HOWARD, ELSTON GENE	D. DECEMBER 14, 1980 NEW YORK, N. Y.
58- 46 HOWARD, FRANK OLIVER	560 ST MARYS BLVD - GREEN BAY WI 54301
79- 56 HOWARD, FRED IRVING	88 SCAMMAN ST - SOUTH PORTLAND ME 04106
14- 92 HOWARD, IVAN CHESTER	D. MARCH 30, 1967 MEDFORD, ORE.
70- 62 HOWARD, LARRY RAYFORD	OLD ADD: 2201 BROOKHOLLOW - ABILENE TX 79605
46- 49 HOWARD, LEE VINCENT	OLD ADD: 1221 SONOMA DRIVE - ALTADENA CA 91001
81- 58 HOWARD, MICHAEL FREDRIC	OLD ADD: 4981 46TH ST - SACRAMENTO CA 95820
73- 64 HOWARD, WILBUR LEON	OLD ADD: 12500 DUNLAP #423 - HOUSTON TX 77031
71- 52 HOWARTH, JAMES EUGENE	606 SANTINI ST - BILOXI MS 39530
74- 54 HOWE, ARTHUR HENRY	711 KAHLDON COURT - HOUSTON TX 77079
52- 52 HOWE, CALVIN EARL	7325 HESSLER DRIVE NE - ROCKFORD MI 49341
23- 65 HOWE, LESTER CURTIS	D. JULY 16, 1976 WOODMERE, N. Y.
80- 57 HOWE, STEVEN ROY	318 WEST 6TH STREET - WHITEFISH MT 59937
47- 45 HOWELL, HOMER ELLIOTT 'DIXIE'	216 STONEHENGE DRIVE #101 - LOUISVILLE KY 40207
85- 50 HOWELL, JACK ROBERT	822 SOUTH LEHIGH DRIVE - TUCSON AZ 85710
80- 58 HOWELL, JAY CANFIELD	4720 HANCOCK DRIVE - BOULDER CO 80303
84- 56 HOWELL, KENNETH	16845 PLAINVIEW - DETROIT MI 48219
40- 37 HOWELL, MILLARD FILLMORE 'DIXIE'	D. MARCH 18, 1960 HOLLYWOOD, FLA.
41- 47 HOWELL, MURRAY DONALD 'RED'	D. OCTOBER 1, 1950 GREENVILLE, S. C.
12- 82 HOWELL, ROLAND BOATNER	D. MARCH 31, 1973
74- 55 HOWELL, ROY LEE	1201 EAST CYPRESS - LOMPOC CA 93436
49- 38 HOWERTON, WILLIAM RAY	1430 BUCKINGHAM WAY - HAYWARD CA 94544
89- 63 HOWITT, DANN PAUL JOHN	OLD ADD: 420 SOUTH PARK STREET - HASTINGS MI 49058
13- 89 HOWLEY, DANIEL PHILIP	D. MARCH 10, 1944 EAST WEYMOUTH, MASS.
61- 54 HOWSER, RICHARD DALTON	D. JUNE 17, 1987 KANSAS CITY, MO.
52- 53 HOYLE, ROLAND EDISON 'TEX'	695 CHURCH ST - CARBONDALE PA 18407
79- 57 HOYT, DEWEY LAMARR 'LAMARR'	OLD ADD: 329 PINECLIFF COURT - COLUMBIA SC 29209
18- 36 HOYT, WAITE CHARLES	D. AUGUST 25, 1984 CINCINNATI, O.
70- 63 HRABOSKY, ALAN THOMAS	16216 PEPPER VIEW COURT - CHESTERFIELD MO 63017
81- 59 HRBEK, KENT ALAN	OLD ADD: 9109 4TH AVENUE SOUTH - BLOOMINGTON MN 55420
68- 42 HRINIAK, WALTER JOHN	18 STACY DR NORTH - ANDOVER MA 01845
78- 59 HUBBARD, GLENN DEE	127 PEACHTREE ST #808,%CHURCH - ATLANTA GA 30303
28- 49 HUBBELL, CARL OWEN	D. NOVEMBER 21, 1988 SCOTTSDALE, ARIZ.
19- 43 HUBBELL, WILBERT WILLIAM 'BILL'	D. AUGUST 3, 1980 LAKEWOOD, CO..
61- 55 HUBBS, KENNETH DOUGLASS	D. FEBRUARY 15, 1964 UTAH LAKE, UTAH
20- 56 HUBER, CLARENCE BILL	D. FEBRUARY 22, 1965 LAREDO, TEX.
39- 55 HUBER, OTTO	D. APRIL 9, 1989 PASSAIC, N.J.
35- 51 HUCKLEBERRY, EARL EUGENE	RR 2-MAUD OK 74854
83- 74 HUDGENS, DAVID MARK	6550 EAST OSBORN - SCOTTSDALE AZ 85251
23- 66 HUDGENS, JAMES PRICE	D. AUGUST 26, 1955 ST. LOUIS, MO.
84- 57 HUDLER, REX ALLEN	503 EAST MENLO - FRESNO CA 93710
26- 39 HUDLIN, GEORGE WILLIS	14 BETSEY LN - LITTLE ROCK AR 72205

72- 51 HUDSON, CHARLES	RR 5 BOX 50 - COALGATE OK 74538
83- 75 HUDSON, CHARLES LYNN	2124 HEATHER GLEN - DALLAS TX 75232
52- 54 HUDSON, HAL CAMPBELL	16 FARMER STREET - NEWNAN GA 30263
69- 83 HUDSON, JESIE JAMES	OLD ADD: 1101 ELOISE - MANSFIELD LA 71052
36- 40 HUDSON, JOHN WILSON	D. NOVEMBER 7, 1970 BRYAN, TEX.
74- 56 HUDSON, REX HAUGHTON	2519 CASTLEFORD - MIDLAND TX 79705
40- 38 HUDSON, SIDNEY CHARLES	1309 WESTWOOD DR - WACO TX 76710
14- 93 HUENKE, ALBERT A.	D. SEPTEMBER 20, 1974 SAINT MARYS, O.
89- 64 HUFF, MICHAEL KALE	1029 PONTIAC - WILMETTE IL 60091
37- 53 HUFFMAN, BENJAMIN FRANKLIN	2 CEDAR LN-LURAY VA 22835
79- 58 HUFFMAN, PHILLIP LEE	334 CALADIUM ST - LAKE JACKSON TX 77566
74- 57 HUGHES, JAMES MICHAEL	7526 EL MANOR AVE - LOS ANGELES CA 90045
52- 55 HUGHES, JAMES ROBERT	4521 WEST 83RD ST - CHICAGO IL 60652
87- 62 HUGHES, KEITH WILLS	309 FRIENDSHIP DRIVE - PAOLI PA 19301
66- 46 HUGHES, RICHARD HENRY	BOX 598 - STEPHENS AR 71764
35- 52 HUGHES, ROY JOHN	4730 BRANDT PIKE-DAYTON OH 45424
70- 64 HUGHES, TERRY WAYNE	432 PIERPONT AVE EXT - SPARTANBURG SC 29303
59- 39 HUGHES, THOMAS EDWARD	OLD ADD: 5921 SOUTHCREST ST - HOUSTON TX
30- 36 HUGHES, THOMAS FRANKLIN	790 19TH ST - BEAUMONT TX 77706
41- 48 HUGHES, THOMAS OWEN	RR 4-MOUNTAINTOP PA 18707
14- 94 HUGHES, VERNON ALEXANDER	D. SEPTEMBER 26, 1961 SEWICKLEY, PA.
21- 46 HUGHES, WILLIAM NESBERT	D. FEBRUARY 25, 1963 BIRMINGHAM, ALA.
41- 49 HUGHSON, CECIL CARLTON 'TEX'	135 WEST SIERRA C - SAN MARCOS TX 78666
15- 71 HUHN, EMIL HUGO	D. SEPTEMBER 5, 1925 CAMDEN, S.C.
83- 76 HUISMAN, MARK LAWRENCE	1711 F STREET - SCHUYLER NE 68661
83- 77 HULETT, TIMOTHY CRAIG	RR 5 - SPRINGFIELD IL 62707
22- 59 HULIHAN, HARRY JOSEPH	D. SEPTEMBER 11, 1980 RUTLAND, VT.
23- 67 HULVEY, JAMES HENSEL 'HANK'	D. APRIL 9, 1982 MOUNT SIDNEY, VA.
77- 70 HUME, THOMAS HUBERT	OLD ADD: 1803 WEST 7TH STREET - PALMETTO FL 33561
11- 76 HUMPHREY, ALBERT	D. MAY 13, 1961 ASHTABULA, O.
38- 40 HUMPHREY, BYRON WILLIAM 'BILL'	3248 SOUTH CLAY - SPRINGFIELD MO 65807
71- 53 HUMPHREY, TERRYAL GENE	21 ENSUENO WEST - IRVINE CA 92701
62- 58 HUMPHREYS, ROBERT WILLIAM	FARM DEPT., COUNTY STADIUM - MILWAUKEE WI 53246
10- 74 HUMPHRIES, ALBERT	D. SEPTEMBER 21, 1945 ORLANDO, FLA.
38- 41 HUMPHRIES, JOHN WILLIAM	D. JUNE 24, 1965 NEW ORLEANS, LA.
64- 49 HUNDLEY, CECIL RANDOLPH 'RANDY'	122 EAST FOREST LN - PALATINE IL 60067
22- 60 HUNGLING, BERNARD HERMAN	D. MARCH 30, 1968 DAYTON, O.
26- 40 HUNNEFIELD, WILLIAM FENTON	D. AUGUST 28, 1976 NANTUCKET, MASS.
10- 75 HUNT, BENJAMIN FRANKLIN	OLD ADD: 730 K ST - SACRAMENTO CA
85- 51 HUNT, JAMES RANDALL 'RANDY'	117 DESTIN ST - MONTGOMERY AL 36110
59- 40 HUNT, KENNETH LAWRENCE	1464 WEST 170TH ST - GARDENA CA 90247
61- 56 HUNT, KENNETH RAYMOND	268 EAST 300 NORTH - MORGAN UT 84050
31- 41 HUNT, OLIVER JOEL	D. JULY 24, 1978 TEAGUE, TEXAS
63- 60 HUNT, RONALD KENNETH	2806 JACKSON RD - WENTZVILLE MO 63385
33- 26 HUNTER, EDISON FRANKLIN	D. MARCH 14, 1967 COLERAIN TWP., O.
11- 77 HUNTER, FREDERICK CREIGHTON 'NEWT'	D. OCTOBER 26, 1963 COLUMBUS, O.
53- 35 HUNTER, GORDON WILLIAM 'BILLY'	104 EAST SEMINARY AVE - LUTHERVILLE MD 21093
71- 54 HUNTER, HAROLD JAMES 'BUDDY'	5407 SOUTH 15TH ST - OMAHA NE 68107
16- 44 HUNTER, HERBERT HARRISON	D. JULY 26, 1970 ORLANDO, FLA.
65- 48 HUNTER, JAMES AUGUSTUS 'CATFISH'	RR ONE BOX 895 - HERTFORD NC 27944
62- 59 HUNTER, WILLARD MITCHELL	2562 POPPLETON AVE - OMAHA NE 68105
12- 83 HUNTER, WILLIAM ELLSWORTH	D. APRIL 10, 1934 BUFFALO, N.Y.
67- 51 HUNTZ, STEPHEN MICHAEL	22495 HABER - CLEVELAND OH 44126
23- 68 HUNTZINGER, WALTER HENRY	D. AUGUST 11, 1981 UPPER DARBY, PA.
83- 78 HUPPERT, DAVID BLAINE	4134 LOWELL LANE - ZEPHYRHILLS FL 33541
54- 46 HURD, THOMAS CARR	D. SEPTEMBER 5, 1982 WATERLOO, IOWA
77- 71 HURDLE, CLINTON MERRICK	515 MARGARET ST - MERRITT ISLAND FL 32952
80- 59 HURST, BRUCE VEE	471 EAST 650 SOUTH - SAINT GEORGE UT 84770
28- 50 HURST, FRANK O'DONNELL 'DON'	D. DECEMBER 6, 1952 LOS ANGELES, CAL.
88- 69 HUSON, JEFFREY KENT	P.O. BOX 3410 - WEST SEDONA AZ 86340
25- 52 HUSTA, CARL LAWRENCE	D. NOVEMBER 6, 1951 KINGSTON, N. Y.
37- 54 HUSTON, WARREN LLEWELLYN	12 ROBINWOOD ROAD, RR 3 - BUZZARD BAY MA 02532
33- 27 HUTCHESON, JOSEPH JOHNSON	2400 BELL AVE - DENTON TX 76201
40- 39 HUTCHINGS, JOHN RICHARD JOSEPH	D. APRIL 27, 1963 INDIANAPOLIS, IND.
39- 56 HUTCHINSON, FREDERICK CHARLES	D. NOVEMBER 12, 1964 BRADENTON, FLA.
33- 28 HUTCHINSON, IRA KENDALL	D. AUGUST 21, 1973 CHICAGO, ILL.
74- 58 HUTSON, GEORGE HERBERT	7203 WEST SUGARTREE CT - SAVANNAH GA 31410
25- 53 HUTSON, ROY LEE	D. MAY 20, 1957 LAMESA, CAL.
70- 65 HUTTO, JAMES NEAMON	OLD ADD: P.O. BOX 86 - DAYTONA BEACH FL 32015
66- 47 HUTTON, THOMAS GEORGE	1713 LYNDON ST - SOUTH PASADENA CA 91030
55- 60 HYDE, RICHARD ELDE	1506 CAMBRIDGE - CHAMPAIGN IL 61820
73- 65 IGNASIAK, GARY RAYMOND	3084 ANGELUS DRIVE - PONTIAC MI 48055
13- 90 IMLAY, HARRY MILLER 'DOC'	D. OCTOBER 7, 1948 BORDENTOWN, N.J.
86- 66 INCAVIGLIA, PETER JOSEPH	P.O. BOX 526 - PEBBLE BEACH CA 93953
87- 63 INFANTE, FERMIN ALEXIS	EL HATILLO CALLE SVCR #33 - CARACAS VENEZUELA S.A.
14- 95 INGERSOLL, ROBERT RANDOLPH	D. JANUARY 13, 1927 MINNEAPOLIS, MINN.
11- 78 INGERTON, WILLIAM JOHN 'SCOTTY'	D. JUNE 15, 1956 CLEVELAND, O.
29- 53 INGRAM, MELVIN DAVID	D. OCTOBER 28, 1979 MEDFORD, ORE.
87- 64 INNIS, JEFFREY DAVID	3024 GREENLAKE DRIVE - DECATUR IL 62521
77- 72 IORG, DANE CHARLES	1330 NORTH 100 EAST - PLEASANT GROVE UT 84062
78- 60 IORG, GARTH RAY	BOX 1074 - BLUE LAKE CA 95525
41- 50 IOTT, CLARENCE EUGENE 'HOOKS'	D. AUGUST 17, 1980 ST. PETERSBURG, FLA.
14- 96 IRELAN, HAROLD	D. JULY 16, 1944 CARMEL, IND.
81- 60 IRELAND, TIMOTHY NEAL	20932 TIMES AVE - HAYWARD CA 94541
49- 39 IRVIN, MONFORD MERRILL 'MONTE'	104 SYCAMORE CIR - HOMOSASSA FL 32646
12- 84 IRVIN, WILLIAM EDWARD	D. FEBRUARY 18, 1916 PHILADELPHIA, PA.
38- 42 IRWIN, THOMAS ANDREW	508 50TH ST-ALTOONA PA 16602
21- 47 IRWIN, WALTER KINGSLEY	D. AUGUST 18, 1976 SPRING LAKE, MICH.
80- 60 ISALES, ORLANDO	OLD ADD: 16 SE 1171 CABARRA TER - RIO PIEDRAS PR 00921
71- 55 IVIE, MICHAEL WILSON	534 MIDLAND PARK DR - STONE MOUNTAIN GA 30083
67- 52 IZQUIERDO, ENRIQUE ROBERTO 'HANK'	6011 SW 97TH AVE - MIAMI FL 33173
53- 36 JABLONSKI, RAYMOND LEO	D. NOVEMBER 25, 1985 CHICAGO, ILL.
59- 41 JACKSON, ALVIN NEIL	ONE SAINT MARKS PL - DIX HILLS NY 11746
15- 72 JACKSON, CHARLES HERBERT	D. MAY 27, 1968 RATFORD, VA.
87- 65 JACKSON, CHARLES LEO	5727 37TH AVENUE SOUTH - SEATTLE WA 98118
83- 79 JACKSON, DANNY LYNN	31 NEWARK #C - AURORA CO 80012
78- 61 JACKSON, DARRELL PRESTON	1310 JARVIS AVE - LOS ANGELES CA 90061
85- 52 JACKSON, DARRIN JAY	1950 WELLINGTON ROAD - LOS ANGELES CA 90016
11- 79 JACKSON, GEORGE CHRISTOPHER	D. NOVEMBER 25, 1972 CLEBURNE, TEX.

65- 49 JACKSON, GRANT DWIGHT	212 MESA CIRCLE - UPPER SAINT CLAIR PA 15241
33- 29 JACKSON, JOHN LEWIS	D. OCTOBER 24, 1956 SOMERS POINT, N. J.
87- 66 JACKSON, KENNETH BERNARD	P.O. BOX 613 - WASKOM TX 75692
55- 61 JACKSON, LAWRENCE CURTIS	1520 WEST WASHINGTON - BOISE ID 83702
58- 47 JACKSON, LOUIS CLARENCE	D. MAY 27, 1969 TOKYO, JAPAN
86- 67 JACKSON, MICHAEL RAY	7234 WILEY STREET - HOUSTON TX 77016
70- 66 JACKSON, MICHAEL WARREN	626 N. 13TH ST - HUMBOLDT TN 38343
50- 37 JACKSON, RANSOM JOSEPH 'RANDY'	250 HUNNICUT DR - ATHENS GA 30601
67- 53 JACKSON, REGINALD MARTINEZ	22 YANKEE HILL - OAKLAND CA 94816
63- 61 JACKSON, ROLAND THOMAS 'SONNY'	P.O. BOX 42383 - ATLANTA GA 30311
54- 47 JACKSON, RONALD ALLEN	210 RAINTREE CIRCLE - KALAMAZOO MI 49007
75- 55 JACKSON, RONNIE D	519 SAN LEON - IRVINE CA 92714
77- 73 JACKSON, ROY LEE	711 DOGWOOD AVE - OPELIKA AL 36801
22- 61 JACKSON, TRAVIS CALVIN	D. JULY 27, 1987 WALDO, ARK.
88- 68 JACKSON, VINCENT ~~EDWARD~~	P.O. BOX 330466 - BIRMINGHAM AL 35248
16- 97 JACKSON, WILLIAM RILEY	D. SEPTEMBER 26, 1958 PEORIA, ILL.
48- 48 JACOBS, ANTHONY ROBERT	D. DECEMBER 21, 1980 NASHVILLE, TENN.
39- 57 JACOBS, ARTHUR EVAN	D. JUNE 8, 1967 INGLEWOOD, CAL.
54- 48 JACOBS, FORREST VANDERGRIFT 'SPOOK'	BOX 66 - MILFORD DE 19963
60- 49 JACOBS, LAMAR GARY 'JAKE'	BOX 340 - CANFIELD OH 44406
37- 55 JACOBS, NEWTON SMITH 'BUCKY'	1437 GREYCOURT AVE-RICHMOND VA 23227
18- 37 JACOBS, OTTO ALBERT	D. NOVEMBER 19, 1955 CHICAGO, ILL.
28- 51 JACOBS, RAYMOND F.	D. APRIL 5, 1952 LOS ANGELES, CAL.
14- 98 JACOBS, WILLIAM ELMER	D. FEBRUARY 10, 1958 SALEM , MO.
15- 73 JACOBSON, MERWIN JOHN WILLIAM	D. JANUARY 13, 1978 BALTIMORE, MD.
15- 74 JACOBSON, WILLIAM CHESTER 'BABY DOLL'	D. JANUARY 16, 1977 ORION, ILL.
18- 38 JACOBUS, STUART LOUIS 'LARRY'	D. AUGUST 19, 1965 NORTH COLLEGE HILL, OHIO
81- 61 JACOBY, BROOK WALLACE	401 IVYWOOD DRIVE - OXNARD CA 93030
71- 56 JACQUEZ, PATRICK THOMAS	8351 COLONIAL - STOCKTON CA 95209
64- 50 JAECKEL, PAUL HENRY	328 WEST 7TH STREET - CLAREMONT CA 91711
20- 57 JAEGER, JOSEPH PETER	D. DECEMBER 13, 1963 HAMPTON, IA.
25- 54 JAHN, ARTHUR CHARLES	D. JANUARY 9, 1948 LITTLE ROCK, ARK.
36- 41 JAKUCKI, SIGMUND	D. MAY 28, 1979 GALVESTON, TEXAS
24- 54 JAMERSON, CHARLEY DEWEY	D. AUGUST 4, 1980 MOCKSVILLE, N. C.
75- 56 JAMES, ARTHUR	4531 GARLAND AVE - DETROIT MI 48214
60- 50 JAMES, CHARLES WESLEY	104 COLLIER ST - FULTON MO 65221
68- 43 JAMES, CLEO JOEL	6020 KITTYHAWK DR - RIVERSIDE CA 92504
83- 80 JAMES, DION	804 NINTH AVENUE - SACRAMENTO CA 95818
86- 69 JAMES, DONALD CHRISTOPHER 'CHRIS'	RURAL ROUTE 2 BOX 231 - ALTO TX 75925
68- 44 JAMES, JEFFREY LYNN	39095 MOUNTAIN HOME DRIVE - LEBANON OR 97355
58- 48 JAMES, JOHN PHILLIP	6037 EAST LARKSPUR - SCOTTSDALE AZ 85254
77- 74 JAMES, PHILIP ROBERT 'SKIP'	7716 W. 72ND TER - OVERLAND PARK KS 66204
67- 54 JAMES, RICHARD LEE	2358 FOXWORTH DR - PANAMA CITY FL 32405
29- 54 JAMES, ROBERT BYRNE 'BERNIE'	123 EAST RAMPART #108 - SAN ANTONIO TX 78216
78- 62 JAMES, ROBERT HARVEY	7838 KYLE - SUNLAND CA 91040
12- 85 JAMES, WILLIAM A. 'LEFTY'	D. MAY 3, 1933 PORTSMOUTH, O.
11- 80 JAMES, WILLIAM HENRY	D. MAY 24, 1942 VENICE, CALIF.
13- 91 JAMES, WILLIAM LAWRENCE	D. MARCH 10, 1971 OROVILLE, CALOF.
15- 75 JAMIESON, CHARLES DEVINE	D. OCTOBER 27, 1969 PATERSON, N.J.
70- 67 JANESKI, GERALD JOSEPH	OLD ADD: 317 NORTH MISSION DR - SAN GABRIEL CA 91711
53- 37 JANOWICZ, VICTOR FELIX	1966 JERVIS RD - COLUMBUS OH 43221
47- 46 JANSEN, LAWRENCE JOSEPH	RR 2 BOX 413A - FOREST GROVE OR 97116
10- 76 JANSEN, RAYMOND WILLIAM	D. MARCH 19, 1934 ST. LOUIS, MO.
12- 86 JANTZEN, WALTER C. 'HEINIE'	D. APRIL 1, 1948 HINES, ILL.
11- 81 JANVRIN, HAROLD CHANDLER	D. MARCH 1, 1962 BOSTON, MASS.
44- 63 JARVIS, LEROY GILBERT	2605 NORTH HUDSON - OKLAHOMA CITY OK 73103
69- 84 JARVIS, RAYMOND ARNOLD	P.O. BOX 9452 - PROVIDENCE RI 02940
66- 48 JARVIS, ROBERT PATRICK 'PAT'	4425 EAST KINGSPOINTS CIR - DUNWOOD GA 30338
14- 99 JASPER, HARRY W. 'HI'	D. MAY 22, 1937 ST. LOUIS, MO.
65- 50 JASTER, LARRY EDWARD	1105 MATTES DRIVE - MIDLAND MI 48640
72- 52 JATA, PAUL	1598 BIRARD STREET - WANTAGH NY 11793
40- 40 JAVERY, ALVA WILLIAM	D. SEPTEMBER 13, 1977 WOODSTOCK, CONN.
76- 41 JAVIER, IGNACIO ALFREDO	BARRIO LIBRE #96 ING CON-SAN PEDRO DE MACORIS DOM. REP.
60- 51 JAVIER, MANUEL JULIAN	B/12 URB. PINA - SAN FRANCISCO DE MACORIS DOM. REP.
84- 58 JAVIER, STANLEY JULIAN ANTONIO	B/12 URB. PINA-SAN FRANCISCO DE MACORIS DOMINICAN REP.
53- 38 JAY, JOSEPH RICHARD	3660 STATE ROAD 580 #80 - OLDSMAR FL 34677
21- 48 JEANES, ERNEST LEE 'TEX'	D. APRIL 5, 1973 LONGVIEW, TEX.
36- 42 JEFFCOAT, GEORGE EDWARD	D. OCTOBER 13, 1978 LEESVILLE, S. C.
48- 49 JEFFCOAT, HAROLD BENTLEY	4016 WISCONSIN AVE - TAMPA FL 33616
83- 81 JEFFCOAT, JAMES MICHAEL 'MIKE'	RURAL ROUTE 1 BOX 289 - PINE BLUFF AR 71603
87- 67 JEFFERIES, GREGORY SCOTT	70 DUMONT COURT - MILLBRAE CA 94030
73- 66 JEFFERSON, JESSE HARRISON	1421 RAILROAD AVE - MIDLOTHIAN VA 23113
86- 70 JEFFERSON, STANLEY	2420-3E HUNTER AVENUE - BRONX NY 10475
30- 37 JEFFRIES, IRVINE FRANKLIN	D. JUNE 8, 1982 LOUISVILLE, KY.
41- 51 JELINCICH, FRANK ANTHONY	LIBERTY TOWER 99, 890 MAIN ST - SANTA CLARA CA 95050
87- 68 JELKS, GREGORY DION	615 BAY SPRINGS ROAD - CENTRE AL 35960
83- 82 JELTZ, LARRY STEVEN 'STEVE'	615 WEST 28TH PLACE - LAWRENCE KS 66044
65- 51 JENKINS, FERGUSON ARTHUR	P.O. BOX 1202 - GUTHRIE OK 73044
22- 62 JENKINS, JOHN ROBERT	D. AUGUST 3, 1968 COLUMBIA, MO.
14-100 JENKINS, JOSEPH DANIEL	D. JUNE 21, 1974 FRESNO, CALIF.
25- 55 JENKINS, THOMAS GRIFFIN	D. MAY 3, 1979 WEYMOUTH, MASS.
62- 60 JENKINS, WARREN WASHINGTON 'JACK'	3810 OBISPO - TAMPA FL 33609
88- 70 JENNINGS, JAMES DOUGLAS 'DOUG'	7807 EVENING STAR LANE - TALLAHASSEE FL 32312
51- 44 JENNINGS, WILLIAM LEE	7065 FOXCROFORT DR - AFFTON MO 63123
31- 42 JENSEN, FORREST DUCENUS 'WOODY'	1311 NORTH PARKWOOD LANE - WICHITA KS 67206
50- 38 JENSEN, JACK EUGENE	D. JULY 14, 1982 CHARLOTTESVILLE, VA.
12- 87 JENSEN, WILLIAM CHRISTIAN	D. MARCH 27, 1917 PHILADELPHIA, PA.
29- 55 JESSEE, DANIEL EDWARD	D. APRIL 30, 1970 VENICE, FLA.
69- 85 JESTADT, GARRY ARTHUR	825 PARNELL PL - SUNNYVALE CA 94087
52- 56 JESTER, VIRGIL MILTON	8130 RALEIGH PL - WESTMINSTER CO 80030
69- 86 JETER, JOHN	1590 METROPOLITAN AVE #2F - BRONX NY 10462
50- 39 JETHROE, SAMUEL	340 EAST 14TH ST - ERIE PA 16503
83- 83 JIMENEZ, ALFONSO 'HOUSTON'	OLD ADD: NAVOJOA MEXICO
64- 51 JIMENEZ, FELIX ELVIO	SIMON BOLIVAR #24 - SAN PEDRO DE MACORIS DOM. REP.
88- 71 JIMENEZ, GERMAN	OLD ADD: SANTIAGO, IXCUINTLA MEX.
62- 61 JIMENEZ, MANUEL EMILIO	24 SIMON BOLIVAR - SAN PEDRO DE MACORIS DOM. REP.
74- 59 JIMINEZ, JUAN ANTONIO	CALLE 9,CASA 1N EL ENSUENO - SANTIAGO DOMINICAN REP.
63- 62 JOHN, THOMAS EDWARD	32 ADAMS STREET - CRESSKILL NJ 07626

RIGHT-HANDED PITCHERS

Hall of Fame right-handed pitchers are shown on these Perez-Steele autographed Art Post Cards

```
26- 41  JOHNS, AUGUSTUS FRANCIS              D. SEPTEMBER 12, 1975 SAN ANTONIO, TEX.
15- 76  JOHNS, WILLIAM R. 'PETE'             D. AUGUST 9, 1964 CLEVELAND, O.
14-101  JOHNSON, ADAM RANKIN SR              D. JULY 2, 1972 WILLIAMSPORT, PA.
41- 52  JOHNSON, ADAM RANKIN 'RANK' JR.      1308 1/2 WARREN AVENUE - WILLIAMSPORT PA 17701
64- 52  JOHNSON, ALEXANDER                   7650 GRAND RIVER - DETROIT MI 48206
81- 62  JOHNSON, ANTHONY CLAIR               OLD ADD: 4446 JANSSEN DR - MEMPHIS TN 38128
27- 47  JOHNSON, ARTHUR GILBERT              D. JUNE 7, 1982 SARASOTA, FLA.
40- 41  JOHNSON, ARTHUR HENRY                23 HEMLOCK DR-HOLDEN MA 01520
59- 42  JOHNSON, BENJAMIN FRANKLIN           112 LOCKSLEY DR - GREENWOOD SC 29646
81- 63  JOHNSON, BOBBY EARL                  OLD ADD: 3432 SOUTH LOOP 12 - DALLAS TX 75224
46- 50  JOHNSON, CHESTER LILLIS              D. APRIL 10, 1983 SEATTLE, WASH.
69- 87  JOHNSON, CLAIR BARTH 'BART'          904 INDIAN BOUNDARY DRIVE - WESTMONT IL 60559
72- 53  JOHNSON, CLIFFORD                    318 GLEN OAK - SAN ANTONIO TX 78220
53- 39  JOHNSON, CLIFFORD 'CONNIE'           1900 EAST 54TH ST - KANSAS CITY MO 64130
52- 57  JOHNSON, DARRELL DEAN                3 BUSSELL PARK ROAD - ORD NE 68862
65- 52  JOHNSON, DAVID ALLEN                 1064 HOWELL BEACH ROAD - WINTER PARK FL 32789
74- 60  JOHNSON, DAVID CHARLES               2402 MARCHALL ST - ABILENE TX 79605
87- 69  JOHNSON, DAVID WAYNE                 3528 WAGON TRAIN ROAD - BALTIMORE MD 21220
60- 52  JOHNSON, DERON ROGER                 13881 POWAY VALLEY ROAD - POWAY CA 92064
47- 47  JOHNSON, DONALD ROY                  1925 NE 19TH AVENUE #5A - PORTLAND OR 97212
43- 66  JOHNSON, DONALD SPORE                580 BROOKS - LAGUNA BEACH CA 92651
40- 42  JOHNSON, EARL DOUGLAS                9541 25TH AVE NW-SEATTLE WA 98107
20- 58  JOHNSON, EDWIN CYRIL                 D. JULY 3, 1975 MORGANFIELD, KY.
12- 88  JOHNSON, ELLIS WATT                  D. JANUARY 14, 1965 MINNEAPOLIS, MINN.
14-102  JOHNSON, ELMER ELLSWORTH             D. OCTOBER 31, 1966 HOLLYWOOD, FLA.
12- 89  JOHNSON, ERNEST RUDOLPH              D. MAY 1, 1952 MONROVIA, CALIF.
50- 40  JOHNSON, ERNEST THORWALD             500 DORRIS RD - ALPHARETTA GA 30201
66- 49  JOHNSON, FRANK HERBERT               568 NORTH CENTER ST - MESA AZ 85201
22- 63  JOHNSON, FREDERICK EDWARD            D. JUNE 14, 1973 KERRVILLE, TEX.
13- 92  JOHNSON, GEORGE HOWARD 'CHIEF'       D. JUNE 12, 1922 DES MOINES, IA.
25- 56  JOHNSON, HENRY WARD                  D. AUGUST 20, 1982 BRADENTON, FLA.
82- 63  JOHNSON, HOWARD MICHAEL              3105  PINEVIEW AVENUE  - CLEARWATER FL 33516
70- 68  JOHNSON, JAMES BRIAN                 1459 MADISON ST - MUSKEGON MI 49442
68- 45  JOHNSON, JERRY MICHAEL               4566 DEL MAR AVE - SAN DIEGO CA 92107
44- 64  JOHNSON, JOHN CLIFFORD               810 MINE STREET - NORWAY MI 49870
78- 63  JOHNSON, JOHN HENRY                  7578 YOUNG CIR - RENO NV 89511
85- 53  JOHNSON, JOSEPH RICHARD              14 EVERGREEN RD - PLAINVILLE MA 02762
87- 70  JOHNSON, KENNETH LANCE 'LANCE'       230 CEDAR RIDGE #E3 - MOBILE AL 36608
58- 49  JOHNSON, KENNETH TRAVIS              121 MYRTLEWOOD DR - PINEVILLE LA 71360
47- 48  JOHNSON, KENNETH WANDERSEE           326 BROOKFIELD - WICHITA KS 67206
74- 61  JOHNSON, LAMAR                       5105 YUCCA COURT - ARLINGTON TX 76017
72- 54  JOHNSON, LARRY DOBY                  31,15 EAST 98TH ST - CLEVELAND OH 44104
34- 50  JOHNSON, LLOYD WILLIAM               D. OCTOBER 8, 1980 STOCKTON, CALIF.
60- 53  JOHNSON, LOUIS BROWN                 5830 GREEN VALLEY CIR - CULVER CITY CA 90230
74- 62  JOHNSON, MICHAEL NORTON              OLD ADD: RR 1 - FARIBAULT MN 55021
11- 82  JOHNSON, OTIS L.                     D. NOVEMBER 9, 1915 JOHNSON CITY, N. Y.
20-136  JOHNSON, PAUL OSCAR                  D. FEBRUARY 14, 1973 MCALLEN, TEX.
88- 72  JOHNSON, RANDALL DAVID               11418 COTTONTAIL WAY - PENN VALLEY CA 95946
82- 64  JOHNSON, RANDALL GLENN               852 WEST 11TH AVE - ESCONDIDO CA 92025
80- 61  JOHNSON, RANDALL STUART              40 WEST 64TH ST - HIALEAH FL 33012
58- 50  JOHNSON, RICHARD ALLAN               808-B NORTH BEELINE - PAYSON AZ 85541
69- 88  JOHNSON, ROBERT DALE                 12862 MALENA DR - SANTA ANA CA 92705
33- 30  JOHNSON, ROBERT LEE                  D. JULY 6, 1982 TACOMA, WASH.
60- 54  JOHNSON, ROBERT WALLACE              1474 BARCLAY ST - ST PAUL MN 55106
82- 65  JOHNSON, RONALD DAVID                11371 KATHY LN - GARDEN GROVE CA 92640
86- 71  JOHNSON, RONDIN ALLEN                3620 SOUTHWEST 102 ND - SEATTLE WA 98146
29- 56  JOHNSON, ROY CLEVELAND               D. SEPTEMBER 10, 1973 TACOMA, WASH.
82- 66  JOHNSON, ROY EDWARD                  902 NORTH ST. LOUIS - CHICAGO IL 60651
18- 40  JOHNSON, ROY J. 'HARDROCK'           D. JANUARY 10, 1986 SCOTTSDALE, ARIZ.
16- 45  JOHNSON, RUSSELL CONWELL 'JING'      D. DECEMBER 6, 1950 POTTSTOWN, PA.
28- 52  JOHNSON, SILAS KENNETH               600 WEST CHURCH STREET - SHERIDAN IL 60551
60- 55  JOHNSON, STANLEY LUCIUS              56 MORNINGSIDE DR - DALY CITY CA 94015
22- 64  JOHNSON, SYLVESTER                   D. FEBRUARY 20, 1985 PORTLAND, ORE.
74- 63  JOHNSON, THOMAS RAYMOND              1575 HURON STREET - SAINT PAUL MN 55108
73- 67  JOHNSON, TIMOTHY EVALD               1021 AVONDALE ROAD - LAS CRUCES NM 88005
44- 65  JOHNSON, VICTOR OSCAR                1515 DRURY AVE - EAU CLAIRE WI 54701
81- 64  JOHNSON, WALLACE DARNELL             2512 ADAMS ST - GARY IN 46407
83- 84  JOHNSON, WILLIAM CHARLES             OLD ADD: 1701 N. LINCOLN ST - WILMINGTON DE 19806
16- 46  JOHNSON, WILLIAM LAWRENCE            D. NOVEMBER 5, 1950 LOS ANGELES, CALIF.
43- 67  JOHNSON, WILLIAM RUSSEL              2903 LAKE FOREST DR-AUGUSTA GA 30904
79- 59  JOHNSTON, GREGORY BERNARD            1406 PROSPECT DRIVE - POMONA CA 91766
11- 83  JOHNSTON, JAMES HARLE                D. FEBRUARY 14, 1967 CHATTANOOGA, TENN.
13- 93  JOHNSTON, JOHN THOMAS                D. MARCH 7, 1940 SAN DIEGO, CALIF.
64- 53  JOHNSTON, REX DAVID                  15117 ILLINOIS ST - PARAMOUNT CA 90723
24- 55  JOHNSTON, WILFRED IVEY 'FRED'        D. JULY 14, 1959 TYLER, TEX.
66- 50  JOHNSTONE, JOHN WILLIAM 'JAY'        OLD ADD: 1300 WENTWORTH AVE - PASADENA CA 91106
34- 51  JOINER, ROY MERRILL 'POP'            D. DECEMBER 26, 1989 RED BLUFF, CALIF.
54- 49  JOK, STANLEY EDWARD                  D. MARCH 6, 1972 BUFFALO, N. Y.
30- 38  JOLLEY, SMEAD POWELL                 2020 SANTA CLARA AVE #402 - ALAMEDA CA 94501
53- 40  JOLLY, DAVID                         D. MAY 27, 1963 DURHAM, N. C.
83- 85  JONES, ALFORNIA                      RURAL ROUTE 1 BOX 63 - CHARLESTON MS 38921
32- 38  JONES, ARTHUR LENOX                  D. NOVEMBER 25, 1980 COLUMBIA, S. C.
86- 72  JONES, BARRY LOUIS                   411 SOUTH MORTON AVENUE - CENTERVILLE IN 47330
16- 47  JONES, CARROLL ELMER 'DEACON'        D. DECEMBER 28, 1952 PITTSBURG, KAN.
85- 54  JONES, CHRISTOPHER DALE              1821 WESTWARD HO CIR - EL CAJON CA 92021
67- 55  JONES, CLARENCE WOODROW              5146-L EAST PONCE DE LEON - STONE MOUNTAIN GA 30083
63- 63  JONES, CLEON JOSEPH                  751 EDWARD ST - MOBILE AL 36610
28- 53  JONES, COBURN DYAS                   D. JUNE 3, 1969 DENVER, COLO.
41- 53  JONES, DALE ELDON                    D. NOVEMBER 8, 1980 ORLANDO, FLA.
79- 60  JONES, DARRYL LEE                    BOX 175 - HARMONSBURG PA 16422
26- 42  JONES, DECATUR POINDEXTER 'DICK'     125 MCAULEY DR - VICKSBURG MS 39180
82- 67  JONES, DOUGLAS REID                  129 NAVILLA - COVINA CA 91723
45- 50  JONES, EARL LESLIE                   D. JANUARY 24, 1989 FRESNO, CALIF.
70- 69  JONES, GARY HOWELL                   475 S. WESTRIDGE CIR - ANAHEIM HILLS CA 92807
54- 50  JONES, GORDON BASSETT                53 MOONLIT CIR - SACRAMENTO CA 95831
62- 62  JONES, GROVER WILLIAM 'DEACON'       1015 GOLDFINCH - SUGARLAND TX 77478
61- 57  JONES, HAROLD MARION                 4125 PALMYRA RD - LOS ANGELES CA 90008
21- 49  JONES, HOWARD                        D. JULY 15, 1972 JEANNETTE, PA.
```

86- 73	JONES, JAMES CONDIA	3054 NEWCASTLE DRIVE - DALLAS TX 75220
64- 54	JONES, JAMES DALTON	10155 MAMMOTH AVE - BATON ROUGE LA 70814
41- 54	JONES, JAMES MURRELL 'JAKE'	BOX 156-EPPS LA 71237
83- 86	JONES, JEFFERY RAYMOND	311 WHITE HORSE PL - HADDON HEIGHTS NJ 08035
80- 62	JONES, JEFFREY ALLEN	15626 DRAKE - SOUTHGATE MI 48198
23- 69	JONES, JESSE F. 'BROADWAY'	D. SEPTEMBER 7, 1977 LEWES, DEL.
24- 56	JONES, JOHN JOSEPH 'BINKY'	D. MAY 13, 1961 ST. LOUIS, MO.
19- 44	JONES, JOHN PAUL	D. JUNE 5, 1980 RUSTON, LA.
23- 70	JONES, JOHN WILLIAM	D. NOVEMBER 3, 1956 BALTIMORE, MD.
24- 57	JONES, KENNETH FREDERICK	4 RIDGE ROAD - SIMSBURY CT 06070
79- 61	JONES, LYNN MORRIS	BOX 175 - HARMONSBURG PA 16422
61- 58	JONES, MACK	184 NATHAN RD - ATLANTA GA 30331
80- 63	JONES, MICHAEL CARL	OLD ADD: 6182 HILLVIEW COURT - JACKSONVILLE FL 32210
40- 43	JONES, MORRIS E. 'RED'	D. JUNE 30, 1975 LINCOLN, CALIF.
75- 57	JONES, ODELL	17800 LYSANDER DR - CARSON CA 90746
20- 59	JONES, PERCY LEE	D. MARCH 18, 1979 DALLAS, TEXAS
73- 68	JONES, RANDALL LEO	13379 VIA STEPHEN - POWAY CA 92064
86- 74	JONES, RICKY MIRON	OLD ADD: 4071 GREENSTONE COURT - DECATUR GA 30035
74- 64	JONES, ROBERT OLIVER	2107 ABEYTA CT - LOVELAND CO 80537
17- 36	JONES, ROBERT WALTER	D. AUGUST 30, 1964 SAN DIEGO, CAL.
88- 73	JONES, RONALD GLEN	2316 CHAPMAN - SEQUIN TX 78155
84- 59	JONES, ROSS A.	5371 WEST 12TH AVE - HIALEAH FL 33012
76- 42	JONES, RUPPERT SANDERSON	P.O. BOX 1149 - POWAY CA 92064
51- 45	JONES, SAMUEL	D. NOVEMBER 5, 1971 MORGANTOWN, W. VA.
14-103	JONES, SAMUEL POND 'SAD SAM'	D. JULY 6, 1966 BARNESVILLE, O.
46- 51	JONES, SHELDON LESLIE 'AVAILABLE'	1102 WEST WRIGHT ROAD - GREENVILLE NC 27858
60- 56	JONES, SHERMAN JARVIS 'ROADBLOCK'	OLD ADD: WYANDOTTE COUNTY POLICE - KANSAS CITY KS 66101
67- 56	JONES, STEVEN HOWELL	8116 KINGSDALE DR - KNOXVILLE TN 37919
76- 43	JONES, THOMAS FREDERICK ;RICK'	4835 MANVILLE CIRCLE - JACKSONVILLE FL 32210
77- 75	JONES, TIMOTHY BYRON	6204 GREENEYES WAY - ORANGEVALE CA 95662
86- 75	JONES, TRACY DONALD	OLD ADD: 13727 JUDAH AVENUE - HAWTHORNE CA 90250
46- 52	JONES, VERNAL LEROY 'NIPPY'	7322 ALCEDO CIR - SACRAMENTO CA 95823
11- 84	JONES, WILLIAM DENNIS	D. OCTOBER 10, 1946 BOSTON, MASS.
11- 85	JONES, WILLIAM RODERICK 'TEX'	D. FEBRUARY 26, 1938 WICHITA, KAN.
88- 74	JONES, WILLIAM TIMOTHY 'TIM'	206 MILLER ROAD - SUMTER SC 29150
47- 49	JONES, WILLIE EDWARD	D. OCTOBER 18, 1983 CINCINNATI, O.
20- 60	JONNARD, CLARENCE JAMES 'BUBBER'	D. AUGUST 23, 1977 NEW YORK, N. Y.
21- 50	JONNARD, CLAUDE ALFRED	D. AUGUST 27, 1959 NASHVILLE, TENN.
36- 43	JOOST, EDWIN DAVID	245 BELGREEN PLACE - SANTA ROSA CA 95405
27- 48	JORDAN, BAXTER BYERLY 'BUCK'	2004-D LINCOLNTON RD - SALISBURY NC 28144
33- 31	JORDAN, JAMES WILLIAM	D. DECEMBER 4, 1957 GASTONIA, N. C.
53- 41	JORDAN, MILTON MIGNOT	57 LAKESHORE RD - LANSING NY 14881
51- 46	JORDAN, NILES CHAPMAN	1114 METCALF - SEDRO WOOLLEY WA 98284
88- 75	JORDAN, PAUL SCOTT 'RICKY'	11548 SUTTERS MILL CIRCLE - GOLD RIVER CA 95670
12- 90	JORDAN, RAYMOND WILLIS 'RIP'	D. JUNE 5, 1960 MERIDEN, CONN.
88- 76	JORDAN, SCOTT ALLAN	21 NETTLE COURT - COLUMBUS GA 31909
44- 66	JORDAN, THOMAS JEFFERSON	2909 SOUTH WYOMING - ROSWELL NM 88201
29- 57	JORGENS, ARNDT LUDWIG 'ART'	D. MARCH 1, 1980 WILMETTE, ILL.
35- 53	JORGENS, ORVILLE EDWARD	129 SOUTH SPRUCE ST-WOOD DALE IL 60191
47- 50	JORGENSEN, JOHN DONALD 'SPIDER'	8267 KIRKWOOD CT - CUCAMONGA CA 91730
68- 46	JORGENSEN, MICHAEL	1604 LILLIAN AVE - ARLINGTON TX 76013
89- 65	JORGENSEN, TERRY ALLEN	LUXEMBURG WI 54217
37- 56	JORGENSON, CARL 'PINKY'	119 MINNIE ST - SANTA CRUZ CA 95062
88- 77	JOSE, DOMINGO FELIX	CALLE 30 DE MAYO #7A - ING. OZAMA, SAN LUIS DOM. REP.
64- 55	JOSEPH, RICARDO EMELINDO	D. SEPTEMBER 8, 1979 SANTIAGO DOM REP
65- 53	JOSEPHSON, DUANE CHARLES	213 SOUTH CHESTNUT - NEW HAMPTON IA 50659
69- 89	JOSHUA, VON EVERETT	3499 RAINBOW LANE - HIGHLAND CA 92346
16- 48	JOURDAN, THEODORE CHARLES	D. SEPTEMBER 23, 1961 NEW ORLEANS, LA.
62- 63	JOYCE, MICHAEL LEWIS	1609 WHITMAN LN - WHEATON IL 60187
65- 54	JOYCE, RICHARD EDWARD	20 HILLSIDE AVENUE - UPPER SADDLE RIVER NJ 07458
39- 58	JOYCE, ROBERT EMMETT	D. DECEMBER 10, 1981 SAN FRANCISCO, CALIF.
86- 76	JOYNER, WALLACE KEITH	OLD ADD: 2186 TUDOR CASTLE WAY - DECATUR GA 30035
27- 49	JUDD, RALPH WESLEY	D. MAY 6, 1957 LAPEER, MICH.
41- 55	JUDD, THOMAS WILLIAM OSCAR	CATERBURY ST 64 - INGERSOLL ONTARIO CAN.
15- 77	JUDGE, JOSEPH IGNATIUS	D. MARCH 11, 1963 WASHINGTON, D.C.
40- 44	JUDNICH, WALTER FRANKLIN	D. JULY 12, 1971 GLENDALE, CAL.
48- 50	JUDSON, HOWARD KOLLS	239 FAIRWAY CIRCLE NE - WINTER HAVEN FL 33881
35- 54	JUDY, LYLE LEROY	309 RIVERSIDE DRIVE #207 - HOLLY HILL FL 32017
39- 59	JUELICH, JOHN WALTER	D. DECEMBER 25, 1970 ST. LOUIS, MO.
40- 45	JUMONVILLE, GEORGE BENEDICT	5507 WILLIAM & MARY - MOBILE AL 36608
37- 57	JUNGELS, KENNETH PETER	D. SEPTEMBER 9, 1975 WEST BEND, WIS.
82- 68	JURAK, EDWARD JAMES	3650 SOUTH WALKER AVE - SAN PEDRO CA 90731
65- 55	JUREWICZ, MICHAEL ALLEN	17826 IXONIA AVE WEST - LAKEVILLE MN 55044
31- 43	JURGES, WILLIAM FREDERICK	OLD ADD: 7001 142ND AVE #74 - LARGO FL 33541
44- 67	JURISICH, ALVIN JOSEPH	D. NOVEMBER 3, 1981 NEW ORLEANS, LA.
44- 68	JUST, JOSEPH ERWIN	7708 WEST KANGAROO LAKE-BAILEYS HARBOR WI 54202
89- 66	JUSTICE, DAVID CHRISTOPHER	311 GLENWOOD AVENUE - CINCINNATI OH 45217
72- 55	JUTZE, ALFRED HENRY 'SKIP'	3395 ZEPHYR CT - WHEAT RIDGE CO 80033
14-104	JUUL, EARL HERBERT	D. JANUARY 4, 1942 CHICAGO, ILL.
11- 86	JUUL, HERBERT VICTOR	D. NOVEMBER 14, 1928 CHICAGO, ILL.
59- 43	KAAT, JAMES LEE	100 SE 5TH AVENUE #509 - BOCA RATON FL 33432
10- 77	KADING, JOHN FREDERICK	D. JUNE 2, 1964 CHICAGO, ILL.
13- 94	KAFORA, FRANK JACOB 'JAKE'	D. MARCH 23, 1928 CHICAGO, ILL.
22- 65	KAHDOT, ISAAC LEONARD 'IKE'	2218 NW 42ND - OKLAHOMA CITY OK 73112
38- 43	KAHLE, ROBERT WAYNE	D. DECEMBER 16, 1988 INGLEWOOD, CALIF.
10- 78	KAHLER, GEORGE RANNELS	D. FEBRUARY 14, 1924 BATTLE CREEK, MICH.
30- 39	KAHN, OWEN EARLE 'JACK'	D. JANUARY 17, 1981 RICHMOND, VA.
80- 64	KAINER, DONALD WAYNE	10 DARNELL - CONROE TX 77301
11- 87	KAISER, ALFRED EDWARD	D. APRIL 11, 1969 CINCINNATI, O.
55- 62	KAISER, CLYDE DONALD 'DON'	2901 EAST 12TH - ADA OK 74820
85- 55	KAISER, JEFFREY PATRICK	2807 RIVERSIDE - TRENTON MI 48183
71- 57	KAISER, ROBERT THOMAS	1774 TERRAZA - OCEANSIDE CA 92054
14-105	KAISERLING, GEORGE	D. MARCH 2, 1918 STEUBENVILLE, O.
37- 58	KALFASS, WILLIAM PHILIP	D. SEPTEMBER 8, 1968 BROOKLYN, N. Y.
40- 46	KALIN, FRANK BRUNO	D. JANUARY 12, 1975 WEIRTON, W. VA.
53- 42	KALINE, ALBERT WILLIAM	945 TIMBERLAKE DR - BLOOMFIELD HILLS MI 48013
18- 41	KALLIO, RUDOLPH	D. APRIL 6, 1979 NEWPORT, ORE.
23- 71	KAMM, WILLIAM EDWARD 'WILLIE'	D. DECEMBER 21, 1988 BELMONT, CALIF.

78- 64	KAMMEYER, ROBERT LYNN	4711 DEL RIO RD - SACRAMENTO CA 95822
24- 58	KAMP, ALPHONSE FRANCIS	D. FEBRUARY 25, 1955 BOSTON, MASS.
34- 52	KAMPOURIS, ALEX WILLIAM	2776 17TH ST - SACRAMENTO CA 95818
15- 78	KANE, FRANCIS THOMAS	D. DECEMBER 2, 1962 BROCKTON, MASS.
25- 57	KANE, JOHN FRANCIS	D. JULY 25, 1956 CHICAGO, ILL.
38- 44	KANE, THOMAS JOSEPH	D. NOVEMBER 26, 1973 CHICAGO, ILL.
62- 64	KANEHL, RODERICK EDWIN	72600 FRED WARING DRIVE #701 - PALM DESERT CA 92260
14-106	KANTLEHNER, ERVINE LESTER	D. FEBRUARY 3, 1990 SANTA BARBARA, CALIF.
36- 44	KARDOW, PAUL OTTO	D. APRIL 27, 1968 SAN ANTONIO, TEXAS
86- 77	KARKOVICE, RONALD JOSEPH	3400 CHAROW LANE - ORLANDO FL 32806
43- 68	KARL, ANTON ANDREW	D. APRIL 8, 1989 SAN DIEGO, CALIF.
30- 40	KARLON, WILLIAM JOHN 'JACK'	D. DECEMBER 7, 1964 WARE, MASS.
27- 50	KAROW, MARTIN GREGORY	D. APRIL 27, 1986 BRYAN, TEXAS
46- 53	KARPEL, HERBERT	6922 BABCOCK AVE - NORTH HOLLYWOOD CA 91605
20- 61	KARR, BENJAMIN JOYCE	D. DECEMBER 8, 1968 MEMPHIS, TENN.
15- 79	KARST, JOHN GOTTLIEB	D. MAY 21, 1976 CAPE MAY COURT HOUSE, N. J.
57- 35	KASKO, EDWARD MICHAEL	317 BURNWICK RD - RICHMOND VA 23227
52- 58	KATT, RAYMOND FREDERICK	711 RUDELOFF RD - SEGUIN TX 78155
44- 69	KATZ, ROBERT CLYDE	D. DECEMBER 14, 1962 ST. JOSEPH, MICH.
12- 91	KAUFF, BENJAMIN MICHAEL	D. NOVEMBER 17, 1961 COLUMBUS,O.
14-107	KAUFFMAN, HOWARD RICHARD 'DICK'	D. APRIL 17, 1948 LEWISBURG, PA.
21- 51	KAUFMAN, ANTHONY CHARLES	D. JUNE 4, 1982 ELGIN, ILL.
82- 69	KAUFMAN, CURT GERRARD	RR 3 BOX 33 - HARLAN IA 51537
14-108	KAVANAGH, CHARLES HUGH	D. SEPTEMBER 6, 1973 REEDSBURG, WIS.
14-109	KAVANAGH, LEO DANIEL	D. AUGUST 10, 1950 CHICAGO, ILL.
14-110	KAVANAGH, MARTIN JOSEPH	D. JULY 28, 1960 TAYLOR, MICH.
48- 51	KAZAK, EDWARD TERRANCE	802 NEWMAN DR - AUSTIN TX 78703
53- 43	KAZANSKI, THEODORE STANLEY	40008 CROSSWIND - NOVI MI 48050
68- 47	KEALEY, STEVEN WILLIAM	RR 1 BOX 6 - HILLSBORO KS 67063
61- 59	KEANE, JOHN JOSEPH	D. JANUARY 6, 1967 HOUSTON, TEX.
79- 62	KEARNEY, ROBERT HENRY	11611 PICCADILLY CIRCLE - SAN ANTONIO TX 78251
24- 59	KEARNS, EDWARD PAUL 'TED'	D. DECEMBER 21, 1949 TRENTON, N. J.
42- 54	KEARSE, EDWARD PAUL	D. JULY 15, 1968 EUREKA, CALIF.
12- 92	KEATING, RAYMOND HERBERT	D. DECEMBER 28, 1963 SACRAMENTO, CALIF.
13- 95	KEATING, WALTER FRANCIS 'CHICK'	D. JULY 13, 1959 PHILADELPHIA, PA.
81- 65	KEATLEY, GREGORY STEVEN	101 WOODLAND DRIVE - LEXINGTON SC 29072
22- 66	KECK, FRANK JOSEPH 'CACTUS'	D. FEBRUARY 6, 1981 ST. LOUIS, MO.
85- 56	KEEDY, CHARLES PATRICK 'PAT'	1958 BRACKETT LOOP - BIRMINGHAM AL 35214
17- 37	KEEFE, DAVID EDWIN	D. FEBRUARY 4, 1978 KANSAS CITY, MO.
59- 44	KEEGAN, EDWARD CHARLES	BOX 71-A, HARRISONVILLE RD - MULLICA HILL NJ 08067
53- 44	KEEGAN, ROBERT CHARLES	101 SANDSTONE DR - ROCHESTER NY 14616
44- 70	KEELY, ROBERT WILLIAM	313 BRYN MAWR ISLAND - BRADENTON FL 33507
18- 42	KEEN, HOWARD VICTOR	D. DECEMBER 10, 1976 SALISBURY, MD.
11- 88	KEEN, WILLIAM BROWN	D. JULY 16, 1947 SOUTH POINT, O.
20- 62	KEENAN, JAMES WILLIAM	D. JUNE 5, 1980 SEMINOLE, FLA.
82- 70	KEENER, JEFFREY BRUCE	31607 102ND AVE SE - AUBURN WA 98002
76- 44	KEENER, JOSEPH DONALD	STAR ROUTE 79 - ADELANTO CA 92301
25- 58	KEESEY, JAMES WARD	D. SEPTEMBER 5, 1951 BOISE, IDA.
80- 65	KEETON, RICKEY	3433 STATHEM AVE - CINCINNATI OH 45211
42- 55	KEHN, CHESTER LAURENCE	D. APRIL 5, 1984 SAN DIEGO, CALIF.
14-111	KEIFER, SHERMAN CARL	D. FEBRUARY 19, 1927 OUTWOOD, KY.
65- 56	KEKICH, MICHAEL DENNIS	3901 GEORGIA NE #G3 - ALBUQUERQUE NM 87110
11- 89	KELIHER, MAURICE MICHAEL	D. SEPTEMBER 7, 1930 WASHINGTON, D.C.
52- 59	KELL, EVERETT LEE 'SKEETER'	3101 OLIVE - PINE BLUFF AR 71603
43- 69	KELL, GEORGE CLYDE	BOX 158 - SWIFTON AR 72471
16- 49	KELLEHER, ALBERT ALOYSIUS 'DUKE'	D. SEPTEMBER 28, 1947 STATEN ISLAND, N. Y.
42- 56	KELLEHER, FRANCIS EUGENE	D. APRIL 13, 1979 STOCKTON, CALIF.
35- 55	KELLEHER, HAROLD JOSEPH	D. AUGUST 27, 1989 CAPE MAY COURT HOUSE, N. J.
12- 93	KELLEHER, JOHN PATRICK	D. AUGUST 21, 1960 BRIGHTON, MASS.
72- 56	KELLEHER, MICHAEL DENNIS	2429 ANACAPA ST - SANTA BARBARA CA 93105
39- 60	KELLER, CHARLES ERNEST	D. MAY 23, 1990 FREDERICK, MD.
49- 40	KELLER, HAROLD KEFAUVER	2018 245TH AVE SE - ISSAQUAH WA 98027
66- 51	KELLER, RONALD LEE	4280 ROLAND RD - INDIANAPOLIS IN 46208
53- 45	KELLERT, FRANK WILLIAM	D. NOVEMBER 19, 1976 OKLAHOMA CITY, OKLA.
23- 72	KELLETT, ALFRED HENRY	D. JULY 14, 1960 NEW YORK, N. Y.
34- 53	KELLETT, DONALD STAFFORD 'RED'	D. NOVEMBER 5, 1970 FT. LAUDERDALE, ALA.
25- 59	KELLEY, HARRY LEROY	D. MARCH 23, 1958 PARKIN, ARK.
64- 56	KELLEY, RICHARD ANTHONY	OLD ADD: 13630 ADDISON ST - SHERMAN OAKS CA 91423
64- 57	KELLEY, THOMAS HENRY	2933 FINCH DR - DANVILLE VA 24540
19- 45	KELLIHER, FRANCIS MORTIMER	D. MARCH 4, 1956 SOMERVILLE, MASS.
48- 52	KELLNER, ALEXANDER RAYMOND	3716 NORTH JACKSON AVE - TUCSON AZ 85719
52- 60	KELLNER, WALTER JOSEPH	3737 NORTH TUCSON BLVD - TUCSON AZ 85716
14-112	KELLOGG, WILLIAM DEARSTYNE	D. DECEMBER 12, 1971 BALTIMORE, MD.
10- 79	KELLY, ALBERT MICHAEL 'RED'	D. JANUARY 29, 1961 ZEPHYRHILLS, FLA.
86- 78	KELLY, BRYAN KEITH	8012 ROSE AVENUE - ORLANDO FL 32810
80- 66	KELLY, DALE PATRICK 'PAT'	5176 SAN SIMEON DR - SANTA BARBARA CA 93111
14-113	KELLY, EDWARD LEO	D. NOVEMBER 4, 1928 RED LODGE, MONT.
15- 80	KELLY, GEORGE LANGE	D. OCTOBER 13, 1984 BURLINGAME, CALIF.
67- 57	KELLY, HAROLD PATRICK 'PAT'	6748 FRIENDSHIP DRIVE - SARASOTA FL 34241
14-114	KELLY, HERBERT BARRETT	D. MAY 18, 1973 TORRANCE, CALIF.
14-115	KELLY, JAMES ROBERT	D. APRIL 10, 1961 KINGSPORT, TENN.
75- 58	KELLY, JAY THOMAS 'TOM'	9244 133RD LANE NORTH - SEMINOLE FL 34646
14-116	KELLY, JOSEPH HENRY	D. AUGUST 16, 1977 ST. JOSEPH, MO.
26- 43	KELLY, JOSEPH JAMES	D. NOVEMBER 24, 1969 LYNBROOK, N. Y.
26- 44	KELLY, MICHAEL J.	OLD ADD: 5853 VON VESSEN AVE - ST LOUIS MO
23- 73	KELLY, REYNOLDS JOSEPH 'REN'	D. AUGUST 24, 1963 MILLBRAE, CAL.
87- 71	KELLY, ROBERT CONRADO	4 CIUDAD RADIAL - JUANA DIAZ PANAMA C.A.
51- 47	KELLY, ROBERT EDWARD	9 MOHAWK DR - NIENTIC CT 06359
69- 90	KELLY, VAN HOWARD	11 BEAUREGARD DR - SPENCER NC 28159
20- 63	KELLY, WILLIAM HENRY	D. APRIL 8, 1990 SYRACUSE, N. Y.
10- 80	KELLY, WILLIAM JOSEPH	D. JUNE 3, 1940 DETROIT, MICH.
64- 58	KELSO, WILLIAM EUGENE	419 NW BRIARCLIFF ROAD - KANSAS CITY MO 64116
37- 59	KELTNER, KEN FREDERICK	3220 KING ARTHURS CT WEST - GREENFIELD WI 53221
54- 51	KEMMERER, RUSSELL PAUL	6335 COLEBROOK DRIVE - INDIANAPOLIS IN 46220
29- 58	KEMNER, HERMAN JOHN 'DUTCH'	D. JANUARY 16, 1988 QUINCY, ILL.
77- 76	KEMP, STEVE F	12979 CLAYMONT COURT - SAN DIEGO CA 92130
69- 91	KENDALL, FRED LYNN	1219 HICKORY AVE - TORRANCE CA 90503
61- 60	KENDERS, ALBERT DANIEL GEORGE	8744 MATILIJA AVE - VAN NUYS CA 91402

JOHNNY BENCH S.00

MOE BERG

HUGH CASEY

MICKEY COCHRANE

EARLE COMBS

"Pea Ridge" Day
PEA RIDGE DAY

HOWARD EHMKE

PAUL DEAN

LOU GEHRIG
600.

GIL HODGES

CUT
AUTOGRAPHS

MARK FIDRYCH

HARMON KILLEBREW 3.00

WALLY PIPP

BOOG POWELL

BROOKS ROBINSON

GUS SANDBERG

BABE RUTH 6.00.

BILL WAMBSGANSS

PAUL WANER

DAVE WINFIELD

CARL YASTRZEMSKI
3.00

73

28- 54	KENNA, EDWARD ALOYSIUS	D. AUGUST 21, 1972 SAN FRANCISCO, CALIF.
70- 70	KENNEDY, JAMES EARL	OLD ADD: 2573 NW NORTHRUP - PORTLAND OR 97210
62- 65	KENNEDY, JOHN EDWARD	2 RODNEY ROAD - WEST PEABODY MA 01960
57- 36	KENNEDY, JOHN IRVIN	%E.WHITE,4166 LOCKHART-JACKSONVILLE FL 32209
74- 65	KENNEDY, JUNIOR RAYMOND	412 FRONTIER STREET - BAKERSFIELD CA 93308
34- 54	KENNEDY, LLOYD VERNON 'VERN'	RR 1 BOX 164 - MENDON MO 64660
46- 54	KENNEDY, MONTIA CALVIN	5735 BERRYWOOD - RICHMOND VA 23224
16- 50	KENNEDY, RAYMOND LINCOLN	D. JANUARY 18, 1969 CASSELBERRY, FLA.
39- 61	KENNEDY, ROBERT DANIEL	3708 EAST OMEGA CIR - MESA AZ 85205
78- 65	KENNEDY, TERRENCE EDWARD	P.O. BOX 220 - RIDERWOOD MD 21139
48- 53	KENNEDY, WILLIAM AULTON	D. APRIL 8, 1983 SEATTLE, WASH.
42- 57	KENNEDY, WILLIAM GORMAN	2500 N. VAN DORN ST #621 - ALEXANDRIA VA 22304
38- 45	KENNEY, ARTHUR JOSEPH	#3 TIMBER LANE - NORTH READING MA 01864
67- 58	KENNEY, GERALD T	1980 HARRISON - BELOIT WI 53511
12- 94	KENT, MAURICE ALLEN	D. APRIL 19, 1966 IOWA CITY, IA.
62- 66	KENWORTHY, RICHARD LEE	3745 TADE LN - INDIANAPOLIS IN 46234
12- 95	KENWORTHY, WILLIAM JENNINGS 'DUKE'	D. SEPTEMBER 21, 1950 EUREKA, CALIF.
68- 48	KEOUGH, JOSEPH WILLIAM	OLD ADD: 2958 LIBERTY DRIVE - PLEASANTON CA 94566
77- 77	KEOUGH, MATTHEW LON	6281 FRONT SOUTH RD - LIVERMORE CA 94550
56- 47	KEOUGH, RICHARD MARTIN 'MARTY'	18 FABRIANO - IRVINE CA 92720
84- 60	KEPSHIRE, KURT DAVID	27 OAKWOOD DRIVE - SEYMOUR CT 06483
85- 57	KERFELD, CHARLES PATRICK	1001 SONOMA ST - CARSON CITY NV 89701
50- 41	KERIAZAKOS, CONSTANTINE NICHOLAS 'GUS	238 CLAREMONT AVE - MONTCLAIR NJ 07042
39- 62	KERKSIECK, WAYMAN WILLIAM 'BILL'	D. MARCH 11, 1970 LITTLE ROCK, ARK.
15- 81	KERLIN, ORIE MILTON	D. OCTOBER 29, 1974 SHREVEPORT, LA.
74- 66	KERN, JAMES LESTER	6009 AMBERWOOD CT - ARLINGTON TX 76016
62- 67	KERN, WILLIAM GEORGE	625 GREEN ST - ALLENTOWN PA 18102
65- 57	KERNEK, GEORGE BOYD	BOX 1225 - PURCELL OK 73080
20- 64	KERNS, DANIEL P.	B. PHILADELPHIA, PA.
45- 51	KERNS, RUSSELL ELDON	22000 LAWRENCE RD - FIDDLETOWN CA 95629
23- 74	KERR, JOHN FRANCIS	2812 EAST 220TH PL - LONG BEACH CA 90810
14-117	KERR, JOHN JONAS 'DOC'	D. JUNE 9, 1937 BALTIMORE, MD.
43- 70	KERR, JOHN JOSEPH 'BUDDY'	341 GROVE ST-ORADELL NJ 07649
25- 60	KERR, JOHN MELVILLE 'MEL'	D. AUGUST 9, 1980 VERO BEACH, FLA.
19- 46	KERR, RICHARD HENRY	D. MAY 4, 1963 HOUSTON, TEX.
76- 45	KERRIGAN, JOSEPH THOMAS	1018 SAN GABRIEL CIRCLE #521 - DALY CITY CA 94014
64- 59	KESSINGER, DONALD EULON	1010 JUNE ROAD #201 - MEMPHIS TN 38119
68- 49	KESTER, RICHARD LEE	BOX 623 - GARDNERVILLE NV 89410
22- 67	KETCHUM, AUGUST FRANKLIN 'GUS'	D. SEPTEMBER 10, 1980 OKLAHOMA CITY, OKLA.
12- 96	KETTER, PHILIP	B. HUTCHINSON, KAN.
14-118	KEUPPER, HENRY J.	D. AUGUST 14 1960 MARION, ILL.
84- 61	KEY, JAMES EDWARD	OLD ADD: 3301 AVERY AVENUE SW - HUNTSVILLE AL 35805
85- 58	KHALIFA, SAM	8825 EAST SECOND PLACE - TUCSON AZ 85710
25- 61	KIBBIE, HORACE KENT 'HOD'	D. OCTOBER 19, 1975 FORT WORTH, TEX.
12- 97	KIBBLE, JOHN WESTLY	D. DECEMBER 13, 1969 ROUNDUP, MONT.
20- 65	KIEFER, JOSEPH WILLIAM	D. JULY 5, 1975 UTICA, N. Y.
84- 62	KIEFER, STEVEN GEORGE	11822 OLD FASHION - GARDEN GROVE CA 92640
51- 48	KIELY, LEO PATRICK	D. JANUARY 18, 1984 GLEN RIDGE, N. J.
17- 38	KILDUFF, PETER JOHN	D. FEBRUARY 14, 1930 PITTSBURG, KAN.
87- 72	KILGUS, PAUL NELSON	2102 SMALLHOUSE ROAD - BOWLING GREEN KY 42101
14-119	KILHULLEN, JOSEPH ISADORE 'PAT'	D. NOVEMBER 2, 1922 OAKLAND, CALIF.
69- 92	KILKENNY, MICHAEL DAVID	274 HOLLAND ST WEST - BRADFORD ONTARIO CAN.
54- 52	KILLEBREW, HARMON CLAYTON	BOX 626 - ONTARIO OR 97914
59- 45	KILLEEN, EVANS HENRY	123 MAIN ST - WESTHAMPTON NY 11978
11- 90	KILLILAY, JOHN WILLIAM	D. OCTOBER 21, 1968 TULSA, OKLA.
37- 60	KIMBALL, NEWELL W. 'NEWT'	1425 GRIFFITH AVE - LAS VEGAS NV 89104
36- 45	KIMBERLIN, HARRY LYDLE	1028 KINZER ST #201B - POPLAR BLUFF MO 63901
45- 52	KIMBLE, RICHARD LOUIS	3733 LARCHMONT PARKWAY - TOLEDO OH 43613
20- 66	KIME, HAROLD LEE	D. MAY 16, 1939 COLUMBUS, O.
76- 46	KIMM, BRUCE EDWARD	RR 1 BOX 13A - AMANA IA 52203
19- 47	KIMMICK, WALTER LYONS	D. JULY 21, 1989 BOSWELL, PA.
29- 59	KIMSEY, CLYDE ELIAS 'CHAD'	D. DECEMBER 3, 1942 PRYOR, OKLA.
56- 48	KINDALL, GERALD DONALD	ATH DEPT, UNIV OF ARIZONA - TUCSON AZ 85721
46- 55	KINDER, ELLIS RAYMOND	D. OCTOBER 16, 1968 JACKSON, TENN.
46- 56	KINER, RALPH MCPHERRAN	48 271 SILVER SPUR TRAIL - PALM DESERT CA 92260
54- 53	KING, CHARLES GILBERT 'CHICK'	RURAL ROUTE 1 BOX 68B - PARIS TN 38242
44- 71	KING, CLYDE EDWARD	103 STRATFORD RD - GOLDSBORO NC 27530
16- 51	KING, EDWARD LEE	D. SEPTEMBER 16, 1967 SHINNSTOWN, W. VA.
16- 52	KING, EDWARD LEE	D. SEPTEMBER 7, 1938 CHELSEA, MASS.
86- 79	KING, ERIC STEVEN	1063 STANFORD DRIVE - SIMI VALLEY CA 93065
67- 59	KING, HAROLD	1027 WEST SOUTH ST - ORLANDO FL 32805
55- 63	KING, JAMES HUBERT	RR 2 BOX 15 - ELKINS AR 72727
89- 67	KING, JEFFREY WAYNE	9835 KIT CARSON LANE - COLORADO SPRINGS CO 80908
35- 56	KING, LYNN PAUL	D. MAY 11, 1972 ATLANTIC, IA.
54- 54	KING, NELSON JOSEPH	126 JAMES PL - PITTSBURGH PA 15228
32- 39	KINGDON, WESCOTT WILLIAM	D. APRIL 19, 1975 CAPISTRANO, CALIF.
86- 80	KINGERY, MICHAEL SCOTT	411 SOUTH THIRD - ATWATER MN 56209
79- 63	KINGMAN, BRIAN PAUL	11 TOKENEKE TRAIL - DARIEN CT 06820
71- 58	KINGMAN, DAVID ARTHUR	OLD ADD: P.O. BOX 209 - GLENBROOK NV 89413
14-120	KINGMAN, HENRY LEES	D. DECEMBER 27, 1982 OAKLAND, CALIF.
78- 66	KINNEY, DENNIS PAUL	122 ROBERTS DRIVE - SCHNECKSVILLE PA 18078
18- 43	KINNEY, WALTER WILLIAM	D. JULY 1, 1971 ESCONDIDO, CAL.
80- 67	KINNUNEN, MICHAEL JOHN	5818 MCKINLEY PL NORTH - SEATTLE WA 98103
19- 48	KINSELLA, ROBERT FRANCIS	D. DECEMBER 30, 1951 LOS ANGELES, CALIF.
89- 68	KINZER, MATTHEW ROY	5899 NORTH 400 WEST - UNIONDALE IN 46791
34- 55	KINZY, HENRY HENSEL 'HARRY'	3721 ARROYO RD - FORT WORTH TX 76109
57- 37	KIPP, FRED LEO	6510 WEST 69TH ST - OVERLAND PARK KS 66204
85- 59	KIPPER, ROBERT WAYNE	17 HILLCREST DRIVE - AURORA IL 60506
53- 46	KIPPER, THORNTON JOHN	8780 EAST MCKELLOPS #340 - SCOTTSDALE AZ 85257
14-121	KIPPERT, EDWARD AUGUST	D. JUNE 3, 1960 DETROIT, MICH.
69- 93	KIRBY, CLAYTON LAWS	949 NORTH POTOMAC ST - ARLINGTON VA 22205
49- 41	KIRBY, JAMES HERSCHEL	729 DOVER RD - NASHVILLE TN 37211
12- 98	KIRBY, LARUE	D. JUNE 10, 1961 LANSING, MICH.
19- 49	KIRCHER, MICHAEL ANDREW	D. JUNE 26, 1972 ROCHESTER, N. Y.
47- 51	KIRK, THOMAS DANIEL	D. AUGUST 1, 1974 PHILADELPHIA, PA.
61- 61	KIRK, WILLIAM PARTHEMORE	365 FOLKSTONE WAY - YORK PA 17402
10- 81	KIRKE, JUDSON FABIAN 'JAY'	D. AUGUST 31, 1968 NEW ORLEANS, LA.
58- 51	KIRKLAND, WILLIE CHARLES	OLD ADD: 17155 SANTA ROSA - DETROIT MI 48221

62- 68 KIRKPATRICK, EDGAR LEON	24791 VIA LARGA - LAGUNA NIGUEL CA 92677
12- 99 KIRKPATRICK, ENOS CLAIRE	D. APRIL 14, 1964 PITTSBURGH, PA.
74- 67 KIRKWOOD, DONALD PAUL	455 WEST ELMWOOD - CLAWSON MI 48017
50- 42 KIRRENE, JOSEPH JOHN	2557 KILPATRICK COURT - SAN RAMON CA 94583
10- 82 KIRSCH, HARRY LOUIS	D. DECEMBER 25, 1925 PITTSBURGH, PA.
45- 53 KISH, ERNEST ALEXANDER	486-3 BUCK CROSSING - AURORA OH 44202
71- 59 KISON, BRUCE EUGENE	1403 RIVERVIEW CIRCLE - BRADENTON FL 33529
54- 55 KITSOS, CHRISTOPHER ANESTOS	1219 ANCHOR DR - MOBILE AL 36609
82- 71 KITTLE, RONALD DALE	8080 E. 109TH - CROWN POINT IN 46307
34- 56 KLAERNER, HUGO EMIL	D. JANUARY 3, 1982 FREDERICKSBURG, TEXAS
66- 52 KLAGES, FRED ANTHONY	OLD ADD: 261 BERRY ST - BADEN PA 15005
64- 60 KLAUS, ROBERT FRANCIS	10661 GABACHO DR - SAN DIEGO CA 92124
52- 61 KLAUS, WILLIAM JOSEPH	1655 SOUTH DR - SARASOTA FL 33579
85- 60 KLAWITTER, THOMAS CARL	2913 MOHECAN - JANESVILLE WI 53545
25- 52 KLEE, OLLIE CHESTER	D. FEBRUARY 9, 1977 TOLEDO, O.
28- 55 KLEIN, CHARLES HERBERT	D. MARCH 28, 1958 INDIANAPOLIS, IND.
44- 72 KLEIN, HAROLD JOHN	D. DECEMBER 10, 1957 ST. LOUIS, MO.
43- 71 KLEIN, LOUIS FRANK	D. JUNE 20, 1976 METAIRIE, LA.
34- 57 KLEINHANS, THEODORE OTTO	D. JULY 24, 1985 REDINGTON BEACH, FLA.
35- 57 KLEINKE, NORBERT GEORGE 'NUB'	D. MARCH 16, 1950 MARIN, CAL.
11- 91 KLEPFER, EDWARD LLOYD	D. AUGUST 9, 1950 TULSA, OKLA.
76- 47 KLEVEN, JAY ALLEN	118 VIA BOLSA - SAN LORENZO CA 94580
43- 72 KLIEMAN, EDWARD FREDERICK	D. NOVEMBER 15, 1979 HOMOS ASSA, FLA.
58- 52 KLIMCHOCK, LOUIS STEPHEN	1913 EAST MYRNA LANE - TEMPE AZ 85284
69- 94 KLIMKOWSKI, RONALD BERNARDO	791 EDGEWOOD DR - WESTBURY NY 11590
55- 64 KLINE, JOHN ROBERT 'BOBBY'	5924 47TH AVE NORTH -ST PETERSBURG FL 33703
30- 41 KLINE, ROBERT GEORGE	D. MARCH 16, 1987 WESTERVILLE, O.
52- 62 KLINE, RONALD LEE	MAIN ST BOX 155 - CALLERY PA 16024
70- 71 KLINE, STEVEN JACK	BOX 429 - CHELAN WA 98816
27- 51 KLINGER, JOSEPH JOHN	D. JULY 31, 1960 LITTLE ROCK, ARK.
38- 46 KLINGER, ROBERT HAROLD	D. AUGUST 19, 1977 VILLA RIDGE, MO.
87- 73 KLINK, JOSEPH CHARLES	2115 NORTH 35TH AVENUE - HOLLYWOOD FL 33021
50- 43 KLIPPSTEIN, JOHN CALVIN	1176 ABERDEEN RD - PALATINE IL 60067
44- 73 KLOPP, STANLEY HAROLD	D. MARCH 11, 1980 ROBESONIA, PA.
31- 44 KLOZA, JLHN CLARENCE 'NAP'	D. JULY 18, 1951 MOBERLY, MO.
21- 52 KLUGMANN, JOSIE	N67 W27085 SILVER SPRING DRIVE - SUSSEX WI 53089
34- 58 KLUMPP, ELMER EDWARD	D. MARCH 29, 1988 CINCINNATI, O.
47- 52 KLUSZEWSKI, THEODORE BERNARD	20701 BECH BLVD #259-HUNTINGTON BCH CA 92648
76- 48 KLUTTS, GENE ELLIS "MICKEY"	D. MAY 12, 1979 SALISBURY, N. C.
42- 58 KLUTTZ, CLYDE FRANKLIN	1415 CASTLE CT - ST JOSEPH MI 49085
75- 59 KNAPP, ROBERT CHRISTIAN 'CHRIS'	D. JULY 6, 1967 NEW ORLEANS, LA.
10- 83 KNAUPP, HENRY ANTONE 'COTTON'	D. APRIL 6, 1965 BALTIMORE, MD.
26- 45 KNEISCH, RUDOLPH FRANK	2045 OAKHILL ROAD - ROSEBURG OR 97470
76- 49 KNEPPER, ROBERT WESLEY	D. MARCH 23, 1980 LANCASTER, P A.
45- 54 KNERR, WALLACE LUTHER 'LOU'	BOX 433 - DAYTON VA 22821
79- 64 KNICELY, ALAN LEE	P.O. BOX 236 - CLINTON CORNERS NY 12514
47- 53 KNICKERBOCKER, AUSTIN JAY	D. SEPTEMBER 8, 1963 SEBASTOPOL, CALIF.
33- 32 KNICKERBOCKER, WILLIAM HART	2308 TARA DRIVE - ALBANY GA 31707
74- 68 KNIGHT, CHARLES RAY 'RAY'	D. JULY 30, 1976 SAN ANTONIO, TEX.
22- 68 KNIGHT, ELMA RUSSELL 'JACK'	D. JULY 1, 1948 BROWNSVILLE,PA.
12-100 KNISELY, PETER C.	D. DECEMBER 20, 1980 SOUTH BEND, IND.
20- 67 KNODE, KENNETH THOMSON 'MIKE'	D. APRIL 13, 1982 BATTLE CREEK, MICH.
23- 75 KNODE, ROBERT TROXELL 'RAY'	P.O. BOX 981 - FRONTENAC KS 66762
64- 61 KNOOP, ROBERT FRANK	D. JULY 3, 1981 DOVER, N. J.
32- 40 KNOTHE, GEORGE BERTRAM	D. MARCH 22, 1963 PASSAIC, N. J.
32- 41 KNOTHE, WILFRED EDGAR 'FRITZ'	D. OCTOBER 13, 1981 BROWNWOOD, TEXAS
33- 33 KNOTT, JOHN HENRY	5261 42ND ST - ST.PETERSBURG FL 33711
65- 58 KNOWLES, DAROLD DUANE	D. APRIL 11, 1943 MIAMI SHORES, FLA.
15- 82 KNOWLSON, THOMAS HERBERT	D. FEBRUARY 25, 1944 PHILADELPHIA, PA.
20- 60 KNOWLTON, WILLIAM YOUNG	D. SEPTEMBER 24, 1965 OSKALOOSA, IA.
24- 60 KNOX, CLIFFORD HIRAM 'BUD'	OLD ADD: 34 PELL MELL DRIVE - BETHEL CT 06801
72- 57 KNOX, JOHN CLINTON	881 WEST 100TH AVE - NORTHGLENN CO 80221
85- 61 KNUDSON, MARK RICHARD	52 STONEHEDGE DR - NEWINGTON CT 06111
53- 47 KOBACK, NICHOLAS NICHOLIA	EDDY RD - COLDEN NY 14033
73- 69 KOBEL, KEVIN RICHARD	1517 RIDGELAND ROAD EAST - MOBILE AL 36695
63- 64 KOCH, ALAN GOODMAN	D. JUNE 6, 1987 TACOMA, WASH.
44- 74 KOCH, BARNETT	D. JANUARY 13, 1965 WHITE HAVEN, PA.
12-104 KOCHER, BRADLEY WILSON	2000 VALLEY FORGE CIR-KING OF PRUSSIA PA19406
46- 57 KOECHER, RICHARD FINLAY	OLD ADD: 1205 NORTH 48TH - PHOENIX AZ 85008
70- 72 KOEGEL, PETER JOHN	D. DECEMBER 8, 1986 TACOMA, WASH.
25- 63 KOEHLER, HORACE LEVERING 'POP'	D. SEPTEMBER 17, 1935 TORONTO, ONT.
32- 42 KOENECKE, LEONARD GEORGE	RURAL ROUTE 3 #3654 - ORLAND CA 95963
25- 64 KOENIG, MARK ANTHONY	D. JULY 1, 1972 WATERLOO, ILL.
19- 50 KOENIGSMARK, WILLIS THOMAS	D. OCTOBER 27, 1959 FAIRBURY, ILL.
10- 84 KOESTNER, ELMER JOSEPH	D. MARCH 16, 1974 PHILADELPHIA, PA.
37- 61 KOHLMAN, JOSEPH JAMES	D. APRIL 9, 1986 CHICAGO, ILL.
48- 54 KOKOS, RICHARD JEROME	164 CIRCLE DR - CROSS LANE WV 25356
60- 57 KOLB, GARY ALAN	2236 WEST 121ST STREET PL - BLUE ISLAND IL 60406
40- 47 KOLLOWAY, DONALD MARTIN	D. JULY 29, 1967 NEW ORLEANS, LA.
21- 53 KOLP, RAYMOND CARL	D. MAY 3, 1956 CUMBERLAND, MD.
15- 83 KOLSETH, KARL DICKEY	15149 BEL ESCOU DR - SAN JOSE CA 95124
62- 69 KOLSTAD, HAROLD EVERETTE	D. JUNE 14, 1943 CHICAGO, ILL.
13- 96 KOMMERS, FRED RAYMOND	2987 HANOVER DRIVE - LIMA OH 45805
83- 87 KOMMINSK, BRAD LYNN	8341 RIVERLAND DRIVE #6 - STERLING HEIGHTS MI 48078
73- 70 KONIECZNY, DOUGLAS	OLD ADD: 81 BANK STREET - SEYMOUR CT 06483
48- 55 KONIKOWSKI, ALEXANDER JAMES	3212 SOUTH ADAMS - DENVER CO 80210
42- 59 KONOPKA, BRUCE BRUNO	D. JUNE 11, 1976 ONEONTA, N. Y.
44- 75 KONSTANTY, CASIMIR JAMES 'JIM'	D. NOVEMBER 12, 1941 LEMAY, MO.
15- 84 KOOB, ERNEST GERALD	3646 GOLFVIEW DR - HOPE MILLS NC 28348
62- 70 KOONCE, CALVIN LEE	RR 2 BOX 67E - CHASKA MN 55318
67- 60 KOOSMAN, JERRY MARTIN	14150 SOMERSET COURT - ORLAND PARK IL 60462
66- 53 KOPACZ, GEORGE FELIX	D. APRIL 30, 1979 CINCINNATI, O.
21- 54 KOPF, WALTER HENRY	D. OCTOBER 15, 1986 ANDERSON TWP., HAMILTON CO., OHIO
13- 97 KOPF, WILLIAM LORENZ 'LARRY'	623 BOYD ST - OSHKOSH WI 54901
61- 62 KOPLITZ, HOWARD DEAN	D. MAY 7, 1960 SACRAMENTO, CALIF.
15- 85 KOPP, MERLIN HENRY	7887 BEATRICE ST - WESTLAND MI 48185
58- 53 KOPPE, JOSEPH	D. DECEMBER 26, 1934 LYNCHBURG, VA.
23- 76 KOPSHAW, GEORGE KARL	

54- 56	KORCHECK, STEPHEN JOSEPH	P.O. BOX 1849 - BRADENTON FL 33506
15- 86	KORES, ARTHUR EMIL	D. MARCH 26, 1974 MILWAUKEE, WIS.
66- 54	KORINCE, GEORGE EUGENE	OLD ADD: 83 SHORELINE DR - ST. CATHERINES ONT. L2N 5N7
65- 59	KOSCO, ANDREW JOHN	9329 NEW SPRINGFIELD RD - POLAND OH 44514
52- 63	KOSHOREK, CLEMENT JOHN	3951 AMHERST - ROYAL OAK MI 48072
51- 49	KOSKI, WILLIAM JOHN	2656 EL GRECO DR - MODESTO CA 95351
41- 56	KOSLO, GEORGE BERNARD 'DAVE'	D. DECEMBER 1, 1975 MENASHA, WIS.
44- 76	KOSMAN, MICHAEL THOMAS	2110 S. 6TH - LAFAYETTE IN 47904
31- 45	KOSTER, FREDERICK CHARLES	D. APRIL 24, 1979 SAINT MATTHEWS, KY.
62- 71	KOSTRO, FRANK JERRY	36 STEELE STREET #20 - DENVER CO 80206
55- 65	KOUFAX, SANFORD 'SANDY'	1000 ELYSIAN PARK AVE - LOS ANGELES CA 90012
25- 65	KOUPAL, LOUIS LADDIE	D. DECEMBER 8, 1961 SAN GABRIEL, CAL.
32- 43	KOWALIK, FABIAN LORENZ	D. AUGUST 14, 1954 KARNES CITY, TEX.
38- 47	KOY, ERNEST ANYZ	BOX 476 1047 SOUTH OAK-BELLVILLE TX 77418
48- 56	KOZAR, ALBERT KENNETH	3004 VINCENT RD - WEST PALM BEACH FL 33405
39- 63	KRACHER, JOSEPH PETER	D. DECEMBER 25, 1981 SAN ANGELO, TEXAS
89- 69	KRAEMER, JOSEPH WAYNE	510 NORTHWEST 69TH STREET - VANCOUVER WA 98665
14-122	KRAFT, CLARENCE OTTO	D. MARCH 26, 1958 FORT WORTH, TEX.
37- 62	KRAKAUSKAS, JOSEPH VICTOR LAWRENCE	D. DECEMBER 8, 1960 HAMILTON, ONT.
59- 46	KRALICK, JOHN FRANCIS	%J.P. KRALICK,13320 MERCIER - WYANDOTTE MI 48192
53- 48	KRALY, STEVEN CHARLES	12 DAVIS AVENUE - JOHNSON CITY NY 13790
39- 64	KRAMER, JOHN HENRY	2126 PAULINE ST-NEW ORLEANS LA 70117
88- 78	KRAMER, RANDALL JOHN	239 CASTILLON WAY - SAN JOSE CA 95119
62- 72	KRANEPOOL, EDWARD EMIL	177 HIGH POND DRIVE - JERICHO NY 11753
11- 92	KRAPP, EUGENE H.	D. APRIL 13, 1923 DETROIT, MICH.
43- 73	KRAUS, JOHN WILLIAM 'TEX'	D. JANUARY 2, 1976 SAN ANTONIO, TEX.
31- 46	KRAUSSE, LEWIS BERNARD SR.	D. SEPTEMBER 6, 1988 SARASOTA, FLA.
61- 63	KRAUSSE, LOUIS BERNARD JR	RR 1 BOX 572C - HOLT MO 64048
75- 60	KRAVEC, KENNETH PETER	3679 KINGSTON BLVD - SARASOTA FL 33583
56- 49	KRAVITZ, DANIEL	RR1 - DUSHORE PA 18614
84- 63	KRAWCZYK, RAYMOND ALLEN	10032 RIDGLEY DR - GARDEN GROVE CA 92643
31- 47	KREEVICH, MICHAEL ANDREAS	RURAL ROUTE 2 BOX 220 - CECIL WI 54111
43- 74	KREITNER, ALBERT JOSEPH	313 CHURCH ST - NASHVILLE TN 37201
11- 93	KREITZ, RALPH WESLEY	D. JULY 20, 1941 PORTLAND, ORE.
24- 61	KREMER, REMY PETER 'RAY'	D. FEBRUARY 8, 1965 PINOLE, CAL.
73- 71	KREMMEL, JAMES LOUIS	EAST 12021 SPRAGUE - SPOKANE WA 99206
79- 65	KRENCHICKI, WAYNE RICHARD	53 FARRELL AVENUE - TRENTON NJ 08618
47- 54	KRESS, CHARLES STEVEN	3102 DUNCAN - SAINT JOSEPH MO 64507
27- 52	KRESS, RALPH 'RED'	D. NOVEMBER 29, 1962 LOS ANGELES, CALIF.
46- 58	KRETLOW, LOUIS HENRY	3302 GOLDFINCH - ENID OK 73701
75- 61	KREUGER, RICHARD ALAN	1143 POWERS NW - GRAND RAPIDS MI 49504
88- 79	KREUTER, CHAD MICHAEL	32106 HARBOR VIEW - WESTLAKE VILLAGE CA 91361
62- 73	KREUTZER, FRANKLIN JAMES	921 WINDWHISPER LANE - ANNAPOLIS MD 21403
11- 94	KRICHELL, PAUL BERNARD	D. JUNE 4, 1957 NEW YORK, N.Y.
49- 42	KRIEGER, KURT FERDINAND	D. AUGUST 16, 1970 ST. LOUIS, MO.
37- 63	KRIST, HOWARD WILBUR	D. APRIL 23, 1989 DELAVAN, N.Y.
78- 67	KROL, JOHN THOMAS	3012 FLEET ST - WINSTON SALEM NC 27107
64- 62	KROLL, GARY MELVIN	9038 EAST 40TH ST - TULSA OK 74145
35- 58	KRONER, JOHN HAROLD	D. AUGUST 26, 1968 ST. LOUIS, MO.
60- 58	KRSNICH, MICHAEL	1118 GREEN PINE BLVD #B1 - WEST PALM BEACH FL 33409
49- 43	KRSNICH, ROCCO PETER	5701 WEST 92ND STREET - OVERLAND PARK KS 66207
13- 98	KRUEGER, ERNEST GEORGE	D. APRIL 22, 1976 WAUKEGAN, ILL.
83- 88	KRUEGER, WILLIAM CULP	2353 NW 153RD AVENUE - BEAVERTON OR 97006
65- 60	KRUG, EVERETT BEN 'CHRIS'	32225 WESLEY - WILHOMAR CA 92395
81- 66	KRUG, GARY EUGENE	1327 BAYLOR DR - COLORADO SPRINGS CO 80909
12-102	KRUG, MARTIN JOHN	D. JUNE 27, 1966 GLENDALE, CALIF.
86- 81	KRUK, JOHN MARTIN	RURAL ROUTE 4 BOX 31 - KEYSER WV 26726
76- 50	KRUKOW, MICHAEL EDWARD	416 ALABAMA STREET - SAN GABRIEL CA 91775
49- 44	KRYHOSKI, RICHARD DAVID	18855 WARWICK RD - BIRMINGHAM MI 48009
57- 38	KUBEK, ANTHONY CHRISTOPHER	N8323 NORTH SHORE ROAD - MENASHA WI 54952
67- 61	KUBIAK, THEODORE ROGER	12826 OAKFIELD WAY - POWAY CA 92064
61- 64	KUBISZYN, JACK JOSEPH	2306 UNIVERSITY BLVD - TUSCALOOSA AL 35401
80- 68	KUBSKI, GILBERT THOMAS	1565 SUNRISE CIR - CARLSBAD CA 92008
50- 44	KUCAB, JOHN ALBERT	D. MAY 26, 1977 YOUNGSTOWN, O.
74- 69	KUCEK, JOHN ANDREW CHARLES	1219 WARREN RD - NEWTON FALLS OH 44444
55- 66	KUCKS, JOHN CHARLES	15 OAKLAND ST - HILLSDALE NJ 07642
49- 45	KUCZEK, STANISLAW LEO 'STEVE'	769 SACANDAGA RD - SCOTIA NY 12302
43- 75	KUCZYNSKI, BERNARD CARL	1725 NORTH DAUPHIN STREET - ALLENTOWN PA 18103
76- 51	KUEHL, KARL OTTO	8218 VIA DE LA ESCUELA - SCOTTSDALE AZ 85258
52- 64	KUENN, HARVEY EDWARD	D. FEBRUARY 28, 1988 PEORIA, ARIZ.
77- 78	KUHAULUA, FRED MAHELE	89-203 NALAKAHIKI PL - NANAKULI HI 96792
30- 42	KUHEL, JOSEPH ANTHONY	D. FEBRUARY 26, 1984 KANSAS CITY, KAN.
24- 62	KUHN, BERNARD DANIEL 'BUB'	D. NOVEMBER 20, 1956 LANSING, MICH.
55- 67	KUHN, KENNETH HAROLD	69 SKYLINE TERRACE - MILL VALLEY CA 94941
12-103	KUHN, WALTER CHARLES	D. JUNE 14, 1935 FRESNO, CALIF.
74- 70	KUIPER, DUANE EUGENE	% SBROCCO,36931 EAGLE RD - WILLOUGHBY HILLS OH 44094
55- 68	KUME, JOHN MIKE	RR2 WOODARD RD - ANDOVER OH 44003
84- 64	KUNKEL, JEFFREY WILLIAM	1 NAUTILUS DR - LEONARDO NJ 07737
61- 65	KUNKEL, WILLIAM GUSTAVE JAMES	D. MAY 4, 1985 RED BANK, N. J.
79- 66	KUNTZ, RUSSELL JAY 'RUSTY'	834 ANGELA LANE - KISSIMMEE FL 32741
23- 77	KUNZ, EARL DEWEY	D. APRIL 14, 1963 SACRAMENTO, CAL.
75- 62	KUROSAKI, RYAN YOSHITOMO	1324 HIGH VIEW PL - HONOLULU HI 96816
41- 57	KUROWSKI, GEORGE JOHN 'WHITEY'	310 HIPPSIDE DR-SHILLINGTON PA 19607
68- 50	KURTZ, HAROLD JAMES	BELLE POINT - QUEENSTOWN MD 21658
41- 58	KUSH, EMIL BENEDICT	D. NOVEMBER 26, 1969 RIVER GROVE, ILL.
73- 72	KUSICK, CRAIG ROBERT	14228 GARRETT AVENUE - APPLE VALLEY MN 55124
70- 73	KUSNYER, ARTHUR WILLIAM	777 WINTERSIDE CIRCLE - SAN RAMON CA 94583
86- 82	KUTCHER, RANDY SCOTT	35918 42ND STREET EAST - PALMDALE CA 93550
11- 95	KUTINA, JOSEPH PETER	D. APRIL 13, 1945 CHICAGO, ILL.
59- 47	KUTYNA, MARION JOHN 'MARTY'	2711 EAST CAMBRIA ST - PHILADELPHIA PA 19134
46- 59	KUZAVA, ROBERT LEROY	1118 VINEWOOD AVE - WYANDOTTE MI 48192
42- 60	KVASNAK, ALEXANDER	3265 HEMPSTEAD AVE-ARCADIA CA 91006
12-104	KYLE, ANDREW EWING	D. SEPTEMBER 6, 1971 TORONTO, ONT.
37- 64	LAABS, CHESTER PETER	D. JANUARY 26, 1983 WARREN, MICH.
50- 45	LABINE, CLEMENT WALTER	BOX 643 - WOONSOCKET RI 02895
69- 95	LABOY, JOSE ALBERTO 'COCO'	19TH ST. B20 #24 SABANA GDNS - CAROLINA PR 00630
77- 79	LACEY, ROBERT JOSEPH	431 WEST THIRD PLACE - MESA AZ 85201
69- 96	LACHEMANN, MARCEL ERNEST	1449 BOOKMAN AVE - WALNUT CA 91789

65- 61 LACHEMANN, RENE GEORGE	2736 WEST PLATA AVE - MESA AZ 85202
83- 89 LACHOWICZ, ALLEN ROBERT	310 ROOSEVELT AVE - MCKEES ROCK PA 15136
14-128 LACLAIRE, GEORGE LEWIS	D. OCTOBER 10, 1918 FARNHAM, QUE.
72- 58 LACOCK, RALPH PIERRE 'PETE'	9725 RIGGS - OVERLAND PARK KS 66212
75- 63 LACORTE, FRANK JOSEPH	1667 EL DORADO DR - GILROY CA 95020
78- 68 LACOSS, MICHAEL JAMES	4110 LAVIDA - VISALIA CA 93277
72- 59 LACY, LEONDAUS 'LEE'	29025 CATHERWOOD COURT - AGOURA HILLS CA 91301
26- 46 LACY, OSCEOLA GUY	D. NOVEMBER 19, 1953 CLEVELAND, TENN.
79- 67 LADD, PETER LINWOOD	10420 NORTH THORNYDALE - TUCSON AZ 85741
46- 60 LADE, DOYLE MARION	445 NORTH 12TH ST - GENEVA NE 68361
47- 55 LAFATA, JOSEPH JOSEPH	29321 BRITTANY CT WEST - ROSEVILLE MI 48066
45- 55 LAFOREST, BYRON JOSEPH 'TY'	D. MAY 5, 1947 ARLINGTON, MASS.
82- 72 LAFRANCOIS, ROGER VICTOR	28 ASPINOOK ST - JEWETT CITY CT 06351
82- 73 LAGA, MICHAEL RUSSELL	27 CENTER ST - RAMSEY NJ 07446
34- 59 LAGGER, EDWIN JOSEPH	D. NOVEMBER 10, 1981 JOLIET, ILL.
70- 74 LAGROW, LERRIN HARRIS	12271 EAST TURQUOISE - SCOTTSDALE AZ 85259
68- 51 LAHOUD, JOSEPH MICHAEL	HUT HILL ROAD, BOX 165 - BRIDGEWATER CT 06752
82- 72 LAHTI, JEFFREY ALLEN	OLD ADD: 90 SW SIXTH AVE - ONTARIO OR 97914
46- 61 LAJESKIE, RICHARD EDWARD	D. AUGUST 15, 1976 RAMSEY, N. J.
39- 65 LAKE, EDWARD ERVING	1840 NELSON ST - SAN LEANDRO CA 94579
83- 90 LAKE, STEVEN MICHAEL	16445 NORTH 63RD DRIVE - GLENDALE AZ 85306
42- 61 LAKEMAN, ALBERT WESLEY	D. MAY 25, 1976 SPARTANBURG, S. C.
62- 74 LAMABE, JOHN ALEXANDER	16224 ANTIETAM AVE - BATON ROUGE LA 70816
43- 76 LAMACCHIA, ALFRED ANTHONY	13515 VISTA BONITA - SAN ANTONIO TX 78216
40- 48 LAMANNA, FRANK	D. SEPTEMBER 1, 1980 SYRACUSE, N. Y.
41- 59 LAMANNO, RAYMOND SIMON	827 POLK ST-ALBANY CA 94706
35- 59 LAMANSKE, FRANK JAMES	D. AUGUST 4, 1971 OLNEY, ILL.
17- 39 LAMAR, WILLIAM HARMONG	D. MAY 24, 1970 ROCKPORT, MASS.
37- 65 LAMASTER, WAYNE LEE	2525 EAST ELM ST NEW-ALBANY IN 47150
70- 75 LAMB, JOHN ANDREW	SHARON VALLEY RD - SHARON CT 06069
20- 69 LAMB, LAYMAN RAYMOND	D. OCTOBER 5, 1955 FAYETTEVILLE, ARK.
69- 97 LAMB, RAYMOND RICHARD	1741 TUSTIN AVE #17C - COSTA MESA CA 92627
46- 62 LAMBERT, CLAYTON PATRICK	D. APRIL 3, 1981 OGDEN, UTAH
41- 60 LAMBERT, EUGENE MARION	268 MONTELO-MEMPHIS TN 38117
16- 53 LAMBETH, OTIS SAMUEL	D. JUNE 5, 1976 MORAN, KAN.
12-105 LAMLINE, FREDERICK ARTHUR	D. SEPTEMBER 20, 1970 PORT HURON, MICH.
70- 76 LAMONT, GENE WILLIAM	4110 TONGA - SARASOTA FL 33583
20- 70 LAMOTTE, ROBERT EUGENE	D. NOVEMBER 2, 1970 CHATHAM, GA.
77- 80 LAMP, DENNIS PATRICK	12100 MONTECITO RD #161-LOS ALAMITOS CA 90720
69- 98 LAMPARD, CHRISTOPHER KEITH	842 NE 74TH AVE - PORTLAND OR 97213
88- 80 LAMPKIN, THOMAS MICHAEL	9605 NE 14TH STREET - BELLEVUE WA 98004
35- 60 LANAHAN, RICHARD ANTHONY	D. MARCH 12, 1975 ROCHESTER, MINN.
87- 74 LANCASTER, LESTER WAYNE	OLD ADD: 105 EAST EIGHTH - IRVING TX 75060
77- 81 LANCE, GARY DEAN	1802 OMEGA DR - COLUMBIA SC 29206
82- 75 LANCELLOTTI, RICHARD ANTHONY 'RICK'	5190 THOMPSON ROAD - CLARENCE NY 14031
29- 60 LAND, WILLIAM GILBERT 'DOC'	D. APRIL 14, 1986 LIVINGSTON, ALA.
52- 65 LANDENBERGER, KENNETH HENRY	D. JULY 28, 1960 CLEVELAND, O.
77- 82 LANDESTOY, RAFAEL SIVIALDO CAMILO	615 NORTH OCEAN BLVD - POMPANO BEACH FL 33062
57- 39 LANDIS, JAMES HENRY	2439 STONEHOUSE CT - NAPA CA 94558
63- 65 LANDIS, WILLIAM HENRY	525 SYCAMORE - HANFORD CA 93230
77- 83 LANDREAUX, KENNETH FRANCIS	608 NORTH LEDNARD STREET - MONTEBELLO CA 90640
76- 52 LANDRETH, LARRY ROBERT	5 BURRITT ST - STRATFORD ONT. N5A 4W6 CAN.
50- 46 LANDRITH, HOBERT NEAL	4335 QUEENS WAY - BLOOMFIELD HILLS MI 48013
57- 40 LANDRUM, DONALD LEROY	19 BARRIE COURT - PITTSBURG CA 94565
38- 48 LANDRUM, JESSE GLENN	D. JUNE 27, 1983 BEAUMONT, TEX.
50- 47 LANDRUM, JOSEPH BUTLER	RR 5 BOX 339 - COLUMBIA SC 29203
80- 69 LANDRUM, TERRY LEE 'TITO'	1121 KENTUCKY SE - ALBUQUERQUE NM 87108
86- 83 LANDRUM, THOMAS WILLIAM 'BILL'	RURAL ROUTE 5 BOX 339 - COLUMBIA SC 29203
24- 63 LANE, JAMES HUNTER	5720 HERALD SQUARE - MEMPHIS TN 38119
53- 49 LANE, JERALD HAL	D. JULY 24, 1988 CHATTANOOGA, TENN.
71- 60 LANE, MARVIN	17191 ARDMORE - DETROIT MI 48235
49- 46 LANE, RICHARD HARRISON	26609 ACADEMY DR-PALOS VERDES PENIN CA 90274
41- 61 LANFRANCONI, WALTER OSWALD	D. AUGUST 18, 1986 BARRE, VT.
38- 49 LANG, DONALD CHARLES	5700 KIRKSIDE DR #F - BAKERSFIELD CA 93309
30- 43 LANG, MARTIN JOHN	D. JANUARY 13, 1968 LAKEWOOD, COLO.
75- 64 LANG, ROBERT DAVID	985 HOMER AVE - PITTSBURGH PA 15237
14-123 LANGE, ERWIN HENRY	D. APRIL 24, 1971 MAYWOOD, ILL.
10- 85 LANGE, FRANK HERMAN	D. DECEMBER 26, 1945 MADISON, WIS.
72- 60 LANGE, RICHARD OTTO	3387 BROOKS RD, RR 2 - FREELAND MI 48623
26- 47 LANGFORD, ELTON L. 'SAM'	906 OAKLAND - PLAINVIEW TX 79072
76- 53 LANGFORD, JAMES RICK	1119 59TH ST NW - BRADENTON FL 33505
85- 65 LANGSTON, MARK EDWARD	2935 MARIETTA DR - SANTA CLARA CA 95051
64- 63 LANIER, HAROLD CLIFTON	11250 SW RIO VISTA - DUNELLON FL 32630
38- 50 LANIER, HUBERT MAX 'MAX'	11250 SW RIO VISTA DRIVE - DUNNELLON FL 32630
71- 61 LANIER, LORENZO	2928 WOODHILL AVE - CLEVELAND OH 44104
36- 46 LANNING, JOHN YOUNG	28 DEANWOOD CIR - ASHEVILLE NC 28803
16- 54 LANNING, LESTER ALFRED	D. JUNE 13, 1962 BRISTOL, CONN.
38- 51 LANNING, THOMAS NEWTON	D. NOVEMBER 4, 1967 MARIETTA, GA.
78- 69 LANSFORD, CARNEY RAY	RURAL ROUTE 1 BOX 50 - BAKER OR 97814
82- 76 LANSFORD, JOSEPH DALE 'JODY'	RR TWO - EUFAULA OK 74432
22- 69 LANSING, EUGENE HEWETT	D. JANUARY 18, 1945 RENSSELAER, N. Y.
51- 50 LAPALME, PAUL EDMORE	167 SMITH ST - LEOMINSTER MA 01453
22- 70 LAPAN, PETER NELSON	D. JANUARY 5, 1973 NORWALK, CAL.
42- 62 LAPIHUSKA, ANDREW	900 MULBERRY STREET-MILLVILLE NJ 08332
80- 70 LAPOINT, DAVID JEFFREY	2 JUDMAR LANE - GLENS FALLS NY 12801
47- 56 LAPOINTE, RALPH JOHN	D. SEPTEMBER 13, 1967 BURLINGTON, VT.
58- 54 LARKER, NORMAN HOWARD	4701 VILLAGE RD - LONG BEACH CA 90808
86- 84 LARKIN, BARRY LOUIS	6818 ELWYNNE DRIVE - CINCINNATI OH 45236
87- 75 LARKIN, EUGENE THOMAS	916 BELLMORE ROAD - NORTH BELLMORE NY 11710
83- 91 LARKIN, PATRICK CLIBURN	25861 LACUESTA AVENUE - LAGUNA HILLS CA 92653
34- 60 LARKIN, STEPHEN PATRICK	D. MAY 2, 1969 NORRISTOWN, PA.
18- 44 LARMORE, ROBERT MCCAHAN	D. JANUARY 15, 1964 ST. LOUIS, MO.
70- 77 LAROCHE, DAVID EUGENE	420 WEST 8TH - FORT SCOTT KS 66701
78- 70 LAROSE, HENRY JOHN	99 ROLAND - CUMBERLAND RI 02864
68- 52 LAROSE, VICTOR RAYMOND	2908 EAST SYLVIA ST - PHOENIX AZ 85028
14-124 LAROSS, HARRY RAYMOND	D. MARCH 22, 1954 HINES, ILL.
53- 50 LARSEN, DON JAMES	17090 COPPER HILL DR - MORGAN HILL CA 95037

36- 47	LARSEN, ERLING ADELI	2801 SOUTH PALM SPRINGS DR - TUCSON AZ 85730
76- 54	LARSON, DANIEL JAMES	1616 MONTEREY AVE - HERMOSA BEACH CA 90254
63- 66	LARUSSA, ANTHONY	338 GOLDEN MEADOW PLACE - DANVILLE CA 94526
54- 57	LARY, ALFRED ALLEN	RR 8 BOX 139 - NORTHPORT AL 35476
54- 58	LARY, FRANK STRONG	RR 8 BOX 142 - NORTHPORT AL 35476
29- 61	LARY, LYNFORD HOBART	D. JANUARY 9, 1973 DOWNEY, CAL.
63- 67	LASHER, FREDERICK WALTER	HIGHWAY EAST - MERRILLAN WI 54754
82- 77	LASKEY, WILLIAM ALAN	311 EAST WEBER ST - TOLEDO OH 43608
24- 64	LASLEY, WILLARD ALMOND	2565 DEXTER AVE NORTH #201 - SEATTLE WA 98109
54- 59	LASORDA, THOMAS CHARLES	1473 WEST MAXZIM - FULLERTON CA 92633
57- 41	LASSETTER, DONALD O'NEAL	406 GORDY ST - PERRY GA 31069
85- 62	LATHAM, WILLIAM CAROL	1312 BARDSWOOD TERRACE - BIRMINGHAM AL 35235
10- 86	LATHERS, CHARLES TEN EYCK 'CHICK'	D. JULY 26, 1971 PETOSKEY, MICH.
13- 99	LATHROP, WILLIAM GEORGE	D. NOVEMBER 20, 1958 JANESVILLE, WIS.
57- 42	LATMAN, ARNOLD BARRY	13700 TAHITI WAY #340 - MARINA DEL REY CA 90291
56- 50	LAU, CHARLES RICHARD	D. MARCH 18, 1984 KEY COLONY BEACH, FLA.
81- 67	LAUDNER, TIMOTHY JON	6505 VALLEY VIEW ROAD - CORCORAN MN 55340
67- 62	LAUZERIQUE, GEORGE	601 OLEASTER AVE - WEST PALM BEACH FL 33414
34- 61	LAVAGETTO, HARRY ARTHUR 'COOKIE'	46 TARA RD - ORINDA CA 94563
84- 66	LAVALLIERE, MICHAEL EUGENE	12 SCOTT AVE - HOCKSETT NH 03106
13-100	LAVAN, JOHN LEONARD 'DOC'	D. MAY 29, 1952 DETROIT, MICH.
74- 71	LAVELLE, GARY ROBERT	1100 WORTHINGTON CIRCLE - VIRGINIA BEACH VA 23464
12-106	LAVENDER, JAMES SANFORD	D. JANUARY 12, 1960 CARTERSVILLE, GA.
14-125	LAVIGNE, ARTHUR DAVID	D. JULY 18, 1950 WORCESTER, MASS.
69- 99	LAW, RONALD DAVID	OLD ADD: 9000 YUCCA WAY - THORNTON CO
78- 71	LAW, RUDY KARL	4841 LENNOX STREET - INGLEWOOD CA 90304
80- 71	LAW, VANCE AARON	1748 NORTH COBBLESTONE DRIVE - PROVO UT 84604
50- 48	LAW, VERNON SANDERS	1748 NORTH COBBLESTONE DRIVE - PROVO UT 84604
46- 63	LAWING, GARLAND FREDERICK	5710 ORR RD #20 - CHARLOTTE NC 28213
82- 78	LAWLESS, THOMAS JAMES	1736 WEST 25TH ST - ERIE PA 16502
54- 60	LAWRENCE, BROOKS ULYSSES	OLD ADD: 716E NORTHLAND RD - CINCINNATI OH 45240
63- 68	LAWRENCE, JAMES ROSS	BOX 851 - CALEDONIA ONTARIO NOA 1AO CAN.
24- 65	LAWRENCE, ROBERT ANDREW	D. NOVEMBER 6, 1983 JAMAICA, N. Y.
32- 44	LAWRENCE, WILLIAM HENRY	135 GRAND ST - REDWOOD CITY CA 94062
16- 55	LAWRY, OTIS CARROLL	D. OCTOBER 23, 1965 CHINA, ME.
30- 44	LAWSON, ALFRED VOYLE 'ROXIE'	D. APRIL 9, 1977 STOCKPORT, IA.
72- 61	LAWSON, STEVEN GEORGE	3013 LIVE OAK CT - DANVILLE CA 94526
89- 70	LAWTON, MARCUS DWAYNE	1700 J. Q. ADAMS STREET #B - GULFPORT MS 39501
70- 78	LAXTON, WILLIAM HARRY	261 MANSION AVE - AUDUBON NJ 08106
15- 87	LAYDEN, EUGENE FRANCIS	D. DECEMBER 12, 1984 PITTSBURGH, PA.
48- 57	LAYDEN, PETER JOHN	D. JULY 18, 1982 EDNA, TEXAS
27- 53	LAYNE, HERMAN	D. AUGUST 27, 1973 GALLIPOLIS, O.
41- 62	LAYNE, IVORIA HILLIS 'HILLY'	4623 DORISA AVE-CHATTANOOGA TN 37411
48- 58	LAYTON, LESTER LEE	8780 EAST MCKELLIPS RD #27 - SCOTTSDALE AZ 85257
68- 53	LAZAR, JOHN DAN	8444 OAKWOOD AVE - MUNSTER IN 46321
43- 77	LAZOR, JOHN PAUL	8054 S. 116TH ST - SEATTLE WA 98178
84- 67	LAZORKO, JACK THOMAS	44 CANFIELD AVENUE - EAST HANOVER NJ 07936
26- 48	LAZZERI, ANTHONY MICHAEL	D. AUGUST 6, 1946 SAN FRANCISCO, CAL.
80- 72	LEA, CHARLES WILLIAM	4237 FAIRMONT AVENUE - MEMPHIS TN 38108
23- 78	LEACH, FREDERICK M	D. DECEMBER 10, 1981 HAGERMAN, ID.
81- 68	LEACH, RICHARD MAX 'RICK'	4033 WEST COURT - FLINT MI 48504
81- 69	LEACH, TERRY HESTER	5241 WEST 121ST STREET - OVERLAND PARK KS 66209
80- 73	LEAL, LUIS ENRIQUE	CALLE 28 #30-60 - BARQUISMETO,EDO. LARA VENEZ
14-126	LEAR, CHARLES BERNARD 'KING'	D. OCTOBER 31, 1976 GREENCASTLE, PA.
15- 88	LEAR, FREDERICK FRANCIS	D. OCTOBER 13, 1995 EAST ORANGE, N.J.
17- 40	LEARD, WILLIAM WALLACE	D. JANUARY 15, 1970 SAN FRANCISCO, CAL.
14-127	LEARY, JOHN LOUIS	D. AUGUST 18, 1961 WALTHAM, MASS.
81- 70	LEARY, TIMOTHY JAMES	201 OCEAN AVE #1801B - SANTA MONICA CA 90402
20- 71	LEATHERS, HAROLD LANGFORD	D. APRIL 12, 1977 MODESTO, CALIF.
19- 51	LEBOURVEAU, DEWITT WILEY 'BEVO'	D. DECEMBER 19, 1947 NEVADA CITY, CAL.
15- 89	LEDBETTER, RALPH OVERTON 'RAZOR'	D. FEBRUARY 1, 1969 WEST PALM BEACH, FLA.
19- 52	LEE, CLIFFORD WALKER	D. AUGUST 25, 1980 DENVER, COLO.
57- 43	LEE, DONALD EDWARD	9101 PALM TREE DR - TUCSON AZ 85710
20- 72	LEE, ERNEST DUDLEY 'DUD'	D. JANUARY 7, 1971 DENVER, COLO.
30- 45	LEE, HAROLD BURNHAM	D. SEPTEMBER 4, 1989 PASCAGOULA, MISS.
69-100	LEE, LERON	2-2-33 HYAKUNINCHO SHIN JUKO-KU - TOKYO 160 JAPAN
85- 63	LEE, MANUEL LEE	3RA #86 VILLA MAGDALENA - SAN PEDRO DE MACORIS DOM REP.
78- 72	LEE, MARK LINDEN	9722 MCCARDLE - SANTEE CA 92071
88- 81	LEE, MARK OWEN	OLD ADD: 1821 EAST SECOND - CASPER WY 82601
60- 59	LEE, MICHAEL RANDALL	2511 BUENA FLORES - FALLBROOK CA 92028
64- 64	LEE, ROBERT DEAN	P.O. BOX 0346 - TEHACHAPI CA 93461
45- 56	LEE, ROY EDWIN	D. NOVEMBER 11, 1985 ST. LOUIS, MO.
33- 34	LEE, THORNTON STARR	9054 CALLE NORLO EAST - TUCSON AZ 85710
34- 62	LEE, WILLIAM CRUTCHER	D. JUNE 15, 1977 PLAQUEMINE, LA.
69-101	LEE, WILLIAM FRANCIS	RURAL ROUTE 1 BOX 1 - CRAFTSBURG VT 05826
15- 90	LEE, WILLIAM JOSEPH	D. JANUARY 6, 1984 WEST HAZELTON, PA.
59- 48	LEEK, EUGENE HAROLD	3327 BANCROFT ST - SAN DIEGO CA 92104
84- 68	LEEPER, DAVID DALE	1922 FERN - ORANGE CA 92667
21- 55	LEES, GEORGE EDWARD	D. JANUARY 2, 1980 MECHANICSBURG, PA.
65- 62	LEFEBVRE, JAMES KENNETH	9120 NORTH 106TH PLACE - SCOTTSDALE AZ 85258
80- 74	LEFEBVRE, JOSEPH HENRY	9 WELLSWEEP LANE - KILLINGSWORTH CT 06417
38- 52	LEFEBVRE, WILFRID HENRY 'BILL'	7200 ULMERTON RD #1379 - LARGO FL 33541
20- 73	LEFEVRE, ALFREDO MODESTO	D. JANUARY 21, 1982 GLEN COVE, N. Y.
83- 92	LEFFERTS, CRAIG LINDSAY	1035 INSPIRATION LANE - ESCONDIDO CA 92025
24- 66	LEFLER, WADE HAMPTON	D. MARCH 6, 1981 HICKORY, N. C.
74- 72	LEFLORE, RONALD	5126 IROQUOIS - DETROIT MI 48213
29- 62	LEGETT, LOUIS ALFRED 'DOC'	D. MARCH 6, 1988 NEW ORLEANS, LA.
86- 85	LEGG, GREGORY LYNN	4550 ODOM DRIVE - DUNCAN OK 73533
32- 45	LEHENY, REGIS FRANCIS	D. NOVEMBER 2, 1976 PITTSBURGH, PA.
61- 66	LEHEW, JAMES ANTHONY	398 ARMSTRONG LN - BALTIMORE MD 21221
52- 66	LEHMAN, KENNETH KARL	447 COIN LAKE RD -SEDRO WOOLLEY WA 98284
46- 64	LEHNER, PAUL EUGENE	D. DECEMBER 27, 1987 BIRMINGHAM, ALA.
11- 96	LEHR, CLARENCE EMANUEL	D. JANUARY 31, 1948 DETROIT, MICH.
26- 49	LEHR, NORMAN CARL MICHAEL	D. JULY 17, 1968 CONESUS LAKE, N. Y.
33- 35	LEIBER, HENRY EDWARD	RR 2 BOX 811 - TUCSON AZ 85749
13-101	LEIBOLD, HARRY LORAN 'NEMO'	D. FEBRUARY 4, 1977 DETROIT, MICH.
79- 68	LEIBRANDT, CHARLES LOUIS	1424 OVERLOOK DR - GOLF IL 60029
21- 56	LEIFER, ELMER EDWIN	D. SEPTEMBER 26, 1948 EVERETT, WASH.

12-107 LEINHAUSER, WILLIAM CHARLES	D. APRIL 14, 1978 ELKINS PARK, PA.
39- 66 LEIP, EDGAR ELLSWORTH	D. NOVEMBER 24, 1983 ZEPHYRHILLS, FLA.
84- 69 LEIPER, DAVID PAUL	1421 HURON TRAIL - PLANO TX 75075
87- 76 LEISTER, JOHN WILLIAM	OLD ADD: 2901 DELMAR - GREAT FALLS MT 59404
87- 77 LEITER, ALOIS TERRY	37 BROWN AVENUE - PINE BEACH NJ 08741
54- 61 LEJA, FRANK JOHN	118 WILSON RD - NAHANT MA 01908
11- 97 LEJEUNE, SHELDON ALDENBERT 'LARRY'	D. APRIL 21, 1952 CHATTANOOGA, TENN.
65- 63 LEJOHN, DONALD EVERETT	154 EDWARDS ST - BROWNSVILLE PA 15417
73- 73 LEMANCZYK, DAVID LAWRENCE	24 LEHIGH CT - ROCKVILLE CENTRE NY 11570
62- 75 LEMASTER, DENVER CLAYTON	4424 RIVERCLIFF DR - LILBURN GA 30247
75- 65 LEMASTER, JOHNNIE LEE	372 4TH ST - PAINTSVILLE KY 41240
61- 67 LEMAY, RICHARD PAUL	4821 SOUTH FLORENCE AVE - TULSA OK 74105
50- 49 LEMBO, STEPHEN NEAL	D. DECEMBER 4, 1989 FLUSHING, N.Y.
88- 82 LEMKE, MARK ALAN	3 OLENA DRIVE - WHITESBORO NY 13492
75- 66 LEMON, CHESTER EARL 'CHET'	4805 HIGHLANDS PLACE DRIVE - LAKELAND FL 33813
50- 50 LEMON, JAMES ROBERT	95 FAIRWAY LAKES - MYRTLE BEACH SC 29577
41- 63 LEMON, ROBERT GRANVILLE	1141 CLAIBORNE DR-LONG BEACH CA 90807
69-102 LEMONDS, DAVID LEE	5029 JACKSON DRIVE - CHARLOTTE NC 28213
76- 55 LEMONGELLO, MARK	OLD ADD: 251 ATLANTIC ST #30A - KEYPORT NJ 07735
50- 51 LENHARDT, DONALD EUGENE	13317 WOODLAKE VILLAGE CT - ST LOUIS MO 63141
28- 56 LENNON, EDWARD FRANCIS	D. SEPTEMBER 13, 1947 PHILADELPHIA, PA.
54- 62 LENNON, ROBERT ALBERT	8 DUDLEY LANE - DIX HILLS NY 11746
78- 73 LENTINE, JAMES MATTHEW	3363 CALLE LAVETA - SAN CLEMENTE CA 92672
68- 54 LEON, EDUARDO ANTONIO	5616 N. CALLE DE LA REINA - TUCSON AZ 85718
45- 57 LEON, ISIDORO JUAN	CALLE O NO. 260, APT 5 - VADARO HAVANA CUBA
73- 74 LEON, MAXIMINO (MEDINA)	DOMICILIO CONOCIDO - VILLA ACULA VERACRUZ MEX.
74- 73 LEONARD, DENNIS PATRICK	4102 EVERGREEN LN - BLUE SPRINGS MO 64015
11- 98 LEONARD, ELMER ELLSWORTH 'TINY'	D. MAY 27, 1981 NAPA, CALIF.
33- 36 LEONARD, EMIL JOHN "DUTCH"	D. APRIL 17, 1983 SPRINGFIELD, ILL.
13-102 LEONARD, HUBERT BENJAMIN 'DUTCH'	D. JULY 11, 1952 FRESNO, CALIF.
77- 84 LEONARD, JEFFREY N	1626 NORTH FELTON ST - PHILADELPHIA PA 19151
14-129 LEONARD, JOSEPH HOWARD	D. MAY 1, 1920 WASHINGTON, D.C.
67- 63 LEONHARD, DAVID PAUL	87 CORNING ST - BEVERLY MA 01915
28- 57 LEOPOLD, RUDOLPH MATAS	D. SEPTEMBER 3, 1965 BATON ROUGE, LA.
41- 64 LEOVICH, JOHN JOSEPH	3531 NORTH REEF DR - LINCOLN CITY OR 97367
52- 67 LEPCIO, THADDEUS STANLEY 'TED'	263 GREENLODGE ST - DEDHAM MA 02026
55- 69 LEPPERT, DON EUGENE	OLD ADD: 5130 DURANT - MEMPHIS TN 38116
61- 68 LEPPERT, DONALD GEORGE	ROAD #1 BOX AA-7 - NINEVAH IN 46164
75- 67 LERCH, RANDY LOUIS	P.O. BOX 73 - KELSEY CA 95643
10- 87 LERCHEN, BERTRAM ROE	D. JANUARY 7, 1962 DETROIT, MICH.
52- 68 LERCHEN, GEORGE EDWARD	354 EAST ROSE - GARDEN CITY MI 48135
28- 58 LERIAN, WALTER IRVIN	D. OCTOBER 22, 1929 BALTIMORE, MD.
69-103 LERSCH, BARRY LEE	OLD ADD: 1617 1/2 PALMER ST - PUEBLO CO 81004
72- 62 LESHNOCK, DONALD LEE	464 LORA AVE - YOUNGSTOWN OH 44504
82- 79 LESLEY, BRADLEY JAY	BOX 1012 - TURLOCK CA 95381
17- 41 LESLIE, ROY REID	D. APRIL 9, 1972 SHERMAN, TEX.
29- 63 LESLIE, SAMUEL ANDREW	D. JANUARY 21, 1979 PASCAGOULA, MISS.
39- 67 LETCHAS, CHARLIE	1121 HIGHLAND ST - THOMASVILLE GA 31792
47- 57 LEVAN, JESSE ROY	255 LINCOLN RD - READING PA 19606
13-103 LEVERENZ, WALTER FRED	D. MARCH 19, 1973 ATASCADERO, CALIF.
22- 71 LEVERETT, GORHAM VANCE 'DIXIE'	D. FEBRUARY 20, 1957 BEAVERTON, ORE.
20- 74 LEVERETTE, HORACE WILBUR 'HOD'	D. APRIL 10, 1958 ST. PETERSBURG, FLA.
30- 46 LEVEY, JAMES JULIUS	D. MARCH 14, 1970 DALLAS, TEX.
23- 79 LEVSEN, EMIL HENRY 'DUTCH'	D. MARCH 12, 1972 MINNEAPOLIS, MINN.
40- 49 LEVY, EDWARD CAHRLES	%ED WHITNER, 505 RIDGECREST RD - LAGRANGE GA 30240
75- 68 LEWALLYN, DENNIS DALE	2900 BRECKENRIDGE DR - PENSACOLA FL 32506
51- 51 LEWANDOWSKI, DANIEL WILLIAM	370 MOUNT ALBION ROAD - HAMILTON ONTARIO L8K 5T2 CAN.
67- 64 LEWIS, ALLAN SYDNEY	PUERTO ARMUELLAS - CHIRIQUI GRANDE PANAMA C.A.
10- 88 LEWIS, GEORGE EDWARD 'DUFFY'	D. JUNE 17, 1979 SALEM, N. H.
79- 69 LEWIS, JAMES MARTIN	OLD ADD: 16049 NE 8TH AVE - NORTH MIAMI BEACH FL 33162
11- 99 LEWIS, JOHN DAVID	D. FEBRUARY 25, 1956 STEUBENVILLE, O.
35- 61 LEWIS, JOHN KELLY 'BUDDY'	BOX 788-GASTONIA NC 28052
64- 65 LEWIS, JOHNNY JOE	822 CARR #F - ST. LOUIS 63101
24- 67 LEWIS, WILLIAM BURTON	D. MARCH 24, 1950 TONAWANDA, N. Y.
33- 37 LEWIS, WILLIAM HENRY 'BUDDY'	D. OCTOBER 24, 1977 MEMPHIS, TENN.
71- 62 LEY, TERRENCE RICHARD	2914 NE 66TH - PORTLAND OR 97213
86- 86 LEYLAND, JAMES RICHARD	30 MIDWAY ROAD - PITTSBURGH PA 15216
89- 71 LEYVA, NICHOLAS TOMAS	2 ALGONQUIN COURT - WAYNE PA 19087
80- 75 LEZCANO, CARLOS MANUEL	962 ALAMEDA VILLA - GRANADA, RIO PIEDRAS PR 00923
74- 74 LEZCANO, SIXTO JOAQUIN	OLD ADD: 437 SOUTH HAWLEY RD #69-MILWAUKEE WI
45- 58 LIBKE, ALBERT WALTER	1117 SOUTH APPELAND DR - WENATCHEE WA 98801
69-104 LIBRAN, FRANCISCO	CALLE DR ESCADE #202 - MAYAGUEZ PR 00708
81- 71 LICKERT, JOHN WILBUR	922 WILHELM ST - PITTSBURGH PA 15220
53- 51 LIDDLE, DONALD EUGENE	1022 NORTH CHERRY ST - MOUNT CARMEL IL 62863
35- 62 LIEBER, CHARLES EDWIN 'DUTCH'	D. DECEMBER 31, 1961 LOS ANGELES, CAL.
30- 47 LIEBHARDT, GLENN IGNATIUS	2460 TANTELON PL - WINSTON SALEM NC 27107
10- 89 LIESE, FREDERICK RICHARD	D. JUNE 30, 1967 LOS ANGELES, CALIF.
36- 48 LILLARD, ROBERT EUGENE 'GENE'	5676 ENCINA RD - GOLETA CA 93117
39- 68 LILLARD, WILLIAM BEVERLY	340 OLD MILL ROAD #47 - SANTA BARBARA CA 93110
89- 72 LILLIQUIST, DEREK JANSEN	426 33RD AVENUE SW - SARASOTA FL 32962
58- 55 LILLIS, ROBERT PERRY	2216 EAST LORRAINE DRIVE - CARROLLTON TX 75006
51- 52 LIMMER, LOUIS	100-6 DREISER LOOP - BRONX NY 10475
81- 72 LINARES, RUFINO DELACRUZ	QUIS QUEYA,LA LOMA 14 #23-SAN PEDRO DE MACORIS DOM REP.
27- 54 LIND, HENRY CARL	D. AUGUST 2, 1946 NEW YORK, N. Y.
74- 75 LIND, JACKSON HUGH	718 N. LINDEN CIR - MESA AZ 85203
87- 78 LIND, JOSE	VILLA CAITO #18 - DORADO PR 00646
60- 60 LINDBECK, EMERIT DESMOND	210 HILLCREST DRIVE - KEWANEE IL 61443
65- 64 LINDBLAD, PAUL ANTON	2310 GARDEN LN - ARLINGTON TX 76015
47- 58 LINDE, LYMAN GILBERT	607 WEST BURNETT ST - BEAVER DAM WI 53916
41- 65 LINDELL, JOHN HARLAN	D. AUGUST 27, 1985 NEWPORT BEACH, CALIF.
86- 87 LINDEMAN, JAMES WILLIAM	2278 SCOTT STREET - DES PLAINES IL 60018
50- 52 LINDEN, WALTER CHARLES	4432 HARVEY AVE - WESTERN SPRINGS IL 60558
43- 78 LINDQUIST, CARL EMIL	RR 1 BOX 185A - EMPORIUM PA 15834
11-100 LINDSAY, WILLIAM GIBBONS	D. JULY 14, 1963 GREENSBORO, N.C.
22- 72 LINDSEY, JAMES KENDRICK	D. OCTOBER 25, 1963 JACKSON, LA.
87- 79 LINDSEY, WILLIAM DONALD	21410 TOWN LAKES DRIVE #918 - BOCA RATON FL 33432
16- 56 LINDSTROM, AXEL OLAF	D. JUNE 25, 1940 ASHEVILLE, N. C.
58- 56 LINDSTROM, CHARLES WILLIAM	220 PARK PLACE - LINCOLN IL 62656

THE WORKS OF THE PEREZ—STEELE GALLERIES

Although this book is called the Address List, it provides to its readers much more than addresses. It provides a list, alphabetically, of all players, managers, coaches and umpires who have appeared in the Major Leagues since 1910; it tells which year each player played in his first Major League game (the debut year gives this information); it lists which players are living and which ones are deceased — it even list the year and place of death; and it discusses proper, courteous and effective means of obtaining autographs through the mails. It is, to be sure, as its slogan states, "The Autograph Hunter's Best Friend".

The authors have, by design, avoided any reference to autograph values or autographing media through the first five editions of the Address List. However, during the last few years the baseball autographs portion of the sports memorabilia hobby has grown to such a degree that sports memorabilia show are sometimes distinguished by being either "card shows" or "autograph shows". Current and former ball players are often guests at these shows — and they are paid for their signatures. (The policy of ball players charging for autographs has brought on much controversy; but, fortunately or unfortunately, it is now a fact of life.) The mails, the ball parks and the secondary market still provide the lions share of autographs to collectors; still, the autograph shows are frequent and well attended. Remember, legitimacy is assured if one actually sees the autographer sign the item.

One of the things this recent surge in autograph collecting has accomplished is to provide much needed knowledge as to the value collectors place on baseball players autographs, particularly those of current players and Hall of Fame members. It is to the latter group that we wish to direct our attention in this section. But in order to discuss the value of autographs of Hall of Fame members, a suitable medium must be used so that we don't compare apples with oranges (or in the case of autographs, a simple cut autograph of Carl Yastrzemski with a Carl Yastrzemski autograph on an elaborate original, piece of art). As the title of this article suggests, we have chosen the works of the Perez-Steele Galleries as the autographable media for our presentation.

Dick Perez, the artist of the Perez-Steele organization, has gained renown as one of the best renderers of baseball associated art of our times. Born in Puerto Rico, reared in Spanish Harlem, and educated at the Philadelphia College of Art and the University of Pennsylvania, Perez is the official artist for the Philadelphia Phillies, Leaf, Inc.'s Donruss subdivision, and the National Baseball Hall of Fame. In the late 1970s, he became associated with Frank and Peggy Steele, forming Perez-Steele Galleries.

The association of the Perez-Steele Galleries with the Hall of Fame has produced three major card sets (Art Post Cards, Great Moments, and Celebration) which have captured the fancy of autograph collectors as have no previous media. At least three reasons are apparent for the popularity of these Perez-Steele issues. First, the artwork itself is interesting, attractive and presented on high quality card stock. Second, the subject matter of all three issues is the Baseball Hall of Fame and its members — the most popular of all baseball related subjects to autograph collectors. And last, the Perez-Steele issues are all limited editions, lending collectibility to the cards in their own right, with or without autographs. Unfortunately for the collector who wishes to begin collecting the Perez-Steele issues, the two on-going issues, the Art Post Cards and the Great Moments, are sold out, as are the rights to future issues of these two sets. However, all of these Perez-Steele issues are actively traded and available (for a price, of course) — in fact, one of the purposes of this section is to present these issues and the price one might expect to pay for cards of these issues, both autographed and unautographed.

HALL OF FAME ART POST CARDS

In 1980, the Perez-Steele Galleries issued the first set of Hall of Fame Art Post Cards. This series begins with Ty Cobb, the first inductee, and ends with Dan Brouthers, the thirtieth inductee. Nine additional series have since been released, and the Art Post Cards series is now complete through the inductees of 1989. The Art Post Cards are a limited edition with 10,000 of each card being issued. The cards are numbered by the player's induction number into the Hall of Fame. The cards are also serially numbered by the number out of 10,000 that the card represents; e.g., 02405/10000. In all ten series have been released comprising 204 cards of Hall of Fame members and six supplemental cards of Hall of Fame or baseball related subjects (a value has not been placed on these supplemental cards as they do not portray actual Hall of Fame members).

The prices for the Art Post Cards below are for two conditions — unautographed and autographed. The third category below "Cut Autographed" does not refer to the Art Post Cards at all. It is the price of an autograph of the player, cut from a letter, check, 3X5 or other medium, so that all that remains on the medium is the player's signature. In short, the cut autograph is the simpliest of all autographs, and the least valuable. This category is listed here to give a value floor for all Hall of Famer's autographs.

If you see an em dash (—) in the Card Autographed position, it means there are no known examples of this card being autographed (the player was deceased or incapacitated at the time the card was released). To put all prices on an evquivalent basis and to avoid the ridiculousness of a coin dealer's grading system, the condition of the cards and cuts priced shall be as follows:

>Unautographed Cards — Mint as defined in the Sport Americana Baseball Card Price Guide
>
>Autographed Card — A typical, legible, legitimate autograph of the player, using a blue "Sharpie" pen, on a mint card as defined above
>
>Autographed Cut — A typical, legible, legitimate autograph of the player, using a pen if the player is considered a modern player, using a pencil or pen if the player is considered a 19th-Century-type player

All other conditions are left to the judicious evaluation of the collector; e.g., the use of a black rather than a blue Sharpie is not going to change the value significantly, however, a legible autograph is certainly more desirable than an autograph that is smeared. The conditions above apply also to the values of the Great Moments and Celebration cards.

FIRST SERIES	CARD UNAUTO	CARD AUTO	CUT AUTO		CARD UNAUTO	CARD AUTO	CUT AUTO
1. Ty Cobb	50.00	—	200.00	16. Henry Chadwick	2.00	—	1400.00*
2. Walter Johnson	20.00	—	450.00	17. Cap Anson	2.00	—	1700.00*
3. Christy Mathewson	20.00	—	900.00*	18. Eddie Collins	2.00	—	125.00
4. Babe Ruth	60.00	—	600.00	19. Candy Cummings	2.00	—	800.00*
5. Honus Wagner	10.00	—	200.00	20. Charles Comiskey	2.00	—	300.00
6. Morgan Bulkeley	2.00	—	1600.00*	21. Buck Ewing	2.00	—	1500.00*
7. Ban Johnson	2.00	—	175.00	22. Lou Gehrig	50.00	—	600.00
8. Nap Lajoie	5.00	—	175.00	23. Willie Keeler	2.00	—	900.00*
9. Connie Mack	5.00	—	150.00	24. Hoss Radbourne	2.00	—	1200.00*
10. John McGraw	5.00	—	550.00	25. George Sisler	10.00	—	50.00
11. Tris Speaker	10.00	—	175.00	26. A. G. Spalding	2.00	—	700.00
12. George Wright	2.00	—	650.00	27. Rogers Hornsby	20.00	—	150.00
13. Cy Young	10.00	—	200.00	28. Kenesaw Landis	2.00	—	225.00
14. Grover C. Alexander	7.00	—	275.00	29. Roger Bresnahan	2.00	—	400.00
15. Alexander Cartwright	2.00	—	550.00	30. Dan Brouthers	2.00	—	1400.00*

SECOND SERIES

	CARD UNAUTO	CARD AUTO	CUT AUTO
31. Fred Clarke	2.00	—	110.00
32. Jimmy Collins	2.00	—	500.00
33. Ed Delahanty	2.00	—	1750.00*
34. Hugh Duffy	2.00	—	300.00
35. Hughie Jennings	2.00	—	725.00
36. King Kelly	2.00	—	1750.00*
37. Jim O'Rourke	2.00	—	1000.00*
38. Wilbert Robinson	2.00	—	600.00
39. Jesse Burkett	2.00	—	325.00
40. Frank Chance	5.00	—	725.00
41. Jack Chesbro	2.00	—	900.00*
42. Johnny Evers	5.00	—	400.00
43. Clark Griffith	2.00	—	125.00
44. Thomas McCarthy	2.00	—	1500.00*
45. Joe McGinnity	2.00	—	750.00
46. Eddie Plank	5.00	—	1500.00*
47. Joe Tinker	5.00	—	1500.00*
48. Rube Waddell	5.00	—	1600.00*
49. Ed Walsh	2.00	—	150.00
50. Mickey Cochrane	7.00	—	100.00
51. Frankie Frisch	7.00	—	50.00
52. Lefty Grove	20.00	—	25.00
53. Carl Hubbell	15.00	100.00	10.00
54. Herb Pennock	2.00	—	150.00
55. Pie Traynor	7.00	—	75.00
56. Mordecai Brown	2.00	—	300.00
57. Charles Gehringer	50.00	60.00	5.00
58. Kid Nichols	2.00	—	150.00
59. Jimmy Foxx	15.00	—	150.00
60. Mel Ott	10.00	—	150.00

THIRD SERIES

	CARD UNAUTO	CARD AUTO	CUT AUTO
61. Harry Heilmann	2.00	—	250.00
62. Paul Waner	2.00	—	100.00
63. Ed Barrow	2.00	—	100.00
64. Chief Bender	2.00	—	210.00
65. Tom Connolly	2.00	—	250.00
66. Dizzy Dean	15.00	—	50.00
67. Bill Klem	2.00	—	300.00
68. Al Simmons	7.00	—	75.00
69. Bobby Wallace	2.00	—	200.00
70. Harry Wright	2.00	—	1500.00*
71. Bill Dickey	50.00	90.00	25.00
72. Rabbit Maranville	2.00	—	200.00
73. Bill Terry	10.00	95.00	25.00
74. Frank Baker	2.00	—	400.00
75. Joe DiMaggio	160.00	240.00	25.00
76. Gabby Hartnett	2.00	—	40.00
77. Ted Lyons	10.00	300.00	20.00
78. Ray Schalk	2.00	—	30.00
79. Dazzy Vance	2.00	—	100.00
80. Joe Cronin	10.00	1500.00*	10.00
81. Hank Greenberg	20.00	550.00	15.00
82. Sam Crawford	5.00	—	75.00
83. Joe McCarthy	10.00	—	25.00
84. Zack Wheat	7.00	—	40.00
85. Max Carey	2.00	—	15.00
86. Billy Hamilton	2.00	—	800.00*
87. Bob Feller	20.00	30.00	3.00
88. Bill McKechnie	2.00	—	60.00
89. Jackie Robinson	15.00	—	150.00
90. Edd Roush	10.00	125.00	25.00

FOURTH SERIES

	CARD UNAUTO	CARD AUTO	CUT AUTO
91. John Clarkson	2.00	—	1400.00*
92. Elmer Flick	2.00	—	50.00
93. Sam Rice	2.00	—	30.00
94. Eppa Rixey	2.00	—	75.00
95. Luke Appling	40.00	60.00	3.00
96. Red Faber	2.00	—	15.00
97. Burleigh Grimes	10.00	350.00	15.00
98. Miller Huggins	2.00	—	900.00*
99. Tim Keefe	2.00	—	900.00*
100. Heinie Manush	5.00	—	30.00
101. John Monte Ward	2.00	—	1000.00*
102. Pud Galvin	2.00	—	1500.00*
103. Casey Stengel	20.00	—	25.00
104. Ted Williams	160.00	200.00	20.00
105. Branch Rickey	2.00	—	90.00
106. Red Ruffing	10.00	900.00*	15.00
107. Lloyd Waner	10.00	3200.00*	15.00
108. Kiki Cuyler	2.00	—	175.00
109. Goose Goslin	2.00	—	65.00
110. Joe Medwick	10.00	—	30.00
111. Roy Campanella	20.00	625.00	125.00
112. Stan Coveleski	10.00	650.00	20.00
113. Waite Hoyt	10.00	650.00	15.00
114. Stan Musial	40.00	75.00	10.00
115. Lou Boudreau	20.00	25.00	3.00
116. Earle Combs	2.00	—	20.00
117. Ford Frick	2.00	—	25.00
118. Jesse Haines	2.00	—	30.00
119. Dave Bancroft	2.00	—	50.00
120. Jake Beckley	2.00	—	1400.00*

FIFTH SERIES

	CARD UNAUTO	CARD AUTO	CUT AUTO
121. Chick Hafey	2.00	—	30.00
122. Harry Hooper	2.00	—	20.00
123. Joe Kelley	2.00	—	750.00
124. Rube Marquard	10.00	—	15.00
125. Satchel Paige	20.00	3200.00*	30.00
126. George Weiss	2.00	—	50.00
127. Yogi Berra	25.00	35.00	5.00
128. Josh Gibson	2.00	—	1000.00*
129. Lefty Gomez	10.00	90.00	15.00
130. Will Harridge	2.00	—	50.00
131. Sandy Koufax	35.00	40.00	5.00
132. Buck Leonard	25.00	35.00	3.00
133. Early Wynn	20.00	30.00	3.00
134. Ross Youngs	2.00	—	700.00
135. Roberto Clemente	20.00	—	110.00
136. Billy Evans	2.00	—	225.00
137. Monte Irvin	15.00	25.00	3.00
138. George Kelly	10.00	650.00	15.00
139. Warren Spahn	20.00	30.00	3.00
140. Mickey Welch	2.00	—	1400.00*
141. Cool Papa Bell	25.00	90.00	15.00
142. Jim Bottomley	2.00	—	150.00
143. Jocko Conlan	10.00	90.00	15.00
144. Whitey Ford	20.00	35.00	5.00
145. Mickey Mantle	160.00	225.00	20.00
146. Sam Thompson	2.00	—	1500.00*
147. Earl Averill	10.00	900.00*	15.00
148. Bucky Harris	2.00	—	20.00
149. Billy Herman	15.00	25.00	3.00
150. Judy Johnson	10.00	90.00	15.00

SIXTH SERIES

	CARD UNAUTO	CARD AUTO	CUT AUTO
151. Ralph Kiner	20.00	30.00	3.00
152. Oscar Charleston	2.00	—	900.00*
153. Roger Connor	2.00	—	1000.00*
154. Cal Hubbard	2.00	—	25.00
155. Bob Lemon	20.00	30.00	3.00
156. Fred Lindstrom	2.00	—	15.00
157. Robin Roberts	20.00	30.00	3.00
158. Ernie Banks	20.00	30.00	3.00
159. Martin Dihigo	2.00	—	750.00
160. John Henry Lloyd	2.00	—	750.00

	CARD UNAUTO	CARD AUTO	CUT AUTO
161. Al Lopez	15.00	100.00	15.00
162. Amos Rusie	2.00	—	700.00
163. Joe Sewell	15.00	80.00	15.00
164. Addie Joss	2.00	—	1750.00*
165. Larry MacPhail	2.00	—	15.00
166. Eddie Mathews	20.00	30.00	3.00
167. Warren Giles	2.00	—	30.00
168. Willie Mays	45.00	70.00	10.00
169. Hack Wilson	5.00	—	300.00
170. Al Kaline	20.00	30.00	3.00
171. Chuck Klein	2.00	—	125.00
172. Duke Snider	25.00	35.00	5.00
173. Tom Yawkey	2.00	—	100.00
174. Rube Foster	2.00	—	2000.00*
175. Bob Gibson	20.00	30.00	3.00
176. Johnny Mize	15.00	25.00	3.00

SEVENTH SERIES

	CARD UNAUTO	CARD AUTO	CUT AUTO
177. Hank Aaron	25.00	40.00	5.00
178. Happy Chandler	25.00	60.00	5.00
179. Travis Jackson	10.00	110.00	10.00
180. Frank Robinson	15.00	25.00	3.00
181. Walter Alston	20.00	1100.00*	15.00
182. George Kell	15.00	25.00	3.00
183. Juan Marichal	15.00	25.00	3.00
184. Brooks Robinson	15.00	25.00	3.00

EIGHTH SERIES

	CARD UNAUTO	CARD AUTO	CUT AUTO
185. Luis Aparicio	15.00	30.00	3.00
186. Don Drysdale	15.00	25.00	3.00
187. Rick Ferrell	20.00	30.00	3.00
188. Harmon Killebrew	15.00	20.00	3.00
189. Pee Wee Reese	20.00	30.00	3.00
190. Lou Brock	15.00	20.00	3.00
191. Enos Slaughter	15.00	20.00	3.00
192. Arky Vaughn	2.00	—	250.00
193. Hoyt Wilhelm	15.00	20.00	3.00

NINTH SERIES

	CARD UNAUTO	CARD AUTO	CUT AUTO
194. Bobby Doerr	15.00	20.00	3.00
195. Ernie Lombardi	2.00	—	75.00
196. Willie McCovey	15.00	20.00	3.00
197. Ray Dandridge	15.00	20.00	3.00
198. Catfish Hunter	15.00	20.00	3.00
199. Billy Williams	15.00	20.00	3.00

TENTH SERIES

	CARD UNAUTO	CARD AUTO	CUT AUTO
200. Willie Stargell	10.00	20.00	3.00
201. Al Barlick	10.00	20.00	3.00
202. Johnny Bench	20.00	40.00	5.00
203. Red Schoendienst	10.00	20.00	3.00
204. Carl Yastrzemski	20.00	40.00	5.00

* = Prices vary widely on these items

AUTOGRAPHED WHITEY FORD   AUTOGRAPHED CARL HUBBELL   AUTOGRAPHED LOU BROCK

GREAT MOMENTS

Back in 1911, premium baseball cards were offered by Turkey Red cigarettes. These cards could be obtained at the local retail establishments selling Turkey Red cigarettes by redeeming a Turkey Red coupon and paying the merchant one cent. These large cards (cabinets as they are called) have become the most popular of all cabinet-sized baseball cards. In 1985, the Perez-Steele Galleries released the first series of Great Moments baseball cards which emulate the 1911 Turkey Red cards. Although the theme of the card set — a great moment in the career of a Hall of Fame member — is somewhat vague, the cards themselves are some of the most attractive baseball cards ever produced, from the artwork to the texturized card stock. The Great Moments edition is limited to 5,000 of each card. To date, six twelve-card series have been released. All series have been sold out, and the cards are available only in the secondary market.

FIRST SERIES	CARD UNAUTO	CARD AUTO	FOURTH SERIES	CARD UNAUTO	CARD AUTO
1. Babe Ruth	25.00	—	37. Bill Dickey	40.00	90.00
2. Al Kaline	15.00	25.00	38. Willie Stargell	10.00	20.00
3. Jackie Robinson	10.00	—	39. Brooks Robinson	10.00	20.00
4. Lou Gehrig	20.00	—	40. Tinker-Evers-Chance	7.00	—
5. Whitey Ford	20.00	30.00			
			41. Billy Herman	10.00	20.00
6. Christy Mathewson	7.00	—	42. Grover C. Alexander	7.00	—
7. Roy Campanella	20.00	625.00	43. Luis Aparicio	15.00	30.00
8. Walter Johnson	7.00	—	44. Lefty Gomez	10.00	90.00
9. Hank Aaron	20.00	35.00	45. Eddie Collins	7.00	—
10. Cy Young	7.00	—			
			46. Judy Johnson	7.00	—
11. Stan Musial	35.00	60.00	47. Harry Heilmann	7.00	—
12. Ty Cobb	20.00	—	48. Harmon Killebrew	10.00	20.00
SECOND SERIES			FIFTH SERIES		
13. Ted Williams	50.00	90.00	49. Johnny Bench	15.00	40.00
14. Warren Spahn	15.00	25.00	50. Max Carey	7.00	—
15. The Waner Brothers	7.00	—			
			51. Cool Papa Bell	20.00	40.00
16. Sandy Koufax	20.00	40.00	52. Rube Waddell	7.00	—
17. Robin Roberts	15.00	25.00	53. Yogi Berra	15.00	25.00
18. Dizzy Dean	7.00	—	54. Herb Pennock	7.00	—
19. Mickey Mantle	65.00	120.00	55. Red Schoendienst	10.00	20.00
20. Satchel Paige	10.00	—			
			56. Juan Marichal	10.00	20.00
21. Ernie Banks	15.00	25.00	57. Frankie Frisch	7.00	—
22. Willie McCovey	15.00	25.00	58. Buck Leonard	10.00	25.00
23. Johnny Mize	15.00	20.00	59. George Kell	10.00	20.00
24. Honus Wagner	10.00	—	60. Chuck Klein	7.00	—
THIRD SERIES					
			SIXTH SERIES		
25. Willie Keeler	7.00	—			
			61. King Kelly	7.00	—
26. Pee Wee Reese	20.00	35.00	62. Catfish Hunter	10.00	20.00
27. Monte Irvin	10.00	20.00	63. Lou Boudreau	10.00	20.00
28. Eddie Mathews	15.00	25.00	64. Al Lopez	10.00	100.00
29. Enos Slaughter	10.00	20.00	65. Willie Mays	20.00	55.00
30. Rube Marquard	7.00	—			
			66. Lou Brock	10.00	20.00
31. Charles Gehringer	30.00	50.00	67. Bob Lemon	10.00	20.00
32. Roberto Clemente	15.00	—	68. Joe Sewell	7.00	—
33. Duke Snider	20.00	30.00	69. Billy Williams	10.00	20.00
34. Ray Dandridge	15.00	20.00	70. Rick Ferrell	10.00	20.00
35. Carl Hubbell	10.00	90.00			
			71. Arky Vaughn	7.00	—
36. Bobby Doerr	10.00	20.00	72. Carl Yastrzemski	15.00	40.00

AUTOGRAPHED BROOKS ROBINSON   AUTOGRAPHED STAN MUSIAL

CELEBRATION

In 1989, to commemorate the National Baseball Hall of Fame's 50th Anniversary, Perez-Steele Galleries issued a 44-card set entitled Celebration. This limited edition of 10,000 sets sold out in less than a month from the issue date. Besides being an attractive card set, emulating the style of the 1888 issue by the W.S. Kimball company, 41 out of the 44 cards portray living players, an autograph collector's delight. In addition to the card set, there is a supplemental Celebration booklet. The booklet features 11 pages of baseball associated, Dick Perez backgrounds, upon which reduced versions of the Celebration cards have been inset, four cards to a page. The booklet resembles the W.S. Kimball albums of the 19th Century.

	CARD UNAUTO	CARD AUTO		CARD UNAUTO	CARD AUTO
1. Hank Aaron	15.00	60.00	19. Monte Irvin	10.00	20.00
2. Luis Aparicio	15.00	30.00	20. Judy Johnson	10.00	—
3. Ernie Banks	10.00	20.00			
4. Cool Papa Bell	20.00	40.00	21. Al Kaline	10.00	20.00
5. Johnny Bench	20.00	40.00	22. George Kell	10.00	20.00
			23. Harmon Killebrew	10.00	20.00
6. Yogi Berra	15.00	25.00	24. Ralph Kiner	10.00	20.00
7. Lou Boudreau	10.00	20.00	25. Bob Lemon	10.00	20.00
8. Roy Campanella	25.00	625.00			
9. Happy Chandler	15.00	50.00	26. Buck Leonard	15.00	25.00
10. Jocko Conlan	10.00	1000.00*	27. Al Lopez	10.00	150.00
			28. Mickey Mantle	50.00	110.00
11. Ray Dandridge	10.00	20.00	29. Juan Marichal	10.00	20.00
12. Bill Dickey	40.00	80.00	30. Eddie Mathews	10.00	20.00
13. Bobby Doerr	10.00	20.00			
14. Rick Ferrell	10.00	20.00	31. Willie McCovey	10.00	20.00
15. Charlie Gehringer	25.00	55.00	32. Johnny Mize	10.00	20.00
			33. Stan Musial	30.00	60.00
16. Lefty Gomez	10.00	—	34. Pee Wee Reese	15.00	30.00
17. Billy Herman	10.00	20.00	35. Brooks Robinson	10.00	20.00
18. Catfish Hunter	10.00	20.00			

	CARD UNAUTO	CARD AUTO			CARD UNAUTO	CARD AUTO
36. Joe Sewell	10.00	80.00		41. Bill Terry	10.00	—
37. Enos Slaughter	10.00	20.00		42. Billy Williams	10.00	20.00
38. Duke Snider	15.00	30.00		43. Ted Williams	40.00	90.00
39. Warren Spahn	10.00	20.00		44. Carl Yastrzemski	20.00	40.00
40. Willie Stargell	10.00	20.00				

* = Prices vary widely on this item

THE PEREZ-STEELE GALLERIES

Peggy Steele, Frank Steele and artist Dick Perez

PAGE FROM CELEBRATION BOOKLET

The prices for the Perez-Steele works in this section are not those of the authors, the publisher, the advertisers or any particular contributor to this book. They are consensus prices of some of the leading dealers in Perez-Steele material. Neither are the prices meant to be absolute, nor is anyone required or expected to price their Perez-Steele material according to the prices in this section. The values are guidelines generated from the current, most reliable sources for the values. The prices are those of late June 1990 and are subject to rapid change at any given time. As the price of any autograph is directly related to both supply and demand, the passing of any of the men depicted on the material in this section would have a dramatic effect on the price of that material.

The authors express their appreciation to Dave Dane, Jack Heir, Eric Lange, Lew Lipset and Bob Schmierer for providing pricing input to this section. In addition, a particular debt is owed Dick Gordon who provided most of the autographed Perez-Steele material used to illustrate this section and much of this book. Finally, we should like to thank Dick Perez and Peggy and Frank Steele, first for giving the art-appreciative sector of the sports and autograph collecting hobbies the works of the Perez-Steele Galleries, and second, for the cooperation they extended to us in preparing this section.

PEREZ–STEELE
ART POSTCARDS, GREAT MOMENTS, CELEBRATION

JACK HEIR
49 Birmingham Drive
Manalapan, NJ 07726

**Phone
(201) 446-4758**
Evenings 7:00pm to 10:00pm
and Weekends
or leave message anytime

We have one of the largest Perez-Steele selections in the hobby. Send a large envelope, with **45 cents** postage for our Perez-Steele, single signature baseballs and photos pricelist.

24- 68 LINDSTROM, FRED CHARLES	D. OCTOBER 4, 1981 CHICAGO, ILL.
66- 55 LINES, RICHARD GEORGE	OLD ADD: 4220 N. FEDERAL HWY - FORT LAUDERDALE FL 33306
52- 69 LINHART, CARL JAMES	2647 DELMAR AVE - GRANITE CITY IL 62040
10- 90 LINK, FREDERICK THEODORE	D. MAY 22, 1939 HOUSTON, TEXAS
33- 38 LINKE, EDWARD KARL	D. JUNE 21, 1988 CHICAGO, ILL.
54- 63 LINT, ROYCE JAMES	6814 SE JACK RD - MILWAUKIE OR 97222
29- 64 LINTON, CLAUD CLARENCE 'BOB'	D. APRIL 3, 1980 DESTIN, FLA.
73- 75 LINTZ, LARRY	71 LACONIA CT - SAN JOSE CA 95139
62- 76 LINZ, PHILIP FRANCIS	OLD ADD: 1189 FIRST AVE - NEW YORK NY 10021
63- 69 LINZY, FRANK ALFRED	RR 2 BOX 395 - COWETA OK 74429
56- 51 LIPIETRI, MICHAEL ANGELO	150 YOAKUM AVE - FARMINGDALE NY 11735
42- 63 LIPON, JOHN JOSEPH	13315 ALCHESTER - HOUSTON TX 77079
37- 66 LIPSCOMB, GERARD 'NIG'	D. FEBRUARY 27, 1978 HUNTERSVILLE, N. C.
63- 70 LIPSKI, ROBERT PETER	1 SNOOK ST - SCRANTON PA 18505
87- 80 LIRIANO, NELSON ARTURO	MARTIRES 19 DE NOV.#7,ENS LUPERON-PUERTO PLATA DOM REP.
70- 79 LIS, JOSEPH ANTHONY	4055 SECRETARIAT DRIVE - NEWBURGH IN 47630
27- 55 LISENBEE, HORACE MILTON 'HOD'	D. NOVEMBER 14, 1987 CLARKSVILLE, TENN.
81- 73 LISI, RICCARDO PATRICK EMILIO	OLD ADD: 32 RIVERVIEW W. APTS#2-PITTSFIELD MA
29- 65 LISKA, ADOLPH JAMES	3831 NE WASCO - PORTLAND OR 97232
73- 76 LITTELL, MARK ALAN	BOX 35 - DEFIANCE MO 63341
89- 73 LITTLE, DENNIS SCOTT 'SCOTT'	105 PARK LANE - SCOTT CITY MO 63780
80- 76 LITTLE, DONALD JEFFREY 'JEFF'	OLD ADD: 5550 C. R. 44 - WOODVILLE OH 43469
82- 80 LITTLE, RICHARD BRYAN	OLD ADD: 1003 MAGNOLIA - HEARNE TX 77859
12-108 LITTLE, WILLIAM ARTHUR 'JACK'	D. JULY 27, 1961 DALLAS, TEX.
80- 77 LITTLEFIELD, JOHN ANDREW	1214 N. ALAMEDA ST - AZUSA CA 91702
50- 53 LITTLEFIELD, RICHARD BERNARD	14838 KENTFIELD - DETROIT MI 48223
27- 56 LITTLEJOHN, CHARLES CARLISLE	D. OCTOBER 27, 1977 KANSAS CITY, MO.
78- 74 LITTLEJOHN, DENNIS GERALD	OLD ADD: 2244 WEST FREMONT DR - TEMPE AZ
81- 74 LITTLETON, LARRY MARVIN	2318 ARMAND RD NE - ATLANTA GA 30324
89- 74 LITTON, JON GREGORY 'GREG'	6950 HOYT STREET - PENSACOLA FL 32503
52- 70 LITTRELL, JACK NAPIER	7510 FLOYDSBURG RD - CRESTWOOD KY 40014
40- 50 LITWHILER, DANIEL WEBSTER	3810 PLAYER DRIVE - NEWPORT RICHEY FL 33553
47- 59 LIVELY, EVERETT ADRIAN 'BUD'	8605 ESSLINGER CT - HUNTSVILLE AL 35802
11-101 LIVELY, HENRY EVERETT 'JACK'	D. DECEMBER 5, 1967 ARAB, ALA.
39- 69 LIVENGOOD, WESLEY AMOS	2220 ELGIN RD - WINSTON SALEM NC 27103
38- 53 LIVINGSTON, THOMPSON ORVILLE 'MICKEY'	D. APRIL 3, 1983 HOUSTON, TEXAS
68- 55 LLENAS, WINSTON ENRIQUILLO	APARTADO #92 - SANTIAGO DOMINICAN REP.
22- 73 LLEWELLYN, CLEMENT MANLEY	D. NOVEMBER 27, 1969 CHARLOTTE, N. C.
12-109 LOAN, WILLIAM JOSEPH 'MIKE'	D. NOVEMBER 12, 1966 SPRINGFIELD, PA.
39- 70 LOANE, ROBERT KENNETH	BOX 246 - COOL CA 95614
14-130 LOBERT, FRANK JOHN	D. MAY 29, 1932 PITTSBURGH, PA.
62- 77 LOCK, DONALD WILSON	1330 NORTH WALNUT - KINGMAN KS 67068
55- 70 LOCKE, CHARLES EDWARD	P.O. BOX 3925 - POPLAR BLUFF MO 63901
59- 49 LOCKE, LAWRENCE DONALD 'BOBBY'	RR 1 BOX 400 - DUNBAR PA 15431
64- 66 LOCKE, RONALD THOMAS	P.O. BOX 229 - KENYON RI 02836
65- 65 LOCKER, ROBERT AWTRY	3648 HAPPY VALLEY - LAFAYETTE CA 94549
73- 77 LOCKLEAR, GENE	RR1 BOX 213 - PEMBROKE NC 28382
55- 71 LOCKLIN, STUART CARLTON	1823 SOUTH BOUTEN - APPLETON WI 54911
45- 59 LOCKMAN, CARROLL WALTER 'WHITEY'	8234 NORTH 75TH ST - SCOTTSDALE AZ 85253
65- 66 LOCKWOOD, CLAUDE EDWARD 'SKIP'	79 TEHIAS - RYE NH 03870
38- 54 LODIGIANI, DARIO ANTHONY	745 LATHROP ST - NAPA CA 94558
28- 59 LOEPP, GEORGE HERBERT	D. SEPTEMBER 4, 1967 LOS ANGELES, CAL.
50- 54 LOES, WILLIAM 'BILLY'	33-08 84TH ST - JACKSON HEIGHTS NY 11372
26- 50 LOFTUS, FRANCIS PATRICK	D. OCTOBER 27, 1980 BELCHERTOWN, MASS.
24- 69 LOFTUS, RICHARD JOSEPH	D. JANUARY 21, 1972 CONCORD, MASS.
51- 53 LOGAN, JOHN	6115 WEST CLEVELAND AVE - MILWAUKEE WI 53219
35- 63 LOGAN, ROBERT DEAN 'LEFTY'	D. MAY 20, 1978 INDIANAPOLIS, IND.
14-131 LOHR, HOWARD SYLVESTER	D. JUNE 9, 1977 PHILADELPHIA, PA.
47- 60 LOHRKE, JACK WAYNE 'LUCKY'	2817 LUCENA DR - SAN JOSE CA 95132
34- 63 LOHRMAN, WILLIAM LEROY	250 ROUTE 208 - NEW PALTZ NY 12561
78- 75 LOIS, ALBERTO	INGENIO CONSUELO CALLE 5-SAN PEDRO DE MACORIS DOM. REP.
63- 71 LOLICH, MICHAEL STEPHEN 'MICKEY'	6252 ROBINHILL - WASHINGTON MI 48094
71- 63 LOLICH, RONALD JOHN	OLD ADD: 2436 N. SAVIER - PORTLAND OR 97210
46- 65 LOLLAR, JOHN SHERMAN 'SHERM'	D. SEPTEMBER 24, 1977 SPRINGFIELD, MO.
80- 78 LOLLAR, WILLIAM TIMOTHY 'TIM'	P.O. BOX 2798 - BRECKENRIDGE CO 80424
84- 70 LOMAN, DOUGLAS EDWARD	25 LINCOLN STREET - BAKERSFIELD CA 93305
31- 48 LOMBARDI, ERNEST NATALI	D. SEPTEMBER 26, 1977 SANTA CRUZ, CALIF.
86- 88 LOMBARDI, PHILIP ARDEN	12444 CAROL PLACE - GRANADA HILLS CA 91344
45- 60 LOMBARDI, VICTOR ALVIN	5164 EAST ASHLAN #103 - FRESNO CA 93727
48- 59 LOMBARDO, LOUIS	1551 FIRST STREET S. #701 - JACKSONVILLE BEACH FL 32250
85- 64 LOMBARDOZZI, STEPHEN PAUL	2 HAND HEWN WAY - MANLIUS NY 13104
65- 67 LONBORG, JAMES REYNOLD	498 FIRST PARISH RD - SCITUATE MA 02066
11-102 LONERGAN, WALTER E.	D. JANUARY 23, 1958 LEXINGTON, MASS.
22- 74 LONG, JAMES ALBERT	D. SEPTEMBER 14, 1970 FORT DODGE, IA.
63- 72 LONG, JEOFFREY KEITH	11 FLOWER CT - LAKESIDE PARK KY 41017
11-103 LONG, LESTER 'LEP'	D. OCTOBER 21, 1958 BIRMINGHAM, ALA.
51- 54 LONG, RICHARD DALE 'DALE'	22 COLLINGDALE COURT - PALM COAST FL 32037
81- 75 LONG, ROBERT EARL	113 DOWER ROAD - CHATTANOOGA TN 37419
11-104 LONG, THOMAS AUGUSTUS	D. JUNE 15, 1972 MOBILE, ALA.
24- 70 LONG, THOMAS FRANCIS	D. SEPTEMBER 16, 1973 LOUISVILLE, KY.
85- 65 LONG, WILLIAM DOUGLAS	7699 DIMMICK ROAD - CINCINNATI OH 45241
56- 52 LONNETT, JOSEPH PAUL	126 DUNCAN CIR - BEAVER PA 15009
68- 56 LOOK, BRUCE MICHAEL	P.O. BOX 70 - OKEMOS MI 48805
61- 69 LOOK, DEAN ZACHARY	2103 BUTTERNUT - OKEMOS MI 48864
44- 77 LOPAT, EDMUND WALTER	99 OAK TRAIL RD - HILLSDALE NJ 07642
48- 60 LOPATA, STANLEY EDWARD	LEISURE WORLD MANOR #2239 - MESA AZ 85206
45- 61 LOPATKA, ARTHUR JOSEPH	7310 NORTH HARLEM - CHICAGO IL 60648
72- 63 LOPES, DAVID EARL 'DAVEY'	16984 AVE DE SANTA YNEZ-PACIFIC PALISADES CA 90272
28- 60 LOPEZ, ALFONSO RAMON	3601 BEACH DR - TAMPA FL 33609
65- 68 LOPEZ, ARTURO	OLD ADD: 57 WALNUT STREET - OAKLAND NJ 07436
74- 76 LOPEZ, AURELIO RIOS	5 PONIENTE #8 - TEXAMACHALCO PUEBLA MEX.
76- 56 LOPEZ, CARLOS ANTONIO	MEXICI #33A, POINTE - MAZATLAN SINALOA MEX.
55- 72 LOPEZ, HECTOR HEADLEY	666 JANOS LN - WEST HEMPSTEAD NY 11552
66- 56 LOPEZ, JOSE RAMON	D. SEPTEMBER 4, 1982 MIAMI, FLA.
63- 73 LOPEZ, MARCELINO PONS	841 NW LITTLE RIVER DR - MIAMI FL 33150
23- 80 LORD, WILLIAM CARLTON 'CARL'	D. AUGUST 15, 1947 CHESTER, PA.
13-104 LORENZEN, ADOLPH ANDREAS 'LEFTY'	D. MARCH 5, 1963 DAVENPORT, IA.
16- 57 LOTZ, JOSEPH PETER	D. JANUARY 1, 1971 HAYWARD, CAL.

80- 79 LOUCKS, SCOTT GREGORY	1801 VIOLA DR - SIERRA VISTA AZ 85635
10- 91 LOUDELL, ARTHUR	D. FEBRUARY 19, 1961 KANSAS CITY, MO.
67- 65 LOUGHLIN, LAWRENCE JOHN	410 SOUTH 57TH - TACOMA WA 98408
64- 67 LOUN, DONALD NELSON	9095 WEXFORD DR - VIENNA VA 22180
13-105 LOVE, EDWARD HAUGHTON 'SLIM'	D. NOVEMBER 30, 1942 MEMPHIS, TENN.
22- 75 LOVELACE, THOMAS RIVERS	D. JULY 12, 1979 DALLAS, TEX.
88- 83 LOVELACE, VANCE ODELL	5608 TWELFTH AVENUE - TAMPA FL 33610
55- 73 LOVENGUTH, LYNN RICHARD	13565 SW HART RD - BEAVERTON OR 97005
33- 39 LOVETT, MERRITT MARWOOD	1477 PARK BEACH CIR #14 - PUNTA GORDA FL 33950
80- 80 LOVIGLIO, JOHN PAUL 'JAY'	96 COUNTRY VILLAGE LN - EAST ISLIP NY 11730
72- 64 LOVITTO, JOSEPH	3803 SHADY CREEK NORTH - ARLINGTON TX 76013
63- 74 LOVRICH, PETER	19626 BEECHNUT DR - MOKENA IL 60448
88- 84 LOVULLO, SALVATORE ANTHONY	16825 BAJIO ROAD - ENCINO CA 91436
15- 91 LOW, FLETCHER	D. JUNE 6, 1973 HANOVER, N.H.
11-105 LOWDERMILK, LOUIS BAILEY	D. DECEMBER 27, 1975 CENTRALIA, ILL.
20- 75 LOWE, GEORGE WESLEY	D. SEPTEMBER 2, 1981 SOMERS POINT, N. J.
70- 80 LOWENSTEIN, JOHN LEE	1208 STARKY - AUGUSTA KS 67010
51- 55 LOWN, OMAR JOSEPH 'TURK'	1106 VAN BUREN - PUEBLO CO 81004
42- 64 LOWREY, HARRY LEE 'PEANUTS'	D. JULY 2, 1986 INGLEWOOD, CALIF.
84- 71 LOWRY, DWIGHT	P.O. BOX 2382 - PEMBROKE NC 28372
42- 65 LOWRY, SAMUEL JOSEPH	OLD ADD: 263A HERMITAGE ST - PHILADELPHIA PA 19127
86- 89 LOYND, MICHAEL WALLACE	19 RANDALL DRIVE - SHORT HILLS NJ 07078
84- 72 LOZADO, WILLIAM 'WILLIE'	551 EUCLID AVE - BROOKLYN NY 11208
81- 76 LUBRATICH, STEVEN GEORGE	910 CASTLE - SAN LEANDRO CA 94578
36- 49 LUBY, HUGH MAX	D. MAY 4, 1986 EUGENE, ORE.
38- 55 LUCADELLO, JOHN	103 OAKWOOD DR-SAN ANTONIO TX 78228
23- 61 LUCAS, CHARLES FREDERICK 'RED'	D. JULY 9, 1986 NASHVILLE, TENN. .
35- 64 LUCAS, FREDERICK WARRINGTON	D. MARCH 11, 1987 CAMBRIDGE, MD.
80- 81 LUCAS, GARY PAUL	3356 AVENIDA SIERRA - ESCONDIDO CA 92025
31- 49 LUCAS, JOHN CHARLES	D. OCTOBER 31, 1970 MARYVILLE, ILL.
29- 66 LUCAS, RAY WESLEY	D. OCTOBER 9, 1969 HARRISON, MICH.
70- 81 LUCCHESI, FRANK JOSEPH	3027 GLASGOW DR - ARLINGTON TX 76013
23- 62 LUCE, FRANK EDWARD	D. FEBRUARY 3, 1942 MILWAUKEE, WIS.
20- 76 LUCEY, JOSEPH EARL	D. JULY 30, 1980 HOLYOKE, MASS.
43- 79 LUCIER, LOUIS JOSEPH	579 HIGHLAND ST - NORTHBRIDGE MA 01534
24- 71 LUDOLPH, WILLIAM FRANCIS	D. APRIL 8, 1952 OAKLAND, CAL.
25- 66 LUEBBE, ROY JOHN	D. AUGUST 21, 1985 PAPILLION, NEB.
71- 64 LUEBBER, STEPHEN LEE	3302 MOOREHEAD DR - JOPLIN MO 64804
62- 78 LUEBKE, RICHARD RAYMOND	D. DECEMBER 4, 1974 SAN DIEGO, CALIF.
89- 75 LUECKEN, RICHARD FRED	2739 SHADOWDALE - HOUSTON TX 77043
85- 66 LUGO, URBANO RAFAEL	ROOEVELT RES. TIUNA ENT BPH 44 ROSALES - CARACAS VENEZ
13-106 LUHRSEN, WILLIAM FERDINAND	D. AUGUST 15, 1973 NORTH LITTLE ROCK, ARK.
41- 66 LUKON, EDWARD PAUL	RR 3, CHERRY VALLEY RD - BURGETTSTOWN PA15021
67- 66 LUM, MICHAEL KEN-WAI	3476 COCHISE DR NW - ATLANTA GA 30339
57- 44 LUMENTI, RAPHAEL ANTHONY 'RALPH'	P.O. BOX 137 - WORCHESTER MA 01611
56- 53 LUMPE, JERRY DEAN	732 PEARSON DRIVE - SPRINGFIELD MO 65804
54- 64 LUNA, GUILLERMO ROMERO "MEMO"	CARDENAS 50 OTE. - LOS MOCHIS SINOLOA MEX.
45- 62 LUND, DONALD ANDREW	1000 SOUTH STATE ST - ANN ARBOR MI 48109
67- 67 LUND, GORDON T	1717 ROBBIE LN - MOUNT PROSPECT IL 60056
24- 72 LUNDGREN, EBIN DELMAR 'DEL'	D. OCTOBER 19, 1984 LINDSBORG, KAN.
73- 78 LUNDSTEDT, THOMAS ROBERT	8645 HUNTERS WAY - ST. PAUL MN 55124
19- 53 LUNTE, HARRY AUGUST	D. JULY 27, 1965 ST. LOUIS, MO.
40- 51 LUPIEN, ULYSSES JOHN 'TONY'	BOX 351 - NORWICH VT 05055
61- 70 LUPLOW, ALVIN DAVID	2450 STARLITE DR - SAGINAW MI 48603
14-132 LUQUE, ADOLFO	D. JULY 3, 1957 HAVANA, CUBA
87- 81 LUSADER, SCOTT EDWARD	759 CAROLINE AVENUE - WEST PALM BEACH FL 33406
10- 92 LUSH, ERNEST BENJAMIN	D. FEBRUARY 26, 1937 DETROIT, MICH.
56- 54 LUTTRELL, LYLE KENNETH	D. JULY 11, 1984 CHATTANOOGA, TENN.
22- 76 LUTZ, LOUIS WILLIAM	D. FEBRUARY 22, 1984 CINCINNATI, O.
51- 56 LUTZ, ROLLIN JOSEPH 'JOE'	BOX 617 - COHOES NY 12047
23- 83 LUTZKE, WALTER JOHN 'RUBE'	D. MARCH 6, 1938 MILWAUKEE, WIS.
70- 82 LUZINSKI, GREGORY MICHAEL	320 JACKSON RD - MEDFORD NJ 08055
67- 68 LYLE, ALBERT WALTER 'SPARKY'	17 SIGNAL HILL DR - VOORHEES NJ 08043
25- 67 LYLE, JAMES CHARLES	D. OCTOBER 10, 1977 WILLIAMSPORT, PA.
20- 77 LYNCH, ADRIAN RYAN	D. MARCH 16, 1934 DAVENPORT, IA.
80- 82 LYNCH, EDWARD FRANCIS	5940 SW 120TH ST - MIAMI FL 33156
54- 65 LYNCH, GERALD THOMAS	120 DAVIS MILL COURT - LAWRENCEVILLE GA 30245
48- 61 LYNCH, MATT DANNY 'DUMMY'	D. JUNE 30, 1978 PLANO, TEXAS
22- 77 LYNCH, WALTER EDWARD	D. DECEMBER 21, 1976 DAYTONA BEACH, CALIF.
16- 58 LYNN, BYRD	D. FEBRUARY 5, 1940 NAPA, CAL.
74- 77 LYNN, FREDRIC MICHAEL	801 INVERNESS DRIVE - RANCHO MIRAGE CA 92270
39- 71 LYNN, JAPHET MONROE 'RED'	D. OCTOBER 27, 1977 BELLVILLE, TEX.
37- 67 LYNN, JEROME EDWARD	D. SEPTEMBER 25, 1972 SCRANTON, PA.
44- 78 LYON, RUSSELL MAYO	BOX 366 - CALHOUN FALLS SC 29629
44- 79 LYONS, ALBERT HAROLD	D. DECEMBER 20, 1965 INGLEWOOD, CAL.
86- 90 LYONS, BARRY STEPHEN	644 HOPKINS BOULEVARD - BILOXI MS 39530
47- 61 LYONS, EDWARD HOYT	1466 EBERT ST - WINSTON SALEM NC 27103
20- 78 LYONS, GEORGE TONY	D. AUGUST 12, 1981 NEVADA, MO.
41- 62 LYONS, HERSCHEL E	7900 DUNBARTON AVE-LOS ANGELES CA 90045
85- 67 LYONS, STEPHEN JOHN	OLD ADD: 8475 SW PARKVIEW LOOP - BEAVERTON OR 97005
29- 67 LYONS, TERENCE HILBERT	D. SEPTEMBER 9, 1959 DAYTON, O.
23- 84 LYONS, THEODORE AMAR	D. JULY 25, 1986 SULPHUR, LA.
83- 93 LYONS, WILLIAMS ALLEN	2621 GRANDVIEW AVENUE - ALTON IL 62002
80- 83 LYSANDER, RICHARD EUGENE	263 EAST FERNDALE - SUNNYVALE CA 94086
69-105 LYTTLE, JAMES LAWRENCE	751 CAMINO LAKE CIR - BOCA RATON FL 33432
55- 74 MAAS, DUANE FREDRICK 'DUKE'	D. DECEMBER 7, 1976 MOUNT CLEMENS, MICH.
58- 57 MABE, ROBERT LEE	90 BISHOP AVE - DANVILLE VA 24541
76- 57 MACCORMACK, FRANK LOUIS	2 SCHMIDT PLACE - SECAUCUS NJ 07094
28- 61 MACDONALD, HARVEY FORSYTH	D. OCTOBER 4, 1965 MANOA, PA.
50- 55 MACDONALD, WILLIAM PAUL	RR 1 BOX 13 - BELLEVUE ID 83313
87- 82 MACFARLANE, MICHAEL ANDREW	7421 WOODSIDE AVENUE - STOCKTON CA 95207
26- 51 MACFAYDEN, DANIEL KNOWLES	D. AUGUST 26, 1972 BRUNSWICK, ME.
74- 78 MACHA, KENNETH EDWARD	6934 BERKSHIRE DRIVE - EXPORT PA 15632
79- 70 MACHA, MICHAEL WILLIAM	201 COSTA DEL ORO - VICTORIA TX 77904
89- 76 MACHADO, JULIO S.	AV 2 CON C/19 #17-95,P DEL SUR L'CANADA-MARACAIBO VENEZ
71- 65 MACHEMEHL, CHARLES WALTER	RR 5 BOX 234 - BRENHAM TX 77833
78- 76 MACHEMER, DAVID RITCHIE	1359 ST. JOSEPH CIR - ST. JOSEPH MI 49085
10- 93 MACK, EARLE THADDEUS	D. FEBRUARY 4, 1967 UPPER DARBY, PA.

89

22- 78	MACK, FRANK GEORGE	D. JULY 2, 1971 CLEARWATER, FLA.
45- 63	MACK, JOSEPH JOHN	OLD ADD: 2038 MULBERRY LN - ARLINGTON HEIGHTS IL 60004
38- 56	MACK, RAYMOND JAMES	D. MAY 7, 1969 BUCYRUS, O.
87- 83	MACK, SHANE LEE	13708 FELSON STREET - CERITOS CA 90701
85- 68	MACK, TONY LYNN	OLD ADD: 3304 MONTE VESTA #E32 - LEXINGTON KY 40502
73- 79	MACKANIN, PETER	OLD ADD: 2905 HOLLYBROOK DR - WEST COVINA CA 91791
55- 75	MACKENZIE, ERIC HUGH	1224 EMILY ST - MOORETOWN ONTARIO CAN.
61- 71	MACKENZIE, HENRY GORDON 'GORDY'	36535 MICRO RACETRACK ROAD - FRUITLAND PARK FL 32817
60- 61	MACKENZIE, KENNETH PURVIS	15 FAIR STREET - GUILFORD CT 06437
41- 68	MACKIEWICZ, FELIX THADDEUS	33 NANTUCKET LN-OLIVETTE MO 63132
53- 52	MACKINSON, JOHN JOSEPH	D. OCTOBER 17, 1989 RESEDA, CALIF.
79- 71	MACKO, STEVEN JOSEPH	D. NOVEMBER 15, 1981 ARLINGTON, TEX.
62- 79	MACLEOD, WILLIAM DANIEL	136 BASS AVENUE - GLOUCESTER MA 01930
38- 57	MACON, MAX CULLEN	D. AUGUST 5, 1989 JUPITER, FLA.
22- 79	MACPHEE, WALTER SCOTT 'WADDY'	D. JANUARY 20, 1980 CHARLOTTE, N. C.
44- 80	MACPHERSON, HARRY WILLIAM	971 BAY VISTA BLVD - ENGLEWOOD FL 33533
80- 84	MACWHORTER, KEITH	18 SALEM DRIVE - NORTH PROVIDENCE RI 03030
16- 59	MADDEN, EUGENE	D. APRIL 6, 1949 UTICA, N. Y.
14-133	MADDEN, FRANCIS A.	D. APRIL 30, 1952 PITTSBURGH, PA.
12-110	MADDEN, LEONARD JOSEPH	D. SEPTEMBER 9, 1949 TOLEDO, O.
83- 94	MADDEN, MICHAEL ANTHONY	4733 FRANKFORT WAY - DENVER CO 80239
87- 84	MADDEN, MORRIS DEWAYNE	105 JENNINGS - LAURENS SC 29360
46- 66	MADDERN, CLARENCE JAMES	D. AUGUST 9, 1986 TUCSON, ARIZ.
70- 83	MADDOX, ELLIOTT	109 HILTON AVE - VAUXHALL NJ 07088
72- 65	MADDOX, GARRY LEE	OLD ADD: 26 BRIARWOOD - BERLIN NJ 08091
78- 77	MADDOX, JERRY GLENN	5539 BAYWOOD - RIVERSIDE CA 92504
83- 91	MADDUX, GREGORY ALAN	4241 RAWHIDE - LAS VEGAS NV 89120
86- 92	MADDUX, MICHAEL AUSLEY	4241 RAWHIDE - LAS VEGAS NV 89120
85- 69	MADISON, CHARLES SCOTT 'SCOTTI'	830 GEN. GEORGE PATTON ROAD - NASHVILLE TN 37221
50- 56	MADISON, DAVID PLEDGER	D. DECEMBER 9, 1985 MACON, MISS.
32- 46	MADJESKI, EDWARD WILLIAM	%MONTGOMERY,9915 KNOLLWOOD DR - CINCINNATI OH 45242
73- 80	MADLOCK, BILL	453 EAST DECATUR ST - DECATUR IL 62521
87- 85	MADRID, ALEXANDER	1626 WEST FIFTH STREET - MESA AZ 85201
47- 62	MADRID, SALVADOR	D. FEBRUARY 24, 1977 FORT WAYNE, IND.
60- 62	MAESTRI, HECTOR ANIBAL	581 SW 89TH COURT - MIAMI FL 33174
86- 93	MAGADAN, DAVID JOSEPH	4505 NORTH A STREET - TAMPA FL 33609
11-106	MAGEE, LEO CHRISTOPHER	D. MARCH 14, 1966 COLUMBUS, O.
38- 58	MAGGERT, HARL WARREN	D. JULY 10, 1986 CITRUS HEIGHTS, CALIF.
45- 64	MAGLIE, SALVATORE ANTHONY	77 MORNINGSIDE DR - GRAND ISLAND NY 14072
11-107	MAGNER, EDMUND BURKE 'STUBBY'	D. SEPTEMBER 9, 1956 CHILLICOTHE, O.
70- 84	MAGNUSON, JAMES ROBERT	OLD ADD: 1014 EAST WALNUT - GREEN BAY WI 54301
87- 86	MAGRANE, JOSEPH DAVID	361 CIRCLE DRIVE - MOREHEAD KY 40351
89- 77	MAGRANN, THOMAS JOSEPH	910 NORTH 31ST COURT - HOLLYWOOD FL 33021
66- 57	MAGRINI, PETER ALEXANDER	2402 RANCHO CABEZA DR - SANTA ROSA CA 95404
22- 80	MAGUIRE, FRED EDWARD	D. NOVEMBER 3, 1961 BOSTON, MASS.
50- 57	MAGUIRE, JACK	1904 WEST UNIVERSITY DRIVE - GAINESVILLE FL 32601
21- 57	MAHADY, JAMES BERNARD	D. AUGUST 9, 1936 CORTLAND, N. Y.
60- 63	MAHAFFEY, ARTHUR	3545 RHOADS AVE - NEWTOWN SQUARE PA 19073
26- 52	MAHAFFEY, LEE ROY	D. JULY 23, 1969 ANDERSON, S. C.
40- 52	MAHAN, ARTHUR LEO	1002 KENWYN ST-PHILADELPHIA PA 19124
12-111	MAHARG, WILLIAM JOSEPH	D. NOVEMBER 20, 1953 PHILADELPHIA, PA.
78- 78	MAHLBERG, GREGORY JOHN	5100 N. PLACITA DEL LAZO - TUCSON AZ 85715
77- 85	MAHLER, MICHAEL JAMES 'MICKEY'	3080 VALLEY STREET - SALT LAKE CITY UT 84109
79- 72	MAHLER, RICHARD KEITH 'RICK'	7911 QUIRT DR - SAN ANTONIO TX 78227
30- 48	MAHON, ALFRED GWINN	D. DECEMBER 26, 1977 NEW HAVEN, CONN.
10- 94	MAHONEY, CHRISTOPHER JOHN	D. JULY 15, 1954 VISALIA, CALIF.
11-108	MAHONEY, DANIEL JOSEPH	D. SEPTEMBER 28, 1960 UTICA, N.Y.
59- 50	MAHONEY, JAMES THOMAS	150 SYCAMORE TER - GLEN ROCK NJ 07452
51- 57	MAHONEY, ROBERT PAUL	6901 LYNN - LINCOLN NE 68505
45- 65	MAIER, ROBERT PHILIP	334 DUNELLEN AVE - DUNELLAN NJ 08812
36- 50	MAILHO, EMIL PIERRE	566 SCOTT ST - FREMONT CA 94538
15- 92	MAILS, JOHN WALTER 'DUSTER'	D. JULY 5, 1974 SAN FRANCISCO, CALIF.
48- 62	MAIN, FORREST HARRY 'WOODY'	1418 LOS LOMAS DRIVE - BREA CA 92621
14-134	MAIN, MILES GRANT 'ALEX'	D. DECEMBER 29, 1965 ROYAL OAK, MICH.
43- 80	MAINS, JAMES ROYAL	D. MARCH 17, 1969 BRIDGTON, ME.
15-105	MAISEL, CHARLES LOUIS	D. AUGUST 25, 1953 BALTIMORE, MD.
13-107	MAISEL, FREDERICK CHARLES 'FRITZ'	D. APRIL 22, 1967 BALTIMORE, MD.
13-108	MAISEL, GEORGE JOHN	D. NOVEMBER 20, 1968 BALTIMORE, MD.
39- 72	MAJESKI, HENRY	12 ROOSEVELT ST - STATEN ISLAND NY 10304
37- 68	MAKOSKY, FRANK	D. JANUARY 10, 1987 STROUDSBURG, PA.
75- 69	MAKOWSKI, THOMAS ANTHONY	195 ROESCH AVE - BUFFALO NY 14201
33- 40	MALAY, JOSEPH CHARLES	D. MARCH 19, 1989 BRIDGEPORT, CONN.
81- 77	MALDONADO, CANDIDO 'CANDY'	HCO2 BOX 16800 - ARECIBO PR 00612
81- 78	MALER, JAMES MICHAEL	OLD ADD: 14408 SW 143RD CT - MIAMI FL 33186
37- 69	MALINOSKY, ANTHONY JOSEPH	5540 WEST FIFTH ST #60 - OXNARD CA 93030
34- 64	MALIS, CYRUS SOL	D. JANUARY 12, 1971 NORTH HOLLYWOOD, FLA.
57- 45	MALKMUS, ROBERT EDWARD	400 WALLINGFORD TER - UNION NJ 07083
59- 51	MALLETT, GERALD GORDON	7610 FOREST PARK DR - BEAUMONT TX 77707
50- 58	MALLETTE, MALCOLM FRANCIS	2419 SILVER FOX LN - RESTON VA 22091
87- 87	MALLICOAT, ROBBIN DALE	2820 SOUTHEAST BRODIAEA COURT - HILLSBORO OR 97123
31- 50	MALLON, LESLIE CLYDE	702 CIMMARON TRAIL - GRANBURY TX 76048
21- 58	MALLONEE, HOWARD BENNETT 'BEN'	D. FEBRUARY 19, 1978 BALTIMORE, MD.
25- 68	MALLONEE, JULIUS NORRIS	D. DECEMBER 26, 1934 CHARLOTTE, N. C.
40- 53	MALLORY, JAMES BAUGH	1905 FOREST HILLS DR - GREENVILLE NC 27834
77- 86	MALLORY, SHELDON	17604 S. OAKWOOD - HAZELCREST IL 60429
10- 95	MALLOY, ARCHIBALD ALEXANDER	D. MARCH 1, 1961 FERRIS, TEX.
43- 81	MALLOY, ROBERT PAUL	3850 KIRKUP AVE-CINCINNATI OH 45213
87- 88	MALLOY, ROBERT WILLIAM	OLD ADD: DALLAS TX
55- 76	MALMBERG, HARRY WILLIAM	D. OCTOBER 29, 1976 SAN FRANCISCO, CALIF.
49- 47	MALONE, EDWARD RUSSELL	224 AVENIDA MAJORCA #A - LAGUNA HILLS CA 92653
15- 93	MALONE, LEWIS ALOYSIUS	D. FEBRUARY 17, 1972 BROOKLYN, N.Y.
28- 62	MALONE, PERCE LEIGH 'PAT'	D. MAY 13, 1943 ALTOONA, PA.
60- 64	MALONEY, JAMES WILLIAM	2217 WEST KEATS - FRESNO CA 93705
12-112	MALONEY, PATRICK WILLIAM	D. JUNE 27, 1979 PAWTUCKET, R. I.
13-109	MALOY, PAUL AUGUSTUS	D. MARCH 18, 1976 SANDUSKY, O.
43- 82	MALTZBERGER, GORDON RALPH	D. DECEMBER 11, 1974 RIALTO, CALIF.
55- 77	MALZONE, FRANK JAMES	16 ALETHA RD - NEEDHAM MA 02192
13-110	MAMAUX, ALBERT LEON	D. JANUARY 2, 1963 SANTA MONICA, CALIF.

```
28- 63 MANCUSO, AUGUST RODNEY 'GUS'        D. OCTOBER 26, 1984 HOUSTON, TEXAS
44- 81 MANCUSO, FRANK OCTAVIUS            5126 CRIPPLE CREEK - HOUSTON TX 77017
14-135 MANDA, CARL ALAN                   D. MARCH 9, 1983 ARTESIA, N. MEX.
41- 69 MANDERS, HAROLD CARL               BOX 149 - DALLAS CENTER IA 50063
52- 71 MANGAN, JAMES DANIEL               6878 TRINIDAD - SAN JOSE CA 95120
69-106 MANGUAL, ANGEL LUIS                LAS DELICIAS R10,ROD.DEL VALLE-PONCE PR 00731
72- 66 MANGUAL, JOSE MANUEL 'PEPE'        CALLE 41,AC19 LOS CAOBOS - PONCE PR 00731
24- 73 MANGUM, LEON ALLEN                 D. JULY 9, 1974 LIMA, O.
12-113 MANGUS, GEORGE GRAHAM              D. AUGUST 10, 1933 RUTLAND, MASS.
20- 79 MANION, CLYDE JENNINGS             D. SEPTEMBER 4, 1967 DETROIT, MICH.
76- 58 MANKOWSKI, PHILIP ANTHONY          204 ROSEWOOD TER - CHEEKTOWAGA NY 14225
44- 82 MANN, BEN GARTH                    RR 1 BOX 14 - ITALY TX 76651
28- 64 MANN, JOHN LEO                     D. MARCH 31, 1977 TERRE HAUTE, IND.
89- 78 MANN, KELLY JOHN                   239 VIA LACIRCULA - REDONDO BEACH CA 90277
13-111 MANN, LESLIE                       D. JANUARY 14, 1962 PASADENA, CALIF.
14-136 MANNING, ERNEST DEVON              D. APRIL 28, 1973 PENSACOLA, FLA.
62- 80 MANNING, JAMES BENJAMIN            4341 SW 2ND CT - PLANTATION FL 33317
75- 70 MANNING, RICHARD EUGENE 'RICK'     150 MILES RD - CHAGRIN FALLS OH 44022
40- 54 MANNO, DONALD                      1338 ELLIOTT ST-WILLIAMSPORT PA 17701
81- 79 MANRIQUE, FRED ELOI                CARRERA 6 #21 SANTE FE - CIUDAD BOLIVAR VENEZ
56- 55 MANTILLA, FELIX                    6973 NORTH TACOMA ST - MILWAUKEE WI 53224
51- 58 MANTLE, MICKEY CHARLES             42 CENTRAL PARK SOUTH - NEW YORK NY 10019
69-107 MANUEL, CHARLES FUQUA              4930 BOWER RD SW - ROANOKE VA 24018
75- 71 MANUEL, JERRY                      16745 CALDER DRIVE WEST - LOXAHATCHEE FL 33470
23- 85 MANUSH, HENRY EMMETT 'HEINIE'      D. MAY 12, 1971 SARASOTA, FLA.
50- 59 MANVILLE, RICHARD WESLEY           OLD ADD: 479 MONTGOMERY RD - ALTAMONTE SPRINGS FL 49201
87- 89 MANWARING, KIRT DEAN               502 JOHN STREET - HORSEHEADS NY 14845
88- 85 MANZANILLO, RAVELO                 ULISES ESPAILLAT #7 - SAN PEDRO DE MACORIS DOM. REP.
19- 54 MAPEL, ROLLA MAMILTON              D. APRIL 6, 1966 SAN DIEGO, CAL.
48- 63 MAPES, CLIFFORD FRANKLIN           BOX 872 - PRYOR OK 74362
32- 47 MAPLE, HOWARD ALBERT               D. NOVEMBER 9, 1970 PORTLAND, ORE.
60- 65 MARANDA, GEORGES HENRI             13 THIBEAULT #1 - LEVIS QUEBEC G6V 2J6 CAN.
12-114 MARANVILLE, WALTER JAMES VINCENT   D. JANUARY 5, 1954 NEW YORK, N.Y.
23- 86 MARBERRY, FREDRICK 'FIRPO'         D. JUNE 30, 1976 MEXIA, TEX.
13-112 MARBET, WALTER WILLIAM             D. SEPTEMBER 24, 1956 HOHENWALD, TENN.
40- 57 MARCHILDON, PHILIP JOSEPH          3 COURTWRIGHT ROAD - ETOBICOKE ONTARIO M9C 4B3 CAN.
35- 69 MARCUM, JOHN ALFRED                D. SEPTEMBER 10, 1984 LOUISVILLE, KY.
65- 69 MARENTETTE, LEO JOHN               4000 SYLVANIA #66 - TOLEDO OH 43623
55- 56 MARGONERI, JOSEPH EMANUEL          RR 1 BOX 177 - WEST NEWTON PA 15089
60- 66 MARICHAL, JUAN ANTONIO             3178 NW 19TH STREET - MIAMI FL 33125
36-137 MARION, DONALD G. 'DAN'            D. JANUARY 18, 1933 MILWAUKEE, WIS.
30- 65 MARION, JOHN WYETH 'RED'           D. MARCH 13, 1975 SAN JOSE, CALIF.
40- 56 MARION, MARTIN WHITEFORD 'SLATS'   8 FORCEE LANE - ST.LOUIS MO 63124
57- 46 MARIS, ROGER EUGENE                D. DECEMBER 14, 1985 HOUSTON, TEX.
55- 59 MARKELL, HARRY DUQUESNE 'DUKE'     D. JUNE 14, 1984 FORT LAUDERDALE, FLA.
55- 60 MARKLAND, CLENETH EUGENE 'GENE'    613 EAST OLEANDER CIRCLE - BAREFOOT BAY FL 32976
25- 94 MARKLE, CLIFFORD MONROE            D. MAY 24, 1974 TEMPLE CITY, CALIF.
51- 60 MARLOWE, RICHARD BURTON            D. DECEMBER 30, 1968 TOLEDO, O.
49- 57 MARNIE, HARRY SYLVESTER 'HAL'      2715 SOUTH SMETLEY-PHILADELPHIA PA 19145
53- 53 MAROLEWSKI, FRED DANIEL            298 BENSLEY - CALUMET CITY IL 60409
69-108 MARONE, LOUIS STEPHEN              663 TYRONE ST - EL CAJON CA 92020
31- 51 MARQUARDT, ALBERT LUDWIG 'OLLIE'   D. FEBRUARY 7, 1968 PORT CLINTON, O.
72- 67 MARQUEZ, GONZALO                   D. DECEMBER 20, 1984 VALENCIA, VENEZUELA
51- 61 MARQUEZ, LUIS ANGEL                D. MARCH 1, 1988 AGUADILLA, P. R.
25- 69 MARQUIS, JAMES MILBURN             BOX F - WEST POINT CA 95255
55- 54 MARQUIS, ROBERT RUDOLPH            2075 LONGFELLOW DR - BEAUMONT TX 77706
55- 78 MARQUIS, ROGER                     5 LINDBERGH AVE - HOLYOKE MA 01040
50- 61 MARRERO, CONRADO EUGENIO RAMOS     205 AVONTAMIENTO #1 - CERRO HAVANA CUBA
17- 42 MARRIOTT, WILLIAM EARL             D. AUGUST 11, 1969 BERKELEY, CALIF.
32- 48 MARROW, CHARLES KENNON 'BUCK'      D. NOVEMBER 21, 1982 NEWPORT NEWS, VA.
11-109 MARSANS, ARMANDO                   D. SEPTEMBER 3, 1960 HAVANA, CUBA
49- 57 MARSHALL, CLARENCE FRANCIS         RR4 - CORRY PA 16407
46- 70 MARSHALL, CHARLES ANDREW           1 RADCLIFF CT-WILMINGTON DE 19804
46- 58 MARSHALL, CLARENCE WESTLY          27642-I SUSAN BETH WAY - SAUGUS CA 91350
67- 69 MARSHALL, DAVID LEWIS              4433 CHARLEMAGNE - LONG BEACH CA 90808
29- 68 MARSHALL, EDWARD HARBERT 'DOC'     1840 FAIRWAY CIR CR - SAN MARCOS CA 92069
58- 58 MARSHALL, JIM RUFE                 5761 N. CASA BLANCA - SCOTTSDALE AZ 85253
73- 81 MARSHALL, KEITH ALAN               RR 2, 334F BECKWITH ROAD - PINE CITY NY 14871
81- 80 MARSHALL, MICHAEL ALLEN            13063 VENTURA BLVD - STUDIO CITY CA 91604
67- 70 MARSHALL, MICHAEL GRANT            ATH DEPT,HENDERSON STATE COL - ARKADELPHIA AR 71923
42- 66 MARSHALL, MILO MAX                 4794 BOLIVAR CT - SALEM OR 97301
12-115 MARSHALL, ROY DEVERNE 'RUBE'       D. JUNE 11, 1980 DOVER, O.
42- 67 MARSHALL, WILLARD WARREN           1090 ARCADIAN WAY - FORT LEE NJ 07024
31- 52 MARSHALL, WILLIAM HENRY            D. MAY 5, 1977 SACRAMENTO, CALIF.
50- 62 MARTIN, ALFRED MANUEL 'BILLY'      D. DECEMBER 25, 1989 JOHNSON CITY, N.Y.
53- 55 MARTIN, BARNEY ROBERT              1617 TALL PINES CIR - COLUMBIA SC 29205
44- 49 MARTIN, BORIS MICHAEL 'BABE'       323 FAWN MEADOWS - BALLWIN MO 63011
79- 73 MARTIN, DONALD RENIE               504 FAIRVIEW AVE - DOVER DE 19901
17- 43 MARTIN, ELWOOD GOOD 'SPEED'        D. JUNE 14, 1983 LEMON GROVE, CALIF.
46- 68 MARTIN, FRED TURNER                D. JUNE 11, 1979 CHICAGO, ILL.
37- 70 MARTIN, HERSHEL RAY                D. NOVEMBER 17, 1980 CUBA, MO.
77- 79 MARTIN, JERRY LINDSEY              918 SOUTH BONHAM RD - COLUMBIA SC 29205
12- 16 MARTIN, JOHN CHRISTOPHER           D. JULY 4, 1980 BRONX, N. Y.
28- 57 MARTIN, JOHN LEONARD ROOSEVELT 'PEPPER'   D. MARCH 5, 1965 MCALESTER, OKLA.
80- 63 MARTIN, JOHN ROBERT                P.O. BOX 7281 - PORT SAINT LUCIE FL 34985
59- 61 MARTIN, JOSEPH CLIFTON 'J. C.'     OLD ADD: 19 SHERWOOD PLACE - WHEATON IL 60187
86- 94 MARTIN, JOSEPH MICHAEL 'MIKE'      6444 EAGLE POINT ROAD - LAS VEGAS NV 89108
49- 49 MARTIN, MORRIS WEBSTER             244 POTTERY RD - WASHINGTON MO 63090
19- 55 MARTIN, PATRICK FRANCIS            D. FEBRUARY 4, 1949 BROOKLYN, N. Y.
55- 79 MARTIN, PAUL CHARLES 'JAKE'        1529 33RD STREET - SAN DIEGO CA 92102
43- 83 MARTIN, RAYMOND JOSEPH             107 PELLANA RD-NORWOOD MA 02062
36- 51 MARTIN, STUART MCGUIRE             BOX 184 - SEVERN NC 27877
68- 57 MARTIN, THOMAS EUGENE 'GENE'       110 STANLEY DR - LEESBURG GA 31763
14-138 MARTIN, WILLIAM GLOYD              D. SEPTEMBER 15, 1949 WASHINGTON, D.C.
36- 52 MARTIN, WILLIAM JOSEPH 'JOE'       D. SEPTEMBER 28, 1960 BUFFALO, N. Y.
24- 74 MARTINA, JOSEPH JOHN               D. MARCH 22, 1962 NEW ORLEANS, LA.
80- 86 MARTINEZ, ALFREDO                  2346 THOMAS - LOS ANGELES CA 90031
88- 86 MARTINEZ, CARLOS ALBERTO ESCOBAR   PROL.,10 MARZO BLQ 5 LET #706-LAGUAIRA,DPO VARGAS VENEZ
```

ALL IN FULL COLOR

8"x10" GLOSSY PHOTOS
CURRENT PLAYERS - IN STOCK

1 to 9 ar $ 3.00 each plus postage & handling
10 to 24 at $ 2.50 each plus postage & handling
25 or more at $ 2.25 each plus postage & handling

MANY MORE PHOTOS FROM WHICH TO CHOOSE

SEND ONLY $ 1.00 for DEN'S BIG CATALOGUE CATALOGUE sent FREE with each ORDER

ANGELS – California
Abbott, Jim
Bichette, Dante
Blyleven, Bert
Davis, Chili
Downing, Brian
Joyner, Wally
Langston, Mark
Parrish, Lance
Ray, Johnny
White, Devon
Witt, Mike

ASTROS – Houston
Anthony, Eric
Biggio, Craig
Davis, Glenn
Deshaies, Jim
Doran, Bill
Scott, Mike

ATHLETICS – Oakland
Canseco, Jose
Eckersley, Dennis
Henderson, Dave
Henderson, Rickey
Hubbard, Glenn
Lansford, Carney
McGwire, Mark
Moore, Mike
Randolph, Willie
Steinbach, Terry
Stewart, Dave
Weiss, Walt

BLUE JAYS – Toronto
Bell, George
Borders, Pat
Fernandez, Tony
Gruber, Kelly
McGriff, Fred
Olerud, John
Stieb, Dave
Stottlemyre, Todd
Wilson, Mookie

BRAVES – Atlanta
Blauser, Jeff
Davis, Jody
Esasky, Nick
Gant, Ron
Glavine, Tom
Gregg, Tommy
Hall, Albert
McDowell, Oddibe
Murphy, Dale
Smith, Lonnie
Treadway, Jeff

BREWERS – Milwaukee
August, Don
Braggs, Glenn
Brock, Greg
Deer, Rob
Hamilton, Darryl
Higuera, Ted
Meyer, Joey
Molitor, Paul
Parker, Dave
Sheffield, Gary
Spiers, Bill
Surhoff, B.J.
Sveum, Dale
Vaughn, Greg
Yount, Robin

CARDINALS – St. Louis
Carpenter, Cris
Coleman, Vince
Guerrero, Pedro
Magrane, Joe
McGee, Willie
Oquendo, Jose
Pendleton, Terry
Smith, Byrn
Smith, Lee
Smith, Ozzie
Thompson, Milt
Tudor, John
Worrell, Todd
Zeile, Todd

CUBS – Chicago
Berryhill, Damon
Bielecki, Mike
Dawson, Andre
Dunston, Shawon
Grace, Mark
Griffin, Ty
Harkey, Mike
Law, Vance
Maddux, Greg
Ryne, Sandberg
Smith, Dwight
Sutcliffe, Rick
Walton, Jerome
Williams, Mitch
Wrona, Rick

DODGERS – Los Angeles
Belcher, Tim
Brooks, Hubie
Daniels, Kal
Gibson, Kirk
Gwynn, Chris
Hatcher, Mickey
Hershiser, Orel
Lasorda, Tom
Martinez, Ramon
Murray, Eddie
Samuel, Juan
Scioscia, Mike
Valenzuela, Fernando

EXPOS – Montreal
Aldrete, Mike
Boyd, Oil Can
Galarraga, Andres
Martinez, Dennis
Owen, Spike
Raines, Tim
Santovenia, Nelson
Smith, Zane
Wallach, Tim

GIANTS – San Francisco
Bass, Kevin
Butler, Brett
Carter, Gary
Clark, Will
Manwaring, Kurt
Mitchell, Kevin
Reuschel, Rick
Thompson, Robby
Uribe, Jose
Williams, Matt

NOTE: Players are traded frequently. Every attempt has been made to list the player with his current team; however, the photos available may picture the player in the uniform of a previous team.

INDIANS – Cleveland
Alomar, Sandy Jr.
Hernandez, Keith
Jacoby, Brook
James, Chris
James, Dion
Jones, Doug
Maldonado, Candy
Medina, Luis
Orosco, Jesse
Snyder, Cory
Swindell, Greg

MARINERS – Seattle
Bankhead, Scott
Bradley, Scott
Buhner, Jay
Davis, Alvin
Griffey, Ken Jr.
Hanson, Erik
Leonard, Jeffrey
O'Brien, Pete
Reynolds, Harold

METS – New York
Carreon, Mark
Cone, David
Darling, Ron
Elster, Kevin
Fernandez, Sid
Gooden, Dwight
Jefferies, Gregg
Johnson, Howard
Magadan, Dave
Marshall, Mike
McReynolds, Kevin
Miller, Keith
Ojeda, Bobby
Samuel, Juan
Sasser, Mackey
Strawberry, Darryl
Viola, Frank

ORIOLES – Baltimore
Anderson, Brady
Ballard, Jeff
Bautista, Jose
Bradley, Phil
Devereaux, Mike
Finley, Steve
Harnisch, Pete
Horn, Sam
Malacki, Bob
McDonald, Ben
Melvin, Bob
Milligan, Randy
Olson, Gregg
Orsulak, Joe
Ripken, Billy
Ripken, Cal Jr.
Stanicek, Pete
Tettleton, Mickey
Traber, Jim
Williamson, Mark
Worthington, Craig

PADRES – San Diego
Alomar, Roberto
Carter, Joe
Clark, Jack
Dunne, Mike
Gwynn, Tony
Hurst, Bruce
Lynn, Fred
Pagliarulo, Mike
Santiago, Benito
Templeton, Garry
Whitson, Ed

PHILLIES – Philadelphia
Dernier, Bob
Dykstra, Lenny
Hayes, Von
Herr, Tommy
Jones, Ron
Jordan, Rickey
Kruk, John
McDowell, Roger

PIRATES – Pittsburgh
Backman, Wally
Bonds, Barry
Bonilla, Bobby
Bream, Sid
Drabek, Doug
LaValliere, Mike
Lind, Jose
Reynolds, R.J.
Terrell, Walt
Van Slyke, Andy

RANGERS – Texas
Baines, Harold
Franco, Julio
Hough, Charlie
Incaviglia, Pete
Palmiero, Rafael
Ryan, Nolan
Sierra, Ruben
Valentine, Bobby
Witt, Bobby

RED SOX – Boston
Barrett, Marty
Boddicker, Mike
Boggs, Wade
Brunansky, Tom
Burks, Ellis
Clemens, Roger
Evans, Dwight
Greenwell, Mike
Pena, Tony
Quintana, Carlos
Reardon, Jeff
Reed, Jody

REDS – Cincinnati
Benzinger, Todd
Browning, Tom
Davis, Eric
Hatcher, Billy
Larkin, Barry
Myers, Randy
O'Neill, Paul
Roomes, Rolando
Sabo, Chris

ROYALS – Kansas City
Boone, Bob
Brett, George
Davis, Mark
Davis, Storm
Gordon, Tom
Gubicza, Mark
Jackson, Bo
Saberhagen, Bret
Seitzer, Kevin
Stillwell, Kurt
Tartabull, Danny
Thurman, Gary
White, Frank

TIGERS – Detroit
Anderson, Sparky
Henneman, Mike
Lemon, Chet
Lovullo, Torey
Morris, Jack
Mosbey, Lloyd
Nokes, Matt
Robinson, Jeff
Sheets, Larry
Trammell, Alan
Whitaker, Lou

TWINS – Minnesota
Aguilera, Rick
Anderson, Allen
Candelaria, John
Gaetti, Gary
Gagne, Greg
Gladden, Dan
Hrbek, Kent
Larkin, Gene
Mack, Shane
Puckett, Kirby
West, David

WHITE SOX – Chicago
Calderon, Ivan
Fisk, Carlton
Fletcher, Scott
Gallagher, Dave
Guillen, Ozzie
Kittle, Ron
Pasqua, Dan
Ventura, Robin
Williams, Eddie

YANKEES – New York
Balboni, Steve
Barfield, Jesse
Brower, Bob
Cerone, Rick
Espinoza, Alvaro
Geren, Bob
Hall, Mel
Hawkins, Andy
Jones, Jimmy
Kelly, Roberto
LaPoint, Dave
Mattingly, Don
Muelens, Hensley
Righetti, Dave
Sanders, Deion
Sax, Steve
Washington, Claudell
Winfield, Dave

GROUP PHOTOS
Brett & Bo Jackson
Brett & Boggs
Brett & Cal Ripken
Cal, Cal Sr. & Billy Ripken
Mattingly, Brett & Boggs
Mattingly & Boggs
Mattingly & Brett
Mattingly & Hernandez
Mattingly & Joyner
Mattingly & Rose
Mattingly & Strawberry
Mattingly & Winfield
McGwire, Canseco & Weiss
Righetti & Stieb
Roberto, Sandy & Sandy Jr. Alomar
Roberto & Sandy Jr. Alomar
Rose & Hernandez
Rose & Ryan
Strawberry & Eric Davis
Strawberry & Dykstra
Strawberry & McGee
Winfield & Reggie Jackson
Will Clark & Kevin Mitchell

DEN'S COLLECTORS DEN
HOME OF SPORT AMERICANA
DEPT. BAL
P.O. BOX 606, LAUREL, MD 20725

MARYLAND RESIDENTS ADD 5% SALES TAX
CANADIAN ORDERS – BOOKS ONLY
Canadian orders, orders outside the contiguous
United States, APO and FPO add 25% additional
U.S. FUNDS ONLY

POSTAGE & HANDLING SCHEDULE
$ .01 to $ 20.00 add $ 2.00
$ 20.01 to $ 29.99 add $ 2.50
$ 30.00 to $ 49.99 add $ 3.00
$ 50.00 or more add $ 4.00

VISA/MASTER CHARGE ACCEPTED

MasterCard   VISA

To order by VISA/Master Charge, simply place your account number and 4 digit expiration date in your order letter. Also, include your authorized signature with the order. You may order by phone by calling (301) 776-3900 on weekdays between 10:00 am and 5:00 pm Eastern Time. No collect calls are accepted. All VISA/Master Charge orders must be for at least $ 10.00 or more. Specify VISA or Master Card.

OLD TIMERS and GROUP PHOTOS

GREAT FOR AUTOGRAPHS

1 to 9 ar $ 3.00 each plus postage & handling
10 to 24 at $ 2.50 each plus postage & handling
25 or more at $ 2.25 each plus postage & handling

NEW LARGER EXPANDED LIST

Aaron, Hank *	Kaline, Al *	Shantz, Bobby
Agee, Tommy	Kell, George *	Sievers, Roy
Allen, Dick	Killebrew, Harmon *	Skowron, Moose
Alston, Walter *	Kiner, Ralph *	Slaughter, Enos *
Aparicio, Luis *	Kluzewski, Ted	Snider, Duke *
Appling, Luke * †	Kooseman, Jerry	Spahn, Warren *
Armas, Tony	Koufax, Sandy *	Stargell, Willie *
Ashburn, Richie	Kranepool, Ed	Staub, Rusty
Bando, Sal	Kubek, Tony	Stottlemyre, Mel
Banks, Ernie *	Labine, Clem †	Sutter, Bruce
Bauer, Hank	Law, Vern	Sutton, Don
Baylor, Don	Lemon, Bob *	Thomson, Bobby
Bell, Cool Papa * †	Lolich, Mickey	Tiant, Luis
Bench, Johnny *	Lonborg, Jim	Virdon, Bill
Berra, Yogi *	Lopat, Eddie	Walker, Harry
Blair, Paul	Lopez, Al *	Weaver, Earl
Blue, Vida	Lyle, Sparky	White, Bill
Bonds, Bobby	Madlock, Bill	Wilhelm, Hoyt *
Boudreau, Lou *	Mantle, Mickey *	Williams, Billy *
Brock, Lou *	Marichal, Juan *	Williams, Ted *
Buhl, Bob	Marion, Marty	Wills, Maury
Bumbry, Al	Maris, Roger	Wynn, Early *
Bunning, Jim	Martin, Billy	Yastrzemski, Carl *
Burdette, Lew	Mathews, Eddie *	
Campanella, Roy *	Mays, Willie *	
Campaneris, Bert	Mazerowski, Bill	
Carew, Rod	McCovey, Willie *	
Carlton, Steve	McDougald, Gil †	
Cepeda, Orlando	McDowell, Sam	
Cey, Ron	McGraw, Tug	
Clemente, Roberto *	McLain, Denny	
Cobb, Ty * (tinted)	McNally, Dave	
Colavito, Rocky	Minoso, Minnie	
Crandell, Del	Mize, Johnny * †	
Cueller, Mike	Morgan, Joe *	
Dandridge, Ray *	Munson, Thurman	
Dark, Alvin	Murcer, Bobby	
Davis, Tommy	Musial, Stan *	
Davis, Willie	Nettles, Graig	
Dent, Bucky	Newcomb, Don	
DiMaggio, Joe *	Newhouser, Hal	
Doby, Larry	Niekro, Phil	
Doerr, Bobby * †	Northrup, Jim	
Dropo, Walt	Oliva, Tony	
Drysdale, Don *	Ott, Mel * †	
Erskine, Carl	Paige, Satchel *	
Face, Elroy	Palmer, Jim *	
Feller, Bob *	Perez, Tony	
Ferrell, Rick * †	Perry, Gaylord	
Fingers, Rollie	Perry, Jim	
Ford, Whitey *	Pierce, Billy	
Foster, George	Piersall, Jim	
Foxx, Jimmy * †	Piniella, Lou	
Freehan, Bill (w/BB card)	Pinson, Vada	
Friend, Bob	Podres, Johnny	
Garvey, Steve	Powell, Boog	
Gehrig, Lou * (tinted)	Radatz, Dick †	
Gibson, Bob *	Reese, Pee Wee *	
Grant, Mud Cat	Rice, Jim	
Groat, Dick	Richardson, Bobby	
Grich, Bobby	Rizzuto, Phil	
Grote, Jerry	Roberts, Robin *	
Guidry, Ron	Robinson, Brooks *	
Haddix, Harvey	Robinson, Frank *	
Hodges, Gil	Robinson, Jackie *	
Howard, Elston	Rojas, Cookie	
Howard, Frank	Rose, Pete	
Hubbell, Carl * †	Rosen, Al †	
Hunter, Catfish *	Ruth, Babe * † (player)	
Irvin, Monte *	Ruth, Babe * † (retired)	
Jackson, Reggie	Ruth, Babe * (tinted as Dodger coach)	
Jenkins, Fergie	Santo, Ron	
John, Tommy	Sauer, Hank	
Johnson, Davy	Schmidt, Mike	
Kaat, Jim	Schoendienst, Red *	
	Score, Herb	
	Seaver, Tom	
	Sewell, Joe * †	

SEND ONLY $ 1.00 for DEN'S BIG CATALOGUE CATALOGUE sent FREE with each ORDER

TEAM & GROUP PHOTOS

1950 Phillies Team
1952 Giants Line Up
1955 Dodgers Team
1956 Dodgers Team
1961 Yankees Sluggers
1962 Yankees
1963 Dodgers Team
1964 Cardinals Infield
1964 Yankees Infield
1969 Mets Outfield
1969 Mets Team

Aaron & Mathews
Aaron & Mays
Bench & Lasorda
Bench & Perez
Bench & Yastrzemski
Brooks Robinson & Clete Boyer
Brooks Robinson & Al Kaline
DiMaggio & Feller †
DiMaggio & Williams †
Downing, Stottlemyre, Ford & Peterson
Gehrig, Foxx & Ruth †
Gehrig, Gehringer, Greenberg & Ruth †
Reggie Jackson & Yastrzemski
Joe & Dom DiMaggio †
Koufax & Killebrew
Mantle & DiMaggio
Mantle, DiMaggio & Williams †
Mantle, Maris & Berra
Mantle, Mays & Killebrew
Mantle & Maris
Mantle & Mays †
Musial & Williams †
Phil & Joe Niekro
Preacher Roe & Johnny Podres
Rose, Morgan, Bench & Perez
Rose & Stargell
Ruth & Gehrig †
Ruth & Foxx †
Seaver, Cardwell & Al Jackson
Spahn & Sain †

* = Hall of Fame member
† = Black & white or sepia photo

NOTE: We have more than one pose of many of the players. When more than one pose of a player is ordered, and we have multiple photos of that player, we send different poses to you.

VISA/MASTER CHARGE ACCEPTED

DEN'S COLLECTORS DEN

HOME OF SPORT AMERICANA

DEPT. BAL
P.O. BOX 606, LAUREL, MD 20725

MARYLAND RESIDENTS ADD 5% SALES TAX
CANADIAN ORDERS – BOOKS ONLY
Canadian orders, orders outside the contiguous
United States, APO and FPO add 25% additional
U.S. FUNDS ONLY

POSTAGE & HANDLING SCHEDULE
$ .01 to $ 20.00 add $ 2.00
$ 20.01 to $ 29.99 add $ 2.50
$ 30.00 to $ 49.99 add $ 3.00
$ 50.00 or more add $ 4.00

To order by VISA/Master Charge, simply place
your account number and 4 digit expiration date
in your order letter. Also, include your authorized signature with the order. You may order by
phone by calling (301) 776-3900 on weekdays
between 10:00 am and 5:00 pm Eastern Time.
No collect calls are accepted. All VISA/Master
Charge orders must be for at least $ 10.00 or
more. Specify VISA or Master Card.

83- 95 MARTINEZ, CARMELO	OLD ADD: BUZON NO. 1297 - DORADO PR 00646
86- 95 MARTINEZ, DAVID	360 TULIP TRAIL - CASSELBERRY FL 32707
87- 90 MARTINEZ, EDGAR	OLD ADD: BO. MAGUAYO BUZON 1295RR - DORADO PR 00646
74- 80 MARTINEZ, FELIX ANTHONY 'TIPPY'	1524 DELLSWAY RD - TOWSON MD 21204
63- 75 MARTINEZ, GABRIEL ANTONIO 'TONY'	OLD ADD: 4599 NW 9TH ST - MIAMI FL 33126
69-109 MARTINEZ, JOHN ALBERT 'BUCK'	6213 VISTA AVE - SACRAMENTO CA 95824
69-110 MARTINEZ, JOSE AZCUIZ	6033 NORTH SHERIDAN ROAD #16E - CHICAGO IL 60660
76- 59 MARTINEZ, JOSE DENNIS 'DENNIS'	9795 SW 62ND STREET - MIAMI FL 33173
62- 82 MARTINEZ, ORLANDO OLIVO 'MARTY'	748 NORTH 23RD WEST AVE - TULSA OK 74127
88- 87 MARTINEZ, RAMON JAIME	BO. SAN MIGUEL #9,MANAGUAYABA - SANTO DOMINGO DOM. REP.
62- 81 MARTINEZ, RODOLFO HECTOR	OLD ADD: MARIANOA - HAVANA CUBA
50- 63 MARTINEZ, ROGELIO ULLOA	9118 5TH AVE - BROOKLYN NY 11209
77- 87 MARTINEZ, SILVIO RAMON	OLD ADD: CARLOS DE LORA 25 - SANTIAGO DOMINICAN REP.
70- 85 MARTINEZ, TEODORO NOEL	J. CONTRERAS #194,ENS. LAPAZ - SANTO DOMINGO DOM. REP.
35- 66 MARTINI, GUIDO JOE 'WEDO'	D. OCTOBER 28, 1970
37- 71 MARTY, JOSEPH ANTON	D. OCTOBER 4, 1984 SACRAMENTO, CALIF.
57- 47 MARTYN, ROBERT GORDON	3365 SW 123RD - BEAVERTON OR 97005
75- 72 MARTZ, GARY ARTHUR	17 NORTH DELAWARE - WENATCHEE WA 98801
80- 87 MARTZ, RANDY CARL	901 NATCHEZ DRIVE - SAINT CHARLES MO 63303
87- 91 MARZANO, JOHN ROBERT	1224 SOUTH 11TH STREET - PHILADELPHIA PA 19147
69-111 MASHORE, CLYDE WAYNE	18680 MARSH CREEK RD - CLAYTON CA 94517
39- 73 MASI, PHILIP SAMUEL	D. MARCH 29, 1990 MOUNT PROSPECT, ILL.
66- 58 MASON, DONALD STETSON	8 FAWN ROAD - SOUTH YARMOUTH MA 02664
58- 59 MASON, HENRY	1136 SOUTH LINCOLN - MARSHALL MO 65340
71- 66 MASON, JAMES PERCY	RR 1 BOX 308 - THEODORE AL 36582
82- 81 MASON, MICHAEL PAUL	4925 SLEEPY HOLLOW ROAD - EXCELSIOR MN 55331
84- 73 MASON, ROGER LEROY	5955 STONEYBROOK DR - MINNETONKA MN 55343
57- 48 MASSA, GORDON RICHARD	5905 KIMBERLY AVE - CINCINNATI OH 45213
18- 45 MASSEY, ROY HARDEE	D. JUNE 23, 1954 ATLANTA, GA.
17- 44 MASSEY, WILLIAM HERBERT 'MIKE'	D. OCTOBER 17, 1971 SHREVEPORT, LA.
31- 53 MASTERS, WALTER THOMAS	151 METCALFE ST #404 - OTTAWA ONTARIO K2P 1N8 CAN.
40- 58 MASTERSON, PAUL NICKALIS	3003 WEST 53RD ST-CHICAGO IL 60632
39- 74 MASTERSON, WALTER EDWARD	4515 CARTERET DRIVE - NEW BERN NC 28562
84- 74 MATA, VICTOR JOSE	AVE DE LOS MARTIRES 131 - SANTO DOMINGO DOMINICAN REP.
52- 72 MATARAZZO, LEONARD	2715 CARLISLE ST - NEW CASTLE PA 16105
67- 71 MATCHICK, JOHN THOMAS 'TOM'	5523 BENTWOOD DRIVE - TOLEDO OH 43615
12-117 MATHES, JOSEPH JOHN	D. DECEMBER 21, 1978 ST. LOUIS, MO.
52- 73 MATHEWS, EDWIN LEE	13744 RECUERDO DR - DEL MAR CA 92014
86- 96 MATHEWS, GREGORY INMAN	OLD ADD: 5682 TAHOE CIRCLE - BUENA PARK CA 90621
60- 67 MATHEWS, NELSON ELMER	211 CRESTVIEW - COLUMBIA IL 62236
60- 68 MATHIAS, CARL LYNWOOD	RR 2 - OLEY PA 19567
85- 70 MATHIS, RONALD VANCE	OLD ADD: 10326 BON OAK DR - ST. LOUIS MO 63136
70- 86 MATIAS, JOHN ROY	98 1616 HOOLAUAE ST - AIEA HI 96701
71- 67 MATLACK, JONATHAN TRUMPBOUR	8100 SHELTON DR - FORT WORTH TX 76112
14-139 MATTESON, HENRY EDSON	D. AUGUST 31, 1943 BROCTON, N.Y.
72- 68 MATTHEWS, GARY NATHANIEL	OLD ADD: 3215 MERCER ST - PACOIMA CA 91331
22- 81 MATTHEWS, JOHN JOSEPH	D. FEBRUARY 8, 1968 HAGERSTOWN, MD.
23- 87 MATTHEWS, WID CURRY	D. OCTOBER 5, 1965 HOLLYWOOD, CAL.
43- 84 MATTHEWSON, DALE WESLEY	D. FEBRUARY 20, 1984 BLAIRSVILLE, GA.
38- 59 MATTICK, ROBERT JAMES	1721 159TH PLACE NE - BELLEVUE WA 98008
12-118 MATTICK, WALTER JOSEPH	D. NOVEMBER 5, 1968 LOS ALTOS, CALIF.
82- 82 MATTINGLY, DONALD ARTHUR	RR 5 BOX 74 - EVANSVILLE IN 47711
31- 54 MATTINGLY, LAURENCE EARL	4007 BEDFORD PLACE - SUITLAND MD 20746
14-140 MATTIS, RALPH L.	D. SEPTEMBER 13, 1960 WILLIAMSPORT, PA.
29- 69 MATTOX, CLOY MITCHELL	D. AUGUST 3, 1985 DANVILLE, VA.
22- 82 MATTOX, JAMES POWELL	D. OCTOBER 12, 1973 MYRTLE BEACH, S. C.
79- 74 MATULA, RICHARD CLINTON	1817 CHAPEL HEIGHTS DR - WHARTON TX 77488
81- 81 MATUSZEK, LEONARD JAMES	7674 GINNALA COURT - CINCINNATI OH 45243
34- 65 MATUZAK, HARRY GEORGE	D. NOVEMBER 26, 1978 HOPE, ALA.
44- 84 MAUCH, EUGENE WILLIAM	46 LA RONDA DR - RANCHO MIRAGE CA 92270
34- 66 MAULDIN, MARSHALL REESE 'MARK'	6545 HANEN ST - UNION CITY GA 30291
24- 75 MAUNEY, ERNEST GERALD	D. JANUARY 1, 1987 CORPUS CHRISTI, TEXAS
45- 66 MAUNEY, RICHARD	D. FEBRUARY 6, 1970 ALBEMARLE, N. C.
58- 60 MAURIELLO, RALPH	23644 DEL CER CIR - CANOGA PARK CA 91304
48- 64 MAURO, CARMEN LOUIS	536 STANFORD DR - SAN LUIS OBISPO CA 93401
49- 50 MAVIS, ROBERT HENRY	300 MARKWOOD DR - LITTLE ROCK AR 72205
69-112 MAXIE, LARRY HANS	296 VERDUSO WAY - UPLAND CA 91786
62- 83 MAXVILL, CHARLES DALLAN 'DAL'	9745 RYAN CREST RD - FLORISSANT MO 63031
50- 64 MAXWELL, CHARLES RICHARD	730 MAPLEVIEW AVENUE - PAW PAW MI 49079
68- 58 MAY, CARLOS	OLD ADD: 1221 N. DEARBORN #8035 - CHICAGO IL 60610
67- 72 MAY, DAVID LAFRANCE	915 GRAY ST - NEW CASTLE DE 19720
17- 45 MAY, FRANK SPRUIELL 'JAKIE'	D. JUNE 3, 1970 WENDELL, N. C.
64- 68 MAY, JERRY LEE	RURAL ROUTE 1 BOX 318 - BRIDGEWATER VA 22812
65- 70 MAY, LEE ANDREW	5533 HILL & DALE DR - CINCINNATI OH 45213
39- 75 MAY, MERRILL GLEND 'PINKY'	5503 DASHING CREEK ST - SAN ANTONIO TX 78247
70- 87 MAY, MILTON SCOTT	6504 RIVERVIEW BLVD NW - BRADENTON FL 34209
65- 71 MAY, RUDOLPH	P.O. BOX 1290 - NORTH FORK CA 93643
88- 88 MAY, SCOTT FRANCIS	EAST 3439 SOUTH APPLETREE LANE - WAUPACA WI 54981
24- 76 MAY, WILLIAM HERBERT 'BUCKSHOT'	D. MARCH 15, 1984 BAKERSFIELD, CALIF.
68- 59 MAYBERRY, JOHN CLAIBORN	11115 WEST 121ST TERRACE - OVERLAND PARK KS 66213
59- 53 MAYE, ARTHUR LEE	OLD ADD: 857 E. 52ND ST - LOS ANGELES CA 90011
57- 49 MAYER, EDWIN DAVID	440 OAKDALE AVE - CORTE MADERA CA 94925
12-119 MAYER, ERSKINE JOHN	D. MARCH 10, 1957 LOS ANGELES, CALIF.
15- 95 MAYER, SAMUEL FRANKEL	D. JULY 1, 1962 ATLANTA, GA.
11-110 MAYER, WALTER A.	D. NOVEMBER 18, 1951 MINNEAPOLIS, MINN.
11-111 MAYES, ADAIR BUSHYHEAD 'PADDY'	D. MAY 28, 1962 FAYETTEVILLE, ARK.
40- 59 MAYNARD, JAMES WALTER	D. SEPTEMBER 7, 1977 DURHAM, N. C.
22- 83 MAYNARD, LEROY EVANS 'CHICK'	D. JANUARY 31, 1957 BANGOR, ME.
36- 53 MAYO, EDWARD JOSEPH	825 OCEAN PINES - BERLIN MD 21811
48- 65 MAYO, JOHN LEWIS 'JACKIE'	719 MAPLERIDGE DR - YOUNGSTOWN OH 44512
15- 96 MAYS, CARL WILLIAM	D. APRIL 4, 1971 EL CAJON, CALIF.
51- 82 MAYS, WILLIE HOWARD	51 MT VERNON LN - ATHERTON CA 94025
56- 57 MAZEROSKI, WILLIAM STANLEY	RR6 BOX 130 - GREENSBURG PA 15601
35- 67 MAZZERA, MELVIN LEONARD	6 WEST DUNMAR LN - STOCKTON CA 95207
76- 60 MAZZILLI, LEE LOUIS	12 CARPENTERS DRK RD - GREENWICH CT 06830
11-112 MCADAMS, GEORGE D. 'JACK'	D. MAY 21, 1937 SAN FRANCISCO, CALIF.
30- 49 MCAFEE, WILLIAM FORT	D. JULY 8, 1958 CULPEPPER, VA.
13-113 MCALLESTER, WILLIAM LUSK	D. MARCH 3, 1970 CHATTANOOGA, TENN.

71- 68	MCANALLY, ERNEST LEE	RR 4 BOX 61-A - MOUNT PLEASANT TX 75455
58- 61	MCANANY, JAMES	11066 RHODA WAY - CULVER CITY CA 90230
68- 60	MCANDREW, JAMES CLEMENT	704 EAST CAMPUS DRIVE - CARBONDALE IL 62901
14-141	MCARTHUR, OLAND ALEXANDER 'DIXIE'	D. MAY 31, 1986 COLUMBUS, MISS.
14-142	MCAULEY, JAMES EARL 'IKE'	D. APRIL 6, 1928 DES MOINES, IA.
60- 69	MCAULIFFE, RICHARD JOHN	BOX 211 - WEST SIMSBURY CT 06092
14-143	MCAVOY, GEORGE H	OLD ADD: ARDMORE OK 73401
13-114	MCAVOY, JAMES EUGENE 'WICKEY'	D. JULY 5, 1973 ROCHESTER, N. Y.
59- 54	MCAVOY, THOMAS JOHN	CLINTON COURT - STILLWATER NY 12118
61- 72	MCBEAN, ALVIN O'NEAL	BOX 4475 - ST THOMAS VI 00801
26- 53	MCBEE, PRYOR EDWARD	D. APRIL 19, 1963 ROSEVILLE, CALIF.
73- 82	MCBRIDE, ARNOLD RAY	P.O. BOX 923 - FLORISSANT MO 63032
59- 55	MCBRIDE, KENNETH FAYE	2138 DAVENPORT AVE - CLEVELAND OH 44114
43- 85	MCBRIDE, THOMAS RAYMOND	3219 CAROL ANN - WICHITA FALLS TX 76309
46- 69	MCCABE, RALPH HERBERT	D. MAY 4, 1974 WINDSOR, ONT.
18- 46	MCCABE, RICHARD JAMES	D. APRIL 11, 1950 BUFFALO, N. Y.
15- 97	MCCABE, TIMOTHY	D. APRIL 12, 1977 IRONTON, MO.
18- 47	MCCABE, WILLIAM FRANCIS	D. SEPTEMBER 2, 1966 CHICAGO, ILL.
64- 69	MCCABEM JOE ROBERT	OLD ADD: 1001 CRESCENT DRIVE - GREENCASTLE IN 46135
46- 70	MCCAHAN, WILLIAM GLENN	D. JULY 3, 1986 FORT WORTH, TEXAS
62- 84	MCCALL, BRIAN ALLEN	105 UNION ST - ALEXANDRIA VA 22314
48- 66	MCCALL, JOHN WILLIAM	2959 PALMER DR - SIERRA VISTA AZ 85635
77- 88	MCCALL, LARRY STEPHEN	RR 5 BOX 354 - CANDLER NC 28715
48- 67	MCCALL, ROBERT LEONARD 'DUTCH'	2600 ASHLEY #A107-NORTH LITTLE ROCK AR 72114
27- 57	MCCALLISTER, JOHN	D. OCTOBER 18, 1946 COLUMBUS, O.
89- 79	MCCAMENT, LARRY RANDALL 'RANDY'	15601 NORTH 60TH AVENUE - GLENDALE AZ 85306
14-144	MCCANDLESS, SCOTT COOK 'JOHN'	D. AUGUST 17, 1961 PITTSBURGH, PA.
20- 80	MCCANN, ROBERT EMMETT	D. APRIL 15, 1937 PHILADELPHIA, PA.
59- 56	MCCARDELL, ROGER MORTON	16 WEST MAIN ST - RISING SUN MD 21911
23- 88	MCCARREN, WILLIAM JOSEPH	D. SEPTEMBER 11, 1983 DENVER, COLO.
10- 96	MCCARTHY, ALEXANDER GEORGE	D. MARCH 12, 1978 SALISBURY, MD.
48- 68	MCCARTHY, JEROME FRANCIS	D. OCTOBER 3, 1965 OCEANSIDE, N. Y.
34- 67	MCCARTHY, JOHN JOSEPH	D. SEPTEMBER 13, 1973 MUNDELEIN, ILL.
26- 54	MCCARTHY, JOSEPH VINCENT	D. JANUARY 13, 1978 BUFFALO,N. Y.
85- 71	MCCARTHY, THOMAS MICHAEL	5 CAROLYN DR, RR 8 - PLYMOUTH MA 02360
13-115	MCCARTY, GEORGE LEWIS	D. JUNE 9, 1930 READING, PA.
59- 57	MCCARVER, JAMES TIMOTHY 'TIM'	1518 YOUNGFORD RD - GLADWYNNE PA 19035
85- 72	MCCASKILL, KIRK EDWARD	25 MIRADOR STREET - IRVINE CA 92715
77- 89	MCCATTY, STEVEN EARL	3595 CROOKS ROAD - TROY MI 48084
61- 73	MCCLAIN, JOE FRED	RR 8 BOX 109 - JOHNSON CITY TN 37601
19- 56	MCCLELLAN, HERVEY MCDOWELL	D. NOVEMBER 6, 1925 CYNTHIANA, KY.
87- 92	MCCLENDON, LLOYD GLENN	2975 EAGLE WAY - BOULDER CO 80303
13-116	MCCLESKEY, JEFFERSON LAMAR	D. MAY 11, 1971 AMERICUS, GA.
36- 54	MCCLOSKEY, JAMES ELLWOOD	D. AUGUST 18, 1971 JERSEY CITY, N. J.
10- 97	MCCLURE, LAWRENCE LEDWITH	D. AUGUST 31, 1948 HUNTINGTON, W. VA.
75- 73	MCCLURE, ROBERT CRAIG	1000 BORDER ROAD - LOS ALTOS CA 94022
15- 98	MCCLUSKEY, HARRY ROBERT	D. JUNE 7, 1962 TOLEDO, O.
33- 42	MCCOLL, ALEXANDER BOYD	1203 SHERMAN ST - GENEVA OH 44041
14-145	MCCONNAUGHEY, RALPH J.	D. JUNE 4, 1966 DETROIT, MICH.
15- 99	MCCONNELL, SAMUEL FAULKNER	D. JUNE 27, 1981 PHOENIXVILLE, PA.
64- 70	MCCOOL, WILLIAM JOHN	1560 FRONTIER COURT - SPRING VALLEY OH 45370
80- 88	MCCORMACK, DONALD ROSS	3910 ORCHARD HILL CIRCLE - PALM HARBOR FL 34684
34- 68	MCCORMICK, FRANK ANDREW	D. NOVEMBER 21, 1982 MANHASSET, N. Y.
56- 58	MCCORMICK, MICHAEL FRANCIS	22330 HOMESTEAD RD #305 - CUPERTINO CA 95014
40- 60	MCCORMICK, MYRON WINTHROP 'MIKE'	D. APRIL 14, 1976 LOS ANGELES, CALIF.
39- 76	MCCOSKY, WILLIAM BARNEY 'BARNEY'	66 WOODLAND DRIVE #102 - VERO BEACH FL 32962
59- 58	MCCOVEY, WILLIE LEE	P.O. BOX 620342 - WOODSIDE CA 94062
38- 60	MCCOY, BENJAMIN JENISON	3932 EAST OMAHA DR SW-GRANDVILLE MI 49418
39- 77	MCCRABB, LESTER WILLIAM	1126 RIVER ROAD - QUARRYVILLE PA 17566
63- 76	MCCRAW, TOMMY LEE	2225 CLYDE #1 - LOS ANGELES CA 90016
25- 70	MCCREA, FRANCIS WILLIAM	D. FEBRUARY 25, 1981 DOVER, N. J.
14-146	MCCREERY, ESLEY PORTERFIELD	D. OCTOBER 19, 1960 SACRAMENTO, CALIF.
22- 84	MCCUE, FRANK ALOYSIUS	D. JULY 5, 1953 EVERGREEN PARK, ILL.
85- 73	MCCULLERS, LANCE GRAYE	14602 VILLAGE GLEN CIRCLE - TAMPA FL 33624
40- 61	MCCULLOUGH, CLYDE EDWARD	D. SEPTEMBER 18, 1982 SAN FRANCISCO, CALIF.
29- 70	MCCULLOUGH, PAUL WILLARD	D. NOVEMBER 7, 1970 NEWCASTLE, PA.
42- 68	MCCULLOUGH, PHILIP LAMAR	25 EXETER RD-AVONDALE ESTATES GA 30002
22- 85	MCCURDY, HARRY HENRY	D. JULY 21, 1972 HOUSTON, TEX.
55- 80	MCDANIEL, LYNDALL DALE	1026 8TH STREET - LAS VEGAS NM 87701
57- 50	MCDANIEL, MAX VON	33202 ROLLING WOOD - PINEHURST TX 7736I
12-120	MCDERMOTT, FRANK A. 'RED'	D. SEPTEMBER 11, 1964 PHILADELPHIA, PA.
48- 69	MCDERMOTT, MAURICE JOSEPH 'MICKEY'	4950 BRILL - PHOENIX AZ 85008
72- 69	MCDERMOTT, TERRENCE MICHAEL	407 NORTH VILLAGE AVE - ROCKVILLE CENTRE NY 11552
57- 51	MCDEVITT, DANIEL EUGENE	2991 SALEM RD SE - CONYERS GA 30207
12-121	MCDONALD, CHARLES E. 'TEX'	D. MARCH 31, 1943 HOUSTON, TEX.
69-113	MCDONALD, DAVID BRUCE	32 NE 22ND AVE #204 - POMPANO BEACH FL 33062
11-113	MCDONALD, EDWARD C.	D. MARCH 11, 1946 ALBANY, N.Y.
31- 56	MCDONALD, HENRY MONROE	D. OCTOBER 17, 1982 HEMET, CALIF.
50- 65	MCDONALD, JIMMIE LEROY	3767 STIRRUP DRIVE - KINGMAN AZ 86401
89- 80	MCDONALD, LARRY BENARD 'BEN'	DENHAM SPRINGS LA 70726
10- 98	MCDONALD, MALCOLM JOSEPH	D. MAY 30, 1963 BAYTOWN, TEXAS
43- 86	MCDONNELL, JAMES WILLIAM	OLD ADD: 14238 SEYMOUR - DETROIT MI 48205
51- 63	MCDOUGALD, GILBERT JAMES	10 WARREN AVE - SPRING LAKE NJ 07762
87- 93	MCDOWELL, JACK BURNS	5443 VANNOORD AVENUE - VAN NUYS CA 91401
85- 74	MCDOWELL, ODDIBE	5240 SW 18TH ST - HOLLYWOOD FL 33023
85- 75	MCDOWELL, ROGER ALAN	OLD ADD: 5973 OAKMOST PLACE - STUART FL 34997
61- 74	MCDOWELL, SAMUEL EDWARD	7727 ST LAWRENCE AVE - PITTSBURGH PA 15218
89- 81	MCELROY, CHARLES DWAYNE	1049 NEDERLAND AVENUE - PORT ARTHUR TX 77640
16- 60	MCELWEE, LELAND STANFORD	D. FEBRUARY 8, 1957 UNION, ME.
74- 81	MCENANEY, WILLIAM HENRY	4051 NE 15TH AVENUE - OAKLAND PARK FL 33334
30- 50	MCEVOY, LOUIS ANTHONY	D. DECEMBER 16, 1953 WEBSTER GROVE, MO.
68- 61	MCFADDEN, LEON	8617 10TH AVENUE - INGLEWOOD CA 90305
45- 67	MCFARLAND, HOWARD ALEXANDER	8321 WILLOWBROOK - WICHITA KS 67207
62- 85	MCFARLANE, ORLANDO DE JESUS	OLD ADD: 33 TAFT AVE - ASHEVILLE NC 28803
81- 82	MCGAFFIGAN, ANDREW JOSEPH	356 SWEET BRIAR LN - LAKELAND FL 33803
17- 46	MCGAFFIGAN, MARK ANDREW 'PATSY'	D. DECEMBER 22, 1940 CARLYLE, ILL.
46- 71	MCGAH, EDWARD JOSEPH	1070 GREEN ST #1900 - SAN FRANCISCO CA 94133
62- 86	MCGAHA, FRED MELVIN 'MEL'	P.O. BOX 273 - DISNEY OK 74340

12-122	MCGARR, JAMES VINCENT	D. JULY 21, 1981 MIAMI, FLA.
12-123	MCGARVEY, DANIEL FRANCIS	D. MARCH 7, 1947 PHILADELPHIA, PA.
34- 69	MCGEE, DANIEL ALOYSIUS	252 BUTTRICK AVE - BRONX NY 10465
25- 71	MCGEE, FRANCIS D. 'TUBBY'	D. JANUARY 30, 1934 COLUMBUS, O.
35- 68	MCGEE, WILLIAM HENRY	D. FEBRUARY 11, 1987 ST. LOUIS, MO.
82- 83	MCGEE, WILLIE DEAN	3008 AUTUMN LAKES COURT - ST. LOUIS MO 63044
11-114	MCGEEHAN, DANIEL DESALES	D. JULY 12, 1955 HAZELTON, PA.
12-124	MCGEHEE, PATRICK HENRY	D. DECEMBER 30, 1946 PADUCAH, KY.
50- 66	MCGHEE, WARREN EDWARD 'ED'	D. FEBRUARY 13, 1986 MEMPHIS, TENN.
44- 85	MCGHEE, WILLIAM MAC	MUSTANG ROAD - GULF BREEZE FL 32561
77- 90	MCGILBERRY, RANDALL KENT	4266 LAFITTE ROAD - SARALAND AL 36571
44- 86	MCGILLEN, JOHN JOSEPH	D. AUGUST 11, 1987 UPLAND, PA.
68- 62	MCGINN, DANIEL MICHAEL	1340 SOUTH 163RD ST - OMAHA NE 68120
72- 70	MCGLOTHEN, LYNN EVERATT	D. AUGUST 14, 1984 DUBACH, LA.
49- 51	MCGLOTHIN, EZRA MAC 'PAT'	2317 COREFIELD RD - KNOXVILLE TN 37919
65- 72	MCGLOTHLIN, JAMES MILTON	D. DECEMBER 23, 1975 UNION, KY.
22- 86	MCGOWAN, FRANK BERNARD 'BEAUTY'	D. MAY 6, 1982 HAMDEN, CONN.
48- 70	MCGOWAN, TULLIS EARL 'MICKEY'	618 SPRATT ST - WAYCROSS GA 31501
12-125	MCGRANER, HOWARD	D. OCTOBER 22, 1952 ZALESKI, O.
65- 73	MCGRAW, FRANK EDWIN 'TUG'	ONE DALE LANE - WALLINGFORD PA 19086
14-147	MCGRAW, JOHN	D. NOVEMBER 14, 1918 CLEVELAND, O.
17- 47	MCGRAW, ROBERT EMMETT	D. JUNE 2, 1978 BOISE, ID.
76- 61	MCGREGOR, SCOTT HOUSTON	STAR ROUTE 1 BOX 2800-133 - TEHACHAPI CA 93561
22- 87	MCGREW, WALTER HOWARD 'SLIM'	D. AUGUST 21, 1967 PORT ARTHUR, TEX.
86- 97	MCGRIFF, FREDERICK STANLEY	16051 PENWOOD DRIVE - TAMPA FL 33647
87- 94	MCGRIFF, TERENCE ROY	2905 LANGSTON DRIVE - FORT PIERCE FL 33450
62- 87	MCGUIRE, M C ADOLFUS 'MICKEY'	4326 DORSET DR - DAYTON OH 45405
14-148	MCGUIRE, THOMAS PATRICK	D. DECEMBER 8, 1959 PHOENIX, AZ.
88- 89	MCGUIRE, WILLIAM PATRICK	4668 DREXEL STREET - OMAHA NE 68117
86- 98	MCGWIRE, MARK DAVID	OLD ADD: 2329 SIENA COURT - CLAREMONT CA 91711
43- 87	MCHALE, JOHN JOSEPH	BOX 500 STATION M - MONTREAL QUEBEC H1V 3P2 CAN.
10- 99	MCHALE, MARTIN JOSEPH	D. MAY 7, 1979 HEMPSTEAD, N. Y.
18- 48	MCHENRY, AUSTIN BUSH	D. NOVEMBER 27, 1922 MT. OREB, O.
81- 83	MCHENRY, VANCE LOREN	2396 BROWN ST--DURHAM CA 95938
21- 59	MCILREE, VANCE ELMER	D. MAY 6, 1959 KANSAS CITY, MO.
57- 52	MCILWAIN, WILLIAM STOVER	D. JANUARY 15, 1966 BUFFALO, N. Y.
74- 82	MCINTOSH, JOSEPH ANTHONY	1002 PARKHILL - BILLINGS MT 59102
11-115	MCIVER, EDWARD OTTO	D. MAY 4, 1954 DALLAS, TEX.
37- 72	MCKAIN, ARCHIE RICHARD	D. MAY 21, 1985 SALINA, KAN.
27- 58	MCKAIN, HAROLD LEROY	D. JANUARY 24, 1970 SACRAMENTO, CAL.
75- 74	MCKAY, DAVID LAWRENCE	6102 EAST SURREY AVE - SCOTTSDALE AZ 85254
15-100	MCKAY, REEVE STEWART	D. JANUARY 18, 1946 DALLAS, TEX.
72- 71	MCKEE, JAMES MARION	OLD ADD: 31 S. HAMILTON - COLUMBUS OH 43213
13-117	MCKEE, RAY 'RED'	D. AUGUST 5, 1972 SAGINAW, MICH.
43- 88	MCKEE, ROGERS HORNSBY	409 FOREST HILL DRIVE - SHELBY NC 28150
32- 49	MCKEITHAN, EMMETT JAMES 'TIM'	D. AUGUST 20, 1969 FOREST CITY, N. C.
15-101	MCKENRY, FRANK GORDON 'LIMB'	D. NOVEMBER 1, 1956 FRESNO, CALIF.
86- 99	MCKEON, JOEL JACOB	1901 PIERCE STREET - HOLLYWOOD FL 33020
73- 83	MCKEON, JOHN ALOYSIUS 'JACK'	9985 RUE CHANTENAR - SAN DIEGO CA 92131
70- 88	MCKINNEY, CHARLES RICHARD 'RICH'	2393 EAST PETERSON - TROY OH 45373
60- 70	MCKNIGHT, JAMES ARTHUR	RR2 - BEE BRANCH AR 72013
89- 82	MCKNIGHT, JEFFERSON ALAN	BOX 325 - CHARLESTON AR 72933
63- 77	MCLAIN, DENNIS DALE	4933 COVENTRY PARKWAY - FORT WAYNE IN 46804
32- 50	MCLARNEY, ARTHUR JAMES	D. DECEMBER 20, 1984 SEATTLE, WASH.
12-126	MCLARRY, HOWARD ZELL 'POLLY'	D. NOVEMBER 4, 1971 BONHAM, TEX.
77- 91	MCLAUGHLIN, BYRON SCOTT	OLD ADD: 3464 SWEETWATER MESA - MALIBU CA 92154
14-149	MCLAUGHLIN, JAMES ANSON 'KID'	D. NOVEMBER 13, 1934 ALLEGANY, N.Y.
32- 51	MCLAUGHLIN, JAMES ROBERT	D. DECEMBER 18, 1968 MOUNT VERNON, ILL.
77- 92	MCLAUGHLIN, JOEY RICHARD	1611 SOUTH TROOST - TULSA OK 74120
31- 57	MCLAUGHLIN, JUSTIN THEODORE 'JUD'	D. SEPTEMBER 27, 1964 CAMBRIDGE, MASS.
76- 62	MCLAUGHLIN, MICHAEL DUANE 'BO'	4500 SOUTH LAKE SHORE DR #345 - TEMPE AZ 85282
37- 73	MCLAUGHLIN, PATRICK ELMER	1535 CHANTILLY LN - HOUSTON TX 77018
35- 69	MCLEAN, ALBERT ELDON	3005 HARNETT DRIVE - GREENSBORO NC 27407
51- 64	MCLELAND, WAYNE GAFFNEY	6622 BELDART - HOUSTON TX 77017
86-100	MCLEMORE, MARK TREMELL	1900 AVE OF THE STARS #1240 - LOS ANGELES CA 90067
38- 61	MCLEOD, RALPH ALTON	30 ACTON ST - WOLLASTON MA 02170
30- 51	MCLEOD, SOULE JAMES 'JIM'	D. AUGUST 3, 1981 LITTLE ROCK, ARK.
44- 87	MCLISH, CALVIN COOLIDGE	700 TIMBER RIDGE RD - EDMOND OK 73034
42- 69	MCLYEA, FRANK	OLD ADD: 4908 CROSS CREEK CT #16 - EVANSVILLE IN 47715
56- 59	MCMAHON, JACK WALLY	1717 TEREASA CIRCLE - BENTON AR 72015
57- 53	MCMAHON, DONALD JOHN	D. JULY 22, 1987 LOS ANGELES, CALIF.
60- 71	MCMANUS, JAMES MICHAEL	1244 BOYLSTON ST,%E.F. HUTTON - CHESTNUT HILL MA 02167
13-118	MCMANUS, JOAB LOGAN	D. DECEMBER 23, 1955 SKELTON, W. VA.
20- 81	MCMANUS, MARTIN JOSEPH	D. FEBRUARY 18, 1966 ST. LOUIS, MO.
68- 63	MCMATH, JIMMY LEE	3321 22ND ST - TUSCALOOSA AL 35401
2- 88	MCMILLAN, NORMAN ALEXIS	D. SEPTEMBER 21, 1969 LATTA, S. C.
- 65	MCMILLAN, ROY DAVID	1200 EAST 9TH ST - BONHAM TX 75418
77- 93	MCMILLAN, THOMAS ERWIN	3810 WEST COOPER LAKE DR - SMYRNA GA 30080
25- 72	MCMULLEN, HUGH RAPHAEL	D. MAY 23, 1986 WHITTIER, CALIF.
62- 88	MCMULLEN, KENNETH LEE	10 ESTABAN - CAMARILLO CA 93010
14-150	MCMULLIN, FREDERICK WILLIAM	D. NOVEMBER 21, 1952 LOS ANGELES, CALIF.
83- 96	MCMURTRY, JOE CRAIG	55 ROSE DRIVE - TROY TX 76579
45- 68	MCNABB, CARL MAC	BOX 203 - JASPER TN 37347
29- 71	MCNAIR, DONALD ERIC	D. MARCH 11, 1949 MERIDIAN, MISS.
62- 89	MCNALLY, DAVID ARTHUR	3305 RAMADA DR - BILLINGS MT 59102
15-102	MCNALLY, MICHAEL JOSEPH	D. MAY 29, 1965 BETHLEHEM, PA.
22- 89	MCNAMARA, GEORGE FRANCIS	D. JUNE 12, 1990 HINSDALE, ILL.
69-114	MCNAMARA, JOHN FRANCIS	1008 WILSON PIKE - BRENTWOOD TN 37021
27- 59	MCNAMARA, JOHN RAYMOND	D. DECEMBER 20, 1963 ARLINGTON, TEXAS
39- 78	MCNAMARA, ROBERT MAXEY	23810 BARONA MESA RD - RAMONA CA 92065
22- 90	MCNAMARA, THOMAS HENRY	D. MAY 5, 1974 DANVERS, MASS.
22- 91	MCNAMARA, TIMOTHY AUGUSTINE	21 SUMMIT AV - WOONSOCKET RI 02895
32- 52	MCNAUGHTON, GORDON JOSEPH	D. AUGUST 6, 1942 CHICAGO, ILL.
83- 97	MCNEALY, ROBERT LEE	3301 BOZEMAN STREET - SACRAMENTO CA 95838
24- 77	MCNEELY, GEORGE EARL	D. JULY 16, 1971 SACRAMENTO, CAL.
19- 57	MCNEIL, NORMAN FRANCIS	D. APRIL 11, 1942 BUFFALO, N. Y.
64- 71	MCNERTNEY, GERALD EDWARD	1719 GRAND AVENUE - AMES IA 50010
22- 92	MCNULTY, PATRICK HOWARD	D. MAY 4, 1963 HOLLYWOOD, CAL.

69-115	MCNULTY, WILLIAM FRANCIS	5408 TIBURON WAY - SACRAMENTO CA 95841
23- 89	MCQUAID, HERBERT GEORGE	D. APRIL 5, 1966 RICHMOND, CAL.
34- 70	MCQUAIG, GERALD JOSEPH	110 SCHOOL DR - BUFORD GA 30518
69-116	MCQUEEN, MICHAEL ROBERT	3206 CAMEO DR - HOUSTON TX 77055
18- 49	MCQUILLAN, HUGH A.	D. AUGUST 26, 1947 NEW YORK, N. Y.
38- 62	MCQUILLEN, GLENN RICHARD	D. JUNE 8, 1989 GARDENVILLE, MD.
36- 55	MCQUINN, GEORGE HARTLEY	D. DECEMBER 24, 1978 ALEXANDRIA, VA.
68- 64	MCRAE, HAROLD ABRAHAM	2531 LANDING CIRCLE - BRADENTON FL 33529
69-117	MCRAE, NORMAN	OLD ADD: 1009 LAURA ST - ELIZABETH NJ 07206
83- 98	MCREYNOLDS, WALTER KEVIN	110 ILLINOIS BAYOU - SHERWOOD AR 72116
11-116	MCTIGUE, WILLIAM PATRICK	D. MAY 11, 1920 NASHVILLE, TENN.
21- 60	MCWEENY, DOUGLAS LAWRENCE	D. JANUARY 1, 1953 MELROSE PARK, ILL.
78- 79	MCWILLIAMS, LARRY DEAN	710 WEST MAIN #2208 - ARLINGTON TX 76013
31- 55	MCWILLIAMS, ROBERT HUGH 'PETE'	D. OCTOBER 28, 1987 MONT BELVIEU, TEXAS
31- 58	MCWILLIAMS, WILLIAM HENRY	1600 RICE ROAD - TYLER TX 75703
83- 99	MEACHAM, ROBERT ANDREW	4314 DRESDEN STREET - COLUMBUS OH 43224
43- 89	MEAD, CHARLES RICHARD	16350 FREMONTIA - HESPERIA CA 92345
20- 82	MEADOR, JOHN DAVIS	D. APRIL 11, 1970 WINSTON-SALEM, N. C.
15-103	MEADOWS, HENRY LEE	D. JANUARY 29, 19E3 DAYTONA BEACH, FLA.
86-101	MEADOWS, MICHAEL RAY 'LOUIE'	20 HADLEY COLLINS ROAD - MAYSVILLE NC 28555
26- 55	MEADOWS, RUFUS RIVERS	D. MAY 10, 1970 WICHITA, KAN.
87- 95	MEADS, DAVID DONALD 'DON'	BOX 70, FEDERAL ROAD - ENGLISHTOWN NJ 07726
12-127	MEANEY, PATRICK	D. OCTOBER 20, 1922 PHILADELPHIA,PA.
14-151	MEARA, CHARLES EDWARD	D. FEBRUARY 8, 1962 KINGSBRIDGE, N. Y.
45- 69	MEDEIROS, RAY ANTON	313 SAN MIGUEL WAY - SAN MATEO CA 94403
72- 72	MEDICH, GEORGE FRANCIS 'DOC'	2332 LINDEN AVE - ALIQUIPPA PA 15001
88- 90	MEDINA, LUIS MAIN	7536 BRUNACHE - DOWNEY CA 90242
49- 52	MEDLINGER, IRVING JOHN	D. SEPTEMBER 3, 1975 WHEELING, ILL.
88- 91	MEDVIN, SCOTT HOWARD	4712 MICHAEL AVENUE - NORTH OLMSTED OH 44070
32- 53	MEDWICK, JOSEPH MICHAEL	D. MARCH 21, 1975 ST. PETERSBURG, FLA.
10-100	MEE, THOMAS WILLIAM	D. MAY 16, 1981 CHICAGO, ILL.
15-104	MEEHAN, WILLIAM THOMAS	D. OCTOBER 8, 1982 DOUGLAS, WYO.
23- 90	MEEKER, CHARLES ROY	D. MARCH 25, 1929 ORLANDO, FLA.
48- 71	MEEKS, SAMUEL MACK	4963 HELENE - MEMPHIS TN 38117
72- 73	MEELER, CHARLES PHILLIP 'PHIL'	OLD ADD: 108 HAWTHORNE LN - LENOIR NC 28645
41- 71	MEERS, RUSSELL HARLAN	56 HICKORY TRAIL - KITTY HAWK NC 27949
84- 75	MEIER, DAVID KEITH	523 WEST STUART - FRESNO CA 93704
22- 93	MEINE, HENRY WILLIAM 'HEINIE'	D. MARCH 18, 1968 ST. LOUIS, MO.
13-119	MEINERT, WALTER HENRY	D. NOVEMBER 9, 1958 DECATUR, ILL..
10-101	MEINKE, ROBERT BERNARD	D. DECEMBER 29, 1952 CHICAGO, ILL.
13-120	MEISTER, KARL DANIEL	D. AUGUST 15, 1967 MARIETTA, O.
12-128	MEIXELL, MERTON MERRILL 'MOXIE'	D. AUGUST 17, 1982 LOS ANGELES, CALIF.
55- 81	MEJIAS, ROMAN GEORGE	3242 WEST 59TH ST - LOS ANGELES CA 90043
76- 63	MEJIAS, SAMUEL ELIAS	CALLE 1ST #67,PRES. G-G-1 - SANTO DOMINGO DOM. REP.
37- 74	MELE, ALBERT ERNEST 'DUTCH'	D. FEBRUARY 12, 1975 HOLLYWOOD, FLA.
47- 63	MELE, SABATH ANTHONY 'SAM'	340 ADAMS ST - QUINCY MA 02169
84- 76	MELENDEZ, FRANCISCO	OLD ADD: RR 3 BOX 590 - RIO PIEDRAS PR 00928
70- 89	MELENDEZ, LUIS ANTONIO	EXT. SAN JOSE D-2 - AIBONITO PR 00609
26- 56	MELILLO, OSCAR DONALD	D. NOVEMBER 14, 1963 CHICAGO, ILL.
27- 60	MELLANA, JOSEPH PETER	D. NOVEMBER 1, 1969 SAN RAFAEL, CALIF.
10-102	MELOAN, PAUL	D. FEBRUARY 11, 1950 TAFT, CALIF.
37- 75	MELTON, CLIFFORD GEORGE	D. JULY 28, 1986 BALTIMORE, MD.
56- 60	MELTON, DAVID OLIN	10253 RICHWOOD DR - CUPERTINO CA 95014
41- 72	MELTON, REUBEN FRANKLIN	D. SEPTEMBER 11, 1971 GREER, S. C.
68- 65	MELTON, WILLIAM EDWIN	OLD ADD: 212 CALLE MARINA - SAN CLEMENTE CA 92672
85- 76	MELVIN, ROBERT PAUL	350 LINFIELD DR - MENLO PARK CA 94025
70- 90	MENDOZA, CRISTOBAL RIGOBERTO 'MINNIE'	4110 BROADVIEW DR - CHARLOTTE NC 28210
74- 83	MENDOZA, MARIO	LATERAL DE PACUAL OROZEO #1123 - CHIHUAHUA CHI. MEX.
79- 75	MENDOZA, MICHAEL JOSEPH	12812 ELMFIELD LN - POWAY CA 92064
62- 90	MENKE, DENIS JOHN	780 MAPLE RIDGE RD - PALM HARBOR FL 33563
14-152	MENOSKY, MICHAEL WILLIAM	D. APRIL 11, 1983 DETROIT, MICH.
12-129	MENSOR, EDWARD	D. APRIL 20, 1970 SALEM, ORE.
18- 50	MENZE, THEODORE CHARLES	D. DECEMBER 23, 1969 ST. LOUIS, MO.
33- 43	MEOLA, EMILE MICHAEL 'MIKE'	D. SEPTEMBER 1, 1976 FAIR LAWN, N. J.
71- 69	MEOLI, RUDOLPH BARTHOLOMEW	3233 EAST GREENLEAF DR - BREA CA 92621
82- 84	MERCADO, ORLANDO (RODRIGUEZ)	BOX 6145 - ARECIBO PR 00613
10-103	MERCER, HARRY VERNON	D. JUNE 25, 1945 DAYTON, OHIO
12-224	MERCER, JOHN LOCKE	D. DECEMBER 22, 1982 SHREVEPORT, LA, 71106
81- 84	MERCER, MARK KENNETH	OLD ADD: 1465 THIRD ST - MINNEAPOLIS MN 55440
75- 75	MERCHANT, JAMES ANDERSON	716 EUCLID AVE - MOBILE AL 36601
89- 83	MERCKER, KENT FRANKLIN	2506 STONELEIGH COURT - DUBLIN OH 43017
34- 71	MERENA, JOHN JOSEPH	D. MARCH 9, 1977 BRIDGEPORT, CONN.
22- 94	MEREWETHER, ARTHUR FRANCIS	37-02 222ND ST - BAYSIDE NY 11361
84- 77	MERIDITH, RONALD KNOX	501 SYDNOR - RIDGECREST CA 93555
49- 53	MERRIMAN, LLOYD ARCHER	6691 NORTH DEWOLF - CLOVIS CA 93612
21- 61	MERRITT, HERMAN G.	D. MAY 26, 1927 KANSAS CITY, MO.
65- 74	MERRITT, JAMES JOSEPH	5924 THELMA AVE - LAPALMA CA 90623
13-121	MERRITT, JOHN HOWARD	D. NOVEMBER 3, 1955 TUPELO, MISS.
57- 54	MERRITT, LLOYD WESLEY	2107 COVENTRY DRIVE - ALLISON PARK PA 15101
51- 66	MERSON, JOHN WARREN	6264 OLD WASHINGTON RD - ELK RIDGE MD 21227
43- 90	MERTZ, JAMES VERLIN	5116 EMORY CIR - JACKSONVILLE FL 32207
41- 73	MERULLO, LEONARD RICHARD	159 SUMMER AVE - READING MA 01867
89- 84	MERULLO, MATTHEW BATES	RIDGEFIELD CT 06877
87- 96	MESA, JOSE RAMON	PROY. ISURA CALLERIO TAVARA #2 - AZUA DOMINICAN REP.
38- 63	MESNER, STEPHEN MATHIAS	D. APRIL 6, 1981 SAN DIEGO, CALIF.
24- 78	MESSENGER, ANDREW WARREN 'BUD'	D. NOVEMBER 4, 1971 LANSING, MICH.
68- 66	MESSERSMITH, JOHN ALEXANDER 'ANDY'	200 LAGUNITA DR - SOQUEL CA 95073
63- 78	METCALF, THOMAS JOHN	1390 WISCONSIN RIVER DR-PORT EDWARDS WI 54469
40- 62	METHA, FRANK JOSEPH 'SCAT'	D. MARCH 2, 1975 FOUNTAIN VALLEY, CALIF.
43- 91	METHENY, ARTHUR BEAUREGARD 'BUD'	2424 NORTH SANDPIPER RD - VIRGINIA BEACH VA 23456
22- 95	METIVIER, GEORGE DEWEY	D. MARCH 2, 1947 CAMBRIDGE, MASS.
43- 92	METKOVICH, DEVONWOOD GEORGE MICHAEL 'CATFISH'	18191 DEVONWOOD CIR-FOUNTAIN VALLEY CA 92708
43- 93	METRO, CHARLES	7890 INDIANA ST-GOLDEN CO 80401
23- 91	METZ, LEONARD RAYMOND	D. FEBRUARY 24, 1953 DENVER, COLO.
74- 84	METZGER, CLARENCE EDWARD 'BUTCH'	132 BLUE WATER CIRCLE - SACRAMENTO CA 95831
70- 91	METZGER, ROGER HENRY	OLD ADD: 202 WESTMORELAND - SAN ANTONIO TX
44- 88	METZIG, WILLIAM ANDREW	2129 57TH ST - LUBBOCK TX 79412
25- 73	METZLER, ALEXANDER	D. NOVEMBER 30, 1973 FRESNO, CAL.

89- 85 MEULENS, HENSLEY FILEMON	KAYA CUPIDO 7 - CURACAO NETHERLANDS ANTILLES S. A.
14-154 MEUSEL, EMIL FREDERICK 'IRISH'	D. MARCH 1, 1963 LONG BEACH, CALIF.
20- 83 MEUSEL, ROBERT WILLIAM	D. NOVEMBER 28, 1977 DOWNEY, CALIF.
13-122 MEYER, BENJAMIN	D. FEBRUARY 6, 1974 FESTUS, MO.
88- 92 MEYER, BRIAN SCOTT	205 SOUTH LAKESIDE DRIVE - MEDFORD NJ 08055
74- 85 MEYER, DANIEL THOMAS	222 REMINGTON LOOP - DANVILLE CA 94526
38- 64 MEYER, GEORGE FRANCIS	537 SOUTH WARREN - PALATINE IL 60067
55- 82 MEYER, JOHN ROBERT	D. MARCH 9, 1967 PHILADELPHIA, PA.
37- 76 MEYER, LAMBERT DALTON 'DUTCH'	2205 PARK HILL DR - FORT WORTH TX 76101
64- 72 MEYER, ROBERT BERNARD	P.O. BOX 3024 - MISSION VIEJO CA 92690
46- 72 MEYER, RUSSELL CHARLES	334 ELM ST - OGLESBY IL 61348
78- 80 MEYER, SCOTT WILLIAM	OLD ADD: 15243 SOUTH HAMLIN AVE - MIDLOTHIAN IL
88- 93 MEYER, TANNER JOE	392 KAIMAKE LOOP - KAILUA HI 96734
13-123 MEYER, WILLIAM ADAM	D. MARCH 31, 1957 KNOXVILLE, TENN.
54- 66 MICELOTTA, ROBERT PETER	295 SAVILLE RD - MINEOLA NY 11501
66- 59 MICHAEL, EUGENE RICHARD	49 UNION AVENUE - UPPER SADDLE RIVER NJ 07458
43- 94 MICHAELS, CASIMIR EUGENE	D. NOVEMBER 12, 1982 GROSSE POINTE, MICH.
32- 54 MICHAELS, JOHN JOSEPH	1825 NICARAGUA WAY - WINTER HAVEN FL 33881
24- 79 MICHAELS, RALPH JOSEPH	BOX 837,TRUST OFFICER 2021 - PITTSBURGH PA 15230
21- 62 MICHAELSON, JOHN AUGUST	D. APRIL 16, 1968 WOODRUFF, WIS.
50- 67 MICKELSON, EDWARD ALLEN	12620 FEE FEE RD - CREVE COUER MO 63141
53- 56 MICKENS, GLENN ROGER	7241 WHITE OAK AVE BOX 583 - RESEDA CA 91335
17- 48 MIDDLETON, JAMES BLAINE	D. JANUARY 12, 1974 ARGOS, IND.
22- 96 MIDDLETON, JOHN WAYNE	D. NOVEMBER 3, 1986 AMARILLO, TEXAS
12-223 MIDKIFF, EZRA MILLINGTON	D. MARCH 21, 1957 HUNTINGDON, W. VA.
38- 65 MIDKIFF, RICHARD JAMES	D. OCTOBER 30, 1956 TEMPLE, TEX.
87- 97 MIELKE, GARY ROGER	OLD ADD: 1300 POHL ROAD #404 - MANKATO MN 56001
45- 70 MIERKOWICZ, EDWARD FRANK	7530 MACOMB #1-A - GROSSE ILE MI 48138
48- 72 MIGGINS, LAWRENCE EDWARD	2405 KINGSTON DR - HOUSTON TX 77019
35- 70 MIHALIC, JOHN MICHAEL	D. APRIL 24, 1987 FORT OGLETHORPE, GA.
64- 73 MIKKELSEN, PETER JAMES	P.O. BOX 187 - PROSSER WA 99350
44- 89 MIKLOS, JOHN JOSEPH	19701 SOUTH 115TH AVE - MOKENA IL 60448
44- 90 MIKSIS, EDWARD THOMAS	3906 WHITMAN RD - HUNTINGDON VALLEY PA 19006
88- 94 MILACKI, ROBERT	P.O. BOX 1471 - LAKE HAVASU AZ 86403
15-106 MILAN, HORACE ROBERT	D. JUNE 29, 1955 TEXARKANA, TEX.
74- 86 MILBOURNE, LAWRENCE WILLIAM	7341 TILDEN WAY - SACRAMENTO CA 95822
40- 63 MILES, CARL THOMAS	806 AUSTIN RD - HORSESHOE BEND AR 72512
58- 62 MILES, DONALD RAY	184 SOUTH DEERFOOT CIRCLE - WOODLANDS TX 77380
68- 67 MILES, JAMES CHARLIE	RR2 - BATESVILLE MS 38606
35- 71 MILES, WILSON DANIEL 'DEE'	D. NOVEMBER 2, 1976 BIRMINGHAM, ALA.
75- 76 MILEY, MICHAEL WILFRED	D. JANUARY 6, 1977 BATON ROUGE, LA.
15-107 MILJUS, JOHN KENNETH	D. FEBRUARY 11, 1976 POLSON, MONT.
66- 60 MILLAN, FELIX BERNARDO	CALLE 13R-14, EL CONQUISTADOR - TRUJILLO ALTO PR 00760
73- 84 MILLER, CHARLES BRUCE	2126 PARKLAND DR - FORT WAYNE IN 46825
12-130 MILLER, CHARLES ELMER	D. APRIL 23, 1972 WARRENSBURG, MO.
15-108 MILLER, CHARLES HESS	D. JANUARY 13, 1951 MILLERSVILLE, PA.
13-124 MILLER, CHARLES MARION	D. JUNE 16, 1961 HOUSTON, TEX.
84- 78 MILLER, DARRELL KEITH	6246 PROMONTORY LN - RIVERSIDE CA 92506
75- 77 MILLER, DYAR K	RURAL ROUTE 9 BOX 421A - GREENSBURG IN 47240
21- 63 MILLER, EDMUND JOHN 'BING'	D. MAY 7, 1966 PHILADELPHIA, PA.
77- 94 MILLER, EDWARD LEE	5014 HARTNETT - RICHMOND CA 94804
36- 56 MILLER, EDWARD ROBERT	204 CYPRESS DRIVE - LAKE WORTH FL 33461
12-131 MILLER, EDWIN	D. APRIL 17, 1980 LEBANON, PA.
12-132 MILLER, ELMER	D. NOVEMBER 28, 1944 BELOIT, WIS.
29- 72 MILLER, ELMER JOSEPH	D. JANUARY 8, 1987 CORONA, CALIF.
13-125 MILLER, FRANK LEE	D. FEBRUARY 19, 1974 ALLEGAN, MICH.
10-104 MILLER, FREDERICK HOLMAN	D. MAY 2, 1953 BROOKVILLE, IND.
11-117 MILLER, HUGH STANLEY	D. DECEMBER 24, 1945 JEFFERSON BARRACKS, MO.
22- 97 MILLER, JACOB GEORGE	D. AUGUST 24, 1974 TOWSON, MD.
44- 91 MILLER, JAMES ELDRIDGE 'HACK'	D. NOVEMBER 21, 1966 DALLAS, TEX
66- 61 MILLER, JOHN ALLEN	20 SWIFT COURT - NEWPORT BEACH CA 92663
43- 95 MILLER, JOHN ANTHONY 'OX'	HCR 3 BOX 122 - GEORGE WEST TX 78022
62- 91 MILLER, JOHN ERNEST	1216 REDCLIFFE RD - BALTIMORE MD 21228
87- 98 MILLER, KEITH ALAN	5432 MEADOWBROOK - BAY CITY MI 48706
44- 92 MILLER, KENNETH ALBERT	9344 RAMBLER DR - AFFTON MO 63123
64- 74 MILLER, LARRY DON	9226 NORTH 33RD WAY - PHOENIX AZ 85028
16- 61 MILLER, LAWRENCE H. 'HACK'	D. SEPTEMBER 17, 1971 OAKLAND, CAL.
84- 79 MILLER, LEMMIE EARL	OLD ADD: 480 LEFF #E - SAN LUIS OBISPO CA 93401
23- 92 MILLER, LEO ALPHONSO 'RED'	D. OCTOBER 20, 1973 ORLANDO, FL.
10-105 MILLER, LOWELL OTTO	D. MARCH 29, 1962 BROOKLYN, N.Y.
88- 95 MILLER, NEAL KEITH	RURAL ROUTE 1 BOX 860 - KAUFMAN TX 75142
65- 75 MILLER, NORMAN CALVIN	P.O. BOX 288 - HOUSTON TX 77001
27- 61 MILLER, OTIS LOUIS 'OTTO'	D. JULY 26, 1959 BELLEVILLE, ILL.
21- 64 MILLER, RALPH HENRY	D. FEBRUARY 18, 1967 WHITE BEAR LAKE, MINN.
20- 84 MILLER, RALPH JOSEPH	D. MARCH 18, 1939 FORT WAYNE, IND.
77- 95 MILLER, RANDALL SCOTT	2502 PLANTERS HOUSE LANE - KATY TX 77449
17- 49 MILLER, RAYMOND PETER	D. APRIL 7, 1927 PITTSBURGH, PA.
85- 77 MILLER, RAYMOND ROGER	P. O. BOX 41 - NEW ATHENS OH 43981
71- 70 MILLER, RICHARD ALAN	130 DRAPER RD - WAYLAND MA 01778
53- 57 MILLER, ROBERT GERALD	104 LAKEWOOD CIR - BURR RIDGE IL 60521
49- 54 MILLER, ROBERT JOHN	17397 GLENMORE - DETROIT MI 48240
57- 55 MILLER, ROBERT LANE	7215 LINDEN TERR - CARLSBAD CA 92008
57- 56 MILLER, RODNEY CARTER	9162 WARFIELD DRIVE - HUNTINGTON BEACH CA 92646
74- 87 MILLER, ROGER WESLEY	RR 1 BOX 130 - MILL RUN PA 15464
41- 74 MILLER, ROLLAND ARTHUR 'RONNIE'	7511 LILA - HAZELWOOD MO 63042
10-106 MILLER, ROY OSCAR 'DOC'	D. JULY 31, 1938 JERSEY CITY, N. J.
29- 73 MILLER, RUDEL CHARLES	2246 TIPPERARY RD - KALAMAZOO MI 49001
27- 62 MILLER, RUSSELL LEWIS	D. AUGUST 30, 1962 BUCYRUS, O.
52- 74 MILLER, STUART LEONARD	3701 OCASO COURT - CAMERON PARK CA 95682
18- 51 MILLER, THOMAS ROYALL	D. AUGUST 13, 1980 RICHMOND, VA.
24- 80 MILLER, WALTER JACOB 'JAKE'	D. AUGUST 20, 1975 VENICE, FLA.
11-118 MILLER, WALTER W.	D. MARCH 1, 1956 MARION, IND.
37- 77 MILLER, WILLIAM FRANCIS	D. FEBRUARY 26, 1982 HANNIBAL, MO.
52- 75 MILLER, WILLIAM PAUL	501 EXTON RD - HATBORO PA 19040
34- 72 MILLIES, WALTER LOUIS	5312 WEST 96TH ST - OAK LAWN IL 60453
28- 66 MILLIGAN, JLHN ALEXANDER	D. MAY 15, 1972 FORT PIERCE, FLA.
87- 99 MILLIGAN, RANDY ANDRE	2911 L STREET - SAN DIEGO CA 92102

ROY CAMPANELLA

CARL HUBBELL

BILLY HERMAN

STRENGTH UP THE MIDDLE

These autographed Great
Moments cards depict a
Hall of Fame middle including
Campy, Hubbell, Herman,
Aparicio and Snider

LUIS APARICIO

DUKE SNIDER

53- 58	MILLIKEN, ROBERT FOGLE	1875 SOUTHWOOD LN - CLEARWATER FL 33516
11-119	MILLS, ABBOTT PAIGE 'JACK'	D. JUNE 3, 1973 WASHINGTON, D.C.
27- 63	MILLS, ARTHUR GRANT	D. JULY 23, 1975 UTICA, N. Y.
34- 73	MILLS, COLONEL BUSTER	BOX 13081 - ARLINGTON TX 76016
14-155	MILLS, FRANK LEMOYNE	D. AUGUST 31, 1983 YOUNGSTOWN, O.
34- 74	MILLS, HOWARD ROBINSON 'LEFTY'	D. SEPTEMBER 23, 1982 RIVERSIDE, CALIF.
80- 89	MILLS, JAMES BRADLEY 'BRAD'	BOX 54 - LEMONCOVE CA 93244
70- 92	MILLS, RICHARD ALAN	OLD ADD: 44 WOOD AVE - SCITUATE MA 02060
15-109	MILLS, RUPERT FRANK	D. JULY 20, 1929 LAKE HOPATCONG, N. J.
44- 93	MILLS, WILLIAM HENRY	BOX 43 - EL JOBEAN FL 33927
36- 57	MILNAR, ALBERT JOSEPH	19520 SHAWNEE AVE-CLEVELAND OH 44119
48- 73	MILNE, WILLIAM JAMES 'PETE'	1905 WEST BEAU TERRA DRIVE - MOBILE AL 36618
78- 81	MILNER, BRIAN TATE	1401 CAIRN CIR - FORT WORTH TX 76134
80- 90	MILNER, EDDIE JAMES	1815 ELDORA DRIVE EAST - COLUMBUS OH 43207
71- 71	MILNER, JOHN DAVID	1351 HOLCOMB AVE - EAST POINT GA 30344
44- 94	MILOSEVICH, MICHAEL	D. FEBRUARY 3, 1966 EAST CHICAGO, IND.
24- 81	MILSTEAD, GEORGE EARL	D. AUGUST 9, 1977 CLEBURNE, TEX.
55- 83	MINARCIN, RUDY ANTHONY	37 NORTH FIRST ST - NORTH VANDERGRIFT PA 15690
60- 72	MINCHER, DONALD RAY	BOX 120 - MERIDIANVILLE AL 35759
21- 65	MINER, RAYMOND THEADORE	D. SEPTEMBER 15, 1963 GLENRIDGE SAN., N. Y.
78- 82	MINETTO, CRAIG STEPHEN	1809 LAKESHORE DRIVE - LODI CA 95240
70- 93	MINGORI, STEPHEN BERNARD	11705 EAST 78TH TERRACE - RAYTOWN MO 64138
46- 73	MINNER, PAUL EDISON	115 GREEN LANE DR - CAMP HILL PA 17011
57- 57	MINNICK, DONALD ATHEY	FRANKLIN HGTS - ROCKY MOUNT VA 24151
49- 55	MINOSO, SATURNINO ORESTES 'MINNIE'	4250 MARIN DR - CHICAGO IL 60613
74- 88	MINSHALL, JAMES EDWARD	3607 27TH AVENUE WEST - BRADENTON FL 33505
75- 78	MINTON, GREGORY BRIAN	2004 EAST CLIPPER LANE - GILBERT AZ 85234
78- 83	MIRABELLA, PAUL THOMAS	550 KNOLL RD - BOONTON MANOR NJ 07005
51- 67	MIRANDA, GUILLERMO PEREZ 'WILLIE'	5502 WHITWOOD RD - BALTIMORE MD 21206
14-156	MISSE, JOHN BEVERLY	D. MARCH 18, 1970 ST. JOSEPH, MO.
10-107	MITCHELL, ALBERT ROY	D. SEPTEMBER 8, 1959 TEMPLE, TEX.
84- 80	MITCHELL, CHARLES ROSS	5017 HASTY DR - NASHVILLE TN 37211
11-120	MITCHELL, CLARENCE ELMER	D. NOVEMBER 6, 1963 GRAND ISLAND, NEB.
75- 79	MITCHELL, CRAIG SETON	BOX 174 - ELK CA 95432
21- 66	MITCHELL, JOHN FRANKLIN	D. NOVEMBER 4, 1965 OAKLAND CO., MICH.
86-102	MITCHELL, JOHN KYLE	5017 HASTY DR - NASHVILLE TN 37211
84- 81	MITCHELL, KEVIN DARRELL	4372 Z STREET - SAN DIEGO CA 92123
46- 74	MITCHELL, LOREN DALE	D. JANUARY 5, 1987 TULSA, OKLA.
23- 93	MITCHELL, MONROE BARR	D. SEPTEMBER 4, 1976 VALDOSTA, GA.
75- 80	MITCHELL, PAUL MICHAEL	23 CARR ROAD - BERLIN MA 01503
70- 94	MITCHELL, ROBERT VANCE	38 EAST ELM ST - NORRISTOWN PA 19401
80- 91	MITCHELL, ROBERT VAN	25691 LUPITA DR - VALENCIA CA 91355
16- 62	MITTERLING, RALPH	D. JANUARY 22, 1956 PITTSBURGH, PA.
66- 62	MITTERWALD, GEORGE EUGENE	1721 MURDOCK BLVD - ORLANDO FL 32807
36- 58	MIZE, JOHN ROBERT	BOX 112 - DEMOREST GA 30535
52- 76	MIZELL, WILMER DAVID 'VINEGAR BEND'	RR 5 BOX 333 - WINSTON SALEM NC 27107
83-100	MIZEROCK, JOHN JOSEPH	P.O. BOX 580 - PUNXSUTAWNEY PA 15767
23- 94	MIZEUR, WILLIAM FRANCIS	D. AUGUST 27, 1976 DANVILLE, ILL.
89- 86	MMAHAT, KEVIN PAUL	3268 CASTLE DRIVE - KENNER LA 70065
74- 89	MOATES, DAVID ALLAN	6401 35TH AVE NW - BRADENTON FL 33529
45- 71	MODAK, MICHAEL JOSEPH ALOYSIUS	OLD ADD: P.O. BOX 6041 - NALCREST FL 33856
62- 92	MOELLER, JOSEPH DOUGLAS	330 33RD STREET - HERMOSA BEACH CA 90254
56- 61	MOELLER, RONALD RALPH	3560 GAILYNN DR - CINCINNATI OH 45211
72- 74	MOFFITT, RANDALL JAMES	110 LAKEOVER DRIVE - ATHENS GA 30606
55- 84	MOFORD, HERBERT	P.O. BOX 12 - MINERVA KY 41062
11-121	MOGRIDGE, GEORGE ANTHONY	D. MARCH 4, 1962 ROCHESTER, N.Y.
22- 98	MOHARDT, JOHN HENRY	D. NOVEMBER 24, 1961 SAN DIEGO, CAL.
20- 85	MOHART, GEORGE BENJAMIN	D. OCTOBER 2, 1970 SILVER CREEK, N.Y.
86-103	MOHORCIC, DALE ROBERT	15501 ROCKSIDE ROAD - MAPLE HEIGHTS OH 44137
53- 59	MOISAN, WILLIAM JOSEPH	BOX 41 - NEWTON NH 03858
21- 67	MOKAN, JOHN LEE	D. FEBRUARY 10, 1985 BUFFALO, N. Y.
49- 56	MOLE, FENTON LEROY	349 ALOHA DR - SAN LEANDRO CA 94578
75- 81	MOLINARO, ROBERT JOSEPH	1 HARBORSIDE #2312 - DELRAY BEACH FL 33483
78- 84	MOLITOR, PAUL LEO	10239 NORTH WATERLEAF DRIVE - MEQUON WI 53092
14-157	MOLLENKAMP, FREDERICK HENRY	D. NOVEMBER 1, 1948 CINCINNATI, O.
13-126	MOLLWITZ, FREDERICK AUGUST 'FRITZ'	D. OCTOBER 3, 1967 BRADENTON, FLA.
70- 95	MOLONEY, RICHARD HENRY	125 MALLARD WAY - WALTHAM MA 02154
17- 50	MOLYNEAUX, VINCENT LEO	D. MAY 4, 1950 STAMFORD, CONN.
37- 78	MONACO, BLAS	410 FROST DR - SAN ANTONIO TX 78201
53- 60	MONAHAN, EDWARD FRANCIS	165 83RD ST - BROOKLYN NY 11209
58- 63	MONBOUQUETTE, WILLIAM CHARLES	271 CLARK HILL RD - NEW BOSTON NH 03070
28- 67	MONCEWICZ, FRED ALFRED	D. APRIL 23, 1969 BROCKTON, MASS.
40- 64	MONCHAK, ALEX	7414 8TH AVENUE WEST - BRADENTON FL 34209
66- 63	MONDAY, ROBERT JAMES 'RICK'	1800 S 1ST %ATH ASSN #112 A/H - CHAMPAIGN IL 61821
68- 68	MONEY, DONALD WAYNE	282 OLD FOREST RD - VINELAND NJ 08360
75- 82	MONGE, ISIDRO PEDROZA 'SID'	9722 AVIARY DR - SAN DIEGO CA 92131
17- 51	MONROE, EDWARD OLIVER	D. APRIL 29, 1969 LOUISVILLE, KY.
21- 68	MONROE, JOHN ALLEN	D. JUNE 19, 1956 CONROE, TEX.
76- 64	MONROE, LAWRENCE JAMES	1916 JAMES COURT - SCHAUMBURG IL 60194
58- 64	MONROE, ZACHARY CHARLES	10 SANDALWOOD LN - BARTONVILLE IL 61607
28- 68	MONTAGUE, EDWARD FRANCIS	D. JUNE 17, 1988 DALY CITY, CALIF.
73- 85	MONTAGUE, JOHN EVANS	6001 VINEYARD LANE - MONTGOMERY AL 36117
86-104	MONTALVO, RAFAEL EDGARDO	CALLE 12 S.O. #1783 LAS LOMES - RIO PIEDRAS PR 00921
66- 64	MONTANEZ, GUILLERMO NARANJO 'WILLIE'	ZONA RURAL 142 BUZON 36# - CAGUAS PR 00625
63- 79	MONTEAGUDO, AURELIO FAUNTINI	CALLE 27 NO. 16-26 - BARQUISIMETO, LARA VENEZUELA S.A.
38- 66	MONTEAGUDO, RENE MIRANDA	D. SEPTEMBER 14, 1973 HIALEAH, FL.
74- 90	MONTEFUSCO, JOHN JOSEPH	24 DOWNING HILL LN - COLTS NECK NJ 07722
61- 75	MONTEJO, MANUEL	CALLE 28 #4415,MUNICIPIO PLAYA - HAVANA CUBA
87-100	MONTELEONE, RICHARD	2515 WEST FERN STREET - TAMPA FL 33614
53- 61	MONTEMAYOR, FELIPE ANGEL	TORREON #308, MITRAS CENTRO - MONTERREY NUEVO LEON MEX.
41- 75	MONTGOMERY, ALVIN ATLAS	D. APRIL 26, 1942 WAVERLY, VA.
87-101	MONTGOMERY, JEFFREY THOMAS	OAK RIDGE ADDISON - WELLSTON OH 45692
71- 72	MONTGOMERY, MONTY BRYSON	807 CORN TASSEL TRAIL - MARTINSVILLE VA 24112
70- 96	MONTGOMERY, ROBERT EDWARD	2 PARKWAY DR - SAUGUS MA 01906
72- 75	MONTREUIL, ALLAN ARTHUR	2016 LAUREL ST - GRETNA LA 70053
54- 67	MONZANT, RAMON SEGUNDO	CALLE 18 NRO 2A-33 - MARACAIBO EDO ZULIA VENEZ
72- 76	MONZON, DANIEL FRANCISCO	912 OLMSTEAD AVE - BRONX NY 10473
67- 73	MOOCK, JOSEPH GEOFFREY	12432 PECOS AVE - GREENWELL LA 70739

```
32- 55 MOON, LEO                               D. AUGUST 25, 1970 NEW ORLEANS, LA.
54- 68 MOON, WALLACE WADE                      1415 ANGELINA CIRCLE - COLLEGE STATION TX 77840
31- 59 MOONEY, JAMES IRVING                    D. APRIL 27, 1979 JOHNSON CITY, TENN.
86-105 MOONEYHAM, WILLIAM CRAIG                9470 WEST OLIVE AVENUE - WINTON CA 95388
25- 74 MOORE, ALBERT JAMES                     D. NOVEMBER 29, 1974 ATLANTIC OCEAN
76- 65 MOORE, ALVIN EARL 'JUNIOR'              3728 WALL AVE - RICHMOND CA 94804
46- 75 MOORE, ANSELM WINN                       245 MARILYN DR - JACKSON MS 39208
64- 75 MOORE, ARCHIE FRANCIS                    69 TOWNSEND DR - FLORHAM PARK NJ 07932
70- 97 MOORE, BALOR LILBON                      OLD ADD: 3317 BOND - PASADENA TX 77503
88- 96 MOORE, BRADLEY ALAN                      1208 EAST 21ST COURT - LOVELAND CO 80538
30- 52 MOORE, CARLOS WHITMAN                    D. JULY 2, 1958 NEW ORLEANS, LA.
12-133 MOORE, CHARLES WESLEY                    5932 DAWSON COURT - GREENDALE WI 53129
73- 86 MOORE, CHARLES WILLIAM                   1801 EIGHTH AVENUE WEST - WILLISTON ND 58801
36- 59 MOORE, D C                               D. JULY 18, 1989 ANAHEIM, CALIF.
75- 83 MOORE, DONNIE RAY                        D. FEBRUARY 12, 1989 TISHOMINGO, OKLA.
34- 75 MOORE, EUEL WALTON                       D. MARCH 12, 1978 JACKSON, MISS.
31- 60 MOORE, EUGENE JR.                        D. MAY 6, 1947 ATLANTIC CITY, N.J.
14-158 MOORE, FERDINAND DEPAGE                  OLD ADD: 5018 AIRLINE - DALLAS TX 75205
70- 98 MOORE, GARY DOUGLAS                      D. FEBRUARY 10, 1976 FORT MYERS, FLA.
23- 95 MOORE, GRAHAM EDWARD 'EDDIE'             509 CHAFFEE - ARLINGTON TX 76010
65- 76 MOORE, JACKIE SPENCER                    D. MAY 19, 1973 SEATTLE, WASH.
28- 69 MOORE, JAMES STANFORD
30- 53 MOORE, JAMES WILLIAM                     D. MAY 7, 1986 MEMPHIS, TENN.
28- 70 MOORE, JOHN FRANCIS                      4A SWAN LAKE VILLAGE - BRADENTON FL 34207
30- 54 MOORE, JOSEPH GREGG                      BOX 65 - GAUSE TX 77857
81- 85 MOORE, KELVIN ORLANDO                    RR 1 BOX 132 - LEROY AL 36548
36- 60 MOORE, LLOYD ALBERT 'WHITEY'             D. DECEMBER 10, 1987 CANTON, O.
82- 85 MOORE, MICHAEL WAYNE                     2020 RIDGEWAY - WEATHERFORD OK 73096
27- 64 MOORE, RANDOLPH EDWARD                   BOX 757 - OMAHA TX 75571
52- 77 MOORE, RAYMOND LEROY                     6801 DOWER HOUSE ROAD - UPPER MARLBORO MD 20772
65- 77 MOORE, ROBERT BARRY                      RR1 BOX 174 - CLEVELAND NC 27013
85- 78 MOORE, ROBERT DEVELL                     2500 WELLINGTON ROAD - LOS ANGELES CA 90016
20- 86 MOORE, ROY DANIEL                        D. APRIL 5, 1951 SEATTLE, WASH.
35- 72 MOORE, TERRY BLUFORD                     501 RIDGEMONT DR - COLLINSVILLE IL 62234
72- 77 MOORE, TOMMY JOE                         OLD ADD: RR 1 - DEKALB TX 75559
17- 52 MOORE, WILLIAM ALLEN 'SCRAPPY'           D. OCTOBER 13, 1964 LITTLE ROCK, ARK.
29- 74 MOORE, WILLIAM AUSTIN 'CY'               D. MARCH 28, 1972 AUGUSTA, GA.
25- 75 MOORE, WILLIAM CHRISTOPHER               D. JANUARY 24, 1984 CORNING, N. Y.
26- 57 MOORE, WILLIAM HENRY                     D. MAY 24, 1972 KANSAS CITY, MO.
86-106 MOORE, WILLIAM ROSS                      419 NORTH ASTELL AVENUE - WEST COVINA CA 91790
27- 65 MOORE, WILLIAM WILCY                     D. MARCH 29, 1963 HOLLIS, OKLA.
62- 93 MOORHEAD, CHARLES ROBERT 'BOB'           D. DECEMBER 3, 1986 LEMOYNE, PA.
67- 74 MOOSE, ROBERT RALPH                      D. OCTOBER 9, 1976 MARTINS FERRY, O.
36- 61 MOOTY, J. T. 'JAKE'                      D. APRIL 20, 1970 FORT WORTH, TEX.
76- 66 MORA, ANDRES (IBARRA)                    GALEANO 567,PTE. - LOS MOCHIS SINOLOA MEX.
73- 87 MORALES, JOSE MANUEL                     10435 ATRISCO - ORLANDO FL 32817
69-118 MORALES, JULIO RUBEN 'JERRY'             VILLA NUEVA CALLE 16-C5 - CAGUAS PR 00625
67- 75 MORALES, RICHARD ANGELO                  1650 ROSITA RD - PACIFICA CA 94044
38- 67 MORAN, ALBERT THOMAS                     88 CONGRESS ST #109 - SARATOGA SPRINGS NY 12866
74- 91 MORAN, CARL WILLIAM 'BILL'               P.O. BOX 3372,%PALM & PINES - PUNTA GORDA FL 33950
12-134 MORAN, HARRY EDWIN                       D. NOVEMBER 28, 1962 BECKLEY, WEST VA
63- 80 MORAN, RICHARD ALAN 'AL'                 34134 BAMBURY - FARMINGTON HILLS MI 48018
12-135 MORAN, ROY ELLIS                         D. JULY 18, 1966 ATLANTA, GA.
58- 65 MORAN, WILLIAM NELSON                    8245 GLEDSTONE WAY - FAIRBURN GA 30213
24- 82 MOREHART, RAYMOND ANDERSON               D. JANUARY 13, 1989 DALLAS, TEXAS
63- 81 MOREHEAD, DAVID MICHAEL                  1342 TIKI CIR - TUSTIN CA 92680
57- 58 MOREHEAD, SETH MARVIN                    8675 GROVER PLACE - SHREVEPORT LA 71115
58- 66 MOREJON, DANIEL TORRES                   OLD ADD: 4401 SW 117TH AVE - MIAMI FL 33165
78- 85 MORELAND, BOBBY KEITH 'KEITH             1815 MONTGOMERY COURT - DEERFIELD IL 60015
81- 86 MORENO, ANGEL                            GOMEZ FARIAZ #604 - AGUASCALIENTES AGUAS. MEX.
80- 92 MORENO, JOSE DE LOS SANTOS               CORREA Y CIDRON 9 - SANTO DOMINGO DOM. REP.
50- 68 MORENO, JULIO GONZALES                   D. JANUARY 2, 1987 MIAMI, FLA.
75- 84 MORENO, OMAR RENAN                       APTD. #5 BALBOA, NCON - PANAMA CITY PAN.
70- 99 MORET, ROGELIO 'ROGER'                   RR 1 #6742 - GUAYAMA PR 00654
13-127 MOREY, DAVID BEALE                       D. JANUARY 4, 1986 OAK BLUFF, MASS.
35- 73 MORGAN, CHESTER COLLINS                  602 ORIOLE LA-PASADENA TX 77502
21- 69 MORGAN, CYRIL ARLON                      D. SEPTEMBER 11, 1946 LAKEVILLE, MASS.
28- 71 MORGAN, EDWARD CARRE                     D. APRIL 9, 1980 NEW ORLEANS, LA.
36- 62 MORGAN, EDWIN WILLIS                     D. JUNE 27, 1982 LAKEWOOD, O.
63- 82 MORGAN, JOSEPH LEONARD                   5588 FERNHOFF ROAD - OAKLAND CA 94619
59- 59 MORGAN, JOSEPH MICHAEL                   15 OAK HILL DRIVE - WALPOLE MA 02081
78- 86 MORGAN, MICHAEL THOMAS                   2008 JANSEN ST - LAS VEGAS NV 89101
11-122 MORGAN, RAYMOND CARYLL                   D. FEBRUARY 15, 1940 BALTIMORE, MD.
50- 69 MORGAN, ROBERT NORRIS                    2212 BARCLAY RD - OKLAHOMA CITY OK 73120
51- 68 MORGAN, TOM STEPHEN                       D. JANUARY 13, 1987 ANAHEIM, CALIF.
54- 69 MORGAN, VERNON THOMAS                     D. NOVEMBER 8, 1975 MINNEAPOLIS, MINN.
61- 76 MORHARDT, MEREDITH GOODWIN 'MOE'          182 WILLIAMS AVE - WINSTED CT 06098
35- 74 MORIARTY, EDWARD JEROME                   485 SOUTH ST #322 - HOLYOKE MA 01040
73- 88 MORLAN, JOHN GLEN                          2348 SALEM AVE - GROVE CITY OH 43123
13-128 MORLEY, (WILLIAM MORLEY JENNINGS)         D. MAY 14, 1985 LUBBOCK, TEXAS
86-107 MORMAN, RUSSELL LEE                        OLD ADD: 17704 CHEYENNE DRIVE - INDEPENDENCE MO 64056
83-101 MOROGIELLO, DANIEL JOSEPH                  2365 EAST 72ND ST - BROOKLYN NY 11234
84- 82 MORONKO, JEFFREY ROBERT                    OLD ADD: 3637 S. SHAVER #309 - PASADENA TX 77504
26- 58 MORRELL, WILLARD BLACKMER                  D. AUGUST 5, 1975 BIRMINGHAM, ALA.
68- 69 MORRIS, DANNY WALKE                        OLD ADD: 216 WILSON STREET - GREENVILLE KY 42345
37- 79 MORRIS, DOYT THEODORE                      D. JULY 4, 1984 GASTONIA, N. C.
86-108 MORRIS, JOHN DANIEL                        2775 KIPPS COLONY DRIVE #105 - GULFPORT FL 33707
77- 96 MORRIS, JOHN SCOTT 'JACK'                  4705 OLD ORCHARD TRAIL - ORCHARD LAKE MI 48033
66- 65 MORRIS, JOHN WALLACE                       5538 E. PARADISE LN - SCOTTSDALE AZ 85254
22-100 MORRIS, WALTER EDWARD                      D. MARCH 3, 1932 CENTURY, FLA.
88- 97 MORRIS, WILLIAM HAROLD 'HAL'               1111 MACARTHUR BLVD - MUNSTER IN 46321
15-110 MORRISETTE, WILLIAM LEE                    D. MARCH 25, 1966 VIRGINIA BEACH, VA.
77- 97 MORRISON, JAMES FOREST                     11202 VERANDA COURT - BRADENTON FL 33529
20- 87 MORRISON, JOHN DEWEY                       D. MARCH 20, 1966 LEXINGTON, KY.
21- 70 MORRISON, PHILIP MELVIN                    D. JANUARY 18, 1955 LEXINGTON, KY.
27- 66 MORRISON, WALTER GUY                       D. AUGUST 14, 1934 GRAND RAPIDS, MICH.
32- 56 MORRISSEY, JOSEPH ANSELM 'JO-JO'           D. MAY 2, 1950 WORCESTER, MASS.
29- 75 MORSE, NEWELL OBEDIAH 'BUD'                D. APRIL 6, 1987 SPARKS, NEV.
```

101

11-123 MORSE, PETER RAYMOND 'HAP'	D. JUNE 19, 1974 ST. PAUL, MINN.
69-119 MORTON, CARL WENDLE	D. APRIL 12, 1983 TULSA, OKLA.
54- 70 MORTON, GUY JR.	969 BLACHLEYVILLE ROAD - WOOSTER OH 44691
14-159 MORTON, GUY SR.	D. OCTOBER 18, 1934 SHEFFIELD, ALA.
61- 77 MORTON, WYCLIFFE NATHAN 'BUBBA'	7429 TIMBERACK ROAD - FALLS CHURCH VA 22043
54- 71 MORYN, WALTER JOSEPH	OLD ADD: 545 CHARLES COURT - GLENDALE HEIGHTS IL 60137
65- 78 MOSCHITTO, ROSAIRO ALLEN 'ROSS'	32 MORTON ST - GARNERSVILLE NY 10923
80- 93 MOSEBY, LLOYD ANTHONY	3400 KINGMONT DR - LOOMIS CA 95650
13-129 MOSELEY, EARL VICTOR	D. JULY 1, 1963 ALLIANCE, O.
37- 80 MOSER, ARNOLD ROBERT	7714 ANTOINE - HOUSTON TX 77088
65- 79 MOSES, GERALD BRAHEEN	797 TURNPIKE STREET - NORTH ANDOVER MA 01845
82- 86 MOSES, JOHN WILLIAM	5343 EAST LAFAYETTE - PHOENIX AZ 85018
35- 75 MOSES, WALLACE	777 W. GERMANTOWN PIKE - PLYMOUTH MEETING PA 19462
77- 98 MOSKAU, PAUL RICHARD	4152 EAST SECOND ST - TUCSON AZ 85711
10-108 MOSKIMAN, WILLIAM BANKHEAD 'DOC'	D. JANUARY 11, 1953 SAN LEANDRO, CALIF.
29- 76 MOSOLF, JAMES FREDERICK	D. DECEMBER 28, 1979 DALLAS, ORE.
34- 76 MOSS, CHARLES CROSBY	2400 40TH AVENUE - MERIDIAN MS 39305
30- 55 MOSS, CHARLES MALCOLM 'MAL'	D. FEBRUARY 5, 1983 SAVANNAH, GA.
42- 70 MOSS, HOWARD GLENN	D. MAY 7, 1989 BALTIMORE, MD.
46- 76 MOSS, JOHN LESTER 'LES'	420 TULLIS AVE - LONGWOOD FL 32750
26- 59 MOSS, RAYMOND EARL	3734 KINGS RD - CHATTANOOGA TN 37416
54- 72 MOSSI, DONALD LOUIS	1340 SANFORD RANCH RD - UKIAH CA 95482
51- 69 MOSSOR, EARL DALTON	3088 S.R. 222 - BETHEL OH 45106
18- 52 MOSTIL, JOHN ANTHONY	D. DECEMBER 10, 1970 MIDLOTHIAN, ILL.
62- 94 MOTA, MANUEL RAFAEL	3926 LOS OLIVOS LN - LA CRESCENTA CA 91214
81- 87 MOTLEY, DARRYL DEWAYNE	1324 NORTH RESSIT - PORTLAND OR 97201
45- 72 MOTT, ELISHA MATTHEW 'BITSY'	P.O. BOX 294 - BLUE RIDGE GA 30513
67- 76 MOTTON, CURTELL HOWARD	1522 25TH AVE - OAKLAND CA 94601
46- 77 MOULDER, GLEN HUBERT	2946 LAVISTA CT - DECATUR GA 30083
11-124 MOULTON, ALBERT THEODORE 'OLLIE'	D. JULY 10, 1968 PEABODY, MASS.
13-130 MOWE, RAYMOND BENJAMIN	D. AUGUST 14, 1968 SARASOTA, FLA.
33- 44 MOWRY, JOSEPH ALOYSIUS	6321 BANCROFT - ST LOUIS MO 63109
10-109 MOYER, CHARLES EDWARD	D. NOVEMBER 18, 1962 JACKSONVILLE, FLA.
86-109 MOYER, JAMIE	409 NORTH FOURTH STREET - SOUDERTON PA 18964
54- 73 MROZINSKI, RONALD FRANK	WASH. ARMS BLDG 100 #D2 - WASHINGTON NJ 07882
63- 83 MUDROCK, PHILIP RAY	2548 EAST 6600 SOUTH-SALT LAKE CITY UT 84121
20- 88 MUELLER, CLARENCE FRANCIS 'HEINIE'	D. JANUARY 23, 1975 DESOTO, MO.
48- 74 MUELLER, DONALD FREDERICK	11224 MUELLER LANE - MARYLAND HEIGHTS MO 63043
38- 68 MUELLER, EMMETT JEROME 'HEINIE'	D. OCTOBER 3, 1986 ORLANDO, FLA.
50- 70 MUELLER, JOSEPH GORDON 'GORDY'	1404 CHESAPEAKE AVE - MIDDLE RIVER MD 21220
41- 76 MUELLER, LESLIE CLYDE	RR 2 BOX 294 - MILLSTADT IL 62260
35- 76 MUELLER, RAY COLEMAN	3205 BROOKFIELD ROAD - HARRISBURG PA 17109
22-101 MUELLER, WALTER JOHN	D. AUGUST 16, 1971 ST. LOUIS, MO.
78- 87 MUELLER, WILLARD LAWRENCE 'WILLIE'	1246 WALLACE LAKE - WEST BEND WI 53095
42- 71 MUELLER, WILLIAM LAWRENCE	1401 BRAEBURN - WHEELING IL 60090
57- 59 MUFFETT, BILLY ARNOLD	5655 ALDINGBROOKE TRIANGLE - WEST BLOOMFIELD MI 48322
24- 83 MUICH, IGNATIUS ANDREW	OLD ADD: 9244 LODGE POLE LN - ST. LOUIS MO 63126
51- 70 MUIR, JOSEPH ALLEN	D. JUNE 25, 1980 BALTIMORE, MD.
35- 77 MULCAHY, HUGH NOYES	175 WAYNE ST - BEAVER PA 15009
86-110 MULHOLLAND, TERENCE JOHN	339 DERRICK AVENUE - UNIONTOWN PA 15401
30- 56 MULLEAVY, GREGORY THOMAS	D. FEBRUARY 1, 1980 ARCADIA, CALIF.
10-110 MULLEN, CHARLES GEORGE	D. JUNE 6, 1963 SEATTLE, WASH.
44- 95 MULLEN, FORD PARKER	7127 MULLEN RD SE - OLYMPIA WA 98503
20- 89 MULLEN, WILLIAM JOHN	D. MAY 4, 1971 ST. LOUIS, MO.
33- 45 MULLER, FREDERICK WILLIAM	D. OCTOBER 20, 1976 DAVIS, CALIF.
15-111 MULLIGAN, EDWARD JOSEPH	D. MARCH 15, 1982 SAN RAFAEL, CALIF.
34- 77 MULLIGAN, JOSEPH IGNATIUS	D. JUNE 5, 1986 WEST ROXBURY, MASS.
41- 77 MULLIGAN, RICHARD CHARLES	1205 EAST WALNUT AVENUE - VICTORIA TX 77901
40- 65 MULLIN, PATRICK JOSEPH	320 CHURCH ST - BROWNSVILLE PA 15417
77- 99 MULLINIKS, STEVEN RANCE 'RANCE'	1560 HERITAGE - PORTERVILLE CA 93257
80- 94 MULLINS, FRANCIS JOSEPH	6180 BROADWAY TERRACE - OAKLAND CA 94618
21- 71 MULRENAN, DOMINICK JOSEPH	D. JULY 27, 1964 MELROSE, MASS.
30- 57 MULRONEY, FRANCIS JOSEPH	D. NOVEMBER 11, 1985 ABERDEEN, WASH.
74- 92 MUMPHREY, JERRY WAYNE	3913 SILVERWOOD - TYLER TX 75701
18- 53 MUNCH, JACOB FERDINAND	D. JUNE 8, 1966 LANSDOWNE, PA.
37- 81 MUNCRIEF, ROBERT CLEVELAND	731 RIDGE CREST - DUNCANVILLE TX 75116
13-131 MUNDY, WILLIAM EDWARD	D. SEPTEMBER 23, 1958 KALAMAZOO, MICH.
43- 96 MUNGER, GEORGE DAVID 'RED'	10121 WINDMILL LAKES BLVD #1407 - HOUSTON TX 77075
31- 61 MUNGO, VAN LINGLE	D. FEBRUARY 12, 1985 PAGELAND, S. C.
71- 73 MUNIZ, MANUEL	CALLE 23-R-12 VILLA NUEVA - CAGUAS PR 00626
80- 95 MUNNINGHOFF, SCOTT ANDREW	1028 PARADROME STREET #1 - CINCINNATI OH 45202
34- 78 MUNNS, LESLIE ERNEST	236 EAST 5TH - WAHOO NE 68066
89- 87 MUNOZ, MICHAEL ANTHONY	2717 ELENA AVENUE - WEST COVINA CA 91792
25- 76 MUNSON, JOSEPH MARTIN NAPOLEON	7274 LAMPORT RD - UPPER DARBY PA 19082
69-120 MUNSON, THURMAN LEE	D. AUGUST 2, 1979 AKRON-CANTON AIRPORT, O.
78- 88 MURA, STEPHEN ANDREW	31892 OLD OAK ROAD - TRABUCO CANYON CA 92679
64- 76 MURAKAMI, MASANORI	1-4-15-1506,NISHO OHI SHINAGAWA - TOKYO JAPAN
65- 80 MURCER, BOBBY RAY	3244 WHIPPOORWILL ROAD - OKLAHOMA CITY OK 73120
17- 53 MURCHISON, THOMAS MALCOM 'TIM'	D. OCTOBER 20, 1962 LIBERTY, N. C.
56- 62 MURFF, JOHN ROBERT "RED"	1005 LAWNDALE - BRENHAM TX 77833
76- 67 MURPHY, DALE BRIAN	12055 HOUZE ROAD - ROSWELL GA 30076
60- 73 MURPHY, DANIEL FRANCIS	33 STONE STREET - BEVERLY MA 01915
89- 88 MURPHY, DANIEL LEE	18516 MARIMBA STREET - ROWLAND HEIGHTS CA 91748
78- 89 MURPHY, DWAYNE KEITH	1132 "W" AVENUE #H6 - LANCASTER CA 93534
42- 72 MURPHY, EDWARD JOSEPH	1319 JEFFERSON STREET - JOLIET IL 60435
14-160 MURPHY, HERBERT COURTLAND 'DUMMY'	D. AUGUST 10, 1962 TALLAHASSEE, FLA.
12-136 MURPHY, JOHN EDWARD	D. FEBRUARY 20, 1969 DUNMORE, PA.
32- 57 MURPHY, JOHN JOSEPH	D. JANUARY 14, 1970 NEW YORK, N. Y.
15-112 MURPHY, LEO JOSEPH	D. AUGUST 12, 1960 RACINE, WIS.
12-137 MURPHY, MICHAEL JEROME	D. OCTOBER 26, 1952 JOHNSON CITY, N.Y.
54- 74 MURPHY, RICHARD LEE	7114 MIAMI HILLS DR - CINCINNATI OH 45243
85- 79 MURPHY, ROBERT ALBERT	P.O. BOX 1600 - MIAMI FL 33143
18- 54 MURPHY, ROBERT R. 'BUZZ'	D. MAY 11, 1938 DENVER, COLO.
68- 70 MURPHY, THOMAS ANDREW	26566 CALLE LORENZO - SAN JUAN CAPISTRANO CA 92675
31- 62 MURPHY, WALTER JOSEPH	16123 AMBERWOOD - DALLAS TX 75248
66- 66 MURPHY, WILLIAM EUGENE	10214 88TH AVE SW - TACOMA WA 98498
36- 63 MURRAY, AMBROSE JOSEPH	8297 SE COCONUT ST - HOBO SOUND FL 33455
23- 96 MURRAY, ANTHONY JOHN	D. MARCH 19, 1974 CHICAGO, ILL.

74- 93 MURRAY, DALE ALBERT	RR 2 BOX 1850 - YORKTOWN TX 78164
77-100 MURRAY, EDDIE CLARENCE	13401 BLYTHENIA ROAD - PHOENIX MD 21131
17- 54 MURRAY, EDWARD FRANCIS	D. NOVEMBER 8, 1970 CHEYENNE, WYO.
22-102 MURRAY, GEORGE KING	D. OCTOBER 18, 1955 MEMPHIS, TENN.
22-103 MURRAY, JAMES FRANCIS	D. JULY 15, 1973 NEW YORK , N. Y.
50- 71 MURRAY, JOSEPH AMBROSE	2719 VIA SANTA TOMAS - SAN CLEMEMTE CA 92672
74- 94 MURRAY, LARRY	OLD ADD: 3544 SOUTH CALUMET AVE - CHICAGO IL 60653
19- 58 MURRAY, PATRICK JOSEPH	D. NOVEMBER 5, 1983 ROCHESTER, N. Y.
48- 75 MURRAY, RAYMOND LEE	BOX 453 - KENNEDALE TX 76060
80- 96 MURRAY, RICHARD DALE	435 EAST 108TH ST - LOS ANGELES CA 90061
23- 97 MURRAY, ROBERT HAYES	D. JANUARY 4, 1979 NASHUA, N. H.
17- 55 MURRAY, WILLIAM ALLENWOOD	D. SEPTEMBER 14, 1943 BOSTON, MASS.
63- 84 MURRELL, IVAN AUGUSTE	OLD ADD: 279 OCEAN AVE $1C - BROOKLYN NY 11226
41- 78 MURTAUGH, DANIEL EDWARD	D. DECEMBER 2, 1976 CHESTER PA.
69-121 MUSER, ANTHONY JOSEPH	11222 MARTHA ANN DR - LOS ALAMITOS CA 90720
65- 81 MUSGRAVES, DENNIS EUGENE	RR FOUR - CENTRALLIA MO 65240
41- 79 MUSIAL, STANLEY FRANK	85 TRENT DR - LADUE MO 63124
86-111 MUSSELMAN, JEFFREY JOSEPH	105 BRICK AVENUE - LANOKA HARBOR NJ 08734
82- 87 MUSSELMAN, RALPH RICHARD	5313 AUTUMN DR - WILMINGTON NC 28401
12-138 MUSSER, PAUL	D. JULY 7, 1973 STATE COLLEGE, PA.
32- 58 MUSSER, WILLIAM DANIEL 'DANNY'	1062 HOMEWOOD CT - DECATUR GA 30033
44- 96 MUSSILL, BERNARD JAMES 'BARNEY'	912 MOORLAND DR -GROSSE POINTE WOODS MI 48236
40- 66 MUSTAIKIS, ALEXANDER DOMINICK	D. JANUARY 17, 1970 SCRANTON, PA.
38- 69 MYATT, GEORGE EDWARD	1623 CANTON AVE-ORLANDO FL 32803
20- 90 MYATT, GLENN CALVIN	D. AUGUST 9, 1969 HOUSTON, TEX.
25- 77 MYER, CHARLES SOLOMON 'BUDDY'	D. OCTOBER 31, 1974 BATON ROUGE, LA.
15-113 MYERS, ELMER GLENN	D. JULY 29, 1976 COLLINGSWOOD, N. J.
87-102 MYERS, GREGORY RICHARD	2815 SHENANDOAH ROAD - RIVERSIDE CA 92506
38- 70 MYERS, LINNWOOD LINCOLN	1111 YVERDON DR #C1 - CAMP HILL PA 17011
10-111 MYERS, RALPH EDWARD 'HAP'	D. JUNE 30, 1967 SAN FRANCISCO, CALIF.
85- 80 MYERS, RANDALL KIRK	P.O. BOX 9900 SUITE 155 - VANCOUVER WA 98668
56- 63 MYERS, RICHARD	5400 SAMPSON BLVD - SACRAMENTO CA 95820
35- 78 MYERS, WILLIAM HARRISON	204 SALT RD-ENOLA PA 17025
76- 68 MYRICK, ROBERT HOWARD	1923 ADELINE STREET - HATTIESBURG MS 39401
15-114 NABORS, HERMAN JOHN 'JACK'	D. OCTOBER 29, 1923 WILTON, ALA.
39- 79 NAGEL, WILLIAM TAYLOR	D. OCTOBER 8, 1981 FREEHOLD, N. J.
12-139 NAGELSON, LOUIS MARCELLUS	D. OCTOBER 22, 1965 FORT WAYNE, IND.
68- 71 NAGELSON, RUSSELL CHARLES	ONE POWDERDHORN CT - LITTLE ROCK AR 72212
11-125 NAGLE, WALTER HAROLD 'JUDGE'	D. MAY 27, 1971 SANTA ROSA, CALIF.
69-122 NAGY, MICHAEL TIMOTHY	8 INDIAN TRAIL - BRONX NY 10465
47- 64 NAGY, STEPHEN	3435 63RD AVE SW - SEATTLE WA 98116
38- 71 NAHEM, SAMUEL RALPH	624 VINCENTE - BERKELEY CA 94704
76- 69 NAHORODNY, WILLIAM GERARD	204 SOUTH COMET - CLEARWATER FL 33515
36- 64 NAKTENIS, PETER ERNEST	125 ADELAIDE RD - MANCHESTER CT 06041
24- 84 NALEWAY, FRANK	D. JANUARY 28, 1949 CHICAGO, ILL.
12-140 NAPIER, SKELTON LEROY 'BUDDY'	D. MARCH 29, 1968 DALLAS, TEX.
49- 57 NAPLES, ALOYSIUS FRANK	OLD ADD: 52 RODGERS COURT - WYCKOFF NJ 07481
65- 82 NAPOLEON, DANIEL	OLD ADD: 116 OLIVE AVE - TRENTON NJ
51- 71 NARAGON, HAROLD RICHARD	1521 HAGEY DR - BARBERTON OH 44203
56- 64 NARANJO, LAZARO RAMON GONZALO	D #270, 10 Y 11 - LAWTON, HAVANA CUBA
54- 75 NARLESKI, RAYMOND EDMOND	1183 CHEWS LANDING RD-LAUREL SPRINGS NJ 08021
29- 77 NARLESKI, WILLIAM EDWARD	D. JULY 22, 1964 LAUREL SPRINGS, N. J.
79- 76 NARRON, JERRY AUSTIN	113 MARIE AVENUE - GOLDSBORO NC 27530
35- 79 NARRON, SAMUEL	RR 1 BOX 125 - MIDDLESEX NC 27557
63- 85 NARUM, LESLIE FERDINAND 'BUSTER'	324 SOUTH GLENWOOD AVE - CLEARWATER FL 33515
67- 77 NASH, CHARLES FRANCIS 'COTTON'	600 SUMMERSHADE CIR - LEXINGTON KY 40502
66- 67 NASH, JAMES EDWIN	37 REGINA DR NE - MARIETTA GA 30067
12-141 NASH, KENNETH LELAND	D. FEBRUARY 16, 1977 EPSOM, N. H.
78- 90 NASTU, PHILIP	119 AUSTIN ST - BRIDGEPORT CT 06604
53- 62 NATON, PETER ALPHONSUS	4136 SPLIT ROCK RD - CAMILLUS NY 13031
89- 89 NAVARRO, JAIME (CINTRON)	ST. 3 B-10 NO. 32, SANTA ROSA - BAYAMON PR 00619
62- 95 NAVARRO, JULIO VENTURA	CALLE 3, BLOQUE 10, #32 - SANTA ROSA, BAYAMON PR 00619
42- 73 NAYLOR, EARL EUGENE	D. JANUARY 16, 1990 WINTER HAVEN, FLA.
17- 56 NAYLOR, ROLEINE CECIL	D. JUNE 18, 1966 FORT WORTH, TEX.
39- 80 NAYMICK, MICHAEL JOHN	8334 BERWICK WAY - STOCKTON CA 95210
56- 65 NEAL, CHARLES LENARD	7251 BAYBERRY LANE - DALLAS TX 75249
16- 64 NEALE, ALFRED EARLE 'GREASY'	D. NOVEMBER 2, 1973 LAKE WORTH, FL.
52- 78 NECCIAI, RONALD ANDREW	201 ROSEWOOD DR - MONONGAHELA PA 15063
57- 60 NEEMAN, CALVIN AMANDUS	93 CHAMPAGNE - LAKE ST. LOUIS MO 63367
14-161 NEFF, DOUGLAS WILLIAM	D. MAY 23, 1932 CAPE CHARLES, VA.
52- 79 NEGRAY, RONALD ALVIN	587 WEST NIMISLIA RD - AKRON OH 44319
12-142 NEHER, JAMES GILMORE	D. NOVEMBER 11, 1951 BUFFALO, N.Y.
15-115 NEHF, ARTHUR NEUKOM	D. DECEMBER 18, 1960 PHOENIX, ARIZ.
69-123 NEIBAUER, GARY WAYNE	7110 VAN DORN #89 - LINCOLN NE 68506
60- 74 NEIGER, ALVIN EDWARD	213 PINEHURST RD - WILMINTON OH 19803
39- 81 NEIGHBORS, ROBERT OTIS	D. AUGUST 8, 1952 NORTH KOREA
46- 78 NEILL, THOMAS WHITE	OLD ADD: 1526 HIDDEN HILL - HOUSTON TX 77064
20- 91 NEIS, BERNARD EDMUND	D. NOVEMBER 29, 1972 INVERNESS, FLA.
29- 78 NEKOLA, FRANCIS JOSEPH 'BOTS'	D. MARCH 11, 1987 ROCKVILLE CENTRE, N. Y.
10-112 NELSON, ALBERT FRANCIS 'RED'	D. OCTOBER 26, 1956 ST PETERSBURG, FLA.
68- 72 NELSON, DAVID EARL	3660 NORTH LAKE SHORE DR #4213 - CHICAGO IL 60613
35- 80 NELSON, GEORGE EMMETT	D. AUGUST 25, 1967 SIOUX FALLS, S. D.
49- 58 NELSON, GLENN ALBERT 'ROCKY'	BOX 35 - PORTSMOUTH OH 45662
70-100 NELSON, JAMES LORIN	671 6TH AVENUE - SACRAMENTO CA 95818
83-102 NELSON, JAMES VICTOR	OLD ADD: 16901 SIMS - HUNTINGTON BEACH CA 92649
19- 59 NELSON, LUTHER MARTIN	D. NOVEMBER 14, 1985 MOLINE, ILL.
30- 58 NELSON, LYNN BERNARD	D. FEBRUARY 15, 1955 KANSAS CITY, MO.
60- 75 NELSON, MELVIN FREDERICK	27420 FISHER ST - HIGHLAND CA 92346
83-103 NELSON, RICKY LEE	7250 SOUTH 46TH ST - PHOENIX AZ 85040
86-112 NELSON, ROBERT AUGUSTUS	312 ALTA VISTA AVENUE - SOUTH PASADENA CA 91030
55- 85 NELSON, ROBERT SIDNEY	10830 WALLBROOK - DALLAS TX 75238
67- 78 NELSON, ROGER EUGENE	OLD ADD: 533 WINDSOR - ARCADIA CA 91006
45- 73 NELSON, TOM COUSINEAU	D. SEPTEMBER 24, 1973 SAN DIEGO, CAL.
81- 88 NELSON, WAYLAND EUGENE 'GENE'	BOX 458 - LACOOCHIE FL 33537
63- 86 NEN, RICHARD LEROY	7122 ORANGETHORPE - BUENA PARK CA 90621
11-126 NESS, JOHN CHARLES	D. DECEMBER 3, 1957 DELAND, FLA.
67- 79 NETTLES, GRAIG	13 NORTH LANE - DEL MAR CA 92014
70-101 NETTLES, JAMES WILLIAM	4632 DARIEN DR - TACOMA WA 98407

74- 95	NETTLES, MORRIS	551 1/2 SAN JUAN - VENICE CA 90291
17- 58	NEU, OTTO ADAM	D. SEPTEMBER 19, 1932 KENTON, O.
25- 78	NEUBAUER, HAROLD CHARLES	D. SEPTEMBER 9, 1949 PROVIDENCE, R. I.
72- 78	NEUMEIER, DANIEL GEORGE	N2635 CITY HIGHWAY U - LODI WI 53555
25- 79	NEUN, JOHN HENRY	D. MARCH 28, 1990 BALTIMORE, MD.
50- 72	NEVEL, ERNIE WYRE	D. JULY 10, 1988 SPRINGFIELD, MO.
26- 60	NEVERS, ERNEST ALONZO	D. MAY 3, 1976 SAN RAFAEL, CALIF.
49- 59	NEWCOMBE, DONALD	22507 PEALE DR - WOODLAND HILLS CA 91364
87-103	NEWELL, THOMAS DEAN	1401 LEONARD - GARDNERVILLE NV 89410
72- 79	NEWHAUSER, DONALD LOUIS	321 SHERYL DR - DELTONA FL 32738
39- 82	NEWHOUSER, HAROLD	2584 MARCY-BLOOMFIELD HILLS MI 48013
34- 79	NEWKIRK, FLOYD ELMO	D. APRIL 15, 1976 CLAYTON, MO.
19- 60	NEWKIRK, JOEL IVAN	D. JANUARY 22, 1966 ELDORADO, ILL.
40- 67	NEWLIN, MAURICE MILTON	D. AUGUST 14, 1978 HOUSTON, TEXAS
85- 81	NEWMAN, ALBERT DWAYNE	1044 LARODA - ONTARIO CA 91761
62- 96	NEWMAN, FREDERICK WILLIAM	D. JUNE 24, 1987 FRAMINGHAM, MASS.
76- 70	NEWMAN, JEFFREY LYNN	537 QUIVIRA CT - DANVILLE CA 94526
71- 74	NEWMAN, RAYMOND FRANCIS	1361 HOWARD - MUSKEGON MI 49442
10-113	NEWNAM, PATRICK HENRY	D. JUNE 20, 1938 SAN ANTONIO, TEX.
29- 79	NEWSOM, NORMAN LOUIS 'BOBO'	D. DECEMBER 7, 1962 ORLANDO, FLA.
41- 80	NEWSOME, HEBER HAMPTON 'DICK'	D. DECEMBER 15, 1965 AHOSKIE, N. C.
35- 81	NEWSOME, LAMAR ASHBY 'SKEETER'	1626 17TH AVE-COLUMBUS GA 31901
46- 79	NIARHOS, CONSTANTINE GREGORY 'GUS'	244 MONUMENT AVE - HARRISONBURG VA 22801
52- 80	NICHOLAS, DONALD LEIGH	12311 CHASE - GARDEN GROVE CA 92645
86-113	NICHOLS, CARL EDWARD	2603 BILLINGS STREET - COMPTON CA 90220
26- 61	NICHOLS, CHESTER RAYMOND SR.	D. JULY 11, 1982 PAWTUCKET, R. I.
51- 72	NICHOLS, CHESTER RAYMOND JR	18 COLONIAL DR - LINCOLN RI 02865
58- 67	NICHOLS, DOLAN LEVON	D. NOVEMBER 20, 1989 TUPELO, MISS.
88- 98	NICHOLS, RODNEY LEA	OLD ADD: 7612 TRAIL RIDGE RD NE - ALBUQUERQUE NM 87109
44- 97	NICHOLS, ROY	104 ARIAS WAY - HOT SPRINGS VILLAGE AR 71901
80- 97	NICHOLS, THOMAS REID 'REID'	721 COUNTRY VIEW COURT - BIRMINGHAM AL 35215
60- 76	NICHOLSON, DAVID LAWRENCE	527 SPRINGINGSGUTH - ROSELLE IL 60172
12-143	NICHOLSON, FRANK COLLINS	D. NOVEMBER 11, 1972 JERSEY SHORE, PA.
17- 57	NICHOLSON, FREDERICK	D. JANUARY 23, 1972 KILGORE, TEXAS
12-144	NICHOLSON, OVID EDWARD	D. MARCH 24, 1968 SALEM, IND.
36- 65	NICHOLSON, WILLIAM BECK	RR 3 - CHESTERTOWN MD 21620
78- 91	NICOSIA, STEVEN RICHARD	8520 HW FIFTH STREET - PEMBROKE PINES FL 33024
21- 73	NIEBERGALL, CHARLES ARTHUR 'NIG'	D. AUGUST 29, 1982 HOLIDAY, FLA.
81- 89	NIEDENFUER, THOMAS EDWARD	9849 DENBIGH DRIVE - BEVERLY HILLS CA 90210
25- 80	NIEHAUS, ALBERT BERNARD	D. OCTOBER 14, 1931 CINCINNATI, O.
13-132	NIEHAUS, RICHARD J.	D. MARCH 12, 1957 ATLANTA, GA.
13-133	NIEHOFF, JOHN ALBERT	D. DECEMBER 8, 1974 INGLEWOOD, CALIF.
67- 80	NIEKRO, JOSEPH FRANKLIN	39 SHADOW LANE - LAKELAND FL 33813
64- 77	NIEKRO, PHILIP HENRY	6382 NICHOLS ROAD - FLOWERY BRANCH GA 30542
86-114	NIELSEN, JEFFREY SCOTT	11910 28TH AVENUE EAST - TACOMA WA 98445
49- 60	NIELSON, MILTON ROBERT	824 MCGILL - ST PETER MN 56082
43- 97	NIEMAN, ELMER LEROY 'BUTCH'	1324 BOSWELL AVE-TOPEKA KS 66604
51- 73	NIEMAN, ROBERT CHARLES	D. MARCH 10, 1985 CORONA, CALIF.
79- 77	NIEMANN, RANDAL HAROLD	233 VALLEY AVENUE - FORTUNA CA 95540
43- 98	NIEMES, JACOB LELAND 'JACK'	D. MARCH 4, 1966 HAMILTON, O.
34- 80	NIEMIEC, ALFRED JOSEPH	BOX 467 - KIRKLAND WA 98033
64- 78	NIESON, CHARLES BASSETT	3209 WEST HIGHLAND DR - BURNSVILLE MN 55374
84- 83	NIETO, THOMAS ANDREW	18002 HORST AVE - ARTESIA CA 90701
21- 72	NIETZKE, ERNEST FREDRICH	D. APRIL 27, 1977 SYLVANIA, O.
86-115	NIEVES, JUAN MANUEL	OLD ADD: 500 OLD FARMS ROAD - AVON CT 06001
38- 72	NIGGELING, JOHN ARNOLD	D. SEPTEMBER 16, 1963 LEMARS, IA.
83-104	NIPPER, ALBERT SAMUEL	5105 VILLE MARIA LANE - HAZELWOOD MO 63042
62- 97	NIPPERT, MERLIN LEE	1015 NORTH MICHIGAN ST - MANGUM OK 73554
61- 78	NISCHWITZ, RONALD LEE	6790 GARBER RD - DAYTON OH 45415
45- 74	NITCHOLAS, OTHO JAMES	1500 ERWIN - MCKINNEY TX 75069
15-116	NIXON, ALBERT RICHARD	D. NOVEMBER 9, 1960 OPELOUSAS, LA.
83-105	NIXON, OTIS JUNIOR	BOX 23 HIGHWAY 74 - EVERGREEN NC 28438
87-104	NIXON, ROBERT DONELL	P.O. BOX 23, OLD HWY 74 - EVERGREEN NC 28438
57- 61	NIXON, RUSSELL EUGENE	BOX 1446 - COVINGTON GA 30209
50- 73	NIXON, WILLARD LEE	OLD ADD: RR 2,335 REECEBURG SE - SILVER CREEK GA 30173
51- 74	NOBLE, RAFAEL MIGUEL 'RAY'	698 CHAUNCEY ST - BROOKLYN NY 11207
84- 84	NOBOA, MILCIADES ARTURO 'JUNIOR'	OLD ADD: EVA MARIA PELLERANO,CASTRO #1-SANTO DOMINGO DR
87-105	NOCE, PAUL DAVID	913 WEST MAUMEE - ADRIAN MI 49221
85- 82	NOKES, MATTHEW DODGE	13011 AVENIDA LA VALENCIA - POWAY CA 92064
67- 81	NOLAN, GARY LYNN	5825 WEST ROCHELLE #204 - LAS VEGAS NV 89103
72- 80	NOLAN, JOSEPH WILLIAM	9515 ALIX DR - MEHLVILLE MO 63123
67- 82	NOLD, RICHARD LOUIS	121 PARK PLAZA DR #6 - DALY CITY CA 94015
79- 78	NOLES, DICKIE RAY	BOX 7575 - PHILADELPHIA PA 19101
87-106	NOLTE, ERIC CARL	682 SEVILLE DRIVE - HEMET CA 92343
33- 46	NONNENKAMP, LEO WILLIAM 'RED'	1 OAKWOOD RD - LITTLE ROCK AR 72202
74- 96	NORDBROOK, TIMOTHY CHARLES	OLD ADD: 302 LORI DRIVE #L - GLEN BURNIE MD 21061
76- 71	NORDHAGEN, WAYNE OREN	25896 RAMILLO WAY - VALENCIA CA 91355
50- 74	NOREN, IRVING ARNOLD	3215 VALLEY GLEN ROAD - OCEANSIDE CA 92056
69-124	NORIEGA, JOHN ALAN	2 EAST 900 SOUTH - KAYSVILLE UT 84037
77-101	NORMAN, DANIEL EDMUND	1336 MESA DR - BARSTOW CA 92311
62- 98	NORMAN, FREDIE ROBERT	OLD ADD: 6560 BAYWOOD LANE - CINCINNATI OH 45224
31- 63	NORMAN, HENRY WILLIS PATRICK 'BILL'	D. APRIL 21, 1962 MILWAUKEE, WIS.
78- 92	NORMAN, NELSON AUGUSTO	EMILIO MOREL #54 - SAN PEDRO DE MACORIS DOM. REP.
77-102	NORRIS, JAMES FRANCIS	5524 MANSFIELD RD - ARLINGTON TX 76017
36- 66	NORRIS, LEO JOHN	D. FEBRUARY 13, 1987 ZACHARY, LA.
75- 85	NORRIS, MICHAEL KELVIN	1003 IMPERIAL DR - HAYWARD CA 94541
13-134	NORTH, LOUIS ALEXANDER	D. MAY 16, 1974 SHELTON, CONN.
71- 75	NORTH, WILLIAM ALEX	OLD ADD: 3303 E. MADISON - SEATTLE WA 98102
10-114	NORTHEN, HUBBARD ELWIN	D. OCTOBER 1, 1947 SHREVEPORT, LA.
42- 74	NORTHEY, RONALD JAMES	D. APRIL 16, 1971 PITTSBURGH, PA.
69-125	NORTHEY, SCOTT RICHARD	OLD ADD: 481 RIVIERA BLVD WEST - NAPLES FL
18- 55	NORTHROP, GEORGE HOWARD 'JAKE'	D. NOVEMBER 16, 1945 MONROETON, PA.
64- 79	NORTHRUP, JAMES THOMAS	1326 OTTER DR - PONTIAC MI 48054
72- 81	NORTON, THOMAS JOHN	4900 SOUTHWOOD - SHEFFIELD LAKES OH 44054
77-103	NORWOOD, WILLIE	17721 NORWALK BLVD #50 - ARTESIA CA 90701
89- 90	NOSEK, RANDALL WILLIAM	1025 ARCADIA ROAD - CHILLICOTHE MO 64601
64- 80	NOSSEK, JOSEPH RUDOLPH	437 TERRA LN - AMHERST OH 44001
60- 77	NOTTEBART, DONALD EDWARD	ROUTE 153 BOX 42 - EAST WAKEFIELD NH 03830

Luis
Aparicio

1984 HALL OF FAME INDUCTION

This page features the five players who were inducted into the Hall of Fame in 1984 on their autographed Perez-Steele Art Post Cards — Aparicio, Drysdale, Ferrell, Killebrew and Reese

Don
Drysdale

Harmon
Killebrew

Rick
Ferrell

Pee Wee
Reese

41- 81 NOVIKOFF, LOUIE ALEXANDER	D. SEPTEMBER 30, 1970 SOUTH GATE, CAL.
49- 61 NOVOTNEY, RALPH JOSEPH 'RUBE'	2311 WEST 165TH ST - TORRANCE CA 90504
13-135 NOYES, WINFIELD CHARLES	D. APRIL 8, 1969 CASHMERE, WASH.
11-127 NUNAMAKER, LESLIE GRANT	D. NOVEMBER 14, 1938 HASTINGS, NEB.
82- 88 NUNEZ, EDWIN	OLD ADD: BO. RIO ABAJO BUZON 2762 - HUMACAO PR 00661
87-107 NUNEZ, JOSE	MAURICIO BAEZ #40 VILLA JUANA - SANTO DOMINGO DOM. REP.
59- 60 NUNN, HOWARD RALPH	RR1 - WESTFIELD NC 27053
19- 61 NUTTER, EVERETT CLARENCE 'DIZZY'	D. JULY 25, 1958 BATTLE CREEK, MICH.
44- 98 NUXHALL, JOSEPH HENRY	5706 LINDENWOOD LN - FAIRFIELD OH 45014
66- 68 NYE, RICHARD RAYMOND	1923 S. MANNHEIM RD - WESTCHESTER IL 60153
82- 89 NYMAN, CHRISTOPHER CURTIS	719 FLORENCE STREET - NOKOMIS FL 33555
68- 73 NYMAN, GERALD SMITH	P.O. BOX 153 - MOUNTAIN CITY NV 89831
74- 97 NYMAN, NYLS WALLACE REX	300 KEOKUK - LINCOLN IL 62656
34- 81 OANA, HENRY KAUHANE 'PRINCE'	D. JUNE 19, 1976 AUSTIN, TEX.
70-102 OATES, JOHNNY LANE	1704 LAKE AVE - WILMETTE IL 60091
77-104 OBERKFELL, KENNETH RAY	305 SOUTH DONK ST - MARYVILLE IL 62062
79- 79 OBERRY, PRESTON MICHAEL 'MIKE'	1100 DEARING DOWNS DR - HELENA AL 35017
78- 93 OBRADOVICH, JAMES THOMAS	1853B CHATSWORTH - LEXINGTON KY 40505
85- 83 OBRIEN, CHARLES HUGH	4932 EAST 38TH PLACE - TULSA OK 74135
78- 94 OBRIEN, DANIEL JOGUES	9930 BROADMOOR #4 - SAINT LOUIS MO 63114
53- 63 OBRIEN, EDWARD JOSEPH	3414 108TH PL NE #1 - BELLEVUE WA 98004
23- 98 OBRIEN, FRANK ALOYSIUS 'MICKEY'	D. NOVEMBER 4, 1971 MONTEREY PARK, CAL.
15-117 OBRIEN, GEORGE JOSEPH	D. MARCH 24, 1966 COLUMBUS, O.
53- 64 OBRIEN, JOHN THOMAS	938 21ST ST EAST - SEATTLE WA 98112
82- 90 OBRIEN, PETER MICHAEL	BOX 1037 - PEBBLE BEACH CA 93953
16- 65 OBRIEN, RAYMOND JOSEPH	D. MARCH 31, 1942 ST. LOUIS, MO.
71- 76 OBRIEN, ROBERT ALLEN	3628 NORTH SHIRLEY - FRESNO CA 93727
69-126 OBRIEN, SYDNEY LLOYD	9646 BLOOMFIELD - CYPRESS CA 90630
43- 99 OBRIEN, THOMAS EDWARD	D. NOVEMBER 5, 1978 ANNISTON, ALA.
11-128 OBRIEN, THOMAS JOSEPH 'BUCK'	D. JULY 25, 1959 BOSTON, MASS.
35- 82 OCK, HAROLD DAVID 'WHITEY'	D. MARCH 18, 1975 MOUNT KISCO, N. Y.
44- 99 OCKEY, WALTER ANDREW	D. DECEMBER 4, 1971 STATEN ISLAND, N.Y.
50- 75 OCONNELL, DANIEL FRANCIS	D. OCTOBER 2, 1969 CLIFTON, N. J.
23- 99 OCONNELL, JAMES JOSEPH	D. NOVEMBER 11, 1976 BAKERSFIELD, CALIF.
28- 72 OCONNELL, JOHN CHARLES	1611 19TH ST NE - CANTON OH 44714
81- 90 OCONNOR, JACK WILLIAM	BOX 430 - YUCCA VALLEY CA 92284
16- 66 OCONNOR, JOHN CHARLES	D. MAY 30, 1982 BONNER SPRINGS, KAN.
35- 83 ODEA, JAMES KENNETH 'KEN'	D. DECEMBER 17, 1985 LIMA, N. Y.
44-100 ODEA, PAUL	D. DECEMBER 11, 1978 CLEVELAND, O.
54- 76 ODELL, WILLIAM OLIVER	RR 1 BOX 60 - NEWBERRY SC 29108
21- 74 ODENWALD, THEODORE JOSEPH	D. OCTOBER 23, 1965 SHAKOPEE, MINN.
43-100 ODOM, DAVID EVERETT	5705 BROOKS LANE - GREENSBORO NC 27410
25- 81 ODOM, HERMAN BOYD 'HEINIE'	D. AUGUST 31, 1970 RUSK, TEXAS
64- 81 ODOM, JOHN LEE 'BLUE MOON'	10343 SLATER #204 - FOUNTAIN VALLEY CA 92708
54- 77 ODONNELL, GEORGE DANA	121 HIGH STREET - WINCHESTER IL 62694
27- 67 ODONNELL, HARRY HERMAN	D. JANUARY 31, 1958 PHILADELPHIA, PA.
63- 87 ODONOGHUE, JOHN EUGENE	153 KIRKCALDY DRIVE - ELKTON MD 21921
19- 62 ODOUL, FRANCIS JOSEPH 'LEFTY'	D. DECEMBER 7, 1969 SAN FRANCISCO, CAL.
12-145 ODOWD (JOHN LEO DOWD)	D. JANUARY 31, 1981 FORT LAUDERDALE, FLA.
83-106 OELKERS, BRYAN ALOIS	2700 LINK - OVERLAND MO 63114
58- 68 OERTEL, CHARLES FRANK	BOX 90 - PONTIAC MI 48055
14-162 OESCHGER, JOSEPH CARL	D. JULY 28, 1986 ROHNERT PARK, CALIF.
78- 95 OESTER, RONALD JOHN	3780 NINEMILE ROAD - CINCINNATI OH 45255
15-118 OFARRELL, ROBERT ARTHUR	D. FEBRUARY 20, 1988 WAUKEGAN, ILL.
72- 82 OFFICE, ROWLAND JOHNNIE	4200 21ST STREET - SACRAMENTO CA 95822
18- 56 OGDEN, JOHN MAHLON	D. NOVEMBER 9, 1977 PHILADELPHIA, PA.
22-104 OGDEN, WARREN HARVEY 'CURLY'	D. AUGUST 6, 1964 CHESTER, PA.
36- 67 OGLESBY, JAMES DORN	D. SEPTEMBER 1, 1955 TULSA, OKLA.
71- 77 OGLIVIE, BENJAMIN AMBROSIO	917 BODARK LANE - AUSTIN TX 78745
36- 68 OGRODOWSKI, AMBROSE FRANCIS 'BRUSIE'	D. MARCH 5, 1956 SAN FRANCISCO, CAL.
25- 82 OGRODOWSKI, JOSEPH ANTHONY	D. JUNE 24, 1959 ELMIRA, N. Y.
80- 98 OJEDA, ROBERT MICHAEL	14884 ROAD 312 - VISALIA CA 93277
20- 92 OKRIE, FRANK ANTHONY	D. OCTOBER 16, 1959 DETROIT, MICH.
48- 76 OKRIE, LEONARD JOSEPH	4603 STRATHMORE - FAYETTEVILLE NC 28304
14-163 OLDHAM, JOHN CYRUS 'RED'	D. JANUARY 28,1961 COSTA MESA, CALIF.
56- 66 OLDHAM, JOHN HARDIN	1845 ANNE WAY - SAN JOSE CA 95124
53- 65 OLDIS, ROBERT CARL	306 VIRGINIA DR - IOWA CITY IA 52240
89- 91 OLERUD, JOHN GARRETT	OLD.ADD: BELLEVUE WA
89- 92 OLIN, STEVEN ROBERT	11835 SW WAGONWHEEL COURT - BEAVERTON OR 97005
62- 99 OLIVA, PEDRO 'TONY'	212 SPRING VALLEY DR - BLOOMINGTON MN 55420
60- 78 OLIVARES, EDWARD BALZAC	HC02 BOX 12887 - SAN GERMAN PR 00753
68- 74 OLIVER, ALBERT	1598 CLEVELAND - COLUMBUS OH 43211
77-105 OLIVER, DAVID JACOB	3604 NEWTON RD - STOCKTON CA 95205
59- 61 OLIVER, EUGENE GEORGE	2805 35TH ST - ROCK ISLAND IL 61201
89- 93 OLIVER, JOSEPH MELTON	4540 FORELAND PLACE - ORLANDO FL 32806
63- 88 OLIVER, NATHANIEL	1320 104TH AVE - OAKLAND CA 94603
65- 83 OLIVER, ROBERT LEE	2772 ROWLAND CIRCLE - ANAHEIM CA 92804
30- 59 OLIVER, THOMAS NOBLE	D. FEBRUARY 26, 1988 MONTGOMERY, ALA.
89- 94 OLIVERAS, FRANCISCO JAVIER	CAIMITO BAJO K1 H3 BUZON 1476 - RIO PIEDRAS PR 00928
60- 79 OLIVO, DIOMEDES ANTONIO	D. FEBRUARY 15, 1977 SANTO DOMINGO, DOM. REP.
61- 79 OLIVO, FEDERICO EMILIO 'CHI-CHI'	D. FEBRUARY 3, 1977 GUAYUBIN, DOMINICAN REP.
66- 69 OLLOM, JAMES DONALD	8601 NINTH AVENUE - EVERETT WA 98204
43-101 OLMO, LUIS FRANCISCO RODRIGUEZ	620 FIGUEROA ST - SANTURCE PR 00907
80- 99 OLMSTED, ALAN RAY	RR 4 BOX 233 - TROY MO 63379
22-105 OLSEN, ARTHUR 'OLE'	D. SEPTEMBER 12, 1980 NORWALK, CONN.
41- 82 OLSEN, BERNARD CHARLES	D. MARCH 30, 1977 EVERETT, MASS.
39- 83 OLSEN, VERN JARL	D. JULY 13, 1989 MAYWOOD, ILL.
88- 99 OLSON, GREGGORY WILLIAM	OLD ADD: OMAHA NE
89- 95 OLSON, GREGORY WILLIAM	5124 INDIANOLA AVENUE - EDINA MN 55424
11-129 OLSON, IVAN MASSIE 'IVY'	D. SEPTEMBER 1, 1965 INGLEWOOD, CALIF.
51- 75 OLSON, KARL ARTHUR	P.O. BOX 1897 - ZEPHYR COVE NV 89448
31- 64 OLSON, MARVIN CLEMENT	BOX 95 - GAYVILLE SD 57031
36- 69 OLSON, THEODORE OTTO	D. DECEMBER 9, 1980 WEYMOUTH, MASS.
86-116 OLWINE, EDWARD R	1100 HOWARD DRIVE - GREENVILLE OH 45331
82- 91 OMALLEY, THOMAS PATRICK	1120 LOCUST ST - MONTOURSVILLE PA 17754
12-146 OMARA, OLIVER EDWARD	D. OCTOBER 24, 1989 RENO, NEV.
25- 83 ONEAL, ORAN HERBERT 'SKINNY'	D. JUNE 2, 1981 SPRINGFIELD, MO.
84- 85 ONEAL, RANDALL JEFFREY	524 E. RAMBLING DR - WEST PALM BEACH FL 33411

19- 63	ONEIL, GEORGE MICHAEL 'MICKEY'	D. APRIL 8, 1964 ST. LOUIS, MO.
46- 80	ONEIL, JOHN FRANCIS	18 CROSS STREET - JAMESTOWN NY 14701
39- 84	ONEILL, HARRY MINK	D. MARCH 8, 1945 IWO JIMA, MARIANAS IS.
20- 93	ONEILL, JAMES LEO	D. SEPTEMBER 5, 1976 CHAMBERSBURG, PA.
22-106	ONEILL, JOSEPH HENRY 'HARRY'	D. SEPTEMBER 5, 1969 RIDGETOWN, ONT.
85- 84	ONEILL, PAUL ANDREW	9359 OLD VILLAGE DRIVE - CINCINNATI OH 45140
43-103	ONEILL, ROBERT EMMETT	748 RANCHO VISTA - SPARKS NV 89431
11-130	ONEILL, STEPHEN FRANCIS	D. JANUARY 26, 1962 CLEVELAND, O.
35- 84	ONIS, MANUEL DOMINGUEZ 'CURLY'	1515 RIVER LA-TAMPA FL 33603
12-147	ONSLOW, EDWARD JOSEPH	D. MAY 8, 1981 DENNISON, O.
12-148	ONSLOW, JOHN JAMES	D. DECEMBER 22, 1960 WEST ACTON, MASS.
85- 85	ONTIVEROS, STEVEN	10195 EAST WOOD DRIVE - SCOTTSDALE AZ 85261
73- 89	ONTIVEROS, STEVEN ROBERT	20 LIGGET - BAKERSFIELD CA 93307
83-107	OQUENDO, JOSE MANUEL	CALLE M-1M R.B. HILLSED - RIO PIEDRAS PR 00926
55- 86	ORAVETZ, ERNEST EUGENE	4417 PAUL AVE - TAMPA FL 33611
43-104	ORDENANA, ANTONIO RODRIGUEZ	D. SEPTEMBER 29, 1988 MIAMI, FLA.
39- 85	ORENGO, JOSEPH CHARLES	D. JULY 24, 1988 SAN FRANCISCO, CALIF.
69-127	ORILEY, DONALD LEE	OLD ADD: 915 PACIFIC - KANSAS CITY MO 64106
20- 94	ORME, GEORGE WILLIAM	D. MARCH 16, 1962 INDIANAPOLIS, IND.
79- 80	OROSCO, JESSE RUSSELL	1359 TOMOL DRIVE - CARPINTERIA CA 93013
12-149	OROURKE, JAMES FRANCIS	D. MAY 14, 1986 CHATHAM, N. J.
59- 62	OROURKE, JAMES PATRICK	N 15612 LITTLE SPOKANE DR - SPOKANE WA 99208
29- 80	OROURKE, JOSEPH LEO	3151 ARAMINGO AVE - PHILADELPHIA PA 19134
13-136	ORR, WILLIAM JOHN	D. MARCH 10, 1967 ST. HELENA, CALIF.
43-105	ORRELL, FORREST GORDON 'JOE'	420 PARKWAY - CHULA VISTA CA 92010
27- 68	ORSATTI, ERNEST RALPH	D. SEPTEMBER 4, 1968 CANOGA PARK, CAL.
61- 80	ORSINO, JOHN JOSEPH	11501 INDIAN SPRING TRAIL - BOYNTON BEACH FL 33437
83-108	ORSULAK, JOSEPH MICHAEL	29 KEANSBURG RD - PARSIPPANY NJ 07054
72- 83	ORTA, JORGE	SAL CREEL 165,LOS MARGARITAS-TORREON COAHUILA MEX.
60- 80	ORTEGA, FILOMENO CORONADO 'PHIL'	OLD ADD: 4242 SPRING ST - LA MESA CA 92041
73- 80	ORTENZIO, FRANK JOSEPH	723 WEST GETTYSBURG - FRESNO CA 93705
82- 92	ORTIZ, ADALBERTO	OLD ADD: BO. CANDELARO ARRIBA BUZON 590 - HUMACAO PR
69-128	ORTIZ, JOSE LUIS	CALLE 14 HH-57,VILLA DEL CARMEN - PLAYA PONCE PR 00731
44-101	ORTIZ, OLIVRIO NUNEZ 'BABY'	D. MARCH 27, 1984 CENTRAL SENADO, CAMAGUEY, CUBA
41- 83	ORTIZ, ROBERTO GONZALO NUNEZ	D. SEPTEMBER 15, 1971 MIAMI, FLA.
89- 96	ORTON, JOHN ANDREW	100 NORTH RODEO GULCH RD #5 - SOQUEL CA 95073
28- 73	ORWOLL, OSWALD CHRISTIAN	D. MAY 8, 1967 DECORAH, IA.
75- 86	OSBORN, DANNY LEON	7620 KNOX CT - WESTMINSTER CO 80030
25- 84	OSBORN, ROBERT	D. APRIL 19, 1960 PARIS, ARK.
22-107	OSBORNE, ERNEST PRESTON 'TINY'	D. JANUARY 5, 1969 ATLANTA, GA.
57- 62	OSBORNE, LAWRENCE SIDNEY	1969 SEABOARD PLACE NW - ATLANTA GA 30318
35- 85	OSBORNE, WAYNE HAROLD	D. MARCH 13, 1987 VANCOUVER, WASH.
74- 98	OSBURN, LARRY PAT	RR 2 BOX 308 - BRADENTON FL 33508
44-102	OSGOOD, CHARLES BENJAMIN	3 SOUTH MEADOW VLG #22 - CARVER MA 02330
62-100	OSINSKI, DANIEL	3735 WEST 215TH STREET - MATTESON IL 60443
57- 63	OSTEEN, CLAUDE WILSON	1959 WEXFORD ROAD - PALMYRA PA 17078
65- 84	OSTEEN, MILTON DARRELL	1213 LAS POSAS - SAN CLEMENTE CA 92672
14-164	OSTENDORF, FREDERICK	D. MARCH 9, 1965 HAMPTON, VA.
54- 78	OSTER, WILLIAM CHARLES	9 HARBOR HEIGHTS - CENTERPORT NY 11721
21- 75	OSTERGARD, ROY LUND 'RED'	D. JANUARY 13, 1977 HEMET, CALIF.
34- 82	OSTERMUELLER, FREDERICK RAYMOND	D. DECEMBER 17, 1957 QUINCY, ILL.
73- 91	OSTROSSER, BRIAN LEONARD	OLD ADD: 21 LAKE AVENUE SOUTH-STONEY CREEK ONTARIO CAN.
43-106	OSTROWSKI, JOHN THADDEUS	4943 SOUTH KOMENSKY AVE-CHICAGO IL 60632
48- 77	OSTROWSKI, JOSEPH PAUL	441 TRIPP ST - WEST WYOMING PA 18644
45- 75	OTERO, REGINO JOSE GOMEZ	D. OCTOBER 21, 1988 HIALEAH, FLA.
67- 83	OTIS, AMOS JOSEPH	13558 FREEPORT ROAD - SAN DIEGO CA 92129
12-150	OTIS, PAUL FRANKLIN 'BILL'	2310 EAST THIRD ST - DULUTH MN 55817
69-129	OTOOLE, DENNIS JOSEPH	3453 RIDGEWOOD DR - ERLANGER KY 41018
58- 69	OTOOLE, JAMES JEROME	1010 LANETTE DR - CINCINNATI OH 45230
26- 62	OTT, MELVIN THOMAS	D. NOVEMBER 21, 1958 NEW ORLEANS, LA.
74- 99	OTT, NATHAN EDWARD 'ED'	RR 2 BOX 62AA - COUDERSPORT PA 16915
62-101	OTT, WILLIAM JOSEPH	OLD ADD: 25 DONGAN PL - NEW YORK NY 10040
74-100	OTTEN, JAMES EDWARD	BOX 242 - KALISPELL MT 59901
87-108	OTTO, DAVID ALAN	239 TANGLEWOOD DRIVE - ELK GROVE IL 60007
86-117	OUELLETTE, PHILIP ROLAND	4771 JONES ROAD SE - SALEM OR 97302
33- 47	OULLIBER, JOHN ANDREW	D. DECEMBER 26, 1980 NEW ORLEANS, LA.
33- 48	OUTEN, WILLIAM AUSTIN 'CHICK'	D. SEPTEMBER 11, 1961 DURHAM, N. C.
37- 82	OUTLAW, JAMES PAULUS	118 JAMES ST - JACKSON AL 36545
43-107	OVERMIRE, FRANK 'STBBY'	D. MARCH 3, 1977 LAKELAND, FLA.
76- 72	OVERY, HARRY MICHAEL	101 FAIRVIEW PL - CLINTON IL 61727
11-131	OVITZ, ERNEST GAYHART	D. SEPTEMBER 11, 1980 GREEN BAY, WISC.
76- 73	OWCHINKO, ROBERT DENNIS	8355 EAST RAINTREE #110 - SCOTTSDALE AZ 85260
37- 83	OWEN, ARNOLD MALCOLM 'MICKEY'	2731 E.LOMBARD - SPRINGFIELD MO 65802
83-109	OWEN, DAVE	RURAL ROUTE 5 BOX 281 - CLEBURNE TX 76031
81- 91	OWEN, LAWRENCE THOMAS	804 WHITE PINE ST - NEW CARLISLE OH 45344
31- 65	OWEN, MARVIN JAMES	1230 MAIN STREET - SANTA CLARA CA 95050
83-110	OWEN, SPIKE DEE	RURAL ROUTE 5 BOX 281 - CLEBURNE TX 76031
35- 86	OWENS, FURMAN LEE 'JACK'	D. NOVEMBER 14, 1958 GREENVILLE, S. C.
55- 87	OWENS, JAMES PHILIP	1761 CROTON DR - VENICE FL 33595
72- 84	OWENS, PAUL FRANCIS	RR 2 BOX 689 - MULLICA HILL NJ 08062
82- 93	OWNBEY, RICHARD WAYNE	627 SPRINGBROOK NORTH - IRVINE CA 92714
65- 85	OYLER, RAYMOND FRANCIS	D. JANUARY 26, 1981 REDMOND, WASH.
73- 92	OZARK, DANIEL LEONARD	BOX 6666 - VERO BEACH FL 32960
23-100	OZMER, HORACE ROBERT 'DOC'	D. DECEMBER 28, 1970 ATLANTA, GA.
77-106	PACELLA, JOHN LEWIS	6586 SUNBURY RD - WESTERVILLE OH 43081
87-109	PACILLO, PATRICK MICHAEL	15 ADDISON AVENUE - RUTHERFORD NJ 07070
87-110	PACIOREK, JAMES JOSEPH	OLD ADD: 13432 MOENART - DETROIT MI 48212
63- 89	PACIOREK, JOHN FRANCIS	8400 HUNTINGTON DR - SAN GABRIEL CA 91775
70-103	PACIOREK, THOMAS MARIAN	2389 BROAD CREEK DRIVE - STONE MOUNTAIN GA 30087
49- 62	PACK, FRANKIE	BOX 1623 - HENDERSONVILLE NC 28739
12-151	PACKARD, EUGENE MILO	D. MAY 19, 1959 RIVERSIDE, CALIF.
75- 87	PACTWA, JOSEPH MARTIN	232 154TH PL - CALUMET CITY IL 60409
32- 59	PADDEN, THOMAS FRANCIS	D. JUNE 11, 1973 MANCHESTER, N. H.
12-152	PADDOCK, DELMAR HAROLD	D. FEBRUARY 6, 1952 REMER, MINN.
37- 84	PADGETT, DON WILSON	D. DECEMBER 9, 1980 HIGH POINT, N. C.
23-101	PADGETT, ERNEST KITCHEN	D. APRIL 15, 1957 EAST ORANGE, N. J.
69-130	PAEPKE, DENNIS RAY	DRAWER #CE - CRESTLINE CA 92325
43-108	PAFKO, ANDREW	1420 BLACKHAWK DR - MOUNT PROSPECT IL 60056

73- 93 PAGAN, DAVID PERCY	BOX 1819 - NIPAWIN SASK. SOE 1EO CAN.
59- 63 PAGAN, JOSE ANTONIO	CALLE JASPE #15 - CAGUAS PR 00625
44-103 PAGE, JOSEPH FRANCIS	D. APRIL 21, 1980 LATROBE, PA.
68- 75 PAGE, MICHAEL RANDY	BOX 334 - WOODRUFF SC 29388
77-107 PAGE, MITCHELL OTIS	OLD ADD: 125 EAST 93RD STREET - LOS ANGELES CA 90003
28- 74 PAGE, PHILIPPE RAUSAC	D. JUNE 27, 1958 SPRINGFIELD, MASS.
39- 86 PAGE, SAMUEL WALTER	BOX 204-WOODRUFF SC 29388
38- 73 PAGE, VANCE LINWOOD	D. JULY 14, 1951 WILSON, N. C.
78- 96 PAGEL, KARL DOUGLAS	812 WEST OBISPO - MESA AZ 85202
55- 88 PAGLIARONI, JAMES VINCENT	10388 PARTRIDGE DR - GRASS VALLEY CA 95945
84- 86 PAGLIARULO, MICHAEL TIMOTHY	164 WEST WYOMING AVENUE - MELROSE MA 02176
87-111 PAGNOZZI, THOMAS ALAN	6046 EAST 16TH - TUCSON AZ 85711
11-132 PAIGE, GEORGE LYNN 'PAT'	D. JUNE 8, 1939 BERLIN, WIS.
48- 78 PAIGE, LEROY "SATCHEL"	D. JUNE 8, 1982 KANSAS CITY, MO.
51- 76 PAINE, PHILLIPS STEERE	D. FEBRUARY 19, 1978 LEBANON, PA.
88-100 PALACIOS, ROBERT REY	359 VAN BRUNT STREET - BROOKLYN NY 11321
87-112 PALACIOS, VICENTE	DOMICILIO CONOCIDO - MATALOMA VERACRUZ MEX.
39- 87 PALAGYI, MICHAEL RAYMOND	167 14TH ST-CONNEAUT OH 44030
45- 76 PALICA, ERVIN MARTIN	D. MAY 29, 1982 HUNTINGTON BEACH, CALIF.
88-101 PALL, DONN STEVEN	11541 VIENNA - PALOS PARK IL 60464
48- 79 PALM, RICHARD PAUL 'MIKE'	63 NICHOLS RD - COHASSET MA 02025
86-118 PALMEIRO, RAFAEL CORRALES	223 NORTHWEST 32ND STREET - MIAMI FL 33127
78- 97 PALMER, DAVID WILLIAM	1395 EASTGATE DRIVE - STONE MOUNTAIN GA 30087
89- 97 PALMER, DEAN WILLIAM	205 CACTUS STREET - TALLAHASSEE FL 32304
17- 59 PALMER, EDWIN HENRY	D. JANUARY 9, 1983 MARLOW, OKLA.
65- 86 PALMER, JAMES ALVIN	BOX 145 - BROOKLANDVILLE MD 21022
69-131 PALMER, LOWELL RAYMOND	P.O. BOX 1704 - ORANGEVALE CA 95662
15-119 PALMERO, EMILIO ANTONIO	D. JULY 15, 1970 TOLEDO, O.
31- 66 PALMISANO, JOSEPH	D. NOVEMBER 5, 1971 ALBUQUERQUE, N. M.
60- 81 PALMQUIST, EDWIN LEE	1921 16TH STREET - KINGSBURG CA 93631
53- 66 PALYS, STANLEY FRANCIS	RR ONE - MOSCOW PA 18444
84- 87 PANKOVITS, JAMES FRANKLIN	9419 BONNIE DALE RD - RICHMOND VA 23229
71- 78 PANTHER, JAMES EDWARD	1125 SHARI LN - LIBERTYVILLE IL 60048
61- 81 PAPA, JOHN PAUL	29 PHILLIPS DR - SHELTON CT 06484
48- 80 PAPAI, ALFRED THOMAS	2553 SOUTH 7TH ST - SPRINGFIELD IL 62703
76- 74 PAPE, KENNETH WAYNE	2714 OAK FIRE - SAN ANTONIO TX 78217
74-101 PAPI, STANLEY GERARD	1111 WEST SIERRA MADRE - FRESNO CA 93705
45- 77 PAPISH, FRANK RICHARD	D. AUGUST 30, 1965 PUEBLO, COLO.
57- 64 PAPPAS, MILTON STEPHEN	RR 1, BOX 154, ASHLAND AVE. — BEECHER, IL 60401
85- 86 PARDO, ALBERTO JUDAS	614 WEST BUFFALO AVE - TAMPA FL 33603
88-102 PAREDES, JOHNNY ALFONSO	OLD ADD: MARACAIBO VENEZ
86-119 PARENT, MARK ALAN	P.O. BOX 591 - COTTONWOOD CA 96022
82- 94 PARIS, KELLY JAY	OLD ADD: 19961 SANTA RITA ST - WOODLAND HILLS CA 91364
43-109 PARISSE, LOUIS PETER	D. JUNE 2, 1956 PHILADELPHIA, PA.
15-120 PARK, JAMES	D. DECEMBER 17, 1970 LEXINGTON, KY.
37- 85 PARKER, CLARENCE MCKAY 'ACE'	210 SNEAD'S FAIRWAY-PORTSMOUTH VA 23701
15-121 PARKER, CLARENCE PERKINS 'PAT'	D. MARCH 21, 1967 CLAREMONT, N.H.
73- 94 PARKER, DAVID GENE	7864 RIDGE ROAD - CINCINNATI OH 45237
23-102 PARKER, DOUGLAS WOOLLEY 'DIXIE'	D. MAY 15, 1972 GREEN POND, ALA.
36- 70 PARKER, FRANCIS JAMES 'SALTY'	9201 CLAREWOOD #121 - HOUSTON TX 77036
70-104 PARKER, HARRY WILLIAM	3324 SOUTH ASH PLACE - BROKEN ARROW OK 74012
87-113 PARKER, JAMES CLAYTON 'CLAY'	1112 CHARWOOD LANE - HIXSON TN 37343
64- 82 PARKER, MAURICE WESLEY 'WES'	P.O. BOX 550 - SANTA MONICA CA 90406
19- 64 PARKER, ROY W.	B. 1897
71- 79 PARKER, WILLIAM DAVID	OLD ADD: 1975 EL PARQUE DRIVE - TEMPE AZ 85282
21- 76 PARKINSON, FRANK JOSEPH	D. JULY 4, 1960 TRENTON, N.J.
37- 86 PARKS, ARTIE WILLIAM	D. DECEMBER 6, 1989 LITTLE ROCK, ARK.
21- 77 PARKS, VERNON HENRY 'SLICKER'	D. FEBRUARY 21, 1978 ROYAL OAK, MICH.
29- 81 PARMELEE, LEROY EARL	D. AUGUST 31, 1981 MONROE, MICH.
47- 65 PARNELL, MELVIN LLOYD	700 TURQUOISE ST - NEW ORLEANS LA 70124
16- 67 PARNHAM, JAMES ARTHUR 'RUBE'	D. NOVEMBER 25, 1963 MCKEESPORT, PA.
86-120 PARRETT, JEFFREY DALE	722 SEATTLE DRIVE - LEXINGTON KY 40503
70-105 PARRILLA, SAMUEL	163 BAY SEVENTH STREET - BROOKLYN NY 11228
77-108 PARRISH, LANCE MICHAEL	22370 STARWOOD DRIVE - YORBA LINDA CA 92686
74-102 PARRISH, LARRY ALTON	4989 EAST STATE RD #544 - HAINES CITY FL 33844
77-109 PARROTT, MICHAEL EVERETT ARCH	2784 MAGNOLIA ST - CAMARILLO CA 93010
10-115 PARSON, WILLIAM EDWIN 'JIGGS'	D. MAY 19, 1967 INGLEWOOD, CALIF.
81- 92 PARSONS, CASEY ROBERT	EAST 12124 25TH - SPOKANE WA 99206
39- 88 PARSONS, EDWARD DIXON 'DIXIE'	4723 WEST MARSHALL ST - LONGVIEW TX 75601
63- 90 PARSONS, THOMAS ANTHONY	LINCOLN CITY ROAD - LAKEVILLE CT 06039
71- 80 PARSONS, WILLIAM RAYMOND	2725 SOUTH AZALEA - TEMPE AZ 85281
43-110 PARTEE, ROY ROBERT	DRAWER 730 - TRINIDAD CA 95570
13-137 PARTENHEIMER, HAROLD PHILIP 'STEVE'	D. JUNE 16, 1971 MANSFIELD, O.
44-104 PARTENHEIMER, STANWOOD WENDELL	D. JANUARY 28, 1989 NASHUA, N. H.
27- 69 PARTRIDGE, JAMES BUGG 'JAY'	D. JANUARY 4, 1974 NASHVILLE, TENN.
15-122 PASCHAL, BENJAMIN EDWIN	D. NOVEMBER 10, 1974 CHARLOTTE, N. C.
78- 98 PASCHALL, WILLIAM HERBERT	OLD ADD: 4557 PRINCESS ANNE RD - VIRGINIA BEACH VA 2346
54- 79 PASCUAL, CAMILO ALBERTO	7741 SW 32ND ST - MIAMI FL 33155
50- 76 PASCUAL, CARLOS ALBERTO	2540 SW 92ND COURT - MIAMI FL 33165
33- 49 PASEK, JOHN PAUL	D. MARCH 13, 1976 NIAGARA FALLS, N. Y.
82- 95 PASHNICK, LARRY JOHN	9625 BLACKBURN - LIVONIA MI 48150
74-103 PASLEY, KEVIN PATRICK	4423 EAST SHARON - PHOENIX AZ 85032
85- 87 PASQUA, DANIEL ANTHONY	46 GAIL DRIVE - NEW CITY NY 10956
19- 65 PASQUELLA, MICHAEL JOHN	D. APRIL 5, 1965 BRIDGEPORT, CONN.
35- 87 PASSEAU, CLAUDE WILLIAM	113 LONDON ST - LUCEDALE MS 39452
79- 81 PASTORE, FRANK ENRICO	1542 NORTH FRAMIS WAY - UPLAND CA 91786
83-111 PASTORNICKY, CLIFFORD SCOT	490 NORTH CIVIC DRIVE #104 - WALNUT CREEK CA 94596
26- 63 PATE, JOSEPH WILLIAM	D. DECEMBER 26, 1948 FORT WORTH, TEX.
80-100 PATE, ROBERT WAYNE	12330 OSBORNE STREET #30 - PACOIMA CA 91331
68- 76 PATEK, FREDERICK JOSEPH	GRANDY'S,14221 E. 40TH HWY - KANSAS CITY MO 64101
41- 84 PATRICK, ROBERT LEE	107 NORTH 18TH-FORT SMITH AR 72901
68- 77 PATTERSON, DARYL ALAN	20145 TOLLHOUSE RD - CLOVIS CA 93612
79- 82 PATTERSON, DAVID GLENN	8425 EVANSTON AVENUE - RAYTOWN MO 64138
77-110 PATTERSON, GILBERT THOMAS	8185 NW 8 MANOR - PLANT FL 33324
32- 60 PATTERSON, HENRY JOSEPH	D. SEPTEMBER 30, 1970 PANORAMA CITY, CAL.
88-103 PATTERSON, KENNETH BRIAN	RURAL ROUTE 2 BOX 99 - MCGREGOR TX 76657
81- 93 PATTERSON, MICHAEL LEE	2419 RIDGELEY DR #9 - LOS ANGELES CA 90016
81- 94 PATTERSON, REGINALD ALLEN	2900 ARLINGTON AVE - BESSEMER AL 35020

TONY LARUSSA

FRED LYNN

FRED LYNN

JOHN ANTHONY MILLER

ED MORIARTY

JOE ORSULAK

JOE ORSULAK

GEORGE PIPGRAS

EWALD PYLE

NOLAN RYAN P

NOLAN RYAN

NELSON SANTOVENIA

85- 88	PATTERSON, ROBERT CHANDLER	RURAL ROUTE 10 BOX 787P - HICKORY NC 28601
21- 78	PATTERSON, WILLIAM JENNINGS BRYAN	D. OCTOBER 1, 1977 ST. LOUIS, MO.
68- 78	PATTIN, MARTIN WILLIAM	RURAL ROUTE 4 BOX 186A - LAWRENCE KS 66044
29- 82	PATTISON, JAMES WELLS	883 VANCE CIRCLE NE - PALM BAY FL 32905
44-105	PATTON, GENE TUNNEY	60 SOUTH 17TH AVE - COATESVILLE PA 19320
35- 88	PATTON, GEORGE WILLIAM	D. MARCH 15, 1986 PHILADELPHIA, PA.
10-116	PATTON, HARRY CLAUDE	D. JUNE 9, 1930 ST. LOUIS, MO.
57- 65	PATTON, THOMAS ALLEN	RR 4 BOX 335 - HONEY BROOK PA 19344
68- 79	PAUL, MICHAEL GEORGE	5121 CIRCULO SOBRIO - TUCSON AZ 85718
54- 80	PAULA, CARLOS (CONNILL)	D. APRIL 25, 1983 MIAMI, FLA.
11-133	PAULETTE, EUGENE EDWARD	D. FEBRUARY 8, 1966 LITTLE ROCK, ARK.
25- 85	PAULSON, PAUL GUILFORD	5904 119TH AVENUE EAST - PUYALLUP WA 98372
57- 66	PAVLETICH, DONALD STEPHEN	13645 ADELAIDE LANE - BROOKFIELD WI 53005
46- 81	PAWELEK, THEODORE JOHN	D. FEBRUARY 12, 1964 CHICAGO HEIGHTS, ILL.
55- 89	PAWLOSKI, STANLEY WALTER	1013 GORMAN ST - PHILADELPHIA PA 19116
87-114	PAWLOWSKI, JOHN	9 LINDA DRIVE - BINGHAMTON NY 13905
77-111	PAXTON, MICHAEL DEWAYNE	OLD ADD: 345 LINCOLN #10 - BOSTON MA 02111
20- 95	PAYNE, GEORGE WASHINGTON	D. JANUARY 24, 1959 BELLFLOWER, CALIF.
84- 88	PAYNE, MICHAEL EARL	BOX 712 - WILLISTON FL 32696
75- 88	PAZIK, MICHAEL JOSEPH	8413 COMANCHE COURT - BETHESDA MD 20817
37- 87	PEACOCK, JOHN GASTON	D. OCTOBER 17, 1981 WILSON, N. C.
33- 50	PEARCE, FRANKLIN THOMAS	D. SEPTEMBER 3, 1950 VAN BUREN, N. Y.
12-153	PEARCE, GEORGE THOMAS	D. OCTOBER 11, 1935 JOLIET, ILL.
17- 60	PEARCE, HARRY JAMES	D. JANUARY 8, 1942 PHILADELPHIA, PA.
49- 63	PEARCE, JAMES MADISON	RR 5 BOX 404 - ZEBULON NC 27597
58- 70	PEARSON, ALBERT GREGORY	%CCF, RURAL ROUTE 1 BOX 109 - LINDALE TX 75771
39- 89	PEARSON, ISSAC OVERTON	D. MARCH 17, 1985 SARASOTA, FLA.
32- 61	PEARSON, MONTGOMERY MARCELLUS	D. JANUARY 27, 1978 FRESNO, CALIF.
10-117	PEASLEY, MARVIN WARREN	D. DECEMBER 27, 1948 SAN FRANCISCO, CALIF.
15-123	PECHOUS, CHARLES EDWARD	D. SEPTEMBER 13, 1980 KENOSHA, WIS.
43-111	PECK, HAROLD ARTHUR	1037 WEST SHAW COURT #3 - WHITEWATER WI 53190
10-118	PECKINPAUGH, ROGER THORPE	D. NOVEMBER 17, 1977 CLEVELAND, O.
86-121	PECOTA, WILLIAM JOSEPH	471 LIQUID AMBER WAY - SUNNYVALE CA 94086
53- 67	PEDEN, LESLIE EARL	17437 ELSINORE DRIVE - JACKSONVILLE FL 32226
85- 89	PEDERSON, STUART RUSSELL	24848 SKYLAND - LOS GATOS CA 95030
87-115	PEDRIQUE, ALFREDO JOSE	6684 CRESCENT GREEN - WEST BLOOMFIELD MI 48322
41- 85	PEEK, STEPHEN GEORGE	204 WEST HAMILTON AVE-SHERRILL NY 13461
27- 70	PEEL, HOMER HEFNER	3757 GREENWAY - SHREVEPORT LA 71105
35- 89	PEERSON, JACK CHILES	D. OCTOBER 23, 1966 FT. WALTON BEACH, FLA.
27- 71	PEERY, GEORGE A. 'RED'	D. MAY 6, 1985 SALT LAKE CITY, UTAH
56- 67	PEETE, CHARLES	D. NOVEMBER 27, 1956 CARACAS, VENEZ.
46- 82	PELLAGRINI, EDWARD CHARLES	103 WEBB ST - WEYMOUTH MA 02188
74-104	PEMBERTON, BROCK	1012 SOUTH FLORENCE - TULSA OK 74104
81- 95	PENA, ADALBERTO	19-2-0-5, BAIROA MIRABEL-CAGUAS PR 00625
81- 96	PENA, ALEJANDRO	1713 GERMAIN DR - MONTEBELLO CA 90640
80-101	PENA, ANTONIO FRANCISCO	COMP HAB 30 DEMARZO,MAN #1 ED 14-SANTIAGO DOM. REP.
86-122	PENA, HIPOLITO (CONCEPCION)	PEREZ RODRIGUEZ #13 - SANTO DOMINGO DOMINICAN REP.
69-132	PENA, JOSE	A.FLORES #1116 NTE,C.JIQUILPAN-LOS MOCHIS SINOLOA MEX.
58- 71	PENA, ORLANDO	1750 WEST 46TH STREET #416 - HIALEAH FL 33012
89- 98	PENA, RAMON ARTURO	PALO VERDE - MONTECRISTI DOMINICAN REP.
65- 87	PENA, ROBERT CESAR	D. JULY 23, 1982 SANTIAGO DOMINICAN REPUBLIC
22-108	PENCE, ELMER CLAIR	D. SEPTEMBER 17, 1968 SAN FRANCISCO, CAL.
21- 79	PENCE, RUSSELL WILLIAM	D. AUGUST 11, 1971 HOT SPRINGS, ARK.
53- 68	PENDLETON, JAMES EDWARD	6622 HARTWICK - HOUSTON TX 77016
84- 89	PENDLETON, TERRY LEE	512 NORTH VENTURA ROAD - PORT HUENEME CA 93041
16- 68	PENNER, KENNETH WILLIAM	D. MAY 28, 1959 SACRAMENTO, CAL.
17- 61	PENNINGTON, GEORGE LOUIS 'KEWPIE'	D. MAY 5, 1953 NEWARK, N. J.
12-154	PENNOCK, HERBERT JEFFERIS	D. JANUARY 30, 1948 NEW YORK, N.Y.
54- 81	PENSON, PAUL EUGENE	711 LAKE OF THE FOREST-BONNER SPGS KS 66012
75- 89	PENTZ, EUGENE DAVID	207 RAINBOW DRIVE - JOHNSTOWN PA 15904
62-102	PEPITONE, JOSEPH ANTHONY	OLD ADD: LIGHTHOUSE RD - SAUGERTIES NY 12477
29- 83	PEPLOSKI, HENRY STEPHEN	D. JANUARY 28, 1982 DOVER, N. J.
13-139	PEPLOSKI, JOSEPH ANTHONY 'PEPPER'	D. 1946 OR 1947
66- 70	PEPPER, DONALD HOYTE	70 WORTH ROAD - GANSEVOORT NY 12831
54- 82	PEPPER, HUGH MCLAURIN 'LAURIN'	123 HOLCOMB BLVD - OCEAN SPRINGS MS 39564
32- 62	PEPPER, RAYMOND WATSON	BOX 40 - MOORESVILLE AL 35649
15-124	PEPPER, ROBERT ERNEST	D. APRIL 8, 1968 FORD CLIFF, PA.
69-133	PERAZA, LUIS	CALLE 6 C.F. 13 RES. BAIROA-CAGUAS PR 00625
88-104	PERAZA, OSWALD JOSE	CLE BARBUAL #19-36 - PUERTO CABELLO EDO. CARABOBO VENEZ
80-102	PERCONTE, JOHN PATRICK	6197 HINTERLONG COURT - LISLE IL 60532
11-134	PERDUE, HERBERT RODNEY 'HUB'	D. OCTOBER 31, 1968 GALLATIN, TENN.
64- 83	PEREZ, ATANASIO RIGAL 'TONY'	LOS FLORES 113 - SANTURCE PR 00911
58- 72	PEREZ, GEORGE THOMAS	39646 87TH ST WEST - LEONA VALLEY CA 93550
69-134	PEREZ, MARTIN ROMAN	30 WILLOWICK DR - DECATUR GA 30034
87-116	PEREZ, MELIDO TURPEN	NIGUA KM 21 1/2 - SANTO DOMINGO DOMINICAN REP.
80-103	PEREZ, PASCUAL (GROSS)	SALVADOR, CUCURULO #105 - SANTIAGO DOMINICAN REP.
88-105	PEREZCHICA, ANTONIO LLAMAS	33760 VIA ECHO - PALM SPRINGS CA 92264
78- 99	PERKINS, BRODERICK PHILLIP	2110 BURTON AVE - PITTSBURG CA 94565
67- 84	PERKINS, CECIL BOYCE	RR 1 BOX 100-P - MARTINSBURG WV 25401
30- 60	PERKINS, CHARLES SULLIVAN	D. MAY 25, 1988 SALEM, ORE.
15-125	PERKINS, RALPH FOSTER 'CY'	D. OCTOBER 2, 1963 PHILADELPHIA, PA.
50- 77	PERKOVICH, JOHN JOSEPH	16 ATHENA CT - LITTLE ROCK AR 72207
47- 66	PERKOWSKI, HAROLD WALTER	211 MCGINNIS - BECKLEY WV 25801
85- 90	PERLMAN, JONATHAN SAMUEL	1019 FORREST LANE - CARTHAGE TX 75633
77-112	PERLOZZO, SAMUEL BENEDICT	129 RACE - CUMBERLAND MD 21502
42- 75	PERME, LEONARD JOSEPH	3350 D ST - HAYWARD CA 94541
10-119	PERNOLL, HENRY HUBBARD	D. FEBRUARY 18, 1944 GRANTS PASS, ORE.
61- 82	PERRANOSKI, RONALD PETER	3805 INDIAN RIVER DRIVE - VERO BEACH FL 32963
21- 80	PERRIN, JOHN STEPHENSON	D. JUNE 24, 1969 DETROIT, MICH.
34- 83	PERRIN, WILLIAM JOSEPH	D. JUNE 30, 1974 NEW ORLEANS, LA.
12-155	PERRITT, WILLIAM DAYTON 'POL'	D. OCTOBER 15, 1947 SHREVEPORT, LA.
41- 86	PERRY, BOYD GLENN	RR 1 - SNOW CAMP NC 27349
62-103	PERRY, GAYLORD JACKSON	320 EAST JEFFERIES STREET - GAFFNEY SC 29342
83-112	PERRY, GERALD JUNE	BOX 1403 - HILTON HEAD SC 29928
15-126	PERRY, HERBERT SCOTT	D. OCTOBER 27, 1959 KANSAS CITY, MO.
59- 64	PERRY, JAMES EVAN	5720 DUNCAN LANE - MINNEAPOLIS MN 55436
63- 91	PERRY, MELVIN GAY "BOB"	621 HOLIDAY CITY - NEW BERN NC 28562
12-156	PERRY, WILLIAM HENRY 'HANK'	D. JULY 18, 1956 PONTIAC, MICH.

85- 91 PERRY, WILLIAM PATRICK 'PAT'	1115 WEST FRANKLIN - TAYLORVILLE IL 62568
15-127 PERRYMAN, EMMETT KEY 'PARSON'	D. SEPTEMBER 12, 1966 STARKE, FLA.
18- 57 PERTICA, WILLIAM ANDREW	D. DECEMBER 28, 1967 LOS ANGELES, CAL.
71- 81 PERZANOWSKI, STANLEY	324 SARATOGA DRIVE - GREER SC 29651
42- 76 PESKY, JOHN MICHAEL	25 PARSONS DR-SWAMPSCOTT MA 01907
89- 99 PETEREK, JEFFREY ALLEN	P.O. BOX 5 - HARBERT MI 49115
42- 77 PETERMAN, WILLIAM DAVID	9823 WISTERIA ST - PHILADELPHIA PA 19115
59- 65 PETERS, GARY CHARLES	2626 ESPANOLA AVE - SARASOTA FL 33580
15-128 PETERS, JOHN WILLIAM	D. FEBRUARY 21, 1932 KANSAS CITY, MO.
12-157 PETERS, OTTO CASPER	D. FEBRUARY 7, 1965 PEQUANNOCK, N. J.
70-106 PETERS, RAYMOND JAMES	1317 NORTH BARKLEY STREET - MESA AZ 85203
79- 83 PETERS, RICHARD DEVIN 'RICKY'	12601 SOUTH HALO DRIVE - COMPTON CA 90221
36- 71 PETERS, RUSSELL DIXON 'RUSTY'	BOX 751 - BEDFORD VA 24523
87-117 PETERS, STEVEN BRADLEY	OLD ADD: RR 11 BOX 531A - OKLAHOMA CITY OK 73170
87-118 PETERSON, ADAM CHARLES	6401 NE 144TH STREET - VANCOUVER WA 98686
55- 90 PETERSON, CARL FRANCIS 'BUDDY'	8665 FLORIN RD #101 - SACRAMENTO CA 95828
62-104 PETERSON, CHARLES ANDREW 'CAP'	D. MAY 16, 1980 TACOMA WA
66- 71 PETERSON, FRED INGELS 'FRITZ'	P.O. BOX 31206 - PALM BEACH GARDENS FL 33410
55- 91 PETERSON, HARDING WILLIAM 'PETE'	1406 CAMELOT COURT - PALM HARBOR FL 34684
31- 67 PETERSON, JAMES NIELS	D. APRIL 8, 1975 PALM BEACH, FLA.
44-106 PETERSON, KENT FRANKLIN	P.O. BOX 164 - PROVO UT 84603
43-112 PETERSON, SIDNEY HERBERT	4604 UNIVERSITY AVENUE - WICHITA FALLS TX 76308
34- 84 PETOSKEY, FREDERICK LEE 'TED'	RR 4 BOX 109 - HOPKINS SC 29061
82- 96 PETRALLI, EUGENE JAMES	2605 LAUREL VALLEY LANE - ARLINGTON TX 76006
63- 92 PETROCELLI, AMERICO PETER 'RICO'	19 TOWNSEND RD - LYNNFIELD MA 01940
79- 84 PETRY, DANIEL JOSEPH	1808 CARTLEN DRIVE - PLACENTIA CA 92670
83-113 PETTIBONE, HARRY JONATHAN 'JAM'	OLD ADD: 1261 WEST CATALPA - ANAHEIM CA 92801
14-165 PETTIGREW, JIM NED	D. AUGUST 20, 1952 DUNCAN, OKLA.
80-104 PETTINI, JOSEPH PAUL	112 LOGAN COURT - BETHANY WV 26032
82- 97 PETTIS, GARY GEORGE	5475 WADEAN PLACE - OAKLAND CA 94601
51- 77 PETTIT, GEORGE WILLIAM PAUL	25313 WOODWARD - LOMITA CA 90717
35- 90 PETTIT, LEON ARTHUR	D. NOVEMBER 21, 1974 COLUMBIA, TENN.
21- 81 PETTY, JESSE LEE	D. OCTOBER 23, 1971 ST. PAUL, MINN.
89-100 PEVEY, MARTY ASHLEY	207 CIRCLE DRIVE - STATESBORO GA 30458
14-166 PEZOLD, LORENZ JOHANNES 'LARRY'	D. OCTOBER 22, 1957 BATON ROUGE, LA.
35- 91 PEZZULLO, JOHN 'PRETZLES'	D. MAY 16, 1990 DALLAS, TEXAS
11-135 PFEFFER, EDWARD JOSEPH 'JEFF'	D. AUGUST 15, 1972 CHICAGO, ILL.
13-138 PFEFFER, MONTE	D. SEPTEMBER 27, 1941 NEW YORK, N. Y.
69-135 PFEIL, ROBERT RAYMOND	P.O. BOX 4025 - STOCKTON CA 95204
61- 83 PFISTER, DANIEL ALBIN	3600 NW 91ST AVE - WEST HOLLYWOOD FL 33024
41- 87 PFISTER, GEORGE EDWARD	215 JOHN ST - BOUND BROOK NJ 08805
45- 78 PFUND, LEROY HERBERT 'LEE'	1421 PRINCETON COURT #A - WHEATON IL 60187
36- 72 PHEBUS, RAYMOND WILLIAM 'BILL'	930 LAKEVIEW AVE-BARTOW FL 33830
10-120 PHELAN, ARTHUR THOMAS	D. DECEMBER 27, 1964 FORT WORTH, TEX.
31- 68 PHELPS, ERNEST GORDON 'BABE'	1417 HALE ST - ODENTON MD 21113
80-105 PHELPS, KENNETH ALLEN	7531 EAST TURQUOISE AVE - SCOTTSDALE AZ 85258
30- 61 PHELPS, RAYMOND CLIFFORD	D. JULY 7, 1971 FT. PIERCE, FLA.
41- 88 PHILLEY, DAVID EARL	1336 EAST POLK ST-PARIS TX 75460
64- 84 PHILLIPS, ADOLFO EMILIO	APARTADO 6109 CHORILLA - PANAMA CITY PAN.
30- 62 PHILLIPS, ALBERT ABERNATHY 'BUZZ'	D. NOVEMBER 6, 1964 BALTIMORE, MD.
34- 85 PHILLIPS, CLARENCE LEMUEL 'RED'	D. FEBRUARY 1, 1988 WICHITA, KANSAS
42- 78 PHILLIPS, DAMON RUSSELL	BOX 805 - HENDERSON TX 75652
24- 85 PHILLIPS, EDWARD DAVID	D. JANUARY 26, 1968 BUFFALO, N.Y.
69-136 PHILLIPS, HAROLD ROSS 'LEFTY'	D. JUNE 12, 1972 FULLERTON, CAL.
53- 69 PHILLIPS, HOWARD EDWARD 'ED'	WEST ELY - HANNIBAL MO 63401
47- 67 PHILLIPS, JACK DORN	MAY RD #2 - POTSDAM NY 13676
45- 79 PHILLIPS, JOHN	D. JUNE 16, 1958 ST. LOUIS, MO.
55- 92 PHILLIPS, JOHN MELVIN 'BUBBA'	2704 MIMOSA LN - HATTIESBURG MS 39401
82- 98 PHILLIPS, KEITH ANTHONY 'TONY'	P.O. BOX 602 - ROSWELL GA 30075
73- 95 PHILLIPS, MICHAEL DWAINE	3322 RIDGEFIELD - IRVING TX 75060
70-107 PHILLIPS, NORMAN EDWIN 'EDDIE'	2207 EDGEHILL RD - LOUISVILLE KY 40205
62-105 PHILLIPS, RICHARD EUGENE	6280 MARLBOROUGH #302 - BURNABY BRIT. COL. V5H 3L8 CAN.
15-129 PHILLIPS, THOMAS GERALD	D. APRIL 12, 1929 PHILIPSBURG, PA.
56- 68 PHILLIPS, WILLIAM TAYLOR	BOX 13 - AUSTELL GA 30001
66- 72 PHOEBUS, THOMAS HAROLD	1825 SE VESTHAVEN COURT - PORT SAINT LUCIE FL 34952
77-113 PICCIOLO, ROBERT MICHAEL 'ROB'	6421 FIREBRAND ST - LOS ANGELES CA 90045
45- 80 PICCIUTO, NICHOLAS THOMAS	261 ELMWOOD AVE - MAPLEWOOD NJ 07040
60- 82 PICHE, RONALD JACQUES	100 RUE DE GASPE #1208 - VERDUN QUEBEC H3E 1E5 CAN.
16- 69 PICINICH, VALENTINE JOHN	D. DECEMBER 5, 1942 NOBLEBORO, ME.
14-167 PICK, CHARLES THOMAS	D. JUNE 26, 1954 LYNCHBURG, VA.
23-103 PICK, EDGAR EVERETT	D. MAY 13, 1967 WEST LOS ANGELES, CAL.
31- 69 PICKERING, URBANE HENRY 'DICK'	D. MAY 13, 1970 MODESTO, CALIF.
10-121 PICKETT, CHARLES ALBERT	D. MAY 20, 1969 SPRINGFIELD, O.
33- 51 PICKREL, CLARENCE DOUGLAS	D. NOVEMBER 4, 1983 ROCKY MOUNT, VA.
18- 58 PICKUP, CLARENCE WILLIAM 'TY'	D. AUGUST 2, 1974 OAKLEY CA 94561
88-106 PICO, JEFFREY MARK	4304 BEECHNUT LANE - OAKLEY CA 94561
47- 68 PICONE, MARIO PETER	8876 BAY 16 - BROOKLYN NY 11214
40- 68 PIECHOTA, ALOYSIUS EDWARD	1656 NORTH MAYFIELD AVE-CHICAGO IL 60639
13-140 PIEH, EDWIN JOHN 'CY'	D. SEPTEMBER 12, 1945 JACKSONVILLE, FLA.
73- 96 PIERCE, LAVERN JACK	314 SALAMANCA-COL INDUSTRIAL - LEON GUANAJUANTO MEX.
24- 86 PIERCE, RAYMOND LESTER	D. MAY 4, 1963 DENVER, COLO.
67- 85 PIERCE, TONY MICHAEL	5002 WILLOWBROOK DR - COLUMBUS GA 31909
45- 81 PIERCE, WALTER WILLIAM 'BILLY'	9000 SOUTH FRANCISCO - EVERGREEN PARK IL60642
17- 62 PIERCY, WILLIAM BENTON	D. AUGUST 28, 1951 LONG BEACH, CAL.
45- 82 PIERETTI, MARINO PAUL	D. JANUARY 30, 1981 SAN FRANCISCO, CALIF.
20- 96 PIEROTTI, ALBERT FELIX	D. FEBRUARY 12, 1964 EVERETT, MASS.
50- 78 PIERRO, WILLIAM LEONARD	1751 74TH ST - BROOKLYN NY 11204
50- 79 PIERSALL, JAMES ANTHONY	1105 OAKVIEW DR - WHEATON IL 60187
18- 59 PIERSON, WILLIAM MORRIS	D. FEBRUARY 20, 1959 ATLANTIC CITY, N. J.
31- 70 PIET, ANTHONY FRANCIS	D. DECEMBER 1, 1981 HINSDALE, ILL.
14-168 PIEZ, CHARLES WILLIAM 'SANDY'	D. DECEMBER 29, 1930 ATLANTIC CITY, N.J.
57- 67 PIGNATANO, JOSEPH BENJAMIN	150 78TH ST - BROOKLYN NY 11209
46- 83 PIKE, JAMES WILLARD	D. MARCH 28, 1984 SAN DIEGO, CALIF.
56- 69 PIKTUZIS, GEORGE RICHARD	12051 PARAMOUNT BLVD #9 - DOWNEY CA 90242
56- 70 PILARCIK, ALFRED JAMES	BOX 185 - ST JOHN IN 46373
49- 64 PILLETTE, DUANE XAVIER	165 BLOSSOM HILL RD #404 - SAN JOSE CA 95123
17- 63 PILLETTE, HERMAN POLYCARP	D. APRIL 30, 1960 SACRAMENTO, CAL.
15-130 PILLION, CECIL RANDOLPH 'SQUIZ'	D. SEPTEMBER 30, 1962 PITTSBURGH, PA.

36- 73 PILNEY, ANDREW JAMES	3309 RIDGEWAY DR-METAIRIE LA 70002
68- 80 PINA, HORACIO GARCIA	OLD ADD: VENUSTIANA CARRANZA 207-COAHUILA MEX
18- 60 PINELLI, RALPH ARTHUR 'BABE'	D. OCTOBER 22, 1984 DALY CITY, CALIF.
64- 85 PINIELLA, LOUIS VICTOR	103 MACINTYRE LN - ALLENDALE NJ 07401
58- 73 PINSON, VADA EDWARD	710 31ST ST - OAKLAND CA 94609
22-109 PINTO, WILLIAM LERTON	D. MAY 13, 1983 OXNARD, CALIF.
32- 63 PIPGRAS, EDWARD JOHN	D. APRIL 13, 1964 CURRIE, MINN.
23-104 PIPGRAS, GEORGE WILLIAM	D. OCTOBER 19, 1986 GAINESVILLE, FLA.
13-141 PIPP, WALTER CHARLES	D. JANUARY 11, 1965 GRAND RAPIDS, MICH.
36- 74 PIPPEN, HENRY HAROLD 'COTTON'	D. FEBRUARY 15, 1981 WILLIAMS, CALIF.
78-100 PIRTLE, GERALD EUGENE	9403 SOUTH 236TH EAST AVE - BROKEN ARROW OK 74012
53- 70 PISONI, JAMES PETE	10832 MUELLER RD - ST. LOUIS MO 63123
38- 74 PITKO, ALEXANDER	8001 E. BROADWAY #6512 - MESA AZ 85208
17- 64 PITLER, JACOB ALBERT	D. FEBRUARY 3, 1968 BINGHAMTON, N. Y.
70-108 PITLOCK, LEE PATRICK THOMAS 'SKIP'	513 NORTH SAN MARCOS - SEGUIN TX 78155
85- 92 PITTARO, CHRISTOPHER FRANCIS	42 PINTINALLI DRIVE - TRENTON NJ 08619
21- 82 PITTENGER, CLARKE ALONZO 'PINKY'	D. NOVEMBER 4, 1977 FORT LAUDERDALE, FLA.
81- 97 PITTMAN, JOSEPH WAYNE	809 MCKINNON DR - COLUMBUS GA 31907
74-105 PITTS, GAYLEN RICHARD	2082 SOUTH HELENA STREET #C - AURORA CO 80013
57- 68 PITULA, STANLEY	D. AUGUST 16, 1965 HACKENSACK, N. J.
57- 69 PIZARRO, JUAN CORDOVA	278 DEL RIO - SANTURCE PR 00912
79- 85 PLADSON, GORDON CECIL	OLD ADD: 11375 84TH AVE - DELTA BC
31- 71 PLANETA, EMIL JOSEPH	D. FEBRUARY 2, 1963 ROCKY HILL, CONN.
78-101 PLANK, EDWARD ARTHUR	3005 MILL STREET - RENO NV 89502
55- 93 PLARSKI, DONALD JOSEPH	D. DECEMBER 29, 1981 ST. LOUIS, MO.
62-106 PLASKETT, ELMO ALEXANDER	BOX 1764 - FREDERIKSTED VI 00840
42- 79 PLATT, MIZELL GEORGE 'WHITEY'	D. JULY 27, 1970 WEST PALM BEACH, FLA.
13-142 PLATTE, ALFRED FREDERICK JOSEPH	D. AUGUST 29, 1976 GRAND RAPIDS, MICH.
61- 84 PLEIS, WILLIAM	6844 COUNTRY LAKES CIRCLE - SARASOTA FL 34243
86-123 PLESAC, DANIEL THOMAS	717 PETTIBONE STREET - CROWN POINT IN 46307
56- 71 PLESS, RANCE	RURAL ROUTE 2 BOX 258 - GREENEVILLE TN 37743
56- 72 PLEWS, HERBERT EUGENE	1460 NORTHWESTERN RD - LONGMONT CO 80501
18- 61 PLITT, NORMAN WILLIAM	D. FEBRUARY 1, 1954 NEW YORK, N. Y.
72- 85 PLODINEC, TIMOTHY ALFRED	2201 MCMINN - ALIQUIPPA PA 15001
68- 81 PLUMMER, WILLIAM FRANCIS	3582 RHONDA ROAD - COTTONWOOD CA 96022
86-124 PLUNK, ERIC VAUGHN	14725 BRUCE AVENUE - BELLFLOWER CA 90706
42- 80 POAT, RAYMOND WILLIS	D. APRIL 29, 1990 OAK LAWN, ILL.
75- 90 POCOROBA, BIFF BENEDICT	7002 DESHON RIDGE DRIVE - LITHONIA GA 30058
49- 65 PODBIELAN, CLARENCE ANTHONY 'BUD'	D. OCTOBER 26, 1982 SYRACUSE, N. Y.
40- 69 PODGAJNY, JOHN SIGMUND	D. MARCH 2, 1971 CHESTER, PA.
53- 71 PODRES, JOHN JOSEPH	1 COLONIAL COURT - GLENS FALLS NY 12801
75- 91 POEPPING, MICHAEL HAROLD	RR 2 - PIERZ MN 56364
26- 64 POETZ, JOSEPH FRANK	D. FEBRUARY 7, 1942 ST. LOUIS, MO.
40- 70 POFAHL, JAMES WILLARD	D. SEPTEMBER 14, 1984 OWATONNA, MINN.
79- 86 POFF, JOHN WILLIAM	78 BROWNS LN - FAIRFIELD CT 06430
37- 88 POFFENBERGER, CLETUS ELWOOD 'BOOTS'	13 1/2 NORTH CONOCOCHEAGUE-WILLIAMSPORT MD 21795
50- 80 POHOLSKY, THOMAS GEORGE	177 HORSESHOE DR - KIRKWOOD MO 63122
36- 75 POINDEXTER, CHESTER JENNINGS 'JINKS'	D. MARCH 3, 1983 NORMAN, OKLA.
63- 93 POINTER, AARON ELTON	4406 ARBORDALE AVE WEST - TACOMA WA 98466
43-113 POLAND, HUGH REID	D. MARCH 30, 1984 GUTHRIE, KY.
73- 97 POLE, RICHARD HENRY	21012 WHITLOCK DRIVE - DEARBORN HEIGHTS MI 48127
85- 93 POLIDOR, GUSTAVO ADOLFO	LA AV.DE PRO-PATRIA BLOQ.3 PATRIA B#9-CARACAS VENEZ
47- 69 POLIVKA, KENNETH LYLE	D. JULY 23, 1988 AURORA, ILL.
41- 89 POLLET, HOWARD JOSEPH	D. AUGUST 8, 1974 HOUSTON, TEX.
32- 64 POLLI, LOUIS AMERICO	BOX 45 - GRANITEVILLE VT 05654
37- 89 POLLY, NICHOLAS JOSEPH	2331 NORTH LEAVITT AVE-CHICAGO IL 60647
77-114 POLONI, JOHN PAUL	3205 ELLIS - CHANDLER AZ 85224
87-119 POLONIA, LUIS ANDREW	TURIDEPORTES SA EDCIO HACHETER PISO-LADO ESTE DOM. REP.
34- 86 POMORSKI, JOHN LEON	D. DECEMBER 6, 1977 BRAMPTON, ONTARIO
85- 94 PONCE, CARLOS ANTONIO	51-15 44TH ST,VILLA CAROLINA - CAROLINA PR 00630
10-122 POND, RALPH BENJAMIN	D. SEPTEMBER 8, 1947 CLEVELAND, O.
17- 65 PONDER, CHARLES ELMER	D. APRIL 20, 1974 ALBUQUERQUE, N. M.
34- 87 POOL, HARLIN WELTY	D. FEBRUARY 15, 1963 RODEO, CAL.
25- 86 POOLE, JAMES RALPH	D. JANUARY 2, 1975 HICKORY, N. C..
41- 90 POOLE, RAYMOND HERMAN	RR 10 BOX 655-SALISBURY NC 28144
52- 81 POPE, DAVID	9020 PARMELEE AVE - CLEVELAND OH 44108
64- 86 POPOVICH, PAUL EDWARD	3578 COLLINS FERRY ROAD - MORGANTOWN WV 26501
69-137 POPOWSKI, EDWARD JOSEPH	P.O. BOX 45 - SAYREVILLE NJ 08872
73- 98 POQUETTE, THOMAS ARTHUR	4624 WOODRIDGE DRIVE - EAU CLAIRE WI 54701
14-169 PORRAY, EDMUND JOSEPH	D. JULY 13, 1954 LACKAWAXEN, PA.
81- 98 PORTER, CHARLES WILLIAM	9321 SNYDER LN - PERRY HALL MD 21128
51- 78 PORTER, DANIEL EDWARD	7360 COWLES MT BLVD - SAN DIEGO CA 92119
71- 82 PORTER, DARRELL RAY	19 NE DAYVIEW DRIVE - LEES SUMMIT MO 64063
14-170 PORTER, IRVING MARBLE	D. FEBRUARY 20, 1971 LYNN, MASS.
52- 82 PORTER, J. W. 'JAY'	9677 HEATHER CIR W-PALM BCH GARDENS FL 33410
26- 65 PORTER, NED SWINDELL	D. JUNE 30, 1968 GAINESVILLE, FLA.
29- 84 PORTER, RICHARD TWILLEY	D. SEPTEMBER 24, 1974 PHILADELPHIA, PA.
81- 99 PORTER, ROBERT LEE	4 EDITH COURT PARK BLVD - NAPA CA 94558
48- 81 PORTERFIELD, ERWIN COOLIDGE 'BOB'	D. APRIL 28, 1980 CHARLOTTE, N. C.
48- 82 PORTO, ALFRED	40943 13TH STREET WEST - PALMDALE CA 93551
54- 83 PORTOCARRERO, ARNOLD MARIO	D. JUNE 21, 1986 KANSAS CITY, KAN.
85- 95 PORTUGAL, MARK STEVEN	11843 ORANGE #A - NORWALK CA 90650
60- 83 POSADA, LEOPOLDO JESUS	8200 GRAND CANAL - MIAMI FL 33126
38- 75 POSEDEL, WILLIAM JOHN	D. NOVEMBER 28, 1989 LIVERMORE, CALIF.
32- 65 POSER, JOHN FALK 'BOB'	551 WEST SCHOOL - COLUMBUS WI 53925
46- 84 POSSEHL, LOUIS THOMAS	715 EL CENTRO - LONGBOAT KEY FL 34228
22-110 POST, SAMUEL GILBERT	D. MARCH 31, 1971 PORTSMOUTH, VA.
49- 66 POST, WALTER CHARLES	D. JANUARY 6, 1982 SAINT HENRY, O.
22-111 POTT, NELSON ADOLPH	D. DECEMBER 3, 1963 MACK,O.
38- 76 POTTER, MARYLAND DYKES	3024 WEST MUDDY BRANCH ROAD - ASHLAND KY 41101
76- 75 POTTER, MICHAEL GARY	21582 ARCHER CIR - HUNTINGTON BEACH CA 92646
36- 76 POTTER, NELSON THOMAS	408 SOUTH MCKENDRIE AVE #110 - MOUNT MORRIS IL 61054
23-105 POTTER, SQUIRE	D. JANUARY 27, 1983 ASHLAND, KY.
14-171 POTTS, JOHN FREDERICK	D. SEPTEMBER 5, 1962 CLEVELAND, O.
67- 86 POULSEN, KEN STERLING	684 EAST WEAVER - SIMI VALLEY CA 93065
87-120 POWELL, ALONZO SIDNEY	620 GARFIELD STREET - SAN FRANCISCO CA 94132
30- 63 POWELL, ALVIN JACOB 'JAKE'	D. NOVEMBER 4, 1948 WASHINGTON, D. C.
85- 96 POWELL, DENNIS CLAY	P. O. BOX 133 - NORMAN PARK GA 31771
63- 94 POWELL, GROVER DAVID	D. MAY 21, 1985 RALEIGH, N. C.
78-102 POWELL, HOSKEN	1289 TAMARA STREET - PENSACOLA FL 32503

61- 85 POWELL, JOHN WESLEY 'BOOG'	U. S. ANGLERS MARINE - KEY WEST FL 33040
71- 83 POWELL, PAUL RAY	810 NORTH MYERS - ELOY AZ 85231
13-143 POWELL, RAYMOND REATH	D. OCTOBER 16, 1962 CHILLICOTHE, O .
13-144 POWELL, REGINALD BERTRAND 'JACK'	D. MARCH 12, 1930 MEMPHIS, TENN.
55- 94 POWELL, ROBERT LEROY	5366 STAMPA ST - LAS VEGAS NV 89102
81-100 POWER, TED HENRY	3490 TIFFANY RIDGE LN - CINCINNATI OH 45241
54- 84 POWER, VICTOR PELLOT	CONDOMINEO TORRE,MOLINOS 703-GUAYNABO PR00657
32- 66 POWERS, ELLIS FOREE 'MIKE'	D. DECEMBER 2, 1983 LOUISVILLE, KY.
55- 95 POWERS, JOHN CALVIN	6727 FIRST AVE SOUTH - BIRMINGHAM AL 35206
27- 72 POWERS, JOHN LLOYD 'IKE'	D. DECEMBER 22, 1968 HANCOCK, MD.
38- 77 POWERS, LESLIE EDWIN	D. NOVEMBER 13, 1978 SANTA MONICA, CALIF.
57- 70 POWIS, CARL EDGAR	OLD ADD: 8502 EASTON COMMONS #104 - HOUSTON TX 77095
75- 92 PRALL, WILFRED ANTHONY 'WILLIE'	38 HIGHLAND DRIVE - KINNELON NJ 07405
49- 67 PRAMESA, JOHN STEVEN	111 INLET OAKS VILLAGE - MURRELLS INLET SC 29576
12-158 PRATT, DERRILL BURNHAM 'DEL'	D. SEPTEMBER 30, 1977 TEXAS CITY, TEX.
21- 83 PRATT, FRANCIS BRUCE	D. APRIL 8, 1974 CENTREVILLE, ALA.
14-172 PRATT, LESTER JOHN 'LARRY'	D. JANUARY 8, 1969 PEORIA, ILL.
63- 95 PREGENZER, JOHN ARTHUR	6314 104TH ST EAST - PUYALLUP WA 98373
40- 71 PREIBISCH, MELVIN ADOLPHUS	D. APRIL 12, 1980 SEALY, TEXAS
48- 83 PRENDERGAST, JAMES BARTHOLOMEW	330 FAIRFIELD AVE - BUFFALO NY 14223
14-173 PRENDERGAST, MICHAEL THOMAS	D. NOVEMBER 18, 1967 OMAHA, NEB.
61- 86 PRESCOTT, GEORGE BERTRAND 'BOBBY'	ESTAFETA PARQUE LEFEVRE ENTREGA GENERAL-PANAMA 10, PAN.
51- 79 PRESKO, JOSEPH EDWARD	1612 NE 77TH TER - KANSAS CITY MO 64118
84- 90 PRESLEY, JAMES ARTHUR	1108 HUNTSMAN CIRCLE - PENSACOLA FL 32514
38- 78 PRESSNELL, FOREST CHARLES 'TOT'	329 EAST LIMA ST-FINDLAY OH 45840
67- 87 PRICE, JIMMIE WILLIAM	1183 ROLLING HILLS - BLOOMFIELD HILLS MI 48013
46- 85 PRICE, JOHN THOMAS REID 'JACKIE'	D. OCTOBER 2, 1967 SAN FRANCISCO, CAL.
28- 75 PRICE, JOSEPH PRESTON	D. JANUARY 15, 1961 WASHINGTON. D. C.
80-106 PRICE, JOSEPH WALTER	OLD ADD: BOX 1696 - LAKESIDE CA 92040
39- 90 PRICHARD, ROBERT ALEXANDER	523 SUNSET DRIVE - STAMFORD TX 79553
41- 91 PRIDDY, GERALD EDWARD	D. MARCH 3, 1980 NORTH HOLLYWOOD, CALIF.
62-107 PRIDDY, ROBERT SIMPSON	OLD ADD: 519 NORTH CASCADE TER-SUNNYVALE CA94087
11-136 PRIEST, JOHN GOODING	D. NOVEMBER 4, 1979 WASHINGTON, D. C.
33- 52 PRIM, RAYMOND LEE	19120 D STREET - MONTE RIO CA 95462
62-108 PRINCE, DONALD MARK	5 BAHAMA DR - WRIGHTSVILLE BEACH NC 28480
87-121 PRINCE, THOMAS ALBERT	277 NORTH DOUGLAS - BRADLEY IL 60915
57- 71 PRITCHARD, HAROLD WILLIAM 'BUDDY'	507 EAST SUNNY HILL RD - FULLERTON CA 92635
59- 66 PROCTOR, JAMES ARTHUR	OLD ADD: 609 COUNT FLEET COURT - NAPERVILLE IL 60540
23-106 PROCTOR, NOAH RICHARD 'RED'	D. DECEMBER 17, 1954 RICHMOND, VA.
76- 76 PROLY, MICHAEL JAMES	2585 FRISCO DR - CLEARWATER FL 33519
23-107 PROPST, WILLIAM JACOB 'JAKE'	D. FEBRUARY 24, 1967 COLUMBUS, MISS.
20- 97 PROTHRO, JAMES THOMPSON 'DOC'	D. OCTOBER 14, 1971 MEMPHIS, TENN.
12-160 PROUGH, HERSCHEL CLINTON 'BILL'	D. NOVEMBER 29, 1936 RICHMOND, IND.
29- 85 PRUDHOMME, JOHN OLGUS	5935 FAIRFIELD AVE - SHREVEPORT LA 71106
20- 98 PRUESS, EARL HENRY 'GIBBY'	D. AUGUST 28, 1979 BRANSON, MO.
22-112 PRUETT, HUBERT SHELBY	D. JANUARY 28, 1982 LADUE, MO.
44-107 PRUETT, JAMES CALVIN	1906 MADERA ST - WAUKESHA WI 53186
75- 93 PRUITT, RONALD RALPH	909 JOHNSON AVENUE - FLINT MI 48504
76- 77 PRYOR, GREGORY RUSSELL	P.O. BOX 34523 - NORTH KANSAS CITY MO 64116
30- 64 PUCCINELLI, GEORGE LAWRENCE	D. APRIL 16, 1956 SAN FRANCISCO, CAL.
84- 91 PUCKETT, KIRBY	8924 ASHLEY TERRACE - BROOKLYN PARK MN 55443
11-137 PUCKETT, TROY LEVI	D. APRIL 13, 1971 WINCHESTER, IND.
70-109 PUENTE, MIGUEL ANTONIO	COBRE 106,COL MORALES-SAN LUIS POTOSI SAN LUIS POT MEX.
77-115 PUHL, TERRENCE STEPHEN	3523 GOLDEN TEE LN - MISSOURI CITY TX 77459
74-106 PUIG, RICHARD GERALD	16708 FOOTHILL DR - TAMPA FL 33624
77-116 PUJOLS, LUIS BIENVENIDO	NICOLAS HEREDIA - BANI DOMINICAN REP.
81-101 PULEO, CHARLES MICHAEL	8208 CORTELAND DRIVE - KNOXVILLE TN 37909
83-114 PULIDO, ALFONSO	H.RICARDO MERCADO,CASILLAS 26-27-TIERRA BLANCA VER MEX.
25- 87 PUMPELLY, SPENCER ARMSTRONG	D. DECEMBER 5, 1973 SAYRE, PA.
64- 87 PURDIN, JOHN NOLAN	4748 GEORGE AVE - SARASOTA FL 33583
26- 66 PURDY, EVERETT VIRGIL 'PID'	D. JANUARY 16, 1951 BEATRICE, NEB.
54- 85 PURKEY, ROBERT THOMAS	5767 KING SCHOOL RD - BETHEL PARK PA 15102
76- 78 PUTMAN, EDDY WILLIAM	23 GLORIETA WEST - IRVINE CA 92720
77-117 PUTNAM, PATRICK EDWARD	309 MORSE PLAZA - TICE FL 33905
55- 96 PYBURN, JAMES EDWARD	RR 13 BOX 265 - JASPER AL 35501
54- 86 PYECHA, JOHN NICHOLAS	107 NOTTINGHAM DRIVE - CHAPEL HILL NC 27514
39- 91 PYLE, EWALD	538 HALLIDAY AVENUE - DUQUOIN IL 62832
28- 76 PYLE, HARLAN ALBERT	BOX 307 - LIBERTY NE 68381
32- 67 PYTLAK, FRANK ANTHONY	D. MAY 8, 1977 BUFFALO, N. Y.
86-125 PYZNARSKI, TIMOTHY MATTHEW	10716 SOUTH AUSTIN - CHICAGO RIDGE IL 60415
69-138 QUALLS, JAMES ROBERT	OLD ADD: RR 4 BOX 710 - LODI CA 95240
53- 72 QUALTERS, THOMAS FRANCIS	RR 2 BOX 39 - SOMERSET PA 15501
64- 88 QUEEN, MELVIN DOUGLAS	2130 NORTH MAIN - MORRO BAY CA 93442
42- 81 QUEEN, MELVIN JOSEPH	D. APRIL 4, 1982 FORT SMITH, ARK.
54- 87 QUEEN, WILLIAM EDDLEMAN	1616 EAST PERRY STREET - GASTONIA NC 28052
31- 72 QUELLICH, GEORGE WILLIAM	D. AUGUST 31, 1958 JOHNSVILLE, CALIF.
39- 92 QUICK, JAMES HAROLD	D. MARCH 9, 1974 SWANSEA, ILL.
65- 88 QUILICI, FRANK RALPH	9336 NESBITT ROAD - BLOOMINGTON MN 55437
13-145 QUINLAN, THOMAS ALOYSIUS 'FINNERS'	D. FEBRUARY 17, 1966 SCRANTON, PA.
49- 68 QUINN, FRANK WILLIAM	OLD ADD: 530 SW 27TH WAY - BOYNTON BEACH FL 33435
11-138 QUINN, JOHN EDWARD PICK	D. APRIL 9, 1956 MARLBORO, MASS.
41- 92 QUINN, WELLINGTON HUNT 'WIMPY'	D. SEPTEMBER 1, 1954 LOS ANGELES, CAL.
83-115 QUINONES, LUIS RAUL	URB STA TERESITA CALLE 1 AE11-PONCE PR 00731
86-126 QUINONES, REY FRANCISCO	CLE RONDA 216 VILLA ANADALUCIA - RIO PIEDRAS PR 00926
88-107 QUINTANA, CARLOS NARCIS	558 RIVER STREET - MAMPORAL,MIRANDA VENEZUELA S.A.
74-107 QUINTANA, LUIS JOAQUIN	CASCRIO CATONI ED. 11 #70 - VEGA BAJA PR 00763
62-109 QUIRK, ARTHUR LEONARD	90 SOUTH MILL DRIVE - SOUTH GLASTONBURG CT 06073
75- 94 QUIRK, JAMES PATRICK	8412 WEST 113TH TERRACE - OVERLAND PARK KS 66210
79- 87 QUISENBERRY, DANIEL RAYMOND	12208 BUENA VISTA - LEAWOOD KS 66209
82- 99 RABB, JOHN ANDREW	1321 WEST 106TH STREET - LOS ANGELES CA 90044
22-113 RABBITT, JOSEPH PATRICK	D. DECEMBER 5, 1969 NORWALK, CONN.
57- 72 RABE, CHARLES HENRY	7725 LINDEN AVE - DARIEN IL 60559
40- 72 RACHUNOK, STEPHEN STEPANOVICH	2660 WEST BALL ROAD #3 - ANAHEIM CA 92804
47- 70 RACKLEY, MARVIN EUGENE	HIRAM-ACWORTH DRIVE - DALLAS GA 30132
62-110 RADATZ, RICHARD RAYMOND	P.O. BOX 348,ATL. CONTAINER - BRAINTREE MA 02184
34- 88 RADCLIFF, RAYMOND ALLEN 'RIP'	D. MAY 23, 1962 ENID, OKLA.
11-139 RADEBAUGH, ROY	D. JANUARY 17, 1945 CEDAR RAPIDS, IA.
71- 84 RADER, DAVID MARTIN	2114 OAKWOOD DR - BAKERSFIELD CA 93304

13-146	RADER, DONALD RUSSELL	D. JUNE 26, 1983 WALLA WALLA, WASH.
67- 88	RADER, DOUGLAS LEE	112-7 CEDAR POINT - STUART FL 33494
21- 84	RADER, DREW LEON	D. JUNE 5, 1975 CATSKILL, N. Y.
36- 77	RADTKE, JACK WILLIAM	289 SOUTH LOCUST - TWIN FALLS ID 83301
54- 88	RAETHER, HAROLD HERMAN	5920 MEROLD DR - EDINA MN 55436
39- 93	RAFFENSBERGER, KENNETH DAVID	418 CLOVER DRIVE, RR 7 - YORK PA 17402
69-139	RAFFO, ALBERT MARTIN	BOX 866 - JASPER TN 37347
32- 68	RAGLAND, FRANK ROLAND	D. JULY 28, 1959 PARIS, MISS.
71- 85	RAGLAND, THOMAS	20201 GREENLAWN ST - DETROIT MI 48224
75- 95	RAICH, ERIC JAMES	OLD ADD: 1625 WOODRUFF #45 - BELL CA 90201
57- 73	RAINES, LAWRENCE GLENN HOPE	D. JANUARY 28, 1978 LANSING, MICH.
79- 88	RAINES, TIMOTHY	2316 AIRPORT BLVD - SANFORD FL 32771
79- 89	RAINEY, CHARLES DAVID	13340 GRANDVIA POINT - SAN DIEGO CA 92130
78-103	RAJSICH, DAVID CHRISTOPHER	5324 NORTH SIXTH ST - PHOENIX AZ 85012
82-100	RAJSICH, GARY LOUIS	5324 NORTH 6TH ST - PHOENIX AZ 85012
60- 84	RAKOW, EDWARD CHARLES	12259 HILLMAN CIR - LAKE PARK FL 33403
10-123	RALSTON, SAMUEL BERYL 'DOC'	D. AUGUST 29, 1950 LANCASTER, PA.
46- 86	RAMAZOTTI, ROBERT LOUIS	1111 SOUTH 26TH ST - ALTOONA PA 16602
39- 94	RAMBERT, ELMER DONALD 'PEP'	D. NOVEMBER 16, 1974 WEST PALM BEACH, FLA.
26- 67	RAMBO, WARREN DAWSON 'PETE'	CROWN POINT RD - THOROFARE NJ 08086
83-116	RAMIREZ, DANIEL ALLAN	2806 ERWIN - VICTORIA TX 77901
80-107	RAMIREZ, MARIO	OLD ADD: RR 2 BOX 7 - YAUCO PR 00768
70-110	RAMIREZ, MILTON	7 TULIO LARRINAGA ST - MAYAGUEZ PR 00708
74-108	RAMIREZ, ORLANDO	TORICES PASO ABADIO #1325-CARTAGENA COLOMBIA S.A.
80-108	RAMIREZ, RAFAEL EMILIO	M.P. GAZETT #8,ENS. PRIMAVERA-SAN PEDRO DE MACORIS D.R.
78-104	RAMOS, DOMINGO ANTONIO	CARR DUARTE KM 8 1/2,LICEY AL MEDIO-SANTIAGO DOM. REP.
44-108	RAMOS, JESUS MANUEL GARCIA 'CHUCHO'	AVE SANTADER, LAPINTA #4 - EL PARAISO VENEZ
55- 97	RAMOS, PEDRO	9367 FONTAINEBLEAU BLVD #G119 - MIAMI FL 33172
78-105	RAMOS, ROBERTO	8945 LAKE IRMA POINT - ORLANDO FL 32817
47- 71	RAMSDELL, JAMES WILLARD 'WILLIE'	D. OCTOBER 8, 1969 WICHITA, KAN.
87-122	RAMSEY, MICHAEL JAMES	STAR ROUTE BOX 36F - HARLEM GA 30814
78-106	RAMSEY, MICHAEL JEFFREY	OLD ADD: 2900 CEDAR KNOLL DR - ROSWELL GA 30076
45- 83	RAMSEY, WILLIAM THRACE	769 ROSEBANK RD - MEMPHIS TN 38116
53- 73	RAND, RICHARD HILTON	25612 SAN LUPE AVENUE - MORENO VALLEY CA 92388
88-108	RANDALL, JAMES ODELL 'SAP'	711 CRANE AVENUE - WHISTLER AL 36612
76- 79	RANDALL, ROBERT LEE	308 OPAL CIR - AMES IA 50010
71- 86	RANDLE, LEONARD SHENOFF	15741 SLEEPY OAK ROAD - CHINO HILLS CA 91709
75- 96	RANDOLPH, WILLIE LARRY	648 JUNIPER PLACE - FRANKLIN LAKES NJ 07417
62-111	RANEW, MERRITT THOMAS	P.O. BOX 6281 - OCALA FL 32678
49- 69	RANEY, FRANK ROBERT DONALD 'RIBS'	11242 CHARLES DR - WARREN MI 48093
81-102	RANSOM, JEFFERY DEAN	2131 CURTIS ST - BERKELEY CA 94702
49- 70	RAPP, EARL WELLINGTON	301A SECOND STREET - SWEDESBORO NJ 08085
21- 85	RAPP, JOSEPH ALOYSIUS 'GOLDIE'	D. JULY 1, 1966 LAMESA, CALIF.
77-118	RAPP, VERNON FRED	14800 N. LOWELL BLVD - BLOOMFIELD CO 80020
46- 87	RASCHI, VICTOR JOHN ANGELO	D. OCTOBER 14, 1988 GROVELAND, N. J.
83-117	RASMUSSEN, DENNIS LEE	16210 WRIGHT CIRCLE - OMAHA NE 68130
75- 97	RASMUSSEN, ERIC RALPH	8829 NORTHWEST AVE - RACINE WI 53406
15-131	RASMUSSEN, HENRY FLORIAN	D. JANUARY 1, 1949 CHICAGO, ILL.
68- 82	RATH, FRED HELSHER	7308 PELICAN ISLAND DR - TAMPA FL 33614
65- 89	RATLIFF, KELLY EUGENE 'GENE'	3403 MILLERFIELD RD - MACON GA 31201
63- 96	RATLIFF, PAUL HAWTHORNE	408 EAST 15TH #7 - BEAUMONT CA 92223
80-109	RATZER, STEVEN WAYNE	1671 SOUTH SALIDA WAY - AURORA CO 80012
72- 86	RAU, DOUGLAS JAMES	RR 1 BOX 154-A - COLUMBUS TX 78934
72- 87	RAUCH, ROBERT JOHN	OLD ADD: 1149 OLIVE RD - VIRGINIA BEACH VA 23462
66- 73	RAUDMAN, ROBERT JOYCE 'SHORTY'	OLD ADD: 17529 CHATSWORTH - GRANADA HILLS CA 91344
77-119	RAUTZHAN, CLARENCE GEORGE 'LANCE'	RR 4 BOX 4454 - POTTSVILLE PA 17901
78-107	RAWLEY, SHANE WILLIAM	6315 APPROACH ROAD - SARASOTA FL 33583
14-174	RAWLINGS, JOHN WILLIAM	D. OCTOBER 16, 1972 INGLEWOOD, CALIF.
15-132	RAY, CARL GRADY	D. APRIL 3, 1970 WALNUT COVE, N.C.
65- 90	RAY, JAMES FRANCIS	OLD ADD: 7530 PROMPTON - HOUSTON TX 77025
81-103	RAY, JOHN CORNELIAS	RR 1 BOX 64 - CHAUTEAU OK 74337
82-101	RAY, LARRY DOYLE	OLD ADD: RR 3 - VEVAY IN 47043
10-124	RAY, ROBERT HENRY 'FARMER'	D. MARCH 11, 1963 ELECTRA, TEX.
58- 74	RAYDON, CURTIS LOWELL	1515 SOUTH BUNN ST - BLOOMINTON IL 61701
80-110	RAYFORD, FLOYD KINNARD	OLD ADD: 1010 LARCH STREET #12 - INGLEWOOD CA 90301
59- 67	RAYMOND, JOSEPH CLAUDE	3 DE LA CITIERE, B.P. 911 - ST. LUC QUEBEC J0J 2A0 CAN.
19- 66	RAYMOND, LOUIS ANTHONY	D. MAY 2, 1979 ROCHESTER, N. Y.
73- 99	RAZIANO, BARRY JOHN	1315 4TH ST - KENNER LA 70062
83-118	READY, RANDY MAX	4050 NORTH HIDDEN COVE PLACE - TUCSON AZ 85749
69-140	REAMS, LEROY	1638 85TH AVE - OAKLAND CA 94621
79- 90	REARDON, JEFFREY JAMES	4 MARLWOOD LN - PALM BEACH GARDENS FL 33410
38- 79	REBEL, ARTHUR ANTHONY	1726 WEST FORE DR-TAMPA FL 33610
68- 83	REBERGER, FRANK BEALL	2132 NW 204TH STREET - SEATTLE WA 98177
12-161	REDDING, PHILIP HAYDEN	D. MARCH 30, 1929 GREENWOOD, MISS.
32- 69	REDER, JOHN ANTHONY	BOX 1892 - FALL RIVER MA 02722
28- 77	REDFERN, GEORGE HOWARD 'BUCK'	D. SEPTEMBER 8, 1964 ASHEVILLE, N. C.
76- 80	REDFERN, PETER IRVINE	15131 PADDOCK - SYLMAR CA 91342
88-109	REDFIELD, JOSEPH RANDALL	31273 GANADO DRIVE - RANCHO PALOS VERDES CA 90274
74-109	REDMON, GLENN VINCENT	BETHESDA BAPTIST CHURCH - BROWNSBURG IN 46112
65- 91	REDMOND, HOWARD WAYNE	OLD ADD: 16557 HEYDEN - DETROIT MI 48235
35- 92	REDMOND, JACKSON MCKITTRICK	D. JULY 28, 1968 GARLAND, TEX.
82-102	REDUS, GARY EUGENE	BOX 202 - TANNER AL 35671
78-108	REECE, ROBERT SCOTT	1654 BONITA - FOLSOM CA 95630
58- 75	REED, HOWARD DEAN	D. DECEMBER 7, 1984 CORPUS CHRISTI, TEX.
84- 92	REED, JEFF SCOTT	RR 7 BOX 3570 - ELIZABETHTON TN 37643
81-104	REED, JERRY MAXWELL	21 GRANDVIEW RD - ASHEVILLE NC 28806
87-123	REED, JODY ERIC	OLD ADD: 2319 MERROLY CIRCLE NORTH - SEFFNER FL 33584
61- 87	REED, JOHN BURWELL	BOX 97 - SILVER CITY MS 39166
11-140	REED, MILTON D.	D. JULY 27, 1938 ATLANTA, GA.
15-133	REED, RALPH EDWIN 'TED'	D. FEBRUARY 16, 1959 BEAVER, PA.
88-110	REED, RICHARD ALLEN	2205 JEFFERSON AVENUE - HUNTINGTON WV 25704
69-141	REED, ROBERT EDWARD	108 ESSEX DRIVE - LONGWOOD FL 32750
66- 74	REED, RONALD LEE	2613 CLIFFVIEW DR - LILBURN GA 30247
52- 83	REED, WILLIAM JOSEPH	11807 MARRS - HOUSTON TX 77065
49- 71	REEDER, WILLIAM EDGAR	BOX 812 - WHITNEY TX 76692
18- 62	REES, STANLEY MILTON	D. AUGUST 29, 1937 LEXINGTON, KY.
27- 73	REESE, ANDREW JACKSON	D. JANUARY 10, 1966 TUPELO, MISS.
40- 73	REESE, HAROLD HENRY 'PEE WEE'	3211 BEALS BRANCH RD-LOUISVILLE KY 40206

Johnny Mize

Bobby Doerr

Charlie Gehringer

Red Schoendienst

Lou Boudreau

Joe Sewell

George Kell

DELUXE INFIELD

Imagine an infield with the Hall of Famers included on this page of autographed Perez-Steele Art Post Cards — Mize, Doerr, Gehringer, Schoendienst, Boudreau, Sewell, Kell and Brooks Robinson

Brooks Robinson

REESE   RICHARDSON

30- 65 REESE, JAMES HERMAN	10797 ASHTON AVE - LOS ANGELES CA 90024
64- 89 REESE, RICHARD BENJAMIN 'RICH'	OLD ADD: 4210 DEVONSHIRE COURT - NORTHBROOK IL 60062
26- 68 REEVES, ROBERT EDWIN	702 BELVOIR AVE - CHATTANOOGA TN 37412
54- 89 REGALADO, RUDOLPH VALENTINO	5f22 LOS ALTOS COURT - SAN DIEGO CA 92109
17- 66 REGAN, MICHAEL JOHN	D. MAY 23, 1961 ALBANY, N. Y.
60- 85 REGAN, PHILIP RAYMOND	1375 108TH ST - BYRON CENTER MI 49315
26- 69 REGAN, WILLIAM WRIGHT	D. JUNE 11, 1968 PITTSBURGH, PA.
24- 87 REGO, ANTONE	D. JANUARY 6, 1978 TULSA, OKLA.
12-162 REHG, WALTER PHILLIP	D. AUGUST 5, 1946 BURBANK, CALIF.
33- 53 REIBER, FRANK BERNARD	BOX 6284 - SARASOTA FL 33578
49- 72 REICH, HERMAN CHARLES	3779 PALA MESA DR - FALLBROOK CA 92028
64- 90 REICHARDT, FREDERIC CARL 'RICK'	2605 NW 90TH TER - GAINESVILLE FL 32606
22-114 REICHLE, RICHARD WENDELL	D. JUNE 13, 1967 ST. LOUIS, MO.
46- 88 REID, EARL PERCY	D. MAY 11, 1984 CULLMAN, ALA.
87-124 REID, JESSIE THOMAS	3614 CEDAR AVENUE - LYNWOOD CA 90262
69-142 REID, SCOTT DONALD	3611 EAST NAMBE COURT - PHOENIX AZ 85044
17- 67 REILLY, ARCHER EDWIN	D. NOVEMBER 29, 1963 COLUMBUS, O.
19- 67 REILLY, HAROLD J.	
88-111 REIMER, KEVIN MICHAEL	1206 WEST SALMON ARM RD-ENDERBY BRIT. COL. VOE 1V0 CAN.
74-110 REINBACH, MICHAEL WAYNE	% CREAMER, 9459 SLOPE ST - SANTEE CA 92071
19- 68 REINHART, ARTHUR CONRAD	D. NOVEMBER 11, 1946 HOUSTON, TEX.
28- 78 REINHOLZ, ARTHUR AUGUST	D. DECEMBER 29, 1980 NEWPORT RICHEY, FLA.
15-134 REINICKER, WALTER JOSEPH	D. APRIL 18, 1957 PITTSBURGH, PA.
11-141 REIS, HARRIE CRANE 'JACK'	D. JULY 20, 1939 CINCINNATI, O.
31- 73 REIS, ROBERT JOSEPH THOMAS	D. MAY 1, 1973 ST. PAUL, MINN.
38- 80 REIS, THOMAS EDWARD	41 HOLLY LN - FORT THOMAS KY 41075
40- 74 REISER, HAROLD PATRICK 'PETE'	D. OCTOBER 25, 1981 PALM SPRINGS, CALIF.
11-142 REISIGL, JACOB 'BUGGS'	D. FEBRUARY 24, 1957 AMSTERDAM, N.Y.
32- 70 REISS, ALBERT ALLEN	D. MAY 13, 1989 RED BANK, N.J.
72- 88 REITZ, KENNETH JOHN	7541 WARNER - SAINT LOUIS MO 63117
79- 91 REMMERSWAAL, WILHELMUS ABRAHAM	DOKTOR VAN PRAAG ST 16 - WASSENAAR HOLLAND EUROP
12-163 REMNEAS, ALEXANDER NORMAN	D. AUGUST 27, 1975 PHOENIX, ARIZ.
75- 98 REMY, GERALD PETER	5 DENNIS DR - WESTPORT MA 02790
13-147 RENFER, ERWIN ARTHUR	D. OCTOBER 26, 1957 SYCAMORE, ILL.
59- 68 RENFROE, MARSHALL DALTON	D. DECEMBER 10, 1970 PENSACOLA, FLA.
68- 84 RENICK, WARREN RICHARD 'RICK'	4374 MEADOWLAND CIR - SARASOTA FL 33583
61- 88 RENIFF, HAROLD EUGENE	424 STAFFORD - SCRANTON PA 18505
38- 81 RENINGER, JAMES DAVID	BOX 9051 - SHAWNEE MISSION KS 66201
69-143 RENKO, STEVEN	3408 WEST 129TH - LEAWOOD KS 66209
53- 74 RENNA, WILLIAM BENEDITTO	1476 LESHER CT - SAN JOSE CA 95125
30- 66 RENSA, GEORGE ANTHONY 'TONY'	D. JANUARY 4, 1987 WILKES-BARRE, PA.
86-127 RENTERIA, RICHARD AVINA	P.O. BOX 8053 - SUN CITY CA 92380
39- 95 REPASS, ROBERT WILLIS	169 BRIMFIELD RD-WETHERSFIELD CT 06109
78-109 REPLOGLE, ANDREW DAVID	1115 YELLOWWOOD CIR - NOBLESVILLE IN 46060
64- 91 REPOZ, ROGER ALLEN	1106 IRVING ST - BELLINGHAM WA 98225
53- 75 REPULSKI, ELDON JOHN 'RIP'	1541 8TH AVE NORTH - ST CLOUD MN 56301
43-114 RESCIGNO, XAVIER FREDERICK	163E FALMOUTH COURT - RIDGE NY 11961
49- 73 RESTELLI, DINO PAUL	1860 SAN CARLOS AVE - SAN CARLOS CA 94070
68- 85 RETTENMUND, MERVIN WELDON	16670 ESPOLA RD - POWAY CA 92064
22-115 RETTIG, ADOLPH JOHN 'OTTO'	D. JUNE 16, 1977 STUART, FLA.
61- 89 RETZER, KENNETH LEO	137 HICKORY STREET - WOOD RIVER IL 62095
75- 99 REUSCHEL, PAUL RICHARD	RR 1 BOX 76 - CAMP POINT IL 62320
72- 89 REUSCHEL, RICKY EUGENE	1403 PICADILLY CIRCLE - MOUNT PROSPECT IL 60056
69-144 REUSS, JERRY	324 WEST 35TH STREET - CHICAGO IL 60616
78-110 REVERING, DAVID ALVIN	9050 EAST PARADISE DRIVE - SCOTTSDALE AZ 85260
83-119 REYES, GILBERTO ROLANDO	CALLE 2DA. #7 LOS MAMEYES - SANTO DOMINGO DOM. REP.
43-115 REYES, NAPOLEON AGUILERA	2203 NW 33RD STREET - MIAMI FL 33142
42- 82 REYNOLDS, ALLIE PIERCE	2525 CASHION PL-OKLAHOMA CITY OK 73112
68- 86 REYNOLDS, ARCHIE EDWARD	601 PHEASANT RUN - BURLESON TX 76028
27- 74 REYNOLDS, CARL NETTLES	D. MAY 29, 1978 HOUSTON, TEX.
45- 84 REYNOLDS, DANIEL VANCE	BOX 55 - SCOTTS NC 28699
78-111 REYNOLDS, DONALD EDWARD	2605 SOUTHEAST RYAN - CORVALLIS OR 97330
75-100 REYNOLDS, GORDON CRAIG	5906 PARADISE VALLEY COURT - HOUSTON TX 77069
83-120 REYNOLDS, HAROLD CRAIG	2605 SE RYAN ST - CORVALLIS OR 97330
70-111 REYNOLDS, KENNETH LEE	182 GREENWOOD - MARLBOROUGH MA 01752
69-145 REYNOLDS, ROBERT ALLEN	1910 SW 311TH STREET - FEDERAL WAY WA 98023
83-121 REYNOLDS, ROBERT JAMES	7076 EL SORENO CIR - SACRAMENTO CA 95831
82-103 REYNOLDS, RONN DWAYNE	133 LONGWOOD AVENUE - AUSTIN TX 78748
14-175 REYNOLDS, ROSS ERNEST	D. JUNE 23, 1970 ADA, OKLA.
63- 97 REYNOLDS, THOMAS D	1577 SAN ALTOS - LEMON GROVE CA 92045
13-148 REYNOLDS, WILLIAM DEE	D. JUNE 5, 1924 CARNEGIE, OKLA.
47- 72 RHAWN, ROBERT JOHN	D. JUNE 9, 1984 DANVILLE, PA.
14-176 RHEAM, KENNETH JOHNSTON 'CY'	D. OCTOBER 23, 1947 PITTSBURGH, PA.
24- 88 RHEM, CHARLES FLINT	D. JULY 30, 1969 COLUMBIA, S. C.
29- 86 RHIEL, WILLIAM JOSEPH	D. AUGUST 16, 1946 YOUNGSTOWN, O.
74-111 RHODEN, RICHARD ALAN	235 SW 12TH AVENUE - BOYNTON BEACH FL 33435
52- 84 RHODES, JAMES LAMAR "DUSTY"	245 DIXON AVE - STATEN ISLAND NY 10303
29- 87 RHODES, JOHN GORDON	D. MARCH 22, 1960 LONG BEACH, CAL.
82-104 RHOMBERG, KEVIN JAY	5786 BEACH DR - MENTOR ON THE LAKE OH 44060
26- 70 RHYNE, HAROLD J.	D. JANUARY 7, 1971 ORANGEVALE, CAL.
64- 92 RIBANT, DENNIS JOSEPH	18201 VON KARMAN AVE #900 - IRVINE CA 92715
76- 81 RICCELLI, FRANK JOSEPH	103 LINCOLN PARK DRIVE - SYRACUSE NY 13203
45- 85 RICE, DELBERT W	D. JANUARY 26, 1983 BUENA PARK, CALIF.
15-135 RICE, EDGAR CHARLES 'SAM'	D. OCTOBER 13, 1974 ROSSMOR, MD.
48- 84 RICE, HAROLD HOUSTON	%RON RICE,1008 W. HAINES AVE-MUNCIE IN 47303
23-108 RICE, HARRY FRANCIS 'SAM'	D. JANUARY 1, 1971 PORTLAND, ORE.
74-112 RICE, JAMES EDWARD	135 WODEN WAY - WINTER HAVEN FL 33880
44-109 RICE, LEONARD OLIVER	BOX 54 - ARNOLD CA 95223
26- 71 RICE, ROBERT TURNBULL	D. FEBRUARY 20, 1986 ELIZABETHTOWN, PA.
39- 96 RICH, WOODROW EARL	D. APRIL 18, 1983 MORGANTON, N.C.
71- 87 RICHARD, JAMES RODNEY	10235 SAGEDALE - HOUSTON TX 77089
71- 88 RICHARD, LEE EDWARD 'BEE BEE'	1621 EAST 14TH ST - PORT ARTHUR TX 77640
60- 86 RICHARDS, DUANE LEE	BOX 54 - PALESTINE OH 45352
77-120 RICHARDS, EUGENE	4360 PANORAMA DRIVE - LAMESA CA 92041
51- 80 RICHARDS, FRED CHARLES	1760 DODGE NW - WARREN OH 44485
32- 71 RICHARDS, PAUL RAPIER	D. MAY 5, 1986 WAXAHACHIE, TEXAS
89-101 RICHARDS, RUSSELL EARL 'RUSTY'	10014 VILLA LEA - HOUSTON TX 77071
29- 88 RICHARDSON, CLIFFORD NOLEN	D. SEPTEMBER 25, 1951 ATHENS, GA.

116

64- 93 RICHARDSON, GORDON CLARK — RR 3 BOX 217 - COLQUITT GA 31737
89-102 RICHARDSON, JEFFREY SCOTT — 3550 COUNTRY SQUIRE DR #405 - CARROLLTON TX 75005
15-136 RICHARDSON, JOHN WILLIAM — D. JANUARY 18, 1970 MARION, ILL.
42- 83 RICHARDSON, KENNETH FRANKLIN — D. DECEMBER 7, 1987 WOODLAND HILLS, CALIF.
55- 98 RICHARDSON, ROBERT CLINTON — 47 ADAMS - SUMTER SC 29150
17- 68 RICHARDSON, THOMAS MITCHELL — D. NOVEMBER 15, 1939 ONAWA, IA.
80-111 RICHARDT, MICHAEL ANTHONY — 5054 WEST DONNER AVENUE - FRESNO CA 93722
21- 86 RICHBOURG, LANCE CLAYTON — D. SEPTEMBER 10, 1975 CRESTVIEW, FLA.
62-112 RICHERT, PETER GERARD — 5932 PARADISE PLAZA - PALM SPRINGS CA 92264
89-103 RICHIE, ROBERT EUGENE — 2175 EDGEMAR CIRCLE - RENO NV 89512
33- 54 RICHMOND, BERYL JUSTICE — D. APRIL 24, 1980 CAMERON, W. VA.
41- 93 RICHMOND, DONALD LESTER — D. MAY 24, 1981 ELMIRA, N. Y.
20- 99 RICHMOND, RAYMOND SINCLAIR — D. OCTOBER 21, 1969 DESOTO, MO.
51- 81 RICHTER, ALLEN GORDON — P.O. BOX 41 - VIRGINIA BEACH VA 23451
11-143 RICHTER, EMIL HENRY 'REGGIE' — D. AUGUST 3, 1934 CHICAGO, ILL.
42- 84 RICKERT, MARVIN AUGUST — D. JUNE 3, 1978 OAKVILLE, WASH.
63- 98 RICKETTS, DAVID WILLIAM — 12860 POLO PARC DRIVE - ST.LOUIS MO 63146
59- 89 RICKETTS, RICHARD JAMES — D. MARCH 6, 1988 ROCHESTER, N.Y.
69-146 RICO, ALFREDO CRUZ 'FRED' — 27315 MANZANITA #102 - CANYON COUNTRY CA 91351
16- 70 RICO, ARTHUR RAYMOND — D. JANUARY 3, 1919 BOSTON, MASS.
23-109 RICONDA, HARRY PAUL — D. NOVEMBER 15, 1958 MAHOPAC, N. Y.
39- 97 RIDDLE, ELMER RAY — D. MAY 14, 1984 COLUMBUS, GA.
30- 67 RIDDLE, JOHN LUDY — 4017 MONACO DRIVE #B - INDIANAPOLIS IN 46220
70-112 RIDDLEBERGER, DENNIS MICHAEL — 200 WEST 31ST #5A - NORFOLK VA 23504
14-177 RIDGWAY, JACOB A. 'JOHN' — D. FEBRUARY 23, 1928 PHILADELPHIA, PA.
50- 81 RIDZIK, STEPHEN GEORGE — 910 TROPICAL DRIVE - BRADENTON FL 33508
42- 85 RIEBE, HARVEY DONALD 'HANK' — 28031 LAKE SHORE BLVD-CLEVELAND OH 44132
10-125 RIEGER, ELMER JAY — D. OCTOBER 21, 1959 LOS ANGELES, CALIF.
11-144 RIGGERT, JOSEPH ALOYSIUS — D. DECEMBER 10, 1973 KANSAS CITY, MO.
34- 89 RIGGS, LEWIS SIDNEY — D. AUGUST 12, 1975 DURHAM, N. C.
79- 92 RIGHETTI, DAVID ALLAN — 1574 KOCH LN - SAN JOSE CA 95125
22-116 RIGNEY, EMORY ELMO 'TOPPER' — D. JUNE 6, 1972 SAN ANTONIO, TEX.
37- 90 RIGNEY, JOHN DUNGAN — D. OCTOBER 21, 1984 LOMBARD, ILL.
46- 89 RIGNEY, WILLIAM JOSEPH — 3136 ROUND HILL RD - ALAMO CA 94507
84- 93 RIJO, JOSE ANTONIO — CENTRAL CABRAL #66 - SAN CRISTOBAL DOMINICAN REP.
41- 94 RIKARD, CULLEY — 50 HWY 304 - OLIVE BRANCH MS 38654
85- 97 RILES, ERNEST — RR 1 BOX 38 - WHIGHAM GA 31797
79- 93 RILEY, GEORGE MICHAEL — 12 SOUTH 20TH STREET - READING PA 19606
10-126 RILEY, JAMES JOSEPH — D. MARCH 25, 1949 BUFFALO, N.Y.
21- 87 RILEY, JAMES NORMAN — D. MAY 25, 1969 SEQUIN, TEXAS
44-110 RILEY, LEON FRANCIS — D. SEPTEMBER 13, 1970 SCHENECTADY, N. Y.
80-112 RINCON, ANDREW JOHN — 5425 LOS TOROS - PICO RIVERA CA 90660
79- 94 RINEER, JEFFREY ALAN — OLD ADD: 3608C ORKNEY ROAD - MOUNTVILLE PA 17554
17- 69 RING, JAMES JOSEPH — D. JULY 2, 1965 NEW YORK, N. Y.
50- 82 RINKER, ROBERT JOHN — 10 NORTH MADISON - MCADOO PA 18237
69-147 RIOS, JUAN ONOFRE VELEZ — OLD ADD: 95 TANCA STREET - SAN SEBASTIAN PR 00755
81-105 RIPKEN, CALVIN EDWIN JR. — 410 CLOVER ST - ABERDEEN MD 21001
85- 98 RIPKEN, CALVIN EDWIN, SR. — 410 CLOVER ST - ABERDEEN MD 21001
87-125 RIPKEN, WILLIAM OLIVER — 322 LIMESTONE VALLEY DR #H - COCKEYSVILLE MD 21030
78-112 RIPLEY, ALLEN STEVENS — BOX 349 %A. COOPER - NORTH ATTLEBORO MA 02760
35- 93 RIPLEY, WALTER FRANKLIN — 55 WEST ST - NORTH ATTLEBORO MA 02760
62-113 RIPPELMEYER, RAYMOND ROY — RR 2 BOX 34 - VALMEYER IL 62295
44-111 RIPPLE, CHARLES DAWSON — D. MAY 6, 1979 WILMINGTON, N. C.
36- 78 RIPPLE, JAMES ALBERT — D. JULY 16, 1959 GREENSBURG, PA.
17- 70 RISBERG, CHARLES AUGUST 'SWEDE' — D. OCTOBER 13, 1975 RED BLUFF, CAL.
64- 94 RITCHIE, JAY SEAY — 1108 TERRACE DR - SALISBURY NC 28144
87-126 RITCHIE, WALLACE REID — 341 WONDERVIEW DRIVE - GLENDALE CA 91202
86-128 RITTER, REGGIE BLAKE — RURAL ROUTE 1 BOX 297 - DONALDSON AR 71941
12-164 RITTER, WILLIAM HERBERT 'HANK' — D. SEPTEMBER 3, 1964 AKRON, O.
70-113 RITTWAGE, JAMES MICHAEL — 23931 COLUMBUS RD - BEDFORD HEIGHTS OH 44146
89-104 RITZ, KEVIN D. — RURAL ROUTE 5 - BLOOMFIELD IA 52537
83-122 RIVERA, GERMAN — OLD ADD: VIA LETICIA #4E-24,V.FONTANA-CAROLINA PR 00630
75-101 RIVERA, JESUS 'BOMBO' — VILLA DEL CARMEN CALLE 30 P-18 - PONCE PR 00731
86-129 RIVERA, LUIS ANTONIO — LAZARO RAMOS #16 - CIDRA PR 00639
52- 85 RIVERA, MANUEL JOSEPH 'JIM' — RURAL ROUTE 5 BOX 100 - ANGOLA IN 46703
70-114 RIVERS, JOHN MILTON 'MICKEY' — 350 NW 48TH ST - MIAMI FL 33127
21- 88 RIVIERE, ARTHUR BERNARD 'TINK' — D. SEPTEMBER 27, 1965 LIBERTY, TEX.
12-165 RIXEY, EPPA — D. FEBRUARY 28, 1963 TERRACE PARK, O.
38- 82 RIZZO, JOHN COSTA — D. DECEMBER 4, 1977 HOUSTON, TEX.
41- 95 RIZZUTO, PHILIP FRANCIS — 912 WESTMINSTER AVE-HILLSIDE NJ 07205
53- 76 ROACH, MELVIN EARL — 106 WEST 30TH ST - RICHMOND VA 23225
10-127 ROACH, WILBUR CHARLES 'ROXY' — D. DECEMBER 26, 1947 BAY CITY, MICH.
61- 90 ROARKE, MICHAEL THOMAS — 11 ROSEVIEW DR - CRANSTON RI 02910
79- 95 ROBBINS, BRUCE DUANE — 3813 CHADAM LANE #1C - MUNCIE IN 47304
33- 55 ROBELLO, THOMAS VARDASCO 'TONY' — 3504 WESLEY AV - FORT WORTH TX 76111
79- 96 ROBERGE, BERTRAND ROLAND — 267 SUNDERLAND AVE - AUBURN ME 04210
41- 96 ROBERGE, JOSEPH ALBERT ARMAND 'SKIPPY' — 173 CRAWFORD - LOWELL MA 01854
43-116 ROBERTS, CHARLES EDWARD — 4705 WEST HIGHWAY 166 - CARROLLTON GA 30117
13-149 ROBERTS, CLARENCE ASHLEY 'SKIPPER' — D. DECEMBER 24, 1963 LONG BEACH, CALIF.
54- 90 ROBERTS, CURTIS BENJAMIN — D. NOVEMBER 14, 1969 OAKLAND, CALIF.
67- 89 ROBERTS, DALE — 206 BERRY AVE - VERSAILLES KY 40383
69-148 ROBERTS, DAVID ARTHUR — OLD ADD: 6629 MAYARD - HOUSTON TX 77041
62-114 ROBERTS, DAVID LEONARD — 17510 MAYALL ST - NORTHRIDGE CA 91324
72- 90 ROBERTS, DAVID WAYNE — 2785 NW CIRCLE DRIVE #A - PORTLAND OR 97229
24- 89 ROBERTS, JAMES NEWSOM — D. JUNE 24, 1984 COLUMBUS, MISS.
86-130 ROBERTS, LEON JOSEPH 'BIP' — 3500 MALCOLM AVENUE - OAKLAND CA 94605
74-113 ROBERTS, LEON KAUFFMAN — 3316 REDSTONE DRIVE - ARLINGTON TX 76017
19- 69 ROBERTS, RAYMOND — D. JANUARY 30, 1962 CRUGER, MISS.
48- 85 ROBERTS, ROBIN EVAN — 504 TERRACE HILL DR - TEMPLE TERRACE FL 33617
54- 91 ROBERTSON, ALFRED JAMES 'JIM' — 3342 AYITA CIR - LAS VEGAS NV 89109
81-106 ROBERTSON, ANDRE LEVETT — 2229 CROSS LN ST - ORANGE TX 77360
19- 70 ROBERTSON, CHARLES CULBERTSON — D. AUGUST 23, 1984 FORT WORTH, TEX.
62-115 ROBERTSON, DARYL BERDINE — 755 PRINCTON DR - MIDVALE UT 84047
12-166 ROBERTSON, DAVIS AYDELOTTE — D. NOVEMBER 5, 1970 VIRGINIA BEACH, VA.
54- 92 ROBERTSON, DONALD ALEXANDER — 422 DOGWOOD ST - PARK FOREST IL 60466
19- 99 ROBERTSON, EUGENE EDWARD — D. OCTOBER 21, 1981 FALLON, NEV.
69-149 ROBERTSON, JERRY LEE — 3251 PLASS - TOPEKA KS 66611
13-150 ROBERTSON, PRESTON — D. OCTOBER 2, 1944 NEW ORLEANS, LA.

66- 75 ROBERTSON, RICHARD PAUL — 5823 RANDLESWOOD COURT - SAN JOSE CA 95129
67- 90 ROBERTSON, ROBERT EUGENE — RR 1 SHINNAMON DR - LAVALE MD 21502
40- 75 ROBERTSON, SHERRARD ALEXANDER — D. OCTOBER 23, 1970 HOUGHTON, S. D.
85- 99 ROBIDOUX, WILLIAM JOSEPH 'BILLY JOE' — RR BOX 148 - WARE MA 01082
43-117 ROBINSON, AARON ANDREW — D. MARCH 9, 1966 LANCASTER, O.
55- 99 ROBINSON, BROOKS CALBERT — 1506 SHERBROOK RD - LUTHERVILLE MD 21093
78-113 ROBINSON, BRUCE PHILLIP — 3968 SAN AUGUSTINE WAY - SAN DIEGO CA 92130
72- 91 ROBINSON, CRAIG GEORGE — OLD ADD: P.O. BOX 814 - PULASKI VA 24301
70-115 ROBINSON, DAVID TANNER — 6140 CAMINO DEL RINSON - SAN DIEGO CA 92120
79- 97 ROBINSON, DEWEY EVERETT — 1733 WEST ARTHUR AVE - CHICAGO IL 60626
78-114 ROBINSON, DON ALLEN — 2012 POPLAR ST - KENOVA WV 25530
58- 76 ROBINSON, EARL JOHN — 6895 OAKWOOD DRIVE - OAKLAND CA 94611
60- 87 ROBINSON, FLOYD ANDREW — 2660 HELIX STREET - SPRING VALLEY CA 92097
56- 73 ROBINSON, FRANK — 15557 AQUA VERDE DR - LOS ANGELES CA 90077
55-100 ROBINSON, HUMBERTO VALENTINO — 1695 BROOKLYN AVE - BROOKLYN NY 11210
47- 73 ROBINSON, JACK ROOSEVELT — D. OCTOBER 24, 1972 STAMFORD, CONN.
84- 94 ROBINSON, JEFFREY DANIEL — 701 PARKLAND COURT - WEXFORD PA 15090
87-127 ROBINSON, JEFFREY MARK — 1579 SAXON PLACE - EL CAJON CA 92021
49- 74 ROBINSON, JOHN EDWARD — 210 FLORIDA SHORE BLVD - DAYTONE BEACH SHORE FL 32018
11-145 ROBINSON, JOHN HENRY 'HANK' — D. JULY 3, 1965 NORTH LITTLE ROCK, ARK.
84- 95 ROBINSON, RONALD DEAN — 473 PINE ST - WOODLAKE CA 93286
42- 86 ROBINSON, WILLIAM EDWARD 'EDDIE' — 6104 CHOLLA DR - FORT WORTH TX 76102
66- 76 ROBINSON, WILLIAM HENRY — P.O. BOX 8143 - TURNERSVILLE NJ 08012
69-150 ROBLES, RAFAEL RADAMES — INGENIO QUISQUEYA-SAN PEDRO DE MACORIS DOM. REP.
72- 92 ROBLES, SERGIO — CERRO CHIQUIHUITE #148-C.CHURUBUSCO,MEXICO CITY 21 MEX.
74-114 ROBSON, THOMAS JAMES — 611 EAST ALAMEDA DR - TEMPE AZ 85282
43-118 ROCCO, MICHAEL DOMINICK 'MICKEY' — 868 WEST IOWA AVE - ST PAUL MN 55117
45- 86 ROCHE, ARMANDO BAEZ — OLD ADD: AVE LOS PINOS - HAVANA CUBA
14-178 ROCHE, JOHN JOSEPH — D. MARCH 31, 1983 PEORIA, ARIZ.
14-179 ROCHEFORT, BENNETT HAROLD — D. APRIL 2, 1981 RED BANK, N. J.
44-112 ROCHELLI, LOUIS JOSEPH — 501 RATTON - VICTORIA TX 77901
88-112 ROCHFORD, MICHAEL JOSEPH — 9 YANDOW DRIVE - SOUTH BURLINGTON VT 05401
36- 79 ROCK, LESTER HENRY — 1027 OLIVE DR #6 - DAVIS CA 95616
76- 82 ROCKETT, PATRICK EDWARD — 1335 VIEWRIDGE - SAN ANTONIO TX 78213
83-123 RODAS, RICHARD MARTIN — 1180 TILSON DRIVE - CONCORD CA 94520
57- 74 RODGERS, KENNETH ANDRE IAN — BOX N386 - NASSAU BAHAMAS W.I.
61- 91 RODGERS, ROBERT LEROY — 5181 WEST KNOLL DR - YORBA LINDA CA 92686
15-137 RODGERS, WILBUR KINCAID — D. DECEMBER 24, 1978 GOLIAD, TEX.
44-113 RODGERS, WILLIAM SHERMAN — 1433 NAUDAIN - HARRISBURG PA 17104
54- 93 RODIN, ERIC CHAPMAN — 947 GARFIELD AVE - BRIDGEWATER TOWNSHIP NJ 08807
67- 91 RODRIGUEZ, AURELIO ITUARTE — BAHIA DE TOPOLOBAMPO,#197 SUR - LOS MOCHIS SONORA MEX.
73-100 RODRIGUEZ, EDUARDO — URB. CATALINA CALLE 4 #E34 - BARCELONETA PR 00617
82-105 RODRIGUEZ, EDWIN (MORALES) — JARDINES CARIBE 28 ST #Z-3 - PONCE PR 00731
68- 87 RODRIGUEZ, ELISEO C.'ELLIE' — LAGO VISTA #2 BLDG 29 #C - LEVITTOWN LAKES PR 00619
58- 77 RODRIGUEZ, FERNANDO PEDRO 'FREDDY' — OLD .ADD: 555 MAYIA RODRIGUEZ - HAVANA CUBA
52- 86 RODRIGUEZ, HECTOR ANTONIO — OLD ADD: %A.CANIZARES,CERT. 99-A COL. POSTAL-MEXICO DF
16- 71 RODRIGUEZ, JOSE — D. MARCH 23, 1948 HAVANA, CUBA
86-131 RODRIGUEZ, RICARDO — 5014 PROCTOR ROAD - CASTRO VALLEY CA 94546
67- 92 RODRIGUEZ, ROBERTO MUNOZ — CORTIJITO DESARRIAS,8 CJN RECOBE 30 - CARACAS VENEZ
89-105 RODRIGUEZ, ROSARIO ISABEL — OLD ADD: LOS MOCHIS MEXICO
86-132 RODRIGUEZ, RUBEN DARIO — 10 #17 ENSANCHE LUPERON - SANTO DOMINGO DOMINICAN REP.
84- 96 RODRIGUEZ, VICTOR MANUEL — OLD ADD: BO. MAIZALES APTO. 464K - NAGUABO PR 00718
38- 83 ROE, ELWIN CHARLES 'PREACHER' — 204 WILDWOOD TER - WEST PLAINS MO 65775
23*110 ROE, JAMES CLAY — D. APRIL 3, 1956 CLEVELAND, MISS.
55-101 ROEBUCK, EDWARD JACK — 3434 WARWOOD RD - LAKEWOOD CA 90712
76- 83 ROENICKE, GARY STEVEN — 10800 MILL SPRINGS DRIVE - NEVADA CITY CA 95959
81-107 ROENICKE, RONALD JON — 829 MANCHESTER COURT - CLAREMONT CA 91711
89-106 ROESLER, MICHAEL JOSEPH — OLD ADD: 3305 MONOGENE DRIVE - FORT WAYNE IN 46806
23-111 ROETTGER, OSCAR FREDERICK LOUIS — D. JULY 4, 1986 ST. LOUIS, MO.
27- 75 ROETTGER, WALTER HENRY — D. SEPTEMBER 14, 1951 CHAMPAIGN, ILL.
29- 89 ROETZ, EDWARD BERNARD — D. MARCH 16, 1965 PHILADELPHIA, PA.
38- 84 ROGALSKI, JOSEPH ANTHONY — D. NOVEMBER 20, 1951 ASHLAND, WIS.
25- 88 ROGELL, WILLIAM GEORGE — 1700 GARNET DRIVE #206 - NEWPORT RICHEY FL 34652
14-180 ROGERS, JAY LOUIS — D. JULY 18, 1964 CARLISLE, PA.
89-107 ROGERS, KENNETH SCOTT — 14653 LAKE AVENUE - DOVER FL 33527
38- 85 ROGERS, LEE OTIS — 4920 HAWTHORNE RD-LITTLE ROCK AR 72207
35- 94 ROGERS, ORLIN WOODROW 'BUCK' — RR ONE BOX 222 - BLAIRS VA 24527
38- 86 ROGERS, STANLEY FRANK 'PACKY' — 964 WALNUT ST-ELMIRA NY 14901
73-101 ROGERS, STEPHEN DOUGLAS — 7548 EAST 65TH PLACE - TULSA OK 74133
17- 71 ROGERS, THOMAS ANDREW — D. MARCH 7, 1936 NASHVILLE, TENN.
15-138 ROGGE, FRANCIS CLINTON — D. JANUARY 6, 1969 MOUNT CLEMENS, MICH.
63- 99 ROGGENBURK, GARRY EARL — 18828 CANYON ROAD - CLEVELAND OH 44126
73-102 ROGODZINSKI, MICHAEL GEORGE — 1 EMLYN COURT - LAUREL SPRINGS NJ 08021
49- 75 ROGOVIN, SAUL WALTER — 420 WEST 24TH DR - NEW YORK NY 10011
83-124 ROHN, DANIEL JAY — 9247 WEST LONG LAKE RD - ALPENA MI 49707
67- 93 ROHR, LESLIE NORVIN — 1340 WICKS LANE - BILLINGS MT 59105
67- 94 ROHR, WILLIAM JOSEPH — 429 HELIOTROPE - NEWPORT BEACH CA 92661
21- 89 ROHWER, RAY — D. JANUARY 24, 1988 DAVIS, CALIF.
53- 77 ROIG, ANTON AMBROSE — 23310 INLET DR #12 - LIBERTY LAKE WA 99019
66- 77 ROJAS, MINERVINO ALEJANDRO 'MINNIE' — 7101A PLASKA - HUNTINGTON PARK CA 90255
62-116 ROJAS, OCTAVIO 'COOKIE' — 10317 SW 118TH STREET - MIAMI FL 33176
42- 87 ROJEK, STANLEY ANDREW — 895 PAYNE AVE - NORTH TONAWANDA NY 14120
62-117 ROLAND, JAMES IVAN — 5000 COUNTRY LANE - HIGH POINT NC 27263
31- 74 ROLFE, ROBERT ABIAL 'RED' — D. JULY 8, 1969 GILFORD, N. H.
12-167 ROLLINGS, RAYMOND COPELAND — D. AUGUST 25, 1966 ST.PAUL, MINN.
27- 76 ROLLINGS, WILLIAM RUSSELL 'RED' — D. DECEMBER 31, 1964 MOBILE, ALA.
61- 92 ROLLINS, RICHARD JOHN — 2751 EAST WALLINGS RD - BROADVIEW HGTS OH 44147
84- 97 ROMAN, JOSE RAFAEL — VISTA ALEGRE #10 SANCHES LUPERON-PUERTO PLATA DOM. REP.
64- 95 ROMAN, WILLIAM ANTHONY — IBM,TOWER 3,FL-9,1701 GOLF RD-ROLLING MEADOWS IL 60008
84- 98 ROMANICK, RONALD JAMES — 4221 135TH PL SE - BELLEVUE WA 98006
50- 83 ROMANO, JAMES KING — 233 BURLINGTON AVE - DEER PARK NY 11729
58- 78 ROMANO, JOHN ANTHONY — 7 TANGLEWOOD HOLLOW - UPPER SADDLE RIVER NJ 07458
87-128 ROMANO, THOMAS MICHAEL — 15 SLATE CREEK DRIVE #5 - CHEEKTOWAGA NY 14227
54- 94 ROMBERGER, ALLEN IRVING — D. MAY 26, 1983 WEIKERT, PA.
77-121 ROMERO, EDGARDO — 1380 WOOD ROW WAY - WEST PALM BEACH FL 33414
84- 99 ROMERO, ROMAN — CLE ULISES ESPAILLOT #60-SAN PEDRO DE MACORIS DOM. REP.
85-100 ROMINE, KEVIN ANDREW — 8750 ROGUE RIVER AVE - FOUNTAIN VALLEY CA 92708
20-100 ROMMEL, EDWIN AMERICUS — D. AUGUST 26, 1970 BALTIMORE, MD.

77-122 ROMO, ENRIQUE	AVENIDA SN, CARLOS #923 - TORREON COAHUILA MEX.
68- 88 ROMO, VICENTE	CALLE 32 AVENIDA 17 #45 - GUAYMAS SONORA MEX.
53- 78 ROMONOSKY, JOHN	5090 BIXBY ROAD - GROVEPORT OH 43125
13-151 RONDEAU, HENRI JOSEPH	D. MAY 28, 1943 WOONSOCKET , R.I.
76- 84 RONDON, GILBERT	339 BLEAKER STREET #2L - BROOKLYN NY 11237
81-108 ROOF, EUGENE LAWRENCE	4571 WESTCHESTER LANE - PADUCAH KY 42001
61- 93 ROOF, PHILLIP ANTHONY	RR 1 BOX 402 - BOAZ KY 42027
68- 89 ROOKER, JAMES PHILIP	1684 CITATION DR - LIBRARY PA 15129
88-113 ROOMES, ROLANDO AUDLEY	OLD ADD: 330 SOUTH BECK AVE - TEMPE AZ 85281
14-181 ROONEY, FRANK	D. APRIL 6, 1977 BESSEMER, MICH.
81-109 ROONEY, PATRICK EUGENE	925 SOUTH WALNUT - ARLINGTON HEIGHTS IL 60005
23-112 ROOT, CHARLES HENRY	D. NOVEMBER 5, 1970 HOLLISTER, CAL.
70-116 ROQUE, JORGE	BO SAN ANTON #135 - PONCE PR 00731
77-123 ROSADO, LUIS (ROBLES)	CALLE 508 B-213 #13 5TH-CAROLINA PR 00630
39- 98 ROSAR, WARREN VINCENT 'BUDDY'	733 EGGERT RD-BUFFALO NY 14215
71- 89 ROSARIO, ANGEL RAMON	CALLE 1 #421 HERNANDES DAVILA-BAYAMON PR00619
65- 92 ROSARIO, SANTIAGO	OLD ADD: VILLA GRILLASCA D.5B - PONCE PR
71- 90 ROSE, DONALD GARY	1133 HUNTINGDON - SAN JOSE CA 95129
63-100 ROSE, PETER DAVID	100 RIVERFRONT STADIUM - CINCINNATI OH 45202
89-108 ROSE, ROBERT RICHARD	OLD ADD: 554 PISTOL CREEK - SAN DIMAS CA 91773
57- 75 ROSEBORO, JOHN JUNIOR	1703 VIRGINIA RD - LOS ANGELES CA 90019
55-102 ROSELLI, ROBERT EDWARD	1548 HEMLOCK AVE - SAN MATEO CA 94401
72- 93 ROSELLO, DAVID	PAZ 160 - BO PARIS - MAYAGUEZ PR 00708
47- 74 ROSEN, ALBERT LEONARD	611 WASHINGTON STREET - SAN FRANCISCO CA 94111
37- 91 ROSEN, GOODWIN GEORGE	120 SHELBURNE AVE #1205 - TORONTO ONTARIO M6B 2M7 CAN.
30- 68 ROSENBERG, HARRY	23 MEADOWBROOK DR - SAN FRANCISCO CA 94127
23-113 ROSENBERG, LOUIS C	320 ALEMANY BLVD - SAN FRANCISCO CA 94110
88-114 ROSENBERG, STEVEN ALLEN	8425 FOREST HILLS DRIVE - CORAL SPRINGS FL 33065
31- 75 ROSENFELD, MAX	D. MARCH 10, 1969 MIAMI, FLA.
36- 80 ROSENTHAL, LAWRENCE JOHN	3 KOVE - SAINT PAUL MN 55119
25- 89 ROSENTHAL, SIMON	D. APRIL 7, 1969 BOSTON, MASS.
44-114 ROSER, EMERSON COREY 'STEVE'	CAMP ROAD, CEDAR LAKE - CLAYVILLE NY 13322
22-118 ROSER, JOHN JOSEPH 'BUNNY'	D. MAY 6, 1979 ROCKY HILL, CONN.
24- 90 ROSS, CHESTER FRANKLIN 'BUSTER'	D. APRIL 24, 1982 MAYFIELD, KY.
39- 99 ROSS, CHESTER JAMES	D. FEBRUARY 21, 1989 BUFFALO, N.Y.
54- 95 ROSS, CLIFFORD DAVID	2581 ROSEWOOD - ROSLYN PA 19001
38- 87 ROSS, DONALD RAYMOND	416 SOUTH OLD RANCH RD-ARCADIA CA 91006
50- 84 ROSS, FLOYD ROBERT 'BOB'	2010 WEST SAN MARCOS BLVD #19 - SAN MARCOS CA 92069
68- 90 ROSS, GARY DOUGLAS	OLD ADD: 7985 LABRUSCA WAY - CARLSBAD CA 92008
18- 63 ROSS, GEORGE SIDNEY	D. APRIL 22, 1935 AMITYVILLE, N. Y.
36- 81 ROSS, LEE RAVON 'BUCK'	D. NOVEMBER 23, 1978 CHARLOTTE, NORTH . C.
82-106 ROSS, MARK JOSEPH	7951 GLENHEATH - HOUSTON TX 77061
52- 87 ROSSI, JOSEPH ANTHONY	934 STANNAGE AVE - ALBANY CA 94706
44-115 ROSSO, FRANCIS JAMES	D. JANUARY 26, 1980 SPRINGFIELD, MASS.
48- 86 ROTBLATT, MARVIN	1354 WEST OHIO,1ST FLOOR - CHICAGO IL 60622
14-182 ROTH, ROBERT FRANK 'BRAGGO'	D. SEPTEMBER 11, 1936 CHICAGO, ILL.
45- 87 ROTHEL, ROBERT BURTON	D. MAY 21, 1984 HURON, O.
25- 90 ROTHROCK JOHN HOUSTON	D. FEBRUARY 2, 1980 SAN BERNARDINO, CALIF.
81-110 ROTSCHILD, LAWRENCE LEE	21 SCHNECK #1CC - GREAT NECK NY 11021
70-117 ROUNSAVILLE, VIRL GENE	2901 LONE TREE WAY #A - ANTIOCH CA 94509
13-152 ROUSH, EDD J	D. MARCH 21, 1988 BRADENTON, FLA.
11-146 ROWAN, DAVID	D. JULY 30, 1955 TORONTO, ONT.
84-100 ROWDON, WADE LEE	OLD ADD: 12929 SW 64TH CT - MIAMI FL 33156
63-101 ROWE, DONALD HOWARD	19791 SCENIC BAY LN-HUNTINGTON BEACH CA 92648
16- 72 ROWE, HARLAND STIMSON	D. MAY 26, 1969 SPRINGVALE, ME.
63-102 ROWE, KENNETH DARRELL	708 GREENLEAF DRIVE - NORCROSS GA 30092
33- 56 ROWE, LYNWOOD THOMAS 'SCHOOLBOY'	D. JANUARY 8, 1961 EL DORADO, ARK.
39-100 ROWELL, CARVEL WILLIAM 'BAMA'	RR 1 BOX 456 - CITRONELLE AL 36522
23-114 ROWLAND, CHARLIE LELAND	HIGHWAY 64 RR 2 - WENDELL NC 27591
15-139 ROWLAND, CLARENCE HENRY 'PANTS'	D. MAY 17, 1969 CHICAGO, ILL.
80-113 ROWLAND, MICHAEL EVAN	OLD ADD: 6425 EAST VIRGINIA - SCOTTSDALE AZ 85257
33- 57 ROY, EMILE ARTHUR	146 SOUTH COUNTRY CLUB ROAD - CRYSTAL RIVER FL 32629
46- 90 ROY, JEAN PIERRE	8969 VERVILLE - MONTREAL QUEBEC CAN.
24- 91 ROY, LUTHER FRANKLIN	D. JULY 24, 1963 GRAND RAPIDS, MICH.
50- 85 ROY, NORMAN BROOKS	53 CENTRAL ST - WEST CONCORD MA 01781
73-103 ROYSTER, JERON KENNIS	9 SHELDRAKE LANE - PALM BEACH GARDENS FL 33418
81-111 ROYSTER, WILLIE ARTHUR	229 55TH ST NE - WASHINGTON DC 20019
50- 86 ROZEK, RICHARD LOUIS	BOX 249 - CEDAR RAPIDS IA 52406
77-124 ROZEMA, DAVID SCOTT	4434 OREGON ROAD - LAPEER MI 48446
64- 96 ROZNOVSKY, VICTOR JOSEPH	1686 WEST BULLARD - FRESNO CA 93711
40- 76 RUBELING, ALBERT WILLIAM	D. JANUARY 28, 1988 BALTIMORE, MD.
69-151 RUBERTO, JOHN EDWARD 'SONNY'	7354 WHITE HALL COLONIAL LN - ST. LOUIS MO 63119
66- 78 RUBIO, JORGE JESUS	1001 LERDO AVE - MEXICALI BAJA CALIF. MEX.
27- 77 RUBLE, WILLIAM ARTHUR	D. NOVEMBER 1, 1983 MARYVILLE, TENN.
81-112 RUCKER, DAVID MICHAEL	P.O. BOX 559 - PINION HILLS CA 92372
40- 77 RUCKER, JOHN JOEL	D. AUGUST 7, 1985 MOULTRIE, GA.
67- 95 RUDI, JOSEPH ODEN	RR 1 BOX 66 - BAKER OR 97814
45- 88 RUDOLPH, ERNEST WILLIAM	RR 2 BOX 14A - BLACK RIVER FALLS WI 54615
57- 76 RUDOLPH, FREDERICK DONALD 'DON'	D. SEPTEMBER 12, 1968 ENCINO, CAL.
69-152 RUDOLPH, KENNETH VICTOR	2604 SOUTH SANTA BARBARA - MESA AZ 85202
10-128 RUDOLPH, RICHARD	D. OCTOBER 20, 1949 BRONX, N.Y.
15-140 RUEL, HEROLD DOMINIC 'MUDDY'	D. NOVEMBER 13, 1963 PALO ALTO, CALIF.
17- 72 RUETHER, WALTER HENRY 'DUTCH'	D. MAY 16, 1970 PHOENIX, ARIZ.
49- 76 RUFER, RUDOLPH JOSEPH	649 CORNWELL AVE - MALVERNE NY 11565
86-133 RUFFIN, BRUCE WAYNE	15610 FERN BASIN - HOUSTON TX 77084
24- 92 RUFFING, CHARLES HERBERT 'RED'	D. FEBRUARY 17, 1986 MAYFIELD HEIGHTS, O.
74-115 RUHLE, VERNON GERALD	5716 MIGUEL WAY - LONG BEACH CA 90814
64- 97 RUIZ, HIRALDO SABLON 'CHICO'	D. FEBRUARY 9, 1972 SAN DIEGO, CALIF.
78-115 RUIZ, MANUEL 'CHICO'	TAPIA 267 - SANTURCE PR 00912
43-119 RULLO, JOSEPH VINCENT	D. OCTOBER 28, 1969 PHILADELPHIA, PA.
14-183 RUMLER, WILLIAM GEORGE	D. MAY 26, 1966 LINCOLN, NEB.
81-113 RUNGE, PAUL WILLIAM	646 DELAWARE AVE - KINGSTON NY 12401
85-101 RUNNELLS, THOMAS WILLIAM	1017 29TH AVENUE COURT - GREELEY CO 80631
51- 82 RUNNELS, JAMES EDWARD 'PETE'	1106 MAPLE-LOIS ST - PASADENA TX 77502
25- 91 RUSH, JESS HOWARD 'ANDY'	D. MARCH 16, 1969 FRESNO, CAL.
48- 87 RUSH, ROBERT RANSOM	1358 EAST 1ST PLACE - MESA AZ 85201
15-141 RUSSELL, ALLAN E.	D. OCTOBER 20, 1972 BALTIMORE, MD.
10-129 RUSSELL, CLARENCE DICKSON 'LEFTY'	D. JANUARY 22, 1962 BALTIMORE, MD.

13-153	RUSSELL, EWELL ALBERT 'REB'	D. SEPTEMBER 30, 1973 INDIANAPOLIS, IND.
39-101	RUSSELL, GLEN DAVID 'RIP'	D. SEPTEMBER 26, 1976 LOS ANGELES CAL.
14-184	RUSSELL, HARVEY HOLMES	D. JANUARY 8, 1980 ALEXANDRIA, VA.
26- 72	RUSSELL, JACK ERWIN	919 OSCEOLA ROAD #204 - BELAIR FL 33516
42- 88	RUSSELL, JAMES WILLIAM	D. NOVEMBER 24, 1987 PITTSBURGH, PA.
83-125	RUSSELL, JEFFREY LEE	28 BRANDYWINE DR - CINCINNATI OH 45246
17- 73	RUSSELL, JOHN ALBERT	D. NOVEMBER 19, 1930 ELY, NEV.
84-101	RUSSELL, JOHN WILLIAM	412 FOREMAN AVE - NORMAN OK 73069
38- 88	RUSSELL, LOYD OPAL	D. MAY 24, 1968 WACO, TEX.
69-153	RUSSELL, WILLIAM ELLIS	11430 SOUTH FULTON AVENUE - TULSA OK 74137
39-102	RUSSO, MARIUS UGO	27 NORFOLK DR - ELMONT NY 11003
66- 79	RUSTECK, RICHARD FRANK	OLD ADD: 6315 SW PEYTON RD-PORTLAND OR 97219
44-116	RUSZKOWSKI, HENRY ALEXANDER	8815 HARVARD AVE - CLEVELAND OH 44105
14-185	RUTH, GEORGE HERMAN 'BABE'	D. AUGUST 16, 1948 NEW YORK, N.Y.
10-130	RUTHERFORD, JAMES HOLLIS	D. SEPTEMBER 18, 1956 LAKEWOOD, O.
52- 88	RUTHERFORD, JOHN WILLIAM	911 HENRIETTA - BIRMINGHAM MI 48009
73-104	RUTHVEN, RICHARD DAVID	39779 BENEVENTE AVE - FREMONT CA 94538
47- 75	RUTNER, MILTON MICKEY	14 SHOTGUN LN - LEVITTOWN NY 11756
82-107	RYAL, MARK DWAYNE	BOX 291 - DEWAR OK 74431
42- 89	RYAN, CORNELIUS JOSEPH	626 NORTH BEAUCHENE DRIVE - MANDEVILLE LA 70448
12-168	RYAN, JOHN BUDD	D. JULY 9, 1956 SACRAMENTO, CALIF.
30- 69	RYAN, JOHN COLLINS 'BLONDY'	D. NOVEMBER 28, 1959 SWAMPSCOTT, MASS.
29- 90	RYAN, JOHN FRANCIS	D. SEPTEMBER 2, 1967 ROCHESTER, MINN.
66- 80	RYAN, LYNN NOLAN	719 DEZZO DR - ALVIN TX 77511
64- 98	RYAN, MICHAEL JAMES	126 NORTH MAIN ST - PLAISTOW NH 03865
19- 71	RYAN, WILFRED PATRICK DOLAN 'ROSY'	D. DECEMBER 10, 1980 PHOENIX, ARIZ.
35- 95	RYBA, DOMINIC JOSEPH 'MIKE'	D. DECEMBER 13, 1971 SPRINGFIELD, MO.
31- 76	RYE, EUGENE RUDOLPH	D. JANUARY 21, 1980 PARK RIDGE, ILL.
72- 94	RYERSON, GARY LAWRENCE	1059 TERRACE COURT - EL CAJON CA 92019
84-102	SABERHAGEN, BRET WILLIAM	19229 ARMINTA ST - RESEDA CA 91335
36- 82	SABO, ALEXANDER	816 ANCHOR DRIVE - FORKED RIVER NJ 08731
88-115	SABO, CHRISTOPHER ANDREW	17300 SUNDERLAND - DETROIT MI 48219
51- 83	SACKA, FRANK	968 SYCAMORE ST - WYANDOTTE MI 48192
60- 88	SADECKI, RAYMOND MICHAEL	7710 EVERETT - KANSAS CITY KS 66112
73-105	SADEK, MICHAEL GEORGE	6632 SPRUCE LANE - DUBLIN CA 94568
60- 89	SADOWSKI, EDWARD ROMAN	11181 CLARISSA ST - GARDEN GROVE CA 92640
74-116	SADOWSKI, JAMES MICHAEL	914 HANSEN - PITTSBURGH PA 15209
63-103	SADOWSKI, ROBERT F.	4053 ASHENTREE DR - CHAMBLEE GA 30341
60- 90	SADOWSKI, ROBERT FRANK	1465 CREEKSIDE DRIVE - HIGH RIDGE MO 63049
60- 91	SADOWSKI, THEODORE	196 ALMA ST - PITTSBURGH PA 15223
49- 77	SAFFELL, THOMAS JUDSON	1503 CLOWER CREEK DRIVE #262 - SARASOTA FL 33581
11-147	SAIER, VICTOR SYLVESTER	D. MAY 14, 1967 EAST LANSING, MICH.
42- 90	SAIN, JOHN FRANKLIN	2 SOUTH 707 AVENUE LATOUR - OAKBROOK IL 60521
51- 84	SAINTCLAIRE, EDWARD JOSEPH 'EBBA'	D. AUGUST 22, 1982 WHITEHALL, N. Y.
84-103	SAINTCLAIRE, RANDY ANTHONY	174 COOPER STREET - LAKE GEORGE NY 12845
77-125	SAKATA, LENN HARUKI	333 SHAMROCK PLACE - MERCED CA 95340
84-104	SALAS, MARK BRUCE	330 BARCA AVE - LAPUENTE CA 91744
83-126	SALAZAR, ARGENIS ANTONIO	RODRIGUEZ DOMINGUES MANZANA G#7-VARINA VENEZ
80-114	SALAZAR, LUIS ERNESTO	PRINC. DE HUACARAPA 34-HUARENAS MIRANDA VENEZ
24- 93	SALE, FREDERICK LINK	D. MAY 27, 1956 HERMOSA BEACH, CAL.
45- 89	SALKELD, WILLIAM FRANKLIN	D. APRIL 22, 1967 LOS ANGELES, CAL.
12-169	SALMON, ROGER ELLIOTT	D. JUNE 17, 1974 BELFAST, ME.
64- 99	SALMON, RUTHERFORD EDUARDO 'CHICO'	ALMIRANTE, BOCAS DEL TORO - PANAMA PANAMA C.A.
32- 72	SALTZGAVER, OTTO HAMLIN 'JACK'	D. FEBRUARY 2, 1978 KEOKUK, IA.
33- 58	SALVESON, JOHN THEODORE	D. DECEMBER 28, 1974 NORWALK, CALIF.
39-103	SALVO, MANUEL	3541 WOODBROOK DR - NAPA CA 94558
76- 85	SAMBITO, JOSEPH CHARLES	9041 BAYWOOD PARK DR - SEMINOLE FL 33543
51- 85	SAMCOFF, EDWARD WILLIAM	8153 MADEIRA PORT LN - FAIR OAKS CA 95628
54- 96	SAMFORD, RONALD EDWARD	1325 WEST CANTERBURY CT - DALLAS TX 75208
78-116	SAMPLE, WILLIAM AMOS	10 PASCACK ROAD - WESTWOOD NJ 07675
62-118	SAMUEL, AMADO RUPERTO	1931 YALE DR - LOUISVILLE KY 40205
83-127	SAMUEL, JUAN MILTON	CALLE I #22 RESTAURACION-SAN PEDRO DE MACORIS DOM. REP.
30- 70	SAMUELS, JOSEPH JONES	34 BUELL STREET - BATH NY 14810
88-116	SAMUELS, ROGER HOWARD	4865 TAMPICO WAY - SAN JOSE CA 95118
23-115	SANBERG, GUSTAVE E.	D. FEBRUARY 3, 1930 LOS ANGELES, CAL.
82-108	SANCHEZ, ALEJANDRO	BOCA CHICA GATEY GAUTIR-SANTO DOMINGO DOMINICAN REP.
89-109	SANCHEZ, ALEJANDRO ANTHONY	100 CLAUDIA COURT #32 - ANTIOCH CA 94509
72- 95	SANCHEZ, CELERINO	MUTUALISMO #222-A - CELAYA GUANAJUATO MEX.
88-117	SANCHEZ, ISRAEL	OLD ADD: 5300 NORTH CHRISTIANA - CHICAGO IL 60625
81-114	SANCHEZ, LUIS MERCEDES	CALLE SAN FELIPE 11-CARIACO,EST. SUCRE VENEZ
81-115	SANCHEZ, ORLANDO	BOX SAN ISODRO P-52 - CANOVANAS PR 00629
52- 89	SANCHEZ, RAUL GUADALUPE	17821 NW 56TH AVE - CORAL CITY FL 33054
23-116	SAND, JOHN HENRY 'HEINIE'	D. NOVEMBER 3, 1958 SAN FRANCISCO, CAL.
81-116	SANDBERG, RYNE DEE	2357 IROQUOIS DRIVE - GLENVIEW IL 60025
45- 90	SANDERS, DEE WILMA	1312 COUNTRY CLUB RD - MCALESTER OK 74501
89-110	SANDERS, DEION LUWYNN	1625 HENDERSON AVENUE - FORT MYERS FL 33916
65- 93	SANDERS, JOHN FRANK	6112 SOUTH 25TH ST - LINCOLN NE 68512
64-100	SANDERS, KENNETH GEORGE	12141 PARKVIEW LN - HALES CORNERS WI 53130
42- 91	SANDERS, RAYMOND FLOYD	D. OCTOBER 28, 1983 WASHINGTON, MO.
74-117	SANDERS, REGINALD JEROME	5281 NEWPORT - DETROIT MI 48213
17- 74	SANDERS, ROY GARVIN	D. JANUARY 17, 1950 KANSAS CITY, MO.
18- 64	SANDERS, ROY L.	OLD ADD: 525 SOUTH THIRD ST - LOUISVILLE KY 40202
78-117	SANDERSON, SCOTT DOUGLAS	OLD ADD: 1271 WENDY DR - NORTHBROOK IL 60062
42- 92	SANDLOCK, MICHAEL JOSEPH	18 ROCK LAND PL-OLD GREENWICH CT 06870
67- 96	SANDS, CHARLES DUANE	2250 LONI CERA WAY - CHARLOTTESVILLE VA 22906
75-102	SANDT, THOMAS JAMES	25 ORIOLE LANE - LAKE OSWEGO OR 97034
40- 78	SANFORD, JOHN DOWARD	1001 KINON ST-WILSON NC 27893
43-120	SANFORD, JOHN FREDERICK 'FRED'	1046 WEST 600 NORTH - SALT LAKE CITY UT 84116
56- 74	SANFORD, JOHN STANLEY 'JACK'	2300 PRESIDENTIAL WAY - WEST PALM BEACH FL 33401
67- 97	SANGUILLEN, MANUEL DE JESUS	1200 FEDERAL HWY #204 - BOCA RATON FL 33432
49- 78	SANICKI, EDWARD ROBERT	12 BARTON RD - OLD BRIDGE NJ 08857
29- 91	SANKEY, BENJAMIN TURNER	RR 3 BOX 603B - WASHINGTON GA 30673
83-128	SANTANA, RAFAEL FRANCISCO	VILLA PEREYRA CALLE IRA #99 - LAROMANA DOMINICAN REP.
86-134	SANTIAGO, BENITO	URB. VILLA JAUCA #B21 - SANTA ISABEL PR 00757
54- 97	SANTIAGO, JOSE GUILLERMO	56-SE-NO. 1167 - RIO PIEDRAS PR 00921
63-104	SANTIAGO, JOSE RAFAEL	YOGRAMO 2-12,ARECIBO HEIGHTS - CAROLINA PR 00630
60- 92	SANTO, RONALD EDWARD	1303 SOMERSET - GLENVIEW IL 60025
79- 98	SANTODOMINGO, RAFAEL	BOX 277 - OROCOVIS PR 00720

Historic Limited Editions, publisher of "Z" Silk Cachets, is now accepting a limited number of membership applications in the history making, "Great Moments in Baseball" Program.

These "Great Moments" will be selected by a panel of renowned baseball experts and recorded for all eternity in a special series of Commemorative Covers.

Act now and take advantage of this history making opportunity. Provided we can accept your application, here's what you get:

1. Whenever a baseball event of historic significance occurs Historic Limited Editions will issue a Commemorative Cover in honor of the event. (Pete Rose tying and breaking Ty Cobbs lifetime hit record, Tom Seaver winning his 300th game, Rod Carew getting his 3024th hit; memorable events like a no-hitter, four home-runs in a game, or record breaking occurrences)

2. These special Commemorative Covers will be postmarked at the event site. Please note the difficulty in getting to many of these places in time for postmarking—therefore some events might be missed. However, every effort will be made to secure a postmark in time.

3. Following your third purchase, you will also receive—FREE of charge—a handsome, padded collector's album to house your Commemorative Covers—a full $24.95 value.

Baseball lovers, this is the perfect opportunity to collect something of great interest and personal value. When you enter this program, Historic Limited Editions assumes the responsibility for your Collection—we guaranty each Personally Autographed Cover to represent a truly significant and historic baseball event.

This is the first time in baseball history that an authentic Autographed Baseball Commemorative Cover Program has been inaugurated.

Each issue, published about once a month, will celebrate a great event and promises to be a work of art, brilliantly illustrated by noted baseball artist Rini and will bear an official U.S. stamp designed by a prominent American artist. Hurry! Limited quantities of approximately 600 each, make these truly limited editions.

These Covers will cost $15.95 plus $1.00 postage and handling (on rare occasions the price may vary). With each month's offering we will try to bring you 2 or 3 alternate choices. You can purchase the featured offer, the alternate choices, all Covers or none. Whatever your selection, only 600 of each cover will exist.

Important Note: To preserve the issue value the Baseball Commemorative Cover Program must be limited. Be sure you don't miss out on this special first-of-its-kind offering, place your order promptly. (immediate refund if your application cannot be accepted)

HISTORIC LIMITED EDITIONS
P.O. Box 400, Williston Park, NY 11596

YES! I accept this opportunity to participate in the Historic Limited Editions Autographed Cover Club. I am guaranteed that I will be offered a minimum of 12 Autographed Baseball Covers, worthy of historic significance. Also following the purchase of my third selection I will receive FREE OF CHARGE the collectors album to house my Commemorative Covers.

Enclosed is payment for my initial Autographed Commemorative Baseball Cover for $15.95 plus $1.00 shipping and handling (Total $16.95). I may cancel my subscription at any time.

Visa, Mastercard, or American Express Card Number

Expiration Date_____

Name_____

Address_____

City_____ State_____ Zip_____

A DIVISION OF JOHN ZASO, INC., Z SILK CACHET

68- 91 SANTORINI, ALAN JOEL	RR 2, ARTHUR RD - BELLE MEADE NJ 08502
87-129 SANTOVENIA, NELSON GIL	12350 SW 185TH STREET - MIAMI FL 33177
21- 90 SARGENT, JOSEPH ALEXANDER	D. JULY 5, 1950 ROCHESTER, N. Y.
76- 86 SARMIENTO, MANUEL EDUARDO	AVE DIAZ MORENO #90-13-VALENCIA CARABOBO VENEZUELA S.A.
51- 86 SARNI, WILLIAM FLORINE	D. APRIL 15, 1983 CREVE COEUR, MO.
87-130 SASSER, MACK DANIEL	OLD ADD: 4D WELLINGTON PLACE APTS - MIDLAND AL 36350
61- 94 SATRIANO, THOMAS VICTOR	11661 SAN VICENTE BLVD #615 - LOS ANGELES CA 90049
51- 87 SAUCIER, FRANCIS FIELD	1615 BRYAN PL #9 - AMARILLO TX 79102
78-118 SAUCIER, KEVIN ANDREW	4170 ROMMITCH LANE - PENSACOLA FL 32504
43-121 SAUER, EDWARD	D. JULY 1, 1988 THOUSAND OAKS, CALIF.
41- 97 SAUER, HENRY JOHN	207 VALLEJO CT - MILLBRAE CA 94030
70-118 SAUNDERS, DENNIS JAMES	OLD ADD: 19971 AVE DEL REY-ROWLAND HEIGHTS CA
27- 78 SAUNDERS, RUSSELL COLLIER 'RUSTY'	D. NOVEMBER 24, 1967 DOVER TWP.,OCEAN CO,N.J.
86-135 SAUVEUR, RICHARD DANIEL	4008 15TH AVENUE WEST - BRADENTON FL 34205
44-117 SAVAGE, DONALD ANTHONY	D. DECEMBER 25, 1961 MONTCLAIR, N. J.
12-170 SAVAGE, JAMES HAROLD	D. JUNE 26, 1940 NEW CASTLE, PA.
87-131 SAVAGE, JOHN JOSEPH	4402 LANDSIDE COURT - LOUISVILLE KY 40220
42- 93 SAVAGE, JOHN ROBERT 'BOB'	RURAL ROUTE 1 BOX 1140 - RANDOLPH NH 03570
62-119 SAVAGE, THEODORE EPHESIAN	4311 DRYDEN COURT - ST. LOUIS MO 63115
59- 70 SAVERINE, ROBERT PAUL	228 SLICE DR - STAMFORD CT 06907
29- 92 SAVIDGE, DONALD SNYDER	D. MARCH 22, 1983 SANTA BARBARA, CALIF.
54- 98 SAVRANSKY, MORRIS 'MOE'	2178 CEDARVIEW DR - CLEVELAND OH 44121
48- 88 SAWATSKI, CARL ERNEST	10201 MARKHAM ST WEST #214 - LITTLE ROCK AR 72205
15-142 SAWYER, CARL EVERETT	D. JANUARY 17, 1957 LOS ANGELES, CALIF.
48- 89 SAWYER, EDWIN MILBY	BOX 296 - VALLEY FORGE PA 19481
74-118 SAWYER, RICHARD CLYDE	3100 CREST DRIVE - BAKERSFIELD CA 93306
82-109 SAX, DAVID JOHN	2980 SAGEMILL WAY - SACRAMENTO CA 95833
28- 79 SAX, ERIK OLIVER 'OLLIE'	D. MARCH 21, 1982 NEWARK, N. J.
81-117 SAX, STEPHEN LOUIS	OLD ADD: 11 WESTPORT - MANHATTAN BEACH CA 90266
39-104 SAYLES, WILLIAM NISBETH	2830 NE LAKE DR - LINCOLN CITY OR 97367
48- 90 SCALA, GERARD DANIEL	OLD ADD: 19 BERNADETTE CT - PERRY HALL MD 21128
39-105 SCALZI, FRANK JOSEPH	D. AUGUST 25, 1984 PITTSBURGH, PA.
31- 77 SCALZI, JOHN ANTHONY	D. SEPTEMBER 27, 1962 PORT CHESTER, N. Y.
74-119 SCANLON, JAMES PATRICK 'PAT'	7400 PORTLAND AVE SOUTH - RICHFIELD MN 55423
56- 75 SCANTLEBURY, PATRICIO ATHELSTAN	47 WOODLAND AVE - MONTCLAIR NJ 07042
79- 99 SCARBERY, RANDY JAMES	5010 EAST LEWIS - FRESNO CA 93727
42- 94 SCARBOROUGH, RAY WILSON	D. JULY 1, 1982 MOUNT OLIVE NC
72- 96 SCARCE, GUERRANT MCCURDY 'MAC'	1708 BROADMOOR DR - RICHMOND VA 23221
29- 93 SCARRITT, RUSSELL MALLORY	429 POU STATION RD - PENSACOLA FL 32507
35- 96 SCARSELLA, LESLIE GEORGE	D. DECEMBER 16, 1958 SAN FRANCISCO, CAL.
64-101 SCHAAL, PAUL	10545 REDWING CIRCLE - OLATHE KS 66061
19- 72 SCHACHT, ALEXANDER	D. JULY 14, 1984 WATERBURY, CONN.
50- 87 SCHACHT, SIDNEY	783 NW 30TH AVE - DELRAY BEACH FL 33445
45- 91 SCHACKER, HAROLD	4609 NORTH MATANZAS AVE - TAMPA FL 33614
52- 90 SCHAEFFER, HARRY EDWARD	412 WHEATLAND AVE - SHILLINGTON PA 19607
72- 97 SCHAEFFER, MARK PHILIP	18261 PARTHENIA ST - NORTHRIDGE CA 91324
89-111 SCHAFER, JEFFREY SCOTT	20 BRIGHTWOOD STREET - PATCHOGUE NY 11772
61- 95 SCHAFFER, JIMMIE RONALD	655 BIRCH TER - COOPERSBURG PA 18036
59- 71 SCHAFFERNOTH, JOSEPH ARTHUR	20 MARIAN AVE - BERKLEY HEIGHTS NJ 07922
58- 79 SCHAIVE, JOHN EDWARD	RR 2 BOX 55 - DAWSON IL 62520
32- 73 SCHALK, LEROY JOHN	1100 LAWRENCE #21 - GAINESVILLE TX 76240
12-171 SCHALK, RAYMOND WILLIAM	D. MAY 19, 1970 CHICAGO, ILL.
11-148 SCHALLER, WALTER 'BIFF'	D. OCTOBER 9, 1939 EMERYVILLE, CALIF.
51- 88 SCHALLOCK, ARTHUR LAWRENCE	BOX 711 - SAN RAFAEL CA 94902
14-186 SCHANG, ROBERT MARTIN	D. AUGUST 29, 1966 SACRAMENTO, CALIF.
13-154 SCHANG, WALTER HENRY	D. MARCH 6, 1965 ST. LOUIS, MO.
44-118 SCHANZ, CHARLEY MURRELL	2217 MEER WAY - SACRAMENTO CA 95822
11-149 SCHARDT, WILBURT	D. JULY 20, 1964 VERMILION, O.
32- 74 SCHAREIN, ARTHUR OTTO	D. JULY 3, 1969 SAN ANTONIO, TEX.
37- 92 SCHAREIN, GEORGE ALBERT	D. DECEMBER 22, 1981 DECATUR, ILL.
81-118 SCHATTINGER, JEFFERY CHARLES	1322 WEST SAN MADELE - FRESNO CA 93711
77-126 SCHATZEDER, DANIEL ERNEST	33 EAST MADISON ST - VILLA PARK IL 60181
13-155 SCHAUER, ALEXANDER JOHN 'RUBE'	D. APRIL 15, 1957 MINNEAPOLIS, MINN.
13-156 SCHEER, ALLAN G.	D. MAY 6, 1959 LOGANSPORT, IND.
22-119 SCHEER, HENRY 'HEINIE'	D. MARCH 21, 1976 NEW HAVEN, CONN.
14-187 SCHEEREN, FREDERICK 'FRITZ'	D. JUNE 17, 1973 OIL CITY, PA.
43-122 SCHEETZ, OWEN FRANKLIN	275 ROBIN LN - REYNOLDSBURG OH 43068
41- 98 SCHEFFING, ROBERT BODEN	D. OCTOBER 26, 1985 PHOENIX, ARIZ.
12-172 SCHEGG, (GILBERT EUGENE PRICE) 'LEFTY'	D. FEBRUARY 27, 1963 NILES, O.
43-123 SCHEIB, CARL ALVIN	2922 OLD RANCH RD - SAN ANTONIO TX 78217
65- 94 SCHEINBLUM, RICHARD ALAN	3140 EAST BRADBURY COURT - ORANGE CA 92667
54- 99 SCHELL, CLYDE DANIEL 'DANNY'	D. MAY 11, 1972 MAYVILLE, MICH.
39-106 SCHELLE, GERARD ANTHONY 'JIM'	OLD ADD: 115 EAST MELROSE AVE - BALTIMORE MD 21212
23-117 SCHEMANSKE, FREDERICK GEORGE	D. FEBRUARY 18, 1960 DETROIT, MICH.
45- 92 SCHEMER, MICHAEL "LEFTY"	D. APRIL 22, 1983 MIAMI, FLA.
13-157 SCHENEBERG, JOHN BLUFORD	D. SEPTEMBER 7, 1950 HUNTINGTON, W. VA.
46- 91 SCHENZ, HENRY LEONARD 'HANK'	D. MAY 12, 1988 CINCINNATI, O.
19- 73 SCHEPNER, JOSEPH MARTIN	D. JULY 25, 1959 MOBILE, ALA.
50- 88 SCHERBARTH, ROBERT ELMER	5280 EAST BAY ROAD, OXBOW LAKE - PRESQUE ISLE WI 54557
69-154 SCHERMAN, FREDERICK JOHN	11546 STECK RD RT#1 - BROOKVILLE OH 45309
82-110 SCHERRER, WILLIAM JOSEPH	1149 CONCORD AVENUE - SPRING HILL FL 34606
31- 78 SCHESLER, CHARLES 'DUTCH'	D. NOVEMBER 19, 1953 HARRISBURG, PA.
10-131 SCHETTLER, LOUIS MARTIN	D. MAY 1, 1960 YOUNGSTOWN, O.
17- 75 SCHICK, MAURICE FRANCIS	D. OCTOBER 25, 1979 HAZEL CREST, ILL.
61- 96 SCHILLING, CHARLES THOMAS	5 CARLISLE ROAD - MILLER PLACE NY 11764
88-118 SCHILLING, CURTIS MONTAGUE	OLD ADD: 3935 EAST WILLOW AVENUE - PHOENIX AZ 85032
22-120 SCHILLINGS, ELBERT ISAIAH 'RED'	D. JANUARY 7, 1954 OKLAHOMA CITY, OKLA.
20-101 SCHINDLER, WILLIAM GIBBONS	D. FEBRUARY 6, 1979 PERRYVILLE, MO.
84-105 SCHIRALDI, CALVIN DREW	2102 SAN JUAN - AUSTIN TX 78746
14-188 SCHIRICK, HARRY ERNEST 'DUTCH'	D. NOVEMBER 12, 1968 KINGSTON, N.Y.
65- 95 SCHLESINGER, WILLIAM CORDES	5708 ABELIA COURT - CINCINNATI OH 45213
23-118 SCHLIEBNER, FREDERICK PAUL 'DUTCH'	D. APRIL 15, 1975 TOLEDO, O.
71- 91 SCHLUETER, JAYD	5203 E. SAHUARO DRIVE - SCOTTSDALE AZ 85254
38- 89 SCHLUETER, NORMAN JOHN	4211 GULL COVE - NEW SMYRNA BEACH FL 32069
15-143 SCHMANDT, RAYMOND HENRY	D. FEBRUARY 1, 1969 ST. LOUIS, MO.
52- 91 SCHMEES, GEORGE EDWARD	2803 MONTE CRESTA WAY - SAN JOSE CA 95132
67- 98 SCHMELZ, ALAN GEORGE	4638 EAST DESERT COVE - PHOENIX AZ 85028
81-119 SCHMIDT, DAVID FREDERICK	26636 PORTALES - MISSION VIEJO CA 92675

81-120	SCHMIDT, DAVID JOSEPH	5144 EAST WAGNER WAY - AGOURA CA 91301
44-119	SCHMIDT, FREDERICK ALBERT	1940 WINFIELD ST - EMMAUS PA 18049
13-158	SCHMIDT, HERMAN FREDERICK 'PETE'	D. NOVEMBER 11, 1973 PEMBROKE, ONT.
72- 98	SCHMIDT, MICHAEL JACK	24 LAKEWOOD DR - MEDIA PA 19063
58- 80	SCHMIDT, ROBERT BENJAMIN	9 HARDWOOD ST - ST CHARLES MO 63301
16- 73	SCHMIDT, WALTER JOSEPH	D. JULY 4, 1973 CERES, CALIF.
52- 92	SCHMIDT, WILLARD RAYMOND	1242 LOMA DRIVE - NORMAN OK 73069
41- 99	SCHMITZ, JOHN ALBERT	526 EAST UNION AVE-WAUSAU WI 54401
43-124	SCHMULBACH, HENRY ALRIVES	29 DALE ALLEN DR - BELLEVILLE IL 62223
14-189	SCHMUTZ, CHARLES OTTO	D. JUNE 27, 1962 SEATTLE, WASH.
72- 99	SCHNECK, DAVID LEE	3891 LEHIGH DR - NORTHAMPTON PA 18067
10-132	SCHNEIBERG, FRANK FREDERICK	D. MAY 18, 1948 MILWAUKEE, WIS.
63-105	SCHNEIDER, DANIEL LOUIS	11315 EAST MICHELLE LN - TUCSON AZ 85715
81-121	SCHNEIDER, JEFFERY THEODORE	2340 41ST - ROCK ISLAND IL 61201
14-190	SCHNEIDER, PETER JOSEPH	D. JUNE 1, 1957 LOS ANGELES, CALIF.
22-121	SCHNELL, KARL OTTO	130 MELVILLE AVE - PALO ALTO CA 94301
68- 92	SCHOEN, GERALD THOMAS	OLD ADD: 8588 DE INDIAN SCHOOL-SCOTTSDALE AZ
45- 93	SCHOENDIENST, ALBERT FRED 'RED'	331 LADUE WOODS CT - CREVE COEUR MO 63141
53- 79	SCHOFIELD, JOHN RICHARD 'DICK'	138 CIRCLE DR - SPRINGFIELD IL 62703
83-129	SCHOFIELD, RICHARD CRAIG	138 CIRCLE DRIVE - SPRINGFIELD IL 62703
88-119	SCHOOLER, MICHAEL RALPH	OLD ADD: 238 WEST SIRIUS AVENUE - ANAHEIM CA 92802
55-103	SCHOONMAKER, JERALD LEE	8343 SCHREIDER AVE - MUNSTER IN 46321
15-144	SCHORR, EDWARD WALTER	D. SEPTEMBER 12, 1969 ATLANTIC CITY, N.J.
35- 97	SCHOTT, ARTHUR EUGENE 'GENE'	703 WARD CIRCLE - SUN CITY CENTER FL 33570
53- 80	SCHRAMKA, PAUL EDWARD	13111 WEST LUCILLE LANE - BUTLER WI 53007
11-150	SCHREIBER, DAVID HENRY 'BARNEY'	D. OCTOBER 6, 1964 CHILLICOTHE, O.
14-191	SCHREIBER, HENRY WALTER	D. FEBRUARY 23, 1968 INDIANAPOLIS, IND.
22-122	SCHREIBER, PAUL FREDERICK	D. JANUARY 28, 1982 SARASOTA, FLA.
63-106	SCHREIBER, THEODORE HENRY	144 JEROME ROAD - STATEN ISLAND NY 10305
65- 96	SCHRODER, ROBERT JAMES	4 DELOND PL - HATTIESBURG MS 39401
83-130	SCHROEDER, ALFRED WILLIAM 'BILL'	116 EXTONVILLE ROAD - TRENTON NJ 08620
58- 81	SCHROLL, ALBERT BRINGHURST	1504 EVARIST - ALEXANDRIA LA 71301
80-115	SCHROM, KENNETH MARVIN	713 ROSINANTE - EL PASO TX 79922
84-106	SCHU, RICHARD SPENCER	4607 CHARLESTON DR - CARMICHAEL CA 95608
27- 79	SCHUBLE, HENRY GEORGE 'HEINIE'	1802 FLORIDA ST - BAYTOWN TX 77520
72-100	SCHUELER, RONALD RICHARD	646 SWEET COURT - LAFAYETTE CA 94549
79-100	SCHULER, DAVID PAUL	12656 HOLMES STREET - OMAHA NE 68137
31- 79	SCHULMERICH, EDWARD WESLEY 'WES'	D. JUNE 26, 1985 CORVALLIS, ORE.
53- 81	SCHULT, ARTHUR WILLIAM	231 EAST LANTANA RD - LANTANA FL 33462
27- 80	SCHULTE, FRED WILLIAM	D. MAY 20, 1983 BELVIDERE, ILL.
40- 79	SCHULTE, HERMAN JOSEPH	1655 SOUTH RIVER RD-SAINT CHARLES MO 63301
23-119	SCHULTE, JOHN CLEMENT	D. JUNE 28, 1978 ST. LOUIS, MO.
44-120	SCHULTE, LEONARD WILLIAM	D. MAY 6, 1986 ORLANDO, FLA.
75-103	SCHULTZ, CHARLES BUDD	6201 EAST VOLTAIRE AVENUE - SCOTTSDALE AZ 85254
55-104	SCHULTZ, GEORGE WARREN 'BARNEY'	790 WOODLANE RD - BEVERLY NJ 08010
43-125	SCHULTZ, HOWARD HENRY	1333 MCKUSICK ROAD LANE WEST - STILLWATER MN 55082
12-173	SCHULTZ, JOSEPH CHARLES SR	D. APRIL 13, 1941 COLUMBIA, S.C.
39-107	SCHULTZ, JOSEPH CHARLES	838 COALPORT - ST LOUIS MO 63141
51- 89	SCHULTZ, ROBERT DUFFY	D. MARCH 31, 1979 NASHVILLE, TENN.
24- 94	SCHULTZ, WEBB CARL	D. JULY 26, 1986 DELAVAN, WISC.
47- 76	SCHULTZ, WILLIAM MICHAEL 'MIKE'	502 ROBY AVE - EAST SYRACUSE NY 13057
12-174	SCHULZ, ALBERT CHRISTOPHER	D. DECEMBER 13, 1931 TOLEDO, O.
89-112	SCHULZ, JEFFREY ALAN	1167 SOUTH STOCKWELL ROAD - EVANSVILLE IN 47715
20-102	SCHULZ, WALTER FREDERICK	D. FEBRUARY 27, 1928 PRESCOTT, ARIZ.
83-131	SCHULZE, DONALD ARTHUR	313 EAST PINE - ROSELLE IL 60172
31- 80	SCHUMACHER, HAROLD HENRY	90 SOUTH MAIN ST - DOLGEVILLE NY 13329
13-159	SCHUPP, FERDINAND MAURICE	D. DECEMBER 16, 1971 LOS ANGELES, CALIF.
64-102	SCHURR, WAYNE ALLEN	RR ONE - HUDSON IN 46747
37- 93	SCHUSTER, WILLIAM CHARLES	D. JUNE 28, 1987 EL MONTE, CALIF.
89-113	SCHWABE, MICHAEL SCOTT	OLD ADD: ORANGE CA
61- 97	SCHWALL, DONALD BERNARD	2000 LAKE MARSHALL DR - GIBSONIA PA 15044
48- 91	SCHWAMB, RALPH RICHARD	D. DECEMBER 21, 1989 LANCASTER, CALIF.
65- 97	SCHWARTZ, DOUGLAS RANDALL 'RANDY'	757 EL RANCHO DR - EL CAJON CA 92021
14-192	SCHWARZ, WILLIAM DEWITT	D. JUNE 24, 1949 JACKSONVILLE BEACH, FLA.
13-160	SCHWENK, HAROLD EDWARD	D. SEPTEMBER 3, 1955 KANSAS CITY, MO.
14-193	SCHWERT, PIUS LOUIS	D. MARCH 11, 1941 WASHINGTON, D.C.
12-175	SCHWIND, ARTHUR EDWIN	D. JANUARY 13, 1968 SULLIVAN ,ILL.
55-105	SCHYPINSKI, GERALD ALBERT	10830 BALFOR AVE - DETROIT MI 48224
80-116	SCIOSCIA, MICHAEL LORRI	3447 NORTH YANKTON AVENUE - CLAREMONT CA 91711
36- 83	SCOFFIC, LOUIS	600 WEST 5TH ST-JOHNSTON CITY IL 62951
13-161	SCOGGINS, JAMES LYNN	D. AUGUST 16, 1923 COLUMBIA, S.C.
81-122	SCONIERS, DARYL ANTHONY	15918 TORREY AVENUE - FONTANA CA 92335
55-106	SCORE, HERBERT JUDE	OLD ADD: RADIO STATION WWWE - CLEVELAND OH 44101
73-106	SCOTT, ANTHONY	1526 DIXMONT AVE - CINCINNATI OH 45207
83-132	SCOTT, DONALD MALCOLM	OLD ADD: 705 W. HENRY - TAMPA FL 33604
26- 73	SCOTT, FLOYD JOHN 'PETE'	D. MAY 3, 1953 DALY CITY, CAL.
66- 81	SCOTT, GEORGE	1316 GOODRICH ST - GREENVILLE MS 38701
20-103	SCOTT, GEORGE WILLIAM	OLD ADD: CORSICANA TX 75110
14-194	SCOTT, JAMES WALTER	D. MAY 12, 1972 SOUTH PASADENA, FLA.
74-120	SCOTT, JOHN HENRY	D. NOVEMBER 30 1959 DURHAM, N. C.
16- 74	SCOTT, JOHN WILLIAM	RR 1 BOX 2168 - SHELBY AL 35143
39-108	SCOTT, LEGRANT EDWARD	D. NOVEMBER 2, 1960 FORT WAYNE, IND.
14-195	SCOTT, LEWIS EVERETT	D. MARCH 3, 1964 HOUSTON, TEX.
45- 94	SCOTT, MARSHALL 'LEFTY'	5417 WEST 134TH PLACE - HAWTHORNE CA 90250
79-101	SCOTT, MICHAEL WARREN	1134 VESTAL AVE - BINGHAMTON NY 13903
72-101	SCOTT, RALPH ROBERT 'MICKEY'	56 PINE STREET - ELLSWORTH ME 04605
89-114	SCOTT, RICHARD EDWARD	124 SHORTLEAF PL - THOMASVILLE GA 31792
63-107	SCOTT, RICHARD LEWIS	4206 PRISCILLA - INDIANAPOLIS IN 46226
75-104	SCOTT, RODNEY DARRELL	27500 HAMMACK AVE - PERRIS CA 92370
84-107	SCRANTON, JAMES DEAN	23673 S. VILLAGE HOUSE #3A - SOUTHFIELD MI 48034
75-105	SCRIVENER, WAYNE ALLISON	P.O. BOX 6 - BLOSSOM TX 75416
89-115	SCUDDER, WILLIAM SCOTT 'SCOTT'	OLD ADD: 130 PRATER WAY - SPARKS NV 89431
80-117	SCURRY, RODNEY GRANT	1941 COUNTY RD 207 - DURANGO CO 81301
64-103	SEALE, JOHNNIE RAY	4212 KREOLE AVE - MOSS POINT MS 39563
79-102	SEAMAN, KIM MICHAEL	658 SOUTH 5TH STREET - BRAWLEY CA 92227
89-116	SEANEZ, RUDY CABALLERO	1234 EAST CALIFORNIA AVENUE - GLENDALE CA 91206
81-123	SEARAGE, RAYMOND MARK	4113 FULTON DRIVE - KNOXVILLE TN 37918
88-120	SEARCY, WILLIAM STEPHEN 'STEVE'	

123

Code	Name	Address / Death Info
74-121	SHELDON, BOB MITCHELL	25370 LACEBARK DRIVE - MURRIETTA CA 92362
61- 98	SHELDON, ROLAND FRANK	614 NE CORONADO - LEES SUMMIT MO 64063
18- 66	SHELLENBACK, FRANK VICTOR	D. AUGUST 17, 1969 NEWTON, MASS.
66- 82	SHELLENBACK, JAMES PHILIP	BOX 614 - BAKER OR 97814
35- 98	SHELLEY, HUBERT LENEIRRE 'HUGH'	D. JUNE 16, 1978 BEAUMONT, TEX.
15-149	SHELTON, ANDREW KEMPER 'SKEETER'	D. JANUARY 9, 1954 HUNTINGTON, W. VA.
44-121	SHEMO, STEPHEN MICHAEL 'STAN'	RR 1 BOX 290A - MADISON NC 27025
45- 95	SHEPARD, BERT ROBERT	8014 BANGOR AVENUE - HESPERIA CA 92345
53- 82	SHEPARD, JACK LEROY	2450 EL CAMINO RD #108 - PALO ALTO CA 94306
68- 94	SHEPARD, LAWRENCE WILLIAM	1716 PINEDALE - LINCOLN NE 68520
24- 95	SHEPHARDSON, RAYMOND FRANCIS	D. NOVEMBER 8, 1975 LITTLE FALLS, N. Y.
84-109	SHEPHERD, RONALD WAYNE	RR 2 BOX 53X - KILGORE TX 75662
18- 67	SHERDEL, WILLIAM HENRY	D. NOVEMBER 14, 1968 MCSHERRYSTOWN, PA.
29- 95	SHERID, ROYDEN RICHARD	D. FEBRUARY 28, 1982 PARKER FORD, PA.
18- 68	SHERIDAN, EUGENE ANTHONY 'RED'	D. NOVEMBER 25, 1975 QUEENS VILLAGE, N. Y.
48- 93	SHERIDAN, NEILL RAWLINS	150 CHAUCER DR - PLEASANT HILL CA 94523
81-126	SHERIDAN, PATRICK ARTHUR	31654 TAFT- WAYNE MI 48184
24- 96	SHERLING, EDWARD CREECH	D. NOVEMBER 16, 1965 ENTERPRISE, ALA.
30- 72	SHERLOCK, JOHN CLINTON 'MONK'	D. NOVEMBER 26, 1985 BUFFALO, N. Y.
35- 99	SHERLOCK, VINCENT THOMAS	237 SUMMIT AVE-BUFFALO NY 14214
15-150	SHERMAN, JOEL POWERS	D. DECEMBER 21, 1987 CAPE CORAL, FLA.
14-197	SHERMAN, LESTER DANIEL 'BABE'	D. SEPTEMBER 16, 1955 HIGHLAND PARK, MICH.
78-119	SHERRILL, DENNIS LEE	OLD ADD: 240 SW 63RD CT - MIAMI FL 33144
11-152	SHERRY, FRED PETER	D. JULY 27, 1975 HONESDALE, PA.
58- 83	SHERRY, LAWRENCE	27181 ARENA LN - MISSION VIEJO CA 92675
59- 73	SHERRY, NORMAN BURT	4383-89 NOBEL DRIVE - SAN DIEGO CA 92122
59- 74	SHETRONE, BARRY STEVAN	10 8TH AVENUE NW - GLEN BURNIE MD 21061
30- 73	SHEVLIN, JAMES CORNELIUS	D. OCTOBER 30, 1974 FORT LAUDERDALE, FLA.
24- 97	SHIELDS, BENJAMIN COWAN	D. JANUARY 24, 1982 WOODRUFF, S. C.
15-151	SHIELDS, FRANCIS LEROY 'PETE'	D. FEBRUARY 11, 1961 JACKSON, MISS.
85-104	SHIELDS, STEPHEN MACK	LYNDA AVE, RR 11 - GADSDEN AL 35903
24- 98	SHIELDS, VINCENT WILLIAM	D. NOVEMBER 24, 1952 PLASTER ROCK, NEB.
57- 79	SHIFFLETT, GARLAND JESSIE	1095 CODY - LAKEWOOD CO 80215
39-109	SHILLING, JAMES ROBERT	D. SEPTEMBER 12, 1986 TULSA, OKLA.
21- 94	SHINAULT, ENOCH ERSKINE 'GINGER'	D. DECEMBER 29, 1930 DENVER, COLO.
83-133	SHINES, ANTHONY RAYMOND 'RAZOR'	2135 SUFFOLK LANE - INDIANAPOLIS IN 46260
22-125	SHINNERS, RALPH PETER	D. JULY 23, 1962 MILWAUKEE, WIS.
85-105	SHIPANOFF, DAVID NOEL	3 SALINA DRIVE - SAINT ALBERT, ALBERTA CAN.
86-138	SHIPLEY, CRAIG BARRY	52 BEAMISH ROAD - NORTHMEAD, N.S.W. AUSTRALIA 2152
58- 84	SHIPLEY, JOSEPH CLARK	OLD ADD: 29 HONEY LOCUST #7 - ST CHARLES MO
28- 83	SHIRES, CHARLES ARTHUR 'ART'	D. JULY 13, 1967 ITALY, TEX.
20-107	SHIREY, CLAIR LEE 'DUKE'	D. SEPTEMBER 1, 1962 HAGERSTOWN, MD.
41-101	SHIRLEY, ALVIS NEWMAN 'TEX'	416 LOWRENCE ROAD - RED OAK TX 75154
64-104	SHIRLEY, BARTON ARVIN	1237 LOGAN - CORPUS CHRISTI TX 78404
24- 99	SHIRLEY, ERNEST RAEFORD 'MULE'	D. AUGUST 3, 1955 GOLDSBORO, N. C.
77-131	SHIRLEY, ROBERT CHARLES	9641 SOUTH SANDUSKY STREET - TULSA OK 74137
82-113	SHIRLEY, STEVEN BRIAN	9200 JAMES PLACE NE - ALBUQUERQUE NM 87111
31- 81	SHIVER, IVEY MERWIN	D. AUGUST 31, 1972 SAVANNAH, GA.
16- 76	SHOCKER, URBAN JAMES	D. SEPTEMBER 9, 1928 DENVER, COLO.
64-105	SHOCKLEY, JOHN COSTEN	405 WALTER ST - GEORGETOWN DE 19947
61- 99	SHOEMAKER, CHARLES LANDIS	2310 FAIRVIEW AVE - MOUNT PENN PA 19606
29- 96	SHOFFNER, MILBURN JAMES 'MILT'	D. JANUARY 19, 1978 MADISON, O.
47- 78	SHOFNER, FRANK STRICKLAND 'STRICK'	816 MAJESTIC - HEWITT TX 76643
41-102	SHOKES, EDWARD CHRISTOPHER	222 SPRING STREET - WINCHESTER VA 22601
16- 77	SHOOK, RAYMAND CURTIS	D. SEPTEMBER 16, 1970 SOUTH BEND, IND.
59- 76	SHOOP, RONALD LEE	BOX 92 - RURAL VALLEY PA 16249
67-101	SHOPAY, THOMAS MICHAEL	17923 SW 77TH CT - MIAMI FL 33157
12-180	SHORE, ERNEST GRADY	D. SEPTEMBER 24, 1980 WINSTON-SALEM, N.C.
46- 92	SHORE, RAYMOND EVERETT	675 SILVER LEDGE LN - CINCINNATI OH 45231
28- 84	SHORES, WILLIAM DAVID	D. FEBRUARY 19, 1984 PURCELL, OKLA.
59- 76	SHORT, CHRISTOPHER JOSEPH	1609 BARNABY ST - NEWARK DE 19702
40- 82	SHORT, DAVID ORVIS	D. NOVEMBER 22, 1983 SHREVEPORT, LA.
60- 93	SHORT, WILLIAM ROSS	2975 57TH ST - SARASOTA FL 33580
15-152	SHORTEN, CHARLES HENRY 'CHICK'	D. OCTOBER 23, 1965 SCRANTON, PA.
35-100	SHOUN, CLYDE MITCHELL	D. MARCH 20, 1968 MOUNTAIN HOME, TENN.
11-153	SHOVLIN, JOHN JOSEPH	D. FEBRUARY 16, 1976 BETHESDA, MD.
81-127	SHOW, ERIC VAUGHN	P.O. BOX 29009 - SAN DIEGO CA 92124
22-126	SHRIVER, HARRY GRAYDON	D. JANUARY 21, 1970 MORGANTOWN, W. VA.
48- 94	SHUBA, GEORGE THOMAS	3421 BENT WILLOW LN - YOUNGSTOWN OH 44511
11-154	SHULTZ, WALLACE LUTHER 'TOOTS'	D. JANUARY 30, 1959 MCKEESPORT, PA.
42- 96	SHUMAN, HARRY	7402 MALVERN AVE - PHILADELPHIA PA 19151
45- 96	SHUPE, VINCENT WILLIAM	D. APRIL 5, 1962 CANTON, O.
16- 78	SICKING, EDWARD JOSEPH	D. AUGUST 30, 1978 CINCINNATI, O.
56- 76	SIEBERN, NORMAN LEROY	4951 NORTH TAMIAMI TRAIL #2 - NAPLES FL 33940
74-122	SIEBERT, PAUL EDWARD	4804 WEST 70TH ST - EDINA MN 55135
32- 76	SIEBERT, RICHARD WALTHER	D. DECEMBER 9, 1978 MINNEAPOLIS, MINN.
64-106	SIEBERT, WILFRED CHARLES 'SONNY'	2555 BRUSH CREEK - SAINT LOUIS MO 63129
63-109	SIEBLER, DWIGHT LEROY	231 SOUTH WESGAYE - GRETNA NE 68028
25- 92	SIEMER, OSCAR SYLVESTER	D. DECEMBER 5, 1959 ST. LOUIS, MO.
86-139	SIERRA, RUBEN ANGEL	EDIF. 25 #2501, JARDINES SELLES - RIO PIEDRAS PR 00924
88-125	SIERRA, ULISES 'CANDY'	BO. TORRECILLA,BAJA BUZON 108 - LOIZA PR 00672
49- 81	SIEVERS, ROY EDWARD	11505 BELLEFONTAINE RD-SPANISH LAKE MO 63138
26- 74	SIGAFOOS, FRANCIS LEONARD	D. APRIL 12, 1968 INDIANAPOLIS, IND.
14-198	SIGLIN, WESLEY PETER 'PADDY'	D. AUGUST 5, 1956 OAKLAND, CALIF.
29- 97	SIGMAN, WESLEY TRIPLETT 'TRIPP'	D. MARCH 8, 1971 AUGUSTA, GA.
43-130	SIGNER, WALTER DONALD ALOYSIUS	D. JULY 23, 1974 GREENWICH, CONN.
37- 94	SILBER, EDWARD JAMES	D. OCTOBER 26, 1976 DUNEDIN, FLA.
19- 75	SILVA, DANIEL JAMES	D. APRIL 4, 1974 HYANNIS, MASS.
55-107	SILVERA, AARON ALBERT 'AL'	723 NORTH SIERRA DR - BEVERLY HILLS CA 90210
48- 95	SILVERA, CHARLES ANTHONY RYAN	1240 MANZANITA DR - MILLBRAE CA 94030
78-120	SILVERIO, LUIS PASCUAL	CALLE 4 CASA #2,REP. LALOTERIA-SANTIAGO DOMINICAN REP.
70-121	SILVERIO, TOMAS ROBERTO	CALLE 9#14 COLINAS - SANTO DOMINGO DOMINICAN REP.
39-110	SILVESTRI, KENNETH JOSEPH	3328 WEST LAKE SHORE DR - TALLAHASSEE FL 32303
50- 89	SIMA, ALBERT	813 CENTER ST - BRANDON FL 33511
24-100	SIMMONS, ALOYSIUS HARRY	D. MAY 26, 1956 MILWAUKEE, WIS.
47- 79	SIMMONS, CURTIS THOMAS	200 PARK RD - PROSPECTVILLE PA 19002
10-134	SIMMONS, GEORGE WASHINGTON 'HACK'	D. APRIL 26, 1942 ARVERNE, N.Y.
49- 82	SIMMONS, JOHN EARL	9 LEE DR - FARMINGDALE NY 11735

84-110	SIMMONS, NELSON BERNARD	209 CEDARIDGE DR - SAN DIEGO CA 92114
28- 85	SIMMONS, PATRICK CLEMENT	D. JULY 3, 1968 ALBANY, N. Y.
68- 95	SIMMONS, TED LYLE	P.O. BOX 26 - CHESTERFIELD MO 63006
23-121	SIMON, SYLVESTER ADAM	D. FEBRUARY 28, 1973 CHANDLER, IND.
31- 82	SIMONS, MELBERN ELLIS	D. OCTOBER 11, 1974 PADUCAH, KY.
51- 91	SIMPSON, HARRY LEON	D. APRIL 3, 1979 AKRON, O.
75-106	SIMPSON, JOE ALLEN	66 SHAKER PLACE - VALLEY NE 68064
62-122	SIMPSON, RICHARD CHARLES	696 SAN JUAN AVE - VENICE CA 90291
72-103	SIMPSON, STEVEN EDWARD	D. NOVEMBER 2, 1989 OMAHA, NEB.
53- 83	SIMPSON, THOMAS LEO	22640 JAMESON DR - WOODLAND HILLS CA 91364
70-122	SIMPSON, WAYNE KIRBY	330 COLLAMER DR - CARSON CA 90744
15-153	SIMS, CLARENCE 'PETE'	D. DECEMBER 2, 1968 DALLAS, TEX.
64-107	SIMS, DUANE B. 'DUKE'	6 GALLOPING HILL ROAD - BROOKFIELD CENTER CT 06805
66- 83	SIMS, GREGORY EMMETT	6700 RANCHO PICO WAY - SACRAMENTO CA 95828
81-128	SINATRO, MATTHEW STEPHEN	68 MONTRE SQUARE NW - ATLANTA GA 30327
64-108	SINGER, WILLIAM ROBERT	1712 ANTIGUA WAY - NEWPORT BEACH CA 92660
45- 97	SINGLETON, BERT ELMER	2489 NORTH 4425 WEST - PLAIN CITY UT 84404
22-122	SINGLETON, JOHN EDWARD	D. OCTOBER 23, 1937 DAYTON, O.
70-123	SINGLETON, KENNETH WAYNE	5 TREMBLANT CT - LUTHERVILLE MD 21093
34- 91	SINGTON, FREDERIC WILLIAM	2017 5TH AVE NORTH - BIRMINGHAM AL 35203
45- 98	SIPEK, RICHARD FRANCIS	1611 JACKSON ST - QUINCY IL 62301
69-157	SIPIN, JOHN WHITE	328 HERMAN AVE - WATSONVILLE CA 95076
82-114	SISK, DOUGLAS RANDALL	1408 BEACH DRVE NE - TACOMA WA 98422
62-123	SISK, TOMMIE WAYNE	15 NORTH 100 EAST #200 - PROVO UT 84606
56- 77	SISLER, DAVID MICHAEL	11 HACIENDA DR - ST LOUIS MO 63124
15-154	SISLER, GEORGE HAROLD	D. MARCH 26, 1973 ST. LOUIS, MO.
46- 93	SISLER, RICHARD ALLEN	2315 ABBOTT MARTIN ROAD - NASHVILLE TN 37215
39-111	SISTI, SEBASTIAN DANIEL 'SIBBY'	39 CLIFFORD HEIGHTS - AMHERST NY 14226
36- 86	SIVESS, PETER	RR 1 BOX 555 - ST. MICHAELS MD 21663
82-115	SIWY, JAMES GERARD	103 DARLING ST - CENTRAL FALLS RI 02863
69-158	SIZEMORE, TED CRAWFORD	OLD ADD: 1059 FRUIT TREE LN - CREVE COEUR MO 63141
35-101	SKAFF, FRANCIS MICHAEL	D. APRIL 12, 1988 TOWSON, MD.
77-132	SKAGGS, DAVID LINDSEY	911 DAUGHERTY RD - NORCO CA 91760
89-117	SKALSKI, JOSEPH DOUGLAS	14348 BENSLEY AVENUE - BURNHAM IL 60633
57- 80	SKAUGSTAD, DAVID WENDALL	1113 N. MAR-LES DR - SANTA ANA CA 92706
10-135	SKEELS, DAVID	D. DECEMBER 2, 1926 SPOKANE, WASH.
42- 97	SKETCHLEY, HARRY CLEMENT 'BUD'	D. DECEMBER 19, 1979 LOS ANGELES, CALIF.
70-124	SKIDMORE, ROBERT ROE	815 SOUTH STONE - DECATUR IL 62521
21- 95	SKIFF, WILLIAM FRANKLIN	D. DECEMBER 25, 1976 BRONXVILLE, N. Y.
22-128	SKINNER, ELISHA HARRISON 'CAMP'	D. AUGUST 4, 1944 DOUGLASVILLE, GA.
83-134	SKINNER, JOEL PATRICK	4259 MANCHESTER AVENUE - ENCINITAS CA 92024
54-101	SKINNER, ROBERT RALPH	1576 DIAMOND ST - SAN DIEGO CA 92109
56- 78	SKIZAS, LOUIS PETER	2101 WEST WHITE - CHAMPAIGN IL 61821
73-110	SKOK, CRAIG RICHARD	105 ARBOUR RUN - SUWANEE GA 30174
54-102	SKOWRON, WILLIAM JOSEPH 'MOOSE'	1118 BEACHCOMBER DR - SCHAUMBURG IL 60193
82-116	SKUBE, ROBERT JACOB	OLD ADD: 3569 GREENVILLE DRIVE - SIMI VALLEY CA 93063
30- 74	SLADE, GORDON LEIGH	D. JANUARY 2, 1974 LONG BEACH, CALIF.
79-104	SLAGLE, ROGER LEE	536 WEST THIRD ST - LARNED KS 67550
10-136	SLAGLE, WALTER JENNINGS	D. JUNE 17, 1974 SAN GABRIEL, CALIF.
11-155	SLAPNICKA, CYRIL CHARLES	D. OCTOBER 20, 1979 CEDAR RAPIDS, IA.
20-108	SLAPPEY, JOHN HENRY	D. JUNE 10, 1957 MARIETTA, GA.
71- 93	SLATON, JAMES MICHAEL	43515 28TH ST WEST - LANCASTER CA 93534
15-155	SLATTERY, PHILIP RYAN	D. MARCH 2, 1968 LONG BEACH, CAL9F.
82-117	SLAUGHT, DONALD MARTIN	5420 MEADOWDALE LN - RANCHO PALOS VD CA 90274
10-137	SLAUGHTER, BYRON ATKINS 'BARNEY'	D. MAY 17, 1961 PHILADELPHIA PA.
38- 90	SLAUGHTER, ENOS BRADSHER	RR 2-ROXBORO NC 27573
64-109	SLAUGHTER, STERLING FEORE	742 EAST AVENIDA SIERRA MADRE - GILBERT AZ 85234
26- 75	SLAYBACK, ELBERT 'SCOTTIE'	D. NOVEMBER 30, 1979 CINCINNATI, O.
72-104	SLAYBACK, WILLIAM GROVER	21900 ROSCOE BLVD - CANOGA PARK CA 91304
28- 86	SLAYTON, FOSTER HERBERT 'STEVE'	D. DECEMBER 20, 1984 MANCHESTER, N. H.
50- 90	SLEATER, LOUIS MORTIMER	48 ALDERMAN COURT - LUTHERVILLE MD 21093
44-122	SLOAN, BRUCE ADAMS	D. SEPTEMBER 24, 1973 OKLAHOMA CITY, OKLA.
13-164	SLOAN, YALE YEASTMAN 'TOD'	D. SEPTEMBER 12, 1956 AKRON, O.
48- 96	SLOAT, DWAIN CLIFFORD	2101 EAST 5TH ST - ST PAUL MN 55119
69-159	SLOCUM, RONALD REECE	OLD ADD: 5715 BALTIMORE DR #82 - LAMESA CA 92041
88-126	SMAJSTRLA, CRAIG LEE	P.O. BOX 32 - PEARLAND TX 77581
30- 75	SMALL, CHARLES ALBERT	D. JANUARY 14, 1953 LEWISTON, ME.
78-121	SMALL, GEORGE HENRY 'HANK'	P.O. BOX 763 - MOUNT PLEASANT SC 29464
55-108	SMALL, JAMES ARTHUR	9420 TAYLORS TURN - STANWOOD MI 49346
48- 97	SMALLEY, ROY FREDERICK JR	534 WEST ARBOR VITAE - INGLEWOOD CA 90301
75-107	SMALLEY, ROY FREDERICK III	5739 LONG BRAKE CIRCLE - MINNEAPOLIS MN 55435
17- 78	SMALLWOOD, WALTER CLAYTON	D. APRIL 29, 1967
46- 94	SMAZA, JOSEPH PAUL	D. MAY 30, 1979 ROYAL OAK, MICH.
86-140	SMILEY, JOHN PATRICK	208 WEST THIRD AVENUE - TRAPPE PA 19426
34- 92	SMITH, ALFRED JOHN	D. APRIL 28, 1977 BROWNSVILLE, TEX.
26- 76	SMITH, ALFRED HENDRICKS	23928 GREEN HAVEN - RAMONA CA 92065
53- 84	SMITH, ALPHONSE EUGENE	8440 INDIANA 3RD FLOOR - CHICAGO IL 60619
12-182	SMITH, ARMSTRONG FREDERICK 'KLONDIKE'	D. NOVEMBER 15, 1959 SPRINGFIELD, MASS.
32- 77	SMITH, ARTHUR LAIRD	73 OENOKE RIDGE #307 - NEW CANAAN CT 06840
75-108	SMITH, BILLY ED	OLD ADD: 5439 TIMBER POST - SAN ANTONIO TX 78250
81-129	SMITH, BILLY LAVERN	8407 NEFF - HOUSTON TX 77036
57- 81	SMITH, BOBBY GENE	11808 WOODBINE LANE SW - TACOMA WA 98499
87-134	SMITH, BRICK DUDLEY	4743 AMITY PLACE - CHARLOTTE NC 28212
81-130	SMITH, BRYN NELSON	812 EAST FELSER - SANTA MARIA CA 93454
70-125	SMITH, CALVIN BERNARD 'BERNIE'	BOX 513 - LUTCHER LA 70071
66- 84	SMITH, CARL REGINALD 'REGGIE'	11764 DORAL AVENUE - NORTHRIDGE CA 91326
60- 94	SMITH, CHARLES WILLIAM	3060 SPROUT WAY - SPARKS NV 89431
81-131	SMITH, CHRISTOPHER WILLIAM	8713 EAST CLUBHOUSE WAY - SCOTTSDALE AZ 85255
13-165	SMITH, CLARENCE OSSIE	D. FEBRUARY 16, 1924 SWEETWATER, TEX.
38- 91	SMITH, CLAY JAMIESON	RR 1 BOX 9 - CAMBRIDGE KS 67023
38- 92	SMITH, DAVID MERWIN	BOX 671-WHITEVILLE NC 28472
80-119	SMITH, DAVID STANLEY	1225 RANCHO ENCINITAS DR - ENCINITAS CA 92024
84-111	SMITH, DAVID WAYNE	16330 JERSEY DR - HOUSTON TX 77040
12-181	SMITH, DOUGLASS WELDON	D. SEPTEMBER 18, 1973 GREENFIELD, MASS.
55-109	SMITH, EARL CALVIN	2764 NORTH LEONARD - FRESNO CA 93727
16- 79	SMITH, EARL LEONARD	D. MARCH 14, 1943 PORTSMOUTH, O.
19- 76	SMITH, EARL SUTTON	D. JUNE 8, 1963 LITTLE ROCK, ARK.
36- 87	SMITH, EDGAR	ROUTE 130 KINKORA - BORDENTOWN NJ 08505

Willie
McGovey

Hank
Aaron

Frank
Robinson

500 HOME RUN CLUB

**Several living members of
the 500 Home Run Club
are featured on these
autographed Great Moments
and Art Post Cards of
Perez-Steele**

EDDIE MATHEWS

ERNIE BANKS

HARMON KILLEBREW

127

```
45- 99  SMITH, EDWARD MAYO                        D. NOVEMBER 24, 1977 BOYNTON BEACH, FLA.
14-199  SMITH, ELMER JOHN                         D. AUGUST 3, 1984 COLUMBIA, KY.
26- 77  SMITH, ELWOOD HOPE 'MIKE'                 D. MAY 31, 1981 CHESAPEAKE, VA.
23-122  SMITH, EMANUEL CARR                       D. APRIL 14, 1989 MIAMI, FLA.
30- 76  SMITH, ERNEST HENRY                       D. APRIL 6, 1973 BROOKLYN, N. Y.
50- 91  SMITH, FRANK THOMAS                       120 89TH AVE - ST PETERSBURG FL 33702
13-166  SMITH, FREDERICK VINCENT                  D. MAY 28, 1961 CLEVELAND, O.
16- 80  SMITH, GEORGE ALLEN                       D. JANUARY 7, 1965 GREENWICH, CONN.
63-110  SMITH, GEORGE CORNELIUS                   D. JUNE 15, 1987 ST. PETERSBURG, FLA.
26- 78  SMITH, GEORGE SELBY                       D. MAY 26, 1981 RICHMOND, VA.
89-118  SMITH, GREGORY ALAN                       12612 HOWARD LODGE DRIVE - SYKESVILLE MD 21784
32- 78  SMITH, HAROLD LAVERNE                     5200 N. OCEAN BLVD #612 - FORT LAUDERDALE FL 33308
56- 79  SMITH, HAROLD RAYMOND                     6602 WINKLEMAN - HOUSTON TX 77083
55-110  SMITH, HAROLD WAYNE                       2322 MAPLE CREST DRIVE - MISSOURI CITY TX 77459
12-183  SMITH, HARRISON M                         D. JULY 26, 1964 DUNBAR, NEB.
10-138  SMITH, HENRY JOSEPH 'HAP'                 D. FEBRUARY 26, 1961 SAN JOSE, CALIF.
62-124  SMITH, JACK HATFIELD                      OLD ADD: 621 TAHOE CIR - STONE MOUNTAIN GA 30083
11-156  SMITH, JACOB 'BIG JAKE'                   D. NOVEMBER 7, 1948 EAST MCKEESPORT, PA.
11-157  SMITH, JAMES CARLISLE 'RED'               D. OCTOBER 11, 1966 ATLANTA, GA.
14-200  SMITH, JAMES HARRY                        D. APRIL 1, 1922 CHARLOTTE, N.C.
14-201  SMITH, JAMES LAWRENCE                     D. JANUARY 1, 1974 PITTSBURGH, PA.
82-118  SMITH, JAMES LORNE                        8345 WESTLAWN AVENUE - LOS ANGELES CA 90045
15-156  SMITH, JOHN                               D. MAY 2, 1972 WESTCHESTER, ILL.
89-119  SMITH, JOHN DWIGHT 'DWIGHT'               P.O. BOX 98 - VARNVILLE SC 29944
31- 83  SMITH, JOHN MARSHALL                      D. MAY 9, 1982 SILVER SPRING, MD.
13-167  SMITH, JOHN WILLIAM 'CHICK'               D. OCTOBER 11, 1935 DAYTON, KY.
77-133  SMITH, KEITH LAVARNE                      OLD ADD: 522 11TH ST NORTH - PALMETTO FL 33561
81-132  SMITH, KENNETH EARL                       100 LANDSDOWNE BLVD - YOUNGSTOWN OH 44506
20-109  SMITH, LAWRENCE PATRICK 'PADDY'           P.O. BOX 775 - QUECHEE VT 05059
80-120  SMITH, LEE ARTHUR                         OLD ADD: 4170 N. MARINE #4L - CHICAGO IL 60613
84-112  SMITH, LEROY PURDY 'ROY'                  472 GRAMATON AVE - MOUNT VERNON NY 10552
78-122  SMITH, LONNIE                             185 RIDGEWOOD DRIVE - SPARTANBURG SC 29303
83-135  SMITH, MARK CHRISTOPHER                   OLD ADD: 711 SOUTH 19TH ST - ARLINGTON VA 22202
25- 93  SMITH, MARVIN HAROLD 'RED'                D. FEBRUARY 19, 1961 LOS ANGELES, CAL.
84-113  SMITH, MICHAEL ANTHONY                    3226 LIVINGSTON RD - JACKSON MS 39210
89-120  SMITH, MICHAEL ANTHONY 'TEXAS'            7605 ANTIQUE OAK - SAN ANTONIO TX 78233
55-111  SMITH, MILTON                             535 KLINE ROAD - WAHIAWA HI 96786
62-125  SMITH, NATHANIEL BEVERLY                  OLD ADD: 5303 ENNIS ST - HOUSTON TX 77004
78-123  SMITH, OSBORNE EARL 'OZZIEI'              P.O. BOX 8787 - SAINT LOUIS MO 63102
84-114  SMITH, PATRICK KEITH                      37418 OXFORD DRIVE - PALMDALE CA 93550
53- 85  SMITH, PAUL LESLIE                        27 RAVENSWORTH RD - CONROE TX 77301
16- 81  SMITH, PAUL STONER                        D. JULY 3, 1958 DECATUR, ILL.
87-135  SMITH, PETER JOHN                         OLD ADD: BURLINGTON MA
62-126  SMITH, PETER LUKE                         52 FAIRVIEW AVENUE - NATICK MA 01760
81-133  SMITH, RAYMOND EDWARD                     OLD ADD: 1063 OAK DR - VISTA CA 92083
63-111  SMITH, RICHARD ARTHUR                     2252 TABLE ROCK ROAD #143 - MEDFORD OR 97501
51- 92  SMITH, RICHARD HARRISON                   1926 NORWOOD LN - STATE COLLEGE PA 16801
69-160  SMITH, RICHARD KELLY                      RR 7 BOX 200 - LINCOLNTON NC 28092
27- 83  SMITH, RICHARD PAUL 'RED'                 D. MARCH 8, 1978 TOLEDO, O.
13-169  SMITH, ROBERT ASHLEY                      1914 ADD: HARDWICK VT
23-123  SMITH, ROBERT ELDRIDGE                    D. JULY 19, 1987 WAYCROSS, GA.
55-112  SMITH, ROBERT GILCHRIST                   47 FERNWOOD - TEXARKANA TX 75503
58- 85  SMITH, ROBERT WALKAY 'RIVERBOAT'          RR 1 BOX 21 - CLARENCE MO 63437
27- 84  SMITH, RUFUS FRAZIER                      D. AUGUST 21, 1984 AIKEN, S. C.
13-168  SMITH, SALVATORE GIUSEPPE 'JOE'           D. JANUARY 12, 1974 YONKERS, N. Y.
11-158  SMITH, SHEROD MALONE                      D. SEPTEMBER 12, 1949 REIDSVILLE, GA.
73-111  SMITH, TOMMIE ALEXANDER                   1299 EAST CANNON AVE - ALBEMARIE NC 28001
41-103  SMITH, VINCENT AMBROSE                    D. DECEMBER 14, 1979 VIRGINIA BEACH, VA.
11-159  SMITH, WALLACE H.                         D. JUNE 10, 1930 FLORENCE, ARIZ.
17- 79  SMITH, WILLARD JEHU 'RED'                 D. JULY 17, 1972 NOBLESVILLE, IND
58- 86  SMITH, WILLIAM GARLAND                    4265 BRANCH SE AVENUE - TEMPLE HILLS MD 20748
63-112  SMITH, WILLIE                             607 BRADFORD ST - HOBSON CITY AL 36201
84-115  SMITH, ZANE WILLIAM                       RR 4 BOX 138-C1 - NORTH PLATTE NE 69101
82-119  SMITHSON, BILLY MIKE                      BOX 204 - CENTERVILLE TN 37033
40- 83  SMOLL, CLYDE HETRICK                      D. AUGUST 31, 1985 QUAKERTOWN, PA.
88-127  SMOLTZ, JOHN ANDREW                       1415 MAYCROFT - LANSING 48917
12-184  SMOYER, HENRY NEITZ                       D. FEBRUARY 28, 1958 DUBOIS, PA.
16- 82  SMYKAL, FRANK JOHN                        D. AUGUST 11, 1950 CHICAGO, ILL.
44-123  SMYRES, CLARENCE MELVIN 'CLANCY'          11470 ORCAS AVE - SAN FERNANDO CA 91342
15-157  SMYTH, JAMES DANIEL 'RED'                 D. APRIL 14, 1958 INGLEWOOD, CALIF.
29- 98  SMYTHE, WILLIAM HENRY 'HARRY'             D. AUGUST 28, 1980 AUGUSTA, GA.
12-185  SNELL, CHARLES ANTHONY                    D. APRIL 4, 1988 READING, PA.
84-116  SNELL, NATHANIEL                          RR 2 BOX 42 - HOLLY HILL SC 29059
13-170  SNELL, WALTER HENRY                       D. JULY 23, 1980 PROVIDENCE, R. I.
47- 80  SNIDER, EDWIN DONALD 'DUKE'               3037 LAKEMONT DR - FALLBROOK CA 92028
88-128  SNIDER, VAN VOORHEES                      621 19TH AVENUE SOUTH - BIRMINGHAM AL 35205
23-124  SNIPES, WYATT EURE 'ROXY'                 D. MAY 1, 1941 FAYETTEVILLE, N. C.
73-112  SNOOK, FRANK WALTER                       OLD ADD: RR2 - WHITEHOUSE STATION NJ
19- 77  SNOVER, COLONEL LESTER                    D. APRIL 30, 1969 ROCHESTER, N. Y.
35-102  SNYDER, BERNARD AUSTIN                    2415 WAVERLY - PHILADELPHIA PA 19146
85-106  SNYDER, BRIAN ROBERT                      14834 WOOD HOME ROAD - CENTERVILLE VA 22020
59- 77  SNYDER, EUGENE WALTER                     1960 NORTH SHERMAN ST - YORK PA 17402
12-186  SNYDER, FRANK ELTON                       D. JANUARY 5, 1962 SAN ANTONIO, TEX.
88-141  SNYDER, JAMES CORY                        816 AILEEN STREET - CAMARILLO CA 93010
61-100  SNYDER, JAMES ROBERT                      OLD ADD: 8613 BACKWOOD - TAMPA FL 33615
52- 95  SNYDER, JERRY GEORGE                      2420 GULFCREST BLVD - PEARLAND TX 77581
14-202  SNYDER, JOHN WILLIAM                      D. DECEMBER 13, 1981 REDSTONE TWP., PA.
59- 78  SNYDER, RUSSELL HENRY                     P.O. BOX 264 - NELSON NE 68961
19- 78  SNYDER, WILLIAM NICHOLAS                  D. OCTOBER 8, 1934 VICKSBURG, MICH.
37- 95  SODD, WILLIAM                             3845 DIAMON LOCK WEST - FORT WORTH TX 76118
71- 94  SODERHOLM, ERIC THANE                     10 SOUTH 360 HAMPSHIRE LN WEST - HINSDALE IL 60521
86-142  SOFF, RAYMOND JOHN                        9015 RODESILER HIGHWAY - RIGA MI 49276
79-105  SOFIELD, RICHARD MICHAEL 'RICK'           BASEBALL OFFICE, JMH CENTER - SALT LAKE CITY UT 84112
68- 96  SOLAITA, TOLIA 'TONY'                     D. FEBRUARY 10, 1990 TAFUNA, AMERICAN SAMOA
83-136  SOLANO, JULIO CESAR                       VILLA ESPANA C.O. 31 - LAROMANA DOMINICAN REP.
58- 87  SOLIS, MARCELINO                          OLD ADD: CALLE VIDREA 8370 - MONTEREY MEXICO
73-113  SOLOMON, EDDIE 'BUDDY'                    D. JANUARY 12, 1986 MACON, GA.
23-125  SOLOMON, MOSES HIRSCH                     D. JUNE 25, 1966 MIAMI, FLA.
```

34- 93 SOLTERS, JULIUS JOSEPH 'MOOSE'	D. SEPTEMBER 28, 1975 PITTSBURGH, PA.
10-139 SOMERLOTT, JOHN WESLEY 'JOCK'	D. APRIL 21, 1965 BUTLER, IND.
12-187 SOMMERS, RUDOLPH	D. MARCH 18, 1949 LOUISVILLE,KY.
50- 92 SOMMERS, WILLIAM DUNN	2550 SW BOBOLINK COURT - PALM CITY FL 34990
24-101 SONGER, DON	D. OCTOBER 3, 1962 KANSAS CITY, MO.
77-134 SORENSEN, LARY ALAN	22145 DALEVIEW DRIVE - NOVI MI 48050
28- 87 SORRELL, VICTOR GARLAND	D. MAY 4, 1972 RALEIGH, N. C.
65-102 SORRELL, WILLIAM	%A.WINTON,16476 BERNARDO CTR DR - SAN DIEGO CA 92128
22-129 SORRELLS, RAYMOND EDWIN 'CHICK'	D. JULY 20, 1983 TERRELL, TEXAS
89-121 SORRENTO, PAUL ANTHONY	7 JOSEPH AVENUE - PEABODY MA 01960
72-105 SOSA, ELIAS	35 ESTE #25 ENS. LUPERON - SANTO DOMINGO DOMINICAN REP.
75-109 SOSA, JOSE YNOCENCIO	HAINA KM12 CARRETERA SANCHEZ - SANTO DOMINGO DOM. REP.
89-122 SOSA, SAMUEL	MELLO CENTRO - SAN PEDRO DE MACORIS DOMINICAN REP.
26- 79 SOTHERN, DENNIS ELWOOD	D. DECEMBER 7, 1977 DURHAM, N. C.
14-203 SOTHORON, ALLEN SUTTON	D. JUNE 17, 1939 ST. LOUIS, MO
77-135 SOTO, MARIO MELVIN	JOACHS LACHAUSTEGUI #42 SUR - BANI DOMINICAN REP.
46- 95 SOUCHOCK, STEPHEN	441 SOUTHWEST 55TH TERRACE - PLANTATION FL 33317
11-160 SOUTHWICK, CLYDE AUBRA	D. OCTOBER 14, 1961 FREEPORT, ILL.
13-171 SOUTHWORTH, WILLIAM HARRISON	D. NOVEMBER 15, 1969 COLUMBUS, O.
64-110 SOUTHWORTH, WILLIAM FREDERICK	320 DOBBEN RD - WEBSTER GROVES MO 63119
80-121 SOUZA, KENNETH MARK	11145 SOUTH ALTA MESA CIRCLE - SANDY UT 84092
42- 98 SPAHN, WARREN EDWARD	RR 2 - HARTSHORNE OK 74547
27- 85 SPALDING, CHARLES HARRY 'DICK'	D. FEBRUARY 3, 1950 PHILADELPHA, PA.
59- 79 SPANGLER, ALBERT DONALD	27202 AFTON WAY - HUFFMAN TX 77336
64-111 SPANSWICK, WILLIAM HENRY	159 BRAINARD ROAD #5 - ENFIELD CT 06082
64-112 SPARMA, JOSEPH BLASE	D. MAY 14, 1986 COLUMBUS, O.
55-113 SPEAKE, ROBERT CHARLES	4742 SW URISH RD - TOPEKA KS 66604
86-143 SPECK, ROBERT CLIFFORD 'CLIFF'	7975 SOUTHWEST 83RD AVENUE - PORTLAND OR 97223
24-102 SPEECE, BYRON FRANKLIN	D. SEPTEMBER 29, 1974 ELGIN, ORE.
75-110 SPEED, HORACE ARTHUR	1301 BANKERS DRIVE - CARSON CA 90746
43-131 SPEER,VERNIE FLOYD	D. MARCH 22, 1969 LITTLE ROCK, ARK.
71- 95 SPEIER, CHRIS EDWARD	6114 EAST MONTECITO - SCOTTSDALE AZ 85251
69-161 SPENCE, JOHN ROBERT 'BOB'	2521 SAN MARCOS - SAN DIEGO CA 92104
40- 84 SPENCE, STANLEY ORVILLE	D. JANUARY 9, 1983 KINSTON, N. C.
52- 96 SPENCER, DARYL DEAN	2740 LARKIN DRIVE - WICHITA KS 67216
12-188 SPENCER, FRED CALVIN	D. FEBRUARY 5, 1969 ST. ANTHONY, MINN.
50- 93 SPENCER, GEORGE ELWELL	8160 HICKORY AVE - GALENA OH 43021
28- 88 SPENCER, GLENN EDWARD	D. DECEMBER 30, 1958 BINGHAMTON, N. Y.
78-124 SPENCER, HUBERT THOMAS 'TOM'	2021 EAST CONNER STRAV - TUCSON AZ 85716
68- 97 SPENCER, JAMES LLOYD	725A OLD BANFIELD RD - SEVERNA PARK MD 21146
13-172 SPENCER, LLOYD BENJAMIN	D. SEPTEMBER 1, 1970 FINKSBURG, MD.
25- 94 SPENCER, ROY HAMPTON	D. FEBRUARY 8, 1973 PORT CHARLETTE, FLA.
20-110 SPENCER, VERNON MURRAY	D. JUNE 3, 1971 WIXOM, MICH.
20-111 SPERAW, PAUL BACHMAN	D. FEBRUARY 22, 1962 CEDAR RAPIDS, IA.
24-103 SPERBER, EDWIN GEORGE	D. JANUARY 5, 1976 CINCINNATI, O.
74-123 SPERRING, ROBERT WALTER	13302 CHRISWOOD DRIVE - CYPRESS TX 77429
36- 88 SPERRY, STANLEY KENNETH	D. SEPTEMBER 27, 1962 EVANSVILLE,WIS.
55-114 SPICER, ROBERT OBERTON	423 MCPHEE DR - FAYETTEVILLE NC 28305
89-123 SPIERS, WILLIAM JAMES	RURAL ROUTE 2 BOX 108 - CAMERON SC 29030
64-113 SPIEZIO, EDWARD WAYNE	5620 N. BARRINGTON RD - MORRIS IL 60450
72-106 SPIKES, LESLIE CHARLES 'CHARLIE'	OLD ADD: 10921 KINNEIL ROAD - NEW ORLEANS LA 70127
74-124 SPILLNER, DANIEL RAY	27535 SE 154TH - ISSAQUAH WA 98027
78-125 SPILMAN, WILLIAM HARRY	RURAL ROUTE 4 BOX 36 - DAWSON GA 31742
39-112 SPINDEL, HAROLD STEWART	12816 EL MORO AVE-LA MIRADA CA 90638
69-162 SPINKS, SCIPIO RONALD	OLD ADD: 7222 BELLERIVE DR #405 - HOUSTON TX 77036
70-126 SPLITTORFF, PAUL WILLIAM	4204 HICKORY LN - BLUE SPRING MO 64015
32- 79 SPOGNARDI, ANDREA ETTORE	4394 WASHINGTON ST - ROSLINDALE MA 02131
28- 89 SPOHRER, ALFRED RAY	D. JULY 21, 1972 CARMEL, N. Y.
54-103 SPOONER, KARL BENJAMIN	D. APRIL 10, 1984 VERO BEACH, FLA.
30- 77 SPOTTS, JAMES RUSSELL	D. JUNE 15, 1964 MEDFORD, N. J.
47- 81 SPRAGINS, HOMER FRANK	BOX 113 - MINTER CITY MS 38944
68- 98 SPRAGUE, EDWARD NELSON	2316 NORTH DAVID ROAD - LODI CA 95240
11-161 SPRATT, HENRY LEE 'JACK'	D. JULY 3, 1969 WASHINGTON, PA.
65-103 SPRIGGS, GEORGE HERMAN	336 WEST BAY FRONT ROAD - LOTHIAN MD 20711
55-115 SPRING, JACK RUSSELL	8506 EAST DALTON - SPOKANE WA 99206
25- 95 SPRINGER, BRADFORD LOUIS	D. JANUARY 4, 1970 BIRMINGHAM, MICH.
30- 78 SPRINZ, JOSEPH CONRAD	1359 33RD AVE - SAN FRANCISCO CA 94122
45-100 SPROULL, CHARLES WILLIAM	D. JANUARY 13, 1980 ROCKFORD, ILL.
61-101 SPROUT, ROBERT SAMUEL	2858 FLEETWOOD DR - LANCASTER PA 17601
78-126 SPROWL, ROBERT JOHN	114 EAST 144TH AVE - TAMPA FL 33612
24-104 SPURGEON, FRED	D. NOVEMBER 5, 1970 KALAMAZOO, MICH.
75-111 SQUIRES, MICHAEL LYNN	879 HONEY LANE - CRETE IL 60417
80-122 STABLEIN, GEORGE CHARLES	9839 LA AMAPOLA AVE - FOUNTAIN VLY CA 92708
10-140 STACK, WILLIAM EDWARD	D. AUGUST 28, 1958 CHICAGO, ILL.
64-114 STAEHLE, MARVIN GUSTAVE	570 CHECKER DRIVE - BUFFALO GROVE IL 60089
60- 95 STAFFORD, BILL CHARLES	6108 COURTLAND - PLYMOUTH MI 48170
16- 83 STAFFORD, HENRY ALEXANDER 'HEINIE'	D. JANUARY 29, 1972 LAKE WORTH, FLA.
77-136 STAGGS, STEPHEN ROBERT	4213 QUIVAS STREET - DENVER CO 80211
64-115 STAHL, LARRY FLOYD	300 NORTH PENNSYLVANIA - BELLEVILLE IL 62220
75-112 STAIGER, ROY JOSEPH	8127 SOUTH 77TH EAST AVE #301 - TULSA OK 74133
34- 94 STAINBACK, GEORGE TUCKER 'TUCK'	1000 ELYSIAN AVE - LOS ANGELES CA 90012
25- 96 STALEY, GEORGE GAYLORD 'GALE'	1935 GOLDEN RAIN RD - WALNUT CREEK CA 94529
47- 82 STALEY, GERALD LEE	2600 NE 99TH ST - VANCOUVER WA 98665
60- 96 STALLARD, EVAN TRACY	HC05 BOX 316 - COEBURN VA 24230
47- 83 STALLCUP, THOMAS VIRGIL 'VIRGIL'	D. MAY 2, 1989 GREENVILLE, S. C.
43-132 STALLER, GEORGE WALBORN	321 NORTH 67TH ST - HARRISBURG PA 17111
41-104 STANCEU, CHARLES	D. APRIL 3, 1969 CANTON, O.
25- 97 STANDAEART, JEROME JOHN	D. AUGUST 4, 1964 CHICAGO, ILL.
11-162 STANDRIDGE, ALFRED PETER	D. AUGUST 2, 1963 SAN FRANCISCO, CALIF.
63-113 STANEK, AL	96 ALLYN ST - HOLYOKE MA 01070
79-106 STANFIELD, KEVIN BRUCE	7565 NEWCOMB ST - SAN BERNARDINO CA 92410
61-102 STANGE, ALBERT LEE 'LEE'	2837 WINGED FOOT COURT - WINTER HAVEN FL 33882
72-107 STANHOUSE, DONALD JOSEPH	4231 NASHWOOD - DALLAS TX 75244
87-136 STANICEK, PETER LOUIS	118 CHESTNUT - PARK FOREST IL 60466
87-137 STANICEK, STEPHEN BLAIR	118 CHESTNUT - PARK FOREST IL 60466
59- 80 STANKA, JOE DUBLIN	1109 CONRAD SAUER - HOUSTON TX 77043
43-133 STANKY, EDWARD RAYMOND	2100 SPRING HILL RD - MOBILE AL 36607
69-163 STANLEY, FREDRICK BLAIR	8711 E. PINNACLE PEAK RD - SCOTTSDALE AZ 85255
14-204 STANLEY, JAMES F.	B. 1889

11-163	STANLEY, JOHN LEONARD 'BUCK'	D. AUGUST 13, 1940 NORFOLK, VA.
64-116	STANLEY, MITCHELL JACK 'MICKEY'	53510 GRAND RIVER #11B - NEW HUDSON MI 48165
86-144	STANLEY, ROBERT MICHAEL	1108 NORTHEAST 10TH AVENUE - FORT LAUDERDALE FL 33304
77-137	STANLEY, ROBERT WILLIAM	WM. FAIRFIELD DR - WENHAM MA 01984
18- 69	STANSBURY, JOHN JAMES	D. DECEMBER 26, 1970 EASTON, PA.
31- 84	STANTON, GEORGE WASHINGTON 'BUCK'	401 WINDING WAY DR - SAN ANTONIO TX 78232
70-127	STANTON, LEROY BOBBY	1751 NORWOOD LN - FLORENCE SC 29501
75-113	STANTON, MICHAEL THOMAS	BOX 2573 - PHENIX CITY AL 36867
89-124	STANTON, WILLIAM MICHAEL 'MIKE'	16102 RILL LANE - HOUSTON TX 77062
87-138	STAPLETON, DAVID EARL	P.O. BOX 702 - CLAYPOOL AZ 85532
80-123	STAPLETON, DAVID LESLIE	RR 1 BOX 600 - LOXLEY AL 36551
62-127	STARGELL, WILVER DORNEL	113 ASHLEY PLACE - STONE MOUNTAIN GA 30083
87-139	STARK, MATTHEW SCOTT	3641F OAK CREEK DRIVE - ONTARIO CA 91761
32- 80	STARR, RAYMOND FRANCIS	D. FEBRUARY 9, 1963 BAYLISS, ILL.
47- 84	STARR, RICHARD EUGENE	613 NORTH CRESCENT DR - KITTANNING PA 19201
35-103	STARR, WILLIAM 'CHICK'	666 UPAS ST #1801 - SAN DIEGO CA 92103
63-114	STARRETTE, HERMAN PAUL	208 HERMITAGE ROAD - STATESVILLE NC 28677
72-108	STATON, JOSEPH	P.O. BOX 28582 - SEATTLE WA 98118
19- 79	STATZ, ARNOLD JOHN 'JIGGER'	D. MARCH 16, 1988 CORONA DEL MAR, CALIF.
63-115	STAUB, DANIEL JOSEPH 'RUSTY'	1271 3RD AVE - NEW YORK NY 10021
23-126	STAUFFER, CHARLES EDWARD 'ED'	D. JULY 2, 1979 ST PETERSBURG, FLA.
74-125	STEARNS, JOHN HARDIN	7107 CEDARWOOD CIRCLE - BOULDER CO 80301
16- 84	STEELE, ROBERT WESLEY	D. JANUARY 27, 1962 OCALA, FLA.
10-141	STEELE, WILLIAM MITCHELL	D. OCTOBER 19, 1949 OVERLAND, MO.
87-140	STEELS, JAMES EARL	712 WEST POLK STREET - SANTA MARIA CA 93454
12-189	STEEN, WILLIAM JOHN	D. MARCH 13, 1979 SIGNAL HILL, CALIF.
24-105	STEENGRAFE, MILTON HENRY	D. JUNE 2, 1977 OKLAHOMA CITY, OKLA.
62-128	STEEVENS, MORRIS DALE 'MOE'	14465 CADILLAC DRIVE - SAN ANTONIO TX 78248
83-137	STEFERO, JOHN ROBERT	529 MICHELLE ROAD - ODENTON MD 21113
78-127	STEGMAN, DAVID WILLIAM	316 EAST OAK - LOMPOC CA 93436
32- 81	STEIN, IRVIN MICHAEL	D. JANUARY 7, 1981 COVINGTON, LA.
38- 93	STEIN, JUSTIN MARION	1915 GRAPE AVE - ST LOUIS MO 63136
72-109	STEIN, WILLIAM ALLEN	1340 GLENEAGLE WAY - ROCKLEDGE FL 32955
78-128	STEIN, WILLIAM RANDOLPH	1540 PALMER ST - POMONA CA 91766
86-145	STEINBACH, TERRY LEE	306 SOUTH JEFFERSON - NEW ULM MN 56073
37- 96	STEINBACHER, HENRY JOHN	D. APRIL 3, 1977 SACRAMENTO, CALIF.
12-190	STEINBRENNER, WILLIAM GASS	D. APRIL 25, 1970 PITTSBURGH, PA.
31- 85	STEINECKE, WILLIAM ROBERT	D. JULY 20, 1986 SAINT AUGUSTINE, FLA.
23-127	STEINEDER, RAYMOND	D. AUGUST 25, 1982 VINELAND, N. J.
45-101	STEINER, BENJAMIN SAUNDERS	D. OCTOBER 27, 1988 VENICE, FLA.
45-102	STEINER, JAMES HARRY 'RED'	17700 SOUTH WESTERN AVE #93 - GARDENA CA 90248
82-120	STEIRER, RICKY FRANCIS	2646 DULANY - BALTIMORE MD 21223
16- 85	STELLBAUER, WILLIAM JENNINGS	D. FEBRUARY 16, 1974 HOUSTON, TEX.
71- 96	STELMASZEK, RICHARD FRANCIS	2734 EAST 97TH ST - CHICAGO IL 60617
80-124	STEMBER, JEFFREY ALAN	330 WEST JERSEY ST - ELIZABETH NJ 07202
12-191	STENGEL, CHARLES DILLON 'CASEY'	D. SEPTEMBER 29, 1975 GLENDALE, CAL.
62-129	STENHOUSE, DAVID ROTCHFORD	70 WOODBURY RD - CRANSTON RI 02905
82-121	STENHOUSE, MICHAEL S	70 WOODBURY RD - CRANSTON RI 02905
71- 97	STENNETT, RENALDO ANTONIO	OLD ADD: 1200 FEDERAL HWY #204 - BOCA RATON FL 33432
68- 99	STEPHEN, LOUIS ROBERTS 'BUZZ'	308 NORTH PARKVIEW - PORTERVILLE CA 93257
47- 85	STEPHENS, BRYAN MARIS	10222 WESLEY CIR - HUNTINGTON BEACH CA 92646
52- 97	STEPHENS, GLEN EUGENE 'GENE'	5804 NORTH BELLS ST - OKLAHOMA CITY OK 73112
41-105	STEPHENS, VERNON DECATUR	D. NOVEMBER 4, 1968 LONG BEACH, CAL.
71- 98	STEPHENS, CHESTER EARL	RR 1 BOX 295D - ANGIER NC 27501
21- 96	STEPHENSON, JACKSON RIGGS	D. NOVEMBER 15, 1985 TUSCALOOSA, ALA.
63-116	STEPHENSON, JERRY JOSEPH	1425 MARELEN DR - FULLERTON CA 92635
64-117	STEPHENSON, JOHN HERMAN	105 BELLEWOOD - HAMMOND LA 70401
43-134	STEPHENSON, JOSEPH CHESTER	822 JADE WAY - ANAHEIM CA 92805
89-125	STEPHENSON, PHILLIP RAYMOND	604 NORTH BROAD - GUTHRIE OK 73044
55-116	STEPHENSON, ROBERT LOYD	1518 BROOKHAVEN BLVD - NORMAN OK 73069
35-104	STEPHENSON, WALTER MCQUEEN	3160 REISOR RD - SHREVEPORT LA 71118
74-126	STERLING, RANDALL WAYNE	2516 LINDA AVE - KEY WEST FL 33040
12-192	STERRETT, CHARLES HURLBUT 'DUTCH'	D. DECEMBER 9, 1965 BALTIMORE, MD.
41-106	STEVENS, CHARLES AUGUSTUS	12062 VALLEY VIEW #211-GARDEN GROVE CA 92645
45-103	STEVENS, EDWARD LEE	6211 SOUTH BRAESWOOD - HOUSTON TX 77096
14-205	STEVENS, JAMES ARTHUR	D. SEPTEMBER 25, 1966 BALTIMORE, MD.
58- 88	STEVENS, R. C.	1405 MOUND ST - DAVENPORT IA 52803
31- 86	STEVENS, ROBERT JORDAN	803 ROXBORO RD - ROCKVILLE MD 20850
13-173	STEWART, CHARLES EUGENE 'TUFFY'	D. NOVEMBER 18, 1934 CHICAGO, ILL.
78-129	STEWART, DAVID KEITH	817 MANCHESTER COURT - CLAREMONT CA 91711
41-107	STEWART, EDWARD PERRY	5501 WEST 119TH ST-INGLEWOOD CA 90304
27- 86	STEWART, FRANK	RR 1 BOX 290 - SAINT JOSEPH WI 54082
40- 85	STEWART, GLEN WELDON	60 SOUTH ALICIA-MEMPHIS TN 38112
63-117	STEWART, JAMES FRANKLIN	RURAL ROUTE 1 BOX 503 - LAFAYETTE AL 36862
16- 86	STEWART, JOHN FRANKLIN 'STUFFY'	D. DECEMBER 30, 1980 LAKE CITY, FLA.
13-174	STEWART, MARK	D. JANUARY 17, 1942 MEMPHIS, TENN.
78-130	STEWART, SAMUEL LEE	107 SCENIC VIEW DR - SWANNANOA NC 28778
52- 98	STEWART, VESTON GOFF 'BUNKY'	RAY MCCOTTER REALTY CO - NEW BERN NC28560
21- 97	STEWART, WALTER CLEVELAND 'LEFTY'	D. SEPTEMBER 26, 1974 KNOXVILLE, TENN.
40- 86	STEWART, WALTER NESBITT	5260 ROBERTS MILL RD, RR 5 - LONDON OH 43140
44-124	STEWART, WILLIAM MACKLIN 'MACK'	D. MARCH 21, 1960 MACON, GA.
55-117	STEWART, WILLIAM WAYNE	302 RUMFORD ROAD - LITITZ PA 17543
79-107	STIEB, DAVID ANDREW	1960 JEANNIE LANE - GILROY CA 95020
29- 99	STIELY, FRED WARREN	D. JANUARY 6, 1981 VALLEY VIEW, PA.
60- 97	STIGMAN, RICHARD LEWIS	12914 5TH AVE SOUTH - BURNSVILLE MN 55337
30- 79	STILES, ROLLAND MAYS	10161 SAKURA DR - ST. LOUIS MO 63128
75-114	STILLMAN, ROYLE ELDON	1904 SPRECKLER - REDONDO BEACH CA 90278
86-146	STILLWELL, KURT ANDREW	1417 DOVER AVENUE - THOUSAND OAKS CA 91360
61-103	STILLWELL, RONALD ROY	1417 DOVER - THOUSAND OAKS CA 91360
80-125	STIMAC, CRAIG STEVEN	OLD ADD: 1603 ROBINHOOD LN - LAGRANGE IL 60525
23-128	STIMSON, CARL REMUS	D. NOVEMBER 9, 1936 OMAHA, NEB.
34- 95	STINE, LEE ELBERT	1939 CALLE PASITO - HEMET CA 92343
69-164	STINSON, GORRELL ROBERT 'BOB'	14408 130TH AVENUE NE - KIRKLAND WA 98034
43-135	STIRNWEISS, GEORGE HENRY 'SNUFFY'	D. SEPTEMBER 15, 1958 NEWARK, N. J.
47- 86	STOBBS, CHARLES KLEIN	5150 HONORE AVE - SARASOTA FL 33583
13-175	STOCK, MILTON JOSEPH	D. JULY 16, 1977 MONTROSE, ALA.
59- 81	STOCK, WESLEY GAY	5917 FRANCES AVE NE - TACOMA WA 98422
81-134	STODDARD, ROBERT LYLE	15760 SUNNYSIDE AVE - MORGAN HILL CA 95037

BOBBY SHANTZ

FRANCIS JOSEPH SHEA

DAVE STIEB
pitcher

DAVE STIEB

RICK SUTCLIFFE

RICK SUTCLIFFE

VIRGIL TRUCKS

FRED WALKER

EARL WEAVER

EARL WEAVER

Billy Werber

BILL WERBER

DON ZIMMER

75-115 STODDARD, TIMOTHY PAUL   3928 EAST BUTTERNUT ST - EAST CHICAGO IN 46312
25- 98 STOKES, ALBERT JOHN   OLD ADD: 55 CARNABY HILL RD - WILTON CT 06897
25- 99 STOKES, ARTHUR MELTON   D. JUNE 3, 1962 TITUSVILLE, PA.
45-104 STONE, CHARLES RICHARD 'DICK'   D. FEBRUARY 18, 1980 OKLAHOMA CITY, OKLA.
53- 86 STONE, DARRAH DEAN   1221 7TH AVE CT - SILVIS IL 61282
13-176 STONE, DWIGHT ELY   D. JULY 3, 1976 GLENDALE, CALIF.
23-129 STONE, EDWIN ARNOLD 'ARNIE'   D. JULY 29, 1948 HUDSON FALLS N. Y.
69-165 STONE, EUGENE DANIEL   800 O'SULLIVAN DAM ROAD - OTHELLO WA 99344
67-102 STONE, GEORGE HEARD   1206 EASTLAND AVE - RUSTON LA 71270
66- 85 STONE, HARRY RONALD 'RON'   P.O. BOX 829 - WILSONVILLE OR 97070
83-138 STONE, JEFFREY GLEN   OLD ADD: RR 1 BOX 94C - HAYTI MO 63851
28- 90 STONE, JOHN THOMAS   D. NOVEMBER 30, 1955 SHELBYVILLE, TENN.
43-136 STONE, JOHN VERNON 'VERN'   D. NOVEMBER 12, 1986 FOUNTAIN VALLEY, CALIF.
71- 99 STONE, STEVEN MICHAEL   OLD ADD: 4333 N. BROWN AVE - SCOTTSDALE AZ 85251
23-130 STONE, WILLIAM ARTHUR 'TIGE'   D. JANUARY 1, 1960 JACKSONVILLE, FLA.
33- 59 STONEHAM, JOHN ANDREW   7201 OAK HILL DR - HOUSTON TX 77017
67-103 STONER, WILLIAM HAMBLY   P.O. BOX 500, STATION M - MONTREAL QUEBEC H1V 3P2 CAN.
22-130 STONER, ULYSSES SIMPSON GRANT 'LIL'   D. JUNE 26, 1966 ENID, OKLA.
31- 87 STORIE, HOWARD EDWARD   D. JULY 27, 1968 PITTSFIELD, MASS.
30- 80 STORTI, LINDO IVAN   D. JULY 24, 1982 ONTARIO, CALIF.
64-118 STOTTLEMYRE, MELVIN LEON   9 SOUTH THIRD STREET - YAKIMA WA 98901
88-129 STOTTLEMYRE, TODD VERNON   5804 WEST CHESTNUT - YAKIMA WA 98908
31- 88 STOUT, ALLYN MCCLELLAND   D. DECEMBER 22, 1974 SIKESTON, MO.
38- 94 STOVIAK, RAYMOND THOMAS   2501 SOUTH OCEAN BLVD #208 - BACON RATON FL 33432
60- 98 STOWE, HAROLD RUDOLPH   RR 3 BOX 281 - GASTONIA NC 28052
70-128 STRAHLER, MICHAEL WAYNE   2501 38TH AVE - SACRAMENTO CA 95822
54-104 STRAHS, RICHARD BERNARD   OLD ADD: 3400 NORTH LAKE SHORE DR - CHICAGO IL 60657
79-108 STRAIN, JOSEPH ALLAN   8167 SOUTH PENNSYLVANIA CT - LINCOLN CO 80122
87-141 STRAKER, LESTER PAUL   AVE. REPUBLICA NO. 6 - ESTADO BOLIVAR VENEZ

72-110 STRAMPE, ROBERT EDWIN   SOUTH 24720 LANCE HILL ROAD - CHENEY WA 99004
13-177 STRAND, PAUL EDWARD   D. JULY 2, 1974 SALT LAKE CITY, UT.
15-158 STRANDS, JOHN LAWRENCE   D. JANUARY 19, 1957 FOREST PARK, ILL.
34- 96 STRANGE, ALAN COCHRANE   8239 41ST AVE NE - SEATTLE WA 98115
89-126 STRANGE, JOSEPH DOUGLAS 'DOUG'   7 PEBBLE CREEK WAY - TAYLORS SC 29687
34- 97 STRATTON, MONTY FRANKLIN PIERCE   D. SEPTEMBER 29, 1982 GREENVILLE, TEXAS
83-139 STRAWBERRY, DARRYL EUGENE   1419 RED BLUFF COURT - SAN DIMAS CA 91773
28- 91 STRELECKI, EDWARD HAROLD   D. JANUARY 9, 1968 NEWARK, N. J.
54-105 STREULI, WALTER HERBERT   1107 WESTMINSTER - GREENSBORO NC 27410
50- 94 STRICKLAND, GEORGE BEVAN   6328 CONSTANCE ST - NEW ORLEANS LA 70118
71-100 STRICKLAND, JAMES MICHAEL   1851 SILVANA LANE - SANTA CRUZ CA 95062
37- 97 STRICKLAND, WILLIAM GOSS   4444 US HWY 98 NORTH #532 - LAKELAND FL 33805
59- 82 STRIKER, WILBUR SCOTT 'JAKE'   120 SCHELL AVE - BUCYRUS OH 44820
40- 87 STRINCEVICH, NICHOLAS MIHAILOVICH   1308 CAMELOT MANOR - PORTAGE IN 46368
41-108 STRINGER, LOUIS BERNARD   23442 EL TORO #E112 - EL TORO CA 92630
28- 92 STRIPP, JOSEPH VALENTINE   D. JUNE 10, 1989 ORLANDO, FLA.
70-129 STROHMAYER, JOHN EMERY   4120 BURSELL ST - CENTRAL VALLEY CA 96019
72-111 STROM, BRENT TERRY   P.O. BOX 26267 - ALBUQUERQUE NM 87125
39-113 STROMME, FLOYD MARVIN   3029 SHERIDAN - NORTH BEND OR 97459
29-100 STRONER, JAMES M.   D. NOVEMBER 16, 1971 CHICAGO, ILL.
66- 86 STROUD, EDWIN MARVIN   1696 OAK ST - WARREN OH 44485
10-142 STROUD, RALPH VIVIAN 'SAILOR'   D. APRIL 11, 1970 STOCKTON, CALIF.
82-122 STROUGHTER, STEPHEN LOUIS   323 NE 2ND - VISALIA CA 93277
34- 98 STRUSS, CLARENCE HERBERT 'STEAMBOAT'   D. SEPTEMBER 12, 1985 GRAND RAPIDS, MICH.
24-106 STRYKER, STERLING ALPA 'DUTCH'   D. NOVEMBER 5, 1964 RED BANK, N. J.
22-131 STUART, JOHN DAVIS   D. MAY 13, 1970 CHARLESTON, W. VA.
21- 98 STUART, LUTHER LANE 'LUKE'   D. JUNE 15, 1947 WINSTON-SALEM, N. C.
49- 83 STUART, MARLIN HENRY   RR 1 BOX 133 - PARAGOULD AR 72450
58- 89 STUART, RICHARD LEE   926 WOODSIDE ROAD - REDWOOD CITY CA 94061
84-117 STUBBS, FRANKLIN LEE   RURAL ROUTE 2 BOX 67C - HAMLET NC 28345
67-104 STUBING, LAWRENCE GEORGE 'MOOSE'   10821 SOUTH LACONIA STREET - VILLA PARK CA 92667
21- 99 STUELAND, GEORGE ANTON   D. SEPTEMBER 9, 1964 ONAWA, IA.
50- 95 STUFFEL, PAUL HARRINGTON   13136 VINE STREET NE - ALLIANCE OH 44601
57- 82 STUMP, JAMES GILBERT   939 WESTON - LANSING MI 48906
31- 89 STUMPF, GEORGE FREDERICK   222 STAFFORD AV - NEW ORLEANS LA 70124
12-193 STUMPF, WILLIAM FREDRICK   D. FEBRUARY 14, 1966 CROWNSVILLE, MD.
82-123 STUPER, JOHN ANTON   BUTLER COUNTY COMM. COLLEGE - BUTLER PA 16001
55-118 STURDIVANT, THOMAS VIRGIL   825 SW 113TH STREET - OKLAHOMA CITY OK 73170
27- 87 STURDY, GUY R.   D. MAY 4, 1965 MARSHALL, TEX.
40- 88 STURGEON, ROBERT HARWOOD   3903 LEWIS AVE-LONG BEACH CA 90807
14-206 STURGIS, DEAN DONNELL   D. JUNE 4, 1950 UNIONTOWN, PA.
41-109 STURM, JOHN PETER JOSEPH   3840 FRENCH CT-ST LOUIS MO 63116
26- 80 STUTZ, GEORGE   D. DECEMBER 29, 1930 PHILADELPHIA, PA.
19- 80 STYLES, WILLIAM GRAVES 'LENA'   D. MARCH 14, 1956 HUNTSVILLE, ALA.
66- 87 SUAREZ, KENNETH RAYMOND   1301 FINDLAY DR - ARLINGTON TX 76012
44-125 SUAREZ, LUIS ABELARDO   OLD ADD: AGUILA #4 - HAVANA CUBA
70-130 SUCH, RICHARD STANLEY   2100 LORD ASHLEY DR - SANFORD NC 27330
38- 95 SUCHE, CHARLES MORRIS   D. FEBRUARY 11, 1984 SAN ANTONIO, TEXAS
50- 96 SUCHECKI, JAMES JOSEPH   RR 2 - ZIMMERMAN MN 55398
68-100 SUDAKIS, WILLIAM PAUL   16641 ALGONQUIN - HUNTINGTON BEACH CA 92649
41-110 SUDER, PETER   903 ROOSEVELT AVE - ALIQUIPPA PA 15001
30- 81 SUHR, AUGUST RICHARD   341 HAZEL AVE - MILLBRAE CA 94030
26- 81 SUKEFORTH, CLYDE LEROY   RR 3 BOX 123 - WALDOBORO ME 04572
64-119 SUKLA, EDWARD ANTHONY   16 PERCH - IRVINE CA 92714
80-126 SULARZ, GUY PATRICK   6225-108 SHOUP AVENUE - WOODLAND HILLS CA 91364
36- 89 SULIK, ERNEST RICHARD   D. MAY 31, 1963 OAKLAND, CAL.
44-126 SULLIVAN, CARL MANUEL 'JACK'   %V.CROWDER,602 BARNES ST - MCKINNEY TX 75069
28- 93 SULLIVAN, CHARLES EDWARD   D. MAY 28, 1935 MAIDEN, N. C.
53- 87 SULLIVAN, FRANKLIN LEAL   BOX 1873 - LIHUE HI 96766
55-119 SULLIVAN, HAYWOOD COOPER   FENWAY PARK - BOSTON MA 02215
21-100 SULLIVAN, JAMES RICHARD   D. FEBRUARY 12, 1972 BURTONSVILLE, MD.
35-105 SULLIVAN, JOE   D. APRIL 8, 1985 SEQUIM, WASH.
19- 81 SULLIVAN, JOHN JEREMIAH   D. JULY 7, 1958 CHICAGO, ILL.
20-112 SULLIVAN, JOHN LAWRENCE   D. APRIL 1, 1966 UNION CO., PA.
42- 99 SULLIVAN, JOHN PETER   2301 183RD ST #403A - HOMEWOOD IL 60430
63-118 SULLIVAN, JOHN PETER   24 HIGHLAND AV - DANSVILLE NY 14437
82-124 SULLIVAN, MARC COOPER   134 SPRING LN - CANTON MA 02021
39-114 SULLIVAN, PAUL THOMAS 'LEFTY'   D. NOVEMBER 1, 1988 SCOTTSDALE, ARIZ.
51- 93 SULLIVAN, RUSSELL GUY H   1701 HILL-N-DALE DR - FREDERICKSBURG VA 22401

22-132 SULLIVAN, THOMAS AUGUSTIN	D. SEPTEMBER 23, 1962 BOSTON, MASS.
25-100 SULLIVAN, THOMAS BRANDON	D. AUGUST 16, 1944 SEATTLE, WASH.
31- 90 SULLIVAN, WILLIAM JOSEPH JR.	OLD ADD: 7957 NORTH TAMIAMI TRAIL - SARASOTA FL 33580
20-113 SUMMA, HOMER WAYNE	D. JANUARY 29, 1966 LOS ANGELES, CAL.
74-127 SUMMERS, JOHN JUNIOR	2091 TREVINO - OCEANSIDE CA 92056
28- 94 SUMNER, CARL RINGDAHL	24 WINTERSET DRIVE - CHATHAM MA 02633
74-128 SUNDBERG, JAMES HOWARD	4610 RIVERFOREST DR - ARLINGTON TX 76017
56- 80 SUNDIN, GORDON VINCENT	505 WHISPERING PINE LN - NAPLES FL 33940
36- 90 SUNDRA, STEPHEN RICHARD	D. MARCH 23, 1952 CLEVELAND, O.
37- 98 SUNKEL, THOMAS JACOB	RR 1 BOX 194-A - PARIS IL 61944
85-107 SURHOFF, RICHARD CLIFFORD	239 PURCHASE ST - RYE NY 10580
87-142 SURHOFF, WILLIAM JAMES 'B. J.'	9926 WEST BROOKSIDE DRIVE - HALES CORNER WI 53130
49- 84 SURKONT, MATTHEW CONSTANTINE 'MAX'	D. OCTOBER 8, 1986 LARGO, FLA.
29-101 SUSCE, GEORGE CYRIL METHODIUS SR.	D. FEBRUARY 25, 1986 SARASOTA, FLA.
55-120 SUSCE, GEORGE DANIEL JR	12 JARVIS CIRCLE - NEEDHAM MA 02192
34- 99 SUSKO, PETER JONATHAN	D. MAY 22, 1978 JACKSONVILLE, FLA.
38- 96 SUTCLIFFE, CHARLES INIGO 'BUTCH'	33 MALVEY ST-FALL RIVER MA 02720
76- 87 SUTCLIFFE, RICHARD LEE 'RICK'	313 NW NORTH SHORE DR - PARKVILLE MO 64151
64-120 SUTHERLAND, DARRELL WAYNE	3445 LAS PALMAS AVE - GLENDALE CA 91208
66- 88 SUTHERLAND, GARY LYNN	338 NORTH OAK CLIFF - MONROVIA CA 91016
21-101 SUTHERLAND, HARVEY SCOTT 'SUDS'	D. MAY 11, 1972 PORTLAND, ORE.
49- 85 SUTHERLAND, HOWARD ALVIN 'DIZZY'	D. AUGUST 26, 1979 WASHINGTON, D. C.
80-127 SUTHERLAND, LEONARDO CANTIN	2237 S. OERTLEY DR - ANAHEIM CA 92802
76- 88 SUTTER, HOWARD BRUCE	1368 HAMILTON RD - KENNESAW GA 30144
66- 89 SUTTON, DONALD HOWARD	22952 ALCADE DRIVE #140 - LAGUNA HILLS CA 92653
77-138 SUTTON, JOHNNY IKE	RR 1 BOX 857 - DESOTO TX 75115
86-147 SVEUM, DALE CURTIS	248 DON CASTER DRIVE - VALLEJO CA 94590
83-140 SWAGGERTY, WILLIAM DAVID	OLD ADD: 3542 TERRACE HILL #204 - RANDALLSTOWN MD 21133
73-114 SWAN, CRAIG STEVEN	38 BUTLER STREET - COS COB CT 06807
14-207 SWAN, HARRY GORDON 'DUCKY'	D. MAY 9, 1946 PITTSBURGH, PA.
89-127 SWAN, RUSSELL HOWARD	1108 WEST 27TH AVENUE - KENNEWICK WA 99337
55-121 SWANSON, ARTHUR LEONARD	OLD ADD: 15718 WENDY GLEN - HOUSTON TX 77095
29-102 SWANSON, ERNEST EVAR	D. JULY 17, 1973 GALESBURG, ILL.
28- 95 SWANSON, KARL EDWARD	212 HILLCREST DR - AVON PARK FL 33825
71-101 SWANSON, STANLEY LAWRENCE	P.O. BOX 659 - MARSHALL TX 75671
14-208 SWANSON, WILLIAM ANDREW	D. OCTOBER 14, 1954 NEW YORK, N.Y.
47- 87 SWARTZ, SHERWIN MERLE	1937 NORTH BEVERLY DR - BEVERLY HILLS CA 90210
20-114 SWARTZ, VERNON MONROE 'DAZZY'	D. JANUARY 13, 1980 GERMANTOWN, O.
14-209 SWEENEY, CHARLES FRANCIS	D. MARCH 13, 1955 PITTSBURGH, PA.
44-127 SWEENEY, HENRY LEON	D. MAY 6, 1980 COLUMBIA, TENN.
28- 96 SWEENEY, WILLIAM JOSEPH	D. APRIL 18, 1957 SAN DIEGO, CAL.
78-131 SWEET, RICHARD JOE 'RICK'	7402 MICHIGAN STREET - VANCOUVER WA 98664
27- 88 SWEETLAND, LESTER LEO	D. MARCH 4, 1974 MELBOURNE, FL.
22-133 SWENTOR, AUGUST WILLIAM	D. NOVEMBER 10, 1969 WATERBURY, CONN.
29-103 SWETONIC, STEPHEN ALBERT	D. APRIL 22, 1974 CANONSBURG, PA.
40- 89 SWIFT, ROBERT VIRGIL	D. OCTOBER 17, 1966 DETROIT, MICH.
85-108 SWIFT, WILLIAM CHARLES	13205 122ND PLACE NE - KIRKLAND WA 98003
32- 82 SWIFT, WILLIAM VINCENT	D. FEBRUARY 23, 1969 BARTOW, FLA.
39-115 SWIGART, OADIS VAUGHN	2917 SENECA BLVD - ST. JOSEPH MO 64507
17- 80 SWIGLER, ADAM WILLIAM	D. FEBRUARY 5, 1975 PHILADELPHIA, PA.
86-148 SWINDELL, FOREST GREGORY 'GREG'	7706 TWIN HILLS - HOUSTON TX 77071
11-164 SWINDELL, JOSHUA ERNEST	D. MARCH 19, 1969 FRUITA, COLO.
74-129 SWISHER, STEVEN EDWARD	RR 1 BOX 5A - MINERAL WELLS WV 26150
65-104 SWOBODA, RONALD ALVIN	621 JEFFERSON AVENUE - NEW ORLEANS LA 70115
77-139 SYKES, ROBERT JOSEPH	509 WEST MAIN ST - CARMI IL 62821
53- 88 SZEKELY, JOSEPH	3260 ALLEN - PARIS TX 75460
70-131 SZOTKIEWICZ, KENNETH JOHN	1709 BEECH ST - WILMINGTON DE 19805
76- 89 TABB, JERRY LYNN	4502 RUIDOSO COURT - MIDLAND TX 79707
26- 82 TABER, EDWARD TIMOTHY 'LEFTY'	D. NOVEMBER 5, 1983 LINCOLN, NEB.
81-135 TABLER, PATRICK SEAN	11943 TIMBERLAKE DRIVE - CINCINNATI OH 45249
87-143 TABOR, GREGORY STEPHEN	29317 WHALE BONE WAY - HAYWARD CA 94544
38- 97 TABOR, JAMES REUBIN	D. AUGUST 22, 1953 SACRAMENTO, CAL.
13-178 TAFF, JOHN GALLATIN	D. MAY 15, 1961 HOUSTON, TEX.
28- 97 TAITT, DOUGLAS JOHN	D. DECEMBER 12, 1970 PORTLAND, ORE.
63-119 TALBOT, FREDERICK LEALAND	7701 LUNSEFORD LANE - FALLS CHURCH VA 22043
53- 89 TALBOT, ROBERT DALE	608 WEST KAWEAH - VISALIA CA 93277
43-137 TALCOTT, LEROY EVERETT	5060 SW 82ND AVE - MIAMI BEACH FL 33143
66- 90 TALTON, MARION LEE 'TIM'	RR 2 BOX 255 - PIKEVILLE NC 27863
76- 90 TAMARGO, JOHN FELIX	1425 EAST PARIS - TAMPA FL 33604
34-100 TAMULIS, VITAUTIS CASIMIRUS	D. MAY 5, 1974 NASHVILLE, TENN.
73-115 TANANA, FRANK DARYL	28492 SOUTH HARWICK - FARMINGTON HILLS MI 48018
25-101 TANKERSLEY, LAWRENCE WILLIAM 'LEO'	D. SEPTEMBER 18, 1980 DALLAS, TEXAS
85-109 TANNER, BRUCE MATTHEW	34 MAITLAND LANE EAST - NEW CASTLE PA 16101
55-122 TANNER, CHARLES WILLIAM	34 MAITLAND LN EAST - NEW CASTLE PA 16101
89-128 TAPANI, KEVIN RAY	5301 HYLAND GREEN DRIVE #728 - MINNEAPOLIS MN 55437
54-106 TAPPE, ELVIN WALTER	2021 WILMAR SOUTHEAST - QUINCY IL 62301
50- 97 TAPPE, THEODORE NASH	203 MARR - WENATCHEE WA 98801
14-221 TAPPEN, WALTER VAN DORN	D. DECEMBER 19, 1967 LYNWOOD, CALIF.
27- 89 TARBERT, WILBER ARLINGTON 'ARLIE'	D. NOVEMBER 27, 1946 CLEVELAND, O.
84-118 TARTABULL, DANILO	4105 NW 185TH STREET - CORAL CITY FL 33055
62-130 TARTABULL, JOSE	4105 NW 185TH ST - CORAL CITY FL 33055
86-149 TARVER, LASCHELLE	3175 FINE AVENUE - CLOVIS CA 93612
58- 90 TASBY, WILLIE	1486 12TH ST - OAKLAND CA 94607
46- 96 TATE, ALVIN WALTER	739 WEST 3400 SOUTH - BOUNTIFUL UT 84010
24-107 TATE, HENRY BENNETT 'BENNIE'	D. OCTOBER 27, 1973 FRANKFORT, ILL.
58- 91 TATE, LEE WILLIE	6905 PRATT - OMAHA NE 68131
75-116 TATE, RANDALL LEE	RR 1 BOX 423 - KILLEN AL 35645
89-129 TATE, STUART DOUGLAS	250 MERIDIANVILLE ROAD - MERIDIANVILLE AL 35759
68-101 TATUM, JARVIS	727 SOUTH ARTHUR - FRESNO CA 93706
69-166 TATUM, KENNETH RAY	340 WOODWARD RD - BIRMINGHAM AL 35228
41-111 TATUM, THOMAS VEE TEE	D. NOVEMBER 7, 1989 OKLAHOMA CITY, OKLA.
35-106 TAUBY, FRED JOSEPH	D. NOVEMBER 23, 1955 CONCORDIA, CAL.
28- 98 TAUSCHER, WALTER EDWARD	2600 WESTERN PARKWAY - ORLANDO FL 32803
58- 92 TAUSSIG, DONALD FRANKLIN	BOX 225 - LONG BEACH NY 11561
21-102 TAVENER, JOHN ADAM	D. SEPTEMBER 14, 1969 FT. WORTH, TEX.
76- 91 TAVERAS, ALEJANDRO ANTONIO 'ALEX'	A. MONSANTO 8 TAMBORIL - SANTIAGO DOMINICAN REP.
71-102 TAVERAS, FRANKLIN CRISOSTOMO	CALLE 31 #16 LOS COLINOS - SANTIAGO DOMINICAN REP.
58- 93 TAYLOR, ANTONIO	2772 MARSEILLE CIRCLE - BROUSSARD QUEBEC J4Y 1L1 CAN.

21-103	TAYLOR, ARLAS WALTER	D. SEPTEMBER 10, 1958 DADE CITY, FLA.
12-194	TAYLOR, BENJAMIN HARRISON	D. NOVEMBER 3, 1946 MARTIN COUNTY, IND.
77-140	TAYLOR, BRUCE BELL	8 HIGHLAND PARK RD - RUTLAND MA 01543
25-102	TAYLOR, C. L. 'CHINK'	D. JULY 7, 1980 TEMPLE, TEXAS
68-102	TAYLOR, CARL MEANS	OLD ADD: 530 SOUTH VENICE BY-PASS - VENICE FL
69-167	TAYLOR, CHARLES GILBERT	1619 GEORGETOWN LN - MURFREESBORO TN 37130
26- 83	TAYLOR, DANIEL TURNEY	D. OCTOBER 11, 1972 LATROBE, PA.
87-144	TAYLOR, DONALD CLYDE 'DORN'	1645 FRANKLIN AVENUE - WILLOW GROVE PA 19090
86-150	TAYLOR, DWIGHT BERNARD	OLD ADD: 1230 NORTH PARK AVE #103 - TUCSON AZ 85721
26- 84	TAYLOR, EDWARD JAMES	BOX 2237 - CHULA VISTA CA 92012
51- 94	TAYLOR, EUGENE BENJAMIN 'BEN'	RURAL ROUTE 1 BOX 447A - CLARKSVILLE AR 72830
50- 98	TAYLOR, FREDERICK RANKIN	3144 DRRBY RD - COLUMBUS OH 43221
69-168	TAYLOR, GARY WILLIAM	OLD ADD: 827 N. MARTHA - DEARBORN MI 48128
57- 83	TAYLOR, HARRY EVANS	2125 COOKS LN - FORT WORTH TX 76112
32- 83	TAYLOR, HARRY WARREN	D. APRIL 27, 1969 TOLEDO, O.
46- 97	TAYLOR, JAMES HARRY	RR 13 BOX 111 - WEST TERRE HAUTE IN 47885
20-115	TAYLOR, JAMES WREN 'ZACK'	D. SEPTEMBER 19, 1974 ORLANDO, FLA.
54-107	TAYLOR, JOE CEPHUS	705 WATT LN - PITTSBURGH PA 15219
23-131	TAYLOR, LEO THOMAS	D. MAY 20, 1982 SEATTLE, WASH.
11-165	TAYLOR, PHILIP WILEY	D. JULY 9, 1954 TOPEKA, KAN.
57- 84	TAYLOR, ROBERT DALE 'HAWK'	RR 5 BOX 897 - MURRAY KY 42071
70-132	TAYLOR, ROBERT LEE	27 SUNNYBROOK RD - SPRINGFIELD MA 01109
62-131	TAYLOR, RONALD WESLEY	19 ALVIN AVENUE - TORONTO ONTARIO M4G 1A4 CAN.
58- 94	TAYLOR, SAMUEL DOUGLAS	BOX 152 - WOODRUFF SC 29388
88-130	TAYLOR, TERRY DERRELL	9255 SOUTH MCCLELLAND STREET - CRESTVIEW FL 32536
24-108	TAYLOR, THOMAS LIVINGSTONE CARLTON	D. APRIL 5, 1956 GREENVILLE, MISS.
52- 99	TAYLOR, VERNON CHARLES 'PETE'	823 CEDARCROFT DR - MILLERSVILLE MD 21108
54-108	TAYLOR, WILLIAM MICHAEL	BOX 146 - ACTON CA 93510
30- 82	TEACHOUT, ARTHUR JOHN 'BUD'	D. MAY 11, 1985 LAGUNA BEACH, CALIF.
36- 91	TEBBETTS, GEORGE ROBERT 'BIRDIE'	229 OAK AVE-ANNA MARIA FL 33501
14-211	TEDROW, ALLEN SEYMOUR	D. JANUARY 23, 1958 WESTERVILLE, O.
53- 90	TEED, RICHARD LEROY	45 TAYLOR STREET - WINDSOR CT 06095
86-151	TEJADA, WILFREDO ARISTIDES	J.ALVAREZ ALEJO#8,VILLA CONSUELO-SANTO DOMINGO DOM REP.
74-130	TEKULVE, KENTON CHARLES	1531 SEQUOIA - PITTSBURGH PA 15241
79-109	TELLMANN, THOMAS JOHN	1126A MOUNT VERNON STREET - OSHKOSH WI 54901
52-100	TEMPLE, JOHN ELLIS	RR 2 BOX 293C - IRMO SC 29063
55-123	TEMPLETON, CHARLES SHERMAN	6A BAYSIDE ESTATES - FORT MYERS BEACH FL 33931
76- 92	TEMPLETON, GARRY LEWIS	13552 DEL POMONTE RD - POWAY CA 92064
69-169	TENACE, FURY GENE	15368 MARKER RD - POWAY CA 92064
29-104	TENNANT, JAMES MCDONNELL	D. APRIL 16, 1967 TRUMBULL, CONN.
12-195	TENNANT, THOMAS FRANCIS	D. FEBRUARY 16, 1955 SAN CARLOS, CALIF.
67-105	TEPEDINO, FRANK RONALD	95 DAVIS ST - HAUPPAUGE NY 11787
46- 98	TEPSIC, JOSEPH JOHN	RR3 BOX 164 - TYRONE PA 16686
72-112	TERLECKI, ROBERT JOSEPH	760 NORWAY AVE - TRENTON NJ 08629
75-117	TERLECKY, GREGORY JOHN	2130 CAMINO LAUREL - SAN CLEMENTE CA 92672
74-131	TERPKO, JEFFREY MICHAEL	RR 1 BOX 156 - SAYRE PA 18840
82-125	TERRELL, CHARLES WALTER 'WALT'	630 WESTCHESTER - GROSSE POINTE PARK MI 48230
73-116	TERRELL, JERRY WAYNE	1301 SUNNY CREEK LN - BLUE SPRINGS MO 64015
40- 90	TERRY, LANCELOT YANK	D. NOVEMBER 4, 1979 BLOOMINGTON, IND.
56- 81	TERRY, RALPH WILLARD	801 PARK - LARNED KS 67550
86-152	TERRY, SCOTT RAY	OLD ADD: 123 RICE DRIVE - PORTLAND OR 78374
23-132	TERRY, WILLIAM HAROLD	D. JANUARY 9, 1989 JACKSONVILLE, FLA.
16- 87	TERRY, ZEBULON ALEXANDER	D. MARCH 14, 1988 LOS ANGELES, CALIF.
32- 84	TERWILLIGER, RICHARD MARTIN	D. JANUARY 21, 1969 GREENVILLE, MICH.
49- 86	TERWILLIGER, WILLARD WAYNE	6549 BARTLETT BLVD - MOUND MN 55364
15-160	TESCH, ALBERT JOHN	D. AUGUST 3, 1947 JERSEY CITY, N.J.
12-196	TESREAU, CHARLES MONROE 'JEFF'	D. SEPTEMBER 24, 1946 HANOVER, N.H.
58- 95	TESTA, NICHOLAS	2544 LURTING AVE - BRONX NY 10469
55-124	TETTELBACH, RICHARD MORLEY	295 PRESTON ROAD - CHESHIRE CT 06410
84-119	TETTLETON, MICKEY LEE	10405 LESTER LANE - OKLAHOMA CITY OK 73101
83-141	TEUFEL, TIMOTHY SHAWN	37 BYRAM TERRACE DR - GREENWICH CT 06830
86-153	TEWKSBURY, ROBERT ALAN	48 SUMNER STREET - PENACOOK NH 03301
14-212	TEXTOR, GEORGE	D. MARCH 11, 1954 MASSILLON, O.
58- 96	THACKER, MORRIS BENTON 'MOE'	10206 BLUFFSPRINGS TRACE - LOUISVILLE KY 40223
78-132	THAYER, GREGORY ALLEN	1000 3RD ST NORTH - SAUK RAPIDS MN 56379
20-116	THEIS, JOHN LOUIS	D. JULY 6, 1941 GEORGETOWN, O.
77-141	THEISS, DUANE CHARLES	5 COLUMBUS STREET - SOMERSET OH 43703
71-103	THEOBALD, RONALD MERRILL	9 FLEUTI - MORAGA CA 94556
73-117	THEODORE, GEORGE BASIL	3254 ELGIN DRIVE - SALT LAKE CITY UT 84109
44-128	THESENGA, ARNOLD JOSEPH 'JUG'	3907 COUNTRYSIDE PLAZA - WICHITA KS 67218
24-109	THEVENOW, THOMAS JOSEPH	D. JULY 28, 1957 MADISON, IND.
52-101	THIEL, MAYNARD BERT	RR2 - MARION WI 54950
63-120	THIES, DAVID ROBERT	6140 ARCTIC WAY - MINNEAPOLIS MN 55436
54-109	THIES, VERNON ARTHUR 'JAKE'	4 CORNFLOWER COURT - FLORISSANT MO 63033
46-154	THIGPEN, ROBERT THOMAS	P.O. BOX 87 - MONTICELLO FL 32344
67-106	THOENEN, RICHARD CRISPIN	51 NORTH PEACH ST - MEDFORD OR 97501
26- 85	THOMAS, ALPHONSE THOMAS 'TOMMY'	D. APRIL 27, 1988 YORK COUNTY, PA.
85-110	THOMAS, ANDRES PERES	35 DUARTE #35 - BOCA CHICA DOMINICAN REP.
11-166	THOMAS, BLAINE M.	D. AUGUST 21, 1915 PAYSON, ARIZ.
60- 99	THOMAS, CARL LESLIE	5850 EAST ORANGE BLOSSOM LN - PHOENIX AZ 85018
12-197	THOMAS, CHESTER DAVID 'PINCH'	D. DECEMBER 24, 1953 MODESTO, CALIF.
25-103	THOMAS, CLARENCE FLETCHER 'LEFTY'	D. MARCH 21, 1952 CHARLOTTESVILLE, VA.
16- 88	THOMAS, CLAUDE ALFRED	D. MARCH 6, 1946 SULPHUR, OKLA.
76- 93	THOMAS, DANNY LEE	D. JUNE 12, 1980 MOBILE, ALA.
71-104	THOMAS, DERREL OSBON	236 W. 73RD ST - LOS ANGELES CA 90003
27- 90	THOMAS, FAY WESLEY	10526 ANDORA AVE - CHATSWORTH CA 91311
51- 95	THOMAS, FRANK JOSEPH	118 DORAY DR - PITTSBURGH PA 15237
18- 70	THOMAS, FREDERICK HARVEY	D. JANUARY 15, 1986 RICE LAKE, WISC.
57- 85	THOMAS, GEORGE EDWARD	12733 PORTLAND AVE SOUTH - BURNSVILLE MN 55337
24-110	THOMAS, HERBERT MARK	818 WEST PRATT ST - STARKE FL 32071
73-118	THOMAS, JAMES GORMAN 'GORMAN'	5102 WEST BLUEMOUND ROAD - MILWAUKEE WI 53208
61-104	THOMAS, JAMES LEROY 'LEE'	50 EAST CARDIGAN - ST LOUIS MO 63135
51- 96	THOMAS, JOHN TILLMAN 'BUD'	2607 STEPHENSON ST - SEDALIA MO 65301
52-102	THOMAS, KEITH MARSHALL 'KITE'	112 N. CIRCLE DR #7275 - ROCKY MOUNT NC 27801
50- 99	THOMAS, LEO RAYMOND	2024 SANDCREEK WAY - ALAMEDA CA 94501
32- 85	THOMAS, LUTHER BAXTER 'BUD'	RR 1 BOX 400 - NORTH GARDEN VA 22959
26- 86	THOMAS, MYLES LEWIS	D. DECEMBER 12, 1963 TOLEDO, O.
38- 98	THOMAS, RAYMOND JOSEPH	607 WEST VANCE ST - WILSON NC 27893

21-104 THOMAS, ROBERT WILLIAM 'RED'	D. MARCH 29, 1962 FREMONT, O.
77-142 THOMAS, ROY JUSTIN	4055 HIDDEN VALLEY LN - SAN JOSE CA 95127
74-132 THOMAS, STANLEY BROWN	10827 159TH COURT NE - REDMOND WA 98052
57- 86 THOMAS, VALMY	BOX 9184 - SANTURCE PR 00908
10-143 THOMASEN, ARTHUR WILSON	D. MAY 2, 1944 KANSAS CITY, MO.
74-133 THOMASON, MELVIN ERSKINE	405 SOUTH BROAD ST - CLINTON SC 29325
72-113 THOMASSON, GARY LEAH	4515 EAST ONYX ST - PHOENIX AZ 85028
78-133 THOMPSON, BOBBY LARUE	OLD ADD: 3106 CAPITOL DR #2 - CHARLOTTE NC 28208
54-110 THOMPSON, CHARLES LEMOINE	518 MILLER STREET - LEBANON OH 45036
70-133 THOMPSON, DANNY LEON	D. DECEMBER 10, 1976 ROCHESTER, MINN.
48- 98 THOMPSON, DAVID FORREST	D. FEBRUARY 26, 1979 CHARLOTTE, N. C.
49- 87 THOMPSON, DONALD NEWLIN	87 EAST EUCLID PKWY - ASHEVILLE NC 28804
39-116 THOMPSON, EUGENE EARL	7934 E. CRESTWOOD WAY - SCOTTSDALE AZ 85253
20-117 THOMPSON, FRANK E.	D. JUNE 27, 1940 JASPER CO., MINERAL TWP., MO.
11-167 THOMPSON, FULLER WEIDNER	D. FEBRUARY 19, 1972 LOS ANGELES, CALIF.
19- 82 THOMPSON, HAROLD	D. FEBRUARY 14, 1951 RENO, NEV.
47- 88 THOMPSON, HENRY CURTIS	D. SEPTEMBER 30, 1969 FRESNO, CAL.
14-213 THOMPSON, JAMES ALFRED	D. JANUARY 7, 1990 BLACK MOUNTAIN, N. C.
76- 94 THOMPSON, JASON DOLPH	26351 SORRELL - LAGUNA HILLS CA 92653
21-105 THOMPSON, JOHN DUDLEY 'LEE'	D. FEBRUARY 17, 1965 SANTA BARBARA, CAL.
48- 99 THOMPSON, JOHN SAMUEL 'JOCKO'	D. FEBRUARY 3, 1988 OLNEY, MD.
25-104 THOMPSON, LAFAYETTE FRESCO	D. NOVEMBER 20, 1968 FULLERTON, CAL.
71-105 THOMPSON, MICHAEL WAYNE	7565 TURNER DR - DENVER CO 80221
84-120 THOMPSON, MILTON BERNARD	RR 2 BOX 95 - NINETY SIX, SC 29666
85-111 THOMPSON, RICHARD NEIL	7 CHAMBERS COURT - HUNTINGTON STATION NY 11746
86-155 THOMPSON, ROBERT RANDALL	4438 GUN CLUB ROAD - WEST PALM BEACH FL 33406
33- 60 THOMPSON, RUPERT LUCKHART 'TOMMY'	D. MAY 24, 1971 AUBURN, CAL.
12-198 THOMPSON, THOMAS CARL	D. JANUARY 16, 1963 LAJOLLA, CALIF.
12-199 THOMPSON, THOMAS HOMER	D. SEPTEMBER 19, 1957 ATLANTA, GA.
78-134 THOMPSON, VERNON SCOT	110 BEACON RD - RENFREW PA 16053
46- 99 THOMSON, ROBERT BROWN	122 SUNLIT DR - WATCHUNG NJ 07060
79-110 THON, RICHARD WILLIAM 'DICKIE'	HB-12 LOMBARDIA ST - RIO PIEDRAS PR 00924
17- 81 THORMAHLEN, HERBERT EHLER 'HANK'	D. FEBRUARY 6, 1955 LOS ANGELES, CALIF.
77-143 THORMODSGARD, PAUL GAYTON	884 NORTH FOURTH - BANNING CA 92220
73-119 THORNTON, ANDRE	BOX 395 - CHAGRIN FALLS OH 44022
85-112 THORNTON, LOUIS	115 MCLEAN ROAD - HOPE HULL AL 36043
73-120 THORNTON, OTIS BENJAMIN	BOX 164 - DOCENA AL 35060
51- 79 THORPE, BENJAMIN ROBERT 'BOB'	BOX 46 - WAVELAND MS 39576
13-179 THORPE, JAMES FRANCIS	D. MARCH 28, 1953 LOMITA, CALIF.
55-125 THORPE, ROBERT JOSEPH	D. MARCH 17, 1960 SAN DIEGO, CAL.
16- 89 THRASHER, FRANK EDWARD 'BUCK'	D. JUNE 12, 1938 CLEVELAND, TENN.
55-126 THRONEBERRY, MARVIN EUGENE	12102 MACON RD - COLLIERVILLE TN 38017
52-103 THRONEBERRY, MAYNARD FAYE	12016 MACON RD - COLLIERVILLE TN 38017
75-118 THROOP, GEORGE LYNFORD	672 WEST HIGHLAND AVE - SIERRA MADRE CA 91024
39-117 THUMAN, LOUIS CHARLES FRANK	6117 EDLYNNE RD - BALTIMORE MD 21212
87-145 THURMAN, GARY MONTEZ	OLD ADD: 7222 RUE DE MARGOT - INDIANAPOLIS IN 46260
55-127 THURMAN, ROBERT BURNS	9316 BEDELL - WICHITA KS 67207
83-142 THURMOND, MARK ANTHONY	OLD ADD: 4706 MISTY SHADOWS DR - HOUSTON TX 77041
23-133 THURSTON, HOLLIS JOHN 'SLOPPY'	D. SEPTEMBER 14, 1973 LOS ANGELES, CAL.
64-121 TIANT, LUIS CLEMENTE	150 INDIAN LANE - CANTON MA 02021
84-121 TIBBS, JAY LINDSEY	216 REDSTONE WAY - BIRMINGHAM AL 35215
72-114 TIDROW, RICHARD WILLIAM	324 NE WARRINGTON COURT - LEES SUMMIT MO 64064
52-104 TIEFENAUER, BOBBY GENE	700 POPLAR - DESLOGE MO 63601
62-132 TIEFENTHALER, VERLE MATHEW	1852 QUINT AVE - CARROLL IA 51401
20-118 TIERNEY, JAMES ARTHUR 'COTTON'	D. APRIL 18, 1953 KANSAS CITY, MO.
33- 61 TIETJE, LESLIE WILLIAM	RR 2 BOX 107 - KASSON MN 55944
57- 87 TIGHE, JOHN THOMAS	3201 NE 5TH COURT #4 - POMPANO BEACH FL 33062
15-161 TILLMAN, JOHN LAWRENCE	D. APRIL 7, 1964 HARRISBURG, PA.
62-133 TILLMAN, JOHN ROBERT 'BOB'	403 WADERBROOK DR - GALLATIN TN 37066
82-126 TILLMAN, KERRY JEROME 'RUSTY'	130 JACKSON RD - ATLANTIC BEACH FL 32233
67-107 TILLOTSON, THADDEUS ASA	2399 OLD LAKE ROAD - MERCED CA 95340
69-170 TIMBERLAKE, GARY LEAH	1975 BANNER AVENUE - CORYDON IN 47112
69-171 TIMMERMANN, THOMAS HENRY	4900 COOLEY LAKE - MILFORD MI 48042
14-214 TINCUP, AUSTIN BEN	D. JULY 5, 1980 CLAREMORE, OK.
82-127 TINGLEY, RONALD IRVIN	OLD ADD: 1830 GREENBRAE - SPARKS NV 89431
32- 86 TINNING, LYLE FORREST 'BUD'	D. JANUARY 17, 1961 EVANSVILLE, IND.
15-162 TIPPLE, DANIEL E	D. MARCH 26, 1960 OMAHA, NEB.
39-118 TIPTON, ERIC GORDON	125 NINA LN - WILLIAMSBURG VA 23185
48-100 TIPTON, JOSEPH JOHN	1129 2ND AVE - PLEASANT GROVE AL 35127
69-172 TISCHINSKI, THOMAS ARTHUR	2607 NE 68TH TER - GLADSTONE MO 64119
36- 92 TISING, JOHNNIE JOSEPH	D. SEPTEMBER 5, 1967 LEADVILLE, COLO.
78-135 TOBIK, DAVID VANCE	4852 SOUTH SEDGEWICK RD - LYNDHURST OH 44124
37- 99 TOBIN, JAMES ANTHONY	D. MAY 19, 1969 OAKLAND, CAL.
32- 87 TOBIN, JOHN MARTIN	D. AUGUST 8, 1983 RHINEBECK, N. Y.
45-105 TOBIN, JOHN PATRICK	D. JANUARY 18, 1982 OAKLAND, CALIF.
14-215 TOBIN, JOHN THOMAS	D. DECEMBER 10, 1969 ST. LOUIS, MO.
41-112 TOBIN, MARION BROOKS 'PAT'	D. JANUARY 21, 1975 SHREVEPORT, LA.
32- 88 TODD, ALFRED CHESTER	D. MARCH 8, 1985 ELMIRA, N. Y.
77-144 TODD, JACKSON A	8958 EAST 76TH - TULSA OK 74133
74-134 TODD, JAMES RICHARD JR.	8630 EAST PAWNEE DR - PARKER CO 80134
24-111 TODT, PHILIP JULIUS	D. NOVEMBER 15, 1973 ST. LOUIS, MO.
47- 89 TOENES, WILLIAM HARRELL 'HAL'	5119 BRANCH AVE - TAMPA FL 33603
65-105 TOLAN, ROBERT	4145 OLYMPIAD DRIVE - LOS ANGELES CA 90043
84-122 TOLIVER, FREDDIE LEE	1601 BARTON ROAD #1005 - REDLANDS CA 92373
81-136 TOLLESON, JIMMY WAYNE	352 LANHAM CIRCLE - SPARTANBURG SC 29302
81-137 TOLMAN, TIMOTHY LEE	8601 E. FAIRMOUNT PLACE - TUCSON AZ 85715
25-105 TOLSON, CHESTER JULIUS 'CHICK'	D. APRIL 16, 1965 WASHINGTON, D. C.
53- 91 TOMANEK, RICHARD CARL	165 DUFF DR - AVON LAKE OH 44012
49- 88 TOMASIC, ANDREW JOHN	230 7TH ST - WHITEHALL PA 18052
13-180 TOMER, GEORGE CLARENCE	D. DECEMBER 15, 1984 PERRY, IOWA
72-115 TOMLIN, DAVID ALLEN	2020 CLAYTON ROAD - MANCHESTER OH 45144
12-200 TOMPKINS, CHARLES HERBERT	D. SEPTEMBER 20, 1975 PRESCOTT, ARK.
65-106 TOMPKINS, RONALD EVERETT	1645 HARBOR BLVD #158 - FOUNTAIN VALLEY CA 92708
75-119 TOMS, THOMAS HOWARD	GREENWOOD VA 22943
11-168 TONEY, FRED ALEXANDRA	D. MARCH 11, 1953 NASHVILLE, TENN.
11-169 TONNEMAN, CHARLES RICHARD 'TONY'	D. AUGUST 7, 1951 PRESCOTT, ARIZ.
11-170 TOOLEY, ALBERT	D. AUGUST 17, 1976 MARSHALL, MICH.
21-106 TOPORCER, GEORGE 'SPECS'	D. MAY 17, 1989 HUNTINGTON STATION, N. Y.

62-134	TOPPIN, RUPERTO	OLD ADD: 601 CROWN ST - BROOKLYN NY 11213
64-122	TORBORG, JEFFREY ALLEN	1375 CHAPEL HILL - MOUNTAINSIDE NJ 07092
47- 90	TORGESON, CLIFFORD EARL	2121 RUCKER - EVERETT WA 98201
17- 82	TORKELSON, CHESTER LEROY 'RED'	D. SEPTEMBER 22, 1964 CHICAGO, ILL.
20-119	TORPHY, WALTER ANTHONY 'RED'	D. FEBRUARY 11, 1980 FALL RIVER, MASS.
56- 82	TORRE, FRANK JOSEPH	275 US HIGHWAY ONE - TEQUESTA FL 33469
60-100	TORRE, JOSEPH PAUL	3088 GREENFIELD DR - MARIETTA GA 30067
75-120	TORREALBA, PABLO ARNOLDO	AVE PTE.MEDINA,MARIO 50,PISO 19-CARACAS VENEZ
77-145	TORRES, ANGEL RAFAEL	CALLE 16 DE AGOSTO #19 - AZUA DOMINICAN REP.
40- 91	TORRES, DON GILBERTO NUNEZ 'GIL'	D. JANUARY 11, 1983 REGLA, HAVANA, CUBA
62-135	TORRES, FELIX	HC01 BOX 6424 - SANTA ISABEL PR 00757
68-103	TORRES, HECTOR EPITACIO	56 WINCHESTER DRIVE - LIVERPOOL NY 13088
20-120	TORRES, RICARDO J.	D. HAVANA, CUBA
71-106	TORRES, ROSENDO 'RUSTY'	151-34 136TH AVE - JAMAICA NY 11434
67-108	TORREZ, MICHAEL AUGUSTINE	208 NORTH LAKE ST - TOPEKA KS 66616
88-131	TORVE, KELVIN CURTIS	5611 LONE CEDAR - KINGWOOD TX 77345
42-100	TOST, LOUIS EUGENE	D. FEBRUARY 22,1967 SANTA CLARA, CAL.
62-136	TOTH, PAUL LOUIS	6538 SUDER - ERIE MI 48133
28- 99	TOUCHSTONE, CLAYLAND MAFFITT	D. APRIL 28, 1949 BEAUMONT, TEX.
65-107	TOVAR, CESAR LEONARDO	CALLE REAL PRADO MARIA #58 - CARACAS VENEZ
20-121	TOWNSEND, IRA DANCE	D. JULY 21, 1965 SCHULENBERG, TEX.
20-122	TOWNSEND, LEO ALPHONSE	D. DECEMBER 3, 1976 MOBILE, ALA.
84-123	TRABER, JAMES JOSEPH	11674 LITTLE PATUXENT #203 - COLUMBIA MD 21044
62-137	TRACEWSKI, RICHARD JOHN	5 FLORA DR - PECKVILLE PA 18452
80-128	TRACY, JAMES EDWIN	4785 CELADON AVE - FAIRFIELD OH 45014
13-181	TRAGESSER, WALTER JOSEPH	D. DECEMBER 14, 1970 LAFAYETTE, IND.
40- 92	TRAMBACK, STEPHEN JOSEPH 'RED'	D. DECEMBER 28, 1979 BUFFALO, N. Y.
77-146	TRAMMELL, ALAN STUART	7346 SANDY CREEK LANE - BIRMINGHAM MI 48010
15-163	TRAUTMAN, FREDERICK ORLANDO	D. FEBRUARY 15, 1964 BUCYRUS, O.
88-132	TRAUTWEIN, JOHN HOWARD	452 WEST OAKWOOD DRIVE - BARRINGTON IL 60010
12-201	TRAVERS, ALOYSIUS JOSEPH 'ALLAN'	D. APRIL 21, 1968 PHILADELPHIA, PA.
74-135	TRAVERS, WILLIAM EDWARD	10 SHORELINE DR - FOXBORO MA 02035
33- 62	TRAVIS, CECIL HOWELL	2260 HWY 138 - RIVERDALE GA 30296
20-123	TRAYNOR, HAROLD JOSEPH 'PIE'	D. MARCH 16, 1972 PITTSBURGH, PA.
30- 83	TREADAWAY, EDGAR RAYMOND 'RAY'	D. OCTOBER 12, 1935 CHATTANOOGA, TENN.
87-146	TREADWAY, HUGH JEFFERY 'JEFF'	1413 RAINBOW CIRCLE - GRIFFIN GA 30223
44-129	TREADWAY, THADFORD LEON 'RED'	190 ALPINE DRIVE - ROSWELL GA 30075
86-156	TREBELHORN, THOMAS LYNN	4344 SE 26TH AVENUE - PORTLAND OR 97202
37-100	TRECHOCK, FRANK ADAM	D. JANUARY 16, 1989 MINNEAPOLIS, MINN.
13-182	TREKELL, HARRY ROY	D. NOVEMBER 4, 1963 SPOKANE, WASH.
34-101	TREMARK, NICHOLAS JOSEPH	1906 LAUREL DR - HARLINGEN TX 78550
54-111	TREMEL, WILLIAM LEONARD	315 EAST 23RD AVE - ALTOONA PA 16601
27- 91	TREMPER, CARLTON OVERTON	15777 BOLESTA RD #143 - CLEARWATER FL 33520
38- 99	TRESH, MICHAEL	D. OCTOBER 1, 1966 DETROIT, MICH.
61-105	TRESH, THOMAS MICHAEL	OLD ADD: 4206 EAST WING RD - MT PLEASANT MI 48858
78-136	TREVINO, ALEJANDRO	ALONDRA #103, CUACHTEMOC-MONTERREY NUEVO LAREDO MEX.
68-104	TREVINO, CARLOS CASTRO 'BOBBY'	ALONDRA #102, CUAUHTEMOC - MONTERREY NUEVO LAREDO MEX.
53- 92	TRIANDOS, CONSTANDIN GUS	1207 WOODLAWN AVE - SAN JOSE CA 95128
53- 93	TRICE, ROBERT LEE	D. SEPTEMBER 16, 1988 WEIRTON, W. VA.
73-121	TRILLO, JESUS MANUEL 'MANNY'	CENTRO RES. HUMBOLDT #1B-PRADOS DEL ESTE CARACAS VENEZ
55-128	TRIMBLE, JOSEPH GERARD	12 CONIFER DRIVE - NORTH PROVIDENCE RI 02904
43-138	TRINKLE, KENNETH WAYNE	D. MAY 10, 1976 PAOLI, ILL.
38-100	TRIPLETT, HERMAN COAKER 'COAK'	RURAL ROUTE 1 BOX 551 - BOONE NC 28607
73-122	TROEDSON, RICHARD LAMONTE	505 CHURCHILL PARK DR - SAN JOSE CA 95136
33- 63	TROSKY, HAROLD ARTHUR SR	D. JUNE 18, 1979 CEDAR RAPIDS, IOWA
58- 97	TROSKY, HAROLD ARTHUR JR	1919 HAMILTON ST SW - CEDAR RAPIDS IA 52404
37-101	TROTTER, WILLIAM FELIX	D. AUGUST 26, 1984 ARLINGTON, MASS.
52-105	TROUPPE, QUINCY THOMAS	1908 CHOCTAW STREET - HATTIESBURG MS 39401
39-119	TROUT, PAUL HOWARD 'DIZZY'	D. FEBRUARY 28, 1972 HARVEY, ILL.
78-137	TROUT, STEVEN RUSSELL	919 RIVERVIEW DRIVE - SOUTH HOLLAND IL 60473
56- 83	TROWBRIDGE, ROBERT	D. APRIL 3, 1980 HUDSON, N. Y.
12-202	TROY, ROBERT 'BUN'	D. OCTOBER 7, 1918 MEUSE, FRANCE
41-113	TRUCKS, VIRGIL OLIVER 'FIRE'	2156 GRAYSON VALLEY DRIVE - BIRMINGHAM AL 35235
10-144	TRUESDALE, FRANK DAY	D. AUGUST 27, 1943 ALBUQUERQUE, N. M.
85-113	TRUJILLO, MICHAEL ANDREW	2636 SOUTH STUART WAY - DENVER CO 80219
57- 88	TSITOURIS, JOHN PHILIP	5207 AUSTIN ROAD - MONROE NC 28110
27- 92	TUCKER, OSCAR DINWIDDIE	D. JULY 13, 1940 RADIANT, VA.
42-101	TUCKER, THURMAN LOWELL	2400 SOUTH MACARTHUR #11 - OKLAHOMA CITY OK 73128
79-111	TUDOR, JOHN THOMAS	14 FOREST ST - PEABODY MA 01960
18- 71	TUERO, OSCAR MONZON	D. OCTOBER 21, 1960 HOUSTON, TEXAS
81-138	TUFTS, ROBERT MALCOLM	27 WING RD - LYNNFIELD MA 01940
82-128	TUNNELL, BYRON LEE 'LEE'	17530 KLAMATH FALLS - ROUND ROCK TX 78681
35-107	TURBEVILLE, GEORGE ELKINS	D. OCTOBER 5, 1983 SALISBURY, N. C.
43-139	TURCHIN, EDWARD LAWRENCE	D. FEBRUARY 8, 1982 BROOKHAVEN, N. Y.
23-134	TURGEON, EUGENE JOSEPH 'PETE'	D. JANUARY 24, 1977 WICHITA FALLS, TEX.
22-134	TURK, LUCAS NEWTON	RR 1 - HOMER GA 30547
51- 98	TURLEY, ROBERT LEE	P.O. BOX 786 - MARCO ISLAND FL 33937
48-101	TURNER, EARL EDWIN	OLD ADD: 7 SULLIVAN DR - LENOX MA
37-102	TURNER, JAMES RILEY	1004 WOODMONT BLVD-NASHVILLE TN 37204
74-136	TURNER, JOHN WEBBER 'JERRY'	807 CALIFORNIA - VENICE CA 90291
67-109	TURNER, KENNETH CHARLES	4913 NEBLINA DR - CARLSBAD CA 92008
77-162	TURNER, ROBERT EDWARD 'TED'	1018 PEACHTREE ST NW - ATLANTA GA 30309
88-133	TURNER, SHANE LEE	13104 GLENN COURT #20 - CHINO HILLS CA 91709
20-124	TURNER, THEODORE HOLTOP	D. FEBRUARY 4, 1958 LEXINGTON, KY.
15-164	TURNER, THOMAS LOVATT 'TINK'	D. FEBRUARY 25, 1962 PHILADELPHIA, PA.
40- 93	TURNER, THOMAS RICHARD	D. MAY 14, 1986 KENNEWICK, WASH.
52-106	TUTTLE, WILLIAM ROBERT	115 HARLEM RD #155 - KANSAS CITY MO 64116
11-171	TUTWEILER, GUY ISBELL	D. AUGUST 15, 1930 ANNISTON, ALA.
28-100	TUTWILER, ELMER STRANGE	D. MAY 3, 1976 PENSACOLA, FLA.
16- 90	TWINING, HOWARD EARLE 'TWINK'	D. JUNE 14, 1973 LANSDALE, PA.
70-134	TWITCHELL, WAYNE LEE	7129 SW 33RD PL - PORTLAND OR 97219
80-129	TWITTY, JEFFREY DEAN	1734 C AVENUE - NORTH COLUMBIA SC 29169
20-125	TWOMBLY, CLARENCE EDWARD 'BABE'	D. NOVEMBER 23, 1974 SAN CLEMENTE, CALIF.
21-107	TWOMBLY, EDWIN PARKER 'CY'	D. DECEMBER 3, 1974 SAVANNAH, GA.
14-216	TWOMBLY, GEORGE FREDERICK	D. FEBRUARY 17, 1975 LEXINGTON, MASS.
43-140	TYACK, JAMES FRED	2901 MANOR AVE - BAKERSFIELD CA 93308
14-217	TYLER, FREDERICK FRANKLIN	D. OCTOBER 14, 1945 DERRY, N.H.
10-145	TYLER, GEORGE ALBERT 'LEFTY'	D. SEPTEMBER 29, 1953 LOWELL, MASS.

HALL OF FAME LEFTIES

**Southpaw hurlers are pictured
on these autographed Perez-Steele
Great Moments cards**

34-102	TYLER, JOHN ANTHONY	D. JULY 11, 1972 MOUNT PLEASANT, PA.
14-218	TYREE, EARL CARLTON	D. MAY 17, 1954 RUSHVILLE, ILL.
62-138	TYRIVER, DAVID BURTON	D. OCTOBER 28, 1988 OSHKOSH, WIS.
72-116	TYRONE, JAMES VERNON	423 SOUTH WALDO AVENUE #303 - PASADENA CA 91101
76- 95	TYRONE, OSCAR WAYNE 'WAYNE'	107 ENCINAL STREET - ALICE TX 78332
26- 87	TYSON, ALBERT THOMAS 'TY'	D. AUGUST 16, 1953 BUFFALO, N. Y.
44-130	TYSON, CECIL WASHINGTON 'TURKEY'	RR 1 BOX 202, TYSON LN - ELM CITY NC 27822
72-117	TYSON, MICHAEL RAY	479 THUNDERHEAD CANYON DR-BALDWIN MO 63011
26- 88	UCHRINSCKO, JAMES EMERSON	204 WATER STREET - WEST NEWTON PA 15089
62-139	UECKER, ROBERT GEORGE	N6OW15734 HAWTHORNE DR - MENOMONEE FALLS WI 53051
34-103	UHALT, BERNARD BARTHOLOMEW 'FRENCHY'	231 CROSS RD - OAKLAND CA 94618
65-108	UHLAENDER, THEODORE OTTO	SOUND ADVICE,401 S. 12TH ST - MCALLEN TX 78501
19- 83	UHLE, GEORGE ERNEST	D. FEBRUARY 26, 1985 LAKEWOOD, O.
38-101	UHLE, ROBERT ELLWOOD	8721 LANCASTER DR - ROHNERT PARK CA 94928
14-219	UHLER, MAURICE WILLIAM	D. MAY 4, 1918 BALTIMORE MD.
34-104	UHLIR, CHARLES	OLD ADD: 11 SOUTH LASALLE - CHICAGO IL
80-130	UJDUR, GERALD RAYMOND	3312 BERKELEY RD - DULUTH MN 55811
45-106	ULISNEY, MICHAEL EDWARD	1481 PURITA STREET - DELTONA FL 32725
83-143	ULLGER, SCOTT MATTHEW	4232 WEST CAMBRIDGE - VISALIA CA 92083
44-131	ULLRICH, CARLOS SANTIAGO CASTELLO	3671 NW 15TH ST - MIAMI FL 33125
25-106	ULRICH, FRANK W. 'DUTCH'	D. FEBRUARY 11, 1929 BALTIMORE, MD.
64-123	UMBACH, ARNOLD WILLIAM	655 SOUTH DEAN RD - AUBURN AL 36830
75-121	UMBARGER, JAMES HAROLD	OLD ADD: 181 E.56TH AVE #200 - DENVER CO 80216
59- 83	UMBRICHT, JAMES	D. APRIL 8, 1964 HOUSTON, TEX.
53- 94	UMPHLETT, THOMAS MULLEN	RR 2 BOX 17C - AHOSKIE NC 27910
27- 93	UNDERHILL, WILLIE VERN	D. OCTOBER 26, 1970 BAY CITY, TEXAS
79-112	UNDERWOOD, PATRICK JOHN	1810 WEST JEFFERSON STREET - KOKOMO IN 46901
74-137	UNDERWOOD, THOMAS GERALD	8053 NW 71ST COURT - FORT LAUDERDALE FL 33319
42-102	UNSER, ALBERT BERNARD	2096 NORTH UNION-DECATUR IL 62526
68-105	UNSER, DELBERT BERNARD	495 FERNWOOD DR - MORAGA CA 94556
35-108	UPCHURCH, JEFFERSON WOODROW 'WOODY'	D. OCTOBER 23, 1971 BUIES CREEK, N. C.
67-110	UPHAM, JOHN LESLIE	1100 HURON CHURCH RD - WINDSOR ONTARIO N9C 2K7 CAN.
15-165	UPHAM, WILLIAM LAWRENCE	D. SEPTEMBER 14, 1959 NEWARK, N.J.
53- 95	UPRIGHT, ROY T. 'DIXIE'	D. NOVEMBER 13, 1986 CONCORD, N. C.
66- 91	UPSHAW, CECIL LEE	1828 KELVIN DRIVE - LAWRENCEVILLE GA 30245
78-138	UPSHAW, WILLIE CLAY	BOX 395 - BLANCO TX 78606
50-100	UPTON, THOMAS HERBERT	306 MAY STREET - BISHOP CA 93514
54-112	UPTON, WILLIAM RAY	OLD ADD: BOX 3441 - LAMESA CA 92041
57- 89	URBAN, JACK ELMER	8607 FOWLER - OMAHA NE 68134
27- 94	URBAN, LOUIS JOHN 'LUKE'	D. DECEMBER 7, 1980 SOMERSET, MASS.
31- 91	URBANSKI, WILLIAM MICHAEL	D. JULY 12, 1973 PERTH AMBOY, N. J.
84-124	URIBE, JOSE ALTAGRACIA	CLE D #9 SAB.GRANDE DE PALENQUE - JUAN DOMINICAN REP.
77-147	URREA, JOHN GODBY	12540 YOSEMITE - CERRITOS CA 90701
46-100	USHER, ROBERT ROYCE	1022 NORTH FIFTH ST - SAN JOSE CA 95112
25-107	USSAT, WILLIAM AUGUST 'DUTCH'	D. MAY 29, 1959 DAYTON, O.
25-108	VACHE, ERNEST LEWIS 'TEX'	D. JUNE 11, 1953 LOS ANGELES, CALIF.
75-122	VAIL, MICHAEL LEWIS	278 BUCKINGHAM PLACE - PALM HARBOR FL 34684
57- 90	VALDES, RENE GUTIERREZ	AVENIDA 7A,14511 ALTURAS-MANANA,HAVANA CUBA
44-132	VALDES, ROGELIO LAZARO 'ROY'	241 PONCE DE LEON BLVD - CORAL GABLES FL 33134
65-109	VALDESPINO, HILARIO 'SANDY'	17920 NW 43RD AVE - CAROL CITY FL 33055
80-131	VALDEZ, JULIO JULIAN CASTILLO	MAXIMO GAHEZ #4,NIZAO - BANI DOMINICAN REP.
86-157	VALDEZ, SERGIO SANCHEZ	CAL LA PAZ #14,HERRERA-SANTO DOMINGO DOMINICAN REP.
55-129	VALDIVIELSO, JOSE LOPEZ	14 RITA DR - MOUNT SINAI NY 11766
75-123	VALENTINE, ELLIS CLARENCE	5601 VALLEY GLEN WAY - LOS ANGELES CA 90043
59- 84	VALENTINE, FRED LEE	4838 BLAGDEN AVE NW - WASHINGTON DC 20011
54-113	VALENTINE, HAROLD LEWIS 'CORKY'	RURAL ROUTE 1 FREEHOME ROAD - CANTON GA 30114
69-173	VALENTINE, ROBERT JOHN	2113 GRETA LANE - FORT WORTH TX 76112
54-114	VALENTINETTI, VITO JOHN	271 SUMMIT AVE - MOUNT VERNON NY 10552
58- 98	VALENZUELA, BENJAMIN BELTRAN	BAHIA SAN ESTEBAN #267 SUR - LOS MOCHIS SINOLOA MEX.
80-132	VALENZUELA, FERNANDO	3004 N. BEACHWOOD DR - HOLLYWOOD CA 90068
84-125	VALLE, DAVID	33-15 208TH STREET - BAYSIDE NY 11361
65-110	VALLE, HECTOR JOSE	P.O. BOX 5909 COLLEGE STATION - MAYAGUEZ PR 00708
40- 94	VALO, ELMER WILLIAM	571 COLUMBIA AVE-PALMERTON PA 18071
50-101	VAN CUYK, CHRISTIAN GERALD	14405 AMY LANE - HUDSON FL 33562
27- 95	VANALSTYNE, CLAYTON EMERY	D. JANUARY 5, 1960 HUDSON, N. Y.
33- 64	VANATTA, RUSSELL	D. OCTOBER 10, 1986 ANDOVER, N. J.
54-115	VANBRABANT, CAMILLE OSCAR 'OSSIE'	OLD ADD: 2330 N. WASHINGTON - ROYAL OAK MI 48073
28-101	VANCAMP, ALBERT JOSEPH	D. FEBRUARY 2, 1981 DAVENPORT, IOWA
15-166	VANCE, CLARENCE ARTHUR 'DAZZY'	D. FEBRUARY 16, 1961 HOMOSASSA SPRINGS, FLA.
70-135	VANCE, GENE COVINGTON 'SANDY'	OLD ADD: 953 FOYE DRIVE - LAFAYETTE CA 94549
35-109	VANCE, JOSEPH ALBERT	D. JULY 4, 1978 DEVINE, TEXAS
47- 91	VANCUYK, JOHN HENRY	104 WEST FIRST STREET - KIMBERLY WI 54136
14-220	VANDAGRIFT, CARL WILLIAM	D. OCTOBER 9, 1920 FORT WAYNE, IND.
82-129	VANDEBERG, EDWARD JOHN	1331 CLOCK AVE - REDLANDS CA 92374
35-110	VANDENBURG, HAROLD HARRIS 'HY'	10143 THIRD AVE SOUTH - MINNEAPOLIS MN 55420
37-103	VANDERMEER, JOHN SAMUEL	4005 LEONA AVE-TAMPA FL 33606
55-130	VANDUSEN, FREDERICK WILLIAM	826 ROCKRIMMON RD - STAMFORD CT 06903
19- 84	VANGILDER, ELAM RUSSELL	D. APRIL 30, 1977 CAPE GIRARDEAU, MO.
82-130	VANGORDER, DAVID THOMAS	2712 WEST CALLE ARANDAS - TUCSON AZ 85745
13-183	VANN, JOHN SILAS	D. JUNE 10, 1958 SHREVEPORT, LA.
51- 99	VANNOY, JAY LOWELL	1092 NORTH 1700 EAST - LOGAN UT 84321
39-120	VANROBAYS, MAURICE RENE	D. MARCH 1, 1965 DETROIT, MICH.
83-144	VANSLYKE, ANDREW JAMES	24 HARTFORD TER - NEW HARTFORD NY 13413
50-102	VARGA, ANDREW WILLIAM	1964 ADD: 2429 M - BELLVILLE KS 66935
82-131	VARGAS, HEDIBERTO	BOX 1172 - GUANICA PR 00653
55-131	VARGAS, ROBERTO ENRIQUE	24 BRISAIDA ST,URB. L.M.RIVERA - GUAYNABO PR 00657
25-109	VARGUS, WILLIAM FAY	D. FEBRUARY 12, 1979 HYANNIS, MASS.
52-107	VARNER, GLEN GANN	1737 EAST VARNER RD - HIXSON TN 37343
73-123	VARNEY, RICHARD FRED 'PETE'	14 JUNIPER RIDGE RD - ACTON MA 01720
88-134	VARSHO, GARY ANDREW	310 MAGEE STREET - MARSHFIELD WI 54449
79-113	VASQUEZ, RAFAEL (SANTIAGO)	CALLE JULIO A JARSIA #29 - LA ROMANA DOMINICAN REP.
40- 95	VAUGHAN, CECIL PORTER	2881 BRAIDWOOD RD-RICHMOND VA 23225
66- 92	VAUGHAN, CHARLES WAYNE	1802 FOREST LANE - WESLACO TX 78596
63-121	VAUGHAN, GLENN EDWARD	3050 POST OAK BLVD #300 - HOUSTON TX 77056
32- 89	VAUGHAN, JOSEPH FLOYD 'ARKY'	D. AUGUST 30, 1952 EAGLEVILLE, CAL.
34-105	VAUGHN, CLARENCE LEROY	D. MARCH 1, 1937 MARTINSVILLE, VA.
88-135	VAUGHN, DEWAYNE MATHEW	1404 FORDSON - OKLAHOMA CITY OK 73127
44-133	VAUGHN, FREDERICK THOMAS	D. MARCH 2, 1964 LAKE WALES, FLA.

#	Name	Address / Data
89-130	VAUGHN, GREGORY LAMONT	7482 CANDLEWOOD WAY - SACRAMENTO CA 95822
35-111	VEACH, ALVIS LINDELL	8919 PARK ROAD #133 - CHARLOTTE NC 28210
12-203	VEACH, ROBERT HENRY	D. AUGUST 7, 1945 DETROIT, MICH.
58- 99	VEAL, ORVILLE INMAN 'COOT'	1258 TIMBERLANE - MACON GA 31204
62-140	VEALE, ROBERT ANDREW	1502 LOMB AVE WEST - BIRMINGHAM AL 35208
20-126	VEDDER, LOUIS EDWARD	1201 WEST CORNELL #57 - AVON PARK FL 33825
79-114	VEGA, JESUS ANTONIO	OLD ADD: MAGOLY CENTRAL NH22-LEVITTOWN PR
39-121	VEIGEL, ALLEN FRANCIS	1907 DOVER AVE-DOVER OH 44622
87-147	VELARDE, RANDY LEE	904 NORTH DALLAS STREET - MIDLAND TX 79701
73-124	VELAZQUEZ, CARLOS	OLD ADD: BO MEDINA ALTA - LUIZA ALDEA PR
69-174	VELAZQUEZ, FEDERICO ANTONIO	JOSE AMADO SOLER NO. 70 - SANTO DOMINGO DOMINICAN REP.
73-125	VELEZ, OTONIEL FRONCESCHI 'OTTO'	LOS CAOBOS CALLE #35 T-2 - PONCE PR 00731
26- 89	VELTMAN, ARTHUR PATRICK	D. OCTOBER 1, 1980 SAN ANTONIO, TEXAS
79-115	VENABLE, WILLIAM MCKINLEY 'MAX'	2528 LAS CASAS WAY - RANCHO CORDOVA CA 95670
89-131	VENTURA, ROBIN MARK	751 MABLE COURT - SANTA MARIA CA 94455
45-107	VENTURA, VINCENT	23-54 29TH ST - ASTORIA NY 11102
44-134	VERBAN, EMIL MATTHEW 'THE ANTELOPE'	D. JUNE 8, 1989 QUINCY, ILL.
66- 93	VERBANIC, JOSEPH MICHAEL	85462 LORANE HWY - EUGENE OR 97405
51-100	VERBLE, GENE KERMIT	1091 OLD CHARLOTTE HWY - CONCORD NC 28025
44-135	VERDEL, ALBERT ALFRED	2763 WOODGATE LANE #306 - SARASOTA FL 34231
53- 96	VERDI, FRANK MICHAEL	10961 PEPPERTREE LANE - PORT RICHEY FL 34668
15-167	VEREKER, JOHN JAMES	D. APRIL 2, 1974 BALTIMORE, MD.
89-132	VERES, RANDOLPH RUHLAND	OLD ADD: 9469 FORT WORTH - RANCHO CORDOVA CA 95670
31- 92	VERGEZ, JOHN LOUIS	112 KRISTEE PLACE - OROVILLE CA 95966
76- 96	VERHOEVEN, JOHN C	1950 HORSESHOE CR - PLACENTIA CA 92670
39-122	VERNON, JAMES BARTON 'MICKEY'	100 EAST ROSE VALLEY RD - WALLINGFORD PA 19086
12-204	VERNON, JOSEPH HENRY	D. MARCH 13, 1955 PHILADELPHIA, PA.
59- 85	VERSALLES, ZOILO	8645 FREMONT SOUTH - BLOOMINGTON MN 55420
73-126	VERYZER, THOMAS MARTIN	41 UNION AVE - ISLIP NY 11751
80-133	VESELIC, ROBERT MICHAEL	1111 SOUTH BEUBURY DR - WALNUT CA 91789
22-135	VICK, HENRY ARTHUR 'ERNIE'	D. JULY 16, 1980 ANN ARBOR, MICH.
17- 83	VICK, SAMUEL BRUCE	D. AUGUST 17, 1986 MEMPHIS, TENN.
48-102	VICO, GEORGE STEVE	13100 BEACH - DESERT HOT SPRINGS CA 92240
66- 94	VIDAL, JOSE NICOLAS	1972 ADD: JUAN ERAZO 152 - SANTO DOMINGO D R
24-112	VINES, ROBERT EARL	D. OCTOBER 18, 1982 ORLANDO, FLA.
64-124	VINEYARD, DAVID KENT	RR 2 BOX 83B - LEFT HAND WV 25251
66- 95	VINSON, CHARLES ANTHONY	3821 WALTERS LN - FORESTVILLE MD 20747
82-132	VIOLA, FRANK JOHN	844 SWEETWATER ISLAND CIRCLE - LONGWOOD FL 32779
12-205	VIOX, JAMES HENRY	D. JANUARY 6, 1969 ERLANGER, KY.
55-132	VIRDON, WILLIAM CHARLES	1311 RIVER RD - SPRINGFIELD MO 65804
56- 84	VIRGIL, OSVALDO JOSE SR. 'OZZIE'	4316 WEST MESCAL ST - GLENDALE AZ 85301
80-134	VIRGIL, OSVALDO JOSE JR. 'OZZIE'	4316 WEST MESCAL ST - GLENDALE AZ 85301
44-136	VITELLI, ANTONIO JOSEPH 'JOE'	D. FEBRUARY 7, 1967 PITTSBURGH, PA.
12-206	VITT, OSCAR JOSEPH	D. JANUARY 31, 1963 OAKLAND, CALIF.
89-133	VIZCAINO, JOSE LUIS	DUARTE #107 - PALENQUE DE SAN CRISTOBAL DOM. REP.
89-134	VIZQUEL, OMAR ENRIQUE	BLVD DEL CAFETEL,RES ADRIANA 6 PISA 6 "A"-CARACAS VENEZ
23-135	VOGEL, OTTO HENRY	D. JULY 19, 1969 IOWA CITY, IA.
24-113	VOIGT, OLEN EDWARD	D. APRIL 7, 1970
42-103	VOISELLE, WILLIAM SYMMES	RR 2 BOX 318 - NINETY SIX SC 29666
42-104	VOLLMER, CLYDE FREDERICK	P.O. BOX 3321 - CINCINNATI OH 45201
65-111	VONHOFF, BRUCE FREDERICK	423 RIVER HILLS DR - TEMPLE TERRACE FL 33617
14-222	VONKOLNITZ, ALFRED HOLMES 'FRITZ'	D. MARCH 18, 1948 MOUNT PLEASANT, S.C.
83-145	VONOHLEN, DAVID	OLD ADD: 11-06 128TH STREET - COLLEGE POINT NY 11356
86-158	VOSBERG, EDWARD JOHN	5671 EAST 12TH STREET - TUCSON AZ 85711
30- 84	VOSMIK, JOSEPH FRANKLIN	D. JANUARY 24, 1962 CLEVELAND, O.
65-112	VOSS, WILLIAM EDWARD	OLD ADD: 5882 SIERRA SIENA - IRVINE CA 92650
29-105	VOYLES, PHILIP VANCE	D. NOVEMBER 3, 1972 MARLBORO, MASS.
75-124	VUCKOVICH, PETER DENNIS	6080 SOUTH 118TH ST - HALES CORNER WI 53130
80-135	VUKOVICH, GEORGE STEPHEN	421 .NORTH HARVARD AVE - ARLINGTON HEIGHTS IL60005
70-136	VUKOVICH, JOHN CHRISTOPHER	11 SHERI WAY - PINE HILL NJ 08021
17- 84	WACHTEL, PAUL HORINE	D. DECEMBER 15, 1964 SAN ANTONIO, TEX.
84-126	WADDELL, THOMAS DAVID	47 FIFTH STREET - CLOSTER NJ 07624
31- 93	WADDEY, FRANK ORUM	4505 HARDING ROAD #52E - NASHVILLE TN 37205
48-103	WADE, BENJAMIN STYRON	1165 MEDFORD RD - PASADENA CA 91107
55-133	WADE, GALEARD LEE	RR 1 BOX 766 - NEBO NC 28761
36- 93	WADE, JACOB FIELDS	RR 2 BOX 558 - MOREHEAD CITY NC 28557
23-136	WADE, RICHARD FRANK 'RIP'	D. JUNE 15, 1957 SANDSTONE, MINN.
38-102	WAGNER, CHARLES THOMAS	1523 LINDEN ST-READING PA 19604
65-113	WAGNER, GARY EDWARD	701 PRINCETON ROAD - LANOKA HARBOR NJ 08734
37-104	WAGNER, HAROLD EDWARD	D. AUGUST 7, 1979 RIVERSIDE NJ
15-168	WAGNER, JOSEPH BERNARD	D. NOVEMBER 15, 1948 BRONX, N.Y.
58-100	WAGNER, LEON LAMAR	350 S. MADISON #109,%ABDULLAH - PASADENA CA 91101
76- 97	WAGNER, MARK DUANE	1616 WINTER HAVEN DR - ASHTABULA OH 44004
13-184	WAGNER, WILLIAM GEORGE 'BULL'	D. OCTOBER 2, 1967 MUSKEGON, MICH.
14-223	WAGNER, WILLIAM JOSEPH	D. JANUARY 11, 1951 WATERLOO, IA.
44-137	WAHL, KERMIT EMERSON	D. SEPTEMBER 16, 1987 TUCSON, ARIZ.
41-114	WAITKUS, EDWARD STEPHEN	D. SEPTEMBER 15, 1972 BOSTON, MASS.
73-127	WAITS, MICHAEL RICHARD 'RICK'	OLD ADD: 4750 N. CAMINO CORTO - TUCSON AZ 85718
41-115	WAKEFIELD, RICHARD CUMMINGS	D. AUGUST 26, 1985 REDFORD TWP., WAYNE CO., MICH.
64-125	WAKEFIELD, WILLIAM SUMNER	250 29TH AVENUE - SAN FRANCISCO CA 94121
23-137	WALBERG, GEORGE ELVIN 'RUBE'	D. OCTOBER 27, 1978 TEMPE, ARIZ.
45-108	WALCZAK, EDWIN JOSEPH	544 NEW LONDON - NORWICH CT 06360
17- 85	WALDBAUER, ALBERT CHARLES 'DOC'	D. JULY 16, 1969 YAKIMA, WASH.
12-207	WALDEN, THOMAS FRED	D. SEPTEMBER 27, 1955 JEFFERSON BARRACKS, MO.
87-148	WALEWANDER, JAMES	5133 NORTH OCTAVIA STREET - HARWOOD HEIGHTS IL 60656
80-136	WALK, ROBERT VERNON	%C.SHIELDS,BOX 954 - FRAZIER PARK CA 93225
48-104	WALKER, ALBERT BLUFORD 'RUBE'	342 CUMBERLAND WAY - SMYRNA GA 30080
86-159	WALKER, ANTHONY BRUCE	OLD ADD: 4024 PETERLYNN WAY - SAN DIEGO CA 92154
17- 86	WALKER, CHARLES FRANKLIN	D. SEPTEMBER 16, 1974 BRISTOL, TENN.
11-172	WALKER, CLARENCE WILLIAM 'TILLY'	D. SEPTEMBER 21, 1959 UNICOI, TENN.
80-137	WALKER, CLEOTHA 'CHICO'	5344 SOUTH EMERALD AVENUE - CHICAGO IL 60609
82-133	WALKER, DUANE ALLEN	3108 GRANT ST - PASADENA TX 77503
13-185	WALKER, ERNEST ROBERT	D. APRIL 1, 1965 PELL CITY, ALA.
31- 94	WALKER, FRED "DIXIE"	D. MAY 17, 1982 BIRMINGHAM, ALA.
10-146	WALKER, FREDERICK MITCHELL	D. FEBRUARY 1, 1958 OAK PARK, ILL.
31- 95	WALKER, GERALD HOLMES 'GEE'	D. MARCH 20, 1981 WHITFIELD, MISS.
82-134	WALKER, GREGORY LEE	FOREST CIRCLE DRIVE - DOUGLAS GA 31533
40- 96	WALKER, HARRY WILLIAM	RR 2 BOX 145 - LEEDS AL 35094

31- 96	WALKER, HARVEY WILLOS 'HUB'	D. NOVEMBER 26, 1982 SAN JOSE, CALIF.
65-114	WALKER, JAMES LUKE	316 LOMA LINDA - WAKE VILLAGE TX 75501
12-208	WALKER, JAMES ROY	D. FEBRUARY 10, 1962 NEW ORLEANS, LA.
57- 91	WALKER, JERRY ALLEN	2015 COLLINS BLVD - ADA OK 74820
19- 85	WALKER, JOHN MILES	D. AUGUST 19, 1976 HOLLYWOOD, FLA.
23-138	WALKER, JOSEPH RICHARD	D. JUNE 20, 1959 WEST MIFFLIN, PA.
89-135	WALKER, LARRY KENNETH ROBERT	21642 RIVER ROAD - MAPLE RIDGE BRIT. COL. V2X 2B7 CAN.
28-102	WALKER, MARTIN VAN BUREN	D. APRIL 24, 1978 PHILADELPHIA, PA.
88-136	WALKER, MICHAEL CHARLES	15498 SNOW MEMORIAL HWY - BROOKSVILLE FL 33512
72-118	WALKER, ROBERT THOMAS 'TOM'	234 MONTCLAIR AVE - PITTSBURGH PA 15229
19- 86	WALKER, WILLIAM CURTIS 'CURT'	D. DECEMBER 9, 1955 BEEVILLE, TEX.
27- 96	WALKER, WILLIAM HENRY	D. JUNE 14, 1966 EAST ST. LOUIS, ILL.
34-106	WALKUP, JAMES ELTON	P.O. BOX 124 - HAVANA AR 72842
27- 97	WALKUP, JAMES HUEY	1111 GRAND - DUNCAN OK 73533
50-103	WALL, MURRAY WESLEY	D. OCTOBER 8, 1971 LONE OAK, TEXAS
75-125	WALL, STANLEY ARTHUR	9907 E. 80TH ST - RAYTOWN MO 64138
15-169	WALLACE, CLARENCE EUGENE 'JACK'	D. OCTOBER 15, 1960 WINNFIELD, LA.
73-128	WALLACE, DAVID WILLIAM	63 STONEHEDGE LANE - ATTLEBORO MA 02703
67-111	WALLACE, DONALD ALLEN	23 KRIS LN - MANITOU SPRINGS CO 80829
19- 87	WALLACE, FREDERICK RENSHAW 'DOC'	D. DECEMBER 31, 1964 HAVERFORD TWP, PA.
12-209	WALLACE, HARRY CLINTON 'HUCK'	D. JULY 9, 1951 CLEVELAND, O.
42-105	WALLACE, JAMES HAROLD 'LEFTY'	D. JULY 28, 1982 EVANSVILLE, IND.
73-129	WALLACE, MICHAEL SHERMAN	RR 1 BIX 176AA - MIDLAND VA 22728
80-138	WALLACH, TIMOTHY CHARLES	10762 HOLLY DRIVE - GARDEN GROVE CA 92640
40- 97	WALLAESA, JOHN	D. DECEMBER 27, 1986 EASTON, PA.
45-109	WALLEN, NORMAN EDWARD	3429 NORTH WEIL - MILWAUKEE WI 53212
80-139	WALLER, ELLIOTT TYRONE 'TY'	5146 LAPAZ DR - SAN DIEGO CA 92114
75-126	WALLING, DENNIS	BOX 1312 - WAYNESBORO VA 22980
75-127	WALLIS, HAROLD JOSEPH 'JOE'	1055 NEW BALLWIN ROAD #E - BALLWIN MO 63021
52-108	WALLS, RAYMOND LEE	OLD ADD: 3002 N. 70TH ST - SCOTTSDALE AZ 85251
27- 98	WALSH, AUGUST SOTHLEY	D. NOVEMBER 12, 1985 SAN RAFAEL, CALIF.
14-224	WALSH, AUSTIN EDWARD	D. JANUARY 26, 1955 GLENDALE, CALIF.
28-103	WALSH, EDWARD ARTHUR	D. OCTOBER 31, 1937 MERIDEN, CONN.
12-210	WALSH, JAMES CHARLES	D. JULY 3, 1962 SYRACUSE, N.Y.
46-101	WALSH, JAMES GERALD	RR 1, LAYTON RD - OLYPHANT PA 18447
21-108	WALSH, JAMES THOMAS	D. MAY 13, 1967 BOSTON, MASS.
10-147	WALSH, JOSEPH FRANCIS	D. JANUARY 6, 1967 BUFFALO, N.Y.
38-103	WALSH, JOSEPH PATRICK 'TWEET'	7 ST.LUKE'S RD - ALLSTON MA 02134
13-186	WALSH, LEO THOMAS 'DEE'	D. JULY 14, 1971 ST. LOUIS, MO.
10-148	WALSH, MICHAEL TIMOTHY 'JIMMY'	D. JANUARY 21, 1947 BALTIMORE, MD.
20-127	WALSH, WALTER WILLIAM	D. JANUARY 15, 1966 NEPTUNE, N. J.
85-114	WALTER, GENE WINSTON	6042 SOUTH MONITOR - CHICAGO IL 60638
30- 85	WALTER, JAMES BERNARD 'BERNIE'	D. OCTOBER 30, 1988 NASHVILLE, TENN.
15-170	WALTERS, ALFRED JOHN 'ROXY'	D. JUNE 3, 1956 ALAMEDA, CALIF.
69-175	WALTERS, CHARLES LEONARD	12387 PASEO VERANO - YUMA AZ 85365
45-110	WALTERS, JAMES FREDERICK 'FRED'	D. FEBRUARY 1, 1980 LAUREL, MISS.
60-101	WALTERS, KENNETH ROGERS	9545 BELLE MEADE DR - SAN RAMON CA 94583
83-146	WALTERS, MICHAEL CHARLES	OLD ADD: 80119 PALM CIRCLE DRIVE - INDIO CA 92201
31- 97	WALTERS, WILLIAM HENRY 'BUCKY'	OLD ADD: 515 FOX ROAD - GLENSIDE PA 19038
68-106	WALTON, DANIEL JAMES	1130 SUNKIST AVENUE - LAPUENTE CA 91746
89-136	WALTON, JEROME O'TERRELL	459 COUNTRY CLUB ROAD - NEWNAN GA 30243
80-140	WALTON, REGINALD SHERARD	1142 SOUTH CARSON AVE - LOS ANGELES CA 90019
14-225	WAMBSGANSS, WILLIAM ADOLPH	D. DECEMBER 8, 1985 LAKEWOOD, O.
27- 99	WANER, LLOYD JAMES	D. JULY 22, 1982 OKLAHOMA CITY, OKLA.
26- 90	WANER, PAUL GLEE	D. AUGUST 29, 1965 SARASOTA, FLA.
25-110	WANNINGER, PAUL LOUIS 'PEE WEE'	D. MAY 7, 1981 NORTH AUGUSTA, S. C.
65-115	WANTZ, RICHARD CARTER	D. MAY 13, 1965 INGLEWOOD, CAL.
17- 87	WARD, AARON LEE	D. JANUARY 30, 1961 NEW ORLEANS, LA.
17- 88	WARD, CHARLES WILLIAM	D. APRIL 4, 1969 ST. PETERSBURG, FLA.
72-119	WARD, CHRIS GILBERT	365 BURCHETT STREET #214 - GLENDALE CA 91203
85-115	WARD, COLIN NORVAL	242 SOUTH OLIVE - MESA AZ 85204
79-116	WARD, GARY LAMELL	318 WEST RAYMOND ST - COMPTON CA 90220
63-122	WARD, JOHN FRANCIS 'JAY'	16342 NORTHDALE OAKS - TAMPA FL 33624
12-211	WARD, JOSEPH NICHOLAS 'HAP'	D. SEPTEMBER 13, 1979 ELMER, N. J.
62-141	WARD, PETER THOMAS	575 SOUTHWEST "G" - LAKE OSWEGO OR 97034
48-105	WARD, PRESTON MEYER	4371 DESILVA PLACE - LAS VEGAS NV 89109
34-107	WARD, RICHARD OLE	D. JUNE 1, 1966 FREELAND, WASH.
86-160	WARD, ROY DUANE 'DUANE'	209 WEST 24TH STREET - FARMINGTON NM 87401
68-107	WARDEN, JONATHAN EDGAR	9573 LOVELAND MADEIRA RD - LOVELAND OH 45140
84-127	WARDLE, CURTIS RAY	30886 CURZULLA ROAD - WINCHESTER CA 92396
13-187	WARES, CLYDE ELLSWORTH 'BUZZY'	D. MAY 26, 1964 SOUTH BEND, IND.
16- 91	WARMOTH, WALLACE WALTER 'CY'	D. JUNE 20, 1957 MOUNT CARMEL, ILL.
30- 86	WARNEKE, LONNIE	D. JUNE 23, 1976 HOT SPRINGS, ARK.
12-212	WARNER, EDWARD EMORY	D. FEBRUARY 2, 1954 FITCHBURG, MASS.
16- 92	WARNER, HOKE HAYDEN 'HOOKS'	D. FEBRUARY 19, 1947 SAN FRANCISCO, CAL.
62-142	WARNER, JACK DYER	239 EAST ST. JOHNS - PHOENIX AZ 85022
25-111	WARNER, JOHN JOSEPH 'JACK'	D. MARCH 13, 1986 MOUNT VERNON, ILL.
66- 96	WARNER, JOHN JOSEPH	649 CRESTVIEW DRIVE - GLENDORA CA 91740
35-112	WARNOCK, HAROLD CHARLES	BOX 871 - TUCSON AZ 85702
39-123	WARREN, BENNIE LOUIS	3708 NW 18TH ST-OKLAHOMA CITY OK 73107
83-147	WARREN, MICHAEL BRUCE	12281 DIANE STREET - GARDEN GROVE CA 92640
44-138	WARREN, THOMAS GENTRY	D. JANUARY 2, 1968 TULSA, OKLA.
14-226	WARREN, WILLIAM HACKNEY	D. JANUARY 28, 1960 WHITEVILLE, TENN.
30- 87	WARSTLER, HAROLD BURTON 'RABBIT'	D. MAY 31, 1964 NORTH CANTON,O.
75-128	WARTHEN, DANIEL DEAN	2887 NW WESTERN ROAD - PORTLAND OR 97210
61-106	WARWICK, CARL WAYNE	14102 BONNEY BRIER - HOUSTON TX 77069
21-109	WARWICK, FIRMAN NEWTON 'BILL'	D. DECEMBER 19, 1984 SAN ANTONIO, TEXAS
37-105	WASDELL, JAMES CHARLES	D. AUGUST 6, 1983 NEWPORT RICHEY, FLA.
37-106	WASEM, LINCOLN WILLIAM	D. MARCH 6, 1979 SOUTH LAGUNA, CALIF.
41-116	WASHBURN, GEORGE EDWARD	D. JANUARY 5, 1979 BATON ROUGE, LA.
69-176	WASHBURN, GREGORY JAMES	1685 E. STELLON ST - COAL CITY IL 60416
61-107	WASHBURN, RAY CLARK	16309 JUANITA WOODVILLE WAY NE - BOTHELL WA 98011
74-138	WASHINGTON, CLAUDELL	12 CHARLES HILL RD - ORINDA CA 94563
74-139	WASHINGTON, HERBERT	431 WEST MAIN STREET - ROCHESTER NY 14608
78-139	WASHINGTON, LARUE	709 WEST PLUM ST - COMPTON CA 90222
77-148	WASHINGTON, RONALD	1900 ALLEN STREET - NEW ORLEANS LA 70116
35-113	WASHINGTON, SLOAN VERNON 'VERN'	D. FEBRUARY 17, 1985 LINDEN, TEXAS
77-149	WASHINGTON, U. L.	BOX 164 - STRINGTOWN OK 74569

AUTOGRAPHED UNCUT SHEETS OF PEREZ-STEELE ART POST CARDS

The uncut sheet of Series Seven of the Perez-Steele Art Post Cards (above) features autographs on all cards except the card of Walter Alston
The uncut sheet of Series Eight (left) features every possible autograph — the autograph of Vaughn is not possible on the Art Post Cards

141

86-161 WASINGER, MARK THOMAS	OLD ADD: 523 HOWZE STREET - FORT BLISS TX 79916
67-112 WASLEWSKI, GARY LEE	MCKENZIE DR - SOUTHINGTON CT 06489
76- 98 WATERBURY, STEVEN CRAIG	710 N. GARFIELD - MARION IL 62958
55-134 WATERS, FRED WARREN	D. AUGUST 28, 1989 PENSACOLA, FLA.
76- 99 WATHAN, JOHN DAVID	1401 DEER RUN TRAIL - BLUE SPRINGS MO 64015
69-177 WATKINS, DAVID ROGER	1502 ROOSEVELT RD - OWENSBORO KY 42301
30- 88 WATKINS, GEORGE ARCHIBALD	D. JUNE 1, 1970 HOUSTON, TEX.
69-178 WATKINS, ROBERT CECIL	4417 WEST 58TH PLACE - LOS ANGELES CA 90043
53- 97 WATLINGTON, JULIUS NEAL	BOX 418 - YANCEYVILLE NC 27379
14-227 WATSON, ARTHUR STANHOPE	D. MAY 9, 1950 BUFFALO, N. Y.
13-188 WATSON, CHARLES JOHN 'DOC'	D. DECEMBER 30, 1949 SAN DIEGO, CALIF.
18- 72 WATSON, JOHN REEVES 'MULE'	D. AUGUST 25, 1949 SHREVEPORT, LA.
30- 89 WATSON, JOHN THOMAS	D. APRIL 29, 1965 HUNTINGTON, W. V.
16- 93 WATSON, MILTON WILSON	D. APRIL 10, 1962 PINE BLUFF, ARK.
66- 97 WATSON, ROBERT JOSE	2312 NANTUCKET DRIVE - HOUSTON TX 77057
20-128 WATT, ALBERT BAILEY	D. MARCH 15, 1968 NORFOLK, VA.
66- 98 WATT, EDDIE DEAN	BOX 7 - NORTH BEND NE 68649
31- 98 WATT, FRANK MARION	D. AUGUST 31, 1956 GLEN COVE, MD.
29-106 WATWOOD, JOHN CLIFFORD	D. MARCH 1, 1980 GOODWATER, ALA.
52-109 WAUGH, JAMES ELDEN	3109 OAKRIDGE - CORSICANA TX 75110
27-100 WAY, ROBERT CLINTON	D. JUNE 20, 1974 PITTSBURGH, PA.
24-114 WAYENBERG, FRANK	D. APRIL 16, 1975 ZANESVILLE, O.
89-137 WAYNE, GARY ANTHONY	521 CENTRALIA - DEARBORN HEIGHTS MI 48127
36- 94 WEAFER, KENNETH ALBERT	66 RYCKMAN AVE - ALBANY NY 12208
36- 95 WEATHERLY, CYRIL ROY 'STORMY'	1175 DENTON DRIVE - BEAUMONT TX 77707
62-143 WEAVER, DAVID FLOYD	RR 1 BOX 579 - POWDERLY TX 75473
68-108 WEAVER, EARL SIDNEY	19016 WEST LAKE DR - HIALEAH FL 33015
12-213 WEAVER, GEORGE DANIEL 'BUCK'	D. JANUARY 31, 1956 CHICAGO, ILL.
15-171 WEAVER, HARRY ABRAHAM	D. MAY 30, 1983 ROCHESTER, N. Y.
67-113 WEAVER, JAMES BRIAN	276 RHODA DR - LANCASTER PA 17601
28-104 WEAVER, JAMES DEMENT	D. DECEMBER 12, 1983 LAKELAND, FLA.
85-116 WEAVER, JAMES FRANCIS	212 77TH STREET - HOLMES BEACH FL 33510
31- 99 WEAVER, MONTE MORTON	826 SOUTH LAKE ADAIR BLVD - ORLANDO FL 32804
10-149 WEAVER, ORLIE FOREST	D. NOVEMBER 28, 1970 NEW ORLEANS, LA.
80-141 WEAVER, ROGER EDWARD	BOX 15 - SAINT JOHNSVILLE NY 13452
10-150 WEBB, CLEON EARL 'LEFTY'	D. JANUARY 12, 1958 CIRCLEVILLE, O.
72-120 WEBB, HENRY GAYLON	3100 GULF BLVD #133 - BELLEAIR BEACH FL 33535
32- 90 WEBB, JAMES LEVERNE 'SKEETER'	D. JULY 8, 1986 MERIDIAN, MISS.
48-115 WEBB, SAMUEL HENRY 'RED'	5609 35TH PL - HYATTSVILLE MD 20782
25-112 WEBB, WILLIAM EARL	D. MAY 22, 1965 JAMESTOWN, TENN.
43-141 WEBB, WILLIAM FREDERICK	3758 SHARON DR - POWDER SPRINGS GA 30073
17- 89 WEBB, WILLIAM JOSEPH	D. JANUARY 12, 1943 CHICAGO, ILL.
42-106 WEBBER, LESTER ELMER	D. NOVEMBER 13, 1986 SANTA MARIA, CALIF.
89-138 WEBSTER, LEONARD IRELL 'LENNY'	323 WEIL STREET (P.O. BOX 811) - LUTCHER LA 70071
83-107 WEBSTER, MITCHELL DEAN	4201 SANDPIPER LN - GREAT BEND KS 67530
67-114 WEBSTER, RAMON ALBERTO	BOX 1340 - COLON PANAMA C.A.
59- 86 WEBSTER, RAYMOND GEORGE	410 CENTER ST - YUBA CITY CA 95991
11-173 WEEDEN, CHARLES ALBERT	D. JANUARY 7, 1939 NORTHWOOD, N.H.
62-144 WEEKLY, JOHN	D. NOVEMBER 24, 1974 WALNUT CREEK, CAL.
69-179 WEGENER, MICHAEL DENIS	P.O. BOX 634 - BROOMFIELD CO 80020
85-117 WEGMAN, WILLIAM EDWARD	1720 CLIFTMONT CIRCLE - LAWRENCEBURG IN 47025
30- 90 WEHDE, WILBUR 'BIGGS'	D. SEPTEMBER 21, 1970 SIOUX FALLS,S.D.
45-111 WEHMEIER, HERMAN RALPH	D. MAY 21, 1973 DALLAS, TEX.
76-100 WEHRMEISTER, DAVID THOMAS	4216 DUBBE CT - CONCORD CA 94521
46-102 WEIGEL, RALPH RICHARD	1404 WHEATON RD - MEMPHIS TN 38117
48-107 WEIK, RICHARD HENRY	17532 70TH CT - TINLEY PARK IL 60477
40- 98 WEILAND, EDWIN NICHOLAS	D. JULY 12, 1972 CHICAGO, ILL.
28-105 WEILAND, ROBERT GEORGE	D. NOVEMBER 9, 1988 CHICAGO, ILL.
12-214 WEILMAN, CARL WOOLWORTH	D. MAY 25, 1924 HAMILTON, O.
19- 88 WEINERT, PHILLIP WALTER 'LEFTY'	D. APRIL 17, 1973 ROCKLEDGE, FLA.
45-112 WEINGARTNER, ELMER WILLIAM	13604 LORAIN - CLEVELAND OH 44111
33- 65 WEINTRAUB, PHILIP	D. JUNE 21, 1987 PALM SPRINGS, CALIF.
36- 96 WEIR, WILLIAM FRANKLIN 'ROY'	1521 WEST CRIS PLACE - ANAHEIM CA 92802
62-145 WEIS, ALBERT JOHN	902 SOUTH POPLAR - ELMHURST IL 60126
22-136 WEIS, ARTHUR JOHN 'BUTCH'	209 KINGSVILLE CT - WEBSTER GROVES MO 63119
15-172 WEISER, HARRY BUDSON 'BUD'	D. JULY 31, 1961 SHAMOKIN, PA.
80-142 WEISS, GARY LEE	RR 1 BOX 80 - BRENHAM TX 77833
15-173 WEISS, JOSEPH HAROLD	D. JULY 7, 1967 CEDAR RAPIDS, IA.
87-149 WEISS, WALTER WILLIAM	10 SYLVAN WAY - SUFFERN NY 10901
39-124 WELAJ, JOHN LUDWIG	1519 COLLEGE ST #103 - ARLINGTON TX 76010
14-228 WELCH, FLOYD JOHN	D. JANUARY 6, 1943 GREAT BEND, KAN.
19- 89 WELCH, FRANK TIGUER	D. JULY 25, 1957 BIRMINGHAM, ALA.
25-113 WELCH, HERBERT M.	D. APRIL 13, 1967 MEMPHIS, TENN.
26- 91 WELCH, JOHN VERNON	D. SEPTEMBER 2, 1940 ST. LOUIS, MO.
45-113 WELCH, MILTON EDWARD	2860 TAYLOR ST - EUGENE OR 97405
78-140 WELCH, ROBERT LYNN	4150 DELPHI CIR - HUNTINGTON BEACH CA 92649
82-135 WELCHEL, DONALD RAY	OLD ADD: 10327 GARWOOD DRIVE - DALLAS TX 75238
11-174 WELCHONCE, HARRY MONROE	D. FEBRUARY 26, 1977 ARCADIA, CALIF.
16- 94 WELF, OLIVER HENRY	D. JUNE 25, 1967 CLEVELAND, O.
82-136 WELLMAN, BRAD EUGENE	18081 JOSEPH DR - CASTRO VALLEY CA 94546
48-108 WELLMAN, ROBERT JOSEPH	855 ROLLING WOOD DRIVE - COVINGTON KY 41017
87-150 WELLS, DAVID LEE	OLD ADD: 4944 NEWPORT - SAN DIEGO CA 92107
23-139 WELLS, EDWIN LEE	D. MAY 1, 1986 BIRMINGHAM, ALA.
81-139 WELLS, GREGORY DEWAYNE 'BOOMER'	RR 1 BOX 98 - MCINTOSH AL 36553
44-139 WELLS, JOHN FREDERICK	3115 1/2 WEST STATE RD - OLEAN NY 14760
42-107 WELLS, LEO DONALD	1755 HIGHLAND PKWY - ST PAUL MN 55116
81-140 WELSH, CHRISTOPHER CHARLES	7403 16TH AVENUE NW - BRADENTON FL 34209
25-114 WELSH, JAMES DANIEL	D. OCTOBER 30, 1970 OAKLAND, CAL.
48-109 WELTEROTH, RICHARD JOHN	122 ELDRED ST - WILLIAMSPORT PA 17701
26- 92 WELZER, ANTON FRANK	D. MARCH 18, 1971 MILWAUKEE, WIS.
15-174 WENDELL, LEWIS CHARLES	D. JULY 11, 1953 BRONX, N. Y.
43-142 WENSLOFF, CHARLES WILLIAM 'BUTCH'	8 RYAN AVE - MILL VALLEY CA 94941
45-114 WENTZEL, STANLEY AARON	2900 OLEY TURNPIKE RD #J8 - READING PA 19606
68-109 WENZ, FREDERICK CHARLES	1 CIRCLE DR - SOMERVILLE NJ 08876
27-101 WERA, JULIAN VALENTINE	D. DECEMBER 12, 1975 ROCHESTER, MINN.
30- 91 WERBER, WILLIAM MURRAY	11812 QUAIL VILLAGE WAY - NAPLES FL 33999
64-126 WERHAS, JOHN CHARLES	7420 STONE CREEK LANE - ANAHEIM CA 92807
49- 89 WERLE, WILLIAM GEORGE	833 WEST 28TH AVE - SAN MATEO CA 94403

56- 85 WERLEY, GEORGE WILLIAM	16429 HORSESHOE RIDGE - CHESTERFIELD MO 63017
75-129 WERNER, DONALD PAUL	2204 BRIARWOOD - ARLINGTON TX 76013
63-123 WERT, DONALD RALPH	RR 1 BOX 288 - NEW PROVIDENCE PA 17560
79-117 WERTH, DENNIS DEAN	OLD ADD: BOX 802 - LINCOLN IL 62656
14-229 WERTZ, DWIGHT LYMAN MOODY	D. MAY 26, 1958 SARASOTA, FLA.
26- 93 WERTZ, HENRY LEVI 'JOHNNY'	1704 NANCE ST - NEWBERRY SC 29108
47- 92 WERTZ, VICTOR WOODROW	D. JULY 7, 1983 DETROIT, MICH.
79-118 WESSINGER, JAMES MICHAEL	504 KINGSTON RD - UTICA NY 13502
88-137 WEST, DAVID LEE	5159 FERNLEAF AVENUE - MEMPHIS TN 38134
38-104 WEST, MAX EDWARD	507 SIERRA KEYS DR-SIERRA MADRE CA 91024
38-105 WEST, RICHARD THOMAS	BOX 5095 - FORT WAYNE IN 46805
27-102 WEST, SAMUEL FILMORE	D. NOVEMBER 23, 1985 LUBBOCK, TEXAS
28-106 WEST, WALTER MAXWELL 'MAX'	D. APRIL 25, 1971 HOUSTON, TEX.
44-140 WEST, WELDON EDISON 'LEFTY'	D. JULY 23, 1979 HENDERSONVILLE, N. C.
55-135 WESTLAKE, JAMES PATRICK	909 SEAMAS AVENUE - SACRAMENTO CA 95822
47- 93 WESTLAKE, WALDON THOMAS	3800 61ST - SACRAMENTO CA 95820
29-107 WESTON, ALFRED JOHN	1 ALPINE TER - NEEDHAM MA 02192
89-139 WESTON, MICHAEL LEE 'MICKEY'	3281 HORRELL COURT - FENTON MI 48430
47- 94 WESTRUM, WESLEY NOREEN	1235 NORTH SUNNYVALE #40 - MESA AZ 85205
89-140 WETHERBY, JEFFREY BARRETT	OLD ADD: 15626 HILLVIEW LANE - GRANADA HILLS CA 91344
89-141 WETTELAND, JOHN KARL	638 SARGENT STREET - SAN FRANCISCO CA 94132
27-103 WETZEL, CHARLES EDWARD 'BUZZ'	D. MARCH 7, 1941 GLOBE, ARIZ.
20-129 WETZEL, FRANKLIN BURTON 'BUZZ'	D. MARCH 5, 1942 BURBANK, CAL.
82-137 WEVER, STEFAN MATTHEW	480 MONTICELLO - SAN FRANCISCO CA 94127
23-140 WHALEY, WILLIAM CARL	D. MARCH 3, 1943 INDIANAPOLIS, IND.
13-189 WHALING, ALBERT JAMES	D. JANUARY 21, 1965 LOS ANGELES, CALIF.
54-116 WHEAT, LEROY WILLIAM	6125 PINE TER - FORT LAUDERDALE FL 33317
15-175 WHEAT, MCKINLEY DAVIS 'MACK'	D. AUGUST 14, 1979 LOS BANOS, CALIF.
12-215 WHEATLEY, CHARLES	D. DECEMBER 10, 1982 TULSA, OKLA.
43-143 WHEATON, ELWOOD PIERCE	BOX 7091 - LANCASTER PA 17604
49- 90 WHEELER, DONALD WESLEY	8127 COLFAX AVE SOUTH - MINNEAPOLIS MN 55420
45-115 WHEELER, EDWARD RAYMOND	911 J STREET - CENTRALIA WA 98531
21-110 WHEELER, FLOYD CLARK 'RIP'	D. SEPTEMBER 18, 1968 MARION, KY.
10-151 WHEELER, GEORGE HARRISON	D. JUNE 14, 1918 CLINTON, IND.
18- 73 WHEELER, RICHARD	D. FEBRUARY 12, 1962 LEXINGTON, MASS.
76-101 WHEELOCK, GARY RICHARD	1928E LAKE SAMMAMISH PKWY SE - ISSAQUAH WA 98027
13-190 WHELAN, JAMES FRANCIS	D. NOVEMBER 29, 1929 DAYTON, O.
20-130 WHELAN, THOMAS JOSEPH	D. JUNE 26, 1957 BOSTON, MASS.
71-107 WHILLOCK, JACK FRANKLIN	2007 EDGEBROOK CT - ARLINGTON TX 76015
52-110 WHISENANT, THOMAS PETER 'PETE'	218 WEST GRACE ST - PUNTA GORDA FL 33950
77-150 WHISENTON, LARRY	2507 SLATTERY ST - ST LOUIS MO 63106
77-151 WHITAKER, LOUIS RODMAN	803 PIPE - MARTINSVILLE VA 24112
66- 99 WHITAKER, STEVE EDWARD	OLD ADD: 2501 N. OCEAN DR - HOLLYWOOD BEACH FL 33019
64-127 WHITBY, WILLIAM EDWARD	OLD ADD: RR 1 BOX 491D - HUNTERSVILLE NC 28078
45-116 WHITCHER, ROBERT ARTHUR	156 GRAHAM RD - CUYAHOGA FALLS OH 44223
37-107 WHITE, ADEL 'ABE'	D. OCTOBER 1, 1978 ATLANTA, GA.
40- 99 WHITE, ALBERT EUGENE 'FUZZ'	RR 1 BOX 1049 - BRANSON MO 65616
54-117 WHITE, CHARLES	OLD ADD: 8167 HUDSON ST - VANCOUVER BC
85-118 WHITE, DEVON MARKES	474 WEST 158TH ST #42 - NEW YORK NY 10032
48-110 WHITE, DONALD WILLIAM	D. JUNE 15, 1987 CARLSBAD, CALIF.
55-136 WHITE, EDWARD PERRY	D. SEPTEMBER 28, 1962 LAKELAND, FLA.
62-146 WHITE, ELDER LAFAYETTE	919 COLONY AVE - AHOSKIE NC 27910
40-100 WHITE, ERNEST DANIEL	D. MAY 22, 1974 AUGUSTA, GA.
73-130 WHITE, FRANK	8925 LAMBERT DRIVE - LEE'S SUMMIT MO 64063
41-117 WHITE, HAROLD GEORGE	612 BIRD BAY DR #113C - VENICE FL 33595
74-140 WHITE, JEROME CARDELL	7 HAMILTON COURT - PACIFICA CA 94044
27-104 WHITE, JOHN PETER	D. JUNE 19, 1971 FLUSHING, N. Y.
32- 91 WHITE, JOYNER CLIFFORD 'JO-JO'	D. OCTOBER 9, 1986 TACOMA, WASH.
63-124 WHITE, JOYNER MICHAEL 'MIKE'	1820 284TH EAST - ROY WA 98580
83-149 WHITE, LARRY DAVID	11240 DEHAVEN AVENUE - POLOMA CA 91331
78-141 WHITE, MYRON ALAN	3201 SOUTH DEEGAN DR - SANTA ANA CA 92704
65-116 WHITE, ROY HILTON	30 ASPEN WAY - UPPER SADDLE RIVER NJ 07458
51-101 WHITE, SAMUEL CHARLES	BOX 121 - HANALEI HI 96714
19- 90 WHITE, SAMUEL LAMBETH	D. NOVEMBER 11, 1929 PHILADELPHIA, PA.
12-216 WHITE, STEPHEN VINCENT	D. JANUARY 29, 1975 BRAINTREE, MASS.
45-117 WHITE, WILLIAM BARNEY	3721 DARRELL LN - TYLER TX 75701
56- 86 WHITE, WILLIAM DEKOVA	RURAL ROUTE 1 - CHALFONT PA 18914
89-142 WHITED, EDWARD MORRIS	23 PRINCETON ARMS SOUTH - CRANBURY NJ 08512
33- 66 WHITEHEAD, BURGESS URQUHART	206 KING ST - WINDSOR NC 27983
35-114 WHITEHEAD, JOHN HENDERSON	D. OCTOBER 20, 1964 BONHAM, TEX.
23-141 WHITEHILL, EARL OLIVER	D. OCTOBER 22, 1954 OMAHA, NEB.
14-231 WHITEHOUSE, CHARLES EVIS	D. FEBRUARY 14, 1926 BREWER, ME.
12-217 WHITEHOUSE, GILBERT ARTHUR	D. JULY 19, 1960 INDIANAPOLIS, IND.
81-141 WHITEHOUSE, LEONARD JOSEPH	1874 NORTH AVE - BURLINGTON VT 05401
89-143 WHITEHURST, WALTER RICHARD 'WALLY'	186 ARDMORE - SHREVEPORT LA 71105
62-147 WHITFIELD, FRED DWIGHT	RR 1 BOX 91 - VANDIVER AL 35176
74-141 WHITFIELD, TERRY BERTLAND	793 NINANTIC DRIVE - FOSTER CITY CA 94404
46-103 WHITMAN, DICK CORWIN	184 PETER DR - CAMPBELL CA 95008
46-104 WHITMAN, WALTER FRANKLIN 'FRANK'	44 BELLEVUE #5 - COLLINSVILLE IL 62234
80-143 WHITMER, DANIEL CHARLES	823 ROBINHOOD LN - REDLANDS CA 92373
28-107 WHITNEY, ARTHUR CARTER	D. SEPTEMBER 2, 1987 CENTER, TEXAS
77-152 WHITSON, EDDIE LEE	315 SMITH GRAVEYARD ROAD - ASHEVILLE NC 28806
76-102 WHITT, ERNEST LEO	18330 13 MILE RD - ROSEVILLE MI 48066
16- 95 WHITTAKER, WALTER ELTON	D. AUGUST 7, 1965 PEMBROKE, MASS.
12-218 WHITTED, GEORGE BOSTIC 'POSSUM'	D. OCTOBER 16, 1962 WILMINGTON, N.C.
89-144 WICKANDER, KEVIN DEAN	4319 WEST BANFF LANE - GLENDALE AZ 85306
68-110 WICKER, FLOYD EULISS	RR 2 BOX 166A - SNOW CAMP NC 27349
36- 97 WICKER, KEMP CASWELL	D. JUNE 11, 1973 KERNERSVILLE, N. C.
60-102 WICKERSHAM, DAVID CLIFFORD	9118 WEST 104TH TER - OVERLAND PARK KS 66204
13-191 WICKLAND, ALBERT	D. MARCH 14, 1980 PORT WASHINGTON, WISC.
47- 95 WIDMAR, ALBERT JOSEPH	3919 SOUTH OSWEGO AV - TULSA OK 74135
58-101 WIEAND, FRANKLIN DELANO ROOS. 'TED'	216 WALNUT ST - SLATINGTON PA 18080
34-108 WIEDEMEYER, CHARLES JOHN	D. OCTOBER 27, 1979 LAKE GENEVA, FLA.
79-119 WIEDENBAUER, THOMAS JOHN	25 KNOLLWOOD ESTATES DR - ORMOND BEACH FL 32074
81-142 WIEGHAUS, THOMAS ROBERT	RURAL ROUTE 1 BOX 541 - GRANT PARK IL 60940
21-111 WIENEKE, JOHN	D. MARCH 16, 1933 PLEASANT RIDGE, MICH.
51-102 WIESLER, ROBERT GEORGE	2325 INDIAN CUP DR - FLORISSANT MO 63031
39-125 WIETELMANN, WILLIAM FREDERICK 'WHITEY'	7712 GOLFCREST DR - SAN DIEGO CA 92119

81-143	WIGGINS, ALAN ANTHONY	14326 TWISTED BRANCH ROAD - POWAY CA 92064
46-105	WIGHT, WILLIAM ROBERT	6247 MEADOW VISTA DR - CARMICHAEL CA 95608
23-142	WIGINGTON, FREDERICK THOMAS	D. MAY 8, 1980 MESA, ARIZ.
79-120	WIHTOL, ALEXANDER AMES 'SANDY'	2120 SURREY PLACE - CAMPBELL CA 95008
46-106	WILBER, DELBERT QUENTIN	513 WOODLEAF CT - KIRKWOOD MO 63122
40-101	WILBORN, CLAUDE EDWARD	RR 1 BOX 167 - ROXBORO NC 27573
79-121	WILBORN, THADDEAUS IGLEHART	2722 26TH STREET #2 - SACRAMENTO CA 95818
70-137	WILCOX, MILTON EDWARD	15941 MILLAR - FRASER MI 48026
77-153	WILES, RANDALL E	3600 RUE ANDREE - NEW ORLEANS LA 70114
75-130	WILEY, MARK EUGENE	720 RIO VISTA DRIVE - MIAMI SPRINGS FL 33166
77-154	WILFONG, ROBERT DONALD 'ROB'	2905 HOLLYBROOK DRIVE - WEST COVINA 91791
53- 98	WILHELM, CHARLES ERNEST 'SPIDER'	1490 SANDERLING DR - ENGLEWOOD FL 33533
52-111	WILHELM, JAMES HOYT 'HOYT'	3102 NORTH HIMES AVENUE - TAMPA FL 33607
78-142	WILHELM, JAMES WEBSTER	BOX 99 - BELVEDERE CA 94920
16- 96	WILHOIT, JOSEPH WILLIAM	D. SEPTEMBER 25, 1930 SANTA BARBARA, CALIF.
11-175	WILIE, DENNEY EARNEST	D. JUNE 20, 1966 HAYWARD, CALIF.
27-105	WILKE, HARRY JOSEPH	1302 MILLVILLE AVE - HAMILTON OH 45013
83-150	WILKERSON, CURTIS VERNON	RR 1 BOX 191 - SUTHERLAND VA 23885
41-118	WILKIE, ALDON JAY	P.O. BOX 364, 902 W. 1ST ST - NEWBERG OR 97132
89-145	WILKINS, DEAN ALLAN	8580 HYDRA LANE - SAN DIEGO CA 92126
79-122	WILKINS, ERIC LAMOINE	2233 EAST MILLER - SEATTLE WA 98112
44-141	WILKINS, ROBERT LINWOOD	160 CHARLES - SHREVEPORT LA 71105
11-176	WILKINSON, EDWARD HENRY	D. APRIL 9, 1918 TUCSON, ARIZ.
18- 74	WILKINSON, ROY HAMILTON	D. JULY 2, 1956 LOUISVILLE, KY.
85-119	WILKINSON, WILLIAM CARL	7919 SOUTH POPLAR WAY - ENGLEWOOD CO 80112
44-142	WILKS, TEDDY	D. AUGUST 21, 1989 HOUSTON, TEXAS
57- 92	WILL, ROBERT LEE	OLD ADD: 8 ORIOLE - NAPERVILLE IL 60540
84-128	WILLARD, GERALD DUANE	806 THAYER LANE - PORT HUENEME CA 93041
58-102	WILLEY, CARLTON FRANCIS	BOX 64 - CHERRYFIELD ME 04622
63-125	WILLHITE, JON NICHOLAS 'NICK'	7325 EAST HINSDALE PLACE - ENGLEWOOD CO 80112
80-144	WILLIAMS, ALBERT HAMILTON	PEARL LAGOON, DEPOT ZELOYA - NICARAGUA NICARAGUA C.A.
37-108	WILLIAMS, ALMON EDWARD	D. JULY 19, 1969 GROVES, TEX.
11-177	WILLIAMS, ALVA MITCHEL 'RIP'	D. JULY 23, 1933 KEOKUK, IA.
11-178	WILLIAMS, AUGUST JOSEPH	D. APRIL 16, 1964 STERLING, ILL.
70-138	WILLIAMS, BERNARD	3854 M.L. KING, JR. WAY - OAKLAND CA 94609
59- 87	WILLIAMS, BILLY LEO	3227 RANDOLPH AVENUE - OAKLAND CA 94602
71-108	WILLIAMS, CHARLES PROSEK	259-04 KENSINGTON PL - GREAT NECK NY 11021
13-192	WILLIAMS, CLAUD PRESTON 'LEFTY'	D. NOVEMBER 4, 1959 LAGUNA BEACH, CALIF.
81-144	WILLIAMS, DALLAS MCKINLEY	734 BERKLEY ROAD - INDIANAPOLIS IN 46208
89-146	WILLIAMS, DANA LAMOUNT	1404 OAKTREE COURT - MOBILE AL 36609
49- 91	WILLIAMS, DAVID CARLOUS	4645 COUNTRY CREEK #1101 - DALLAS TX 75236
13-193	WILLIAMS, DAVID CARTER 'MUTT'	D. MARCH 30, 1962 FAYETTEVILLE, ARK.
44-143	WILLIAMS, DEWEY EDGAR	720 13TH STREET WEST - WILLISTON ND 58801
58-103	WILLIAMS, DONALD FRED	11405 ROKEBY AVE - GARRETT PARK MD 20766
63-126	WILLIAMS, DONALD REID	5546 CHATEAU DR - SAN DIEGO CA 92117
28-108	WILLIAMS, EARL BAXTER	D. MARCH 10, 1958 KNOXVILLE, TENN.
70-139	WILLIAMS, EARL CRAIG	OLD ADD: 2900 CAMP CREEK PKWY - COLLEGE PARK GA
86-162	WILLIAMS, EDWARD LAQUAN	4393 MCCLINTOCK STREET - SAN DIEGO CA 92105
30- 92	WILLIAMS, EDWIN DIBRELL 'DIB'	22 MOUNTAIN DRIVE - GREENBRIER AR 72058
21-112	WILLIAMS, EVON DANIEL	D. MARCH 23, 1929 SAN CLEMENTE, CALIF.
84-129	WILLIAMS, FRANK LEE	1121 THIRD STREET - LEWISTON ID 83501
45-118	WILLIAMS, FRED 'PAP'	1120 46TH AVE - MERIDIAN MS 39305
12-219	WILLIAMS, FREDERICK 'CY'	D. APRIL 23, 1974 EAGLE RIVER, WIS.
61-108	WILLIAMS, GEORGE	4267 TYLER ST - DETROIT MI 48238
13-194	WILLIAMS, HARRY PETER	D. DECEMBER 20, 1963 HAYWOOD, CALIF.
69-180	WILLIAMS, JAMES ALFRED	1000 SOUTH COAST DRIVE #E204 - COSTA MESA CA 92626
66-100	WILLIAMS, JAMES FRANCIS 'JIMY'	1630 HONEY BEAR LN - DUNEDIN FL 33528
14-232	WILLIAMS, JOHN BRODIE	D. SEPTEMBER 8, 1963 LONG BEACH, CALIF.
15-176	WILLIAMS, KENNETH ROY	D. JANUARY 22, 1959 GRANTS PASS, ORE.
86-163	WILLIAMS, KENNETH ROYAL	3255 SELVA DRIVE - SAN JOSE CA 95148
26- 94	WILLIAMS, LEON THEO	626 OLD IVY RD NE - ATLANTA GA 30305
77-155	WILLIAMS, MARK WESTLY	RR 1 OLD ROUTE 17 BOX 1031 - WINDSOR NY 13865
16- 97	WILLIAMS, MARSHALL MCDIARMID	D. FEBRUARY 22, 1935 TUCSON, ARIZ.
87-151	WILLIAMS, MATTHEW DERRICK	309 GARDEN GATE - CARSON CIY NV 89706
83-151	WILLIAMS, MATTHEW EVAN	243 MOORE STREET - CLUTE TX 77531
86-164	WILLIAMS, MITCHELL STEVEN	4355 RIVERVIEW #2 - WEST LINN OR 97068
14-233	WILLIAMS, REES GEPHARDT 'STEAMBOAT'	D. JUNE 29, 1979 DEER RIVER, MINN.
85-120	WILLIAMS, REGINALD DWAYNE	6669 PONDSIDE CIRCLE - MEMPHIS TN 38119
78-143	WILLIAMS, RICHARD ALLEN	1217 WESSMITH - MADERA CA 93638
51-103	WILLIAMS, RICHARD HIRSCHFIELD	98 UNION #507 - SEATTLE WA 98101
14-234	WILLIAMS, RINALDO LEWIS	D. APRIL 24, 1966 COTTONWOOD, ARIZ.
11-179	WILLIAMS, ROBERT ELIAS	D. AUGUST 6, 1962 NELSONVILLE, O.
40-102	WILLIAMS, ROBERT FULTON 'ACE'	OLD ADD: CROSS ST - MARSHFIELD MA 02050
58-104	WILLIAMS, STANLEY WILSON	4702 HAYTER AVE - LAKEWOOD CA 90712
39-126	WILLIAMS, THEODORE SAMUEL	P.O. BOX 5127 - CLEARWATER FL 34618
64-128	WILLIAMS, WALTER ALLEN	2417 MONTEREY DR - BROWNWOOD TX 76801
69-181	WILLIAMS, WILLIAM	3227 RANDOLPH AVE - OAKLAND CA 94602
38-106	WILLIAMS, WOODROW WILSON	PAMPLIN VA 23958
87-152	WILLIAMSON, MARK ALAN	1983 FAIRHAVEN STREET - LEMON GROVE CA 92045
28-109	WILLIAMSON, NATHANIEL HOWARD 'HOWIE'	D. AUGUST 15, 1969 TEXARKANA, ARK.
28-110	WILLIAMSON, SILAS ALBERT	D. NOVEMBER 29, 1978 HOT SPRINGS, ARK.
30- 93	WILLINGHAM, THOMAS HUGH	D. JUNE 15, 1988 EL RENO, OKLA.
84-130	WILLIS, CARL BLAKE	RR 1 BOX 274 - YANCEYVILLE NC 27379
25-115	WILLIS, CHARLES WILLIAM 'LEFTY'	D. MAY 10, 1962 BETHESDA, MD.
63-127	WILLIS, DALE JEROME	1110 ESTATEWOOD DR - BRANDON FL 33511
53- 99	WILLIS, JAMES GLADDEN	BOX 35 - BOYCE LA 71409
11-180	WILLIS, JOSEPH DENK	D. DECEMBER 3, 1966 IRONTON, O.
47- 96	WILLIS, LESTER EVANS	D. JANUARY 22, 1982 JASPER, TEXAS
77-156	WILLIS, MICHEAL HENRY	201 WILCREST #2305 - HOUSTON TX 77042
66-101	WILLIS, RONALD EARL	D. NOVEMBER 21, 1977 MEMPHIS, TENN.
25-116	WILLOUGHBY, CLAUDE WILLIAM	D. AUGUST 14, 1973 MCPHERSON, KAN.
71-109	WILLOUGHBY, JAMES ARTHUR	P.O. BOX 143 - POLLOCK PINES CA 95726
77-157	WILLS, ELLIOTT TAYLOR 'BUMP'	OLD ADD: 2409 MIGUEL LN - ARLINGTON TX 76016
83-152	WILLS, FRANK LEE	733 GEN. PERSHING ST - NEW ORLEANS LA 70115
59- 88	WILLS, MAURICE MORNING	30100 TOWN CENTER DRIVE #O209 - LAGUNA NIGUEL CA 92677
59- 89	WILLS, THEODORE CARL	524 CLOVIS AVE - CLOVIS CA 93612
18- 75	WILLSON, FRANK HOXIE 'KID'	D. APRIL 17, 1964 UNION GAP, WASH..
89-147	WILMET, PAUL RICHARD	226 NORTH 6TH STREET - DEPERE WI 54115

DEN'S
COLLECTORS DEN

PLASTIC CARD PROTECTING PAGES
LARGEST SELECTION IN THE HOBBY

FINEST QUALITY PLASTIC SHEETS

Featuring:
NON—MIGRATING PLASTIC IN ALL SHEETS
PLASTIC THAT DOES NOT STICK TOGETHER
STIFFNESS TO RESIST CARD CURLING
INTELLIGENT DESIGN
RESISTANCE TO CRACKING
FULL COVERAGE OF CARDS, PHOTOS, ENVELOPES

DEN'S
COLLECTORS
DEN

HOME OF
SPORT
AMERICANA

Dept. BAL
P.O. BOX 606, LAUREL, MD 20725

SEND
ONLY $ 1.00
for DEN'S
BIG CATALOGUE
CATALOGUE
sent FREE
with each ORDER

NO   MIX   &   MATCH

STYLE	POCKETS CAPACITY	RECOMMENDED FOR	PRICE EACH (Does not include Post. & Hand.)			
			1—24	25—99	100—299	300 plus
9	9 / 18	TOPPS (1957 to present), FLEER, DONRUSS SCORE, SPORTFLICS, TCMA, LEAF (1960), All standard 2½'' X 3½'' cards, SIDE LOAD	.25	.23	.21	.19
9T	9 / 18	SAME AS STYLE 9 ABOVE, TOP LOAD	.25	.23	.21	.19
8	8 / 16	TOPPS (1952—1956, 1988 Big), BOWMAN (1953—1955)	.25	.23	.21	.19
12	12 / 24	BOWMAN (1948—1950), TOPPS (1951), TOPPS (Stickers), FLEER (Minis & Stickers)	.25	.23	.21	.19
1	1 / 2	PHOTOGRAPHS (8'' X 10'')	.25	.23	.21	.19
2	2 / 4	PHOTOGRAPHS (5'' X 7''), TOPPS (1984, 1985 & 1986 Supers)	.25	.23	.21	.19
4	4 / 8	POSTCARDS, EXHIBITS, PEREZ—STEELE (Hall of Fame postcards), DONRUSS (1983—1987 All-Stars), TOPPS (1964,70,71 Supers)	.25	.23	.21	.19
6P	6 / 12	POLICE AND SAFETY CARDS (All sports)	.25	.23	.21	.19
18	18 / 36	T206 and most other T CARDS, BAZOOKA (1963—1967 Individual cards), Many 19th Century cards (N Cards)	.40	.40	35	.35
9G	9 / 18	GOUDEY, DIAMOND STARS, LEAF (1948)	.40	.40	.35	.35
9PB	9 / 18	PLAY BALL, BOWMAN (1951-52), All GUM, INC. Cards, TOPPS (Minis), DOUBLE PLAY	.40	.40	.35	.35
1C	1 / 2	TURKEY RED (T3), PRESS GUIDES, PEREZ—STEELE (Greatest Moments), Many WRAPPERS (Sport & non-sport)	.40	.40	.35	.35
3	3 / 6	3—CARD PANELS (Hostess, Star, Zeller's)	.40	.40	.35	.35
6V	6 / 12	TOPPS (Double Headers, Greatest Moments, 1951 Connie Mack, Current All-Stars, Team, 1965 Football and Hockey, Bucks, 1969—1970 Basketball, T201 (Mecca Double folders), T202 (Hassan Triple folders), DADS (Hockey), DONRUSS (1986—87 Pop—Ups)	.40	.40	.35	.35
6D	6 / 12	RED MAN (With or without tabs), DISCS, KAHN'S (1955—1967)	.40	.40	.35	.35
1Y	1 / 1	YEARBOOKS, PROGRAMS, MAGAZINES, Pocket Size is 9'' X 12''	.40	.40	.35	.35
1S	1 / 2	MAGAZINE PAGES and PHOTOS, SMALL PROGRAMS, CRACKER JACK (1982 sheets), Pocket Size is 8½'' X 11''	.40	.40	.35	.35
10	10 / 10	MATCHBOOK COVERS (Standard 20 match)	.40	.40	.35	.35
3E	3 / 3	FIRST DAY COVERS, BASEBALL COM—MEMORATIVE ENVELOPES	.40	.40	.35	.35
3L	3 / 6	SQUIRT PANELS, PEPSI (1963), FLEER (Stamps in strips)	.40	.40	.35	.35

POSTAGE & HANDLING SCHEDULE
$ .01 to $ 20.00 add $ 2.00
$ 20.01 to $ 29.99 add $ 2.50
$ 30.00 to $ 49.99 add $ 3.00
$ 50.00 or more add $ 4.00

VISA/MASTER CHARGE ACCEPTED

MasterCard   VISA

MARYLAND RESIDENTS ADD 5% SALES TAX
CANADIAN ORDERS – BOOKS ONLY
Canadian orders, orders outside the contiguous
United States, APO and FPO add 25% additional
U.S. FUNDS ONLY

34-109 WILSHERE, VERNON SPRAGUE 'WHITEY'	D. MAY 23, 1985 COOPERSTOWN, N. Y.
73-131 WILSHUSEN, TERRY WAYNE	1207 EAST 222ND STREET - CARSON CA 90745
51-104 WILSON, ARCHIE CLIFTON	1620 WOODLAND ST SE - DECATUR AL 35601
51-105 WILSON, ARTHUR LEE	2226 NE 10TH AVE - PORTLAND OR 97212
31-100 WILSON, CHARLES WOODROW	D. DECEMBER 19, 1970 ROCHESTER, N. Y.
89-148 WILSON, CRAIG	22 PAROLE STREET - ANNAPOLIS MD 21401
66-102 WILSON, DONALD EDWARD	D. JANUARY 5, 1975 HOUSTON, TEX.
58-105 WILSON, DUANE LEWIS	1522 COOLIDGE - WICHITA KS 67203
59- 90 WILSON, EARL LAWRENCE	BOX 662 - PONCHATOULA LA 70454
36- 98 WILSON, EDWARD FRANCIS	D. APRIL 11, 1979 HAMDEN, CONN.
14-235 WILSON, FINIS ELBERT	D. MARCH 9, 1959 CORAL GABLES, FLA.
24-115 WILSON, FRANCIS EDWARD	D. NOVEMBER 25, 1974 LEICESTER, MASS.
79-123 WILSON, GARY STEVEN	RURAL ROUTE 2 BOX 644 - CAMDEN AR 71701
11-181 WILSON, GEORGE FRANCIS 'SQUANTO'	D. MARCH 26, 1967 WINTHROP, ME.
34-110 WILSON, GEORGE PEACOCK 'ICEHOUSE'	D. OCTOBER 13, 1973 MORAGA, CAL.
52-112 WILSON, GEORGE WASHINGTON	D. OCTOBER 29, 1974 GASTONIA, N.C.
82-138 WILSON, GLENN DWIGHT	3303 PINE CHASE - MONTGOMERY TX 77356
24-116 WILSON, GOMER RUSSELL 'TEX'	D. SEPTEMBER 15, 1946 SULPHUR SPRINGS, TEX.
48-111 WILSON, GRADY HERBERT	5512 ORCHARD DR - COLUMBUS GA 31904
23-143 WILSON, JAMES	D. JUNE 1, 1947 PALMETTO, FLA.
45-119 WILSON, JAMES ALGER	D. SEPTEMBER 2, 1986 NEWPORT BEACH, CALIF..
85-121 WILSON, JAMES GEORGE	2400 NW 88TH STREET - VANCOUVER WA 98665
34-111 WILSON, JOHN FRANCIS 'JACK'	4111 164TH ST SW #62 - LYNNWOOD WA 98037
13-195 WILSON, JOHN NICODEMUS	D. SEPTEMBER 23, 1954 ANNAPOLIS, MD.
27-106 WILSON, JOHN SAMUEL	D. AUGUST 27, 1980 CHATTANOOGA, TENN.
11-182 WILSON, LESTER WILBUR	D. APRIL 4, 1969 EDMONDS, WASH.
23-144 WILSON, LEWIS ROBERT 'HACK'	D. NOVEMBER 23, 1948 BALTIMORE, MD
40-103 WILSON, MAX	D. JANUARY 2, 1977 GREENSBORO, N. C.
83-153 WILSON, MICHAEL "TACK"	1832 EAST 15TH STREET - OAKLAND CA 94606
58-106 WILSON, ROBERT	D. APRIL 23, 1985 DALLAS, TEXAS
51-106 WILSON, ROBERT JAMES 'RED'	806 CABOT LN - MADISON WI 53711
28-111 WILSON, ROY EDWARD	D. DECEMBER 3, 1969 CLARION, IA.
60-103 WILSON, SAMMY O'NEIL 'NEIL'	RR1 BOX 285 - LEXINGTON TN 38351
21-113 WILSON, SAMUEL MARSHALL 'MIKE'	D. MAY 16, 1978 BOYNTON BEACH, FLA.
88-138 WILSON, STEPHEN DOUGLAS	8446 AQUA DRIVE - VANCOUVER BRIT COL V5P 4S2 CAN.
14-236 WILSON, THOMAS C.	D. MARCH 7, 1953 SAN PEDRO, CALIF.
88-139 WILSON, TREVOR KIRK	892 LAURAL WOOD - OREGON CITY OR 97045
45-120 WILSON, WALTER WOOD	RR 1 BOX 676A - FRANKLIN GA 30217
20-131 WILSON, WILLIAM CLARENCE 'MUTT'	D. AUGUST 31, 1962 WILDWOOD, FLA.
50-104 WILSON, WILLIAM DONALD	17126 WOODRUFF AVENUE #A - BELLFLOWER CA 90706
69-182 WILSON, WILLIAM HARLAN	10108 S. 198TH EAST AVE - BROKEN ARROW OK 74012
80-145 WILSON, WILLIAM HAYWOOD 'MOOKIE'	OLD ADD: 150 HIGHLAND AVE - STATEN ISLAND NY 10301
76-103 WILSON, WILLIE JAMES	3905 WEST 110TH TERRACE - LEAWOOD KS 66211
26- 95 WILTSE, HAROLD JAMES	D. NOVEMBER 2, 1983 BUNKIE, LA.
56- 87 WINCENIAK, EDWARD JOSEPH	10828 SOUTH AVE "O" - CHICAGO IL 60617
59- 91 WINDHORN, GORDON RAY	145 BENT CREEK RD - DANVILLE VA 24540
28-112 WINDLE, WILLIS BREWER	D. DECEMBER 8, 1981 CORPUS CHRISTI TX.
86-165 WINE, ROBERT PAUL JR.	2614 WOODLAND AVENUE - NORRISTOWN PA 19403
60-104 WINE, ROBERT PAUL SR.	2612 WOODLAND AVE - NORRISTOWN PA 19401
29-108 WINEAPPLE, EDWARD	960 PARK AVE - NEW YORK NY 10028
30- 94 WINEGARNER, RALPH LEE	D. APRIL 14, 1988 WICHITA, KAN.
73-132 WINFIELD, DAVID MARK	367 W. FOREST - TEANECK NJ 07666
32- 92 WINFORD, JAMES HEAD	D. DECEMBER 16, 1970 MIAMI, OKLA.
24-117 WINGARD, ERNEST JAMES	D. JANUARY 17, 1977 PRATTVILLE, ALA.
23-145 WINGFIELD, FREDERICK DAVIS 'TED'	D. JULY 18, 1975 JOHNSON CITY, TENN.
19- 91 WINGO, ABSALOM HOLBROOK 'AL'	D. OCTOBER 9, 1954 DETROIT, MICH.
20-132 WINGO, EDMOND ARMAND	D. DECEMBER 5, 1964 LACHINE, QUE.
11-183 WINGO, IVEY BROWN	D. MARCH 1, 1941 NORCROSS, GA.
73-133 WINKLES, BOBBY BROOKS	P.O. BOX 1158 - LAQUINTA CA 92680
19- 92 WINN, GEORGE BENJAMIN	D. NOVEMBER 1, 1969 ROBERTA, GA.
83-154 WINN, JAMES FRANCIS	RURAL ROUTE 1 - CLEVER MO 65631
84-131 WINNINGHAM, HERMAN SON	1542 BELLEVILLE RD - ORANGEBURG SC 29115
30- 95 WINSETT, JOHN THOMAS 'TOM'	BOX 32183 - PALM BEACH GARDENS FL 33410
33- 67 WINSTON, HENRY RUDOLPH	D. FEBRUARY 7, 1974 JACKSONVILLE, FLA.
24-118 WINTERS, CLARENCE JOHN	D. JUNE 29, 1945 DETROIT, MICH.
19- 93 WINTERS, JESSE FRANKLIN 'BUCK'	D. JUNE 5, 1986 ABILENE, TEXAS
89-149 WINTERS, MATTHEW LITTLETON	16 HUNTINGTON COURT - WILLIAMSVILLE NY 14221
78-144 WIRTH, ALAN LEE	1012 WEST MOUNTAIN VIEW - MESA AZ 85201
21-114 WIRTS, ELWOOD VERNON 'KETTLE'	D. JULY 12, 1968 SACRAMENTO, CAL.
32- 93 WISE, ARCHIBALD EDWIN	D. FEBRUARY 2, 1978 WAXAHACHIE, TEX.
30- 96 WISE, HUGH EDWARD	D. JULY 21, 1987 PLANTATION, FLA.
57- 93 WISE, KENDALL COLE 'CASEY'	3631 RUM ROW - NAPLES FL 33940
64-129 WISE, RICHARD CHARLES 'RICK'	8235 SW 184TH STREET - BEAVERTON OR 97007
44-144 WISE, ROY OGDEN	11841 MELODY LN DR - GARDEN GROVE CA 92640
19- 94 WISNER, JOHN HENRY	D. DECEMBER 15, 1981 JACKSON, MICH.
64-130 WISSMAN, DAVID ALVIN	20 WELLINGTON ST - SHELBURNE FALLS MA 01370
34-112 WISTERT, FRANCIS MICHAEL 'WHITEY'	D. APRIL 23, 1985 PAINESVILLE, OHIO
14-230 WISTERZIL, GEORGE JOHN 'TEX'	D. JUNE 27, 1964 SAN ANTONIO, TEX.
40-104 WITEK, NICHOLAS JOSEPH 'MICKEY'	30 WEST RIDGE ST - SHAVERTOWN PA 18708
20-133 WITHROW, FRANK BLAINE	D. SEPTEMBER 5, 1966 OMAHA, NEB.
63-128 WITHROW, RAYMOND WALLACE 'CORKY'	1730 QUEENSWAY COURT - OWENSBORO KY 42301
57- 94 WITT, GEORGE ADRIAN	2209 CATALINA ST - LAGUNA BEACH CA 92651
16- 98 WITT, LAWTON WALTER 'WHITEY'	D. JULY 14, 1988 SALEM COUNTY, N. J.
81-145 WITT, MICHAEL ATWATER	8042 SAN LEON CIR DR - BUENA PARK CA 90620
86-166 WITT, ROBERT ANDREW	30 OAKDALE ROAD - CANTON MA 02021
46-107 WITTE, JEROME CHARLES	7515 OAK VISTA - HOUSTON TX 77087
38-107 WITTIG, JOHN CARL	163 STAFFORD STREET - BALTIMORE MD 21227
74-142 WOCKENFUSS, JOHN BILTON	428 NORTH STREET - ELKTON MD 21921
23-146 WOEHR, ANDREW EMIL	270 SCARLET WAY - EUSTIS FL 32726
72-121 WOHLFORD, JAMES EUGENE	P.O. BOX 6036 - ATASCADERO CA 93422
62-148 WOJCIK, JOHN JOSEPH	33 HAMILTON ST - BUFFALO NY 14207
54-118 WOJEY, PETER PAUL	2359 SOUTH BUENA DR - MOBILE AL 36605
85-122 WOJNA, EDWARD DAVID	48 WILLIAMSBURG DR - MONROE CT 06468
12-220 WOLF, ERNEST A	D. MAY 23, 1964 ATLANTIC HIGHLANDS, N.J.
27-107 WOLF, RAYMOND BERNARD	D. OCTOBER 6, 1979 FORT WORTH, TEXAS
69-183 WOLF, WALTER BECK	17711 TRAIL VIEW - YORBA LINDA CA 92686
21-115 WOLF, WALTER FRANCIS 'LEFTY'	D. SEPTEMBER 25, 1971 NEW ORLEANS, LA.
23-147 WOLFE, CHARLES HENRY	D. NOVEMBER 27, 1957 SCHELLSBURG, PA.

52-113 WOLFE, EDWARD ANTHONY	2240 LIDO - STOCKTON CA 95207
17- 90 WOLFE, HAROLD	D. JULY 28, 1971 FORT WAYNE, IND.
77-158 WOLFE, LAURENCE MARCY	2616 SARDA WAY - RANCHO CORDOVA CA 95670
12-221 WOLFE, ROY CHAMBERLAIN 'POLLY'	D. NOVEMBER 21, 1938 MORRIS, ILL.
41-119 WOLFF, ROGER FRANCIS	1307 KNOTT-CHESTER IL 62233
14-237 WOLFGANG, MELDON JOHN	D. JUNE 30, 1947 ALBANY, N.Y.
66-103 WOMACK, HORACE GUY 'DOOLEY'	209 WEEPING CHERRY LANE - COLUMBIA SC 29212
26- 96 WOMACK, SIDNEY KIRK	D. AUGUST 28, 1958 JACKSON, MISS.
30- 97 WOOD, CHARLES ASHER 'SPADES'	D. MAY 18, 1986 WICHITA, KAN.
23-148 WOOD, CHARLES SPENCER 'DOC'	D. NOVEMBER 3, 1974 NEW ORLEANS, LA.
08 WOOD, HOWARD ELLSWORTH 'SMOKEY JOE'	D. JULY 27, 1985 WEST HAVEN, CONN.
61-109 WOOD, JACOB	851 MAGNOLIA AVE - ELIZABETH NJ 07201
44-145 WOOD, JOE FRANK	BOX 53 - CLINTON CT 06413
43-144 WOOD, JOSEPH PERRY	D. MARCH 25, 1985 HOUSTON, TEXAS
48-112 WOOD, KENNETH LANIER	6337 TERESA AVE - CHARLOTTE NC 28214
13-196 WOOD, ROY WINTON	D. APRIL 6, 1974 FAYETTEVILLE, ARK.
61-110 WOOD, WILBUR FORRESTER	8 WACHUSETT DR - LEXINGTON MA 02173
20-134 WOODALL, CHARLES LAWRENCE 'LARRY'	D. MAY 6, 1963 CAMBRIDGE, MASS.
78-145 WOODARD, DARRELL LEE	1227 EAST 69TH ST - LOS ANGELES CA 90001
85-123 WOODARD, MICHAEL CARY	P.O. BOX 35 - MAYWOOD IL 60153
11-184 WOODBURN, EUGENE STEWART	D. JANUARY 18, 1961 SANDUSKY, O.
44-146 WOODEND, GEORGE ANTHONY	D. FEBRUARY 6, 1980 HARTFORD, CONN.
56- 88 WOODESHICK, HAROLD JOSEPH	803 WYCLIFFE DR - HOUSTON TX 77079
43-145 WOODLING, EUGENE RICHARD	926 REMSEN RD - MEDINA OH 44256
14-239 WOODMAN, DANIEL COURTENAY	D. DECEMBER 14, 1962 TOPSFIELD, MASS.
77-159 WOODS, ALVIS	2518 60TH AVE - OAKLAND CA 94605
14-238 WOODS, CLARENCE COFIELD	D. JULY 2, 1969 RISING SUN, IND.
76-104 WOODS, GARY LEE	2621 NORTH SWAN - TUCSON AZ 85712
43-146 WOODS, GEORGE ROWLAND 'PINKY'	D. OCTOBER 30, 1982 LOS ANGELES, CALIF.
57- 95 WOODS, JAMES JEROME	151 ROSS WAY - SAN BRUNO CA 94066
24-119 WOODS, JOHN FULTON	D. OCTOBER 4, 1946 NORFOLK, VA.
69-184 WOODS, RONALD LAWRENCE	413 PLYMOUTH ST - INGLEWOOD CA 90302
69-185 WOODSON, RICHARD LEE	3416 LONESOME TRAIL - GEORGETOWN TX 78626
87-153 WOODSON, TRACY MICHAEL	6232 SHANNON ROAD - MECHANICSVILLE VA 23111
18- 76 WOODWARD, FRANK RUSSELL	D. JUNE 11, 1961 NEW HAVEN, CONN.
85-124 WOODWARD, ROBERT JOHN	HCR 63 BOX 43A EASTMAN HILL - LEBANON NH 03766
63-129 WOODWARD, WILLIAM FREDERICK 'WOODY'	13 LAMBERT DR - SPARTA NJ 07871
55-137 WOOLDRIDGE, FLOYD LEWIS	214 BARBER ST - GREENFIELD MO 65661
47- 97 WOOTEN, EARL HAZELL	702 WILLIAMS ST - WILLIAMSTON SC 29697
14-240 WORDEN, FREDERICK BAMFORD	D. NOVEMBER 9, 1941 ST. LOUIS, MO.
38-108 WORKMAN, CHARLES THOMAS	D. JANUARY 3, 1953 KANSAS CITY, MO.
24-120 WORKMAN, HARRY HALL 'HOGE'	D. MAY 20, 1972 FORT MYERS, FLA.
50-105 WORKMAN, HENRY KILGARIFF	307 19TH ST - SANTA MONICA CA 90402
85-125 WORRELL, TODD ROLAND	306 HARVARD DRIVE - ARCADIA CA 91006
78-146 WORTHAM, RICHARD COOPER	10302 TIMBERCREST LN - AUSTIN TX 78750
53-100 WORTHINGTON, ALLAN FULTON	1710 MORNING SUN CIRCLE - BIRMINGHAM AL 35242
88-140 WORTHINGTON, CRAIG RICHARD	9431 VAN AKEN - PICO RIVERA CA 90660
31-101 WORTHINGTON, ROBERT LEE 'RED'	D. DECEMBER 8, 1963 LOS ANGELES, CAL.
16- 99 WORTMAN, WILLIAM LEWIS 'CHUCK'	D. AUGUST 19, 1977 LAS VEGAS, NEV.
83-155 WOTUS, RONALD ALLAN	CRESTVIEW DRIVE - COLCHESTER CT 06415
33- 68 WRIGHT, ALBERT EDGAR	4030 PANAMA CT #213 %GLENBROOK - OAKLAND CA 94611
35-115 WRIGHT, ALBERT OWEN 'AB'	P.O. BOX 3 - MUSKOGEE OK 74401
16-100 WRIGHT, CEYLON	D. NOVEMBER 7, 1947 HINES, ILL.
66-104 WRIGHT, CLYDE	528 JEANINE AVE - ANAHEIM CA 92806
24-121 WRIGHT, FOREST GLENN	D. APRIL 6, 1984 OLATHE, KAN.
82-139 WRIGHT, GEORGE DEWITT	3704 PELICAN COURT - ARLINGTON TX 76016
45-121 WRIGHT, HENDERSON EDWARD 'ED'	827 LAKE ROAD - DYERSBURG TN 38024
27-108 WRIGHT, JAMES	D. APRIL 12, 1963 OAKLAND, CAL.
78-147 WRIGHT, JAMES CLIFTON	439 HARRISON ST - COOPERSVILLE MI 49404
81-146 WRIGHT, JAMES LEON	2822 SOUTH 29TH - ST. JOSEPH MO 64503
82-140 WRIGHT, JAMES RICHARD 'RICKY'	3605 WEST HOUSTON - PARIS TX 75460
70-140 WRIGHT, KENNETH WARREN	1416 WISTERIA AVE - PENSACOLA FL 32507
54-119 WRIGHT, MELVIN JAMES	D. MAY 16, 1983 HOUSTON, TEX.
15-177 WRIGHT, ROBERT CASSIUS	5757 CYPRESS AVE #207 - CARMICHAEL CA 95608
56- 89 WRIGHT, ROY EARL	331 PINEHURST CIR - CHICKAMAUGA GA 30707
38-109 WRIGHT, TAFT SHEDRON	D. OCTOBER 22, 1981 ORLANDO, FLA.
48-113 WRIGHT, THOMAS EVERETT	RR 2 BOX 45 - SHELBY NC 28150
17- 91 WRIGHT, WAYNE BROMLEY 'RASTY'	D. JUNE 12, 1948 COLUMBUS, O.
15-178 WRIGHT, WILLARD JAMES 'DICK'	D. JANUARY 24, 1952 BETHLEHEM, PA.
20-135 WRIGHTSTONE, RUSSELL GUY	D. MARCH 1, 1969 HARRISBURG, PA.
88-141 WRONA, RICHARD JAMES	7514 E. 17TH STREET - TULSA OK 74112
29-109 WUESTLING, GEORGE 'YATS'	D. APRIL 26, 1970 ST. LOUIS, MO.
44-147 WURM, FRANK JAMES	P.O. BOX 573 - GLENS FALLS NY 12801
61-111 WYATT, JOHN	605 NW FALK DRIVE - LEES SUMMIT MO 64063
29-110 WYATT, JOHN WHITLOW 'WHIT'	BUCHANAN GA 30113
24-122 WYATT, LORAL JOHN 'JOE'	D. DECEMBER 5, 1970 OBLONG, ILL.
13-197 WYCKOFF, JOHN WELDON	D. MAY 8, 1961 SHEBOYGAN FALLS, WIS.
76-105 WYNEGAR, HAROLD DELANO 'BUTCH'	528 SPRING CREEK DR - LONGWOOD FL 32779
39-127 WYNN, EARLY	P.O. BOX 218 - NOKOMIS FL 34274
63-130 WYNN, JAMES SHERMAN	OLD ADD: 932 1/2 E. 41ST PL - LOS ANGELES CA 90053
83-156 WYNNE, MARVELL	8052 SOUTH CALUMET - CHICAGO IL 60619
67-115 WYNNE, WILLIAM VERNON	7820 TOWER RIDGE COURT - JACKSONVILLE FL 32216
42-108 WYROSTEK, JOHN BARNEY	D. DECEMBER 12, 1986 ST.LOUIS, MO.
42-109 WYSE, HENRY WASHINGTON	1133 SE 14TH ST- PRYOR OK 74361
30- 98 WYSONG, HARLIN 'BIFF'	D. AUGUST 8, 1951 XENIA, O.
72-122 YANCY, HUGH	BOX 9064 - SARASOTA FL 33578
42-110 YANKOWSKI, GEORGE EDWARD	164 CHAPMAN ST-WATERTOWN MA 02172
12-222 YANTZ, GEORGE WEBB	D. FEBRUARY 26, 1967 LOUISVILLE, KY.
26- 97 YARNALL, WALDO WARD 'RUSTY'	D. OCTOBER 9, 1985 LOWELL, MASS.
22-137 YARRISON, BYRON WARDSWORTH 'RUBE'	D. APRIL 22, 1977 WILLIAMSPORT, PA.
21-116 YARYAN, CLARENCE EVERETT 'YAM'	D. NOVEMBER 16, 1964 BIRMINGHAM, ALA.
61-112 YASTRZEMSKI, CARL MICHAEL	4621 SOUTH OCEAN BLVD - HIGHLAND BEACH FL 33431
71-110 YATES, ALBERT ARTHUR	OLD ADD: 11613 WEST YUMA CT - NEW BERLIN WI
24-123 YDE, EMIL OGDEN	D. DECEMBER 4, 1968 LEESBURG, FLA.
19- 95 YEABSLEY, ROBERT WATKINS 'BERT'	D. FEBRUARY 8, 1961 PHILADELPHIA, PA.
72-123 YEAGER, STEPHEN WAYNE	2775 BAYWATER PLACE - THOUSAND OAKS CA 91362
22-138 YEARGIN, JAMES ALMOND	D. MAY 8. 1937 GREENVILLE, S. C.
89-150 YELDING, ERIC GIRARD	P.O. BOX 325 - MONTROSE AL 36559

Entry	Details
17- 92 YELLE, ARCHIE JOSEPH	D. MAY 2, 1983 WOODLAND, CALIF.
63-131 YELLEN, LAWRENCE ALAN	OLD ADD: 67-30 CLYDE ST - FOREST HILLS NY 11375
21-117 YELLOWHORSE, MOSES J. 'CHIEF'	D. APRIL 10, 1964 PAWNEE, OKLA.
27-109 YERKES, CHARLES CARROLL	D. DECEMBER 20, 1950 OAKLAND, CAL.
85-126 YETT, RICHARD MARTIN	1140 N. HIGLEY #109 BOX 161 - MESA AZ 85205
57- 96 YEWCIC, THOMAS	31 CHEORKEE RD - ARLINTON MA 02174
11-185 YINGLING, EARL HERSHEY	D. OCTOBER 2, 1962 COLUMBUS, O.
51-107 YOCHIM, LEONARD JOSEPH	316 NELSON DR - NEW ORLEANS LA 70123
48-114 YOCHIM, RAYMOND AUSTIN ALOYSIUS	5008 FINCH - METAIRIE LA 70001
19- 96 YORK, JAMES EDWARD 'LEFTY'	D. APRIL 9, 1961 YORK, PA.
70-141 YORK, JAMES HARLAN	24671 ATHENA - MISSION VIEJO CA 92691
34-113 YORK, RUDOLPH PRESTON	D. FEBRUARY 5, 1970 ROME, GA.
44-148 YORK, TONY BATTEN	D. APRIL 18, 1970 HILLSBORO, TEXAS
80-146 YOST, EDGAR FREDERICK 'NED'	111 TRAILWAY DRIVE - CLINTON MS 39056
44-149 YOST, EDWARD FRED JOSEPH	48 OAKRIDGE ROAD - WELLESLEY MA 02181
21-118 YOTER, ELMER ELLSWORTH	D. JULY 26, 1966 CAMP HILL, PA.
85-127 YOUMANS, FLOYD EVERETT	591 LANCEWOOD - RIALTO CA 92376
15-179 YOUNG, CHARLES	D. MAY 12, 1952 RIVERSIDE, N. J.
83-157 YOUNG, CURTIS ALLEN	13354 NORTH 100TH PLACE - SCOTTSDALE AZ 85260
37-109 YOUNG, DELMER EDWARD	D. DECEMBER 8, 1979 SAN FRANCISCO, CALIF.
65-117 YOUNG, DONALD WAYNE	OLD ADD: 1350 TRENTON ST - DENVER CO 80220
13-198 YOUNG, GEORGE JOSEPH	D. MARCH 13, 1950 BRIGHTWATERS, N.Y.
87-154 YOUNG, GERALD ANTHONY	1618 WEST BROOK STREET - SANTA ANA CA 92703
11-186 YOUNG, HERMAN JOHN	D. DECEMBER 13, 1966 IPSWICH, MASS.
71-111 YOUNG, JOHN THOMAS	124 WEST 57TH ST - LOS ANGELES CA 90037
78-148 YOUNG, KIP LANE	RR 2 BOX 113-C - WINCHESTER OH 45697
33- 69 YOUNG, LEMUEL FLOYD 'PEP'	D. JANUARY 14, 1962 JAMESTOWN, N. C.
83-158 YOUNG, MATTHEW JOHN	4248 COMMONWEALTH - LACANADA CA 91011
82-141 YOUNG, MICHAEL DARREN	3250 SUNNYBROOK CT - HAYWARD CA 94541
36- 99 YOUNG, NORMAN ROBERT 'BABE'	D. DECEMBER 25, 1983 EVERETT, MASS.
13-199 YOUNG, RALPH STUART	D. JANUARY 24, 1965 PHILADELPHIA, PA.
51-108 YOUNG, RICHARD ENNIS	OLD ADD: 6923 189TH - LYNNWOOD WA 98036
48-115 YOUNG, ROBERT GEORGE	D. JANUARY 28, 1985 BALTIMORE, MD.
31-102 YOUNG, RUSSELL CHARLES	D. MAY 13, 1984 ROSEVILLE, CALIF.
22-139 YOUNGBLOOD, ARTHUR CLYDE 'CHIEF'	D. JULY 6, 1968 AMARILLO, TEX.
76-106 YOUNGBLOOD, JOEL RANDOLPH	8270 EAST WINDROSE - SCOTTSDALE AZ 85254
17- 93 YOUNGS, ROSS MIDDLEBROOK	D. OCTOBER 22, 1927 SAN ANTONIO, TEX.
37-110 YOUNT, FLOYD EDWIN 'EDDIE'	D. OCTOBER 26, 1973 NEWTON, N. C.
14-241 YOUNT, HERBERT MACON 'DUCKY'	D. MAY 9, 1970 WINSTON-SALEM, N. C.
71-112 YOUNT, LAWRENCE KING	OLD ADD: 8101 EAST CLARENDON - SCOTTSDALE AZ 85251
74-143 YOUNT, ROBIN R	5010 EAST SHEA BLVD #D200 - SCOTTSDALE AZ 85254
24-124 YOWELL, CARL COLUMBUS	D. JULY 27, 1985 JACKSONVILLE, TEXAS
52-114 YUHAS, JOHN EDWARD 'EDDIE'	D. JULY 6, 1986 WINSTON-SALEM, N. C.
78-149 YURAK, JEFFREY LYNN	424 SOUTH 188TH STREET - SEATTLE WA 98148
47- 98 YVARS, SALVADOR ANTHONY	1 ALLEN ST - VALHALLA NY 10595
45-122 ZABALA, ADRIAN RODRIGUEZ	11243 ANDREA DR - JACKSONVILLE FL 32218
13-200 ZABEL, GEORGE WASHINGTON 'ZIP'	D. MAY 31, 1970 BELOIT, WIS.
44-150 ZACHARY, ALBERT MYRON 'CHINK'	426 LORRAINE AVE - UTICA NY 13502
18- 77 ZACHARY, JONATHAN THOMPSON WALTON	D. JANUARY 24, 1969 GRAHAM, N. C.
63-132 ZACHARY, WILLIAM CHRIS	P.O. BOX 5093 - KNOXVILLE TN 37928
10-152 ZACHER, ELMER HENRY	D. DECEMBER 20, 1944 BUFFALO, N.Y.
76-107 ZACHRY, PATRICK PAUL	12003 WOODBRIAR CIRCLE - WACO TX 76710
11-187 ZACKERT, GEORGE CARL	D. FEBRUARY 18, 1977 BURLINGTON, IA.
73-134 ZAHN, GEOFFREY CLAYTON	26004 MORENO DRIVE - VALENCIA CA 91355
23-149 ZAHNISER, PAUL VERNON	D. SEPTEMBER 26, 1964 KLAMATH FALLS, ORE.
44-151 ZAK, FRANK THOMAS	D. FEBRUARY 6, 1972 PASSAIC, N.J.
13-201 ZAMLOCH, CARL EUGENE	D. AUGUST 19, 1963 SANTA BARBARA, CALIF.
74-144 ZAMORA, OSCAR JOSE	OLD ADD: 2201 BRICKELL AVE #82 - MIAMI FL 33129
58-107 ZANNI, DOMINICK THOMAS	7 SUSSEX AVE NORTH - MASSAPEQUA NY 11758
33- 70 ZAPUSTAS, JOSEPH JOHN	16 VESEY RD - RANDOLPH MA 02368
45-123 ZARDON, JOSE ANTONIO SANCHEZ	13721 SW 45TH TERRACE - MIAMI FL 33175
43-147 ZARILLA, ALLEN LEE 'ZEKE'	431 NAHUA ST #705 - HONOLULU HI 96815
84-132 ZASKE, LLOYD JEFFREY 'JEFF'	16731 68TH AVE WEST - LYNNWOOD WA 98037
51-109 ZAUCHIN, NORBERT HENRY 'NORM'	818 NORTH MONTEZ DR - THOMAS ACRES AL 35020
89-151 ZAVARAS, CLINTON WAYNE	OLD ADD: DENVER CO
77-160 ZDEB, JOSEPH EDWARD	643 WILTON COURT - PALATINE IL 60067
77-161 ZEBER, GEORGE WILLIAM	9722 RAVENSCROFT RD - SANTA ANA CA 92705
10-153 ZEIDER, ROLLIE HUBERT	D. SEPTEMBER 12, 1967 AUBURN, IND.
89-152 ZEILE, TODD EDWARD	OLD ADD: VALENCIA CA
14-242 ZEISER, MATTHEW J.	D. JUNE 10, 1942 NORWOOD PARK, ILL.
70-142 ZELLER, BARTON WALLACE	5112 IMPERIAL DR - RICHTON PARK IL 60471
69-186 ZEPP, WILLIAM CLINTON	35430 BROOKVIEW - LIVONIA MI 48152
49- 92 ZERNIAL, GUS EDWARD	5902 EAST BELMONT - FRESNO CA 93727
54-120 ZICK, ROBERT GEORGE	24252 BASHIAN - NOVI MI 48050
87-155 ZIEM, STEVEN GRAELING	663 SOUTH 22ND STREET - BANNING CA 92220
41-120 ZIENTARA, BENEDICT JOSEPH	D. APRIL 16, 1985 LAKE ELSINORE, CALIF.
54-121 ZIMMER, DONALD WILLIAM	10124 YACHT CLUB DR - ST PETERSBURG FL 33706
61-113 ZIMMERMAN, GERALD ROBERT	13650 FERNRIDGE - MILWAUKIE OR 97222
45-124 ZIMMERMAN, ROY FRANKLIN	24 NORTH ST - TREMONT PA 17981
15-180 ZIMMERMAN, WILLIAM H.	D. OCTOBER 4, 1952 NEWARK, N.J.
21-119 ZINK, WALTER NOBLE	D. JUNE 12, 1964 QUINCY, MASS.
11-188 ZINN, GUY	D. OCTOBER 6, 1949 CLARKSBURG, W. VA.
19- 97 ZINN, JAMES EDWARD	1050 DEARING ROAD - MEMPHIS TN 38117
44-152 ZINSER, WILLIAM FREDERICK	8834 ROYAL HEIGHTS DR - CINCINNATI OH 45239
61-114 ZIPFEL, MARION SYLVESTER 'BUD'	57 WHITESIDE DR - BELLEVILLE IL 62221
71-113 ZISK, RICHARD WALTER	OLD ADD: 1411 MEADOWLARK DR - PITTSBURGH PA 15243
19- 98 ZITZMANN, WILLIAM ARTHUR	D. MAY 29, 1985 PASSAIC, N. J.
10-154 ZMICH, EDWARD ALBERT	D. AUGUST 20, 1950 CLEVELAND, O.
44-153 ZOLDAK, SAMUEL WALTER	D. AUGUST 25, 1966 MINEOLA, N. Y.
36-100 ZUBER, WILLIAM HENRY	D. NOVEMBER 2, 1982 CEDAR RAPIDS, IA.
57- 97 ZUPO, FRANK JOSEPH	2824 MARIPOSA DR - BURLINGAME CA 94010
82-142 ZUVELLA, PAUL	1396 LASSEN AVE - MILPITAS CA 95305
51-110 ZUVERINK, GEORGE	1721 ELLIS DR - TEMPE AZ 85282
10-155 ZWILLING, EDWARD HARRISON 'DUTCH'	D. MARCH 27, 1978 LA CRESCENTA, CALIF.

COACHES WITH NO MAJOR LEAGUE PLAYING OR MANAGERIAL EXPERIENCE DEBUTING FROM 1910 TO 1989

Code	Name	Address
C89- 1	BERARDINO, RICHARD J	37 EMMELINE AVENUE - WALTHAM MA 02154
C67- 1	BERINGER, CARROLL JAMES 'C.B.'	4917 GRANITE SHOALS - FORT WORTH TX 76103
C89- 2	BEVINGTON, TERRY PAUL	144 COMMONWEALTH - ATTLEBORO MA 02703
C64- 1	BLACKBURN, WAYNE CLARK	1414 OFFNERE ST - PORTSMOUTH OH 45662
C74- 1	BLOOMFIELD, GORDON LEIGH 'JACK'	1310 IRIS - MCALLEN TX 78501
C67- 2	BRAGAN, JAMES ALTON	1059 MARTINWOOD LN - BIRMINGHAM AL 35235
C86- 1	BREEDEN, HAROLD SCOTT	6619 BAYBROOKS CIR - TEMPLE TERRACE FL 33617
C69- 1	CAMACHO, JOSEPH GOMES	48 MASSASOIT AVE - FAIRHAVEN MA 02719
C70- 1	CARNEVALE, DANIEL JOSEPH	161 DORCHESTER RD - BUFFALO NY 14213
C59- 1	CARTER, RICHARD JOSEPH	D. SEPTEMBER 11, 1969 PHILADELPHIA, PA.
C77- 1	CLEAR, ELWOOD ROBERT 'BOB'	120 EAST 234TH ST - CARSON CA 90745
C79- 2	CLUCK, ROBERT	6192 BALTIMORE DRIVE - LAMESA CA 92042
C85- 1	CONNOR, MARK P.	8309 MECKLENBURG COURT - KNOXVILLE TN 37923
C77- 2	CRESSE, MARK EMERY	3840 GOLDENROD ST - SEAL BEACH CA 90740
C79- 1	DEWS, ROBERT WALTER	423 AUDUBON - ALBANY GA 31707
C80- 1	DONNELLY, RICHARD FRANCIS	156 BROCKTON ROAD - STEUBENVILLE OH 43952
C61- 1	DOUGLAS, OTIS WHITFIELD	D. MARCH 21, 1989 KILMARNOCK, PA.
C69- 2	DUNLOP, HARRY ALEXANDER	7470 29TH ST - SACRAMENTO CA 95820
C83- 1	DUSAN, EUGENE	61174 CONCHO ST - BEND OR 97701
C83- 2	EZELL, GLENN WAYNE	1504 LAUREL DR - ARLINGTON TX 76012
C47- 1	FITZGERALD, JOSEPH PATRICK	D. AUGUST 29, 1967 ORLANDO, FLA.
C53- 1	FITZPATRICK, JOHN ARTHUR	5242 GAYLORD PLACE - SAN DIEGO CA 92117
C85- 2	GALANTE, MATTHEW JOSEPH	177 CROSSFIELD AVE - STATEN ISLAND NY 10312
C82- 1	HARMON, THOMAS HAROLD	6101 BON TERRA DRIVE - AUSTIN TX 78731
C84- 1	HINES, BENJAMIN	2709 SECOND ST - LAVERNE CA 91750
C84- 2	HOLMQUIST, DOUGLAS LEONARD	D. FEBRUARY 27, 1988 ALTAMONTE SPRINGS, FLA.
C48- 1	HOLT, GOLDEN DESMOND 'GOLDIE'	4937 STERN AVE - SHERMAN OAKS CA 91423
C68- 1	HOSCHEIT, VERNARD ARTHUR	BOX 36 - PLAINVIEW NE 68769
C88- 1	ISAAC, LUIS	CAROLINA TWRS,1313A ISLA VERDE - CAROLINA PR 00630
C55- 1	KAHN, LOUIS	P.O. BOX 4066 - MESA AZ 85201
C30- 1	KELLY, BERNARD FRANCIS	D. OCTOBER 23, 1968 INDIANAPOLIS, IND.
C89- 3	KIM, WENDELL KEALOHAPAUOLE	5804 EAST FOX STREET - MESA AZ 85205
C69- 3	KISSELL GEORGE MARSHALL	658 MOUNT OAK AVENUE NE - ST. PETERSBURG FL 33702
C71- 1	KITTLE, HUBERT MILTON 'HUB'	3801 RICHLEY ROAD - YAKIMA WA 98902
C70- 2	KOENIG, FRED CARL	6721 EAST 51ST ST - TULSA OK 74145
C88- 2	LETT, JAMES	STAR ROUTE 34 BOX 5751 - WINFIELD WV 25213
C57- 1	LEVY, LEONARD HOWARD	%J. SNELSON,324 COLTART ST-PITTSBURGH PA 15213
C51- 1	LOBE, WILLIAM CHARLES	D. JANUARY 7, 1969 CLEVELAND, O.
C72- 1	LOWE, Q. V.	AUM ATHLETICS - MONTGOMERY AL 36193
C89- 4	MAJTYKA, LEROY W. 'ROY'	RURAL ROUTE 1 BOX 767 - WAGONER OK 74467
C85- 3	MAZZONE, LEO DAVID	RURAL ROUTE 3 BOX 278 - RAWLINGS MD 21557
C51- 2	MCDONNELL, ROBERT 'MAJE'	7423 REVERE ST - PHILADELPHIA PA 19152
C86- 2	MCLAREN, JOHN LOWELL	1518 SEATLES DRIVE - SUGARLAND TX 77478
C85- 4	MERRILL, CARL HARRISON 'STUMP'	18 MERRYMEETING ROAD - TOPSHAM ME 04086
C77- 3	MOZZALI, MAURICE JOSEPH 'MO'	D. MARCH 2, 1987 LAKELAND, FLA.
C85- 5	MULL, JACK	1041 WILSON AVENUE - CHAMBERSBURG PA 17201
C83- 3	NAPOLEON, EDWARD G	1312 73RD ST NW - BRADENTON FL 33529
C83- 4	NOTTLE, EDWARD WILLIAM	6612 PINEHURST DR - EVANSVILLE IN 47711
C58- 1	OCEAK, FRANK JOHN	D. MARCH 19, 1983 JOHNSTOWN, PA.
C62- 1	ONEIL, JOHN B. 'BUCK'	3049 EAST 32ND ST - KANSAS CITY MO 64128
C63- 1	OSBORN, DONALD EDWIN	D. MARCH 23, 1979 TORRANCE, CALIF.
C74- 2	PACHECO, ANTONIO ARISTIDES 'TONY'	D. 1987 MIAMI, FLA.
C61- 2	PAEPKE, JACK	P.O. DRAWER 3039 - CRESTLINE CA 92325
C85- 6	PAVLICK, GREGORY MICHAEL	10136 SEMINOLE ISLE DR - SEMINOLE FL 33343
C84- 4	PETERSON, ERIC HARDING 'RICK'	P.O. BOX 1359 - BRADENTON FL 33506
C69- 4	PLAZA, RONALD EDWARD	2050 68TH AVE SOUTH - ST. PETERSBURG FL 33712
C66- 1	RESINGER, GROVER S.	D. JANUARY 11, 1986 ST. LOUIS, MO.
C81- 1	REYES, BENJAMIN 'CANANEA'	MATAMAROS Y CACATECAS - HERMOSILLO SONORA MEX.
C87- 1	RIDDOCH, GREGORY LEE	1711 GLEN MEADOWS DRIVE - GREELEY CO 80631
C89- 5	RIGGLEMAN, JAMES	322 38TH AVENUE NE - ST. PETERSBURG FL 33704
C66- 2	ROBINSON, WARREN GRANT 'SHERIFF'	OLD ADD: 305 OAKLEY ST - CAMBRIDGE MD
C73- 1	ROSENBAUM, GLEN OTIS	BOX 1 - UNION MILLS IN 46382
C72- 2	ROWE, RALPH EMANUEL	1120 HILLCREST ROAD - NEWBERRY SC 29108
C76- 2	SAUL, JAMES ALLEN	2405 OSBORNE ST - BRISTOL VA 23201
C70- 3	SCHERGER, GEORGE RICHARD	701 ST JULIEN - CHARLOTTE NC 28205
C87- 2	SLIDER, RACHEL W. 'RAC'	RURAL ROUTE 1 - DEKALB TX 75559
C84- 5	SMITH, BILLLY FRANKLIN	109 POTTER DRIVE - JAMESTOWN NC 27282
C77- 4	SOMMERS, DENNIS JAMES	210 WEST BATH - HORTONVILLE WI 54944
C79- 3	SPARKS, JOSEPH EVERETT	3915 EAST CHOLLA ST - PHOENIX AZ 85028
C22- 1	THOMAS, RAY	
C85- 7	TORCHIA, ANTHONY L	5229 SOUTHWEST 11TH AVENUE - CAPE CORAL FL 33904
C81- 2	VAN ORNUM, JOHN CLAYTON	6624 NORTH HAZEL ST - FRESNO CA 93711
C43- 1	VINCENT, ALBERT LINDER	260 MANOR AVE - BEAUMONT TX 77706
C61- 3	WALKER, VERLON LEE 'RUBE'	D. MARCH 24, 1971 CHICAGO, ILL.
C73- 2	WALTON, JAMES ROBERT	BOX 787 - SHATTUCK OK 73858
C77- 5	WARNER, HARRY CLINTON	106 BELFAIR - REEDERS PA 18352
C77- 6	WILLIAMS, DONALD ELLIS	205 FOXFIRE - PARAGOULD AR 72450
C81- 3	WILLIAMS, JAMES BERNARD	4 OLD SOUND ROAD - JOPPATOWNE MD 21085
C32- 1	WOLGAMOT, CLIFTON EARL	D. APRIL 25, 1970 INDEPENDENCE, IA.

UMPIRES DEBUTING FROM 1910 TO 1989

U14- 1	ANDERSON, OLIVER O	D. JULY 7, 1945 LOS ANGELES, CALIF.
U70- 1	ANTHONY, GEORGE MERLYN	OLD ADD: 2361 WILMPALA ST - MESA AZ 85203
U66- 1	ASHFORD, EMMETT LITTLETON	D. MARCH 1, 1980 MARINA DEL REY, CALIF.
U69- 1	AVANTS, NICK R	5805 WOODLAWN - LITTLE ROCK AR 72205
U36- 1	BALLANFANT, EDWARD LEE	D. JULY 15, 1987 DALLAS, TEXAS
U40- 1	BARLICK, ALBERT JOSEPH	2071 NORTH SIXTH - SPRINGFIELD IL 62702
U68- 1	BARNETT, LAWRENCE ROBERT	6464 HUGHES RD - PROSPECT OH 43342
U31- 1	BARR, GEORGE MCKINLEY	D. JULY 26, 1974 SULPHUR, OKLA.
U28- 1	BARRY, DANIEL	D.
U36- 2	BASIL, STEPHEN JOHN	D. JUNE 24, 1962 GILCHRIST, TEX.
U42- 1	BERRY, CHARLES FRANCIS	PLAYER DEBUT 1925
U76- 1	BETCHER, RALPH	153 PARKFEL AVE - PITTSBURGH PA 15237
U22- 4	BIERHALTER	
U70- 2	BLANDFORD, FRED	1123 CHARLES ST - ELMIRA NY 14904
U44- 1	BOGGESS, LYNTON ROSS 'DUSTY'	D. JULY 8, 1968 DALLAS, TEX.
U85- 1	BONIN, GREGORY	101 PROVIDENCE COURT - LAFAYETTE LA 70506
U44- 2	BOYER, JAMES MURRY	D. JULY 25, 1959 FINKSBURG, MD.
U17- 1	BRANSFIELD, WILLIAM EDWARD 'KITTY'	D. MAY 1, 1947 WORCESTER, MASS.
U74- 1	BREMIGAN, NICHOLAS GREGORY	D. MARCH 29, 1989 GARLAND, TEXAS
U15- 1	BREWER,	
U73- 1	BRINKMAN, JOSEPH NORBERT	1021 INDIAN RIVER DRIVE - COCOA FL 32922
U79- 1	BROCKLANDER, FRED WILLIAM	123-40 83RD AVE #10J - KEW GARDENS NY 11415
U57- 1	BURKHART, WILLIAM KENNETH 'KEN'	PLAYER DEBUT 1945
U11- 1	BUSH, GARNET C.	D. DECEMBER 30, 1919 ST. LOUIS, MO.
U13- 1	BYRON, WILLIAM J. 'LORD'	D. DECEMBER 27, 1955 YPSILANTI, MICH.
U28- 2	CAMPBELL, WILLIAM M	OLD ADD: 676 SOUTH BELVEDERE - MEMPHIS TN
U61- 1	CARRIGAN, HERVE SAMUEL 'SAM'	OLD ADD: 651 MCKINSTRY AVE - CHICOPEE FALLS MA 01020
U14- 2	CHILL, OLIVER P. 'OLLIE'	OLD ADD: MAJESTIC HOTEL - KANSAS CITY MO
U54- 1	CHYLAK, NESTOR	D. FEBRUARY 17, 1982 DUNMORE, PA.
U76- 2	CLARK, ALAN MARSHALL	16 INDEPENDENCE PL - NEWTOWN PA 18940
U30- 1	CLARKE, ROBERT M	
U82- 1	COBLE, GEORGE DREW 'DREW'	3554 BOY WOOD ROAD - GRAHAM NC 27253
U15- 2	COCKILL, GEORGE W	D. NOVEMBER 2, 1937 STEELTOWN, PA.
U76- 3	COHEN, ALFRED	1026 NORTH HIGHLAND AVE - PITTSBURGH PA 15206
U10- 1	COLLIFLOWER, JAMES HARRY	D. AUGUST 14, 1961 WASHINGTON, D. C.
U68- 2	COLOSI, NICHOLAS	68-17 54TH AVE - MASPETH NY 11378
U41- 1	CONLAN, JOHN BERTRAND 'JOCKO'	PLAYER DEBUT 1934
U75- 1	COONEY, TERRANCE JOSEPH	4860 N. WOODROW #101 - FRESNO CA 93726
U14- 3	CORCORAN, THOMAS WILLIAM	D. JUNE 25, 1960 PLAINFIELD, CONN.
U83- 1	COSTELLO, PERRY	406 ROSADELL - LANSING MI 48910
U79- 2	COUSINS, DERRYL	702 4TH STREET - HERMOSA BEACH CA 90254
U89- 1	CRAFT, TERRY	2902 NORTH HILL ROAD - PORTSMOUTH OH 45625
U76- 4	CRAWFORD, GERALD JOSEPH	1 PINZON AVE - HAVERTOWN PA 19083
U56- 1	CRAWFORD, HENRY CHARLES 'SHAG'	1530 VIRGINIA AVE - HAVERTOWN PA 19083
U14- 4	CROSS, MONTFORD MONTGOMERY	D. JUNE 21, 1934 PHILADELPHIA, PA.
U71- 1	DALE, JERRY PARKER	428 W. HUNTINGTON SR #4 - ARCADIA CA 91006
U86- 1	DARLING, GARY R	319 SOUTH ABILENE - GILBERT AZ 85234
U48- 1	DASCOLI, FRANK	BOX 75 - DANIELSON CT 06239
U69- 2	DAVIDSON, DAVID LEROY 'SATCH'	2400 WESTHEIMER ST #209W - HOUSTON TX 77098
U82- 2	DAVIDSON, ROBERT ALLAN	2405 TRAILS END - ALTOONA IA 50009
U83- 2	DAVIS, GERALD	616 CAMELLIA LN - APPLETON WI 54915
U70- 3	DEEGAN, WILLIAM EDWARD JOHN	105 CORDOVA GREEN - LARGO FL 33543
U56- 2	DELMORE, VICTOR	D. JUNE 10, 1960 SCRANTON, PA.
U83- 3	DEMUTH, DANA ANDREW	8388 VIA AIROSA - RANCHO CUCAMONGA CA 91730
U69- 3	DENKINGER, DONALD ANTON	3322 DORAL DRIVE - WATERLOO IA 50701
U66- 2	DEZELAN, FRANK JOHN	1314 WOOD ST - PITTSBURGH PA 15221
U63- 1	DIMURO, LOUIS JOHN	D. JUNE 7, 1982 ARLINGTON, TEX.
U53- 1	DIXON, HAL HAYWORTH	D. JULY 28, 1966 CHURNEE, S.C.
U50- 1	DONATELLI, AUGUST JOSEPH	4681 FIRST ST NE - ST PETERSBURG FL 33703
U31- 2	DONNELLY, CHARLES H	D. DECEMBER 13, 1968 LAKE WORTH, FLA.
U30- 2	DONOHUE, MICHAEL R	D. AUGUST 7, 1968 ST. LOUIS, MO.
U11- 2	DOYLE, JOHN JOSEPH 'DIRTY JACK'	D. DECEMBER 31, 1958 HOLYOKE, MASS.
U63- 2	DOYLE, WALTER JAMES	OLD ADD: 3314 HENDERSON BLVD - TAMPA FL 33609
U60- 1	DRUMMOND, CALVIN TROY	D. MAY 2, 1970 DES MOINES, IOWA
U51- 1	DUFFY, JAMES FRANCIS	165 2ND ST - PAWTUCKET RI 02861
U39- 1	DUNN, THOMAS PATRICK	D. JANUARY 20, 1976 PRINCE GEORGES CO., MD.
U14- 5	ELDRIDGE, CLARENCE E	
U65- 1	ENGEL, ROBERT ALLEN	3500 HARMONY LN - BAKERSFILED CA 93306
U52- 1	ENGELN, WILLIAM RAYMOND	D. APRIL 17, 1968 PALO ALTO, CALIF.
U72- 1	EVANS, JAMES BREMOND	9302 SCENIC BLUFF DRIVE - AUSTIN TX 78733
U13- 2	FERGUSON, CHARLES AUGUSTUS	D. MAY 17, 1931 SAULT SAINTE MARIE, MICH.
U79- 3	FIELDS, STEPHEN HAROLD	216 EAST GLENDALE #2 - ALEXANDRIA VA 22301
U11- 3	FINNERAN, WILLIAM F	D. JULY 30, 1961 ERIE, PA.
U79- 4	FITZPATRICK, MICHAEL	262 LODGE LANE - KALAMAZOO MI 49009
U53- 2	FLAHERTY, JOHN FRANCIS 'RED'	9 FOWLER LN - FALMOUTH MA 02540
U75- 2	FORD, ROBERT DALE 'DALE'	RURAL ROUTE 5 BOX 1260 - JONESBORO TN 37659
U61- 2	FORMAN, ALLEN SANFORD	61 WASHINGTON AVE - MORRISTOWN NJ 07960
U69- 4	FRANTZ, ARTHUR FRANK	OLD ADD: 276 LYCEUM ST - ROCHESTER NY
U11- 4	FRARY, RALPH	D. NOVEMBER 10, 1925 ABERDEEN, WASH.
U20- 1	FRIEL, WILLIAM EDWARD	D. DECEMBER 24, 1959 ST. LOUIS, MO.
U71- 2	FROEMMING, BRUCE NEAL	5045 ELK CT - MILWAUKEE WI 53223
U52- 2	FROESE, GROVER A	D. JULY 20, 1982 BAY SHORE NY
U15- 3	FYFE, LOUIS	
U75- 3	GARCIA, RICHARD RAUL	2633 FIRESTONE DR - CLEARWATER FL 33519
U25- 1	GEISEL, HARRY CHRISTIAN	D. FEBRUARY 20, 1966 INDIANAPOLIS, IND.
U14- 6	GOECKEL, E	
U36- 3	GOETZ, LAWRENCE JOHN	D. OCTOBER 31, 1962 CINCINNATI, O.
U68- 3	GOETZ, RUSSELL LOUIS	1010 VERMONT ST - GLASSPORT PA 15045
U46- 1	GORE, ARTHUR JOSEPH 'ARTIE'	D. SEPTEMBER 29, 1986 WOLFEBORO, N. H.
U51- 2	GORMAN, THOMAS DAVID	PLAYER DEBUT 1939
U77- 1	GREGG, ERIC EUGENE	2635 MIMI CIR - PHILADELPHIA PA 19131
U38- 1	GRIEVE, WILLIAM TURNER	D: AUGUST 17, 1979 YONKERS, N. Y.
U70- 4	GRIMSLEY, JOHN WILLIAM	204 RAVENWOOD DR - GREENVILLE NC 27834
U83- 4	GRINDER, SCOTT	128 NORTH VIEW DR - ZELIONOPLE PA 16063
U14- 7	GROOM, ROBERT	D. FEBRUARY 19, 1948 BELLEVILLE, ILL.
U70- 5	GRYGIEL, GEORGE R.	7620 EAST LINDEN STREET - TUCSON AZ 85715
U76- 5	GUCKERT, ELMER	590 CRANE AVE - PITTSBURGH PA 15216
U52- 3	GUGLIELMO, ANGELO AUGIE	183 JERSEY ST - WATERBURY CT 06706

U13- 3 GUTHRIE, WILLIAM J	D. MARCH 6, 1950 CHICAGO, ILL
U61- 3 HALLER, WILLIAM EDWARD	2013 SOUTH LAKE DR - VANDALIA IL 62471
U85- 2 HALLION, THOMAS FRANCIS	246 ST. MATTHEWS AVENUE - LOUISVILLE KY 40207
U79- 5 HARRIS, LANNY DEAN	3313 COLLEGE CORNER RD - RICHMOND IN 47374
U16- 1 HARRISON, PETER A	D. MARCH 9, 1921 SARANAC LAKE, N. Y.
U12- 1 HART, EUGENE F	D. MAY 10, 1937 LOWELL MASS.
U62- 1 HARVEY, HARVEY DOUGLAS	10231 VERA CRUZ CT - SAN DIEGO CA 92124
U77- 2 HENDRY, EUGENE 'TED'	2709 EAST SHAW BUTTE DR - PHOENIX AZ 85028
U45- 1 HENLINE, WALTER JOHN 'BUTCH'	PLAYER DEBUT 1921
U12- 2 HILDEBRAND, GEORGE ALBERT	D. MAY 30, 1960 WOODLAND HILLS, CALIF.
U83- 5 HIRSCHBECK, JOHN FRANCIS	3135 OLD WINTER TRAIL - POLAND OH 44514
U87- 1 HIRSCHBECK, MARK	497 WOODLAWN AVENUE - STRATFORD CT 06497
U89- 2 HOHN, WILLIAM JOHN	41 COVENTRY COURT - BLUE BELL PA 19422
U23- 1 HOLMES, HOWARD ELBERT 'DUCKY'	D. SEPTEMBER 18, 1945 DAYTON, O.
U49- 1 HONOCHICK, GEORGE JAMES 'JIM'	10 SOUTH OTT ST - ALLENTOWN PA 18104
U15- 4 HOWELL, HENRY 'HANDSOME HARRY'	D. MAY 22, 1956 SPOKANE, WASH.
U22- 5 HOWLEY	
U36- 4 HUBBARD, ROBERT CAL	D. OCTOBER 16, 1977 ST PETERSBURG, FLA.
U83- 6 HUMPHREY, RICHARD	1476 BROWNLEAF DR - RICHMOND VA 23225
U47- 1 HURLEY, EDWIN HENRY	D. NOVEMBER 12, 1969 BOSTON, MASS.
U12- 3 HYATT, ROBERT HAMILTON 'HAM'	D. SEPTEMBER 11, 1963 LIBERTY LAKE, WASH.
U52- 4 JACKOWSKI, WILLIAM ANTHONY	64 CHURCH ST - NORTH WALPOLE NH 03608
U14- 8 JOHNSON, HARRY S	D. FEBRUARY 20, 1951 MEMPHIS, TENN.
U84- 1 JOHNSON, MARK STEPHEN	666 PROSPECT ROAD - HONOLULU HI 96813
U36- 5 JOHNSTON, CHARLES EDWARD	D.
U44- 3 JONES, NICHOLAS ITTNER 'RED'	D. MARCH 19, 1987 MIAMI, FLA.
U27- 1 JORDA, LOUIS DE LAROND	D. MAY 27, 1964 LARGO, FL
U89- 3 JOYCE, JAMES	7440 SW HART PLACE - BEAVERTON OR 97005
U77- 3 KAISER, KENNETH JOHN	56 HOLLY SUE LANE - ROCHESTER NY 14626
U10- 2 KECHER, W. H.	
U63- 3 KIBLER, JOHN WILLIAM	3046 SONIA CT - OCEANSIDE CA 92056
U60- 2 KINNAMON, WILLIAM ERVIN	8240 BRENTWOOD RD - LARGO FL 33543
U33- 1 KOLLS, LOUIS CHARLES	D. FEBRUARY 23, 1941 HOOPPOLE, ILL.
U76- 6 KOSC, GREGORY JOHN	3900 FERN ROAD - MEDINA OH 44256
U68- 4 KUNKEL, WILLIAM GUSTAVE JAMES	PLAYER DEBUT 1961
U55- 1 LANDES, STANLEY ALBERT	OLD ADD: 4062 N. MARYLAND AVE - MILWAUKEE WI 53211
U15- 5 LANGEVIN, JOSEPH	D. MARCH 18, 1953 BINGHAMTON, N. Y.
U79- 6 LAWSON, WILLIAM	7228 EAST EASTVIEW DR - TUCSON AZ 85710
U89- 4 LAYNE, JERRY B.	308 FIFTH STREET SE - WINTER HAVEN FL 33880
U85- 3 LEPPERD, THOMAS	5460 NE SIXTH STREET - DES MOINES IA 50313
U14- 9 LINCOLN, FREDERICK H	4017 WASHINGTON ST - HOLLYWOOD FL 33021
U61- 4 LINSALATA, JOSEPH N	P.O. BOX 631 UNION STATION - ENDICOTT NY 13760
U69- 5 LUCIANO, RONALD MICHAEL	D. MARCH 13, 1929 PHILADELPHIA, PA.
U28- 2 MAGEE, SHERWOOD ROBERT 'SHERRY'	D. OCTOBER 7, 1966 ROCK ISLAND, ILL.
U29- 1 MAGERKURTH, GEORGE LEVI 'MAJOR'	3745 NE 171ST ST #60 - NORTH MIAMI FL 33160
U70- 6 MALONEY, GEORGE PATRICK	PLAYER DEBUT 1923
U35- 1 MARBERRY, FRED 'FIRPO'	3271 MADONNA DR - COVINGTON KY 41017
U82- 3 MARSH, RANDALL GILBERT	D. DECEMBER 10, 1961 BRADY, TEX.
U14-10 MAXWELL, JAMES ALBERT 'BERT'	5405 WOODLAND AVENUE - WEST DES MOINES IA 50265
U83- 7 MCCLELLAND, TIMOTHY REID	D. JANUARY 28, 1956 CINCINNATI, O.
U14-11 MCCORMICK, WILLIAM J. 'BARRY'	RR 1 - GREENWAY AR 72430
U71- 3 MCCOY, LARRY SANDERS	
U10- 3 MCGINNIS,	D. DECEMBER 9, 1954 SILVER SPRING, MD.
U25- 2 MCGOWAN, WILLIAM ALOYSIUS	
U12- 4 MCGREEVY, EDWARD	D. JUNE 29, 1969 BEDFORD, VA
U30- 3 MCGREW, HARRY HANCOCK 'TED'	4601 DOVER ST NE - ST PETERSBURG FL 33703
U74- 2 MCKEAN, JAMES GILBERT	D. AUGUST 1, 1980 MOUNT PLEASANT, PA.
U46- 2 MCKINLEY, WILLIAM FRANCIS	D. NOVEMBER 28, 1965 PHILADELPHIA, PA.
U29- 2 MCLAUGHLIN, EDWARD J	OLD ADD: 99 POPLAR ST - WATERTOWN MA
U24- 1 MCLAUGHLIN, PETER J	31 OGDEN PLACE WEST - DOBBS FERRY NY 10522
U71- 4 MCSHERRY, JOHN PATRICK	6535 PREMIER DRIVE #D6 - NASHVILLE TN 37209
U89- 5 MERIWETHER, JULIUS 'CHICK'	BOX 115 - HOOKS TX 75561
U77- 4 MERRILL, EDWIN DURWOOD	2047 KINGS LN - SAN MATEO CA 94402
U76- 7 MONTAGUE, EDWARD MICHAEL	D. JUNE 13, 1949 HORSE CAVE, KY.
U17- 2 MORAN, CHARLES BARTHEL	33 BOGERT ST - TEANECK NJ 07666
U70- 7 MORGENWECK, HENRY CHARLES	D. APRIL 8, 1964 MIAMI, FLA.
U17- 3 MORIARTY, GEORGE JOSEPH	9223 122ND WAY NORTH - SEMINOLE FL 33542
U84- 2 MORRISON, DAN G.	D. AUGUST 21, 1964 JACKSONVILLE, FLA.
U15- 6 MULLANEY, DOMINIC J	OLD ADD: 95 MALCOLM ST - MINNEAPOLIS MN
U14-12 MURRAY, J. A.	D. SEPTEMBER 7, 1956 FREDERICK, MD.
U15- 7 NALLIN, RICHARD F	200 NW BEL AIR DR - FORT LAUDERDALE FL 33314
U51- 3 NAPP, LARRY ALBERT	RR 2 BOX 129E - PERRYVILLE AR 72126
U79- 7 NELSON, RICHARD	700 BRIAN CIR - MARY ESTHER FL 32569
U66- 3 NEUDECKER, JEROME A	
U22- 1 O'SULLIVAN, JOHN J	D. NOVEMBER 5, 1925 TROY, N. Y.
U12- 5 OBRIEN, JOSEPH	
U14-13 OCONNOR, ARTHUR	D. JANUARY 18, 1989 BENNETTSVILLE, S.C.
U64- 1 ODOM, JAMES CECIL	OLD ADD: 204 NORTH DIAMOND ST - CLIFTON HEIGHTS PA
U68- 5 ODONNELL, JAMES MICHAEL	
U15- 8 OHARA,	451 93RD AVE NORTH - ST PETERSBURG FL 33702
U68- 6 OLSEN, ANDREW HOLGER	D. OCTOBER 11, 1962 CHICAGO, ILL.
U23- 2 ORMSBY, EMMETT T. 'RED'	7921 WEST 118TH - OVERLAND PARK KS 66210
U77- 5 PALERMO, STEPHEN MICHAEL	1365 YORK AVE #37L - NEW YORK NY 10021
U79- 8 PALLONE, DAVID MICHAEL	RR 1, CRYSTAL LAKE - CARBONDALE PA 18407
U46- 3 PAPARELLA, JOSEPH JAMES	OLD ADD: 18320 NE 20TH PL-NORTH MIAMI BEACH FL
U36- 6 PARKER, GEORGE LAMBACH	
U11- 5 PARKER, HARLEY P	P.O. BOX 6503 - LINCOLN NE 68506
U79- 9 PARKS, DALLAS FINNEY	D. OCTOBER 12, 1981 HEMET, CALIF.
U41- 2 PASSARELLA, ARTHUR MATTHEW	D. NOVEMBER 30, 1984 SUNNYVALE, CALIF.
U60- 3 PELEKOUDAS, CHRISTOS GEORGE	D. MAY 16, 1937 NEW ORLEANS, LA.
U22- 2 PFIRMAN, CHARLES H. 'CY'	D. JANUARY 31, 1942 EAST GREENBUSH, N. Y.
U12- 6 PHELPS, EDWARD JAYKILL	29 HOLLOWAY DRIVE - LAKE ST. LOUIS MO 63367
U71- 5 PHILLIPS, DAVID ROBERT	PLAYER DEBUT 1918
U35- 2 PINELLI, RALPH ARTHUR 'BABE'	PLAYER DEBUT 1923
U38- 2 PIPGRAS, GEORGE WILLIAM	407 MAGDALEN - SAN CLEMENTE CA 92672
U85- 4 PONCINO, LARRY LOUIS	D. JULY 25, 1971 LYNWOOD, CALIF.
U23- 3 POWELL, CORNELIUS JOSEPH	

U61- 5	PRYOR, JOHN PAUL	1088 45TH AVE NE - ST PETERSBURG FL 33703
U72- 2	PULLI, FRANK VICTOR	4898 CARDINAL TRAIL - PALM HARBOR FL 33563
U76- 8	PUSKARIC, JOSEPH	429 35TH AVE - MCKEESPORT PA 15132
U76- 9	QUICK, JAMES EDWARD	P.O. BOX 6538 - INCLINE VILLAGE NV 89450
U35- 3	QUINN, JOHN ALOYSIUS	D. JULY 4, 1968 PHILADELPHIA, PA.
U14-14	QUISSER, ARTHUR	
U26- 1	REARDON, JOHN EDWARD 'BEANS'	D. JULY 31, 1984 LONG BEACH, CALIF.
U79-10	REED, RICK ALAN	6190 BLUEHILL - DETROIT MI 48224
U77- 6	REILLY, MICHAEL EUGENE	44 LAKESIDE DR - BATTLE CREEK MI 49015
U73- 2	RENNERT, LAURENCE HENRY 'DUTCH'	306 NORTH LARK ST - OSHKOSH WI 54901
U55- 2	RICE, JOHN LA CLAIRE	2666 EAST 73RD ST #A12W - CHICAGO IL 60649
U83- 8	RIPPLEY, THOMAS STEVEN 'STEVE'	11505 7TH WAY NORTH #2308 - ST. PETERSBURG FL 33702
U47- 2	ROBB, DOUGLAS W. 'SCOTTY'	D. APRIL 10, 1969 MONTCLAIR, N.J.
U53- 3	ROBERTS, LEONARD WYATT	OLD ADD: 5505 SPRUCE VIEW - DALLAS TX 75232
U74- 3	RODRIGUEZ, ARMANDO HUMBERTO	OLD ADD: INDEPENCIA 1375 - VERACRUZ VERACRUZ MEXICO
U80- 1	ROE, JOHN 'ROCKY'	2846 TAMWOOD CT - MILFORD MI 48042
U38- 3	ROMMEL, EDWIN AMERICUS	PLAYER DEBUT 1920
U23- 4	ROWLAND, CLARENCE HENRY 'PANTS'	D. MAY 17, 1969 CHICAGO, ILL.
U38- 4	RUE, JOSEPH WILLIAM	D. DECEMBER 1, 1984 LAGUNA HILLS, CALIF.
U54- 2	RUNGE, EDWARD PAUL	4949 CRESITA DR - SAN DIEGO CA 92115
U72- 3	RUNGE, PAUL EDWARD	649 CALLE DE LA SIERRA - EL CAJON CA 92021
U62- 2	SALERNO, ALEX JOSEPH	1913 TILDEN AVE - NEW HARTFORD NY 13413
U70- 8	SATCHELL, DAROLD L	OLD ADD: 1613 NORTH DUKE ST - DURHAM NC 27701
U60- 4	SCHWARTS, HARRY CLARK	D. FEBRUARY 22, 1963 CLEVELAND, O.
U85- 5	SCOTT, DALE ALLAN	25 SW CANBY STREET - PORTLAND OR 97219
U30- 4	SCOTT, JAMES 'DEATH VALLEY JIM'	D. APRIL 7, 1957 PALM SPRINGS, CALIF.
U34- 1	SEARS, JOHN WILLIAM 'ZIGGY'	D. DECEMBER 16, 1956 HOUSTON, TEX.
U52- 5	SECORY, FRANK EDWARD	PLAYER DEBUT 1940
U14-15	SHANNON, WILLIAM PORTER 'SPIKE'	D. MAY 16, 1940 MINNEAPOLIS, MINN.
U79-11	SHULOCK, JOHN RICHARD	445 38TH SQUARE SW - VERO BEACH FL 32962
U57- 2	SMITH, VINCENT AMBROSE	PLAYER DEBUT 1941
U60- 5	SMITH, WILLIAM ALARIC 'AL'	609 DELHI ST - BOSSIER CITY LA 71111
U50- 2	SOAR, ALBERT HENRY 'HANK'	60 CONCH RD - NARRAGANSETT RI 02882
U77- 7	SPENN, FREDERICK CHARLES	81 VILLAGE BLVD - BRADENTON FL 33507
U66- 4	SPRINGSTEAD, MARTIN JOHN	5 BRUCE CT - SUFFERN NY 10901
U28- 3	STARK, ALBERT D. 'DOLLY'	D. AUGUST 24, 1948 NEW YORK, N.Y.
U61- 6	STEINER, MELVIN JAMES	1701 HARBOR WAY - SEAL BEACH CA 90740
U68- 7	STELLO, RICHARD JACK	D. NOVEMBER 18, 1987 LAKELAND, FLA.
U48- 2	STEVENS, JOHN WILLIAM	D. SEPTEMBER 9, 1981 PHILADELPHIA PA.
U41- 3	STEWART, ERNEST DRAPER	OLD ADD: 107 SAN MARCOS - DEL RIO TX 77840
U59- 1	STEWART, ROBERT WILLIAM	D. 1982 WOONSOCKET RI
U33- 2	STEWART, WILLIAM JOSEPH	D. FEBRUARY 18, 1964 JAMAICA PLAIN, MASS.
U15- 9	STOCKDALE, M. J.	OLD ADD: 314 WEST 42ND ST - NEW YORK NY
U57- 3	SUDOL, EDWARD LAWRENCE	415 REVILO BLVD - DAYTONA BEACH FL 32014
U33- 3	SUMMERS, WILLIAM REED	D. SEPTEMBER 12, 1966 UPTON, MASS.
U24- 2	SWEENEY, JAMES M	D. JANUARY 29, 1950 TYLER, TEX.
U56- 3	TABACCHI, FRANK TULE	D. OCTOBER 26, 1983 HOBOKEN, N. J.
U73- 3	TATA, TERRY ANTHONY	300 VILLAGE DRIVE - CHESHIRE CT 06410
U70- 9	TREMBLAY, RICHARD HENRY	D. JUNE 12, 1987 LITTLETON, N. H.
U85- 6	TSCHIDA, TIMOTHY J.	2296 BENSON AVENUE - ST. PAUL MN 55116
U54- 3	UMONT, FRANK WILLIAM	2116 NE 63RD CT - FORT LAUDERDALE FL 33308
U63- 4	VALENTINE, WILLIAM TERRY	BOX 5599 - LITTLE ROCK AR 72215
U27- 2	VAN GRAFLAN, ROY	D. SEPTEMBER 4, 1953 ROCHESTER, N. Y.
U14-16	VAN SICKLE, CHARLES F	D. 1950
U60- 6	VARGO, EDWARD PAUL	101 FREEDOM RD - BUTLER PA 16001
U57- 4	VENZON, ANTHONY	D. SEPTEMBER 20, 1971 PITTSBURGH PA
U77- 8	VOLTAGGIO, VITO HENRY 'VIC'	646 BRENTWOOD DR - VINELAND NJ 08360
U22- 3	WALSH, EDWARD AUGUSTIN 'BIG ED'	D. MAY 26, 1959 POMPANO BEACH, FLA.
U61- 7	WALSH, FRANCIS D.	D. 1985 SAN ANTONIO, TEX.
U49- 2	WARNEKE, LONNIE	PLAYER DEBUT 1930
U43- 1	WEAFER, HAROLD LEON	D. AUGUST 23, 1978 RICHMOND, VA.
U83- 9	WELKE, TIMOTHY JAMES	5843 THUNDER BAY - KALAMAZOO MI 49002
U66- 5	WENDELSTEDT, HARRY HUNTER	88 SOUTH ST ANDREWS - ORMOND BEACH FL 32074
U76-10	WEST, JOSEPH HENRY	114 NORTH EASTERN ST - GREENVILLE NC 27834
U11- 6	WESTERVELT, FREDERICK E	D. MAY 4, 1955 DREXEL HILL, PA.
U61- 8	WEYER, LEE HOWARD	D. JULY 4, 1988 SAN MATEO, CALIF.
U72- 4	WILLIAMS, ARTHUR	D. FEBRUARY 8, 1979 BAKERSFIELD, CALIF.
U78- 1	WILLIAMS, CHARLES HERMAN	5020 SOUTH LAKE DR #1715 - CHICAGO IL 60615
U63- 5	WILLIAMS, WILLIAM GEORGE 'BILLY'	RR 2 BOX 822 LOT 0-29 - COCONUT CREEK FL 33073
U21- 1	WILSON, FRANK	D. JUNE, 1928 BROOKLYN, N. Y.
U83-10	YOUNG, LARRY EUGENE	3538 SHADY BLUFF DRIVE - LARGO FL 33540

BILL VIZAS, Owner

Baseball, Football and
All Sports Cards
Programs, Books, Autographs
and other Sports Collectibles

OPEN
SIX DAYS
A WEEK

BILL'S SPORTS
COLLECTIBLES

2335 South Broadway
Denver, Colorado 80210
(303) 733-4878

GLOSSARY

The definitions presented in this glossary are definitions as they are interpreted by autograph collectors. For example, PHOTO refers to an autographed photo and HOFer refers to the autograph of a HOFer. Some of the definitions may appear self-explanatory and hence unnecessary; however, they are included for completeness.

ALL STAR BALL—A ball autographed by most or all members of a particular baseball all star game.

AUTOPEN—A mechanical device used to affix a signature on a document, letter or other paper medium. Autopen autographs are not considered collectible.

BALL POINT—A type of pen through which the ink is delivered by means of a revolving ball tip.

BASEBALL COMMEMORATIVE ENVELOPE—A stamped envelope postmarked on the date of a significant event in baseball history. The envelope contains some graphic or illustrative identification of the event. These envelopes autographed by a participant of the event are quite attractive and popular with autograph collectors. These envelopes should not be confused with first day covers popular with stamp collectors, although a hybrid first day cover/baseball commemorative envelope does exist. (This envelope contains the 1969 commemorative stamp of baseball's first hundred years and is cacheted with many different baseball superstars.)

CARD—A card autographed by the player portrayed on the card. Cards are normally autographed on the front; however, cards autographed on the back still qualify under this definition.

CHECK—A cancelled check or bank note containing the autograph of a ball player. Checks are quite often obtained from the estate of deceased ball players. Official ball club checks in many cases contain more than one autograph.

CLUB ISSUED POSTCARDS—Postcard size pictures of ball players, the older ones normally being in black and white with modern postcards being predominantly in color. They are usually blank backed, sold at ballparks and make excellent autograph media. Many players send autographed copies of these postcards to fans requesting autographs.

CONTRACT—A legal document, for any purpose, including agreements concerning players and management, equipment or other product manufacturers, or personal agreements signed by the sports personality.

CUT—An autograph that has been "cut" from a larger piece of paper, photo, letter or other written or printed matter.

DATED—An autograph which contains both the signature and the date when the signature was written.

DEBUT YEAR—The year in which a player first appeared in a game in the big leagues. For a manager or coach with no player experience the debut year refers to the year he first appeared as a manager or coach.

DEBUT YEAR NUMBER—Within a particular debut year the number for a player obtained by placing in alphabetical order all players who debuted that particular year and placing a number on each, from 1 to "the total number of players debuting that year," based on this alphabetical order.

FACSIMILE—A copy of an original signature. Facsimile autographs are not considered collectible.

FELT TIP—A type of pen which has a felt tip and which provides a smooth unbroken signature.

HOFer—The autograph of a member of baseball's Hall of Fame.

LETTER—A typed or handwritten communication with a heading listing to whom the letter is written and a closing autographed by a sports personality.

ORIGINAL ART—A unique drawing, painting or other piece of artwork portraying a personality or an event and bearing the signature of a participant of the event or the personality portrayed.

PENCIL—A signature in pencil by a sports personality. Pencil signatures predominated during the early parts of this century and are sometimes the only types of signatures available of certain sports personalities. Care should be taken with pencil signatures as they smear quite easily.

PLACQUE—Postcard pictures of the bronzed placques of Hall of Fame baseball players in the Baseball Hall of Fame in Cooperstown, NY. Through the years there have been several different color placques issued by the Hall of Fame, including black and white types.

PERSONALIZED—An autograph which contains a reference to the person for whom the autograph was written.

PHOTO—A glossy picture, normally 5" X 7" or 8" X 10," which contains an autograph of the player portrayed on the photo.

SASE—Self-addressed stamped envelope. When requesting autographs, SASE's should be sent to insure that returned autographs will be sent to the proper place and to provide the autograph giver a convenient means of returning autographed material.

SHARPIE—A brand of ink pen very popular with autograph collectors because of its broad stroke and its rapid drying characteristics on almost any surface.

STAMP—A signature affixed by means of a rubber or wooden device which contains a facsimile of the sports personality's autograph. Stamped signatures are not considered collectible.

TEAM BALL—A ball autographed by most or all members of a particular team.

TEAM SHEET—A single sheet of paper containing the autographs of most or all members of a particular team during a particular year. Many team sheets are on club stationery.

3 X 5—An index card, either lined or unlined, which many collectors use for obtaining autographs. The 3 X 5 refers to the approximate dimensions of the card. 3 X 5's usually contain only one signature.

'TWO' GOOD TO BE TRUE

Two great new magazines in the tradition of
Beckett Baseball Card Monthly.
Up-to-date, accurate, and reliable prices • interesting articles
full-color superstar cover photos • hobby tips • answers to your questions

Beckett Football Card Magazine Subscriptions

Name _____ Age _____
(Please Print)

Address _____

City _____ State _____ Zip _____

Type of Subscription: ☐ New Subscription ☐ Renewal

Payment enclosed via: ☐ Check or Money Order ☐ VISA/MasterCard

Signature _____

Acct. # _____ Exp. _____

Check one please:

	Your Price
8 issues (a savings of $8.65)	**$14.95**
16 issues (a savings of $21.25)	**$25.95**
24 issues (a savings of $33.85)	**$36.95**
32 issues (a savings of $46.45)	**$47.95**

All foreign addresses add $12 per 8 issues for postage. All payments payable in U.S. funds.
Beckett Football Card Magazine is published 8 times a year.

Mail to: Beckett Publications, Football Subscriptions, 4887 Alpha Rd., Suite 200,
Dallas, Texas 75244   DEPT. BAL 6

Beckett Basketball Card Magazine Subscriptions

Name _____ Age _____
(Please Print)

Address _____

City _____ State _____ Zip _____

Type of Subscription: ☐ New Subscription ☐ Renewal

Payment enclosed via: ☐ Check or Money Order ☐ VISA/MasterCard

Signature _____

Acct. # _____ Exp. _____

Check one please:

	Your Price
6 issues (a savings of $4.75)	**$12.95**
12 issues (a savings of $13.45)	**$21.95**
18 issues (a savings of $23.15)	**$29.95**
24 issues (a savings of $33.85)	**$36.95**

All foreign addresses add $9 per 6 issues for postage. All payments payable in U.S. funds.
Beckett Basketball Card Magazine is published 6 times a year.

Mail to: Beckett Publications, Basketball Subscriptions, 4887 Alpha Rd., Suite 200,
Dallas, Texas 75244   DEPT. BAL 6

EVEN MORE FOR LESS!

More color
superstar covers

More collectable
superstar photos

More answers to
your hobby questions

More accurate prices
to all the new sets

**The best-selling magazine in the hobby just got better.
More color, more photos, more enjoyment for less
money. More than just a price guide, *Beckett Monthly*
is a quality baseball entertainment magazine.
Subscribe today!**

Beckett Baseball Card Monthly Subscriptions

Name __MATT CCair__ Age __9__

Address __2937 E.1499TRD OTTAWA ILL,__ (Please Print)

City __Ottawa__ State __ILL__ Zip __61350__

Type of Subscription: [✓] New Subscription   [ ] Renewal

Payment enclosed via: [✓] Check or Money Order   [ ] VISA/MasterCard

Signature __Matt Clair__

Acct. # _____ Exp. _____

Check one please:

		Your Price
⊗	1 year (a savings of $10.05 for 12 issues)	**$19.95**
	2 years (a savings of $24.05 for 24 issues)	**$35.95**
	3 years (a savings of $42.05 for 36 issues)	**$47.95**
	4 years (a savings of $60.05 for 48 issues)	**$59.95**

All foreign addresses add $18 per year
for postage. All payments payable in
U.S. funds. *Beckett Monthly* is
published monthly.

Mail to: Beckett Publications, Subscriptions, 4887 Alpha Rd., Suite 200, Dallas, Texas 75244

DEPT. BAL 6